W9-BZE-898

CAMBRIDGE TEXTBOOKS IN LINGUISTICS

General Editors: B. COMRIE, C. J. FILLMORE, R. LASS, D. LIGHTFOOT,
J. LYONS, P. H. MATTHEWS, R. POSNER, S. ROMAINE,
N. V. SMITH, N. VINCENT.

TRANSFORMATIONAL GRAMMAR

A FIRST COURSE

TRANSFORMATIONAL GRAMMAR

A FIRST COURSE

ANDREW RADFORD

DEPARTMENT OF LANGUAGE AND LINGUISTICS
UNIVERSITY OF ESSEX

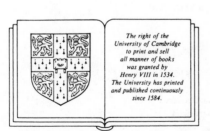

The right of the
University of Cambridge
to print and sell
all manner of books
was granted by
Henry VIII in 1534.
The University has printed
and published continuously
since 1584.

CAMBRIDGE UNIVERSITY PRESS

CAMBRIDGE

NEW YORK   PORT CHESTER   MELBOURNE   SYDNEY

Published by the Press Syndicate of the University of Cambridge
The Pitt Building, Trumpington, Cambridge CB2 1RP
40 West 20th Street, New York, NY 10011, USA
10 Stamford Road, Oakleigh, Melbourne 3166, Australia

First published 1988
Reprinted 1988, 1989

Printed in Great Britain at The Bath Press, Avon

British Library cataloguing in publication data
Radford, Andrew
Transformational grammar: a first course.
1. Generative grammar
I. Title
410   P158

Library of Congress cataloguing in publication data
Radford, Andrew.
Transformational grammar.
(Cambridge textbooks in linguistics)
Bibliography: p.
1. Generative grammar.
2. Grammar, Comparative and general – Syntax.
I. Title. II. Series.
P158.R29 1988   415   87-26831

ISBN 0 521 34506 5 hard covers
ISBN 0 521 34750 5 paperback

EA

CONTENTS

Contents

Contents

PROLOGUE

[This prologue is a short, one-act play for reader and author]

READER [groaning in protest]: Oh no, not another book on Transformational Grammar! I've never done any grammar before: will I be able to follow it?

AUTHOR: Of course you will! I've aimed the book at the absolute beginner who's not done any Syntax before.

READER: What's the general aim of the book?

AUTHOR: To get beginners to the point where they can understand some of the ideas and issues debated in *current* work on Transformational Syntax such as Chomsky's *Knowledge of Language*, or *Barriers*. I've deliberately set out to de-bug the text of the unnecessary technical jargon which plagues so much of the literature in the field. In that respect it's like my earlier *Transformational Syntax* book. But this isn't a second edition of that: the two are very different.

READER: Different how?

AUTHOR: There are three main differences – *theoretical*, *descriptive*, and *pedagogical*. From a theoretical viewpoint, this book is much more up to date than the earlier one, and so uses a more recent framework, which takes into account major works published since 1981 (e.g. Chomsky's *Barriers* monograph). At a descriptive level, the present book has a greater data coverage than its predecessor – i.e. it discusses a wider range of constructions and rules. And from a pedagogical perspective, more care has been devoted in the present book to providing a gentler, more gradual, and more sympathetic introduction to those concepts and constructs which proved mental stumbling blocks to some readers in the old book. In other words, the new book is more up to date, more comprehensive, and more intelligible than the old one.

READER: Is it intended as a reference book or as a coursebook?

Prologue

AUTHOR: It's intended primarily as a *coursebook*, to be used either for class work, or for home study. It's written in a clear enough style that you don't need to rely on having a teacher to explain things to you. But the book also has a detailed bibliographical background section and an extensive bibliography, and these serve an obvious reference function.

READER: Is it a practical book?

AUTHOR: Yes! That's why it has lots and lots of exercise material at the end of every chapter. I want *to get you to be able to do syntax for yourself* – not just to read about how other people do it. Anyone who's read the text should be able to tackle the exercises: they don't require additional background knowledge or reading. There are three different types of exercises.

READER: What are they?

AUTHOR: The first type are *reinforcement* exercises, which give you practice at applying the ideas discussed in the text. The second type are *advancement* exercises, which get you to apply the concepts, structures, or terminology discussed in the chapter to constructions which are not quite the same as (though similar to) those discussed in the text: these are marked by a prefixed single asterisk *. The third type are *problem* exercises, which attempt to get you to look rather more critically at some of the assumptions, arguments and analyses given in the text; these are marked with a prefixed double asterisk **.

READER: Do you have to do the whole of a chapter before you can tackle any of the exercises?

AUTHOR: No, not at all! Each chapter is divided up into about ten different sections. Each exercise relates to ideas discussed in specific sections of the chapter. You'll find at the end of the relevant section of the main text an indication along the following lines:

You should now be able to tackle exercise IV

READER: What's the point of that?

AUTHOR: Well, the whole idea is to cater for both *hares* and *tortoises*! Hares who want to race through a whole chapter at one go, and then tackle the exercises as a block can do so. But tortoises who prefer to plod slowly through each chapter one section at a time, can 'stop' at the end of a particular section, and test themselves with the exercise(s) relating to that section. Likewise, the teacher who wants to cover a whole chapter in a class can ask the class to prepare the whole chapter, and all the exercises relating to it, in a given week. But the teacher who wants to proceed at a more gentle pace can ask the class to 'prepare the first four sections of the next chapter, and the exercises relating to them, for the next session'.

READER: What kind of topics does the book cover?

AUTHOR: It covers four main topics: the goals of linguistic theory; syntactic structure and how it can be represented; the nature and role of the Lexicon; and the function and operation of Transformations. In each case, the emphasis is on current rather than past work.

READER: You mean this isn't a book which traces the history of Transformational Grammar?

AUTHOR: I've included some background historical information, where this relates to 'live' issues which are still being debated in current literature. But I've avoided including 'dead' ideas (i.e. ideas which were once current but have since been abandoned).

READER: Doesn't knowing the way things used to be help you understand the way they are today?

AUTHOR: No, not necessarily. After all, knowing the etymology (= history) of a word doesn't always help you understand its current meaning any better (which is why many dictionaries no longer include etymological information). And in the case of Transformational Grammar, the past few years have seen such a major theoretical reorientation in aims, methods, terminology, and argumentation that it is no longer true that reading yesterday's Linguistics helps you understand today's Linguistics. On the contrary, many beginners find the historicist approach tiresome and bewildering.

READER: When I've finished this book, will I be able to go off and read the primary literature on Transformational Grammar? Will I be able to read through Chomsky's *Knowledge of Language*, for example?

AUTHOR: Well, you'll be able to read and understand parts of it. But not all of it. There are some more technical topics which are not covered in this book – as you'd expect from any *introductory* book.

READER: Is there a book which will serve as a transition between your introductory book, and the primary literature?

AUTHOR: Well, I'm working on a companion volume to this one which is intended to do just that: it's an intermediate/advanced coursebook, and provides a detailed discussion of recent work on Binding,

Bounding, Chains, Empty Categories, Theta Marking, Case Marking, Logical Form, Parameters, etc.

READER: But I don't know what all those technical terms mean.

AUTHOR: Well, the sooner you plough through this volume, the sooner you'll find out! And don't you dare miss out the exercises!

*This book is dedicated to
the memory of a good friend
and colleague of mine
who died in January 1986:*
MICHAEL ANTHONY

ACKNOWLEDGMENTS

My thanks are due to the University College of North Wales for granting me study leave between October and December 1986, during which I wrote a first draft of the manuscript. I'm also grateful to Neil Smith (University College London) for his detailed, painstaking and perspicuous comments on the first draft. I'd further like to thank Bob Borsley (University College Bangor) for helpful comments about overall organisation, and Frits Stuurman (Utrecht) for comments on an early draft of Chapter 4.

1
Goals

1.1 Overview

The aim of this chapter is to give you some idea of the goals of linguistic theory, and to introduce you to some simple concepts which will be used throughout the rest of the book. Among the notions which will be explained in this chapter are terms such as *theory of language, grammar of a language, particular/universal grammar, competence, performance, grammaticality, linguistic intuition, rule-governed creativity, generate, observational/descriptive/explanatory adequacy, constraint, markedness,* and *innateness.*

1.2 Grammatical competence

Linguistics is the study of *Language.* But why should we be interested in the phenomenon of *Language*? Chomsky gives an avowedly *mentalist* answer to this question. For him, the most fundamental reason for studying language is that language is a mirror of the mind – i.e. by detailed study of language, we might hope to reach a better understanding of how the human mind produces and processes language. As Chomsky remarks (*Language and Mind* (1972a), p. 103):

> There are a number of questions which might lead one to undertake a study of language. Personally, I am primarily intrigued by the possibility of learning something, from the study of language, that will bring to light inherent properties of the human mind.

But what aspects of language should be the focus of our study? Chomsky's answer is that there are three inter-related theories which any detailed study of language ultimately seeks to develop, namely:

(1) (i) Theory of Language Structure
   (ii) Theory of Language Acquisition
   (iii) Theory of Language Use

The Theory of Language Structure will concern itself with what are the defining structural properties of natural (i.e. human) languages; the Theory of Language Acquisition with the question of how children acquire their native language(s); and the Theory of Language Use with the question of how linguistic and nonlinguistic knowledge interact in speech comprehension and production. Of the three, the task (i) of developing a Theory of Language Structure is logically prior to the other two, since only if we first know what 'language' is can we develop theories about how it is acquired and used. It is perhaps not surprising, therefore, that most of Chomsky's work has been devoted to the attempt to develop a Theory of Language Structure.

But what exactly is it that such a theory seeks to characterise? The answer is that any adequate Theory of Language Structure must provide answers to questions such as the following:

- What is language?
- What is it that you know when you know a language?
- What are the essential defining characteristics of natural languages which differentiate them from, for example, artificial languages like those used in Mathematics or Computing, or from animal communication systems?
- Do languages differ from each other in unpredictable ways, or do they all share certain common, universal properties?

But how do we attempt to develop a Theory of Language Structure which will answer such questions? The first step is to formulate detailed descriptions (known technically as *grammars*) of particular languages (e.g. English): this is the study of *Particular Grammar*. So, for example, we might try and devise a grammar of English, a grammar of French, a grammar of Swedish, a grammar of Swahili, a grammar of Chinese . . . and so on and so forth. A grammar of a particular language will take the familiar form of a set of rules or principles which tell you how to 'speak' and 'understand' the language: more precisely, a grammar will comprise a set of rules or principles which specify how to form, pronounce, and interpret Phrases and Sentences in the language concerned. The word *grammar* in this technical sense has a much broader sense than that familiar from school textbooks, since it covers not only Morphology (i.e. the internal structure of words) and Syntax (i.e. how words are combined together to form phrases and sentences), but also Phonology (i.e. pronunciation) and some aspects of Semantics (i.e. meaning) as well. When we have compiled detailed grammars of a number of different languages, the second step in our quest for a Theory of Language Structure is to abstract from particular grammars common, universal properties that they all share: this is the study of *Universal Grammar* – i.e. the search for linguistic universals.

Consider first the study of Particular Grammar. What exactly is it that a grammar of a particular language sets out to describe? Chomsky gives an essentially *mentalist* answer to this question: for him, a grammar is a *model* (= systematic description) of those linguistic abilities of native speakers of a language which enable them to speak and understand their language fluently. These linguistic abilities, Chomsky terms the *competence* of the native speaker. Thus, a *grammar* of a language is a model of the linguistic competence of the fluent native speaker of the language. *Competence* (the fluent native speaker's knowledge of the language) is contrasted by Chomsky with *performance* (what people actually say or understand by what someone else says on a given occasion). Competence is 'the speaker–hearer's knowledge of his language', while Performance is 'the actual use of language in concrete situations' (Chomsky, *Aspects* (1965), p. 4). Very often, performance is an imperfect reflection of competence: for example, the fact that people make occasional slips of the tongue in everyday speech does not mean that they don't know their native language, or don't have fluency (i.e. competence) in it. Slips of the tongue and like phenomena are – for Chomsky – *performance errors*, attributable to a variety of performance factors like tiredness, boredom, drunkenness, drugs, external distractions, and so forth. Linguistics is – for Chomsky – primarily concerned with competence, since a Theory of Competence will be a subpart of an eventual Theory of Performance: that is, you have to understand what a native speaker knows about his language before you can study the effects of tiredness, drunkenness, etc. on this knowledge. Thus, what we mean by saying that a grammar is a model of the native speaker's competence is that a grammar tells us what we need to know in order to be fluent in a language.

Chomsky distinguishes two types of competence: (i) *grammatical competence*, and (ii) *pragmatic competence* (see e.g. Chomsky, *Essays* (1977a), p. 40). The former belongs to the Theory of Language Structure, and the latter to the Theory of Language Use. Pragmatics is concerned with the role played by nonlinguistic information such as background knowledge and personal beliefs in our use of sentences. To take one of Chomsky's own examples (from *Essays* (1977a), p. 40), suppose I have a friend who says to me 'Today was a disaster.' If I know (by way of background information) that he was giving a special lecture today, then on the basis of this background knowledge I infer that he probably means that his lecture went down very badly. It is the native speaker's *pragmatic competence* which enables him to bring into play nonlinguistic information in the interpretation of sentences. By contrast, in the case of a sentence such as:

(2)   He thinks that John is wrong

it is the native speaker's *grammatical competence* (his knowledge of the grammar of his language) which tells him that *he* cannot be interpreted as referring to the same person as *John* in a sentence like (2). Since, as we noted earlier, Chomsky has devoted himself primarily to the study of language structure rather than language use, he has focussed almost exclusively on the task of attempting to characterise *grammatical* rather than *pragmatic* competence.

The native speaker's grammatical competence is reflected in two types of *intuition* which speakers have about their native language(s) – (i) intuitions about sentence *well-formedness*, and (ii) intuitions about sentence *structure*. The word *intuition* is used here in a technical sense which has become standardised in Linguistics: by saying that a native speaker has *intuitions* about the well-formedness and structure of sentences, all we are saying is that he has the ability to make *judgments* about whether a given sentence is well-formed or not, and about whether it has a particular structure or not. The term *well-formed* is also a standard technical term in the linguistic literature: for the time being, you can think of it as meaning 'OK' – but a little later, we'll try and define *well-formedness* a little more precisely.

These *intuitions* about sentences span four different aspects of language – namely *Phonology* (= the study of sounds and sound systems), *Morphology* (= the study of how morphemes (grammatical units smaller than the word) are combined together into words), *Syntax* (= the study of how words are combined together to form sentences), and *Semantics* (= the study of meaning). Hence, we can say that native speakers have phonological, morphological, syntactic, and semantic competence, and that this competence is reflected in their intuitions about the phonological, morphological, syntactic, and semantic well-formedness and structure of sentences in their native language(s). We'll look briefly at each of these different aspects of competence in turn.

Let's begin by illustrating typical intuitions reflecting a native speaker's *phonological* competence. All native speakers of English would agree that (3) (a) below is phonologically well-formed in respect of its stress pattern (i.e. it's OK to pronounce the sentence with primary stress on the capitalised syllables), whereas (3) (b) is phonologically ill-formed in respect of its stress pattern (i.e. it isn't OK to pronounce the sentence with primary stress on the capitalised syllables):

(3) (a)   **THIS** is a gra**MMA**tical **SEN**tence
    (b)   This is **A** grammati**CAL** sen**TENCE**

So, we all have intuitions about possible and impossible stress patterns in sentences. Moreover, we all have strong *phonotactic* intuitions – i.e. intuitions about what are possible and impossible sound sequences among native words in English. For instance, we'd probably all agree that *blick* is a possible, but non-occurring English word, whereas *bnick* by contrast is not a possible native English word (an asterisk in front of a word, phrase, or sentence indicates that it is ill-formed in some way): such a word could only occur in English as a foreign borrowing. Phonological competence is also reflected in intuitions about phonological structure: any English speaker intuitively feels, for example, that the sequence 'black bird' can either be a single phonological word (**BLACK**bird, with primary stress on *black* = a species of bird, like thrush, robin, etc.), or two independent phonological words (**BLACK BIRD** or black **BIRD** = bird which is black, as opposed to 'white bird', 'yellow bird', etc.).

In much the same way, *morphological competence* is reflected in the native speaker's intuitions about morphological well-formedness and structure. For example, native speakers of English know that *van* and *can* have the respective plural forms *vans* and *cans*, but that the plural of *man* is *men* and not *mans*. Likewise, native English speakers know that *fold* and *scold* have the respective past tense forms *folded* and *scolded*, but that the past tense form of *hold* is not *holded*, but rather *held*. In the same way, anyone fluent in English knows that the Verbs *approve* and *refuse* have corresponding Nouns *approval* and *refusal*, but that the Noun counterparts of *prove* and *amuse* are not *proval* and *amusal*, but rather *proof* and *amusement*. In addition, native speakers also have intuitions about morphological structure: for example, English speakers intuitively feel that words like *overload*, *overplay*, and *overwork* are structured out of two independent morphemes, a prefix *over* (meaning 'excessively') and a stem *load–play–work*, whereas by contrast *overture* does not comprise the two morphemes *over* and *ture*.

The native speaker's *semantic* competence is reflected in intuitions about semantic well-formedness and structure. For example, any native speaker of English would agree that (4) (a) below is semantically well-formed, but that (4) (b) is semantically ill-formed (i.e. 'odd' in some way, by virtue of its meaning, so that it 'doesn't make sense'):

(4) (a)   I thought that Mary was ill, but it turned out that she wasn't
    (b)   !I realised that Mary was ill, but it turned out that she wasn't

(In this book, we use ! in front of a sentence to show it is 'anomalous' (i.e. semantically or pragmatically 'odd'); generally speaking, we follow the standard practice of using an asterisk * in front of a sentence to indicate that it is *syntactically* ill-formed, though occasionally we extend the use of the asterisk to indicate that a sentence is simply ill-formed in some way, without specifying in what way(s)). A second type of semantic intuition which native speakers have about their language concerns semantic structure and semantic relations. To take an example from Chomsky (*Knowledge* (1986), p. 8), any native speaker of English knows that *them* can be interpreted as being coreferential to (i.e. referring to the same set of individuals as) *the men* in (5) (a) below, but not in (5) (b):

(5) (a)   I wonder who *the men* expected to see *them*

    (b)   *The men* expected to see *them*

Hence, intuitions about coreference relations in sentences are part of the set of intuitions we have about semantic relations in and between sentences.

Having looked briefly at how phonological, morphological, and semantic competence is reflected in intuitions about well-formedness and structure, let's now turn to examine the nature of *syntactic* competence. Here, too, we find that competence is reflected in two types of intuition: intuitions about syntactic well-formedness, and intuitions about syntactic structure. To say that a native speaker has intuitions about syntactic well-formedness in his language is to say that he is able to judge whether such-and-such a sequence of words is a grammatical sentence in his language or not. For example, any native speaker of English would intuitively recognise (leaving aside for the moment differences of style or dialect) that all the examples in (6) below are grammatical (i.e. syntactically well-formed) sentences in English:

(6) (a)   I gave back the car to him
    (b)   I gave the car back to him
    (c)   I gave him back the car
    (d)   I gave him the car back

but that the following are ungrammatical as sentences of English:

(7) (a)   *I gave the car to him back
    (b)   *I gave back him the car

(Recall that an asterisk in front of a sentence means that it is ill-formed in some way (usually, *syntactically ill-formed*, i.e. *ungrammatical*); by convention, any sentence which does not have an asterisk in front of it is assumed to be well-formed; note that asterisks go at the *beginning*, not the *end* of sentences!)

But what does it mean to say that native speakers have intuitions about the *syntactic structure* of sentences in their language? All this means is that native speakers have 'gut feelings' about which words in a sentence 'go with' or 'modify' which other words. For example, in the case of a sentence such as:

(8)   Some people can be very selfish

we'd all agree that *some* 'goes with' *people* (and not, for example, *very*), so that the sequence [*some people*] forms a Phrase of some sort. Likewise, we'd all agree that *very* 'modifies' *selfish* (and not, for example, *be*), so that the sequence [*very selfish*] forms a rather different kind of Phrase. And, if you think about it carefully, you'd probably agree that in a sentence such as:

(9)   You could not go to her party

we could take the word *not* to 'go with' either *could* or *go*, as becomes clearer if we look at the two 'variants' of (9) given in (10) below:

(10) (a)   What you *could not* do is go to her party
    (b)   What you could do is *not go* to her party

Thus, native speakers have an intuitive knowledge of the syntactic relations between the words in sentences in their language; in other words, they intuitively know how words are combined together to form Phrases, and Phrases are combined together to form sentences. We should note, however, that native speakers' intuitions about syntactic structure are often much less sharp (or reliable) than their intuitions about syntactic well-formedness (grammaticality).

1.3   Basic concepts and fundamental misconceptions

Before we go any further, it is useful to clarify some of the basic concepts which we have introduced so far, and to try and eradicate some of the fundamental misconceptions which people sometimes have about these concepts. One basic concept which often gives rise to unfortunate misunderstanding is that of *grammaticality*. In this connection, we should point out that it is important not to confuse the descriptive notion *grammatical* with the corresponding prescriptive notion *correct*. For example, there are many varieties of English in which sentences like:

(11)   Mine is bigger than what yours is

are perfectly grammatical, and for speakers of these dialects such sentences are syntactically well-formed. But at the same time, sentences like (11) are of a type stigmatised as 'incorrect' or 'bad grammar' by a certain self-styled sociocultural elite (= pedants!). This poses an apparent dilemma for the linguist: should he *describe* what people actually say, or should he attempt to *prescribe* what he or others think they ought to say? In other words, should Linguistics be *descriptive* or *prescriptive*?

In actual fact, it is hard to see how anyone could defend the *prescriptive* approach. In any other field of enquiry, it would be seen as patently absurd. What would we say of the social anthropologist who, instead of describing the way a given society is, sets about prescribing the way he thinks it ought to be? (We'd probably suggest he ought to give up Anthropology and take up Politics!) And what would we think of the scientist who, regretting the unfortunate tendency for the moon to orbit round the earth, instead proposes an alternative model in which the earth orbits round the moon, simply because he thinks things *ought* to be that way? No-one these days would take any such enterprise seriously; and the same is true of Linguistics. Modern Linguistics is purely *descriptive*, not prescriptive. Hence, we describe sentences as 'grammatical/ungrammatical', or 'well-formed/ill-formed'; we do not use prescriptive terminology such as 'correct/incorrect' (yes, that is a *prescriptive* statement!)

A related issue which often gives rise to muddled thinking concerns the relative importance of written language on the one hand, and spoken language on the other. There is a tendency for the uninformed to think that written language is a 'purer', 'more correct' form of language than spoken language. As Palmer (1983, p. 27) notes, 'All too often people tend to think of the spoken language as a rather poor version of the written language.' This has been counteracted by the opposite trend in work in Descriptive Linguistics in the last fifty years, which has concerned itself primarily with spoken language, and generally regarded the written language as being of secondary importance. Why should this be? There are a variety of reasons why descriptive linguists might suppose that spoken language is a more fertile and rewarding field of study than written language.

For one thing, spoken language tends to be less subjected to prescriptive pressures than written language, and hence is a less artificial medium of communication (written language is often a kind of 'censored' version of spoken language). Secondly, spoken language is a more spontaneous form of communication than written language: you can spend half an hour composing a sentence in a letter, but not in a conversation! Thirdly, spoken language shows a much greater range of variation between individuals than written language (and hence is more interesting if we want to study how language varies according to social class, etc.). Fourthly, the spoken language generally contains more linguistic information than the written language: for example, all spoken sentences have an associated intonation contour which is not properly represented in the written language. Fifthly, spoken language is far more frequently used as a medium of communication than written language: we talk to friends, etc. all day long, but we don't spend all day writing letters to people! For these and many other reasons, many linguists would argue that Linguistics should concern itself primarily with spoken rather than written language.

There is a sense, however, in which the whole debate about whether we should concentrate on the written or the spoken language is a non-issue. For, after all, what we are seeking to describe is the native speaker's *competence*, i.e. his linguistic knowledge: this is a *mental* property, which commonly has two physical manifestations (in the form of written or spoken language), but which might have alternative physical instantiations (e.g. in sign language, etc.). What we are interested in is the abstract grammatical competence underlying the physical realisations of that competence; to the extent that both written and spoken forms of language (provided we can be sure they are free from prescriptive influences, errors induced by performance factors, etc.) reflect this abstract competence, then both provide us with useful clues to the nature of *competence*. Thus, the linguist doesn't study only the spoken language, or only the written language: rather, he studies *language* (in all its physical instantiations).

A more serious problem which arises with Chomsky's conception of a Grammar as a model of the linguistic intuitions of the fluent native speaker of a given language concerns what to do about disagreements among native speakers about the well-formedness or structure of particular sentences. One of the abstractions that Chomsky makes in studying language is to assume that speech communities are homogeneous: i.e. to assume that all native speakers of a given language will have essentially the same well-formedness and structural intuitions. Chomsky himself remarks (*Aspects* (1965), p. 3) that: 'Linguistic theory is concerned primarily with an ideal speaker–listener, in a completely homogeneous speech community.' But the problem with this abstraction is that it is plainly not the case that speech communities are homogeneous: all native speakers have to some extent their own individual way of speaking (or *idiolect*), and there are, of course, larger linguistic groupings within society. Speakers with a common geographical background may share a common *dialect*, while speakers from a common social background may share a common *sociolect*. We can illustrate the linguistic differences within a given speech community in terms of the examples in (12) below: each of these sentences would probably be accepted as well-formed by only a certain percentage of English speakers (hence the use of the % prefix):

(12) (a)   %Your car wants mending
   (b)   %That's to do tomorrow
   (c)   %I gave it her
   (d)   %Can the both of us come?

(e)   %There's a man sells vegetables in the village

(f)   %It were me what told her

The obvious question is what the linguist is to do in such cases. The broad answer is that in general the problem of linguistic variation within a speech community is one which is more appropriately dealt with in a partially separate discipline (*Sociolinguistics*), and since it is not a problem which is essentially *syntactic* in nature, it is not the kind of problem which ought to be the primary focus of attention in the attempt to develop an adequate theory of *Syntax*. For practical purposes, most linguists describing a language of which they are native speakers rely on their own intuitions, and thus the grammar they devise is essentially a grammar of their own idiolect, which they assume is representative of the language as a whole.

An even more tricky problem which arises with the notion of *well-formedness* concerns the attempt to identify in what way(s) a given ill-formed sentence is 'odd'. Let's first draw a distinction between sentences which are 'pragmatically anomalous' in some way, and those which are 'linguistically ill-formed'. While the distinction may be clear enough in principle, it is often very hard in practice to decide which side of the dividing line a given sentence falls. For example, what is the status of sentences such as the following, (taken from Lakoff (1971), p. 332):

(13) (a)   My uncle realises that I'm a lousy cook

(b)   My cat realises that I'm a lousy cook

(c)   My goldfish realises that I'm a lousy cook

(d)   My pet amoeba realises that I'm a lousy cook

(e)   My frying pan realises that I'm a lousy cook

(f)   My sincerity realises that I'm a lousy cook

(g)   My birth realises that I'm a lousy cook

Intuitively, most people would regard (13) (a) as perfectly well-formed, (13) (b) as slightly less natural, (13) (c) as a bit eccentric, (13) (d) as implausible, (13) (e) as just plain daft, and (13) (f) and (g) as absolutely inconceivable. But what precisely is the nature of the oddity of the more unusual sentences? The answer is that the oddity seems to be largely *pragmatic* (i.e. nonlinguistic) in nature. Thus, whether or not you find expressions like *My goldfish thinks that* . . . well-formed depends on whether or not you believe that goldfish do (or might) possess powers of thought; a sentence like (13) (c) presupposes that goldfish are capable of thought, and a person who rejects sentences like (13) (c) is in effect rejecting the implied proposition that goldfish can think. Why should he reject such a proposition? Presumably because it conflicts with his *personal beliefs about the world*. Thus, sentences like (13) (c) are not *linguistically* ill-formed in any way, but rather simply pragmatically anomalous, in the sense that they express ideas which do not conform to our view of the way the world is.

But surely (13) (f) and (g) are a very different case. Surely nobody in any culture could accept such sentences as well-formed? In this regard, Lakoff (1971, p. 332) remarks:

> (13) (f) and (13) (g) are another matter. That properties and events have mental powers might seem to be an impossible belief, not just a strange one. If this were true, it would follow that (13) (f) and (13) (g) were universally impossible. However, Kenneth Hale informs me that, among the Papagos, events are assumed to have minds (whatever that might mean), and that sentences like (13) (g) would be perfectly normal.

In other words, our judgments about the ill-formedness of sentences like (13) depend entirely on our cultural, religious, or personal beliefs – not on any *linguistic* knowledge that we have about our language. Sentences like (13) are thus linguistically well-formed: they are neither ungrammatical (e.g. they don't involve a plural verb with a singular subject), nor semantically ill-formed (e.g. it is not the case that we find such sentences as completely incomprehensible or meaningless as a sentence from a language we do not speak).

Thus, it is easy to be deceived into thinking that a sentence is linguistically ill-formed in some way, when in fact very often the sentence is merely 'pragmatically anomalous' – i.e. it expresses an idea which (to people with certain beliefs, culture, education, etc.) may seem unacceptable. We can underline this crucial point by drawing a distinction between *acceptability* (a term introduced by Chomsky in *Aspects* (1965), pp. 10–15) and *well-formedness*: this distinction is related to the earlier distinctions we drew between Competence and Performance on the one hand, and Pragmatics and Grammar on the other. Native speakers give judgments about the *acceptability* of sentences (i.e. they indicate whether they find them *acceptable* or *unacceptable*); acceptability is a *performance* notion. If a native speaker says that a sentence is unacceptable in his language, this may be for a variety of reasons. One possibility – discussed earlier in relation to (13) – is that the sentence is simply *pragmatically* odd in some way (i.e. it expresses an idea which the speaker finds distasteful, or otherwise unacceptable): as we have already seen, sentences which are pragmatically odd are not necessarily linguistically ill-formed. However, it may be that a speaker will find unacceptable a sentence which is not pragmatically odd in any way: does this mean that the sentence concerned is linguistically ill-

11

formed? Not necessarily. It may be that the *informant* (= a person who provides you with information about some aspect of his native language) is confused, or tired, or bored with all those silly questions about his language, and hence makes a hasty and perhaps erroneous judgment. In such a case, performance is a poor reflection of competence. Or it may be that the informant is influenced by prescriptive notions inculcated at school: thus, some English speakers, when asked about a sentence like:

(14)   Who did you meet at the party?

would reply that such a sentence is *unacceptable* because it is 'bad grammar' and should be 'corrected' to:

(15)   *Whom* did you meet at the party?

But of course this is nonsense: a sentence like (14) is perfectly well-formed, and is characteristic of everyday conversation. In this case, a performance factor (prescriptive education) is interfering with the natural competence of the native speaker, with the result that the *acceptability* judgments which the informant gives are not an accurate reflection of the well-formedness or otherwise of such sentences in his language.

The nature of the problem is emphasised by Chomsky in *Knowledge* (1986a) p. 36, in the following terms:

> Linguistics as a discipline is characterised by attention to certain kinds of evidence that are, for the moment, readily accessible and informative: largely, the judgments of native speakers. Each such judgment is, in fact, the result of an experiment, one that is poorly designed but rich in the evidence it provides. In practice, we tend to operate on the assumption, or pretence, that these informant judgments give us 'direct evidence' as to the structure of the I-language [= internalised language, i.e. language which the speaker has internalised], but, of course, this is only a tentative and inexact working hypothesis, and any skilled practitioner has at his or her disposal an armoury of techniques to help compensate for the errors introduced. In general, informant judgments do not reflect the structure of the language directly; judgments of acceptability, for example, may fail to provide direct evidence as to grammatical status because of the intrusion of numerous other factors. The same is true of other judgments concerning form and meaning.

To summarise: native speakers of a language have the ability to make performance judgments about sentence acceptability. Because of performance factors, these judgments cannot always be taken to be reliable: e.g. what an informant dismisses as an unacceptable sentence may in fact be perfectly well-formed in an appropriate context. By abstracting out known performance factors (using what Chomsky refers to in the quotation above as 'techniques to help compensate for the errors introduced'), the linguist can translate these *acceptability judgments* into the underlying intuitions about sentence well-formedness which provide the key to understanding the nature of competence. To avoid excessive terminological tedium, we shall henceforth assume that we are working with ideal native speakers who are not subject to performance limitations, and hence whose performance directly mirrors their competence, so that their acceptability judgments directly reflect their intuitive knowledge of the well-formedness of sentences: in other words, we shall somewhat naively assume that native speakers make perfect well-formedness judgments about sentences.

However, even if we assume that we are working with ideal speakers who never make performance errors, it can still be extraordinarily difficult to establish in what way(s) an ill-formed sentence is 'odd' – e.g. whether it is pragmatically, semantically, or syntactically 'odd'. It might seem that the natural way to resolve this issue is to appeal to the intuitions of the native speaker. 'Do native speakers feel that such-and-such a sentence is pragmatically, semantically, or syntactically ill-formed?' we might ask. However, as Chomsky has repeatedly emphasised, this is an unrealistic and unreasonable question to ask of an informant: for the simple fact is that very often all an informant can tell you is that one sentence 'sounds OK', and another 'sounds odd' – without being able to say how or why it sounds odd. As Chomsky remarks:

> We may make an intuitive judgement that some linguistic expression is odd or deviant. But we cannot in general know, pretheoretically, whether this deviance is a matter of syntax, semantics, pragmatics, belief, memory limitations, style, etc., or even whether these are appropriate categories for the interpretation of the judgement in question. It is an obvious and uncontroversial fact that informant judgements and other data do not fall neatly into clear categories: syntactic, semantic, etc.
>
> (Chomsky, *Essays* (1977a), p. 4)

Indeed, it is hardly surprising that informants should not be able to tell you whether a sentence is pragmatically, semantically, or syntactically ill-formed: for these very notions are terms borrowed from linguistic theory: and like all

13

theoretical terms, they are meaningless to those not familiar with the theory. An informant simply gives judgments about acceptability, which the linguist translates into judgments about well-formedness: it is up to the linguist to decide, on the basis of the internal organisation of his own theory, what category a particular type of ill-formedness represents within his theory.

Let's clarify the issues involved with some practical examples. Consider the status of a phrase such as:

(16)   an honest geranium

We'd all agree that this is 'odd' in some way – but in what way? The oddity doesn't seem to be *syntactic*: for example, (16) seems to conform to the rules of English word-order (unlike **geranium honest a*). But is the oddity semantic, or pragmatic? Katz and Postal (1964, p. 16) describe the phrase as 'meaningless', thereby implying that it is semantically ill-formed. But this doesn't seem to be right, as most of us would have no difficulty in assigning a meaning to the phrase *an honest geranium*: we might paraphrase it (in typical lexicographical jargon) as 'a flower of the genus pelargonium which is upright in word and deed'. Of course, those narrow-minded bigots (or linguists) who can't imagine geraniums having essentially human properties like 'not telling fibs' would doubtless feign to be mystified by such a phrase. They *ought* to stare in blank incomprehension at the following extract from a fictitious episode of *The Magic Roundabout*:

> Dougal was looking for his dog biscuits. 'Have you been nibbling my Kanine Krunchy-Munchies again?' he asked Gerald the geranium. 'I'm awfully sorry, old chap,' replied Gerald, 'but I was so hungry . . .' 'Oh well,' growled Dougal doggedly, 'at least you're an honest geranium.'

In such a context (i.e. a 'fairy story' context in which one's beliefs about the real world are suspended), such a phrase is clearly meaningful to anyone with a little imagination. But this is precisely the point: whether or not you find a phrase like *an honest geranium* well-formed depends on your powers of imagination, not on any linguistic fact. In other words, the oddity of such a phrase seems to be essentially *pragmatic*.

Let's take another problematic case. What is the status of a sentence like:

(17)   The boy next door never loses her temper with anyone

Many people would find such a sentence unacceptable. But why? We might claim that the oddity here is *syntactic* in nature: that is, the possessive pronoun *her* is feminine, and hence does not agree in gender with its antecedent (i.e. the expression it refers back to), namely the Noun Phrase [*the boy next door*], which is masculine in gender. Or, we might claim that the oddity is *semantic* in nature: thus, part of the meaning of the word *boy* is that it denotes a male human being, whereas part of the meaning of *her* is that it refers to an entity thought of as being female: hence we have a *contradiction* which gives rise to semantic anomaly. So, is sentence (17) semantically or syntactically ill-formed? Well, perhaps neither. After all, (17) would be a perfectly appropriate way of insinuating that [*the boy next door*] denotes an individual who is effeminate. Of course, a person who finds any such insinuation distasteful may well object to such a sentence – but for nonlinguistic reasons.

Now consider the status of expressions such as:

(18)   the christian which we threw to the lions

At first sight, this phrase might seem to be linguistically ill-formed. After all, it violates the rule given by Quirk *et al.* (1985, p. 314) that *which* requires a [NON-PERSONAL] antecedent (i.e. must refer back to an expression which does not denote a person): since christians are people, the rule is obviously flouted here. So, we might say that (18) is *syntactically* ill-formed (because *which* does not 'agree' in gender with *christian*), or that it is *semantically* ill-formed (because *christian* implies that the entity referred to is a person, whereas *which* implies that it is not, so we have a contradiction). But is this the right way of thinking about things? After all, it's easy enough to think of contexts in which (18) would be acceptable. For example, suppose the christian was dead before being thrown to the lions; or suppose that (18) was uttered by a Roman guard who despised christians . . . The fact that it is possible to think of contexts in which (18) would be acceptable suggests that (18) is not a straightforward case of syntactic or semantic ill-formedness.

Much the same point could be made about a phrase such as:

(19)   the tree who we saw

Once again, there is violation of the rule given by Quirk *et al.* (1985, p. 314) that *who* requires a [PERSONAL] antecedent (i.e. must refer back to an expression denoting a person), since trees are not people: so, we might be tempted to conclude that (19) is *ungrammatical* (because *who* doesn't agree in gender with *tree*), or *semantically ill-formed* (because *who* refers to a person, whereas *tree* denotes a non-human object). But this is surely a very myopic view. We might alternatively suggest that the use of *who* referring back to *tree* carries with it the implication that the tree concerned is thought of as having, for example, human qualities (i.e. in traditional terminology, it is 'personified'). As such, (19) would be fully acceptable in a 'fairy story' context (where beliefs about the real world are suspended) – as in the following fictitious extract from *The Magic Forest*:

> The lascivious tree who we saw in the magic forest waved his luxuriant branches lustfully at Mary, and said: 'You can fondle my foliage anytime, darling.'

Support for this way of looking at phrases like (19) (i.e. as grammatical and meaningful, but pragmatically odd in some way) comes from the title of Pamela McCorduck's (1979) book *Machines Who Think* (W. H. Freeman and Co., San Francisco).

The overall point we are making is thus that it can often be very difficult to decide in what way(s) a sentence is ill-formed, or indeed whether it is. As Quirk *et al.* (1985, p. 16) note:

> The borderline between grammar and semantics is unclear, and linguists will draw the line variously ... Similarly, the borderline between grammar and pragmatics (and even more so between semantics and pragmatics) is unclear.

Of course, we have deliberately concentrated on problematic cases here: it should perhaps be underlined that in the vast majority of cases, the distinction between sentences which are pragmatically, semantically, and syntactically odd will be relatively straightforward. Consider, for example, the following:

(20) (a)   John killed the stone
     (b)   John killed Mary, but she didn't die
     (c)   Killed Mary John

Thus, (20) (a) is pragmatically anomalous because it presupposes that the stone was alive at some stage (and most of us don't believe that stones are living entities); hence, (20) (a) would be acceptable only in a fairy-story context where the stone was treated as a living entity. Likewise, (20) (b) is a straightforward case of semantic ill-formedness, because it expresses a contradiction; and (20) (c) is a simple case of ungrammaticality, since English does not permit verb-initial word order in declarative sentences (= statements). Given the distinction between *ungrammaticality* and *semantic ill-formedness*, we have to beware of making (contradictory) statements like: 'Such and such sentence is ungrammatical *because it doesn't make sense*.'

We can summarise our discussion so far in the following terms. The native speaker's competence in his native language(s) is reflected in his intuitions about sentence well-formedness (derived from his acceptability judgments) on the one hand, and his intuitions about sentence-structure on the other. We have discussed in some detail the problems of deciding whether a given sentence is *grammatical* or not, arguing that it is important not to confuse the descriptive notion of *grammaticality* with the corresponding prescriptive notion of *correctness*. We also emphasised the problems of determining whether a sentence is *ungrammatical*, rather than pragmatically or semantically anomalous in some way.

You should now be able to tackle exercises I and II

1.4   Competence as infinite rule-governed creativity

In section 1.2, we argued that native speakers' syntactic competence is reflected in their ability to give judgments about syntactic wellformedness (i.e. grammaticality) on the one hand, and syntactic structure on the other. But the remarkable fact about these abilities – as Chomsky has emphasised in numerous works – is that they hold not only for familiar sentences that we have heard before, but equally for sentences that we have never heard before (or, as Chomsky calls them in his early work, *novel utterances*). Herein lies what Chomsky refers to as the essential *creativity* of language. He remarks:

> The most striking aspect of linguistic competence is what we may call the 'creativity' of language, that is, the speaker's ability to produce new sentences, sentences that are immediately understood by other speakers although they bear no physical resemblance to sentences which are familiar.
>
> (Chomsky, *Topics* (1966), p. 11)

(By *resemblance* here, Chomsky means *identity*: i.e. he is saying that we can produce and understand sentences which are not word-for-word exact repetitions of any sentences we have ever heard before.) To cite one of Chomsky's own examples (from *Logical Structure* 1955 (1975), p. 132), you have probably never encountered any of the following sentences before:

(21) (a)   Look at the cross-eyed elephant
    (b)   Look at the cross-eyed kindness
    (c)   Look at the cross-eyed from

And yet – if you are a speaker of English – you intuitively know that (21) (a) is linguistically well-formed in English (though of course, the zoo-keepers among you might object that it's pragmatically anomalous because elephants can't be cross-eyed!). By contrast, (21) (b) is anomalous, and (21) (c) almost inconceivable. Any native speaker is capable of producing and understanding 'novel utterances' like (21) (a), or making judgments about their acceptability and structure. What is the significance of the fact that all native speakers have the ability to form, interpret, and pronounce sentences that they have not come across before? Chomsky argues that this essential creativity of language shows that language can't simply be learned by imitation: i.e. learning a language doesn't simply involve rote-learning a list of sentences produced by others, and repeating them parrot-fashion. On the contrary, as Chomsky notes:

> The normal use of language is innovative in the sense that much of what we say in the course of normal language use is entirely new, not a repetition of anything that we have heard before, and not even similar in pattern – in any useful sense of the terms 'similar' and 'pattern' – to sentences or discourse that we have heard in the past.
>
> (Chomsky, *Language and Mind* (1972a), p. 12)

The novelty of most utterances that we produce or hear provides a strong argument against the claim made by behavioural psychologists that language-learning simply involves the acquisition of a set of 'linguistic habits'. As Chomsky remarks in *The Listener* (1968, p. 687):

> This creative use of language is quite incompatible with the idea that language is a habit-structure. Whatever a habit-structure is, it's clear that you can't innovate by habit, and the characteristic use of language, both by a speaker and a hearer, is innovative. You're constantly producing new sentences in your lifetime – that's the normal use of language.

So, if language isn't acquired by imitation, how is it acquired? Chomsky argues that in order to account for the native speaker's ability to produce and understand new sentences, we must postulate that the child learning a language and faced with a certain set of data (i.e. the speech of people around him) abstracts from the data a set of general principles about how sentences are formed, interpreted, and pronounced. These principles (or *rules*) must be of a sufficiently general nature to allow the child to form, interpret, and pronounce new sentences that he hasn't come across before. In other words, acquisition of a language involves acquisition of (*inter alia*) the following:

(22) (i)   a set of *syntactic* rules which specify how sentences are built up out of phrases, and phrases out of words

(ii)   a set of *morphological* rules which specify how words are built up out of morphemes (i.e. grammatical units smaller than the word)

(iii)   a set of *phonological* rules which specify how words, phrases, and sentences are pronounced

(iv)   a set of *semantic* rules which specify how words, phrases, and sentences are interpreted (i.e. what their meaning is)

This is what Chomsky means by saying that language is *rule-governed*. The task of the linguist in seeking to account for this creative aspect of grammatical competence is thus to formulate appropriate sets of syntactic, morphological, phonological, and semantic rules.

In Chomsky's view, then, acquiring a language involves formulating an appropriate set of syntactic, morphological, phonological, and semantic rules. But is there any evidence that language acquisition is indeed *rule-governed*? Some evidence in support of this assumption comes from studies of child language acquisition. Jean Berko in her (1958) paper 'The child's learning of English morphology' describes a simple experiment designed to prove the point. She showed a group of children a picture of an imaginary animal, and told them that it was called a *wug*; she then showed them a picture of two of the same animals, and asked them what they were. The children replied 'Wugs'. The significance of this was that the children had produced the plural form, even though they could never have heard the plural form *wugs* before, since this was an invented nonsense word. What does this tell us? The only way to account for the elicitation of the form *wugs* is to assume that on the basis of hearing pairs such as *dog–dogs, log–logs, rod–rods, flood–floods*, etc., the children formulate a morphological rule which in effect says 'You form the plural of Nouns by adding an -*s* on the end.'

Another source of evidence supporting the conclusion that children learn language by formulating a set of rules comes from *errors* that they produce. A case in point are overgeneralised past tense forms like *comed, goed, seed, buyed, bringed*, etc. frequently used by young children. Such forms cannot have been learned by imitation of adult speech, since they do not occur in adult speech (instead, we find *came, went, saw, bought, brought*). So how is it that children produce such forms? The obvious answer is that, on the basis of pairs such as *love–loved, close–closed, use–used*, etc., the child formulates for himself a rule to the effect that 'You form the past tense by adding -(*e*)*d* to the stem of the verb'; the rule is then overgeneralised to 'irregular' verbs like *come, go, see, buy, bring*, etc.

The observations above suggest that children learn morphology (i.e. to construct past tenses, plural forms, etc.) by formulating for themselves (albeit

19

subconsciously) a set of morphological rules. There is parallel evidence that the same is also true of Syntax. For example, Akmajian and Heny (1975, p. 17) report one three-year-old girl producing direct yes–no questions like:

(23) (a) Is I can do that?
   (b) Is you should eat the apple?
   (c) Is Ben did go?
   (d) Is the apple juice won't spill?

Clearly, no adult English speaker would produce sentences like (23). So how does the child come to produce them? The obvious answer is that on the basis of sentences such as:

(24) (a) Is daddy staying out tonight?
   (b) Is Uncle Harry spending the night here?
   (c) Is mummy going shopping again?

the child formulates for herself a rule to the effect that 'You form a question by putting *is* as the first word in the sentence.' Of course, the rule is 'wrong' to the extent that it doesn't correspond to the adult rule, and will be corrected at a later stage of acquisition by the child. But these 'novel utterances' produced by young children provide strong evidence that acquiring a language does indeed involve acquiring a set of linguistic rules – and hence that language is indeed *rule-governed*.

A further illustration of children formulating rules of their own comes from the speech of my own daughter; between the ages of 48 and 54 months, she consistently produced sentences such as:

(25) (a) I can't *undone* it
   (b) I want daddy to *undone* it for me
   (c) Will you *undone* it for me?

Equally revealing is the following conversation between her and me when she was 49 months of age:

(26)   Suzy: Don't make me lost it
           Daddy: No, don't make me *lose* it
           Suzy: No, not *lose* . . . *losed*!

It is quite clear that she is systematically replacing adult infinitives by perfective/passive participles: she seems to have formulated for herself a rule to the effect that all nonfinite clauses in English contain participles. Once again, it is clear that sentences like (25) cannot have been produced by imitation of any adult pattern, since they do not occur in adult speech. Rather,

Suzy is formulating rules of her own – 'guessing' at the rules of sentence-formation for English, and occasionally making the 'wrong guess', and hence producing sentences which are ungrammatical in adult speech. Another of Suzy's 'creations' from the same period is the following sentence-type (which lasted for about three months):

(27)   What was that noise was?

What seems to be going on here is that she has confused statements like (28) (a) below with the corresponding question (28) (b):

(28) (a)   That noise was the television
     (b)   What was that noise?

Thus, on the basis of (28) (a) she has formulated a rule to the effect that Verbs like *was* are positioned after subject expressions like [*that noise*]; and on the basis of (28) (b) she has devised a rule that Verbs like *was* are positioned before their subjects in questions. In producing her question (27), she seems to have applied both rules, and thus positions *was* both before and after the subject [*that noise*]. What she hasn't yet learned is that in adult grammar, the 'question rule' over-rides and cancels the 'after-the-subject' rule which applies in statements.

   To summarise: there is a certain amount of evidence from studies of child language acquisition that learning a language involves learning a set of syntactic, semantic, morphological, phonological, etc. rules. The *grammatical competence* of the fluent native speaker of a language is therefore characterisable in terms of just such a system of rules of sentence-formation, sentence-interpretation, sentence-pronunciation, and so forth. In the words of Chomsky:

> The person who has acquired knowledge of a language has internalised a system of rules that relate sound and meaning in a particular way. The linguist constructing a grammar of a language is in effect proposing a hypothesis concerning the internalised system.
>
> (Chomsky, *Language and Mind* (1972), p. 29)

We can introduce some technical terminology here. A grammar incorporating an explicitly formulated set of syntactic, semantic, morphological, and phonological rules which specify how to form, interpret, and pronounce a given set of sentences is said to *generate* that set of sentences. Such a grammar is called a *generative grammar*. For a grammar to be adequate, it must *generate* (i.e. specify how to form, interpret, and pronounce) *all and only the well-formed*

Goals

sentences of the language (i.e. the grammar must generate all the well-formed sentences, and no ill-formed sentences).

But this raises the question of how many well-formed sentences there are in a given language. Chomsky argues that the set of well-formed sentences in any natural language is *infinite*. This follows from the fact that there is no theoretical upper limit on the length of sentences in any language (though there are of course *performance* limitations – e.g. you might die before you finished a sentence of more than a million words!). For example, we can have indefinitely many Adjectives qualifying a Noun in English, so that in (29) below, the Noun *man* can be modified by a potentially infinite number of italicised Adjectives:

(29) (a) John is a *handsome* man
     (b) John is a *dark, handsome* man
     (c) John is a *tall, dark, handsome* man
     (d) John is a *sensitive, tall, dark, handsome* man
     (e) John is an *intelligent, sensitive, tall, dark, handsome* man
     (f) Etc.

And likewise, we can have indefinitely many Prepositional Phrases modifying a Noun: thus, in (30) below, each of the italicised Prepositional Phrases modifies the Noun *girl*:

(30) (a) I like the girl *in jeans*
     (b) I like the girl *in jeans with long hair*
     (c) I like the girl *in jeans with long hair at the back of the room*
     (d) I like the girl *in jeans with long hair at the back of the room on the stage*
     (e) Etc.

Nor is there any limit on the number of *that*-clauses we can string together in a sentence:

(31) (a) John said *that Mary was ill*
     (b) Fred said *that John said that Mary was ill*
     (c) Harry said *that Fred said that John said that Mary was ill*
     (d) Etc.

And there is no limit on the number of expressions we can conjoin together by *and* (or *or*):

(32) (a) I like *Madonna*, and *Tina Turner*
     (b) I like *Madonna*, and *Tina Turner*, and *Joan Collins*
     (c) I like *Madonna*, and *Tina Turner*, and *Joan Collins*, and *Bo Derek*,

22

and *Glynis Barber*, and *Debbie Harry*, and *Samantha Fox*, and *Kim Wilde* . . . (etc.: fill in as appropriate!)

In other words, given any sentence of English, we can always form a longer one by adding another Adjective, Prepositional Phrase, Clause, Adverb, Conjunct, etc. In consequence, it is literally true that there is an infinite set of well-formed sentences in English (or any other natural language, for that matter). And the native speaker is capable of making acceptability judgments about any of these; hence, his competence ranges over an infinite set of sentences. And yet, this infinite competence is acquired on the basis of a finite experience (i.e. a child learns a language in a finite period of time, on the basis of having been exposed to a finite sample of speech), as Chomsky observes:

> A speaker of a language has observed a certain limited set of utterances in his language. On the basis of this finite linguistic experience, he can produce an infinite number of new utterances which are immediately acceptable to other members of his speech community.
>
> (Chomsky, *Logical Structure*, 1955 (1975), p. 6)

Thus, the task of the linguist devising a grammar which models the linguistic competence of the fluent native speaker is to devise a *finite* set of rules which are capable of specifying how to form, interpret, and pronounce an *infinite* set of well-formed sentences.

1.5   Discovering the rules

In the previous section, we argued that acquiring competence in a language involves acquiring a finite set of rules which generate (i.e. tell you how to form, pronounce, and interpret) an infinite set of sentences. But how do we establish what the rules are? It might seem that the obvious approach is to ask a native speaker what the rules are which he has internalised, and which enable him to speak and understand his language fluently. But this is not of course possible, because the speaker has only *tacit* (i.e. subconscious) knowledge of the rules, and cannot bring them to consciousness: as Chomsky remarks:

> A person who knows a language has mastered a system of rules that assigns sound and meaning in a definite way for an infinite class of sentences ... Of course, the person who knows the language has no consciousness of having mastered these rules or of putting them to use, nor is there any reason to suppose that this knowledge of the rules can be brought to consciousness.
>
> (Chomsky, *Language and Mind* (1972a), pp. 103–4)

So, if we cannot get direct evidence about the nature of linguistic rules by asking native speakers what the rules are, how can we establish what they are? The linguist who asks this question is in essentially the same position as the physicist who wants to study the laws (i.e. rules) which determine the motion of the planets. Of course, the laws of planetary motion are not themselves directly observable: only the effects produced by the operation of the laws can be observed. So, the physicist who wants to determine what these laws are has to proceed indirectly: i.e. first collect a set of data about the observed motion of the planets, then hypothesise principles which might explain this motion. The linguist is in an exactly parallel position, and has therefore to proceed in the same way, namely:

(33) (i) collect a set of data relevant to the phenomena being studied
  (ii) hypothesise a set of principles (i.e. rules) which account for the data
  (iii) test the hypothesised rule(s) against further data

Natural questions to ask are: 'What counts as *data*? How do you collect *data*?' There are two different types of data which linguists typically work with in formulating grammars. The first is a recorded sample of speech or text (such a sample is known technically as a *corpus of utterances*); we assume (perhaps simplistically) that in general people speak and write well-formed sentences. The second type of data that linguists work with are *informant intuitions*: for example, we might ask a Swahili speaker questions like: 'Can you say '—' in Swahili? If so, what does it mean? What's the corresponding negative? What effect does it have if I alter the word-order?', and so forth. The purpose of these questions is to attempt to *elicit* well-formedness judgments from the native speaker, and so the relevant technique is known as *elicitation*. There are lengthy, but rather sterile debates in the linguistic literature about which is the 'best' method of collecting data. The most commonly used method these days is elicitation, though for practical purposes most linguists accept that it is sensible to use both types of data, and to check one against the other.

Suppose that we have now collected our data, and want to analyse it. How do we determine what are the explanatory principles which account for the data? Unfortunately, there is no known set of inductive procedures which the linguist (or anyone else) can apply to a given set of data to find generalisations. The simple answer is that you have to make an intelligent, informed 'guess' about what principle or rule might be needed to account for a particular phenomenon (linguists like to intellectualise their endeavours by talking about *formulating hypotheses* rather than 'making guesses', however!).

To avoid the discussion becoming excessively abstract, let's take a concrete example. Suppose we are interested in the use of *reflexives* in English – i.e. *-self* forms such as *myself/yourself/himself/herself/itself/ourselves/yourselves/ themselves*. How do we go about 'discovering' the rules or principles which determine how we use and interpret reflexives? Well, we begin by collecting examples of sentences in which reflexives can and can't be used, and we then try and formulate some principle which determines when they are used. For example, suppose we collect pairs of sentences such as the following:

(34) (a)   The government won't commit *itself*

    (b)   *Itself won't be committed

We might then ask ourselves why it's OK to use the reflexive *itself* in (34) (a), but not in (34) (b). An obvious answer would be that the word *itself* refers back to the expression *the government* in (34) (a), but has nothing to refer back to in (34) (b). We might then suggest that reflexives like *itself* can't have *independent reference* (i.e. they cannot be used to refer directly to entities in the outside world), but rather have to take their reference from some other linguistic expression. In traditional grammar, the expression which a reflexive refers to (or takes its reference from) is called the *antecedent* of the reflexive. So, one tentative principle concerning the use of reflexives might be formulated along the following lines:

(35)   Reflexives cannot have independent reference, but require an *antecedent* to take their reference from

Given the 'rule' which we have suggested in (35), it follows that (34) (a) is perfectly well-formed, because the reflexive *itself* has an antecedent in the form of the expression [*the government*]; whereas (34) (b) will be ill-formed, because there is no antecedent for *itself*.

Well, having formulated a simple rule to account for the use of reflexives, we now go on to collect new data about sentences in which reflexives can and can't be used, and 'test' our rule against this new data, and against our existing data as well. For example, suppose that our new data tells us that sentences such as the following are ill-formed:

(36)   *Some governments won't commit itself

At first sight, there might seem to be no reason to expect that (36) should be ill-formed: after all, why can't the expression [*some governments*] serve as the antecedent for the reflexive *itself*? Well, the answer seems to be that [*some governments*] is (in some way or other) not *compatible* with *itself*. But in what way? Traditional grammarians would argue that the two expressions differ with respect to their grammatical *number*: that is, *itself* is *singular in number*, whereas [*some governments*] is *plural* in number. So, we might suppose that a reflexive has to refer back to an antecedent which is *compatible* with it in respect of grammatical *number* (singular/plural). In the light of this observation, we might revise our earlier rule (35) above along the lines of (37) below:

(37)   Reflexives cannot have independent reference, but require a *compatible antecedent* to take their reference from

Since the expression [*some governments*] is plural in (36), it is not compatible with (and hence cannot be the antecedent of) the singular reflexive *itself*. But since there is no other possible antecedent for *itself* in the sentence, (36) is ruled out as an ill-formed sentence by virtue of the fact that it violates the requirement in (37) for reflexives to have a compatible antecedent.

Now that we've come up with our 'new' rule (37), we might test it against 'new' data such as (38) below:

(38) (a)   *He won't commit itself
(b)   *She won't commit itself

For some reason, it seems that a reflexive like *itself* isn't compatible with expressions like *he* or *she*. Why should this be? Traditional grammarians argue that the incompatibility is one of *gender*: that is, it is traditionally said that *he* is an expression which is *masculine* in gender, *she* is *feminine* in gender, and *itself* is *neuter* in gender (though many grammarians prefer to replace the term *neuter* by alternatives such as 'inanimate', 'non-personal', or 'non-human'). If this is so, then we might suppose that *he* and *she* cannot serve as the antecedent of *itself* because they are incompatible in *gender* with the reflexive. In other words, we might suppose that a reflexive must be compatible in both *number* and *gender* with its antecedent.

But is compatibility of number and gender enough? Sentences such as the following suggest that it is not:

(39) (a)   They congratulated themselves
(b)   *We congratulated themselves
(c)   *You congratulated themselves

Since *they* and *we* are plural expressions, and since *you* can function as a plural expression, there is no *number* incompatibility here between the plural reflexive *themselves* and the forms *they/we/you*. Moreover, since *themselves* can be masculine, feminine, or neuter in gender, there is no *gender* incompatibility either. And yet, *themselves* can refer back to *they*, but not to *we* or *you*. Why? The traditional answer is that expressions such as *we*, *you*, and *they* differ in grammatical *person*. More precisely, expressions which refer to the speaker (e.g. *I*) or include the speaker in their reference (e.g. *we*) are said to be *first person* expressions: those which refer to the person(s) being addressed or a group of people including the person(s) being addressed but excluding the speaker (i.e. *you*) are said to be *second person forms*; and expressions which refer to some individual(s) other than the speaker or addressee are called *third person* forms. Using this terminology, we might say about (39) that the reflexive *themselves* is a *third person* form and hence is compatible only with a *third person* expression such as *they*, and not with a *first person* form such as *we*, or a *second person* form such as *you*. If this is so, then it follows that the antecedent of a reflexive must be compatible with the reflexive in *number*, *gender*, and *person*. Hence, we might revise our earlier rule (37) above along the lines of (40) below:

(40)   Reflexives cannot have independent reference, but must take their reference from an antecedent which is *compatible in number, gender, and person* with the reflexive

In actual fact, we could easily demonstrate that there are numerous other conditions which need to be built into our provisional REFLEXIVE RULE (40), and in later chapters we shall revise the rule accordingly. But that is not the point of our discussion. The point we have been making is a methodological one, relating to the question of how we 'discover' the rules which underlie the native speaker's competence. What the linguist does is collect a set of data relevant to a particular aspect of competence, formulate a hypothesis, test the hypothesis against further data, modify the hypothesis as necessary, test it against yet more data . . . and so on and so forth. By repeating this process time and again for a range of different phenomena, the linguist gradually builds up a set of rules of sentence formation, pronunciation, and interpretation which form the basis of his eventual *grammar* of the language.

You should now be able to tackle exercises III and IV

1.6   Levels of adequacy

We can summarise what we've said so far in the following terms. A Grammar is a model of the grammatical competence of the native speaker of a language. It comprises a finite system of rules which generate (i.e. specify how to form, interpret, and pronounce) the infinite set of well-formed sentence-structures in the language. Accordingly, the task of the linguist devising a particular grammar is to formulate a finite system of rules of sentence-formation, interpretation, and pronunciation that will generate the infinite set of well-formed sentences in the language.

One theoretical question which we have not so far addressed ourselves to, however, is how you know whether the grammar you propose for a particular language is adequate or not. Chomsky has proposed a number of *criteria of adequacy* for grammars (and for the linguistic theories associated with them). The weakest requirement for any grammar of a language is that it attain *observational adequacy*: this we might define as follows:

(41)   A grammar of a language is *observationally adequate* if it correctly specifies which sentences are (and are not) syntactically, semantically, morphologically, and phonologically well-formed in the language.

A higher level of adequacy is *descriptive adequacy*, which we can define as:

(42)   A grammar of a language is *descriptively adequate* if it correctly specifies which sentences are (and are not) syntactically, semantically, morphologically, and phonologically well-formed in the language, *and also* properly describes the syntactic, semantic, morphological, and phonological structure of the sentences in the language in such a way as to provide a principled account of the native speaker's intuitions about this structure

We can illustrate the differences between *observational* and *descriptive* adequacy in Syntax in terms of the following example:

(43)   These boys don't like those girls

Any grammar of English which specifies that the sequence of words in (43) forms a grammatical sentence of English would attain observational adequacy (at least, in respect of this one example!). To attain descriptive adequacy, the grammar would have to specify in addition what the syntactic structure of the sentence (43) is – i.e. it would have to specify that *these* modifies *boys* and not *girls*, and that *those* modifies *girls* and not *don't* . . . and so on and so forth.

While it might seem obvious enough how we evaluate the adequacy of grammars of particular languages, it is less immediately obvious by what criteria we judge the adequacy of linguistic theories. Before attempting to answer this question, perhaps we should first remind ourselves of the relationship between *grammars of languages* and a *theory of language*. A theory of language is essentially a set of hypotheses about the nature of possible and impossible grammars of natural languages: e.g. a linguistic theory answers questions like: 'What kind of theoretical constructs (e.g. types of rules or principles) are necessary to describe the Phonology, Morphology, Syntax, and Semantics of natural languages?' Given this, it seems that one obvious condition which has to be imposed on any adequate linguistic theory is that it should attain *universality*: in other words, it should provide us with a powerful enough theoretical apparatus to enable us to describe the grammar of any natural language adequately: thus, a linguistic theory would be totally inadequate if it enabled us to describe English and French, but not Swahili or Chinese. So, what we mean by saying that an adequate linguistic theory must attain *universality* is that it must be able to provide us with a *descriptively adequate grammar* for every natural language.

However, recall that one of the questions we want our theory of language to be able to answer is how natural languages differ from artificial languages on the one hand, and from animal communication systems on the other. It therefore follows that the theoretical constructs provided by our theory for the formulation of natural language grammars must not be so powerful that they can be used to describe not only natural languages, but also computer languages, or animal languages (since any such excessively powerful theory wouldn't be able to pinpoint the essential defining differences between natural language and other types of language). In other words, a second condition which we have to impose on our theory of language is that it be *maximally constrained*: that is, we want our theory to provide us with technical devices which are so restricted in their expressive power that they can only be used to describe human languages, and are not appropriate for the description of other communication systems. Any such *constrained* (i.e. restricted) theory would then enable us to characterise the very essence of human language.

A third condition which any adequate linguistic theory must meet is that of *psychological reality*. Why so? Well, recall Chomsky's claim (cited at the very beginning of this chapter) that our reason for studying language is that language is a mirror of the mind, so that by analysing language we hope to learn something about the way the mind produces and processes language. In the terminology introduced by Chomsky in *Knowledge* (1986a, pp. 19–56), we're studying language as an *internalised* system, as a product of the human brain/mind; our ultimate goal is to characterise the nature of the internalised linguistic system (or *I-language*, as Chomsky terms it) which enables humans to speak and understand their native language. This *I-language* Chomsky takes to have some (as yet undiscovered) physical realisation in terms of brain mechanisms; thus, for Chomsky, the ultimate aim is to uncover the neurophysiological mechanisms which make language possible. But once we commit ourselves to the study of language as an *internalised* phenomenon (i.e. as a product of the human mind/brain), then we thereby commit ourselves to developing a theory of language which is based on principles which are psychologically plausible. In other words, it's no good developing a linguistic theory which makes use of technical devices which are not compatible with known neurophysiological mechanisms.

We might subsume these three conditions which we have imposed on a theory of language under the term *explanatory adequacy*. What we mean by saying that a theory must attain the level of *explanatory adequacy* is (in effect) that a theory must explain why grammars contain certain types of technical devices and not others; it must explain what exactly are the defining characteristics of human languages that differentiate them from other communication systems; and it must explain how it is that human beings come to acquire their native languages. Accordingly, we might define the term *explanatory adequacy* as follows:

(44)   A linguistic theory attains *explanatory adequacy* just in case it provides a descriptively adequate grammar for every natural language, and does so in terms of a maximally constrained set of universal principles which represent psychologically plausible natural principles of mental computation

Thus, to attain explanatory adequacy, a theory must in effect be *universally valid*, *psychologically real*, and *maximally constrained*.

1.7   Constraining grammars

We saw in the previous section that for any linguistic theory to achieve explanatory adequacy it must be maximally constrained. But what does it mean for a linguistic theory to be *constrained*? And why should a theory have to be *constrained* in any case?

To understand this, let's look at the problems associated with the alternative – namely, a totally *unconstrained* theory. In such a theory, where no constraints are put on what could be a 'possible syntactic rule of some grammar of some language', there would be no reason not to expect to find some language whose grammar contained a syntactic rule along the lines of:

(45)   Invert any word beginning with /p/ with any word meaning 'tree' or 'car' on Sundays after 6 p.m. in a leap year

And yet no linguist describing any language has ever proposed any syntactic rule even remotely resembling (45): and in fact all of us would agree, I'm sure, that we would want to rule out (45) as an 'impossible rule' in any grammar of any language. But this amounts to saying that we want to *constrain* our theory in such a way as to ban rules like (45) as universally 'impossible'.

But what's wrong with (45) – i.e. how can we constrain our theory so as to bar such rules? One obvious thing that seems to be wrong with (45) is that here we have a syntactic rule whose application depends on *pragmatic* information (in this case, information about the date and time when a sentence is uttered). So, one way of banning rules like (45) would be to build into our linguistic theory the following *constraint*:

(46)   No syntactic rule can make reference to pragmatic information

However, condition (46) is not strong enough, since it would not preclude 'absurd' rules like:

(47)   Invert any word beginning with /p/ with any word meaning 'tree' or 'car'

How can we rule out (47)? One possibility would be to suggest a constraint along the lines of:

(48)   No syntactic rule can make reference to phonological information (e.g. whether or not a word beings with /p/)

But even (48) would fail to rule out intuitively implausible rules like:

(49)   Invert any word meaning 'tree' with any word meaning 'car'

How can we ban (49) as an 'impossible' rule? One answer would be in terms of a constraint along the lines of:

(50)   No syntactic rule can make reference to semantic information

Conflating the three constraints (46), (48), and (50) gives us:

(51)   AUTONOMOUS SYNTAX PRINCIPLE
             No syntactic rule can make reference to pragmatic, phonological, or semantic information

This principle is defended at length in Chomsky's *Essays* (1977a), pp. 36–59 (not for the faint-hearted!). Chomsky repeatedly emphasises that this claim is an *empirical* one – i.e. a working hypothesis to be judged solely on the basis of whether it leads to interesting generalisations about language: cf. his remarks in *Essays* (1977a), p. 42:

> The thesis ... constitutes an empirical hypothesis about the organisation of language, leaving ample scope for systematic form–meaning connections while excluding many imaginable possibilities.

As a further illustration of ways in which we might propose to *constrain* syntactic rules, consider the problem of how to deal with 'inversion' in direct questions. The difference between a simple declarative (=statement) like (52) (a) below, and the corresponding interrogative (=question) (52) (b):

(52) (a)   *John will* get the prize
     (b)   *Will John* get the prize?

lies in the relative order of the italicised words: we might say that the question counterpart of (52) (a) is formed by 'inverting' the two italicised words. One way in which we might seek to formulate the relevant 'inversion' rule might be along the lines of (53) below:

(53)   SECOND WORD PREPOSING
         Move the second word in a sentence in front of the first word

A rule such as (53) operates independently of the syntactic structure of the sentence, in the sense that you don't need to know what the syntactic structure of the sentence is (i.e. which words modify which other words, and which words belong to which categories) in order to apply the rule. Hence, a rule like (53) might be called a *structure-independent* rule. Now, it's easy enough to show that a rule such as (53) would fail to achieve observational adequacy in anything but the most elementary cases: for example, it would wrongly predict that the interrogative counterpart of (54) (a) below would be (54) (b):

(54) (a)   The boy will get the prize
     (b)   *Boy the will get the prize

Why doesn't rule (53) work? The most principled answer is that languages simply don't work like that: that is to say, we might impose a constraint to the effect that languages never contain structure-independent rules. This constraint might be formulated along the following lines:

(55)   STRUCTURE-DEPENDENCE PRINCIPLE
         All grammatical rules are structure-dependent

And we might assume that (55) is a basic principle of our Theory of Language, so that (55) holds for all grammars of all natural languages.

But what exactly does it mean to say that a rule is *structure-dependent*? Well, by way of example, consider how we might handle *inversion* in questions like (52) (b) in terms of a structure-dependent rule. One such rule which we might propose is the following:

(56)   NP–AUX INVERSION
         Invert a Noun Phrase (=NP) with an immediately following Auxiliary Verb (=AUX)

A rule like (56) is *structure-dependent* in the sense that you can't apply the rule to a given sentence unless you know what the syntactic structure of the sentence is, and what *grammatical categories* the words and phrases in the sentence belong to. For example, in order to know whether we can apply rule (56) in a sentence, we need to know whether the sentence contains an expression belonging to the category Noun Phrase immediately followed by an expression belonging to the category Auxiliary Verb (these are technical terms which we'll explain in the next chapter, so don't worry if you don't know what they mean). In (52) (a), *John* is an NP (i.e. Noun Phrase, or Noun expression), and it is indeed immediately followed by an AUX (= Auxiliary Verb), since *will* is traditionally described as a 'Modal Auxiliary Verb' in English (cf. chapter 3 for a full discussion of this terminology). Thus, our structure-dependent rule (56) correctly predicts that (52) (b) is the interrogative counterpart of (52) (a). And likewise, it correctly predicts that the interrogative counterpart of (54) (a) is *Will the boy get the prize?'* in which we have an NP (= the Noun Phrase [*the boy*]) inverted with an immediately following AUX (= the Modal Auxiliary Verb *will*). Hence, the structure-dependent account makes correct predictions about both sets of sentences.

But no less importantly, our structure-dependent rule (56) also correctly predicts that inversion is not possible in cases such as those below:

(57) (a)   Down will come taxes
     (b)   *Will down come taxes?
(58) (a)   John received a prize
     (b)   *Received John a prize?

In (57) (a) we have the prepositional expression *down* immediately followed by the Auxiliary *will*; whereas in (58) (a) we have the Noun expression *John* immediately followed by the non-Auxiliary Verb ('full Verb') *received*. Since in neither case do we have the required (NP AUX . . .) sequence, then our structure-dependent rule (56) correctly predicts that inversion cannot take place here. By contrast, our structure-independent rule (53) wrongly predicts that inversion is possible in both cases.

So, the phenomenon of 'inversion' in questions provides us with clear empirical (i.e. factual) evidence in support of constraining all grammatical rules in terms of the STRUCTURE-DEPENDENCE PRINCIPLE (55), which stipulates that all grammatical rules are sensitive to the structure of the sentences they apply to. If we incorporate the principle (55) into our Theory of Language, then we thereby impose a very restrictive constraint on the nature of 'possible' and 'impossible' rules in natural language grammars. For, given the constraint that all grammatical rules (or *grammatical transformations*, to adopt the terminology used by Chomsky in the quotation immediately below) must be structure-dependent, it follows that:

> Only certain kinds of formal operations on strings [viz. of words] can appear in grammars – operations that, furthermore, have no a priori justification. For example, the permitted operations cannot be shown in any sense to be the most 'simple' or 'elementary' ones that might be invented. In fact, what might in general be considered 'elementary operations' on strings do not qualify as grammatical transformations at all, while many of the operations that do qualify are far from elementary, in any general sense. Specifically, grammatical transformations are necessarily 'structure-dependent' in that they manipulate substrings only in terms of their assignments to categories. Thus it is possible to formulate a transformation that can insert . . . the Auxiliary Verb to the left of a Noun Phrase that precedes it, independently of what the length or internal complexity of the strings belonging to these categories may be. It is impossible, however, to formulate as a transformation such a simple operation as reflection of an arbitrary string [viz. speaking a sentence backwards] . . . or interchange of the $(2n-1)^{th}$ word with the $2n^{th}$ word [viz. interchanging odd and even words], or insertion of a symbol in the middle of a string of even length.
>
> (Chomsky, *Aspects* (1965), pp. 55–6)

Thus, any Theory of Language incorporating the STRUCTURE-DEPENDENCE PRINCIPLE (55) imposes very strong constraints on the notion 'possible grammatical rule'.

1.8 Constraints, universals, and acquisition

Even if the idea of constraining a grammar or theory is relatively easy to understand, we might still ask *why* it is important to do so. Chomsky's answer is that only a maximally constrained theory of language can lead to the development of an adequate theory of language acquisition. That is, he argues that we can only explain the phenomenon of language acquisition in children if we assume that grammars contain a highly constrained set of principles, and that the child is born with a 'language faculty' which innately endows him with the knowledge of what these principles are which determine the nature of 'possible' and 'impossible' linguistic rules and structures. Chomsky's belief that the language faculty is 'narrowly constrained' is affirmed (for example) in the following sentence from *Knowledge* (1986a), p. 43:

The language faculty appears to be, at its core, a computational system that is rich and narrowly constrained in structure and rigid in its essential operations.

But why should we conclude that the language faculty is heavily constrained, simply in order to account for the rapidity of language acquisition? Chomsky argues that the evidence which the child has to rely on in acquiring his native language (= the speech of those around him) is *degenerate* (i.e. incomplete and imperfect). In consequence, the linguistic rules which the child attempts to formulate are *underdetermined* by this evidence: that is, the evidence on its own is not sufficient for the child to be able to work out the relevant rules.

So, how does the child devise an appropriate set of rules, if not on the basis of the evidence of the speech around him alone? Chomsky's answer is that the child must have 'genetic help', in the sense that he is born (i.e. genetically endowed) with some *Language Acquisition Device* (LAD) or *Language Faculty* which provides an abstract specification of the range of possible and impossible rules and structures in natural language. Given the linguistic knowledge that this Language Acquisition Device endows the child with, he is able to discount some potential rules as 'linguistically impossible'. For example, Chomsky argues that the STRUCTURE-DEPENDENCE PRINCIPLE (which specifies that all grammatical rules are structure-dependent) is part of the innate system of biologically endowed principles of Universal Grammar which constitute the human 'Language Faculty'. Thus he remarks that:

> The reliance on structure-dependent operations must be predetermined for the language-learner by a restrictive initial schematism of some sort that directs his attempts to acquire linguistic competence.
>
> (Chomsky, *Language and Mind* (1972a), p. 63)

(NB 'initial' here is used in the sense of *innate*.) If this is so, then the child would be born with the knowledge that there are no structure-independent rules in natural language grammars. This innate linguistic knowledge considerably reduces the acquisition burden placed on the child, and makes it possible for him to acquire his native language in what is (bearing in mind the complexity of human language) a relatively short period of time (a few years).

But if human beings are genetically 'preprogrammed' with a Language Faculty which provides some 'blueprint' of the range of possible grammars of natural languages, how can we determine just what kind of linguistic information might be contained in that 'genetic blueprint'? Chomsky argues that the key to this question lies in the study of *Universal Grammar* (UG) – i.e. in the search for linguistic universals. For, if there are genetic constraints on the form of grammars of natural languages, then we should expect that all languages will share certain universal properties in common – properties determined by these genetic constraints. Hence, if we discover abstract universal properties of language which cannot plausibly be accounted for in other terms, it seems reasonable (in Chomsky's view) to conclude that these universals must be part of the innate, biologically endowed Language Acquisition Device that the child is born with. But if the child is born with an innate knowledge of universals, then clearly those properties of language which are universal (and hence innate) do not have to be acquired by the child; the child's acquisition task is reduced to that of mastering the idiosyncratic, language-particular properties of the target language, on the basis of his linguistic *experience* (i.e. on the basis of the speech he hears around him). Thus, the answer to the question of how language is acquired

> is given by a specification of UG along with an account of the ways in which its principles interact with experience to yield a particular language: UG is a theory of the 'initial state' of the language faculty, prior to any linguistic experience.
>
> (Chomsky, *Knowledge* (1986a), pp. 3–4)

The position that the child has an innate knowledge of Universal Grammar (UG) is popularly known as the *Innateness Hypothesis*. Chomsky's belief in this hypothesis (and in an intimate connection between UG (= Universal Grammar) and the biologically endowed LAD (= Language Acquisition Device)) has been consistently reaffirmed over the years, as the following quotations illustrate:

> I think it reasonable to postulate that the principles of general linguistics regarding the nature of rules, their organisation, the principles by which they function, the kinds of representations to which they apply and which they form, all constitute part of the innate condition that 'puts a limit on admissible hypotheses'. If this suggestion is correct, then there is no more point in asking how these principles are learned than there is in asking how a child learns to breathe, or, for that matter, to have two arms.
>
> (Chomsky, *Language and Mind* (1972a), p. 171)

> In many cases that have been carefully studied in recent work, it is a near certainty that fundamental properties of the attained grammars are radically underdetermined by evidence available to the language learner and must therefore be attributed to UG [Universal Grammar] itself.
>
> (Chomsky, *Lectures* (1981d), p. 3)

UG may be regarded as a characterisation of the genetically-determined language faculty. One may think of this faculty as a 'language acquisition device', an innate component of the human mind that yields a particular language through interaction with presented experience, a device that converts experience into a system of knowledge attained: knowledge of one or other language.

(Chomsky, *Knowledge* (1986a), p. 3)

The inter-relatedness of universals and innate knowledge leads to the (seemingly paradoxical) conclusion that we can uncover universal properties of language by detailed studies of Particular Grammar (i.e. of the grammar of one particular language). Chomsky reasons that whatever knowledge a native speaker has about his language which he cannot have acquired through experience must be attributable to innate knowledge; and whatever is innate must therefore be universal (at least, if we assume that the innate language faculty does not vary significantly from one individual to another). We can make the discussion less abstract by returning to consider our earlier pair of examples (5), repeated here as (59) below:

(59) (a)   I wonder who *the men* expected to see *them*
 (b)   *The men* expected to see *them*

In the first example, the pronoun *them* can be interpreted as referring to *the men*, but not in the second example. Chomsky argues that neither children acquiring English as their first language nor those learning it as a second language have to learn the principles governing the interpretation of pronouns in such cases. He asks rhetorically (*Knowledge* (1986a), p. 8) 'How does every child know, unerringly, to interpret the clause differently in the two cases? And why does no pedagogic grammar have to draw the learner's attention to such facts?' The implicit answer is that the relevant principles of interpretation are innate, and hence 'known without relevant experience'.

A further apparent paradox which follows from these assumptions about UG is that 'the study of one language may provide crucial evidence concerning the structure of some other language' (Chomsky, *Knowledge* (1986a), p. 37). How can this be? Given that we are interested in developing a *universal* theory of language, then the resultant theory has to be compatible with all known facts about all languages. Hence, a grammar of one language based on a particular theoretical framework will have to be discarded if facts from another language turn out to be incompatible with the assumed theoretical framework.

To summarise: on the basis of a detailed study of particular grammars, the linguist hypothesises a set of linguistic universals which form the basis of his proposed theory of language. This theory of language in turn constitutes an essential subpart of the theory of language acquisition that Chomsky seeks to develop. Universals provide the key to understanding language acquisition, since – in Chomsky's view – only if we hypothesise that the child has innate knowledge of these universals can we account for the rapidity of language acquisition. Universals also provide the key to *explanation* since (according to Chomsky) explanation can only proceed from universal (and hence hypothesised-to-be-innate) principles.

Chomsky distinguishes two types of universal: (i) *absolute* universals (sometimes referred to as *nonstatistical universals*), and (ii) *relative* universals (sometimes referred to as *statistical universals*). An absolute universal is a property which all languages share without any exception: for example, Chomsky would claim that the STRUCTURE-DEPENDENCE PRINCIPLE is an absolute universal. By contrast, a relative universal represents a general tendency in language, but one which has some exceptions (which further research might ultimately show to be attributable to other universal principles). As an example of a *relative* universal, consider the following principle (from Hawkins (1983), p. 2):

(60)   CONSISTENT SERIALISATION PRINCIPLE
         Languages tend to place modifying elements either consistently before or consistently after modified elements (or heads)

(NB *serialisation* means 'ordering of words and phrases'.) So, for example, Japanese is a language which generally places Modifiers before Heads, and hence positions Possessive Phrases, Adjectives, and Relative Clauses before the head Nouns they modify, as we see from Hawkins' (ibid.) examples in (61) below, where the modifying expressions are italicised, and the head Noun is capitalised:

(61) (a)   *Taroo no* IE (*Possessive* + NOUN)
         Taroo's HOUSE
   (b)   kono *omosiroi* HON (Adjective + NOUN)
         this *interesting* BOOK
   (c)   *Taroo ga*   *issyoni benkyoosita* HITO (*Relative* + NOUN)
         Taroo PRT *together studied*   PERSON
         'the person with whom Taroo studied'

(PRT = grammatical Particle). By contrast, Samoan is a language in which Modifiers follow their Heads, so that Possessive Phrases, Adjectives, and Relative Clauses are all positioned after the Nouns they modify, as the following examples (from Hawkins (1983), pp. 2–3) illustrate:

(62) (a)   o le PAOPAO *o* *Tavita* (NOUN + *Possessive*)

             the CANOE   *of David* ('David's canoe')

    (b)   o le TEINE *puta* (NOUN + Adjective)

             the GIRL *fat*   ('the fat girl')

    (c)   le TEINE *o le sa moe i lona fale* (NOUN + Relative)

             the GIRL *who was asleep in her house*

Clearly, principle (60) represents a general word-order tendency in natural languages, so that we find numerous 'consistently premodifying' languages like Japanese (e.g. Burushaki, Kannada, and Turkish), and numerous 'consistently postmodifying' languages like Samoan (e.g. Berber, Fulani, Hebrew, Malay, Maori, Masai, Swahili, Thai, Yoruba, and Zapotec). However, although principle (60) represents a general word-order tendency in natural languages, it has numerous exceptions: thus, there are some 'mixed' languages which position some modifiers before and others after their head Noun. For example, Basque places Relative and Possessive modifiers before their head Noun, but Adjectives after; Greek places Relative and Possessive modifiers after the Noun, but Adjectives before; Hindi places Adjectives and Possessives before the Noun, but Relative Clauses after; Guarani places Relatives and Adjectives after the Noun, but Genitives before ... and so on and so forth. Hence, it is clear that the CONSISTENT SERIALISATION PRINCIPLE cannot be an *absolute* universal, but rather is (at best) a *relative* universal (see Hawkins 1983 for a detailed discussion of numerous proposed word-order universals of this type).

1.9 Markedness and Core Grammar

Intimately connected with the search for universals is the attempt to develop a *Theory of Markedness*, within which we distinguish between *marked* and *unmarked* phenomena. An *unmarked* phenomenon is one which accords with universal principles (whether absolute or relative) in language: a *marked* phenomenon is one which goes against some relative universal (i.e. general tendency in language), and hence is 'exceptional' in some way. To some extent, we can equate the term 'unmarked' with 'regular', 'normal', or 'usual'; and 'marked' with 'irregular', 'abnormal', 'exceptional', or 'unusual'.

Before our discussion gets too abstract, let's illustrate the notion of *markedness* with a concrete example, and return to our earlier *relative universal* (60), repeated as (63) below:

(63)   CONSISTENT SERIALISATION PRINCIPLE

        Languages tend to place modifying elements either consistently before or consistently after modified elements (or heads)

                                  (Hawkins (1983), p. 2)

Goals

As we see from examples such as (64) below, English is a language which generally places Modifiers (italicised) before Heads:

(64) (a)   *good* food (Modifier + Noun)
   (b)   *very* interesting (Modifier + Adjective)
   (c)   *rather* quickly (Modifier + Adverb)
   (d)   *right* inside (Modifier + Preposition)

The reverse order of Head + Modifier is generally not grammatical in English, as we see from the ill-formedness of (65) below:

(65) (a)   *food *good* (Noun + Modifier)
   (b)   *interesting *very* (Adjective + Modifier)
   (c)   *quickly *rather* (Adverb + Modifier)
   (d)   *inside *right* (Preposition + Modifier)

Thus, we might say that the order [Modifier + Head] is the *unmarked* word order in English phrases of the relevant type.

This in turn means that any phrase type in English which shows the 'reverse' order [Head + Modifier] will be a *marked* construction. Accordingly, examples such as those in (66) below (in which an italicised Adjectival Modifier follows the head Noun it modifies) might be said to represent a *marked construction* in English (examples from Quirk *et al.* (1985), p. 418):

(66) (a)   court *martial*
   (b)   heir *apparent*
   (c)   attorney *general*
   (d)   time *immemorial*
   (e)   vice-chancellor *designate*
   (f)   postmaster *general*
   (g)   president *elect*
   (h)   notary *public*
   (i)   body *politic*

The *markedness* of the examples in (66) is reflected in two immediate characteristics of the construction. First, the examples in (66) are *stylistically marked* in the sense that they have a 'literary' and 'archaic' flavour to them. And secondly, the expressions in (66) have something of the character of 'set phrases', so that the construction illustrated in (66) is very far from being productive in English. For example, although the Adjective *martial* can be positioned after the Noun *court*, when used to modify other Nouns it must be positioned before rather than after the Noun concerned: for example, cf.

40

(67) (a)   *martial* law/*law *martial*
   (b)   *martial* arts/*arts *martial*
   (c)   *martial* music/*music *martial*

And conversely, although the word *court* can be followed by the Adjectival Modifier *martial*, other Adjectives used to modify the same word must generally be positioned before rather than after the head: cf.

(68) (a)   *judicial* court/*court *judicial*
   (b)   *criminal* court/*court *criminal*
   (c)   *civil* court/*court *civil*

Hence, it seems appropriate to characterise (66) as a *marked* construction in English.

Related to the Theory of Markedness is the *Theory of Core Grammar* which Chomsky seeks to develop. This represents the attempt to establish a common, universal 'core' of linguistic principles which characterise the full range of unmarked linguistic phenomena found in natural language. Thus, any rule which conforms to these principles is a 'rule of Core Grammar' (or 'core rule'), whereas any marked rule which does not obey the principles concerned is a *peripheral* rule (i.e. a noncore rule). The grammar of any language will thus contain a *core* of unmarked rules and structures, together with a *periphery* of marked rules and structures. As Chomsky remarks:

> It is reasonable to suppose that UG (Universal Grammar) determines a set of core grammars and that what is actually represented in the mind of an individual even under the idealization to a homogeneous speech community would be a core grammar with a periphery of marked elements and constructions.
>
> (Chomsky, *Lectures* (1981d), p. 8)

Since our discussion is beginning to get rather abstract again, let's take a concrete example of a principle of *Core Grammar*, and a *peripheral rule* which seems to violate that principle.

We might assume that the STRUCTURE-DEPENDENCE PRINCIPLE (55) is one such principle of Core Grammar: it follows, therefore, that a rule such as NP–AUX INVERSION rule (56) would be a *core rule*, whereas any structure-independent rule violating this principle would be a *peripheral rule*. Comrie ((1981), pp. 21–2) suggests that the rule of CLITIC PLACEMENT in Serbo-Croat can operate in a structure-independent fashion: he observes (ibid.):

> A number of languages have a rule whereby clitics – constituents that have no independent stress of their own, but are pronounced

41

as part of the adjacent word – must appear in sentence-second position. One such language is Serbo-Croatian. We may illustrate this by starting with a sentence that has no clitics, e.g. *Petar čita knjigu danas* 'Peter reads (the) book today'. If we want to include a clitic in the sentence, for instance the unstressed first person singular dative pronoun *mi* 'to me', then this must come after the first word: *Petar mi čita knjigu danas*. Serbo-Croatian word order is relatively free, so that in the sentence given first any of the possible 24 permutations of the four words is grammatical, with the same cognitive meaning. However, if the clitic *mi* is inserted, it will always appear after the first word, whatever the syntactic function of that word, e.g. *Danas mi Petar čita knjigu, Knjigu mi čita danas Petar*. In this simple example, each major constituent [= structural unit] of the sentence is a single word, so the question naturally arises what happens if the first constituent [is a phrase which] consists of two words, as when we replace *Petar* by *taj pesnik* 'that poet' to get *Taj pesnik čita knjigu danas*. In such a sentence, it is possible to place the clitic quite literally after the first word of the sentence, to give *Taj mi pesnik čita knjigu danas*, despite the virtual incomprehensibility of a literal translation into English: 'That to me poet reads the book today'. However, it is also possible to place the clitic after the first major constituent, i.e. in this case after the whole Noun Phrase *taj pesnik*, to give *Taj pesnik mi čita knjigu danas*.

What Comrie seems to be saying here is that the Serbo-Croat rule of CLITIC PLACEMENT can either apply in a structure-dependent fashion (in which case the clitic *mi* will be positioned after the first complete Phrase in the sentence), or may apply in a structure-independent fashion (in which case the clitic is positioned after the first word in the sentence). If Comrie's interpretation of the facts is correct, then it means that CLITIC PLACEMENT is a *peripheral* rule, because it may apply in such a way as to violate the STRUCTURE-DEPENDENCE PRINCIPLE. (We should point out, however, that there are alternative analyses of the relevant facts: for example, we might argue that CLITIC PLACEMENT should be formulated as a rule which positions a clitic after the first *word-category* or *phrase-category* in the *containing Clause*; and any such alternative account would be structure-dependent in the sense that the three italicised expressions referred to in the rule are structural terms.)

Since the middle of the 1970s, Chomsky has increasingly focussed his attention on the attempt to develop (i) a particular 'core grammar' for English, and

(ii) a universal Theory of Core Grammar. This inevitably means concentrating on the search for greater generalisations, often at the expense of any attempt to account for apparent 'exceptions'. Chomsky justifies this approach in the following terms:

> Linguistics would perhaps profit by taking to heart a familiar lesson of the natural sciences. Apparent counterexamples and unexplained phenomena should be carefully noted, but it is often rational to put them aside pending further study when principles of a certain degree of explanatory adequacy are at stake.
>
> (Chomsky, 'On Binding' (1980b), p. 2)

In discussing Universal Grammar, we have so far laid emphasis on the potential *similarities* between languages; but an obvious question to ask is how we deal with apparent *differences* between languages. As Chomsky himself observes, 'Plainly, rules can vary from language to language . . .' ('On Wh-movement' (1977b), p. 75). However, this variation is by no means random – for example, there is no language with any rule like (45). On the contrary, languages seem to vary 'within fixed limits' (Chomsky, ibid.). Accordingly, one of the essential tasks for linguistic theory is to define the set of possible *parameters of variation* across languages. The Theory of Core Grammar will have to allow for such parametric variation, so that different languages will have different core grammars (though each such grammar will fall within the range of possible core grammars permitted by the associated linguistic theory).

The Theory of Markedness and Core Grammar plays an essential role in Chomsky's Theory of Language Acquisition. He suggests that children are innately endowed with just such a Theory of Markedness and Core Grammar which defines for them the set of 'unmarked' rules which could be found in natural language; children would then have genetic help in learning unmarked (i.e. core) rules, and hence would master these relatively quickly. Their task in arriving at the set of core rules for their native language would be to select from the range of 'possible core rules' defined by the Theory of Core Grammar, the specific subset found in the language they are learning. This they would do on the basis of their linguistic *experience*. This experience would lead them to discard some possible core rules as incompatible with the evidence that they are confronted with, and to select instead other core rules compatible with that evidence. The relevant evidence which constitutes their 'experience' may be either positive or negative (cf. Chomsky, *Lectures* (1981d), pp. 8–9), though Chomsky believes that the relevant evidence is generally positive in nature, observing that 'There is good reason to believe that children learn language from positive evidence only' (*Knowledge* (1986a), p. 55). Positive evidence would comprise a set of observed sentences illustrating a particular phenomenon: for example, if a child hears in the speech around him hundreds or even thousands of examples of simple declarative sentences (i.e. statements) with Subject-Verb-Object word order, this provides him with *positive* evidence that this is a possible word-order for statements in the language he is learning. Negative evidence may be of two kinds – *direct* and *indirect*. Direct evidence comprises the correction of the child's errors by other speakers of the language. However, this type of evidence (contrary to what is often imagined) plays a relatively insignificant role in language acquisition, for two reasons. First, this type of correction is relatively infrequent: adults simply don't correct all the errors children make (if they did, the poor child would soon become inhibited and discouraged from speaking); and secondly, children are notoriously unresponsive to correction, as the following dialogue (from McNeil (1966), p. 69) illustrates:

(69)   CHILD: Nobody don't like me
         ADULT: No, say: 'Nobody likes me'
         CHILD: Nobody don't like me
         (*eight repetitions of this dialogue*)
         ADULT: No, now listen carefully. Say 'Nobody likes me'
         CHILD: Oh, nobody don't likes me

Direct negative evidence might also take the form of *self-correction* by other speakers. Such *self-corrections* tend to have a characteristic intonation and rhythm of their own, and may be signalled by a variety of 'fillers' (such as those italicised in (70) below):

(70) (a)   The picture was hanged ... *or rather* HUNG ... in the Tate Gallery
   (b)   The picture was hanged ... *sorry* HUNG ... in the Tate Gallery
   (c)   The picture was hanged ... *I mean* HUNG ... in the Tate Gallery

However, *self-correction* is probably too infrequent a phenomenon to play a major role in the acquisition process.

Much more significant than direct negative evidence is *indirect negative evidence*. Suppose that a child learning English never hears any example of sentences with the word-order Verb-Object-Subject (e.g. **Like Linguistics they*). On the basis of this *indirect negative evidence*, the child can infer that Verb-Object-Subject is not a possible word-order in English.

Since the grammar of any language comprises both a Core and a Periphery, the child's task is not just to acquire the relevant set of core rules for the language he is learning, but also to acquire the peripheral rules of the language (i.e. the set of marked rules which don't conform to 'general tendencies' found in language). Because of their marked (i.e. exceptional) character, we might expect that (all other things being equal) peripheral rules would generally take longer to acquire than core rules. However, the picture is not quite as simple as this, since numerous factors may 'distort' this idealised view of acquisition. As Chomsky observes:

> We would expect the order of appearance of structures in language acquisition to reflect the structure of markedness in some respects, but there are many complicating factors: e.g. processes of maturation may be such as to permit certain unmarked structures to be manifested only relatively late in language acquisition, frequency effects may intervene, etc.
>
> (Chomsky, *Lectures* (1981d), p. 9)

You should now be able to tackle exercise V

1.10   Summary

This chapter has been concerned with introducing you to the broad aims of Transformational Grammar, and with explaining some basic concepts. In 1.2 we argued that the overall task of the linguist is to formulate *grammars* of particular languages (= the study of *Particular Grammar*), and to abstract from these sets of common principles which form the basis for the study of *Universal Grammar*. A grammar of a language is a *model* of the *competence* of the fluent native speaker of the language. Competence subsumes both *intuitions about sentence well-formedness* and *intuitions about sentence structure*. In 1.3 we argued that the descriptive notion of *grammaticality* should not be confused with notions such as *correctness, acceptability, pragmatic anomaly*, and *semantic ill-formedness*. In 1.4 we argued that language acquisition is a creative activity, and that acquiring a language involves acquiring a finite set of rules with infinite capacity: accordingly, the task of the linguist devising a grammar of a language is to formulate a *finite* set of syntactic, semantic, phonological, and morphological rules which will *generate* the *infinite* set of well-formed sentence structures in the language. In 1.5 we noted that there is no known inductive procedure for 'discovering' linguistic rules; the linguist has to collect a set of data relating to native speaker intuitions about well-formedness and structure, and attempt to formulate hypotheses about the nature of the principles which account for the data. In 1.6 we examined a number of criteria of adequacy for grammars and linguistic theories: we suggested that grammars should attain not only observational but also descriptive adequacy; and we went on to argue that linguistic theories must attain the higher goal of explanatory adequacy. We saw that to attain explanatory adequacy, a theory must be universally valid, psychologically real, and maximally constrained. In 1.7 we examined the reasons why linguistic theories must be constrained; and we looked at two such constraints which have been proposed – the AUTONOMOUS SYNTAX PRINCIPLE, and the STRUCTURE-DEPENDENCE PRINCIPLE. In 1.8 we outlined Chomsky's belief that the form of language is genetically constrained, and that the key to uncovering the nature of these constraints lies in the study of Universal Grammar (on the assumption that what is universal in language may be innate). In 1.9 we introduced the concepts of *markedness* and *Core Grammar*, suggesting that markedness may provide the key to acquisition, if Chomsky is right in arguing that (all things being equal) unmarked structures are acquired before marked structures.

EXERCISES

Exercise I

Discuss the question of whether any or all of the following sentences are ill-formed, and if so, what the nature of the ill-formedness is (pragmatic, syntactic, semantic, etc.).

(1)   John's a living dead man
(2)   My wife is not my wife
(3)   This is a five-sided hexagon
(4)   This oats is of rather poor quality
(5)   You can see the taste in a Fox's glacier mint
(6)   Two and two is five
(7)   I order you to know the answer
(8)   My toothbrush is pregnant again
(9)   Colourless green ideas sleep furiously
(10)   I eat much cereal for breakfast

Exercise II

Discuss why the sentences below would be stigmatised by prescriptive grammarians as involving 'bad grammar', and say how they would be corrected. Are these corrections appropriate?

(1)   The mission of the USS Enterprise is to boldly go where no man has ever been before
(2)   Answer either question 1, or question 2, or question 3
(3)   Hopefully, the weather will clear up by tomorrow

(4)   It's me who gets the blame for everything
(5)   We had to come home early, due to bad weather
(6)   John and Mary love one another
(7)   What are you up to?
(8)   You are taller than me
(9)   Nobody said nothing
(10)   I ought to go there, didn't I / shouldn't I?
(11)   Everyone loses their cool now and then
(12)   Those kind of people get on my nerves
(13)   His last two previous plays were a huge success
(14)   I was literally over the moon about it
(15)   If I was you, I'd resign
(16)   Between you and I, him and her are quite good friends

Exercise III

Agreement is a concept which plays an important role in traditional grammars. Among the various *Agreement Rules* which such grammars posit are the following:

(1)   A reflexive must agree with its antecedent in Number, Person, and Gender
(2)   A finite Verb must agree with its Subject in Person and Number
(3)   A Determiner must agree with its head Noun in Number

We have already illustrated (1) in the text. Rule (2) accounts for paradigms such as:

(4) (a)   I/we/you/they *annoy* Mary
    (b)   He/she/it *annoys* Mary

and the usual generalisation which is made is that a Present Tense Verb carries the inflection -s just in case it has a *Third Person Singular Subject*. Rule (3) accounts for contrasts such as:

(5) (a)   *this/that/*these/*those* book
    (b)   *these/those/*this/*that* books

where we see that the italicised Determiners have to agree in number with the head Nouns which they modify. It is also assumed in traditional grammars that any violation of Agreement Rules such as (1–3) above will result in an ungrammatical sentence.

Show how sentences such as the following suggest that the Agreement Rules given above are observationally inadequate, and try to suggest alternative rules, inventing further examples of your own as necessary. Assume the grammaticality judgments given (which in some cases represent colloquial usage) for the purposes of the exercise.

(6)   This/*these government dislike(s) change
(7)   This/*these England team have put themselves/has put itself in a good
         position to win the championship

Goals

(8)   Someone is/*are going to hurt themselves/himself on that nail one of these days

(9)   That nasty little boy next door hurt himself/herself/itself this morning

Exercise IV

Below are typical utterances produced by two to three-year-old children. Try and work out what 'rule' the children appear to have devised in each case, and (if you can!) how it differs from the corresponding adult 'rule' (treat each numbered set of examples separately). The examples in (1) represent typical negative sentences produced by children at around two years of age; those in (2) represent negative structures typical of two and a half-year-olds. (3) gives examples of typical children's interrogatives (= questions) at around two and a half years; while (4) gives typical questions produced by three-year-olds; and (5) gives examples of a rather less common type of interrogative structure found in some three-year-olds:

(1) (a)   No the sun shining
    (b)   No Fraser drink all tea
    (c)   No mum sharpen it
(2) (a)   He no bite you
    (b)   I no want envelope
    (c)   I no taste them
(3) (a)   Where me sleep?
    (b)   What me think?
    (c)   What the dolly have?
(4) (a)   What he can ride in?
    (b)   Why kitty can't stand up?
    (c)   Where I should put it?
(5) (a)   Where does the wheel goes?
    (b)   What did you bought?

You may find it useful to consult a good reference grammar of English (e.g. Quirk *et al.* 1985) to get a good description of the Syntax of adult negatives and questions.

Exercise V

Define the following terms, commenting on their importance, and illustrating them *with examples of your own*, where appropriate:

(1)   particular/universal grammar
(2)   competence/performance
(3)   linguistic intuitions
(4)   descriptive/prescriptive grammar
(5)   acceptability/well-formedness
(6)   syntactic/semantic/pragmatic ill-formedness
(7)   infinite rule-governed creativity

48

(8)   generative grammar
(9)   corpus/elicitation
(10)   observational/descriptive/explanatory adequacy
(11)   structure dependence
(12)   autonomous Syntax
(13)   innateness hypothesis
(14)   markedness
(15)   core/peripheral rule

2
Structure

2.1 Overview

In the previous chapter, we argued that native speakers' competence in their native language(s) is reflected in their intuitions about sentence well-formedness (derived from their acceptability judgments) on the one hand, and their intuitions about sentence-structure on the other. We have argued that the ability to make judgments about well-formedness and structure holds at all four major linguistic levels – Phonology, Morphology, Syntax, and Semantics. Hence, it follows that a native speaker's *syntactic competence* will be reflected in his intuitions about the *grammaticality* (= syntactic well-formedness) of sentences on the one hand, and their *syntactic structure* on the other. We have discussed in some detail the problems of deciding whether a given sentence is *grammatical* or not. In this chapter, we examine the question of what it means to say that a sentence has a *syntactic structure*; we discuss the evidence in support of that claim; and we look at ways of representing syntactic structure.

2.2 Intuitions about Structure

Part of the evidence for claiming that sentences have a syntactic structure in language comes from the native speaker's intuitions about the structure of sentences in his language. The structural intuitions which native speakers have about the Syntax of their languages are of two types, namely (i) intuitions about how sound-sequences in sentences are structured into successively larger structural units which we call *constituents*; and (ii) intuitions about whether particular sets of constituents (i.e. structural units) belong to the same *category* or not. We can illustrate the nature of these intuitions about *constituents* and *categories* in relation to a sentence such as:

(1)   This boy must seem incredibly stupid to that girl

Consider first our intuitions about the way in which the words in (1) are grouped into successively larger *constituents*. For example, we'd all agree that *incredibly* 'goes with' or 'modifies' *stupid* in (1), so that the sequence [*incredibly stupid*] is a (phrasal) constituent of the sentence. Likewise, *this* modifies *boy* in (1), so that the sequence [*this boy*] forms a single structural unit, a *constituent* of the sentence; in much the same way, we might argue that *that* modifies *girl*, so that the sequence [*that girl*] is also a constituent of the sentence. Furthermore, it is intuitively obvious that *to* goes with the phrase [*that girl*], so that [*to that girl*] is also a constituent. And we might also claim that since the phrases [*incredibly stupid*] and [*to that girl*] both modify *seem*, then the whole sequence [*seem incredibly stupid to that girl*] is also a constituent. What we need is some way of representing all this information about constituent structure in diagrammatic form. In fact, this can be done in terms of a *tree diagram* such as (2) below:

(2)
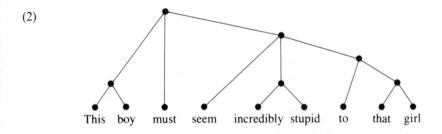

    This boy   must   seem   incredibly stupid   to   that   girl

Each point in the tree is called a *node*; and each *node* represents a *constituent* (i.e. a syntactic unit). Thus, (2) tells us that not only are all the individual words in (2) syntactic units (i.e. *constituents*) of the sentence, but so too are the phrases [*this boy*], [*incredibly stupid*], [*that girl*], [*to that girl*], and [*seem incredibly stupid to that girl*]. In the diagram (2), we have indicated the *nodes* by large dots: however, since *nodes* are predictable (they occur at the top and bottom of the tree, and at points where two or more branches intersect) we shall suppress them in subsequent tree-diagrams.

But while a tree-diagram such as (2) provides a convenient pictorial representation of our intuitions about the *constituent structure* of a sentence such as (1) (i.e. what the basic syntactic units in the sentence are), it does not provide any representation of our intuitions about which constituents are *constituents of the same type*. So if someone asked us whether we feel intuitively that *boy* and *this* in (1) are constituents of the same type, we'd probably say 'No, *boy* is the same kind of word as *girl, man, woman*, etc., whereas *this* is the same kind of word as *that, a, the*, etc.' The traditional way of describing the similarities and differences between constituents is to say that they belong to *categories* of various types. Thus, words like *boy, girl, man, woman*, etc. are traditionally said to belong to the category of Nouns, whereas words like *a, the, this*, and *that* are traditionally said to belong to the category of Determiners. Similarly, we'd probably recognise that *seem* is the same kind of word as *appear, feel, become*, etc. – the kind of word that traditional grammarians call a ('main', 'full', or 'lexical') Verb. By contrast, *must* is the same kind of constituent as *may, might, can, could, will, would, shall*, and *should* – i.e. is a constituent of the type traditionally called a Modal (Auxiliary) (Verb). And we'd intuitively recognise that *to* is the same kind of constituent as *with, from, by, at, in, for*, etc. – namely a Preposition. In addition, we'd probably agree that *incredibly* is a word like *really, fundamentally, potentially*, etc. – i.e. a word traditionally labelled an *Adverb*. In much the same way, we might feel that *stupid* is the same kind of word as *clever, kind, randy, mad, nice*, etc. – i.e. the kind of word traditionally called an Adjective.

Just as *words* belong to different categories, so too do phrases. For instance, we might capture the fact that [*this boy*] and [*that girl*] seem to be phrases of the same type, and that in both cases the *head* (i.e. key constituent) of the phrase is a Noun, by assigning these two constituents the categorial status of Noun Phrases. And in order to capture the fact that the phrase [*incredibly stupid*] is a constituent of the same type as [*rather nice*], [*very handsome*], [*quite trendy*], [*somewhat rude*] etc. – i.e. a phrase whose head in each case is an Adjective (*stupid, nice, handsome, trendy, rude*) – we might call such constituents Adjectival Phrases. Similarly, in order to mark the fact that [*to that girl*] is a phrase of the same type as e.g. [*with his mother*], [*from the professor*], [*into the room*], [*for Mary*] etc., and that in each case the head of the phrase is a Preposition (*to, with, from, into, for*), we might call such phrases Prepositional Phrases. And to capture our intuition that [*seem incredibly stupid to that girl*] is a phrase of the same type as [*speak rather rudely to his mother*], [*give a present to Mary*], [*run back home*], [*close the door*], [*die tomorrow*] – i.e. a constituent whose head is a Verb – we might classify such constituents as Verb Phrases. Finally, we might want to recognise the fact that the whole sequence [*This boy must seem incredibly stupid to that girl*] is a special type of constituent traditionally termed a Clause or Sentence.

Note that none of this vital *categorial* information is contained in the tree diagram (2) which we earlier gave to represent the constituent structure of (1). However, the relevant categorial information can be included in this type of diagram if we simply attach an appropriate *category label* to each of the nodes in the tree: the resultant structure is then known as a *labelled tree diagram*. Given this assumption, we can represent the *categorial constituent structure* of sentence (1) in terms of the labelled tree diagram (3) below:

(3)

(Abbreviations: S = Clause/Sentence; M = Modal; D = Determiner; ADV =
Adverb; P = Preposition, PP = Prepositional Phrase; N = Noun, NP = Noun
Phrase; V = Verb, VP = Verb Phrase; A = Adjective; AP = Adjectival Phrase).

A diagram such as (3) provides a visual representation of the *categorial constituent structure* of sentence (1). Equivalently, we might say that since (3)
shows us how sentence (1) is structured out of its constituent phrases, and how
each of the phrases is structured out of its component words, (3) provides a
visual representation of the *Phrase Structure* of sentence (1). Hence, the type
of labelled tree diagram used in (3) is referred to as a *Phrase-marker*
(P-marker), because it marks the hierarchical grouping of words into phrases,
and phrases into sentences. The P-marker (3) thus provides a visual representation of the superficial syntactic structure (or *S-structure*, as Chomsky calls it)
of the sentence (1).

The method of representing syntactic structure visually by the use of
labelled tree diagrams (P-markers) such as that in (3) is in fact only one of
many alternative systems which have been devised in order to provide a visual
representation of structure. Another (logically equivalent) method of visual
display frequently used in the linguistic literature is to make use of *labelled
bracketing* rather than labelled tree-diagrams. Within this alternative system,
we could represent the categorial status of each of the words in (1) as in (4)
below:

(4)   [D this] [N boy] [M must] [V seem] [ADV incredibly] [A stupid]
         [P to] [D that] [N girl]

Likewise, we could use the system of labelled bracketing to represent the fact
that [*this boy*] and [*that girl*] are NPs (Noun Phrases), that [*to that girl*] is a PP
(Prepositional Phrase), that [*incredibly stupid*] is an AP (Adjectival Phrase),
that [*seem incredibly stupid to that girl*] is a VP (Verb Phrase), and that [*This*

boy must seem incredibly stupid to that girl] is an S (Clause) as follows:

(5)   [S [NP [D this] [N boy]] [M must] [VP [V seem] [AP [ADV incredibly] [A stupid]] [PP [P to] [NP [D that] [N girl]]]]]]

(By convention, only one member of any pair of brackets is usually labelled with the relevant category label, generally the lefthand one.) The resultant diagram (5) is entirely equivalent to (3) – i.e. the two diagrams contain exactly the same information as each other. Generally speaking, tree-diagrams are easier to read (because the information they contain is less condensed), and this is the reason why they are frequently preferred by many linguists as a form of visual representation of syntactic structure.

Diagrams like (3) and (5) provide a virtually complete representation of the syntactic structure of a sentence like (1). Quite often, however, the linguist may prefer to give a less detailed account of the structure of a sentence, where he does not want to include absolutely every minute detail of the structure, but rather just wants to give a partial representation of the structure. It sometimes happens that the linguist will simply want to indicate the major phrases within a sentence, without worrying about the internal structure of those phrases. For this reason, it is quite common to find in the relevant literature partial tree-diagrams, or partial labelled bracketings. For example, suppose that, for the purposes of some point that I am making, it is essential to assume that a sentence like (1) contains three major constituents, the Noun Phrase [*this boy*], a Modal Auxiliary Verb *must*, and a Verb Phrase [*seem incredibly stupid to that girl*], but that it is irrelevant to my argument what the internal structure of the Noun Phrase and Verb Phrase may be. In such a case, in place of the full tree diagram (3), I might prefer the partial P-marker (6) below:

(6)

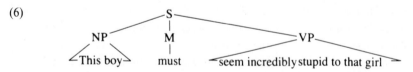

(In partial P-markers like (6), it is quite common to use a 'triangle' to represent constituents with a complex internal structure that you don't choose to represent.) Or, in place of the detailed labelled bracketing (5), we might prefer the partial bracketing (7) below:

(7)   [S [NP this boy] [M must] [VP seem incredibly stupid to that girl]]

Generally speaking, linguists tend to use labelled tree-diagrams (P-markers) for a full representation of the syntactic structure of a sentence (because at that level of detail they are easier to read), and labelled bracketings for partial representation of structure (because they occupy less space on the printed page). But recall that the two systems of representation are logically equivalent (whatever structure can be represented in the one system can be represented in the other and vice-versa), so that the question of whether you adopt one or the other is entirely a matter of typographical convenience, *not* a matter of theoretical significance. Accordingly, we shall use both systems freely in our exposition here.

We can summarise our discussion so far in the following terms. Sentences are not just unstructured sequences of sounds; rather, they have a hierarchical *constituent structure* in which sounds are grouped together into words, words into phrases, and phrases into sentences. Each *constituent* (word or phrase) in a sentence belongs to a specific *syntactic category*. Overall, then, we can say that sentences have a *categorial constituent structure*; or in other words, sentences are built up out of sets of constituents, each of which belongs to a specific category. This categorial constituent structure can be represented schematically in the form of a Phrase-marker (= labelled tree-diagram), or labelled bracketing.

A key assumption which we are making here is that all sentences have a *categorial constituent structure* – i.e. that all sentences are hierarchically structured out of words and phrases, and that each of the component words and phrases in a sentence belongs to a specific *category*. Thus far, we have implicitly assumed that the evidence in support of this claim comes from native speakers' intuitions about the syntactic structure of sentences within their language. But this is only a very small part of the available evidence; moreover, it is a type of evidence which can be rather unreliable. For while experienced linguists over a period of years tend to acquire fairly strong intuitions about syntactic structure, untrained informants by contrast tend to have very weak, uncertain, and unreliable intuitions. For this reason, it is more satisfactory (and more accurate) to regard *constituents* and *categories* as having the status of *theoretical constructs*. That is to say, they are part of the grammatical apparatus which the linguist finds he needs in order to explain certain facts about language (just as 'molecules', 'atoms', and 'subatomic particles' are part of the apparatus which the physicist finds he needs in order to explain the nature of matter in the universe). Inevitably, then, much of the evidence for constituents and categories hangs on heavily theory-internal arguments – arguments of an essentially *empirical* character (i.e. arguments based on observed facts about language). In the remainder of this chapter, we shall present a substantial body of empirical evidence in defence of the assumption that sentences have a categorial constituent structure. We'll begin (in the next section) by looking at the evidence that there are a variety of different *word-*

55

level categories: and in subsequent sections, we'll go on to look at the evidence in support of saying that words are grouped together to form *phrase-level categories* of various sorts.

You should now be able to tackle exercise I

2.3   Word-level categories

What evidence is there that words belong to various categories of different types – categories like Noun, Verb, Adjective, Adverb, Preposition, Modal, Determiner, and so forth? As we shall see, evidence in support of this assumption comes from a wide range of sources.

Part of the evidence is *phonological* in nature: that is to say, constituents and categories prove essential constructs for any adequate description of the phonology of natural language sentences. Consider, for example, the problem of formulating a phonological rule which will provide a principled account of word-stress in cases such as the following (where the primary-stressed syllable is capitalised):

(8) (a)   We need to inCREASE productivity
    (b)   We need an INcrease in productivity
(9) (a)   Why do you torMENT me?
    (b)   Why do you leave me in TORment?
(10) (a)   We might transFER him to another club
    (b)   He's asked for a TRANSfer

In each of the (a) sentences, the stress falls on the second syllable (capitalised) of the relevant word; whereas in each of the (b) sentences, the stress falls on the first syllable. Why should this be? An obvious answer is that in each case the relevant word (*increase, torment, transfer*) has the categorial status of a *Verb* in the (a) sentences, but the categorial status of a *Noun* in the (b) sentences. That is, the relevant generalisation is that words like *increase* carry primary stress on the second syllable when used as Verbs, but on the first syllable when used as Nouns. However, any such generalisation presupposes that phonological rules have access to categorial information: i.e. that such rules have to 'know' what the category of a constituent is before they can apply to it. Overall, then, the claim that words belong to a variety of different *categories* seems to have strong empirical support from phonological facts.

A second type of evidence in support of positing that words belong to categories is *semantic* in nature. More particularly, such an assumption makes it possible to provide a principled account of certain types of *ambiguity* characteristic of natural languages. In this connection, it is important to distinguish between two very different types of ambiguity: (i) *lexical* ambiguity, and (ii) *structural* ambiguity. Lexical ambiguity is ambiguity attributable to the fact that some particular lexical item (= word) has more than one meaning. For example, the word *ball* is ambiguous as between one sense in which it means a 'round object used for playing games', and a second sense in which it means a 'dance'; the ambiguity here is purely lexical. But there is a second type of ambiguity characteristic of natural languages, illustrated by the sentence:

(11)   Mistrust wounds

In a case such as (11), the ambiguity might be argued to be *structural* in nature: that is to say, how we interpret (11) depends on whether we take it to be a Noun + Verb sequence parallel to 'Suspicion wounds', or a Verb + Noun sequence parallel to 'Mistrust sores'.

In fact, traditional grammars typically go much further than this, and claim that categories can be defined (in part) in terms of their *semantic* properties (i.e. meaning), along the lines indicated in (12) below:

(12) (i)   Verbs denote actions (*go, destroy, buy, eat,* etc.)
  (ii)   Nouns denote entities (*car, cat, hill, Reagan,* etc.)
  (iii)   Adjectives denote states (*ill, happy, rich,* etc.)
  (iv)   Adverbs denote the manner in which something is done (*badly, slowly, painfully, cynically,* etc.)
  (v)   Prepositions denote location (*under, over, outside, in, on,* etc.)
  (vi)   Determiners serve to specify (e.g. in '*this* book', *this* serves to specify which book)

Semantically-based criteria for identifying categories such as those in (12) above are generally referred to as *notional* criteria. They are, however, extremely unreliable: for example, *assassination* denotes an action, but is a Noun (not a Verb); *illness* denotes a state, but is a Noun (not an Adjective); in *fast food, fast* indicates the manner in which the food is prepared, but is an Adjective (not an Adverb); in *tall women, tall* serves to specify what kind of women we are talking about, but is an Adjective (not a Determiner); and *Cambridge* denotes a location, but is a Noun (not a Preposition). Not surprisingly, therefore, we shall not make much use of *notional* criteria here!

Far more reliable are *morphological* and *syntactic* criteria: and in fact, the bulk of the evidence in support of postulating that words belong to categories is either morphological or syntactic in nature. Let's examine first the *morphological* evidence. This concerns the fact that certain types of *inflection* (i.e.

grammatical ending) attach only to specific categories: we can thus identify individual categories according to the range of inflections which they permit. For example, Verbs in English can be recognised by the fact that they have up to five distinct forms: they have an uninflected *base* form, and may take as many as four different inflections (the present tense -*s*, past tense -*d*, participle -*n*, and gerund -*ing* inflections), as illustrated in the Table of Verb Forms (13) below:

(13)

Base	*Participle*	*Past*	*Present*	*Gerund*
hew	hewn	hewed	hews	hewing
mow	mown	mowed	mows	mowing
prove	proven	proved	proves	proving
sew	sewn	sewed	sews	sewing
shave	shaven	shaved	shaves	shaving
show	shown	showed	shows	showing
strew	strewn	strewed	strews	strewing

Like most morphological criteria, however, this one is complicated by the *irregularity* of English inflectional morphology: for example, many Verbs have irregular PAST or PARTICIPLE forms, and in some cases either or both of these forms may not in fact be distinct from the base form, so that a single form may serve two or three functions, as illustrated in the Table of Irregular Verbs (14) below:

(14)

Base	*Participle*	*Past*	*Present*	*Gerund*
go	gone	went	goes	going
speak	spoken	spoke	speaks	speaks
see	seen	saw	sees	seeing
-------- come --------		came	comes	coming
meet	-------- met --------		meets	meeting
------------- cut -------------			cuts	cutting

The picture becomes even more complicated if we take into account the Verb *be*, which has *eight* distinct forms! In fact, the most regular Verb inflection in English is the -*ing* inflection, which can be attached to the base form of almost any Verb in English to form a gerund (though cf. minor exceptions such as *beware*).

This morphological property of having five (potentially distinct) forms differentiates Verbs from so-called *Modals* (or *Modal Auxiliaries*), which have no PARTICIPLE (-*n*) or GERUND (-*ing*) forms (and may also lack other forms): cf.

(15)   can – could – *cans – *cannen *canning
         shall – should – *shalls – *shallen – *shalling
         may – might – *mays – *mayen – *maying
         must – *musted – *musts – *musten – *musting

So, in other words, we can justify our distinction between *Verbs* and *Modals* on morphological grounds (though, as we shall see later, this distinction is supported by syntactic evidence as well).

We can also use morphological criteria to identify Adjectives and Adverbs, since these are the only categories (a subset of) which have a comparative form in *-er*: cf.

(16)   tall – taller; fat – fatter; fast – faster; etc.

(The criterion is complicated by the fact that Adjectives and Adverbs longer than two syllables have no *-er* form, so that we don't find Adjective forms like **intelligenter*.) And we can differentiate the two morphologically in that Adverbs generally carry a distinctive *-ly* inflection, as the paradigm in (17) below illustrates:

(17)   *Adjective*   *Adverb*
         sad   sad*ly*
         lucky   lucki*ly*
         desperate   desperate*ly*
         arrogant   arrogant*ly*
         nonchalant   nonchalant*ly*
         aggressive   aggressive*ly*

(It should be noted, however, that there is a handful of 'irregular' Adverbs like *fast, hard*, etc. in English which do not end in *-ly*, and may have the same form as the corresponding Adjectives.) Moreover, we can differentiate Nouns from (for example) Adjectives morphologically by virtue of the fact that only Nouns – not Adjectives – take a plural inflection (usually *-s*): hence the contrast in:

(18)   They are *idiots* (Noun)/**idiotics* (Adjective)

Finally, we can define *Prepositions* (somewhat negatively!) by saying that they are *invariable* forms which cannot take the Verb inflections *-s, -d, -n*, or *-ing*, or the comparative inflection *-er*, or the Adverb inflection *-ly*, or the Noun plural *-s* inflection: hence, a Preposition like *at* always remains completely uninflected: cf.

(19)   at/*ats/*atted/*atten/*atting/*atter/*atly

And as for Determiners – well, I was rather hoping you wouldn't ask! Morphologically speaking, they are a heterogeneous bunch: most are invariable, though *this* has the plural form *these*, and *that* has the plural form *those*: but as an overall category, they have no single defining morphological characteristic which they all share. (Determiners are best defined in *syntactic* terms, as we shall see shortly.)

Having seen that there is ample *morphological* evidence in support of positing that words belong to categories, let's now turn to examine the relevant syntactic evidence. This is *distributional* in nature: that is to say, it rests on the assumption that categories are *distributional classes*. The *distribution* of a word in this sense is the set of sentence-positions it can occur in. For example, if we want to complete the sentence in (20) below by inserting a single word at the beginning of the sentence, in the position marked — :

(20)   — can be a pain in the neck

we can use a Noun (in either its singular form, or plural form, or both), but not a Verb, Preposition, Adjective, Adverb, or Determiner, as we see from (21) below:

(21) (a)   *Linguistics/John/Girls/Television* [Noun] can be a pain in the neck
     (b)   **Went* [Verb]/**For* [Preposition]/**Older* [Adjective]/**Conscientiously* [Adverb]/**The* [Determiner] can be a pain in the neck

Thus, using our distributional criterion, we might define the class of Nouns as the set of words which can occur in the position marked — in (20). However, it's important to be clear about what we mean by this. What we *do* mean is that any word which can occur in the position marked — is a Noun; what we emphatically *don't* mean is that the — position in (20) is the only position which Nouns can occur in. Any such claim would clearly be preposterous, since a typical Noun such as *Linguistics* can occur in a wide variety of sentence positions, as we see from (22) below:

(22) (a)   Is *Linguistics* a spectator sport?
     (b)   Some people consider *Linguistics* kinky
     (c)   Has anyone ever been known to die from *Linguistics*?
     (d)   Do you hate *Linguistics* more than monetarism?
     (e)   Etc.

Hence, it's important to be clear about the logic of the distributional argumentation here: there's an obvious difference between 'Only X occurs in Y' and 'X occurs only in Y': if you don't see the difference, try an elementary Logic textbook!

Using the same type of distributional criterion, we could argue that only a Verb (in its *base* form) can occur in the position marked — in (23) below to complete the sentence:

(23)   They/it can —

And support from this claim comes from the contrasts in (24) below:

(24) (a)   They can *stay/leave/hide/die/starve/cry* [Verb]
     (b)   *They can *gorgeous/cute/grotty/trendy* [Adjective]
     (c)   *They can *up/down/round/in/out/off/on* [Preposition]
     (d)   *They can *woman/door/bible/gold/camera* [Noun]
     (e)   Etc.

Conversely, the only type of word which could be used to begin a three-word sentence such as (25) below:

(25)   — I be frank?

is a Modal: cf.

(26) (a)   *Can/Could/Shall/Should/Must* I be frank? [Modal]
     (b)   **Go/*Wanted/*Tried/*Am* I be frank? [Verb]
     (c)   **Slow/*Ready/*Keen/*Proud* I be frank? [Adjective]
     (d)   Etc.

And the only category of word which can occur after *very* (in its sense of *extremely*) is an Adjective or Adverb, as we see from (27) below:

(27) (a)   He is very *slow* [very + Adjective]
     (b)   He walks very *slowly* [very + Adverb]
     (c)   *Very *girls* love to have fun [very + Noun]
     (d)   *He very *adores* her [very + Verb]
     (e)   *It happened very *after* the party [very + Preposition]

Moreover, we can differentiate Adjectives from Adverbs in distributional terms. For example, only Adverbs can be used to complete a four-word sentence such as 'He treats her —': cf.

(28) (a)   He treats her *badly/politely/arrogantly* [Adverb]
     (b)   *He treats her *nice/proper/good/strange* [Adjective]
     (c)   *He treats her *friend/fool/woman* [Noun]
     (d)   Etc.

And since Adjectives (but not Adverbs) can serve as the complement of the verb *be*, we can delimit the class of Adjectives uniquely by saying that only

Adjectives can be used to complete a four-word sentence of the form 'They are very — ': cf.

(29) (a)   They are very *tall/pretty/kind/nice* [Adjective]
   (b)   *They are very *slowly/innocently/nicely* [Adverb]
   (c)   *They are very *gentlemen/ladies/foxes* [Noun]
   (d)   Etc.

As for the distributional properties of Prepositions, well they alone can be pre-modified (i.e. modified and preceded) by *right* in the sense of 'completely':

(30) (a)   Go right *up* the ladder
   (b)   He fell right *down* the stairs
   (c)   He arrived right *on* time
   (d)   It's right *under* the bed
   (e)   I'm right *out* of matches
   (f)   He went right *inside*
   (g)   He fell right *off* the ledge

By contrast, other categories cannot be intensified by *right* (in standard varieties of English): cf.

(31) (a)   *He right *despaired* [Verb]
   (b)   *Life right *can* be cruel [Modal]
   (c)   *She is right *pretty* [Adjective]
   (d)   *She looked at him right *strangely* [Adverb]
   (e)   *She chose right *this* one [Determiner]

(though in some dialects of English, (31) (c) and (d) are well-formed). Finally, we might delimit the class of *Determiners* in distributional terms by saying that they are the only class of items which can occur in the position marked — below to complete a five-word sentence such as 'He wrote — other work(s)': cf. (32) below:

(32) (a)   He wrote *the/some/few/many/no* other works [Determiner]
   (b)   *He wrote *successful/bad/long* other works [Adjective]
   (c)   *He wrote *be/have/see/hear* other works [Verb]
   (d)   Etc.

Thus, all six of the categories we have encountered so far can be justified on *distributional* grounds.

Given the wide variety of different types of evidence in support of positing that words belong to categories, we might attempt to arrive at a composite definition of a word-level category in the following terms:

(33)   A *word-level category* is a set of words which share a common set
        of linguistic (especially morphological and syntactic) properties

One important point which we should clarify, however, is that individual
words may belong to more than one category. For example, the word *need* can
function as a Verb (in which case it takes the characteristic range of verb inflections such as -*s*), as a Modal (and so can be used in structures such as (25)
above), and as a Noun (and hence can be premodified by a Determiner such as
a): the examples in (34) below illustrate these three uses of *need*:

(34) (a)   He *needs* to see a doctor [Verb]
     (b)   *Need* he be there? [Modal]
     (c)   I feel a *need* to explore my roots [Noun]

Thus far, we have argued that we need to posit that words belong to a restricted set of categories (such as Noun, Adjective, Adverb, Verb, Modal, Preposition, Determiner) in order to attain *observational adequacy* – i.e. in order
to arrive at an accurate description of the facts of English Phonology, Morphology, and Syntax. However, we can go much further than this and suggest
that we cannot attain our ultimate goal of *explanatory adequacy* (accounting
for language acquisition) unless we do recognise that words belong to categories. For, if there were no categories in language, and if every word had its own
utterly idiosyncratic set of linguistic properties, then the task of acquiring
competence in a language would be an impossible one (within the constraints
that the child operates under). By contrast, if words are grouped into a small
finite set of categories, and if phonological, morphological, syntactic and
semantic rules are all category-based, then the child's acquisition task is enormously simplified. For, if in fact all grammatical rules are category-based,
then the task facing the child acquiring (for example) the Syntax of a language
becomes the relatively simple one of identifying which words belong to which
categories in the target language, and which categories can occur in which sentence positions.

To avoid making our discussion too abstract, let's take a concrete example.
Let's suppose that a child learns that in English the words *a, the, this, that, my,
your, his*, etc. all belong to the category D (= Determiner). It follows that if he
hears a sentence like:

(35)   I want *a* toy

then, given the assumption that all syntactic rules are category-based, he can
immediately infer that not only *a* but also all other members of the same category (D) can occur in the italicised position – i.e., having heard (35), he will be

able to infer that the sentences in (36) below are also grammatical in English:

(36) (a)   I want *the* toy
   (b)   I want *this* toy
   (c)   I want *that* toy
   (d)   I want *my* toy
   (e)   I want *your* toy
   (f)   I want *his* toy
   (g)   Etc.

Furthermore, given the same assumption that all syntactic rules are category-based (or *structure-dependent*, to use the equivalent term suggested by Chomsky), he can also infer that in place of *toy* in (36) he can substitute any other item belonging to the same category N (= Noun), and thus generate, for example:

(37) (a)   I want a *ball*
   (b)   I want a *banana*
   (c)   I want a *blackboard*
   (d)   I want a *bike*
   (e)   Etc.

In short, the twin assumptions that syntactic rules are category-based, and that there are a highly restricted finite set of categories in any natural language (perhaps no more than a dozen major categories), together with the assumption that the child either *knows* (innately) or *learns* (by experience) that all rules are structure-dependent (= category-based), provide a highly plausible model of language acquisition, in which languages become learnable in a relatively short, finite period of time (a few years).

You should now be able to tackle exercise II

2.4   Phrasal categories: nonsyntactic evidence

Thus far, we have presented evidence in support of the claim that words in natural language belong to a highly restricted finite set of word-level categories such as Noun, Verb, Modal, Adjective, Adverb, Preposition, Determiner, etc. But recall that in section 2.1 we posited that the major word-level categories can be expanded into the corresponding phrasal categories by the addition of other constituents. For example, Nouns can be expanded into Noun Phrases, Verbs into Verb Phrases, Adjectives into Adjectival Phrases, Adverbs into Adverbial Phrases, and Prepositions into Prepositional Phrases.

In the remaining sections of this chapter, we look at the evidence in support of the assumption that sentences are structured not only out of words belonging to various word-level categories, but also out of *phrases* belonging to the corresponding set of phrasal categories. In this section, we shall briefly outline some non-syntactic evidence in support of this assumption; but the remaining sections of our chapter will be concerned with presenting a vast array of syntactic evidence in support of our claim that sentences are structured out of *phrases* of various different categorial types. The *nonsyntactic* evidence we shall present in this section is of three types: morphological, semantic, and phonological: let's begin by looking at the relevant *morphological evidence*.

Generally speaking, *Morphology* is a property of words rather than phrases: for example, inflections (e.g. plural -*s*, past tense -*d*, comparative -*er*) attach to the end of *words* of a particular type, not to the end of *phrases*. But there is one inflectional morpheme in English which is indeed a *phrasal* inflection – and that is the genitive (= possessive) '*s* inflection. Of course, this is difficult to tell if we take a simple Noun Phrase which ends in a Noun, as in:

(38)   This crown is *the king's*

For in a case like (38), we cannot be sure whether the genitive '*s* inflection is attached to the end of the Noun *king*, or to the end of the whole Noun Phrase *the king*. But if we choose an example of a Noun Phrase in which the head Noun has a postmodifier of some sort (i.e. an expression positioned after the Noun which modifies the Noun), the situation becomes clearer: the genitive '*s* inflection must clearly attach to the end of the whole Noun Phrase, not to the end of the head Noun – precisely as we see from (39) below:

(39) (a)   This crown is [NP *the* [N *king*] *of England*]'s
     (b)   *This crown is [NP the [N *king*]'s of England]

Here, the Noun *king* is followed by the postmodifying PP *of England*: and the genitive inflection '*s* attaches to the end of the whole Noun Phrase [*the king of England*], not to the Noun *king*. So, it seems that genitive '*s* is a Noun Phrase inflection, not a Noun inflection. Moreover, the genitive inflection in English can attach only to a *Noun Phrase*, and not (for example) to an Adjectival Phrase: cf.

(40)   *This crown is [AP *very handsome*]'s

Thus, the postulation of a *Noun Phrase* constituent is justified on morphological grounds, since it is not obvious how we could describe the grammar of the genitive '*s* inflection in English without saying that it's a *Noun Phrase* inflection. More generally still, morphological facts force us to recognise that sentences are structured out of Phrases belonging to various phrasal categories such as (in our present case) *Noun Phrase*.

In addition to *morphological* evidence such as that discussed above, we can also adduce *semantic* evidence in support of our assumption that sentences are structured out of Phrases. Part of the evidence relates to the phenomenon of *structural ambiguity* which we discussed earlier. In simple cases, the structural ambiguity may relate to the categorial status of a particular phrase, as shown in the following example (adapted from Huddleston (1976), p. 11).

(41)   Mary looked *very hard*

the ambiguity concerns the categorial status of the italicised phrase [*very hard*]. On one interpretation, it is an Adjectival Phrase (AP) paraphraseable by 'very severe'; but on the second interpretation, it is an Adverbial Phrase (ADVP) paraphraseable by 'very intensely'.

A rather different kind of structural ambiguity occurs when a given word or phrase (with a given categorial status) can be taken as modifying any one of two (or more) different constituents. For example, consider the following sentence:

(42)   The President could not ratify the treaty

If you think about it very carefully, you'll realise that (42) is ambiguous as between the two interpretations (43) (i) and (ii) below:

(43) (i)   It would not be possible for the President to ratify the treaty
     (ii)   It would be possible for the President not to ratify the treaty

The two different interpretations become clearer if we use (42) in the two different contexts in (44) below:

(44) (a)   Even if he wanted to, the President could not ratify the treaty, because he doesn't have the authority to do so (= (43) (i))
     (b)   If he really wanted to make it clear that he isn't interested in disarmament, the President could not ratify the treaty. By not ratifying it, he would make his opposition to arms reduction patently obvious (= (43) (ii))

The ambiguity of (42) is structural in nature, and relates to the *scope* of the negative particle *not* (i.e. relates to the question of which constituent is being modified by *not*): for this reason, this type of ambiguity is known as *scope ambiguity*. On the first (and most obvious) interpretation (43) (i), *not* might be argued to have within its scope (i.e. to modify) the Modal *could*; whereas on the second (less obvious) interpretation (43) (ii), *not* might be argued to have scope over (i.e. to modify) the Verb Phrase [*ratify the treaty*]. If these assumptions are correct, then (42) would have the simplified structure (45) (i) below on interpretation (43) (i), and the structure (45) (ii) on interpretation (43) (ii):

(45) (i)

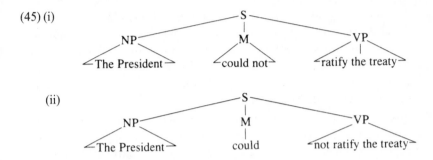

  (ii)

For our present purposes, what is interesting about (45) is that the *negative scope ambiguity* of (42) is represented in *structural* terms. The key premise of our analysis is that clauses like those above have three immediate constituents [NP M VP], and that *not* may have scope either over M, or over VP. Since we are saying that *not* lies outside the VP in (45) (i) but inside the VP in (45) (ii), it is clear that the constituent VP is a key construct in our account of the *scope ambiguity* in (42). Or, to stand the argument on its head, negative scope facts provide strong support for the postulation of a VP constituent.

It is interesting to note that there seems to be some independent *syntactic* evidence in support of the structural ambiguity proposed in (45). For, an Adverb like *simply* would be positioned after *not* on interpretation (43) (i), but before *not* on interpretation (43) (ii): cf.

(46) (i)   The President could not *simply* ratify the treaty (= (43) (i))

   (ii)   The President could *simply* not ratify the treaty (= (43) (ii))

Now, if we suppose that *simply* in such cases is positioned in front of the left-most constituent of the Verb Phrase, then the dual analysis in (45) would provide a very straightforward account of the dual position of *simply*. For, in (45) (i), *ratify* is the leftmost constituent of VP, so that *simply* is positioned in front of *ratify* in (46) (i). But in (45) (ii), *not* is the first constituent of the VP, so that *simply* is positioned in front of *not* in (46) (ii).

Further support for the claim that *not* modifies the Modal *could* on interpretation (43) (i) but modifies the VP [*ratify the treaty*] on interpretation (43) (ii) comes from the fact that the sentence (42) has two different *pseudo-cleft* counterparts. (Pseudo-cleft sentences are sentences of the schematic form 'What X did was Y'.) Thus, the pseudo-cleft counterpart of sentence (42) is

Structure

(47) (i) below on interpretation (43) (i), and (47) (ii) on interpretation (43) (ii):

(47) (i)   What the President could not do is ratify the treaty (= (43) (i))

    (ii)   What the President could do is not ratify the treaty (= (43) (ii))

And it seems clear that *not* goes with the Modal *could* in (47) (i), but with the VP [*ratify the treaty*] in (47) (ii). Thus, although the structural difference between (45) (i) and (45) (ii) is not reflected in a word-order difference in our original sentence (42), there are variants of (42) in which this structural difference does indeed directly correlate with a word-order difference – e.g. in sentence pairs such as (46) and (47) above.

Just as differences in syntactic structure between sentences correlate with semantic differences (i.e. if two sentences differ in syntactic structure, then they will also differ in semantic structure), so too they correlate with phonological differences (so that, for example, sentences with different superficial syntactic structure will have different stress patterns, etc.). By way of example, let's consider a phonological rule in English which I shall call NEGATIVE CONTRACTION. Modals in English generally have contracted negative forms, so that alongside the 'full forms' in the lefthand column in (48) below, we find the corresponding contracted forms in the righthand column:

(48)

Full form	*Contracted form*
would not	wouldn't
should not	shouldn't
could not	couldn't
might not	mightn't

However, NEGATIVE CONTRACTION appears to be subject to a structural condition, which we can gloss informally along the lines of (49) below:

(49)   NEGATIVE CONTRACTION is usually only possible where the negative modifies the Modal, and not where it modifies the following Verb Phrase

If this is so, then we should expect contraction to be possible in a structure like (45) (i) above, but not in (45) (ii). And this does indeed seem to be the case: for, a sentence such as:

(50)   The President couldn't ratify the treaty

can only have interpretation (43) (i) (= 'It would not be possible for the President to ratify the treaty'), and not interpretation (43) (ii) (= 'It would be possible for the President not to ratify the treaty'). What this means is that our NEGATIVE CONTRACTION rule is sensitive to the structure of the sentence to which it applies. More precisely, the rule applies to contract a negative which modifies a Modal, but not to a negative which modifies a VP. But any such account of NEGATIVE CONTRACTION presupposes that sentences have as their immediate constituents [NP M VP], and thus requires us to posit the existence of phrasal categories such as (in particular) VP. More generally still, we can say that the claim that sentences are structured out of Phrases of various sorts receives independent support from phonological facts.

Overall, then, we can conclude this section by saying that the claim that sentences are structured out of Phrases is supported by morphological, semantic, and phonological evidence. But it should be remembered (as we pointed out at the beginning of this section) that the bulk of the evidence in favour of this assumption is *syntactic* in nature: and accordingly, the rest of our chapter is devoted to presenting various different kinds of syntactic evidence in support of this claim.

> *You should now be able to tackle exercise III*

2.5   Phrasal categories: distributional evidence

So far, we have seen that there is morphological, semantic, and phonological evidence in support of the assumption that sentences have a categorial constituent structure. However, it should be repeated that the bulk of the relevant empirical evidence is *syntactic* in nature. Many such syntactic arguments relate to facts about the *distribution* of various sequences of words (recall that many of the arguments we gave in support of positing *word-level* categories were of this kind): i.e. the argumentation takes the form: 'Unless we postulate that sentences are structured out of Phrases belonging to various categories, we cannot account for which sequences of words can occur in which positions in which types of sentence.' And the whole of this section will be devoted to considering *distributional* arguments in support of our claim that sentences are structured out of Phrases belonging to categories of various kinds.

One such distributional argument concerns a phenomenon which we shall refer to simply as *Preposing*. Under appropriate stylistic conditions (e.g. to achieve a particular rhetorical effect), certain parts of a sentence may be preposed 'for emphasis' (especially where the preposed sequence is being contrasted with some other sequence). For example, one way of emphasising the sequence *your elder sister* in a sentence like:

(51)   I can't stand [*your elder sister*]

is to prepose it – i.e. position it at the front of the rest of the sentence, as in:

(52)   [*Your elder sister*], I can't stand (though your brother's OK)

However, it turns out that while some parts of sentences can be preposed in this way, others cannot. For example, various types of phrasal constituent (such as those bracketed in (53) below) can freely undergo preposing: cf.

(53) (a)   [*That kind of behaviour*], I simply will not tolerate (Noun Phrase)
(b)   I went to see the new James Bond film yesterday, and [*very exciting*] it was, too (Adjectival Phrase)
(c)   [*Very shortly*], he's going to be leaving for Paris (Adverbial Phrase)
(d)   [*Down the hill*] John ran, as fast as he could (Prepositional Phrase)
(e)   [*Give in to blackmail*], I never will! (Verb Phrase)

But only a *whole phrase* (and not just *part of* a phrase) can be preposed in this way: thus, in a sentence such as (51) above *I can't stand your elder sister*, only the whole NP (Noun Phrase) [*your elder sister*] can be preposed for emphasis, not just part of the phrase: cf.

(54) (a)   *Your elder sister*, I can't stand
(b)   **Your elder*, I can't stand sister
(c)   **Elder sister*, I can't stand your
(d)   **Sister*, I can't stand your elder
(e)   **Your*, I can't stand elder sister

Likewise, a nonconstituent sequence (i.e. a string of words which do not together form a (phrasal) constituent, but which belong to two or more separate constituents) cannot be preposed: hence, in the case of sentences such as:

(55) (a)   John rang up his mother
(b)   John stood up his date
(c)   John looked up her phone number

we cannot prepose *up* together with the rest of the sentence, as we see from the ungrammaticality of:

(56) (a)   **Up his mother*, John rang
(b)   **Up his date*, John stood
(c)   **Up her phone number*, John looked

The reason is that in each of the sentences in (55), the particle *up* forms a constituent together with the Verb (giving us the so-called 'Phrasal Verbs' *ring up*, *stand up*, and *look up*), not with the immediately following Noun Phrase: since the *up* + NP sequence does not form a phrasal constituent, it cannot therefore be preposed 'for emphasis'. So, it would seem that the relevant generalisation governing Preposing is that:

(57)   Only phrasal constituents (i.e. whole phrases) can undergo Preposing

But note that this account of *Preposing* presupposes that sentences have a categorial constituent structure.

A parallel argument can be formulated in relation to the converse phenomenon of *Postposing*. Under particular circumstances, it may be possible (or necessary) for a particular expression in a sentence to be postposed. This is particularly frequent with expressions which are (in some vague intuitive sense) felt to be especially 'heavy' or 'long'. For example, the bracketed expression in (58) (a) below can optionally be postposed – i.e. moved to the position it occupies in (58) (b):

(58) (a)   He explained [*all the terrible problems that he had encountered*] to her

   (b)   He explained to her [*all the terrible problems that he had encountered*]

However, not just any random string of words can be postposed in this way; for example, in (58) (a) above, it would not have been possible to postpose the string *terrible problems that he had encountered*, as we see from the ungrammaticality of:

(59)   *He explained all the to her *terrible problems that he had encountered*

Why should it be that we can postpose the string *all the terrible problems that he had encountered*, but not the string *terrible problems that he had encountered*? The obvious answer is that *all the terrible problems that he had encountered* is a complete Noun Phrase, whereas *terrible problems that he had encountered* is not (rather, it is a subpart of the larger containing Noun Phrase). And we might assume that just as only complete phrases can undergo *Preposing*, so too only complete phrasal constituents can undergo *Postposing*. In other words, we might revise our earlier principle (57) as:

(60)   Only phrasal constituents can undergo Preposing or Postposing

Since *Preposing* and *Postposing* are both types of *Movement*, we can refine (60) further as:

(61)   Only phrasal constituents can undergo *Movement* (from one posi-
         tion in a sentence to another)

But once again, note that this account of *Movement* presupposes that sentences have a hierarchical constituent structure.

A further *distributional* argument in support of constituent structure can be
formulated in relation to facts relating to what are traditionally known as *sentence-fragments*. Consider the following dialogue:

(62)   SPEAKER A: Where did he go?
         SPEAKER B: *Up the hill*

Instead of replying with a full sentence like 'He went up the hill', speaker B
chooses to give a 'short-form' reply using the sentence-fragment 'Up the hill'.
Any adequate grammar of English will clearly have to specify what kinds of
sequences can and cannot be used as sentence-fragments in this way, since
some sequences cannot be so used: cf.

(63)   SPEAKER A: Who were you ringing up?
         SPEAKER B: *Up my elder sister*

Why the contrast between (62) and (63)? An obvious answer is to suggest that
up the hill is a constituent of the sentence *He went up the hill*, whereas *up my
sister* is not a constituent of a sentence such as *I was ringing up my sister*. We
might then propose that only *constituents* can serve as sentence-fragments.
Moreover, it seems likely that only complete *phrases* can function in this way,
not parts of phrases; thus, for example, speaker B could have replied with the
Noun Phrase *my elder sister* in (63), though not with the simple Noun *sister*.
The relevant restriction would therefore appear to be that:

(64)   Only phrasal constituents (i.e. whole phrases) can serve as sen-
         tence-fragments (in an appropriate context)

Thus, any account of the use of *sentence-fragments* also requires us to assume
that sentences have a categorial constituent structure.

However, it might at first sight seem as if there are some obvious potential
counter-examples to the claim in (64) that only complete phrases can be used
as sentence-fragments. Consider, for example, the following dialogue:

(65)   SPEAKER A: Where are you going to?
         SPEAKER B: *To the cinema/The cinema*

Here, speaker B can reply either with the complete Prepositional Phrase *to the
cinema*, or simply with *the cinema*. But – we might object – in using the shorter

reply *the cinema*, isn't he using just *part of* the Prepositional Phrase *to the cinema*, in apparent violation of the principle (64) that only *complete phrases* can be used as sentence-fragments? The objection is an interesting one (shows you're beginning to think like a syntactician at last!), but entirely misconceived! To see why, consider the structure of the Prepositional Phrase [*to the cinema*], which we might represent as in (66) below:

(66)

```
                  PP
          _____
        /                     \
       P                       NP
       |              _____
       to           /                     \
                   D                       N
                   |                       |
                  the                    cinema
```

While it is perfectly true that *the cinema* is part of the PP *to the cinema* (it is the *object* or *complement* of the Preposition *to*), it is equally true that *the cinema* is itself a *Phrase* – namely, a Noun Phrase (NP). So in replying simply 'The cinema' in (65), speaker в is in fact using a complete Phrase (to be more precise, a complete Noun Phrase), and hence there is no violation of our earlier principle (64).

Let's now turn to look at one final *distributional* argument in support of the assumption that sentences have a categorial constituent structure. This particular argument relates to the distribution of adverbial expressions. From a syntactic point of view, there are two different classes of Adverbials in English; one including Adverbs such as *certainly*, and the other including Adverbs such as *completely*. If we consider a simple sentence such as:

(67)   The team can rely on my support

we find that these two classes of Adverbs can occupy rather different positions in the sentence, as (68) below illustrates:

(68) (a)   *Certainly/*completely*, the team can rely on my support
    (b)   *The *certainly/completely* team can rely on my support
    (c)   The team *certainly/*completely* can rely on my support
    (d)   The team can *certainly/completely* rely on my support
    (e)   The team can rely *completely/*certainly* on my support
    (f)   *The team can rely on *certainly/completely* my support
    (g)   *The team can rely on my *certainly/completely* support
    (h)   The team can rely on my support *completely/certainly*

How can we account for the different distribution of Adverbs such as *certainly* on the one hand, and *completely* on the other? We can provide a simple answer to this question in constituent structure terms, along the lines of (69) below:

(69) (i)   Adverbs like *certainly* are S-adverbs, and hence can only be attached to an S-node

(ii)   Adverbs like *completely* are VP-adverbs, and so can only be attached to a VP-node

Let's assume that sentence (67) has the structure (70) below:

(70)

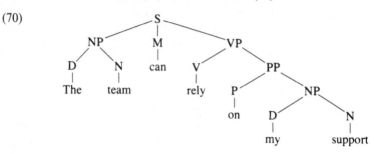

Now, since *certainly* is an S-adverb, it can occur in positions where it is directly attached to S (viz. at the beginning or end of the overall sentence, between *team* and *can*, and between *can* and *rely*), but not in positions where it would be directly attached to VP (e.g. between *rely* and *on*), or to PP (e.g. between *on* and *my*), or to NP (e.g. between *my* and *support*). Possible positions for S-adverbs can be indicated schematically by the asterisks in (71) below:

(71)   Possible positions for S-adverbs like *certainly*

[S * The team * can * [VP rely on my support VP] * S]

Conversely, since *completely* is a VP-adverb, it can occur only in positions where it is immediately attached to VP (viz. at the beginning of the whole VP as in (68) (d), at the end of the whole VP as in (68) (h), and in the middle of the VP between *rely* and *on* as in (68) (e)), and cannot occur in positions where it is directly attached to S (e.g. before *the*, or between *team* and *can*), or to PP (e.g. between *on* and *my*), or to NP (e.g. between *my* and *support*). Possible positions for VP-adverbs can be indicated schematically by the asterisks in (72) below:

(72)   Possible positions for VP-adverbs like *completely*

[S The team can [VP * rely * [PP on my support] * VP] S]

The preceding discussion about Adverbials serves to illustrate very clearly the fundamental principle that any statement about the distribution of particular types of expression requires reference to *constituents* and *categories* –

i.e. presupposes that sentences are hierarchically structured out of word-level and phrase-level constituents, and that such constituents belong to categories such as N – NP, V – VP, P – PP, A – AP, ADV – ADVP, etc.

You should now be able to tackle exercise IV

2.6 Phrasal categories: other syntactic evidence

Thus far, we have argued that *distributional* evidence provides strong syntactic support for our claim that sentences are structured out of Phrases belonging to various categories (NP, VP, PP, AP, ADVP, etc.). In this section, we are going to look at three other types of syntactic evidence supporting this claim.

The first such evidence comes from a phenomenon known as *Coordination*. English and other languages have a variety of *Coordinating Conjunctions* (CONJ) like *and, or, but*, etc. which can be used to *coordinate* or *conjoin* words or phrases: cf.

(73) (a)   He has *a cat* and *a dog*
     (b)   I met your *mother* and *father*
     (c)   Is she *in the kitchen* or *in the bathroom*?
     (d)   He speaks *very slowly* but *very articulately*

In each of the sentences in (73), a Coordinating Conjunction has been used to conjoin the italicised pairs of words or phrases. Clearly, any observationally adequate grammar of English will have to provide a principled answer to the questions:

(74)   What kinds of elements can and cannot be coordinated in English?

Now, it turns out that we can't just coordinate any random set of elements in English, as we see from the ungrammaticality of:

(75)   *John rang *up his mother* and *up his sister*

Why can the italicised items be conjoined in (73), but not in (75)? One possible answer could be that the italicised elements can be conjoined in (73) because they are constituents, whereas the coordinated sequences in (75) are not constituents (because *up* in (75) forms part of the Phrasal Verb *ring up*, so that the sequence *up his mother* is not a constituent). That is, we might suggest a principle along the lines of:

(76)   Only *constituents* can be conjoined; nonconstituent sequences cannot be conjoined

Structure

But can a constituent of one type (or category) be coordinated with a constituent of a different type? Consider the following paradigm:

(77) (a) John wrote *to Mary* and *to Fred* (= PP and PP)
(b) John wrote *a letter* and *a postcard* (= NP and NP)
(c) *John wrote *a letter* and *to Fred* (= NP and PP)
(d) *John wrote *to Fred* and *a letter* (= PP and NP)

(77) shows us that we can conjoin two PPs or two NPs quite freely, but that any attempt to conjoin an NP with a PP, or a PP with an NP leads to an unnatural, unidiomatic, and 'forced' sentence (the type of sentence which, precisely because of its very unnaturalness, may sometimes be used for humorous effect). This suggests that we might revise our principle (76) as:

(78)   Only identical categories can be conjoined, idiomatically

Let's now test the predictions made by the principle (78) for a wider range of categories; it predicts that the following sentences will all be grammatical, because in each case the italicised pairs of words belong to the same category:

(79) (a) Good *linguists* and *philosophers* are rare (N and N)
(b) John is a very *kind* and *considerate* person (A and A)
(c) There are arguments *for* and *against* this claim (P and P)
(d) J.R. *walks* and *talks* like a true Texan (V and V)
(e) You can bring *these* and *those* books (D and D)
(f) He opened the door quite *slowly* and *deliberately* (ADV and ADV)

In each case in (79) we have conjoined identical *word-level categories*; but the principle (78) also predicts that we should be able to conjoin identical *phrasal categories* as well. And this prediction appears to be borne out by sentences such as those in (80) below:

(80) (a) [NP *The man next door*] and [NP *his wife*] are very nice
(b) He is a [AP *very shy*] and [AP *rather inarticulate*] man
(c) He went [PP *to London*] and [PP *to Paris*]
(d) He may [VP *go to London*] and [VP *visit his mother*]
(e) John drives [ADVP *very slowly*] and [ADVP *very carefully*]

It thus seems that the principle (78) has considerable empirical support. But note that the principle makes crucial reference to constituent structure and category membership: in other words, it is not clear how we could provide any principled account of Coordination if we did not posit that sentences are structured into sets of *constituents*, each of which belongs to a particular *cat-*

76

egory. This discussion serves to underline our remark at the beginning of this chapter that the real status of constituents and categories is that of *theoretical constructs* – i.e. abstract elements without which it is not obvious how we could provide a principled explanation of linguistic phenomena such as *Coordination*.

The type of Coordination illustrated in sentences like (79) and (80) above is what we might call *Ordinary Coordination*. However, there is a second (rather different) type of Coordination which we shall call *Shared Constituent Coordination* (though for irrelevant historical reasons it is more widely known in the literature as *Right Node Raising*). This second type of Coordination can be illustrated by sentences such as:

(81) (a)   John walked (and Mary ran) [*up the hill*]
     (b)   John denied – but Fred admitted – [*complicity in the crime*]
     (c)   John will, and Mary may, [*go to the party*]

In a sense which we shall not attempt to make precise here, the italicised sequence in each example is *shared* (so to speak) between the two conjuncts. Thus, for example, *up the hill* seems to go with both *John walked* and *Mary ran* in (81) (a). What is more important for our present purposes is that there are restrictions on this type of Coordination – as illustrated by the ungrammaticality of examples such as:

(82)   *John rang (and Harry picked) *up Mary's sister*

Why are sentences like (81) grammatical, but those like (82) ungrammatical? We might seek an answer to this question along the following lines. We might argue that a sentence like (81) (a) is (in an obvious sense) somehow an elliptical (i.e. 'short') form of:

(83)   *John walked up the hill and Mary ran up the hill*

and that in both of the italicised conjuncts, the sequence *up the hill* is a constituent of the italicised clause containing it. By contrast, we might say that (82) is an elliptical form of:

(84)   *John rang up Mary's sister and Harry picked up Mary's sister*

and that in neither of the italicised conjuncts is *up Mary's sister* a constituent of the Clause containing it: for, in the first conjunct *up* 'goes with' the Verb *rang* to form the Phrasal Verb *rang up*, and in the second conjunct *up* 'goes with' the Verb *picked*, forming the Phrasal Verb *picked up*). So, it seems that we might try and answer the question: 'Why is *Shared Constituent Coordina-*

tion possible in cases like (81) but not in (82)?' in terms of a principle such as the following:

(85)   *Shared Constituent Coordination* is only possible where the shared string is a possible constituent of each of the conjuncts

But note that the answer we have given to our question about when this type of Coordination is and is not possible makes crucial reference to the constituent structure of sentences: i.e. in order to provide a proper account of Shared Constituent Coordination, we have to posit that sentences have a categorial constituent structure.

Let's now turn to another linguistic phenomenon whose systematic description also seems to require the postulation of an abstract categorial constituent structure associated with sentences – namely, *Pronominalisation*. It is a general property of natural languages that they possess devices for referring to entities mentioned elsewhere in the same sentence or discourse. Consider, by way of example, the following discourse:

(86)   SPEAKER A: What do you think of the guy who wrote that unbelievably boring book on Transformational Grammar?
         SPEAKER B: I can't stand *him*

In (86) the italicised *Pronoun* provides a handy way of referring to the individual concerned without the need to repeat the full phrase [*the guy who wrote that unbelievably boring book on Transformational Grammar*]. Using traditional terminology, we can say that [*the guy who wrote that unbelievably boring book on Transformational Grammar*] is the *antecedent* of the Pronoun *him*. However, the term *Pronoun* (although a traditional one) is peculiarly inappropriate here, simply because the antecedent of a Pronoun like *him* is not in fact a Noun, but rather a whole Noun Phrase: that is, *him* refers to the whole Noun Phrase [*the guy who wrote that unbelievably boring book on Transformational Grammar*], and not to any individual Noun within the Noun Phrase. Likewise, the position occupied by so-called 'Personal Pronouns' like *him* in sentences is not that of a Noun, but rather that of a Noun Phrase – hence the fact that we could not replace the Nouns *guy*, *book*, and *Grammar* in speaker A's utterance in (86) by the corresponding Pronouns *him* and *it*, as we see from the ungrammaticality of:

(87)   *What do you think of the *him* who wrote that unbelievably boring *it* on Transformational *it*?

But precisely because pronouns like *him* occur in typical NP positions in sentences, we could replace the whole NP [*the guy who wrote that unbelievably boring book on Transformational Grammar*] by *him*, so that speaker A could equally have asked:

(88)   What do you think of *him*?

Thus, the term *Pronoun* is doubly inappropriate, since it is not an accurate description either of the distribution of such items (i.e. they don't occur in sentence positions typically occupied by a Noun), or of the class of expressions which can serve as their antecedents (since Pronouns typically refer back to Noun Phrases, not to individual Nouns). Words like *him*, *it*, etc. are more accurately described as *pro-NP* (pro-Noun Phrase) constituents, since they occur in NP positions in a sentence, and generally have NPs as their antecedents (though we shall shortly qualify this remark).

In more general terms, since Pronouns 'replace' or 'refer' back to other constituents, we might refer to them as *pro-constituents*, or *proforms*. Not all pro-constituents are pro-NPs, however. One might argue, for example, that in a discourse such as:

(89)   SPEAKER A: Have you ever been to Paris?
          SPEAKER B: No, I have never been *there*

the word *there* is a *pro-PP* (pro-Prepositional Phrase), in that it occupies the same sentence-position as the Prepositional Phrase *to Paris*. In much the same way, we might argue that in sentences such as the following, the italicised words function as pro-VP constituents, and hence refer back to the bracketed VP:

(90) (a)   John might [VP go home], and *so* might Bill
     (b)   John might [VP resign his post], *as* might Bill
     (c)   If John can [VP speak French fluently] – *which* we all know he can – why is he shy with French girls?

And in (91) below, we might argue that *so* functions as a pro-AP (pro-Adjectival Phrase) constituent:

(91)   Many people consider John [AP *extremely rude*], but I've never found him *so*

Thus, there's more to proforms than at first meets the eye! In fact, there seem to be almost as many different kinds of proform as there are Phrases (so, for example, *him* is a pro-NP, *there* can be a pro-PP, *as* can be a pro-VP, *so* can be a pro-AP or a pro-VP, and so on). It is interesting to note that proforms generally replace *phrase-level* constituents, not *word-level* constituents.

Any adequate description of pro-constituents or proforms will have to be concerned with both the syntax and semantics of them. Any adequate syntax of proforms will have to specify which sentence-positions particular proforms can occur in; while any adequate account of the semantics of proforms will have to specify what kind of expressions can be construed as the antecedent of a given proform. But it turns out that any adequate description of either the syntax or the semantics of proforms will have to make crucial reference to *constituents* and *categories*.

We can make this discussion more concrete in relation to the proform *it*. An adequate syntax for *it* will have to answer the question: 'What range of sentence-positions can *it* occupy in English?' The answer is that *it* can occupy the same range of sentence-positions as a typical Noun Phrase like *the book on the table*, as we see from (92):

(92)
(a) $\left\{ \begin{array}{l} \textit{The book on the table} \\ \textit{It} \end{array} \right\}$ is interesting

(b) Is $\left\{ \begin{array}{l} \textit{the book on the table} \\ \textit{it} \end{array} \right\}$ yours

(c) I like $\left\{ \begin{array}{l} \textit{the book on the table} \\ \textit{it} \end{array} \right\}$

(d) I've read about $\left\{ \begin{array}{l} \textit{the book on the table} \\ \textit{it} \end{array} \right\}$

Syntactically, then, *it* has the same distribution as a typical Noun Phrase: i.e. syntactically, *it* functions as a pro-NP.

But what about the semantics of *it*? What kinds of expression can be interpreted as the antecedent of *it*? All the italicised expressions in (93) below are possible antecedents for *it*:

(93) (a)　　[*My car*] is OK when it works
(b)　　[*The back seat of my car*] has got books on it
(c)　　The trouble with [*the table*] is that it's too small
(d)　　If I find [*the lid of the kettle*], I'll give it to you
(e)　　I never use [*that bone-handled knife*], because it's blunt

What have the italicised expressions in (93) got in common? The obvious answer is that they are all Noun Phrases, since they can all occur in the (bracketed) NP positions in (93). Thus, an obvious generalisation about the semantics of *it* is that *it* can be interpreted as having an (inanimate, singular) NP as its antecedent.

But is it only Noun Phrases which can serve as the antecedent of proforms like *it*? Data like (94) below cast doubt on this:

(94) (a)   SPEAKER A: *Mary has finished her assignment*
           SPEAKER B: I don't believe it
    (b)   *Jean is pregnant again*, I just know it
    (c)   If *I don't turn up*, it won't be fair on you
    (d)   SPEAKER A: *Is there snow outside?*
           SPEAKER B: Does it matter?
    (e)   They say *he's planning to resign*, but it may not be true

Each of the italicised phrases in (94) can serve as the antecedent of *it*, and each appears to have the categorial status of S (= Clause). So it would appear that not only an NP, but also an S can be interpreted as the antecedent of the proform *it*.

This shows up an important discrepancy between the *syntax* and *semantics* of certain types of proform: syntactically, *it* occurs only in typical NP positions, not in typical S positions. Thus, for example, a verb like *hope* can take a following *S* complement, but not a following NP complement: cf.

(95) (a)   I hope [*you will come*] (= hope S)
    (b)   *I hope [*the pen on the table*] (= hope NP)

Significantly, *it* cannot be used as a direct complement of *hope*:

(96)   *I hope *it*

Example (96) shows us that *it* cannot occur in a typical S position in a sentence; on the contrary, syntactically *it* occurs only in NP positions. But examples like (94) show us that semantically *it* can have an S as its antecedent. This reveals an obvious discrepancy between the syntax and semantics of *it*.

There are two conclusions to emerge from our discussion of Pronominalisation. The first is that Syntax is autonomous of Semantics, so that in consequence, any adequate description of proforms must include both a syntactic and a semantic characterisation of their function (since these two functions may be distinct). It's not much use simply specifying that such-and-such a form is a pro-NP, pro-PP, pro-S, or whatever: is that meant to be a description of its syntactic distribution, or of the class of expressions which can serve as its antecedent, or both? The second (and more general) conclusion to be drawn from our discussion is that any adequate account of either the syntax or semantics of pro-constituents will have to make crucial reference to structural properties of sentences. For it turns out that proforms have the same distribution as certain phrasal categories on the one hand, and that the class of expressions which can serve as their antecedents is most simply characterised in categorial terms on the other. Once again, then, we find a linguistic phenomenon (i.e. Pronominalisation) which cannot be described adequately without appealing to notions of constituent structure.

Now let's turn to further empirical evidence supporting the same conclusion. Under certain discourse conditions, it is possible in English (and other languages) for some part of a sentence to undergo *Ellipsis* (i.e. to be omitted), provided that the missing part of the sentence can be 'understood from the context'. For example, in a discourse such as (97) below, it is possible to omit the slashed material, since it is identical to something said by the previous speaker, and is thus in some sense 'redundant':

(97)   SPEAKER A: John won't *wash the dishes*
         SPEAKER B: I bet he will ~~wash the dishes~~ if you're nice to him

The same type of Ellipsis is also found in (98):

(98)   John won't *help me with the dishes*, but his brother will ~~help me with the dishes~~

In a fairly obvious sense, the slashed material in (97) and (98) can be omitted because it is identical to the italicised material, and is thus in some sense 're-coverable'. An obvious question which any observationally adequate grammar of English is going to have to answer is:

(99)   What kind of elements can undergo Ellipsis (i.e. be omitted) in this way, and under what conditions?

In actual fact, we can't just omit *any* random set of words in a sentence when they are identical to another set, as we see from the fact that the following sentences are ungrammatical if the slashed material is omitted:

(100) (a)   *John won't put the vodka into the drink, but his brother will put the vodka into the ~~drink~~

     (b)   *John won't put the vodka into the drink, but his brother will put the vodka into ~~the drink~~

     (c)   *John won't put the vodka into the drink, but his brother will put the vodka ~~into the drink~~

     (d)   *John won't put the vodka into the drink, but his brother will put the ~~vodka into the drink~~

     (e)   *John won't put the vodka into the drink, but his brother will put ~~the vodka into the drink~~

Although we can't omit any of the slashed sequences in (100) above, we can omit that in (101) below:

(101)   John won't put the vodka into the drink, but his brother will p̶u̶t̶
          t̶h̶e̶ v̶o̶d̶k̶a̶ i̶n̶t̶o̶ t̶h̶e̶ d̶r̶i̶n̶k̶

Why is it that the slashed material can be omitted in (101) but not in (100)? We
can give a principled answer to this question in terms of constituent structure.
Let us assume that the structure of a sentence such as *His brother will put the
vodka into the drink* is as follows:

(102)

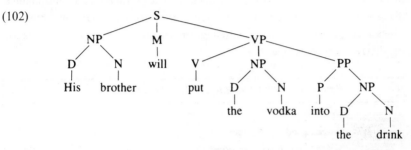

Given the assumption of a constituent structure such as (102) above, we can
suggest a tentative answer to the question we asked earlier about what word-
sequences can and cannot undergo Ellipsis, namely:

(103)   Only VPs (Verb Phrases) can undergo Ellipsis (under appropriate
          discourse conditions)

Principle (103) would provide a ready account of why omission of the slashed
material was possible in (101), but not in (100); for in (101) the slashed material constitutes a VP constituent, whereas in (100) (a) it was an N(oun), in
(100) (b) an NP (Noun Phrase), in (100) (c) a PP (Prepositional Phrase), in
(100) (d) a nonconstituent N PP sequence, and in (100) (e) it was a nonconstituent NP PP sequence. Further support for the principle (103) comes from the
fact that it correctly predicts that the slashed VPs in (104) below can be omitted since they are identical to the italicised VPs (and hence are 'recoverable',
or 'redundant', in some sense):

(104) (a)   He may *come home early*, but then again he may not c̶o̶m̶e̶ h̶o̶m̶e̶
              e̶a̶r̶l̶y̶
      (b)   Mary wants to *close the shop*, but I don't want to c̶l̶o̶s̶e̶ t̶h̶e̶ s̶h̶o̶p̶
      (c)   *Fetch me an apple*, if you can f̶e̶t̶c̶h̶ m̶e̶ a̶n̶ a̶p̶p̶l̶e̶
      (d)   SPEAKER A: Could you *have a look at the car*?
              SPEAKER B: OK, I will h̶a̶v̶e̶ a̶ l̶o̶o̶k̶ a̶t̶ t̶h̶e̶ c̶a̶r̶

What's interesting about the above discussion is that it tells us that we cannot
attain any adequate description of the phenomenon of *Ellipsis* unless we
recognise that sentences have a categorial constituent structure.

In our discussion in sections 2.3–2.6 in this chapter, we have presented a substantial body of empirical arguments in support of the key claim that sentences are hierarchically structured into word- and phrase-level constituents, each of which is assigned to a particular category. In general, these twin assumptions are uncontroversial – i.e. virtually any linguist working on Syntax from any theoretical perspective will accept the need to recognise the existence of an abstract syntactic structure associated with sentences. Where linguists disagree with each other is over the question of just how many different categories there are in a particular language or universally – *not* over the question of whether there are categories.

You should now be able to tackle exercises V and VI

2.7 Words used as Phrases

So far, we have assumed that there are essentially two different *levels* of categories in language: on the one hand there are word-level categories like N, V, P, A, ADV, etc., and on the other hand there are phrase-level categories such as NP, VP, PP, AP, ADVP, etc.; and the distinction between the two seems obvious enough: e.g. *dog* is a Noun, and [*this dog*] is a Noun Phrase. However, empirical evidence which we shall present in this section leads us to the conclusion that the relationship between word-level categories and their phrasal counterparts is by no means as straightforward as one might imagine. By way of illustration, consider a sentence such as:

(105)   Cars can be useful

There doesn't seem to be anything controversial in saying that *cars* is an N (= Noun) in (105), *can* is an M (= Modal), *be* is a V (= Verb), and *useful* is an A (= Adjective); in addition, given the assumptions we have been making, we might argue that *be useful* is a VP (= Verb Phrase), and that the whole sequence *Cars can be useful* is an S (= Clause/Sentence). Hence it might seem reasonable to suppose that (105) has the S-structure (106) below:

(106)

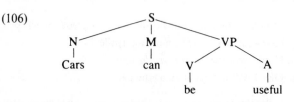

But in fact, this analysis would probably be rejected by most linguists; instead, they would want to say that *cars*, in addition to being an N (= Noun) is also an NP (= Noun Phrase); and that *useful*, in addition to being an A (= Adjective) is also an AP (= Adjectival Phrase); thus, in place of (106) above, they would prefer the analysis (107) below:

(107)

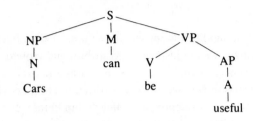

But – we might object – surely it is absurd to say that *cars* is a Noun Phrase and *useful* an Adjectival Phrase when each of these constituents contains only one word: after all, isn't it in the very nature of things that a *Phrase* is a sequence of two or more words? The answer to this is simply: 'No, not the way that we use the term *Phrase* here.' Any theory defines the technical terms it uses in relation to the way in which it uses them: and within the kind of model we are discussing, the term *Phrase* is used to mean simply 'a *set* of elements which form a constituent', with no restriction on the number of elements that the set may or must contain. So, for example 'Noun Phrase' can be taken as meaning something like: 'an expression containing a head Noun', without any implication that a Noun Phrase must necessarily contain anything other than the head Noun.

But of course it isn't enough merely to say that if we define the notion *Phrase* in the appropriate way, then we *could* call expressions consisting of a single Noun like *cars* Noun Phrases. The real question posed by such an analysis is: 'What is the empirical justification for doing so?' – i.e. what set of facts could we explain thereby which might otherwise go unexplained? One set of facts concerns the *distribution* of expressions like *cars*. Notice that in place of *cars* in a sentence like (105) above we could also have any of the italicised expressions in (108) below:

(108) (a)   [*Fast cars*] can be useful
  (b)   [*Very fast cars*] can be useful
  (c)   [*Those very fast cars*] can be useful

And the same is true of other sentence-positions: wherever we can have a full Noun Phrase like [*very fast cars*], we can also have the simple Noun *cars*, as the paradigm in (109) below illustrates:

(109)
  (a)   Do $\begin{Bmatrix} very\,fast\,cars \\ cars \end{Bmatrix}$ turn you on?

(b)   I really enjoy $\begin{Bmatrix} \textit{very fast cars} \\ \textit{cars} \end{Bmatrix}$

(c)   I'm just crazy about $\begin{Bmatrix} \textit{very fast cars} \\ \textit{cars} \end{Bmatrix}$

In other words, a single unmodified Noun can have the same distribution as a Noun Phrase. Accordingly, we are justified on distributional grounds in saying that unmodified Nouns have the status of Noun Phrases (as well as that of Noun): and this is the reason why we posited that *cars* in (107) above is not only an N but also an NP. Consequently, we define 'Noun Phrase' as meaning 'Phrase containing a head Noun' (irrespective of whether or not it also contains nominal modifiers of one sort or another).

The same kind of reasoning can be extended to arguing that an Adjective like [*useful*] is actually also an Adjectival Phrase in sentences like (105) [*Cars can be useful*]. For, of course, here [*useful*] is occurring in exactly the position in which we could find an Adjectival Phrase like [*very useful*] (cf. *Cars can be very useful*). And more generally, wherever we can have a full Adjectival Phrase, we can have a simple unmodified Adjective on its own, as we see from the paradigm in (110) below:

(110) (a)   She is $\begin{Bmatrix} \textit{very keen on sport} \\ \textit{keen} \end{Bmatrix}$

(b)   I've always found her $\begin{Bmatrix} \textit{very keen on sport} \\ \textit{keen} \end{Bmatrix}$

(c) $\begin{Bmatrix} \textit{Very keen on sport} \\ \textit{Keen} \end{Bmatrix}$ though she is, she's hopeless

Thus, we might say that because a single unmodified Adjective has the same distribution as a full Adjectival Phrase, then it follows that an unmodified A should be assigned the status of AP as well as A – precisely as with *useful* in (107) above. Accordingly, we might define an Adjectival Phrase as: 'a Phrase which contains a head Adjective' (with or without modifiers).

Of course, exactly the same reasoning also extends to other constituents: for example, we could argue on distributional grounds that in:

(111)   John must speak clearly

the word *clearly* as well as being an ADV (= Adverb) is also an ADVP (= Adverbial Phrase), since *clearly* here occurs in exactly the kind of sentence-position in which we could find an ADVP like [*rather more clearly*]. Thus, the structure of (111) would be:

(112)

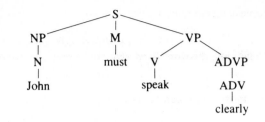

And the same *distributional* argument also extends to the analysis of simple Verbs that lack following complements, e.g. *leave* in a sentence such as:

(113)   John may leave

Here we might be tempted to say that *leave* is simply a Verb; but note that in place of *leave* we could have a Verb Phrase like [*leave home*]: cf.

(114)   John may leave home

Wherever we can have [*leave home*] we can also have simply *leave*: hence, on distributional grounds, we might claim that *leave* in (113) has the same categorial status as [*leave home*] in (114) – i.e. that of VP. Thus, the structure of (113) will be:

(115)

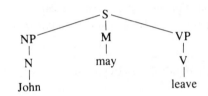

To summarise, then: wherever a *simple category* (like N, V, P, A, ADV, etc.) in a given sentence can be replaced by the corresponding *phrasal category* (e.g. NP, VP, PP, AP, ADVP, etc.), then the simple category is to be regarded as an instance of the corresponding phrasal category. So, for example, an unmodified Noun which can be replaced by a full Noun Phrase is to be taken as an instance of NP; an unaccompanied Adjective which is replaceable by a full Adjectival Phrase is to be regarded as an instance of AP ... and so on, and so forth. What this in effect means is that we regard the key property of a Noun Phrase as being that of containing a head Noun (though not necessarily anything else), the key property of an Adjectival Phrase as being that of containing a head Adjective (though not necessarily anything else) ... and so on and so forth.

In case you are feeling sceptical about this line of reasoning (I sensed you were!), let me try and present more evidence in support of this crucial point of principle. For example, why should I want to say that in a sentence such as:

(116)   Most people can't stand hypocrisy

the word *hypocrisy* is a Noun Phrase comprising simply the head Noun *hypocrisy*? Well, for one thing, the word *hypocrisy* can be preposed for emphasis, as in:

(117)   *Hypocrisy*, most people can't stand

As we saw earlier in relation to sentences such as (54) above, only *full phrases* can be preposed in this way: it therefore follows that *hypocrisy* in (116) must be a full phrase of some sort; and since the phrase concerned is headed by the Noun *hypocrisy*, it must be a Noun Phrase.

Moreover, *hypocrisy* in (116) can serve as a sentence fragment, as we see from the dialogue in (118) below:

(118)   SPEAKER A: What can't most people stand?
          SPEAKER B: *Hypocrisy*

And since we earlier suggested that only full phrases can serve as sentence fragments, this again suggests that *hypocrisy* in (116) must be a full NP.

A third argument leading to the same conclusion can be formulated in relation to *Ordinary Coordination*. For, note that *hypocrisy* can be coordinated with a full Noun Phrase such as [*the kind of glib lies that politicians tell*], as we see from (119) below:

(119)   Most people can't stand [*hypocrisy*] or [*the kind of glib lies that politicians tell*]

Since we earlier posited in (78) that 'Only identical categories can be conjoined', and since it is clear that the second bracketed conjunct in (119) is a full NP, then it follows that the first conjunct must also be a full NP.

Support for this conclusion comes from *Pronominalisation* facts. We suggested earlier in relation to sentences such as (93) above that proforms such as *it* function as pro-NP constituents, and that they replace full Noun Phrases (not individual Nouns). But note that *hypocrisy* in (116) can be replaced by the pro-NP *it*: cf.

(120)   Most people can't stand $\begin{Bmatrix} hypocrisy \\ it \end{Bmatrix}$

This provides still further evidence that *hypocrisy* in (116) must have the categorial status of a full Noun Phrase. In other words, sentence (116) must have the structure (121) below:

(121)

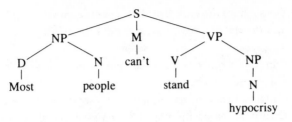

The obvious conclusion is thus that unmodified Nouns have the status of
Noun Phrases (as well as Nouns): and the principle extends from Nouns to all
other categories (so that, for example, wherever an unmodified Adverb can be
replaced by a full Adverbial Phrase, it is assigned the status of an ADVP containing a head ADV).

> ***You should now be able to tackle exercise VII***

2.8 Testing the Structure

What we have argued hitherto is that a whole variety of linguistic
phenomena cannot be described adequately without assuming that every sentence in every natural language has a specific syntactic (constituent) structure.
But an obvious question that arises is:

(122)   How do we determine what the constituent structure of a given
         sentence in a given language is?

Sometimes we can rely on intuition as a first approximation: but while
linguists tend to acquire fairly refined intuitions of this sort over a period of
years, non-linguists may not have particularly firm intuitions about the structure of sentences in their language. So, when our intuitions fail us, how can we
determine what the constituent structure of a given sentence is?

Perhaps we can best answer this question by asking another question: 'Why
do we posit the existence of constituents and categories?' The answer we have
given here is: 'In order to provide a principled account of, for example, Distribution, Preposing, Postposing, Coordination, Adverbials, Pronominalisation,
Ellipsis, etc.' An obvious answer to the question: 'How do we determine
whether a given sequence of words is a constituent of a given type?' is thus:
'On the basis of whether it behaves like a constituent of that type with respect
to Distribution, Preposing, Postposing, Coordination, Adverb position, Pronominalisation, Ellipsis, etc.' More precisely, we might propose the following
diagnostics for determining whether a given set of words in a sentence is a constituent or not, and if so, of what type (= category):

(123) (a) Does it have the same distribution as (i.e. can it be replaced by) an appropriate phrase of a given type? If so, it is a phrase of the relevant type

(b) Can it undergo *movement* (i.e., preposing or postposing)? If so, it is a phrase of some sort

(c) Can it serve as a *sentence-fragment*? If so, it is a phrasal constituent

(d) Does it permit positioning of S- or VP-adverbials internally? If so, it is an S or VP, and not, for example, an NP or PP

(e) Can it undergo *Ordinary Coordination* with another string? If so, it is a constituent of the same type as the one with which it is coordinated

(f) Can it serve as the 'shared constituent' in *Shared Constituent Coordination*? If so, it is a phrase

(g) Can it be replaced by, or serve as the antecedent of an appropriate *proform*? If so, it is a phrase of the same type as the proform

(h) Can it undergo Ellipsis under appropriate discourse conditions? If so, it is a VP

Having outlined our structural diagnostics, let's see how we might apply them to help us determine the constituent structure of the following pair of sentences:

(124) (a) Drunks would get off the bus
(b) Drunks would put off the customers

Now at first sight, the two sentences in (124) might appear to be parallel in structure. After all, both comprise a sequence of a Noun (*drunks*), a Modal (*would*), a Verb (*get/put*), a Preposition (*off*), a Determiner (*the*), and a Noun (*bus/customers*). And yet, what I'm going to suggest here is that the two sentences have very different constituent structures. More precisely, I'm going to try and convince you that (124) (a) has the structure (125) (a) below, whereas (124) (b) has the structure (125) (b):

(125) (a)

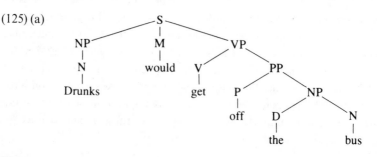

(b)

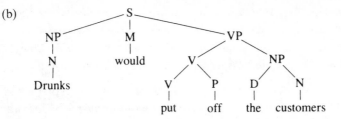

The essential difference between the two structures is that in (125) (a) the Preposition *off* 'goes with' the following Noun Phrase [*the bus*] to form the Prepositional Phrase [*off the bus*]; whereas in (125) (b), the Preposition *off* 'goes with' the Verb *put* to form the complex 'Phrasal Verb' [*put off*]. Thus, in traditional terms, we might say that *get* in (125) (a) is a *Prepositional Verb* (because it is a Verb which takes a Prepositional Phrase after it), whereas *put* in (125) (b) is a *Phrasal Verb* because the sequence [*put off*] seems to form some kind of 'compound verb'.

However, before we examine the *differences* between the two structures in (125), let's look first of all at the obvious *similarities* between the two. For example, in both cases I have claimed that *drunks* is not only a Noun, but also a Noun Phrase: but what justification is there for such an analysis? The simple answer is that the NP analysis can be justified on the basis of the structural diagnostics which we listed in (123) above. For example, if we apply the *distribution* criterion (123) (a), we can argue that *drunks* must be an NP because it has the same distribution as (and hence can be replaced by) a full NP such as [*people who get drunk*]: cf.

(126) (a)   *People who get drunk* would get off the bus
(b)   *People who get drunk* would put off the customers

And if we apply the *movement* criterion (123) (b), we might argue that *drunks* must be a full phrase (i.e. an NP) because it can undergo movement – e.g. it can be postposed in questions such as:

(127) (a)   Would *drunks* get off the bus?
(b)   Would *drunks* put off the customers?

Likewise, the *sentence-fragment* test (123) (c) leads us to the same conclusion, given that only full phrases can occur as sentence-fragments, and that *drunks* can function in this way: cf.

(128) (a)   SPEAKER A: Who would get off the bus?
         SPEAKER B: *Drunks*
(b)   SPEAKER A: Who would put off the customers?
         SPEAKER B: *Drunks*

Since criterion (123) (d) is not directly applicable to the question of the categorial status of *drunks*, let's turn instead to consider the *Ordinary Coordination* test (123) (e). This again supports the NP analysis, since *drunks* can be coordinated with a full NP such as [*other undesirable elements*]: cf.

(129) (a)   *Drunks* and *other undesirable elements* would get off the bus
    (b)   *Drunks* and *other undesirable elements* would put off the customers

The *Shared Constituent Coordination* test (123) (f) is not applicable here, since the test only works with strings which are on the rightmost branch (i.e. at the righthand end) of their containing Phrases or Clauses; and we see from (125) above that *drunks* in each case is the *leftmost* constituent of the S which contains it. However, the *Pronominalisation* test (123) (g) is applicable, and again supports the NP analysis, since *drunks* can be replaced by the pro-NP *they*: cf.

(130) (a)   *They* would get off the bus
    (b)   *They* would put off the customers

Finally, we note that the *Ellipsis* criterion is not applicable to *drunks* here, since *Ellipsis* is a test for VP-hood, not for NP-hood. Thus, all the tests in (123) which are applicable here provide strong empirical support for our claim that *drunks* is not only a Noun, but also a Noun Phrase.

We might use the same set of tests in (123) to check our claim that the sequences [*get off the bus*] in (125) (a) and [*put off the customers*] in (125) (b) are Verb Phrase constituents. For example, note that the VP in either case can undergo 'preposing' for emphasis in an appropriate discourse setting: cf.

(131) (a)   If the driver told the drunks that they had to get off the bus, then [*get off the bus*] they would
    (b)   The restaurant manager thinks that drunks would put off the customers, and [*put off the customers*] they undoubtedly would

Moreover, both VPs can function as sentence-fragments in an appropriate context: cf.

(132)   SPEAKER A: What would drunks do?
       SPEAKER B: { *Get off the bus* / *Put off the customers* }

And both VPs can serve as the antecedent for a pro-VP constituent such as *which*: cf.

(133) (a)   If, whenever they needed to heed the call of nature, drunks would [get off the bus] – *which* they obviously would – then we ought not to allow them on in the first place

(b)   If drunks would [put off the customers] – *which* they obviously would – then we ought not to allow them in the restaurant in the first place

And I leave it to you to verify for yourself that the various other 'diagnostics' which we have devised likewise support the VP analysis for both sentences.

Similarly, we can apply the same set of tests in (123) to support our claim that the three major constituents of the sentence in each case are [NP M VP]. For example, such an analysis would correctly predict that S-adverbs like *certainly* can be positioned between NP and M, or between M and VP, but not between any other pairs of constituents; and this prediction is entirely correct in both cases, as we see from (134) and (135) below:

(134) (a)   Drunks *certainly* would get off the bus
    (b)   Drunks would *certainly* get off the bus
    (c)   *Drunks would get *certainly* off the bus
    (d)   *Drunks would get off *certainly* the bus
    (e)   *Drunks would get off the *certainly* bus

(135) (a)   Drunks *certainly* would put off the customers
    (b)   Drunks would *certainly* put off the customers
    (c)   *Drunks would put *certainly* off the customers
    (d)   *Drunks would put off *certainly* the customers
    (e)   *Drunks would put off the *certainly* customers

By now, you should be excruciatingly familiar with the logic of this type of argument, so I won't subject you to any further mental torture! Suffice it to say that there is abundant evidence in support of the claim in (125) that both sentences comprise an [NP M VP] sequence.

Of course, where the two sentences differ is in the internal structure of the VP which they contain. As we noted earlier, in the case of the VP [*get off the bus*], the Preposition *off* 'goes with' the following Noun Phrase [*the bus*] to form the PP [*off the bus*]; whereas in the case of the VP [*put off the customers*], the Preposition *off* 'goes with' the Verb *put* to form the Phrasal Verb [*put off*]. But at the moment, this claim is based on nothing more substantial than my own personal *structural intuitions*. However, you may well have no more faith in *my* structural intuitions than I have in *yours*, so let's see whether we can find some independent empirical evidence in support of the claimed structural difference!

The *distribution* argument (123) (a) would seem to lend support to our analysis. After all, if the sequence [*off the bus*] in (125) (a) is a Prepositional Phrase, then we should expect that it can be replaced by other PPs with a

93

related meaning: since *on* is the antonym (i.e. 'opposite') of *off*, we might expect to be able to replace the *off*-phrase in (124) (a) by an *on*-phrase. And as (136) below indicates, this is indeed possible:

(136)   Drunks would $\begin{cases} get\ off\ the\ bus \\ get\ on\ the\ bus \end{cases}$

The fact that the sequence [*off the bus*] can be replaced by the PP [*on the bus*] would seem to confirm its PP status. But what is interesting is that in the case of the second example, the sequence *off the customers* has no *on* counterpart: cf.

(137)   Drunks would $\begin{cases} put\ off\ the\ customers \\ *put\ on\ the\ customers \end{cases}$

Why should this be? Well, the answer suggested by analysis (125) above is that the sequence *off the customers* is not a PP (indeed not a constituent at all), and hence cannot be replaced by a PP like [*on the customers*]. Thus, distributional facts seem to support the claim that *put off* is a Phrasal Verb, whereas *get off* is a Prepositional Verb.

However, we are over-simplifying a bit here, by ignoring the fact that the sequence *put on* can indeed be used as a Phrasal Verb, e.g. in sentences such as:

(138)   Mary would *put on* a new dress

But whereas there is a consistent parallelism between *get off* and *get on*, no such parallelism seems to hold between *put off* and *put on*. What kind of parallelism holds in the first case but not the second? Well, for one thing, *get* seems to have a constant meaning (in both cases, it is roughly synonymous with 'climb') irrespective of whether it is combined with *on* or *off*. But this is not at all the case with *put*; thus *put off* means more or less the same as 'deter', whereas *put on* (in its most familiar sense) is roughly synonymous with 'wear'. Generalising somewhat, we could say that *Prepositional Verbs* have a consistent, componential meaning (i.e. the meaning of the whole expression is a simple function of the meaning of its component parts), whereas *Phrasal Verbs* tend to have an idiosyncratic or idiomatic meaning. What I mean by saying that Phrasal Verbs have idiosyncratic meanings is that there's no way of telling what *put off* or *put on* mean simply by knowing the meaning of *put*, and *on*, and *off*.

A second parallelism which we find between different but related uses of Prepositional Verbs is a parallelism of *Selection Restrictions* – i.e. a parallelism in the range of different expressions which can be used after a Prepositional Verb. We see from the examples in (139) below that related Prepositional

Verbs like *get off* and *get on* select the same range of complements (i.e. can be followed by the same range of expressions):

(139) (a)   Drunks would get off *the bus/the train/the table/!the sea/!the wind/ !kindness*

(b)   Drunks would get on *the bus/the train/the table/!the sea/!the wind/ !kindness*

By contrast, no such parallelism of Selection Restrictions holds for Phrasal Verb pairs such as *put off* (in its sense of 'deter') and *put on* (in its sense of 'wear'): cf.

(140) (a)   Drunks would put off *the customers/the waiters/!dirty clothes/ !tattered trousers*

(b)   Drunks would put on *dirty clothes/tattered trousers/!the customers/ !the waiters*

This parallelism of Selection Restrictions in the one case but not in the other seems related to the fact that Prepositional Verb pairs such as *get off* and *get on* have related meanings, whereas Phrasal Verb pairs such as *put off* and *put on* do not.

Let's now turn to further syntactic evidence in support of claiming that Prepositional and Phrasal Verbs have different structures. Our criterion (123) (b) tells us that only full phrases can undergo movement. In this connection, it is interesting to note that in *get off* structures like (125) (a), the whole sequence [*off the bus*] can be preposed for emphasis: cf.

(141)   Every afternoon, the big red bus would stop in front of the village clock, and [*off the bus*] would get a dear old lady carrying a shopping bag

Since only full phrases can undergo movement, it follows that the italicised sequence in (141) must be a full phrase; and since it contains the head Preposition *off*, it clearly must be a Prepositional Phrase. By contrast, note that the sequence *off the customers* can't be preposed in (125) (b): cf.

(142)   *The manager suspects that drunks would put off the customers, and *off the customers* they certainly would put

Why should this be? The answer suggested here is that only full phrases can be preposed in this way, and – as we see from the tree diagram in (125) (b) above – the sequence *off the customers* isn't a phrase: in fact, it isn't even a constituent. So, our *movement* test (123) (b) provides further support for the analysis proposed here.

Not surprisingly, our *sentence-fragment* test (123) (c) yields the same results for, as we see from (143) below, the sequence [*off the bus*] can serve as a sentence-fragment in (125) (a):

(143)   SPEAKER A: Did he get off the train?
          SPEAKER B: No, *off the bus*

Since only full phrases can serve as sentence-fragments, this confirms the PP status of the italicised sequence. By contrast, the string *off the customers* in (125) (b) cannot function as a sentence-fragment, as (144) below illustrates:

(144)   SPEAKER A: Would drunks put off the waitresses?
          SPEAKER B: *No, *off the customers*

Why can't *off the customers* function as a sentence-fragment? The answer suggested by analysis (125) (b) is that the italicised sequence in (144) is not even a constituent, let alone a Phrase (and recall that only full Phrases can function as sentence-fragments). So, our *sentence-fragment* test lends further support to analysis (125).

Our fourth test – (123) (d) – relates to the distribution of Adverbial Phrases. Recall that in 2.5 we drew a distinction between *S-Adverbials* (which occur in positions where they are attached to an S node), and *VP-Adverbials* (which occur in positions where they are attached to a VP node). The class of VP-Adverbials includes expressions such as *quickly, slowly, completely*, etc. Now, since VP-Adverbials can occur internally within VPs, then we should expect that such an Adverbial could be positioned in between the Verb *get* and the Prepositional Phrase [*off the bus*] in (125) (a); and (145) below shows that this is indeed the case:

(145)   Drunks would get *slowly* off the bus

By contrast, it is not possible to position a VP-Adverbial between *put* and *off* in (125) (b), as we see from the ungrammaticality of (146) below:

(146)   *Drunks would put *completely* off the customers

Why should it be possible for a VP-Adverbial to intrude between *get* and *off* in (125) (a), but not between *put* and *off* in (125) (b)? We can see the answer immediately, if we look at the structures which would be assigned to each of the Verb Phrases in (145) and (146) above: these are as in (147) below:

(147) (a)

(b)

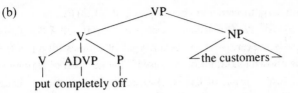

(For brevity here, we omit the fact that *slowly* and *completely* have the status of ADV as well as ADVP: this is a simplifying convention which we shall adopt for other phrasal categories subsequently.) It should now be immediately obvious why (147) (a) is OK, but (147) (b) is not. For, since Adverbials like *slowly* and *completely* are VP-Adverbials, they can only attach to a VP node, as in (147) (a). What's wrong with (147) (b) is that here we have a VP-Adverbial attached to a V node, not to a VP node. In other words, structures like (125) (a) and (b) make precisely the right predictions about the distribution of VP-Adverbials with Prepositional Verbs on the one hand, and Phrasal Verbs on the other.

Let's now turn to our fifth constituent structure test, the *Coordination* test in (123) (e). Given our assumption that [*off the bus*] is a PP constituent in (125) (a), we should expect that it can be coordinated with another PP of the same type: and as (148) below shows, this is indeed the case:

(148)   Drunks would get [*off the bus*] and [*on the train*]

But given our assumption that the sequence *off the customers* is not a constituent of any type in (125) (b), we should expect that it cannot be coordinated with another similar sequence: and this is exactly the right prediction, as the ungrammaticality of (149) below illustrates:

(149)   *Drunks would put *off the customers* and *off the waitresses*

Thus, *Ordinary Coordination* facts support the analysis we proposed in (125).

But what about the *Shared Constituent Coordination* test in (123) (f)? Given our assumption that the sequence [*off the bus*] in (125) (a) is a PP constituent, we should expect that it can function as the 'shared constituent' in sentences involving Shared Constituent Coordination: and we see from (150) below that this is indeed the case:

(150)   Drunks would get – and junkies would fall – *off the bus*

By contrast, the sequence *off the customers* cannot be used in the same way in (125) (b): cf.

(151)   *Drunks would put – and junkies would also put – *off the customers*

So, the *Shared Constituent Coordination* test also supports analysis (125).

Let's move on now to consider the *Ellipsis* test, (123) (h). So far we have looked at one specific type of Ellipsis, which we might call VP ELLIPSIS, for obvious reasons. However, there are other types of Ellipsis found in English. One such type is known as GAPPING, because it has the effect of leaving a 'gap' in the middle of some Phrase or Clause. For example, the second occurrence of the Verb *bought* can be *gapped* in this way in a sentence such as:

(152)   John bought an apple, and Mary b̶o̶u̶g̶h̶t̶ a pear

When a Verb is gapped, any Modal preceding it can also be gapped along with the Verb, even if the two do not form a continuous sequence, as in (153) below:

(153)   Could John close the window, and c̶o̶u̶l̶d̶ Mary c̶l̶o̶s̶e̶ the door?

The exact conditions determining what kind of constituent can and cannot undergo GAPPING in a given sentence are extremely complex, and need not be of concern to us here. What is of more immediate interest to us here is the fact that the Verb *get* can be gapped along with the Modal *would* in structures such as (125) (a), resulting in sentences such as:

(154)   Drunks would get off the bus, and junkies w̶o̶u̶l̶d̶ g̶e̶t̶ off the train

However, what is even more interesting is that we cannot gap the Verb *put* along with the Modal *would* in structures like (125) (b), as illustrated by the ungrammaticality of:

(155)   *Drunks would put off the customers, and junkies w̶o̶u̶l̶d̶ p̶u̶t̶ off the waitresses

By contrast, we can gap the whole expression *put off* along with *would*: cf.

(156)   Drunks would put off the customers, and junkies w̶o̶u̶l̶d̶ p̶u̶t̶ o̶f̶f̶ the waitresses

Thus, it would seem that as far as GAPPING is concerned, the whole expression *put off* is somehow treated as a single 'compound Verb'. But this is the very intuition which we encapsulated in analysis (125) (b), by giving the sequence [*put off*] the status of a single V constituent (i.e. by analysing it as a Phrasal Verb). Thus, facts about GAPPING lend yet further support to analysis (125).

Finally, let's turn to the *Pronominalisation* argument in (123) (g). And here, we find something of a surprise waiting for us. But let me prepare you for the surprise first of all. Just think about the status of the expressions [*the bus*] and [*the customers*] in (125). What are they? Well, by now it should come as a reflex reaction to say: 'They are Noun Phrases consisting of a Determiner and a

Noun'. Quite right! After all, simple Coordination facts tell us that they must be Noun Phrases, since they can be coordinated with other Noun Phrases: cf.

(157) (a)   Drunks would get off [*the bus*] and [*the train*]

    (b)   Drunks would put off [*the customers*] and [*the waitresses*]

Now, if they are Noun Phrases, we should obviously expect that they can be replaced by an appropriate pro-NP constituent such as *it* or *them*. And yet, while this is true of the object of a Prepositional Verb like *get off*: cf.

(158)   The trouble with the bus was that drunks would want to get off *it* every few miles, to exercise their natural bodily functions

it is not true of Phrasal Verbs such as *put off*: cf.

(159)   *What worries me about the customers is whether drunks would put off *them*

So, it would seem that Prepositional Verbs can take pronominal Objects, but Phrasal Verbs require non-pronominal Objects. Why this should be is not entirely clear. However, what does seem clear is that if we draw a systematic structural distinction between *Prepositional* and *Phrasal* Verbs, we can attain the level of *observational adequacy* simply by stipulating that Phrasal Verbs don't permit (certain types of) pronominal Objects. Of course, we would ultimately hope to find a principled explanation for this rather curious restriction, and thereby attain a higher level of adequacy. But the essential point remains that unless we draw some distinction such as that in (125) between Phrasal and Prepositional Verbs, we shall be unable to attain even the level of observational adequacy.

In actual fact, our claim that Phrasal Verbs don't take pronominal objects is something of an oversimplification, as (160) below illustrates:

(160) (a)   *Drunks would put off *them*

    (b)   Drunks would put *them* off

We see in (160) that a Phrasal Verb like *put off* can indeed take a pronominal object, but only when the Preposition is positioned at the end of the sentence. Moreover, it isn't just a pronominal object which can appear between *put* and *off*: as (161) below indicates, an ordinary nominal NP can also appear in this position:

(161)   Drunks would put [*the customers*] off

By contrast, a Prepositional Verb like *get off* does not permit the Preposition to be moved to the end of the VP in this way: cf.

(162)   *Drunks would get the bus *off*

Thus, whereas a Phrasal Verb allows its accompanying Preposition to be positioned either before or after a Noun Phrase Object (though when the Object is pronominal, the Preposition must be positioned after the Object), a Prepositional Verb only allows the Preposition to be positioned *before* the NP Object.

The obvious question to ask at this point is what is the structure of a sentence such as (161), in which the Preposition is positioned at the end of the VP. We shall argue here that (161) has the structure (163) below:

(163)

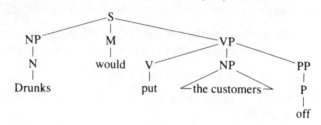

It seems clear that *off* must be a constituent of the VP here, since it can be preposed along with the other constituents of VP for emphasis: cf.

(164)   The manager said that drunks would put the customers off, and [*put the customers off*] they certainly would

But what might seem more controversial here is the claim that *off* in (163) is not just a P, but also a PP. After all, didn't we claim that in (125) (b) *Drunks would put off the customers* that *off* was a P, but not a PP? So, haven't we gone wrong somewhere?

No, not at all (you should know me better by now!). In fact, there is strong empirical evidence in support of saying that in a VP like [*put off the customers*], *off* is merely a P, whereas in [*put the customers off*], *off* has the status of PP. We can defend this analysis on *distributional* grounds (i.e. using criterion (123) (a)). After all, if *off* is a P when immediately adjacent to the Verb, but a PP when separated from the Verb, we should expect that only when it functions as a full Phrase (= PP) will it be able to take a Premodifier (i.e. some preceding expression modifying it), or Postmodifier (i.e. some following expression modifying it), or both. And sure enough, this is exactly what we find: for, when *off* is separated from the Verb, it can take both pre- and postmodifiers such as those italicised below:

(165) (a)   Drunks would put the customers *right* OFF
      (b)   Drunks would put the customers OFF *their food*
      (c)   Drunks would put the customers *right* OFF *their food*

But when *off* occurs immediately adjacent to the Verb, it cannot be premodified or postmodified in any way: cf.

(166) (a) *Drunks would put *right* OFF the customers
     (b) *Drunks would put OFF *their food* the customers
     (c) *Drunks would put *right* OFF *their food* the customers

This is exactly the pattern we should expect to find if *off* has the status of the simple word-level category P in structures like (125)(b), but the status of a phrase-level category PP in structures like (163).

So, our *constituent structure tests* (123) lead us to an interesting conclusion about Phrasal Verbs – namely that the prepositional particle has the status of a simple Preposition when it immediately follows the Verb and precedes the Object, but the status of a full Prepositional Phrase when it follows the Object and is separated from the Verb. This shows the value of *constituent structure tests* like those in (123) in showing up structural differences which we would probably never have arrived at on the basis of intuition alone.

Overall, then, we see that we do not have to rely on (often rather fickle) *intuitions* to support the postulation of a categorial constituent structure associated with sentences. For, it is possible to confirm – or indeed refute – our intuitions using a variety of simple diagnostics. The status of the hypothetical constituent structures which we posit to be associated with sentences is thus not just *intuitive*, but also *empirical* (i.e. open to confirmation or disconfirmation by using empirical procedures such as those outlined in (123) above).

Of course, no 'constituent structure test' can ever be expected to be foolproof; on occasions, a test may fail to yield the anticipated results, simply because some independent factor is 'interfering' with the test and making it inapplicable in some particular context. By way of example, consider the *Adverb distribution* test, in relation to a sentence such as:

(167)   John will finish the assignment

Our standard constituent structure tests lead us to suppose that the sequence *finish the assignment* is a VP: for example, it can be preposed, proformed, coordinated with another VP, and ellipsed: cf.

(168) (a)   John promised that he will finish the assignment, and [*finish the assignment*] he will
     (b)   John will [*finish the assignment*], and *so* will Mary
     (c)   John will [*finish the assignment*] and [*hand it in*]
     (d)   Paul won't [*finish the assignment*], but John will finish the assignment

So it seems reasonable to conclude that the sequence [*finish the assignment*] is a VP containing the V *finish* and an NP object [*the assignment*] (which can be proformed by a pro-NP like it). And yet, *Adverb distribution* facts seem to run partly counter to this analysis, as we see from (169) below:

(169) (a)   John will [VP *completely* finish the assignment]
    (b)   John will [VP finish the assignment *completely*]
    (c)   *John will [VP finish *completely* the assignment]

Given the assumption that *completely* is a VP-adverb, then we should expect that it can occur not only at the beginning of the VP (as in (169) (a)), and at the end of the VP (as in (169) (b)), but also in the middle of the VP (as in (169) (c)). But this latter prediction is incorrect, as the ungrammaticality of (169) (c) shows. Does this mean that the whole *Adverb distribution* argument is flawed? Not at all! It simply means that sometimes perfectly good tests get fouled up by independent factors which interfere with them. What is the factor which is interfering with our *Adverb* test here? Keyser (1968, p. 371) notes that there is a general 'tendency to prevent anything from intervening between a Verb and the following Noun Phrase'. We might describe this restriction in terms of a principle such as (170) below:

(170)   STRICT ADJACENCY PRINCIPLE
        An NP complement of a Verb must be positioned strictly adjacent to (i.e. right next to) its Verb

This restriction against separating a Verb from its NP object accounts for the contrast between (171) and (172) below:

(171) (a)   John argued [about every point] *with the tax-man*
    (b)   John argued *with the tax-man* [about every point]

(172) (a)   John argued [every point] *with the tax-man*
    (b)   *John argued *with the tax-man* [every point]

In (171), the bracketed complement of the Verb *argued* is a PP (= Prepositional Phrase), and can be positioned before or after the other PP [*with the tax-man*]; but in (172), the bracketed complement is an NP, and (in accordance with the STRICT ADJACENCY PRINCIPLE (170)) has to be positioned immediately after the verb *argued*. The same restriction also accounts for contrasts such as that between (173) and (174) below:

(173) (a)   They loaded [hay] *on the cart*
    (b)   *They loaded *on the cart* [hay]

(174) (a)   They loaded [the cart] *with hay*
    (b)   *They loaded *with hay* [the cart]

In both cases, the bracketed expression is an NP complement of the Verb *loaded*, and hence has to be positioned immediately after the Verb, given the restriction (170) that nothing can intervene between a V and its NP object.

In the light of the restriction that an NP object must immediately follow its V, we can now understand why our *Adverb distribution* test appeared to break down in the case of (169) (c); for by attempting to position the Adverb *completely* between the Verb *finish* and its NP object *the assignment*, we were violating the constraint that an NP complement must be positioned immediately after its governing V. This underlines the point made earlier that constituent structure tests sometimes appear to 'break down' because independent factors render them inoperative in special contexts. The simple moral of the story is that we have to make judicious use of constituent structure tests, and bear in mind that their validity may be affected (in particular contexts) by a whole range of syntactic, semantic, pragmatic, stylistic, etc. factors.

We can underline this crucial methodological point by looking briefly at two further cases where traditional constituency 'tests' appear to give the wrong results. Consider for example the following dialogue:

(175)   SPEAKER A: Who will clear up the mess?
          SPEAKER B: The caretaker will

Speaker B's reply here seems at first sight to comprise an NP [*the caretaker*] and an M *will*. Given our postulate in (64) that only complete constituents can function as sentence fragments, then it might seem reasonable to conclude that Speaker B's reply in (175) provides us with empirical evidence that the sequence [NP M] in a sentence forms a constituent of some sort. And yet, any such assumption would fly in the face of all the empirical arguments we presented earlier. So why does our *sentence fragment* test yield the wrong results here? The answer is that it doesn't! For, in applying the test, we failed to take into account the fact that Verb Phrases like [*clear up the mess*] can undergo Ellipsis in certain discourse contexts. Now, suppose we assume that when a VP undergoes Ellipsis, what happens is that it is stripped of all the lexical material (i.e. words) it contains, and survives only in the form of an *empty* category. If we use the symbol 'e' to designate an empty category, then we might suppose that Speaker B's reply in (175) is an S which has the simplified form (176) below:

(176)

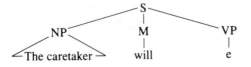

If this is so, then Speaker B's reply in (175) isn't in fact a *sentence fragment* at all, but rather a *full sentence* (S constituent) of the canonical form [NP M VP], in which the VP constituent was 'empty', as in (176) above. So, we have to be careful to differentiate between *sentence fragments* and *elliptical sentences* (= sentences containing empty categories).

Empty categories may also provide the answer to the question of why *co-ordination* tests sometimes appear to give the 'wrong' results. For example, consider the italicised sequence in (177) below:

(177)   John will give his father a shirt and *his mother a skirt*

At first sight, (177) might seem to indicate that the sequences *his father a shirt* and *his mother a skirt* must be constituents, since they have been conjoined by ordinary coordination. But surely this cannot be right: after all, a sequence such as *his father a shirt* cannot be 'preposed for emphasis', or replaced by a single proform, as we see from the ungrammaticality of:

(178) (a)   *His father a shirt* John will give
        (b)   *John will give *it/them*

So, why does our *Ordinary Coordination* test appear to give the wrong results in (177)? Well, we have overlooked the possibility that the italicised conjunct in (177) is in fact a Verb Phrase which contains an 'empty' Verb which has undergone the special kind of Ellipsis which we earlier called GAPPING, so that the VP has the schematic form (179) below:

(179)

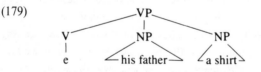

If this is so, then (177) will have essentially the same structure as (180) below:

(180)   John will give his father a shirt, and *give his mother a skirt*

In both cases, the italicised constituent will be a Verb Phrase which has been conjoined with the VP [*give his father a shirt*]: the only difference between the two is that in (180) the Verb is *overt*, whereas in (177) it is *covert* (or *empty*). Given this assumption, then our *Ordinary Coordination* test does indeed work perfectly well. Once again, the moral of the story is that we have to take extreme care in applying constituent structure tests, and try to avoid jumping to hasty conclusions which may turn out to be based on a fundamentally flawed premise.

It is perhaps appropriate that our discussion in this chapter should end with a brief mention of *empty categories*; for, these will come to play an increasingly important role as our discussion develops in later chapters. Indeed, a large part of Volume Two will be devoted to the syntax of *empty categories*.

You should now be able to tackle exercises VIII and IX

2.9 Summary

In this chapter, we have argued in detail that sentences are structured out of words and phrases assigned to various categories. In 2.2 we argued that the native speaker's intuitions about the structural relations between constituents within a sentence can be represented in the form of a tree diagram. However, we pointed out that the true status of constituents and categories is that of theoretical constructs which must therefore be justified on *empirical* grounds (i.e. we have to show that they are necessary in order to provide a principled account of certain linguistic phenomena). In 2.3 we put forward a variety of arguments (mainly morphological and syntactic in nature) in support of claiming that words belong to a variety of categories such as Noun, Verb, Modal, Adjective, Adverb, Determiner, etc. We then went on to show that similar evidence could be adduced in support of positing that sentences are structured out of *Phrases* assigned to categories such as Noun Phrase, Verb Phrase, Adjectival Phrase, Adverbial Phrase, Prepositional Phrase, etc. In 2.4 we examined evidence relating to morphological, semantic, and phonological facts; in 2.5 we put forward a series of distributional arguments; and in 2.6 we examined evidence relating to Coordination, Pronominalisation, and Ellipsis. In 2.7, we argued that individual words can function as Phrases, so that, for example, an unmodified Noun which can be substituted by a full Noun Phrase, or coordinated with a full NP, or pronominalised by a pro-NP, should be assigned the status of a full Noun Phrase. Finally, in 2.8 we suggested a variety of simple diagnostics designed to test whether a given sentence has a given constituent structure or not.

EXERCISES

Exercise I

In the bracketed structures below, the lefthand member of each pair of brackets has been labelled. First, label the righthand member of each pair of brackets, and then convert the bracketed structure into a tree diagram, providing as much (or as little) information in your tree as is provided is the bracketed structure.

(1)   [S [NP His mother] [M might] [VP get [AP very angry]]]

(2)   [S [NP [D The] [N President]] [M may] [VP [V reject] [NP [D their] [N pro-
        posal]]]]

(3)   [S [NP [D The] [N weather]] [M will] [VP [V change] [ADVP [ADV ex-
        tremely] [ADV suddenly]]]]

(4)   [S [NP [D The] [N boys]] [M should] [VP [V buy] [NP [D a] [N present]]
        [PP [P for] [NP [D their] [N teacher]]]]]

Exercise II

Discuss the categorial status of each of the words in the following sentence, giving detailed reasons in support of your analysis.

(1)   That nice young boy in the corner probably will fall off his bed onto the
        cold hard floor early one morning

Now consider the status of the italicised *nonsense words* in the following sentences, giving arguments in support of your analysis.

(2) (a)   John likes to *glonk* in the afternoons
    (b)   He never *glonks* on Sundays
    (c)   He started *glonking* when he was fourteen
    (d)   He once *glonked* an out-of-work actress
    (e)   He's never *glonked* any of his classmates

(3) (a)   John was feeling *nurgy*, but happy
    (b)   He's *nurgier* than anyone I know
    (c)   He's been behaving very *nurgily* all week

(4) (a)   John is a *bong*, and so is Fred
    (b)   In fact, they're both typical *bongs*

(5) (a)   She put the car *ung* the garage
    (b)   She made sure that it was right *ung*

Exercise III

The sentences below might be argued to be structurally ambiguous. Discuss the nature of the ambiguity in each case.

(1)   Mary might seem very keen on the boat
(2)   The police will shoot terrorists with rifles
(3)   John will run down the new road
(4)   They may meet with scepticism

Exercise IV

Account for the contrasts in the following pairs of sentences:

(1) (a)   Up a huge hill John ran
    (b)   *Up a huge bill John ran

| (2) (a) | You can rely on my help entirely, naturally |
| (b) | *You can rely on my help naturally, entirely |

| (3) (a) | He obviously will appeal passionately for support |
| (b) | *He passionately will appeal obviously for support |

| (4) (a) | Pandas live entirely off bamboo shoots |
| (b) | *Poor weather kills entirely off bamboo shoots |

| (5) (a) | He pledged to her all his worldly goods |
| (b) | *He pledged all to her his worldly goods |

Exercise V

Assuming that the following sentences are ill-formed (and hence can be used only for humorous effect, for example), say why they are ill-formed:

(1)   *Could you turn off the fire and on the light?
(2)   *Your mother won't put (and your wife is fed) up with your disgusting behaviour
(3)   *I know the truth, and that you are innocent
(4)   *A nuclear explosion would wipe out plant life and out animal life
(5)   *He ran down the road and down the President

Exercise VI

Discuss the syntax and semantics of the italicised proforms as they are used in the sentences below:

(1)   I don't know whether the President will retire next year, but I certainly hope *so*
(2)   They say he's extremely intelligent, and *so* he may be
(3)   The junkies stashed the hash in the trash-can, but the fuzz found out about *it*
(4)   You should see Paris, if you've never been *there*
(5)   If the Chairman is in Paris (*which* he is), how do we contact *him there*?

Exercise VII

Draw tree diagrams (and the corresponding labelled bracketings) to represent the structure of the following sentences, providing detailed empirical arguments in support of your analysis:

(1)   Parents can treat young children badly
(2)   John will probably go inside

Exercise VIII

Decide whether the Verb in each of the following sentences functions as a Phrasal Verb, or as a Prepositional Verb, giving detailed empirical arguments in support of your analysis:

(1)   He will pick up the ladder
(2)   He will climb up the ladder

Exercise IX

The two sentences below, although superficially similar in form, might be argued to have distinct constituent structures. More precisely, we might argue that in (1), the AP *black* is an entirely separate constituent from the NP [*my coffee*], whereas in (2) the AP *present* is part of the whole Noun Phrase [*the people present*]. What empirical evidence can you find in support of this claim?

(1)   I don't like [NP my coffee] [AP black]
(2)   I don't know [NP the people present]

3

Phrase-markers

3.1 Overview

In the previous chapter, we argued that sentences are not just unstructured sequences of sounds; rather, they have a hierarchical *constituent structure* in which sounds are grouped together into words, words into phrases, and phrases into sentences. Each *constituent* (word or phrase) in a sentence belongs to a specific *syntactic category*. The *categorial constituent structure* of sentences can be represented in the form of a *Phrase-marker*, in which the different nodes are labelled according to the category of the constituent they represent. But what are Phrase-markers? What kind of rules might we devise to generate (i.e. tell us how to form) Phrase-markers? And what exactly is the nature of the categories which are used to label the various constituents which Phrase-markers contain? These are the three essential questions which we address in this chapter.

3.2 The nature of Phrase-markers

In the previous chapter, we used *Phrase-markers* to represent the constituent structure of sentences. But what exactly is a *Phrase-marker*? It's useful to think about this problem for a while, and to devise some appropriate technical terminology for describing the internal structure of P-markers, since this will turn out to be of vital importance in subsequent chapters. But why do we need technical jargon? Well, any adequate description of any phenomenon in any field of enquiry (in our present case, Syntax) must be maximally *explicit*, and to be explicit, it must be *formal* – i.e. make use only of theoretical constructs which have definable formal properties. The use of formal apparatus (involving a certain amount of technical terminology) may seem confusing at first to the unfortunate reader, but as in any other serious field of enquiry (e.g. Molecular Biology) no real progress can be made unless we try to construct formal models of the phenomena we are studying. It would clearly be irrational to accept the use of formalism in one field of enquiry (e.g. Molecular

Biology) while rejecting it in another (e.g. Linguistics). Hence our short ex-
cursus on the formal properties of Phrase-markers!

Essentially, a P-marker is a graph comprising a set of points (or *nodes*, to
use the appropriate technical terminology), connected by *branches* (represented by solid lines). The nodes at the (bottom) end of each complete tree-
structure are called *terminal nodes*; other nodes are *nonterminal*. Each node
carries a *label*. Nonterminal nodes carry category labels (e.g. N, NP, V, VP,
ADV, ADVP, etc.); terminal nodes (unless they are *empty* – a possibility
which we will discuss in a later chapter) are labelled with an appropriate
lexical item (=word). Any given pair of nodes contained in the same
P-marker will be related by one of two different types of relation, namely
either (i) by *dominance*, or (ii) by *precedence*. To say that one node X *dominates* another node Y is simply to say that X occurs higher up the tree than Y,
and is connected to Y by an unbroken set of solid lines (branches). By way of
illustration, consider the S-structure (1) below:

(1)

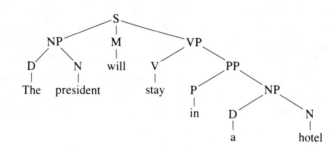

Given the definition above, we can say that, for example, the S node in (1)
dominates all the other nodes in the tree; and the VP node *dominates* the node
labelled V, the terminal node labelled *stay*, the node labelled PP, the node
labelled P, the terminal node labelled *in*, and so on; but VP does not dominate
M, or *will*, or S, or *president*, etc. One node is said to *immediately dominate*
another if it is the next highest node up in the tree, and is connected to the
other by a single branch (solid line). Thus, the S node in (1) immediately
dominates only the NP, M, and VP nodes immediately beneath it. For the
sake of precision, it is essential to be careful in using the term *dominates* on the
one hand, and *immediately dominates* on the other; any confusion between the
two may result in an inaccurate description.

Ignoring a qualification to be made shortly, we can say that one node
precedes another if it occurs to the left of the other node on the printed page.
So, for example, in (1) above, the M node *precedes* the VP, V, PP, P, NP, D,
and N nodes to its right, as well as the words *stay, in, a,* and *hotel*. To say that
one node *immediately precedes* another is to say that it occurs *immediately to*

the left of the other node. So, for example, the M node in (1) *immediately precedes* the VP and V nodes, and the word *stay*; but it does not *immediately precede* (though it does *precede*) the PP node, or the word *in*, etc. There is thus a clear logical distinction between the relation *precedes* on the one hand, and the relation *immediately precedes* on the other. It is therefore important in any explicit description to use these terms appropriately, and not, for example, say 'precedes' when you mean 'immediately precedes'.

Precedence relations are not explicitly indicated in P-markers like (1); rather, they are *tacitly* indicated (by convention) by the relative left-to-right ordering of nodes on a page. Of course, we could indicate precedence relations graphically, for example, by dotted arrows in the manner indicated in (2) below for the NP (= Noun Phrase) *a hotel*:

(2)

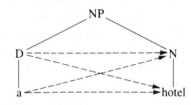

But such diagrams become extraordinarily complex to read once we attempt to represent the precedence relations which hold between sets of (say) more than ten nodes. So, we suppress any explicit visual representation of precedence (= left-to-right linear ordering) relations in favour of a convention that precedence relations are tacitly indicated by relative left-to-right ordering on the printed page. Notice, incidentally, from (2) that nodes may be related *either* by precedence *or* by dominance, but not by both. So, since D is dominated by NP in (2), D does not precede NP (even though it occurs to the left of NP on the printed page); and conversely, since D precedes N in (2), D cannot dominate N, nor N dominate D. Hence, to be rather more precise, we might say that if one node occurs to the left of another, and neither node dominates the other, then the lefthand node *precedes* the righthand one.

We can make use of *dominance* and *immediate dominance* to define two important traditional terms – namely *constituent*, and *immediate constituent*. These we can define in the following way:

(3) (a)   A set of nodes form a *constituent* (of some sentence-structure) iff they are exhaustively dominated by a common node (i.e. iff they all branch out of a single node, and if there are no other nodes branching out of the same single node)

   (b)   X is a *constituent* of Y iff X is dominated by Y

(c)   X is an *immediate constituent* of Y iff X is immediately dominated by Y

(Note *iff* = 'if and only if'; X and Y here stand for nodes.)

In the light of the definitions in (3) above, consider a structure such as (4) below:

(4)

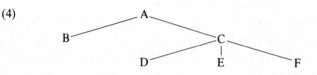

It follows from the definition in (3) (a), that the sequence [D E] does not form a constituent, since although D and E are both dominated by C, they are not *exhaustively* dominated by C, because there is another node (= F) which is also dominated by C. By contrast, the sequence [D E F] does indeed form a constituent, since the nodes D, E, and F are exhaustively dominated by C: thus, the sequence [D E F] forms a constituent of type C. Given the definition in (3) (b), the *constituents* of node A will be all the nodes which A dominates – namely, B, C, D, E, and F. But given (3) (c), the *immediate constituents* of A will be the nodes which are immediately dominated by A, namely B and C.

If we now apply the definitions in (3) to a 'real' tree structure such as (1) above, we see (for example) that the P NP sequence [*in a hotel*] is a constituent in (1), since P and NP are exhaustively dominated by the PP node immediately above them (since this PP node branches only into P and NP, not into any other nodes). But by contrast, the V P sequence *stay in* does not form a constituent in (1), since although they are both dominated by VP, they are not *exhaustively* dominated by VP, since VP also dominates the NP [*the hotel*]. Likewise, given the definitions (3) (b) and (c), it follows that all the nodes in (1) are *constituents* of the overall sentence (S), but that only the NP, M, and VP nodes immediately dominated by S are *immediate constituents* of the sentence. Likewise, the PP [*in a hotel*] is a constituent (though not an immediate constituent) of S, but is both a constituent and an immediate constituent of VP.

Other traditional terms which can be defined in terms of dominance and precedence relations include grammatical relations such as 'Subject', 'Direct (or Primary) Object', 'Secondary Object', 'Prepositional Object', and so on. For example, in a sentence such as:

(5)   Mary could leave John some food in the fridge

we might want to argue that the NP *Mary* is the Subject of the Modal *could* (and indeed of the Verb *leave*, of the Verb Phrase [*leave John some food in the fridge*], and of the whole Sentence), that *John* is the Direct (or Primary) Object of the verb *leave* (and also of the Verb Phrase [*leave John some food in the fridge*], and indeed of the whole Sentence), that [*some food*] is the Secondary Object of the Verb *left* (and of the Verb Phrase and Sentence containing it), and that [*the fridge*] is a Prepositional Object (i.e. Object of the Preposition *in*). How can we incorporate this information about *grammatical relations* or *grammatical functions* into the Phrase-marker diagrams we are using to represent sentence-structure? Chomsky has repeatedly emphasised (most clearly in *Aspects* (1965), pp. 68–74) that relational/functional information of this kind is entirely redundant (and hence should not be directly represented in P-markers), since it can be derived from the primitive information already contained in Phrase-markers, given a very simple set of definitions. Thus, we might define the relevant relations or functions in the following way (in the spirit of Chomsky's proposed definitions in *Lectures* (1981d), p. 42):

(6) (a)   Subject of S = [NP, S]
   (b)   Direct/Primary Object of VP = [NP$_1$, VP]
   (c)   Secondary Object of VP = [NP$_2$, VP]
   (d)   Prepositional Object = [NP, PP]

(The notation [X, Y] should be interpreted as meaning 'A constituent of type X which is immediately dominated by a constituent of type Y'.) Thus, (6) (a) defines the Subject of a Clause as the NP which is immediately dominated by S; (6) (b) defines the Primary (or Direct) Object of a Verb Phrase as the first (i.e. leftmost) NP immediately dominated by VP; (6) (c) defines the Secondary Object of a Verb Phrase as the second NP immediately dominated by VP; and (6) (d) defines a Prepositional Object as an NP immediately dominated by PP. Given the definitions in (6), it is apparent that grammatical relations and functions have no primitive status as 'primes' of syntactic theory; on the contrary, they are purely *derivative* in character – i.e. they can be derived by a simple algorithm (i.e. set of mechanical instructions) from the primitive category-labelling, dominance, and precedence relations already represented in P-markers.

Now for some rather more human terminology! Nodes can have *mothers*, *daughters*, and *sisters* (though interestingly the corresponding relations are known as *fathers*, *sons*, and *brothers* in Italian; I shall leave it to social anthropologists and psychologists to work out what the hidden significance of this cross-cultural terminological transvestism may be!). These terms can be defined as follows:

(7) (a)   If one node X immediately dominates another node Y, then X is the *mother* of Y, and Y is the *daughter* of X

(b)   A set of nodes are *sisters* if they are all immediately dominated by the same (mother) node

(These definitions can be compounded in obvious ways to derive more complex relations like *niece, aunt, grandmother, granddaughter*, etc. in ways which should be obvious: but since only the term *mother, daughter* and *sister* are in common use, we restrict ourselves to these here.) To illustrate these relations, consider a sentence structure like (8) below:

(8)

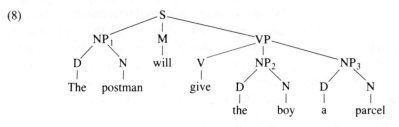

(The subscripts here have no theoretical significance – they are just added for ease of identification.) Let's concentrate in particular on the constituents of the VP (Verb Phrase). Here, we can say that the VP node is the *mother* of three constituents – V, NP_2, and NP_3; these three constituents (V, NP_2, and NP_3) in turn are *daughters* (or, to use our earlier terminology, *immediate constituents*) of the VP node; and furthermore, they are all *sisters* of each other.

Let's summarise what we have said so far. Sentences have a categorial constituent structure, which can be represented in terms of a *Phrase-marker*. A P-marker is a type of graph consisting of a set of points (called *nodes*), with each such point carrying a label, and with each pair of nodes being related either by a *precedence* or a *dominance* relation. Nodes related by dominance are connected by solid lines called *branches*. Each constituent in a sentence carries an appropriate category label. Categories are drawn from a highly restricted finite (and putatively universal) set comprising N – NP, V – VP, P – PP, A – AP, ADV – ADVP, D, M, and a few others which we shall encounter in later chapters.

You should now be able to tackle exercises I and II

3.3   C-command

We can make use of the primitive *dominance* relation discussed in the previous section to define more complex structural relations between constituents which turn out to play an important part in a number of areas of Syntax and Semantics. One such complex structural relation is that of *c-command* (a conventional abbreviation of *constituent-command*: only the abbreviated form is normally used). This we might define as follows:

(9)   X c-commands Y iff (= if and only if) the first branching node dominating X dominates Y, and X does not dominate Y, nor Y dominate X (*a branching node* is a node which branches into two or more immediate constituents)

Quite a mouthful (or do I mean treeful?), you might think! Well, it's not that hard: consider a structure such as (10) below:

(10)

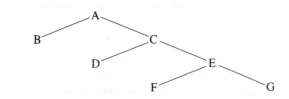

By way of illustration, let's try and work out what the node D c-commands in this structure. The first branching node above D is C: so, by the definition in (9), any other node dominated by C will be c-commanded by D. Now, since C dominates E, F and G (but not A or B), it follows that D c-commands E, F, and G (but not A or B). Since E is the *sister* of D, and since F and G are *nieces* of D (in an obvious sense), then it follows that:

(11)   A node c-commands its sisters, and nieces (and indeed its great nieces, great great nieces, etc.)

Or, more generally:

(12)   A node c-commands its sisters and their descendants (X is a *descendant* of Y if X is dominated by Y)

In more formal terms, what we mean by saying that X c-commands Y is that X is higher up than Y in the tree, or at the same level as Y. Or, if you like, to say that X c-commands Y is to say that X is not *subordinate* to Y, so that X does not occur at a lower level in the tree than Y. You should now be able to work out for yourself what node(s) – if any – each of the nodes in (10) c-commands: namely A c-commands nothing, B c-commands [C, D, E, F, G], C c-commands B, D c-commands [E, F, G], E c-commands D, F c-commands G, and G c-commands F. Simple really, isn't it? Whaddya mean 'No'?

By now, you're probably wondering why I've just dragged you (screaming in protest?) through this terminological quagmire. Well, as we noted above, the relation *c-command* plays an important role in the proper description of a number of syntactic and semantic phenomena. One such phenomenon is *anaphora.* To illustrate what we mean by *anaphora*, contrast the following set of sentences:

(13) (a)   John and Mary think everyone despises *them*
   (b)   John and Mary despise *themselves*
   (c)   John and Mary despise *each other*

In sentence (13 (a), the expression *them* can either refer back to the NP [*John and Mary*], or it can have independent reference and refer to some other group of people (e.g. Jean and Fred). But *themselves* in (13) (b) and *each other* in (13) (c) must be interpreted as referring back to the NP [*John and Mary*], and cannot have *independent reference* (i.e. cannot refer to some other group of people). An expression which cannot have independent reference is called an *anaphor*: thus, *themselves* and *each other* are anaphors, but *them* is not (as the examples in (13) above illustrate). Obviously, then, an anaphor has to take its reference from some other expression: as we saw in Chapter 1, that expression is known as its *antecedent* (= the expression which the anaphor takes its reference from). So, the *antecedent* of the anaphors *themselves* and *each other* in (13) is the NP [*John and Mary*].

Since anaphors cannot have independent reference, it is clear that they must have an appropriate antecedent. As we saw in our discussion of *reflexive anaphors* (i.e. *self*-forms) in Chapter 1, when an anaphor lacks a compatible antecedent, it is uninterpretable, and the resulting sentence is semantically ill-formed. Thus, sentences such as:

(14) (a)   *John despises *each other*
   (b)   *I despise *himself*
   (c)   *Each other* are always arguing
   (d)   *Themselves* are very happy

are ill-formed because the italicised anaphor in each case lacks an appropriate antecedent, and so is uninterpretable. For example, (14) (a) is ruled out by the fact that *each other* requires an antecedent denoting a set of two or more entities, and *John* is a single individual: given that *John* cannot be the antecedent of *each other*, and that there is no other expression which could serve as the antecedent, then the anaphor *each other* is uninterpretable. Likewise, in (14) (b), *I* is not an appropriate antecedent for *himself* (since *I* is a first person Pronoun, and *himself* is a third person form), and there is no other compatible antecedent in the sentence, so that *himself* cannot be assigned reference and is uninterpretable. Likewise, in sentences (14) (c) and (d) there is no possible antecedent at all for the italicised anaphors *each other* and *themselves*, so once again they are uninterpretable.

It seems clear that anaphors like *each other* and *themselves* have obvious semantic properties in common. But they also have syntactic properties in common. For example, both seem to function as NPs, and hence can occupy typical NP positions such as those italicised in (15) below:

(15) (a) They believe [*each other*/*themselves* to be innocent]
   (b) I want [John and Mary to help *each other*/*themselves*]
   (c) I consider [John and Mary to be too preoccupied with *each other*/ *themselves*]

Thus, in (15) (a) *each other* is the Subject of the bracketed infinitival clause, in (15) (b) it is a Verbal Object, and in (15) (c) it is a Prepositional Object: since these are typical NP positions, it seems clear that *each other* and *themselves* are both NPs.

However, in spite of the obvious syntactic and semantic similarities, there are also clear differences between anaphors like *each other* on the one hand, and those like *themselves* on the other. For example, there is a clear meaning difference between the two. Thus, *John and Mary despise themselves* means that John despises John, and Mary despises Mary; whereas *John and Mary despise each other* means that John despises Mary and Mary despises John. Thus, for reasons which should be obvious, *self*-forms (viz. *myself*/*ourselves*/ *yourself*/*yourselves*/*himself*/*itself*/*herself*/*themselves*) are known as *reflexives*, whereas forms like *each other* are known as *reciprocals*.

Thus far, we have established that *each other* is an NP which functions as a reciprocal anaphor requiring to take its reference from some antecedent elsewhere in the sentence, and that *themselves* is an NP which functions as a reflexive anaphor which also requires an antecedent to take its reference from. But what on earth has all of this got to do with the notion of *c-command*? Well, it turns out that there are complex structural conditions which determine whether a given expression can or cannot be interpreted as the antecedent of an anaphor. One such condition can be formulated in terms of the *c-command* relation defined in (9) above: the relevant condition is given in (16) below:

(16)   C-COMMAND CONDITION ON ANAPHORS
        An anaphor must have an appropriate c-commanding antecedent

In the light of this restriction, consider the following contrast:

(17) (a) The soldiers might disgrace *themselves*
   (b) *The soldiers' behaviour might disgrace *themselves*

In (17) (a), the reflexive anaphor can have the NP [*the soldiers*] as its antecedent, whereas in (17) (b) it cannot: moreover, since there is no alternative possible antecedent for *themselves* in (17) (b), the anaphor here is uninterpretable, and the sentence ill-formed. But why can [*the soldiers*] serve as the antecedent of *themselves* in (17) (a), but not in (17) (b)? The answer lies in the fact that the NP [*the soldiers*] c-commands the NP [*themselves*] in (17) (a), but not in (17) (b).

To see this, consider the respective structures of (17) (a) and (b), given as (18) (a) and (b) below (the subscript numerals added to the NP constituents are of no theoretical significance, but are merely added for ease of identification):

(18) (a)

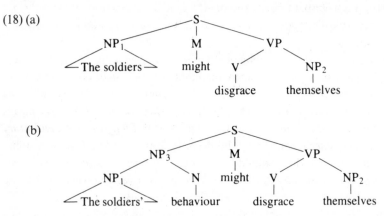

(b)

In (18) (a), NP_1 [*the soldiers*] c-commands the anaphor NP_2 [*themselves*] by virtue of the fact that the first branching node above NP_1 is S, and S dominates NP_2. Since [*the soldiers*] c-commands [*themselves*], and since it is a third person plural NP, then it can function as an appropriate antecedent for the anaphor *themselves*, thereby satisfying the C-COMMAND CONDITION ON ANAPHORS given in (16). But by contrast, in (18) (b), NP_1 [*the soldiers'*] does not c-command NP_2 *themselves*, because the first branching node above NP_1 is NP_3, and NP_3 does not dominate the anaphor NP_2. So, [*the soldiers'*] does not satisfy the structural conditions for being an antecedent imposed in (16). By contrast, NP_3 [*the soldiers' behaviour*] does satisfy this c-command condition (i.e. NP_3 c-commands NP_2), but is ruled out as an antecedent for *themselves* by the *appropriateness* condition in (16): that is, *themselves* requires an antecedent denoting more than one entity, and [*the soldiers' behaviour*] is clearly a single entity. So, the bottom line of the argument is that the c-command condition on anaphors in (16) makes correct predictions about whether a given appropriate NP in a given structural position can or cannot serve as the antecedent of a given anaphor.

We can underline the point made here by showing that our condition (16) correctly predicts that in some cases more than one constituent can be interpreted as the antecedent of an anaphor. Consider for example the following sentence:

(19)   The men will shoot the arrows at each other

What is the antecedent of the reciprocal *each other* here? The answer is that *each other* might either refer back to [*the arrows*] (so that arrows are being shot at other arrows), or to [*The men*] (so that arrows are being shot by men at other men). If we use subscript letters to indicate *coreference* (so that two NPs with the same subscript refer to the same entity, whereas two NPs with different subscripts refer to different entities), then we can say that (19) is ambiguous as between the two interpretations represented in (20) below:

(20) (i)   The men$_i$ will shoot the arrows$_j$ at each other$_j$
    (ii)   The men$_i$ will shoot the arrows$_j$ at each other$_i$

But can our C-COMMAND CONDITION (16) handle the ambiguity of cases such as (19)? Well, let's see! Given the arguments in the previous chapter, (19) will have the structure (21) below:

(21)

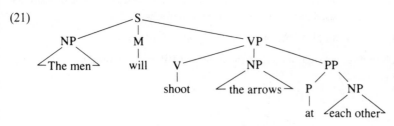

Note that the NP [*the men*] c-commands the reciprocal NP [*each other*] by virtue of the fact that the first branching node above the NP [*the men*] is S, and S dominates the reciprocal NP [*each other*]: hence, we correctly predict that *the men* can function as the antecedent of *each other* in (21), But note that the NP [*the arrows*] also c-commands the reciprocal, since the first branching node above the NP [*the arrows*] is VP, and VP dominates the NP [*each other*]: hence, we correctly predict that *the arrows* can also serve as the antecedent of *each other*. So, overall, our C-COMMAND CONDITION ON ANAPHORS (16) makes exactly the right predictions about the ambiguity of sentences like (19).

The above discussion serves to illustrate two important points. The first is that *dominance* relations play a fundamental role in helping us define more complex structural relations (such as *c-command*) which play an important role in any adequate account of a number of syntactic/semantic phenomena.

And the second is that any adequate description of any linguistic phenomenon must be maximally *explicit*, and to be explicit it must be *formalised* in terms of a primitive set of constructs (in our present case, in terms of Phrase-markers and the dominance relations which hold between the constituents contained within Phrase-markers).

> **You should now be able to tackle exercises III and IV**

3.4 Constraining Phrase-markers

Thus far, we have argued that Phrase-markers are sets of labelled nodes between which specified *precedence*, and *dominance* relations obtain. Now, we argued in Chapter 1 that in order to achieve explanatory adequacy, our linguistic theory must impose severe constraints on the range of technical devices which it makes available for the description of the syntax of natural languages. Accordingly, we might wonder if it is possible to constrain in some way the class of Phrase-markers which can be used to represent natural language sentence structures.

We can illustrate the importance of *constraints* on the well-formedness of P-markers by returning to consider the ungrammaticality of a type of sentence which we discussed in the previous chapter, namely.

(22)   *Drunks would *put completely off the customers*

In Chapter 2, we suggested that the italicised VP in (22) would have the structure (23) below:

(23)

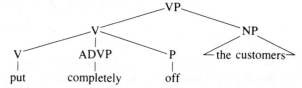

And we argued that such a structure would be ill-formed because a VP-Adverbial like *completely* can only be an immediate constituent of VP, whereas in (23) it is an immediate constituent of V. However, we simplified our discussion at that point by overlooking an alternative possible structure for the italicised VP in (22), namely (24) below:

(24)

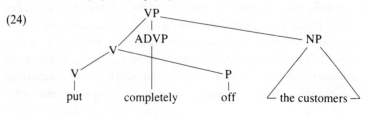

In (24), the ADVP *completely* is indeed an immediate constituent of VP, so that there is no violation of the condition that VP Adverbials can only be attached to VPs. So, unless we find some way of ruling out structures like (24) as ill-formed, our grammar is wrongly going to predict that sentences such as (22) are perfectly grammatical.

But what kind of condition could we invoke which would rule out (24) as an ill-formed structure? If we are to attain our ultimate goal of *Explanatory Adequacy*, we should clearly like to be able to rule out structures such as (24) in terms of some *universal principle* which excludes the possibility of having P-markers like (24) as a representation of the structure of any constituent in any language. But what kind of condition could we devise? Well, perhaps you will already have noticed something rather odd about the tree-diagram in (24) which makes it out of keeping with all the other tree-diagrams that we've drawn so far. What's odd about (24) is that two of the branches (solid lines) intersect each other (i.e. 'cross'). So, the obvious way to rule out structures such as (24) is in terms of a *constraint* to the effect that P-markers cannot contain *crossing branches*. We might formulate the relevant constraint in rather more formal terms as follows:

(25)   NO CROSSING BRANCHES CONSTRAINT
         If one node X precedes another node Y, then X and all descendants of X must precede Y and all descendants of Y (A is a *descendant* of B iff A is dominated by B)

Let's see why a constraint such as (25) would rule out a structure such as (24) as an ill-formed Phrase-marker. To make this clearer, let's attach appropriate subscripts to the offending constituents of the VP in (24) to identify them, as in (26) below:

(26)

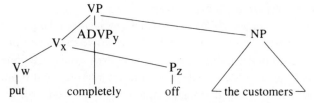

It should now be clear in what way the structure (26) violates the constraint (25). For, in (26), V_x (immediately) precedes $ADVP_y$ (both are immediate constituents of VP): this means that in accordance with the constraint (25), the two constituents of V_x (namely V_w and P_z) must also precede $ADVP_y$. But while V_w satisfies this condition (i.e. *put* precedes *completely*), P_z does not (i.e. *off* does not precede *completely*). Thus, P_z is the offending node here which violates the NO CROSSING BRANCHES CONSTRAINT.

OK – I can hear you objecting – I can see how this 'no crossing branches' constraint can be made to work mechanically, but what on earth is the point of it? Why should it matter whether branches can or cannot cross? A good question (if you asked it for the right reasons, and not just because you're beginning to get exasperated with Syntax!) Well, the motivation behind this constraint is essentially as follows: on general metatheoretical grounds (the desire to develop a maximally constrained theory which provides a plausible basis for developing a model of language acquisition), we want to restrict the class of P-markers which qualify as 'possible natural language sentence-structures' as narrowly as possible, and rule out as many 'impossible' structures as we can. We find that in general the structure of most sentences in most languages can be described quite adequately without the need to posit structures with crossing branches. Hence, in order to *constrain* the class of possible sentence structures in natural languages, we propose to 'ban' the use of P-markers with crossing branches as a representation of sentence structure in natural languages. In what sense is our theory more *constrained* if we impose the 'no crossing branches' condition? The answer is that the set of admissible P-markers if we allow 'crossing branches' is vastly greater than the set of admissible P-markers would be if we impose the 'no crossing branches' condition. Accordingly, in the interests of attaining a more constrained theory of Syntax, we shall impose the 'no crossing branches' restriction (25) on all P-markers used to represent natural language sentence structure. We shall see in the next (and subsequent) chapters that this condition has considerable explanatory force in a number of cases (indeed, we have already seen this in relation to structures such as (24) above). In more traditional terms, the condition amounts to the claim that there cannot be *discontinuous constituents*.

3.5 Generating Phrase-markers

We argued in Chapter 1 that a *grammar* of a language is a model of the grammatical competence of the fluent native speaker of the language. We also argued that acquiring a language involves acquiring a finite system of rules which generate (i.e. specify how to form, interpret, and pronounce) the infinite set of well-formed sentence structures in the language. Accordingly, the task of the linguist describing a particular grammar is to devise a finite system of rules of sentence formation, interpretation, and pronunciation that will generate the infinite set of well-formed sentence structures in the language.

Since our central concern is with Syntax here, let's concentrate on the question of what form *syntactic rules* might take. These rules must comprise a finite system with an infinite capacity, in order to account for the infinite competence (i.e. syntactic knowledge) of the native speaker. This competence is reflected in intuitions about syntactic well-formedness (grammaticality) on the one hand, and syntactic structure on the other. Accordingly, we might suppose that the syntactic rules in a grammar have two tasks to fulfil: namely they must (i) specify which sequences of words form grammatical sentences in a language, and (ii) specify the internal syntactic structure of such sentences. We have seen that the superficial syntactic structure (S-structure) of a sentence can be represented in the form of a labelled tree-diagram or Phrase-marker. Hence, we might reformulate the goal of the syntactic component of a grammar as being that of *generating* (= specifying how to form) all the grammatical sentence-structures in a language. That is, we want to devise a set of rules which specify how grammatical sentences are built up out of phrases, and how phrases are built up out of words. If we further assume that sentence structures can be adequately represented by Phrase-markers, then the problem in effect reduces to devising a set of rules which will generate Phrase-markers of the kind that are used to represent natural language sentence structures.

But what kind of rules could we devise which would generate Phrase-markers? For the sake of concreteness, let's consider how we might generate a tree diagram such as (27) below (taken from example (3) in Chapter 2):

(27)

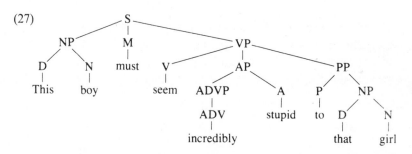

[Abbreviations: S = Clause/Sentence; M = Modal; D = Determiner; ADVP = Adverbial Phrase; ADV = Adverb; P = Preposition, PP = Prepositional Phrase; N = Noun, NP = Noun Phrase; V = Verb, VP = Verb Phrase; A = Adjective; AP = Adjectival Phrase]

The suggestion we shall put forward here is that structures such as (27) could be generated by a set of *Phrase Structure Rules* (= PS rules) – so called because they specify how sentences are structured out of phrases, and phrases out of words. Consider, for example, the following set of Phrase Structure Rules (abbreviations as in (27) above, with [X → Y Z] to be interpreted as specifying that 'X can have a Y immediately followed by a Z as its immediate constituents' – more informally 'You can form an X by taking a Y immediately followed by a Z'):

Phrase-markers

(28) (i)   S → NP M VP   (iv)   ADVP → ADV
     (ii)   VP → V AP PP   (v)   PP → P NP
     (iii)   AP → ADVP A   (vi)   NP → D N

Rule (28) (i) can be regarded as specifying 'You can form a Clause by taking a Noun Phrase immediately followed by a Modal immediately followed by a Verb Phrase'. More formally, we can say that rule (28) (i) will *generate* the partial tree-structure (29) below:

(29)

Rule (28) (ii) specifies that we can form a Verb Phrase by taking a Verb immediately followed by an Adjectival Phrase immediately followed by a Prepositional Phrase; if we apply this rule to expand the VP in (29), we *derive* the structure (30) below:

(30)
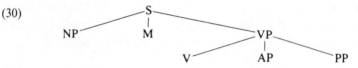

Rule (28) (iii) specifies that we can form a Adjectival Phrase by taking an Adverbial Phrase immediately followed by an Adjective; while rule (28) (iv) tells us that an Adverbial Phrase can consist of an Adverb alone: applying these two rules to the structure (30), we expand (30) into:

(31)
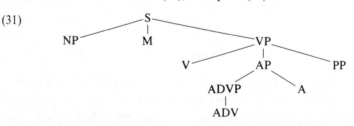

Rule (28) (v) specifies that we can form a Prepositional Phrase out of a Preposition immediately followed by a Noun Phrase; applying rule (28) (v) to the structure (31) will give us:

(32)
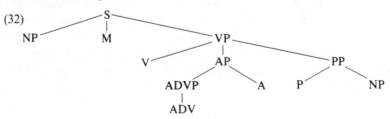

Rule (28) (vi) says that we can form a Noun Phrase by taking a Determiner immediately followed by a Noun; if we apply this rule to expand both Noun Phrases in (32), we derive the structure:

(33)

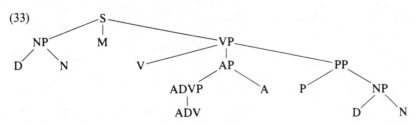

Let's now assume that in addition to the *Categorial Rules* (28) – i.e. rules expanding categories into other categories – the syntactic component of our grammar also contains a *Lexicon* (= dictionary), or list of all the words in the language. And let us further assume that the *Lexical Entry* (= dictionary entry) for each such *Lexical Item* (= item in the dictionary, i.e. 'word') contains – in addition to other information – a specification of the syntactic category that the word belongs to. For present purposes, we might imagine that our Lexicon contains (*inter alia*) the following entries:

(34)   *boy*: N, ...
         girl: N, ...
         incredibly: ADV, ...
         must: M, ...
         seem: V, ...
         stupid: A, ...
         that: D, ...
         this: D, ...
         to: P, ...

(where ... represents other syntactic, semantic, morphological, and phonological information which the relevant dictionary entry contains). And finally, let us also postulate the following principle:

(35)   LEXICALISATION PRINCIPLE
         Any lexical item (= word) listed in the dictionary as belonging to a given word-category can be inserted under any corresponding (terminal) category node in any P-marker

(Recall that a *terminal* node is one at the bottom end of a tree.) All that principle (35) says is that any word listed as a Noun in the Lexicon can be inserted under any N node, any word listed as a Verb under any V node, and so on. Given a LEXICALISATION PRINCIPLE such as (35), we can insert e.g. *this* under the first D in (33), *boy* under the first N, *must* under M, *seem* under V, *incredibly* under ADV, *stupid* under A, *to* under P, *that* under the second D, and *girl* under the second N, thereby deriving from (33) the S-structure (36) below:

(36)

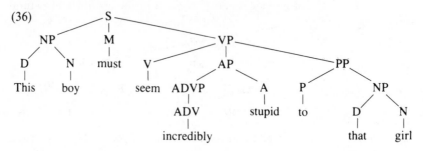

Thus, we see that a set of Categorial Rules like (28) (which specify how categories are formed out of other categories), together with a Lexicon like (34) and an associated LEXICALISATION PRINCIPLE (35) inserting Lexical Items ('real words') into appropriate word-category positions, will prove adequate to generate a sentence structure such as (36), which is the same as (27) above. We have thus now achieved our aim of formulating a set of syntactic rules which will generate S-structures like (27)/(36).

But note that our existing system of rules doesn't just generate the sentence structure (27)/(36): the very same set of rules (together with the same Lexicon) can also be used to generate the S-structures associated with any of the following set of sentences:

(37) (a)   This boy must seem incredibly stupid to this girl
    (b)   That boy must seem incredibly stupid to that girl
    (c)   That boy must seem incredibly stupid to this girl
    (d)   This boy must seem incredibly stupid to this boy
    (e)   This boy must seem incredibly stupid to that boy
    (f)   That boy must seem incredibly stupid to this boy
    (g)   That boy must seem incredibly stupid to that boy
    (h)   This girl must seem incredibly stupid to this girl
    (i)   This girl must seem incredibly stupid to that girl
    (j)   That girl must seem incredibly stupid to that girl
    (k)   That girl must seem incredibly stupid to this girl
    (l)   This girl must seem incredibly stupid to this boy
    (m)   This girl must seem incredibly stupid to that boy
    (n)   That girl must seem incredibly stupid to that boy
    (o)   That girl must seem incredibly stupid to this boy

In other words, the simple grammar we have devised will generate not only the

S-structure (36), but also fifteen other similar sentence structures corresponding to the fifteen sentences listed in (37). Thus, a grammar incorporating a set of Phrase Structure Rules like (28), a Lexicon like (34), and a Lexicalisation Principle like (35) can provide a partial account of the *creativity* of natural language, insofar as the set of rules necessary to generate one S-structure like (36) will also generate 'novel' sentence structures such as those associated with the sentences in (37) above.

Of course, structures like those associated with (36) and (37) constitute only a tiny subset of the infinite set of well-formed sentence structures found in English. We can increase the *Generative Capacity* of our grammar (= the set of structures which it generates) either by expanding the Lexicon on the one hand, or by expanding the Categorial Rules (i.e. Phrase Structure Rules) on the other. For example, we might add to our Lexicon Modals such as *may, might, will, can*, etc., Nouns such as *man, woman, professor, student, person, waiter*, etc., Determiners like *a* and *the*, Adverbs such as *really, decidedly, completely, utterly, surprisingly*, Adjectives like *nice, uncomfortable, randy, generous, trendy, grotty, gorgeous*, etc., Verbs like *feel, appear, become*, etc., Prepositions like *with, on, by, towards*, etc. . . . and so on and so forth. In consequence, our grammar would then generate thousands of sentence structures similar to (36), including those associated with sentences such as:

(38) (a)   This girl might appear really trendy to the waiter
  (b)   A boy must be utterly sincere with a girl
  (c)   The student may feel surprisingly uncomfortable with the professor
  (d)   Etc.

Alternatively, we might modify or expand our existing Categorial Rules so that they generate more types of sentence structure than before. Thus, for example, we might modify our rules so as to take account of the fact that the occurrence of the Prepositional Phrase in sentence structures like (36) is optional, as we see from the grammaticality of sentences such as:

(39)   This boy must seem incredibly stupid

In order to account for this, we might propose to make the Prepositional Phrase an *optional* constituent of the Verb Phrase: this we could do by replacing rule (28) (ii) by rule (40) below:

(40)   VP → V   AP   (PP)

(Note that a constituent in parentheses is, by convention, taken to be optional.) Our revised rule (40) is in fact logically equivalent to the two rules (41) below:

(41) (i)   VP → V AP PP

   (ii)   VP → V AP

And in order to account for sentences such as (42) below:

(42)   [~NP~ *Boys*] must seem incredibly stupid to [~NP~ *girls*]

in which the bracketed Noun Phrases contain no Determiner, we might make the Determiner an optional constituent of NP, so replacing our earlier rule (28) (vi) by rule (43) below:

(43)   NP → (D) N

So, clearly our rules have to be revised in order to take into account the fact that certain constituents are *optional* in certain types of structure.

Moreover, it should be obvious enough that our existing grammar (which contains a handful of rules and a handful of lexical items) will need to be expanded enormously if it is to cope with the hundreds of rules and thousands of lexical items found in English. But the main point that we are concerned to illustrate here is simply that it is possible to devise a system of sentence-formation rules that will indeed generate a wide range of S-structures for any language.

However, we have still not achieved our goal of devising a *finite* set of rules which will generate an *infinite* set of sentence structures. In order to achieve this goal, we need to allow for the fact that natural languages typically have the property that they allow potentially infinite *recursion* of particular structures. For example, one Clause can be *embedded* inside another indefinitely many times, as we see from examples such as (44) below:

(44) (a)   [~S~ John will say nothing]
   (b)   [~S~ Fred may think [~S~ John will say nothing]]
   (c)   [~S~ Jim must realise [~S~ Fred may think [~S~ John will say nothing]]]
   (d)   [~S~ Pete could suspect [~S~ Jim must realise [~S~ Fred may think [~S~ John will say nothing]]]]

Correspondingly, any set of Categorial Rules which we devise to generate sentences like (44) must allow for potentially infinite recursion of S. But how can this be done? Consider the following system of PS rules:

(45) (i)   S → NP M VP

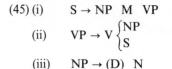

   (ii)   VP → V $\begin{cases} NP \\ S \end{cases}$

   (iii)   NP → (D) N

Rule 45 (i) specifies that we can form a Clause (= S) out of a Noun Phrase, a Modal, and a Verb Phrase; by applying (45) (i), we generate the structure:

(46)

Rule (45) (ii) tells us that we can expand the VP in (46) into a V followed by either an NP, or an S. If we choose the former option and expand VP into the sequence V NP, then by application of (45) (ii) to (46) we obtain:

(47)

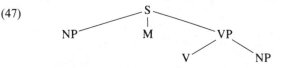

Rule (45) (iii) tells us that we can form a Noun Phrase out of a Noun, with or without a preceding Determiner: we can apply this rule to both NPs in (47), and let's suppose that on both applications we omit the optional Determiner. In this case, rule (45) (iii) will amount simply to [NP → N], and applying the rule to both NPs in (47) above will yield (48) below:

(48)

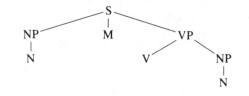

and (48) is precisely the S-structure of sentences like (44) (a), *John will say nothing*.

  But now let's consider an alternative derivation. As before, let's apply rule (45) (i) to generate the subtree (46) above. And let's now look at how we might expand the VP node in (46). Let's suppose that this time, we discard the first option in rule (45) (ii) [VP → V NP], and instead go for the second option [VP → V S]. If we apply this second part of the rule to the VP in (46), we thereby derive (49) below:

(49)

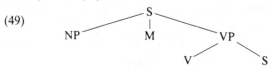

If we now reapply rule (45) (i) to expand the embedded (= lower) S in (49) into
the immediate constituents [NP M VP], we derive:

(50)

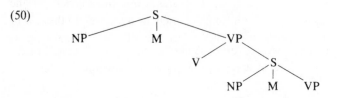

If we next expand the embedded (= lower) VP in (50) into [V NP] by rule
(45) (ii) we obtain:

(51)

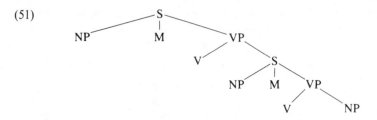

And if we then further expand all the NPs in (51) into N by rule (45) (iii) (omitting the optional Determiner in each case), we derive:

(52)

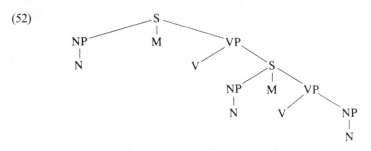

i.e. precisely the categorial constituent structure associated with a sentence
like (44) (b) *Fred may think John will say nothing.* Of course, instead of
expanding VP in (50) into [V NP], we could instead have expanded it into
[V S] by rule (45) (ii): from this (assuming subsequent reapplication of rules
(45) (i), (ii), and (iii)), we could ultimately have derived the structure associated with (44) (c) *Jim must realise Fred may think John will say nothing.*

It should be clear enough from the above discussion that by reapplying the
same set of rules (45) more and more times, we can generate more and more
complex sentences. In fact, there is potentially no limit on the number of times
we can keep reapplying the rules; and in consequence, there is no limit on the
length or number of such sentences that we can generate. In other words, the

rules (45) will generate an infinite set of abstract sentence structures. The interesting property that the rule-system (45) has which enables a finite set of rules to generate an infinite set of sentence structures is that of *recursion* (i.e. the property of being able to be reapplied indefinitely many times). In the case of the rules (45), the recursion resides in the fact that rule (45) (ii) generates as part of its output the category symbol S, which in turn can serve as input to rule (45) (i) ... whose output includes a symbol (VP) which can serve as input to rule (45) (ii): thus (45) (i) and (ii) form a recursive subsystem.

We can summarise our discussion of Syntax thus far as follows. We assume that the task of a *syntax* of a language is to account for the native speaker's intuitions about syntactic well-formedness and structure. We also posit that the syntactic structure of any natural language sentence can be represented in the form of a Phrase-marker (i.e. a labelled tree-diagram). We have seen that there is evidence that acquiring the syntax of a language involves acquiring a set of sentence-formation rules which specify how sentences are built up of phrases, and how phrases are built up of words. In order to account for the fact that native speakers acquire the ability to produce and understand an infinite set of sentences in a finite period of time, we assume that the syntactic component of a grammar must contain a finite recursive set of Categorial Rules (= Phrase Structure Rules, or Constituent Structure Rules) which generate an infinite set of sentence structures.

One question which might usefully be clarified at this point is what exactly we mean by the term *generate*. A seemingly natural enough assumption to make is that a rule which *generates* a certain structure tells you how to form, create, or produce that structure. So, for example, we might interpret a Phrase Structure Rule such as:

(53)   S → NP M VP

as an instruction of the form:

(54)   Plot four distinct points on a graph, and let them be called *nodes*. Let one node be labelled S, another NP, another M, and the other VP. Let the S-node immediately dominate the NP, M, and VP nodes; and let the NP node immediately precede the M node, and let the M node immediately precede the VP node.

Given our earlier conventions about how we represent dominance and precedence relations, (53) – interpreted as (54) – could be regarded as specifying how to produce structures of the form:

(55)

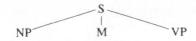

The difficulty with interpreting rules like (53) in the manner outlined in (54) is that it is only too easy to fall into the trap of tacitly imputing to (54) some kind of psychological reality, by reinterpreting (54) as:

(56)   What a native speaker actually does in his mind when he produces a sentence is . . . (cf. 54)

But any claim along the lines of (56) would be patently absurd; we simply have no idea what neurophysiological or psychological processes are involved in the act of creating sentences, and it is absolutely pointless to speculate about them in our present state of knowledge. Hence, the interpretation (56) is misguided. What (56) amounts to is a crude attempt to misconstrue the model of syntactic *competence* we are attempting to develop as a *performance model*.

Perhaps a simple analogy might help to clarify the point. Municipal regulations specify certain structural conditions that houses must meet: they must be built out of certain materials, not others; they must contain so many windows of such-and-such a size, and so many doors; they must have a roof which conforms to certain standards . . . and so on and so forth. What they do not do is tell you *how* to go about building a house; for that, you need a completely different set of instructions, such as might be found e.g. in *Teach Yourself Housebuilding*. Phrase Structure Rules should be thought of as analogous to municipal building regulations: they lay down certain structural conditions which sentences must meet (or, as Chomsky puts it in *Knowledge* (1986a), they *license* certain types of sentence structure as well-formed).

> ### You should now be able to tackle exercise V

3.6   Another look at categories

Hitherto, we have taken a look at some of the formal properties of the kinds of Phrase-markers which are used to represent natural language sentence structures; and we have seen the way in which Phrase Structure Rules can be used to generate the appropriate class of Phrase-markers. Now, Phrase Structure Rules specify how Clauses are built up out of phrasal categories, and how phrasal categories are ultimately built up out of word categories. It is clear, then, that *categories* play a crucial role in our attempt to develop a formal model of natural language Syntax. For this reason, we're going to devote the rest of this chapter to taking a rather closer and more critical look at the system of categories we are employing here.

Let's begin by reviewing the set of categories which we have been assuming hitherto: these include the following:

(57)   N = Noun; NP = Noun Phrase
         V = Verb; VP = Verb Phrase
         P = Preposition; PP = Prepositional Phrase
         A = Adjective; AP = Adjectival Phrase
         ADV = Adverb; ADVP = Adverbial Phrase
         D = Determiner
         M = Modal

There are two obvious questions which arise with any inventory of categories such as (57). The first is whether we have to expand (57) so as to allow for other categories of English which we have not made provision for: this is a question which we shall look at in this section. And the second is the question of whether we could reduce the inventory in (57) by conflating two or more distinct categories into a single category: and this second question we shall turn to in the next section.

Consider first the question of whether we should make provision for additional categories not included in (57). Traditional grammar typically recognises a number of further categories: for example, in his *Reference Book of Terms in Traditional Grammar for Language Students*, Simpson (1982) posits two additional word-level categories which he refers to as *Particle*, and *Conjunction*. Particles include the italicised words in (58) below:

(58) (a)   He put his hat *on*
     (b)   If you pull too hard, the handle will come *off*
     (c)   He was leaning too far over the side, and fell *out*
     (d)   He went *up* to see the manager

while Conjunctions (more specifically, *Subordinating Conjunctions*) include the words italicised in (59) below:

(59) (a)   *After* he had eaten, he fell asleep
     (b)   Matilda was much envied, *for* she was very talented
     (c)   I shall wait *until* you come back
     (d)   There has been no trouble *since* you left

But do we really need to recognise these two additional categories of Particle and Conjunction?

On general metatheoretical grounds (the need to constrain grammars), we clearly want to reduce the set of categories which we posit to the absolute minimum: hence, it would be preferable to subsume 'Particle' and 'Conjunction' under one of our existing categories, if this is at all possible. But under what category? In this connection, it is interesting to note that some traditional grammars analyse Particles as Adverbs (cf. e.g. Quirk *et al.* (1985), p. 516), and refer to the Clauses introduced by the italicised Conjunctions in (59) as Adverbial Clauses (cf. e.g. Simpson (1982), p. 43). But any claim that either Particles or Conjunctions could be analysed as Adverbs seems a doubtful one from a *distributional* point of view: for example, Particles can't generally be replaced by Adverbs, as we see from examples such as (60) and (61) below:

(60)   He put his hat $\begin{cases} on \text{ [Particle]} \\ *carefully \text{ [Adverb]} \end{cases}$

(61)   The handle might come $\begin{cases} off \text{ [Particle]} \\ *suddenly \text{ [Adverb]} \end{cases}$

So, if Particles and Conjunctions are not Adverbs, what are they?

A more promising answer to this question is provided by Emonds ((1976), pp. 172–6): he argues that they are *Prepositions*. In this connection, it is interesting to note that both the Particles in (58) and the Conjunctions in (59) can be used with Noun Phrase objects, as we see from (62) and (63) below:

(62) (a)   He put his hat *on his head*
     (b)   If you pull too hard, the handle will come *off the door*
     (c)   He was leaning too far over the side, and fell *out the window*
     (d)   He went *up the stairs* to see the manager

(63) (a)   *After the meal*, he fell asleep
     (b)   Matilda was much envied *for her talent*
     (c)   I shall wait *until your return*
     (d)   There has been no trouble *since your departure*

There is general agreement that the relevant items function as Prepositions in structures such as (62) and (63) above: it therefore seems plausible to extend this analysis to their use as so-called Particles in (58) and Conjunctions in (59).

The *Preposition* analysis is strengthened by the fact that many items fulfil all three functions, namely that of Preposition, Conjunction, and Particle – as the following examples illustrate:

(64) (a)   I haven't seen him [*since the party*]
     (b)   I haven't seen him [*since the party began*]
     (c)   I haven't seen him [*since*]

(65) (a)   I'd never met her [*before the party*]
     (b)   I'd never met her [*before you held your party*]
     (c)   I'd never met her [*before*]

(66) (a)   You can have some chocolate [*after your dinner*]
  (b)   You can have some chocolate [*after you've eaten your dinner*]
  (c)   You can have some chocolate [*after*]

Clearly, any Theory of Categories which sees the three uses of words like *since*, *before* and *after* as systematically related and can provide a unitary account of them is to be preferred to an atomistic approach (like that of traditional grammarians) which stipulates that they function as Prepositions in the (a) sentences, Conjunctions in the (b) sentences, and (Adverbial) Particles in the (c) sentences. Under the Preposition analysis, we simply say that the relevant items are Prepositions which take a Noun Phrase complement in the (a) sentences, a clausal complement in the (b) sentences, and no complement at all in the (c) sentences. And this is precisely what we would say about the three uses of a Verb such as *know* illustrated in (67) below:

(67) (a)   I don't know the answer
  (b)   I know you are innocent
  (c)   I don't know

Thus in (67) (a), *know* is a Verb which takes a Noun Phrase complement [*the answer*]; in (67) (b) it is a Verb which takes a Clause complement [*you are innocent*]; and in (67) (c) it is a Verb which takes no complement at all. So, the three uses of Prepositions illustrated in (64)–(66) above correspond to the three uses of Verbs illustrated in (67).

Moreover, striking confirmation of the *Preposition* analysis comes from the fact that in all their three uses, Prepositions permit exactly the same range of premodifiers, as (68)–(70) below illustrate:

(68) (a)   He's been difficult *ever* since the party [Preposition]
  (b)   He's been difficult *ever* since the party began [Conjunction]
  (c)   He's been difficult *ever* since [Particle]

(69) (a)   He'd been feeling unwell *a couple of weeks* before his collapse [Preposition]
  (b)   He'd been feeling unwell *a couple of weeks* before he collapsed [Conjunction]
  (c)   He'd been feeling unwell *a couple of weeks* before [Particle]

(70) (a)   There was a drugs raid *immediately* after the party [Preposition]
  (b)   There was a drugs raid *immediately* after the party began [Conjunction]
  (c)   There was a drugs raid *immediately* after [Particle]

So, there seems to be strong empirical support for the Preposition analysis.

The analysis does raise some apparent problems, however. For, it turns out that not all supposed Prepositions can be used in all three ways illustrated above. For example, *until* requires a Noun Phrase or Clause complement, and cannot be used without a complement: cf.

(71) (a)   He waited [*until her departure*]
     (b)   He waited [*until she left*]
     (c)   *He waited [*until*]

During can be used only with an NP complement: cf.

(72) (a)   He left [*during the party*]
     (b)   *He left [*during the party was still going on*]
     (c)   *He left [*during*]

And *while* permits only a clausal complement:

(73) (a)   *He collapsed [*while the party*]
     (b)   He collapsed [*while the party was in full swing*]
     (c)   *He collapsed [*while*]

(though dialectally e.g. in Northern British English *while* is used like *until* in (71), so that 'I'll wait while tomorrow afternoon' means 'I'll wait until tomorrow afternoon'). Surely, the fact that not all supposed Prepositions can occur in all three prepositional constructions undermines the credibility of the Preposition analysis?

No, not at all! After all, precisely the same kind of restrictions are found with Verbs. For example, a Verb like *announce* can only be used with an NP or Clause object, and cannot be used without a complement: cf.

(74) (a)   John announced his resignation
     (b)   John announced he was resigning
     (c)   *John announced

Hence, *until* is little different from *announce* in this respect. Moreover, the Verb *utter* permits only an NP complement (just like the Preposition *during*):

(75) (a)   He uttered a few drunken obscenities
     (b)   *He uttered that he was drunk
     (c)   *He uttered

And the Verb *hope* (like the Preposition *while*) permits only a clausal complement: cf.

(76) (a)   He hoped she would resign
     (b)   *He hoped her resignation
     (c)   *He hoped

So, it seems clear that the idiosyncratic restrictions relating to the range of complements which a Preposition does or does not permit are directly analogous to the parallel restrictions which hold in the case of Verbs. The restrictions concerned are not *categorial* in nature (i.e. they are not associated with every single item belonging to a given category): on the contrary, they are *lexical* in nature (that is to say, they are properties of individual lexical items, so that different words belonging to the same category permit a different range of complements). How these lexical restrictions are to be dealt with is a question which we take up in Chapter 6.

The parallel between Prepositions and Verbs turns out to be even more interesting than you might have expected. For, just as there are Verbs which take complements which are introduced (optionally or obligatorily) by Prepositions, so too there are Prepositions which likewise permit or require a PP complement. For example, there are numerous Verbs which permit or require their complement to be introduced by the Preposition *of*: e.g.

(77) (a) I have a favour to ask (of) you
     (b) I don't know (of) any better solution
     (c) Apparently, some people haven't heard of Debbie Harry
     (d) She'll soon tire of her sexploits

And so too there are a number of Prepositions which permit or require a prepositional complement headed by *of*: e.g.

(78) (a) He stayed at home *because* [of the strike]
     (b) He fell *out* [(of) the window]
     (c) Few people *outside* [(of) the immediate family] know
     (d) It fell *off* [(%of) the table] (of = dialectal)

Thus, the parallel between Verbs and Prepositions is a persuasive one (and we shall explore the significance of this parallelism a little later in this chapter). But the key point that we want to emphasise here is that there really is no reason to expand our existing inventory of categories to include 'Particle' and 'Conjunction', since (as we have shown above) these are simply *Prepositions*: i.e. 'Particles' are Prepositions used without complements, and 'Conjunctions' are Prepositions used with clausal complements.

3.7 Conflating categories

In the previous section, we rejected arguments for *increasing* our existing inventory of categories in (57). We shall now turn to examine the other side of the question, and try to see whether it is possible to *reduce* this inventory by conflating two or more of our existing categories into a single category. More particularly, in this section, we shall examine the possibility of treating first Adverbs and then Determiners as special classes of *Adjective*. We'll begin by looking at Adverbs.

There are numerous reasons for considering the possibility that Adverbs should be analysed as a special class of Adjectives. For one thing, there is a consistent morphological relationship between the two: that is, Adverbs are generally formed from Adjectives by the addition of the suffix *-ly*: cf.

(79)

ADJECTIVE	ADVERB
clever	cleverly
heavy	heavily
beautiful	beautifully
consistent	consistently
careful	carefully
special	specially
nice	nicely
real	really

Moreover, this relationship is a productive one, in the sense that when new Adjectives are created (e.g. *ginormous* concocted out of *gigantic* and *enormous*), then the corresponding Adverb form (in this case *ginormously*) can also be used. And in those exceptional cases where Adverbs do not end in *-ly*, they generally have the same form as the corresponding Adjective, as with *hard, fast*, etc. Moreover, the consistent morphological relationship between Adverbs and Adjectives is underlined by the fact that Adverbs have no *-er* comparative form of their own, but take the corresponding adjectival *-er* form. For example, the Adjective *quick* has the corresponding Adverb form *quickly*. We would thus expect that the *-er* comparative form of the Adverb *quickly* (meaning 'more quickly') would be formed by adding *-er* to the Adverb stem *quickly* to give **quicklier*. But in fact this is not the case at all. Instead, the comparative of the Adverb is formed by adding *-er* to the stem of the corresponding Adjective *quick*, so that the *-er* Adverb corresponding to 'more quickly' is *quicker* (comprising the Adjective stem *quick* and the comparative inflection *-er*), so that both Adjective and Adverb have the same *-er* comparative form: cf.

(80) (a)   He thinks [$_{ADVP}$ *more quickly/quicker/*quicklier* than me]

(b)   His brain is [$_{AP}$ *more quick/quicker* than mine]

And in addition, many dialects of English make no morphological distinction between Adjectives and Adverbs, and thus use Adjectives in contexts where the standard language requires *-ly* Adverbs: cf.

(81) (a)   Tex talks *really quickly* [Adverb + Adverb]
(b)   %Tex talks *real quick* [Adjective + Adjective]

Furthermore, Adjectives and Adverbs permit the same range of premodifiers (such as *very, rather, quite,* etc.): cf.

(82) (a)   His speech is very/rather/quite *slow* [Adjective]
(b)   He talks very/rather/quite *slowly* [Adverb]

And they also permit the same range of following complements: cf.

(83) (a)   Her decision was *independent* of mine [Adjective]
(b)   She decided *independently* of me [Adverb]

(though it should be noted that some Adverbs don't take complements). So, there are many compelling similarities between Adverbs and Adjectives.

In fact, the only obvious difference between the two is in their *distribution*. More precisely, Adjectives like *real* are used to modify nominals, whereas the corresponding Adverb *really* is used to modify Adjectival, Adverbial, Prepositional, and Verbal constituents: cf.

(84) (a)   There is a *real* crisis (A modifying N)
(b)   He is *really* nice (ADV modifying A)
(c)   He walks *really* slowly (ADV modifying ADV)
(d)   He is *really* down (ADV modifying P)
(e)   He must *really* squirm (ADV modifying V)

Now, at first sight, it might seem as if the fact that Adjectives and Adverbs have different distributions provides a strong argument against assigning them to the same category. But this is not in fact the case at all. For the key fact here is that Adjectives and Adverbs are *in complementary distribution*. What on earth does that mean? Well, let's take a simple analogy from a chess board: this comprises a set of black squares and white squares, symmetrically arranged. Suppose you have a chess board in front of you, arranged so that the square in the top lefthand corner is black: and suppose you number all the squares on the board in sequence in the manner indicated in (85) below:

(85)
```
 1  2  3  4  5  6  7  8
16 15 14 13 12 11 10  9
17 18 19 20 21 22 23 24
32 31 30 29 28 27 26 25
33 34 35 36 37 38 39 40
48 47 46 45 44 43 42 41
49 50 51 52 53 54 55 56
64 63 62 61 60 59 58 57
```

Having done all this, you can predict exactly where the black and white squares will occur by a simple formula. That is, odd-numbered squares are black, and even-numbered squares are white. Using the terminology we introduced earlier, we might then say that black and white squares are in *complementary distribution* on a chess-board. By this we mean two things: firstly, black squares and white squares occupy different positions on the board: and secondly, the black and white squares complement each other in the sense that the black squares together with the white squares comprise the total set of 64 squares found on the board (i.e. there is no square on the board which is not either black or white). Of course, given that black and white squares are in complementary distribution, and given that their distribution is symmetrical and determined by a simple formula (odd = black, even = white), then we can predict what colour any given square will be. What colour is square 32? Well, 32 is an even number, and even-numbered squares are white, so square 32 must be white. (I assume you're now going to get your chess-board out to check this!)

But what has chess got to do with Linguistics (apart from the fact that most people find both incomprehensible)? Well, it's generally accepted in all areas of Linguistics (not just Syntax, but also Morphology, Phonology, etc.) that two or more elements which are in systematic complementary distribution with each other should be analysed as units belonging to the same distributional class. We can illustrate this with a traditional argument from Morphology. If we look at the various different ways in which the regular Noun plural inflection (represented by -(*e*)*s* in the spelling) is pronounced, we find the following pattern:

(86)   The regular plural inflection -(*e*)*s* is pronounced as:

    (i)   /ɪz/ when attached to a Noun stem ending in a sibilant consonant (e.g. *class–classes*; *buzz–buzzes*; *bush–bushes*; *mirage–mirages*; *match–matches*; *hedge–hedges*) [in some dialects /ɪz/ = /əz/]

    (ii)   /z/ when attached to Noun stems ending in a vowel, diphthong, or voiced consonant other than a sibilant (e.g. *fee–fees*; *paw–paws*; *plough–ploughs*; *boy–boys*; *cow–cows*; *club–clubs*; *rod–rods*; *bag–bags*; *hive–hives*; *ram–rams*; *plan–plans*; *king–kings*; *ball–balls*; *car–cars*)

    (iii)   /s/ when attached to Noun stems ending in a voiceless consonant other than a sibilant (e.g. *lap–laps*; *rat–rats*; *pack–packs*; *cough–coughs*)

If we adopted the very simplistic position that any units which have different distributions must be different types of elements, then we'd have to say that the three endings /ɪz/, /z/, and /s/ are simply different inflections in English. But this seems counterintuitive: what we really want to say is that they're three different pronunciations of the same inflection, namely the plural -(*e*)*s* inflection. Now, we can do this if we refine our distributional criterion so as to allow for the possibility that elements which are *in systematic complementary distribution* with each other should be assigned to the same distributional class. It is clear that the three plural endings in (86) above are in systematic complementary distribution. This is so for two reasons. Firstly, each of the three endings is attached to different types of Noun stems; and secondly, the three endings together cover the full range of regular Noun stems found in English. Thus, given the assumption that items in systematic complementary distribution should be assigned to the same class, we arrive at the common sense solution of saying that /ɪz/, /z/, and /s/ are simply three *positional variants* of the same plural inflection -(*e*)*s*. By saying that they are *positional variants*, we mean that the choice between them is determined by the position they occur in, viz. whether they are attached to a Noun stem ending in a sibilant, a voiced or voiceless nonsibilant, or a vowel/diphthong.

After a brief trip round the chess-board and a quick dip into Morphology, let's return to our earlier problem relating to the categorial status of Adjectives and Adverbs. The question which concerns us is whether Adjectives and Adverbs can be treated as different members of the same overall category – let's call this category *Advective* (OK, so you don't like the term *Advective* – would you prefer *Adjerb*? I thought not!). Now, bear in mind the principle which we have just established – namely that items which are in systematic complementary distribution should be assigned to the same linguistic class. In this connection, it is interesting to note our earlier observation in relation to the examples in (84) above: these examples showed that Adjectives are used to modify nominal constituents, and Adverbs are used to modify non-nominal constituents. From this, it follows that Adjectives and Adverbs are in systematic complementary distribution, and should therefore be regarded as *positional variants* of each other, and assigned to the same overall category of *Advective*. We can then predict which kind of *Advective* will be required in a given sentence-position from the very simple distributional principle which we gave earlier: namely Adjectives modify nominals, and Adverbs modify non-nominals. So, if you ask me what kind of Advective is used to modify a Verb, the answer is an Adverb (because Verbs are non-nominal): cf. the paradigm in (84) above.

There is thus a very real possibility that our earlier inventory of categories in (57) can be reduced by conflating Adjectives and Adverbs together into a single category of *Advective* (abbreviated to A). But perhaps we can go even further than this, and argue that not only are Adverbs a special type of Adjective, but so too are *Determiners*. If this were so, then we could argue that Adjectives, Adverbs and Determiners all belong to the same category. What could we call such a category? How about *Advecter*? But is it really feasible to conflate Determiners with Advectives? This is the question we shall address ourselves to in the rest of this section.

It might be a good idea to begin our discussion by listing some of the items traditionally considered to be Determiners in English. In his classic work *Language*, Leonard Bloomfield (1935, pp. 203–6) lists the following types of Determiner in English:

(87) (a)   Definite article *the* and Indefinite Article *a*
     (b)   Demonstratives *this/that/these/those*
     (c)   Interrogatives such as *which/what*
     (d)   Quantifiers such as *every/each/any/some/no*, etc.
     (e)   Possessives like *my/your/his/her*, etc.

But in his *Reference Book of Terms in Traditional Grammar for Language Students*, Simpson (1982, p. 12) classifies demonstratives, interrogatives, possessives and quantifiers as *Adjectives*. Now, if we generalise his claim somewhat and treat *all* Determiners as Adjectives, then we can achieve a welcome reduction in our inventory of categories by eliminating the category of Determiner (since all Determiners will be reanalysed as Adjectives). But the obvious question that we have to ask is whether there is empirical support for such a proposal. The answer is that any attempt to analyse Determiners as Adjectives in English runs up against a number of serious problems. Let's see why.

Well, for a start, Adjectives and Determiners have distinct morphological properties. For example, Adjectives generally have a comparative form in *-er* (if they are not more than two syllables in length), whereas Determiners do not: cf.

(88) (a)   ADJECTIVES: quicker, nicer, funnier, narrower, cleverer, prettier, etc.
     (b)   DETERMINERS: *thiser, *everier, *aller, *somer, *anier, etc.

Moreover, Adjectives generally have Adverbial counterparts ending in *-ly*, whereas Determiners do not: cf.

(89) (a)   ADVERBS: quickly,   nicely,   funnily,   narrowly,   cleverly, prettily, etc.
     (b)   DETERMINERS: *thisly, *everily, *ally, *somely, *anily, etc.

In addition, Adjectives and Determiners are syntactically distinct in a variety of ways, in respect of their *distribution*. For example, Adjectives can be recursively 'stacked' to the left of the Noun they modify (i.e. you can go on putting more and more Adjectives in front of the Noun they modify, indefinitely), whereas Determiners cannot be 'stacked' in this way: cf.

(90) (a)   ADJECTIVES: men; *handsome* men; *dark handsome* men; *tall dark handsome* men; *sensitive tall dark handsome* men; *intelligent sensitive tall dark handsome* men, etc.

(b)   DETERMINERS: *the* car; *the my car; *which my cars; *my some cars, etc.

Moreover, Determiners and Adjectives have different distributions, since when they are used together to modify a Noun, the Determiner always has to precede the Adjective: cf.

(91) (a)   [D *the*] [A *big*] bang (Determiner + Adjective)
(b)   *[A *big*] [D *the*] bang (Adjective + Determiner)

(92) (a)   [D *my*] [A *red*] pen (Determiner + Adjective)
(b)   *[A *red*] [D *my*] pen (Adjective + Determiner)

Likewise, Determiners can be coordinated (i.e. joined together by *and*) with other Determiners of the same type (subject to semantic etc. restrictions), as in:

(93) (a)   [*each*] and [*every*] member of the class
(b)   [*these*] and [*those*] books
(c)   [*his*] and [*her*] ideas

And in much the same way, Adjectives can be coordinated with other Adjectives: cf.

(94) (a)   a [*provocative*] and [*contentious*] proposition
(b)   a [*thoughtful*] and [*considerate*] person
(c)   a [*penetrating*] and [*insightful*] discussion

However, Determiners cannot be coordinated with Adjectives: cf.

(95) (a)   *[D *my*] and [A *lazy*] son (Determiner *and* Adjective)
(b)   *[A *silly*] and [D *these*] ideas (Adjective *and* Determiner)

A final argument in support of distinguishing Determiners from Adjectives can be formulated in relation to the different *semantic* properties (i.e. meaning) of Determiners and Adjectives. Because of their semantic properties, Adjectives can generally only be used to modify a restricted class of Nouns, so

that, for example, the bracketed Adjectives in (96) below can be used to
modify some but not all of the italicised Nouns:

(96) (a)   a [thoughtful] *person/cat/?fish/??pan/!problem*
   (b)   an [utter] *fool/bigot/??enemy/!friend/!man/!garden*
   (c)   an [alliterative] *style/poem/!nose/!car*

What's going on in the 'odd' examples in (96) is that the semantic properties
(= meaning) of the Adjective concerned make it somehow incompatible with
the semantic properties of the Noun it is modifying. This *incompatibility*
would seem to be nonlinguistic in nature (e.g. what's odd about *a thoughtful
pan* is that it attributes powers of thought to pans). Restrictions such as those
in (96) are known technically as *Selection Restrictions* (the general idea behind
this rather cumbersome term being that an Adjective like *thoughtful* can only
'select' certain kinds of Noun to modify, e.g. a Noun designating a rational
entity).

By contrast, Determiners seem to be semantically much more 'neutral' or
'transparent' (in some sense), and hence are not selectionally constrained in
the same way, as we see from (97) below:

(97) (a)   [a/the/this] *person/cat/fish/pan/problem*
   (c)   [each/every/any] *fool/bigot/enemy/friend/man/garden*
   (c)   [my/your/no] *style/poem/nose/car*

True, some Determiners do impose restrictions on the choice of head Noun
which they can modify, but these restrictions are *syntactic* in nature, and relate
to *grammatical number*. Thus, as Quirk *et al.* (1985, p. 246) point out, Nouns
can be divided into the following two major syntactic classes:

> Those which, like *book ... bottle, chair, forest, idea*, etc. must be
> seen as denoting individual countable entities and not as an undif-
> ferentiated mass, are called COUNT NOUNS. Nouns which, like
> *furniture, ... bread, grass, warmth, music*, etc. must by contrast be
> seen as denoting an undifferentiated mass or continuum ... are
> called NONCOUNT NOUNS.

Count Nouns can generally be singular or plural (e.g. *tool/tools*), whereas
Noncount Nouns are inherently singular (e.g. *equipment/*equipments*). Determiners in turn can be divided into three classes according to the type of Nouns
they can co-occur with. On the one hand, there are Determiners like *the* which
can modify any kind of Noun, viz. a singular count Noun, a plural count
Noun, and a noncount Noun; then, there are Determiners like *enough* which
can modify plural count Nouns and noncount Nouns; in addition, there are

Determiners like (*a*)*n* which can modify only a singular count Noun: the table below illustrates the relevant Determiner and Noun classes:

(98) DETERMINER CLASSES AND NOUN CLASSES

DETERMINER	NONCOUNT NOUN	PLURAL COUNT NOUN	SINGULAR COUNT NOUN
the	*the* equipment	*the* tools	*the* tool
enough	*enough* equipment	*enough* tools	**enough* tool
a(*n*)	**an* equipment	**a* tools	*a* tool

The grammatical restrictions which hold between Determiners and the Nouns they modify are thus very different in nature from the pragmatic restrictions which hold between Adjectives and the Nouns they modify. Moreover, Adjectives are not generally subject to the kind of *number* restrictions which Determiners are typically subject to: in other words, Adjectives can usually modify *any* grammatical kind of Noun, whether a Mass Noun, a Singular Count Noun, or a Plural Count Noun. So, once again, it seems that we have strong empirical support for drawing a categorial distinction between *Determiners* and *Adjectives*. Of course, our discussion has of necessity been simplified for expository purposes: for example, we have ignored the possibility that some items (e.g. *many*, *few*, etc.) may have dual categorial status, and thus function both as Determiners and as Adjectives.

What we have examined in this section is the question of whether the inventory of categories we presented in (57) above can be reduced by conflating two or more categories together into a single category. In the first half of this section, we argued that Adverbs should be analysed as positional variants of Adjectives (so that the two can be conflated into a single category of *Advective*). But in the second half, we argued against the possibility of analysing Determiners as a subspecies of Adjective, on the grounds that Adjectives and Determiners are both morphologically and syntactically distinct.

You should now be able to tackle exercises VI and VII

3.8 The nature of categories

Thus far, we have considered in some detail the question of the *range* of different categories found in English: for example, we have addressed questions such as 'Do we need to recognise categories such as Particle and Conjunction in English?', 'Are Adverbs really Adjectives in disguise?' and 'Are Determiners adjectival transvestites?'. But we have not addressed ourselves to an even more fundamental theoretical question – namely: 'Are categories *primitive* elements (not reducible to smaller units), or are they *composite* elements built up out of smaller units in much the same way as atoms are composite elements built up out of subatomic particles?'

Perhaps an analogy with Phonology (rather than Atomic Physics) would be more helpful here. A word such as 'bit' comprises the three sound-segments (traditionally called *phonemes*) /b/, /ɪ/, and /t/. But are phonemes primitive sound-units, or are they composites of smaller units? Numerous phonologists have argued that phonemes are not primitive elements at all, but rather are composites of sets of articulatory and acoustic properties known as *distinctive features* (so that within the Distinctive Feature Theory of Phonology, a phoneme is traditionally defined as a 'matrix of distinctive features'). Thus, for example, within the Theory of Distinctive Feature Phonology outlined in Chomsky and Halle's (1968) *The Sound Pattern of English*, the phoneme /p/ would not be a primitive element, but rather would be a composite of the set of thirteen primitive distinctive features outlined in (99) below:

$$(99) \qquad /p/ = \begin{bmatrix} -\text{Vocalic}, +\text{Consonantal}, -\text{High}, -\text{Back}, -\text{Low}, \\ +\text{Anterior}, -\text{Coronal}, -\text{Round}, +\text{Tense}, -\text{Voice}, \\ -\text{Continuant}, -\text{Nasal}, -\text{Strident} \end{bmatrix}$$

Drawing a simple analogy with Phonology, Chomsky (*Aspects* (1965), p. 82) suggests that syntactic categories might not be primitive units, but rather might be composites of primitive syntactic (i.e. categorial) features.

This idea is taken up and further developed in Chomsky's 1970 paper *Remarks on Nominalisation*, and in numerous later works. For example, Chomsky in his 1974 *Amherst Lectures* suggests that the four major word-level categories Verb, Adjective, Noun, and Preposition can be analysed as complexes of just two binary syntactic features, namely [±N] (nominal/non-nominal) and [±V] (verbal/non-verbal). Under this proposal, the four major word-classes would be broken down into feature sets in the manner indicated in (100) below:

$$(100) \qquad \begin{array}{ll} \text{Verb} = [+V, -N] & \text{Adjective} = [+V, +N] \\ \text{Noun} = [-V, +N] & \text{Preposition} = [-V, -N] \end{array}$$

But what is the purpose of breaking down categories into sets of features in this way?

One reason for doing so is in order to capture *supercategorial* generalisations: i.e. generalisations which extend across more than one category. For example, observe that in English only Verbs and Prepositions take NP complements (direct object NPs), not Nouns or Adjectives: cf.

101 (a)   John *loves* [Mary] (V + NP)

   (b)   John bought a present *for* [Mary] (P + NP)

   (c)   *John's *admiration* [Mary] (N + NP)

   (d)   *John is *fond* [Mary] (A + NP)

Thus, in (101) the NP *Mary* can be used as the complement of the Verb *loves* or of the Preposition *for*, but not of the Noun *admiration*, or of the Adjective *fond*. Now, of course, we could account for the data in (101) by simply *listing* the set of categories which take NP complements (viz. Verbs and Prepositions); but lists are arbitrary and have no explanatory value, since a list could in principle contain any random set of elements. A higher level of generality (and explanatory adequacy) would be attained if we could somehow capture the intuition that Verbs and Prepositions form a natural class, a kind of *supercategory*. But how can we do this? Decomposing categories into sets of categorial features in the manner suggested in (100) above provides us with an obvious answer, since we could then say that Verbs and Prepositions form a natural supercategory by virtue of the fact that they both share the feature $[-N]$ (though of course they differ in respect of the feature $[\pm V]$). We could then say in relation to the paradigm in (101) that only $[-N]$ items take NP complements in English.

More generally still, we could argue that the feature analysis proposed above allows us to define a supercategory as a set of categories which share a subset of features (e.g. one feature) in common. Given this assumption, we should expect to find the following types of supercategory in natural languages:

(102) (i)   a supercategory of $[+V]$ categories, comprising V and A

    (ii)   a supercategory of $[-V]$ categories, comprising N and P

    (iii) a supercategory of $[+N]$ categories, comprising N and A

    (iv) a supercategory of $[-N]$ categories, comprising V and P

And indeed it does seem that just such a system of supercategories can be motivated on universalist grounds (in the sense that it is applicable to languages other than English). For example, in Italian, Nouns and Adjectives are inflected for *gender* (masculine or feminine), but not Verbs or Prepositions: cf.

(103) (a)   brav*o* ragazz*o* 'good boy' [Masculine Singular A + N]

    (b)   brav*a* ragazz*a* 'good girl' [Feminine Singular A + N]

    (c)   brav*i* ragazz*i* 'good boys' [Masculine Plural A + N]

    (d)   brav*e* ragazz*e* 'good girls' [Feminine Plural A + N]

Within the system of categorial features outlined in (100) above, the fact that Nouns and Adjectives form a natural class is not an accidental property, but rather follows from the assumption that they form a supercategory, by virtue of sharing the feature [+N]; we can thus say that in Italian, only [+N] categories inflect for gender.

Just as word-level categories are grouped into larger supercategory sets, so too it appears to be true that phrase-level categories also group into supercategory sets; indeed, each of the word-level supercategories in (102) seems to have a phrase-level counterpart. In this connection, it is interesting to note Jackendoff's (1977a, p. 17) observation that only NPs and PPs can appear in the italicised *focus* position in so-called *cleft sentences* such as those below:

(104) (a) It was *a car* that she bought (NP)
    (b) It was *in the shop* that I met her (PP)
    (c) *It is *very pretty* that she is (AP)
    (d) *It is *very quickly* that she writes (ADVP)
    (e) *It is *go home* that I will (VP)

So it seems evident that NP and PP form a natural phrasal supercategory. But we can capture this generalisation quite simply in terms of our proposed feature analysis. Since N and P share the feature [−V], we can say that only phrases headed by a [−V] constituent can be focused in cleft sentences. Thus, NP and PP form a natural phrase-level supercategory in the same way as N and P form a word-level supercategory.

Stowell (1981, p. 24) presents universalist evidence that AP and VP form a natural phrasal supercategory: citing unpublished work by van Riemsdijk, he observes that in German AP and VP can function as prenominal modifiers (though not NP or PP): cf. his examples:

(105) (a) der [AP seiner Freundin überdrüssige] *Student*
        the   of-his girlfriend weary   student
        'the student weary of his girlfriend'
    (b) ein [VP sein Studium seit   langem hassender] *Student*
        a   his studies since long   hating   student
        'a student hating his studies for a long time'

Thus, the class of prenominal modifiers in German can be identified as the supercategory of phrases headed by a [+V] constituent.

Stowell adds a further universalist argument in support of the claim that the proposed categorial feature system defines a natural set of supercategories. He remarks:

The feature system ... can be motivated on the basis of the fact that the pairs of categories which it defines as natural classes are often collapsed into single categories in languages other than English. For instance, in some languages there is no lexical or morphological distinction between Adjectives and Nouns, and so there is just one [+N] categorial phrase-type. In other languages, the categorial distinction between NP and PP is eliminated, and the function served by Prepositions is taken over by case affixes. Moreover, it is not unheard of for the categorial distinction between Adjectives and Verbs to be neutralised, so that a single syntactic category of Predicates results.

(Stowell, 1981, p. 25)

We have seen that one justification for decomposing categories into feature sets is that it enables us to capture *supercategorial* generalisations. But a second type of justification for the feature analysis is a precisely opposite one – namely that it enables us to capture *subcategorial* generalisations. By way of illustration of this general point, let us consider how various subclasses of Verbs can be differentiated by the use of features. In general terms, we might define a Verb as an item which can be morphologically marked for Tense (in an appropriate context, e.g. in a finite clause). Verbs in English have two morphologically distinct tenses, Present and Past – as we see from the paradigm of third person singular forms in (106) below:

(106)

PRESENT	PAST	PRESENT	PAST
works	worked	is	was
goes	went	has	had
sees	saw	may	might
comes	came	will	would
hides	hid	can	could

However, Verbs are traditionally divided into the two major subclasses in (107):

(107) (i) AUXILIARY VERBS = *will/would, shall/should, can/could, may/might, must, ought, used* (and also *be, have, do, need, dare* in some of their uses, not others)

(ii) NONAUXILIARY VERBS = Verbs other than those in (107) (i)

There are a number of idiosyncratic syntactic properties which distinguish Auxiliaries from Nonauxiliary Verbs. Firstly, Auxiliaries can undergo 'inversion' in direct questions, i.e. can be moved into pre-subject position: cf.

149

(108) (a)   *Can* you speak Japanese?
     (b)   *Would* you go there again?
     (c)   *Is* it still raining?
     (d)   *Have* you been anywhere interesting?

whereas by contrast other Verbs do not themselves permit inversion, but rather require *do-support* (i.e. require inverted forms with the Auxiliary *do*): cf.

(109) (a)   **Intends* he to come?
     (b)   *Does* he intend to come?

(110) (a)   **Saw* you the mayor?
     (b)   *Did* you see the mayor?

(111) (a)   **Works* he in the evenings?
     (b)   *Does* he work in the evenings?

Secondly, Auxiliaries can be directly negated by *not/n't*: cf.

(112) (a)   John *could not/couldn't* come to the party
     (b)   I *do not/don't* like her much
     (c)   He *is not/isn't* working very hard
     (d)   They *have not/haven't* finished

whereas other Verbs cannot themselves be negated, but require the use of so-called *do*-periphrasis: cf.

(113) (a)   *They *like not/liken't* me
     (b)   They *do not/don't* like me

(114) (a)   *I *see not/seen't* any point in it
     (b)   I *do not/don't* see any point in it

(115) (a)   *You *tried not/triedn't* hard enough
     (b)   You *did not/didn't* try hard enough

And thirdly, Auxiliaries can appear in sentence-final 'tags': cf.

(116) (a)   You don't like her, *do* you?
     (b)   He'll win, *won't* he?
     (c)   She isn't very clever, *is* she?
     (d)   They can't stand spaghetti, *can* they?

whereas Nonauxiliary Verbs can't themselves be used to form 'tags', but rather require the use of *do*-tags: cf.

(117) (a)   You like her, *do/*like* you?

(b)   They want to go home, *do/*want* they?

(c)   They came back, *did/*came* they?

So, on the basis of these (and other) syntactic properties, it seems that we are justified in positing that there are two major subclasses of Verbs – Auxiliary and Nonauxiliary Verbs.

But how can we formalise the distinction between these two subclasses of Verb? The use of *syntactic features* provides us with an obvious solution to our dilemma. More precisely, we might resort to positing a *minor categorial feature* $[\pm \text{AUX}]$ to differentiate Auxiliary Verbs $(=[+\text{AUX}])$ on the one hand from Nonauxiliary Verbs $(=[-\text{AUX}])$ on the other. Given this assumption, a typical Auxiliary Verb such as *will* would be differentiated from a typical Nonauxiliary Verb such as *want* as in (118) below:

(118) $will = [+V, -N, +\text{AUX}] = $ Auxiliary Verb

$want = [+V, -N, -\text{AUX}] = $ Nonauxiliary Verb

However, the class of Auxiliary Verbs is itself far from homogeneous; more particularly, we can distinguish two major classes of Auxiliaries, along the lines indicated in (119) below:

(119)   MODAL AUXILIARIES = *will/would, shall/should, can/could, may/ might, do/did, must*

NON-MODAL AUXILIARIES = other auxiliaries (*be* and *have*)

Modal Auxiliaries have two defining characteristics, one morphological, one syntactic: namely

(120) (i)   Modals lack nonfinite forms (hence have no infinitive, no gerund form in *-ing*, and no perfective/passive participle form in *-n*)

(ii)   Modals take a 'bare' infinitival Verb Phrase complement (i.e. a VP not introduced by the infinitive marker *to*)

Accordingly, we can define Modals as Verbs which possess *both* properties in (120). The three traditionally recognised Non-modal Auxiliaries are the perfective Auxiliary *have*, the progressive Auxiliary *be*, and the passive Auxiliary *be*. Perfective *have* is so-called because it marks the completion (hence, *perfection*) of an action; it is followed by a VP headed by a perfective *-n* participle, as in:

(121)   The referee has [$_{VP}$ *shown* him the red card]

Progressive *be* is so-called because it marks an action in progress; it is followed by a VP headed by a gerund (i.e. a Verb in the *-ing* form): cf.

(122)   She is [$_{VP}$ *making* a lot of progress]

Perfective *have* and progressive *be* are together known as *Aspectual Auxiliaries*, since they mark *Aspect* (viz. whether an action is in progress or has been completed). The third major Non-modal Auxiliary is the Passive Auxiliary *be*, so called because it is used to form passive structures; it is followed by a VP headed by a passive *-n* participle, as in:

(123)   He was [$_{VP}$ *shown* the red card by the referee]

Given our morphological criterion in (120) (i), it follows that Non-modal Auxiliaries have *infinitive* forms (and so can be used after the infinitive marker *to*), gerund forms in *-ing*, and perfective participle forms in *-n* (and so can be used after the perfective Auxiliary *have*): and, as we see from the examples below, a typical Non-modal Auxiliary such as passive *be* has all these properties: cf.

(124) (a)   He's going to *be* taken home by Mary [infinitive]
    (b)   He is *being* taken home by Mary [gerund]
    (c)   He has *been* taken home by Mary [perfective participle]

But by contrast, a typical Modal such as *can* lacks all three nonfinite forms: cf.

(125) (a)   *It'd be nice to *can* speak Arabic [infinitive]
    (b)   *I can't imagine him *canning* do it [gerund]
    (c)   *He hasn't *cannen/canned* come [perfective participle]

Our second criterion (120) (ii) lends further support to the distinction we are drawing between Modal and Non-modal Auxiliaries; for, whereas Modals are followed by a 'bare' (i.e. *to*-less) infinitival VP complement, as in:

(126)   John may/might/can/could/will/would [$_{VP}$ *go home*]

Non-modal Auxiliaries typically take other types of VP complement: for example, progressive *be* takes a gerund (*-ing*) VP complement, while passive *be* and perfective *have* take a participial (*-n*) VP complement: cf.

(127) (a)   John is [$_{VP}$ *writing a letter to Mary*]
    (b)   The letter was [$_{VP}$ *written by John*]
    (c)   John has [$_{VP}$ *written Mary a letter*]

And a typical Nonauxiliary Verb like *get* tends to take either a gerund (*-ing*) complement, or a participial (*-n*) complement, or an infinitive complement with *to*, or an NP/PP/AP/etc. complement:

(128) (a)   I must get [*working on my book*]

(b)   You might get [*thrown in jail*]

(c)   When will I get [*to see the finished product*]?

(d)   I might get [*a medal*] / [*into trouble*] / [*really angry*]

Thus, we have both morphological and syntactic motivation for drawing a distinction between Modal and Non-modal Auxiliaries.

Of course, the criteria we have used to differentiate between Auxiliary and Nonauxiliary Verbs on the one hand, and between Modal and Non-modal Auxiliaries on the other can be used as 'diagnostics' to test for the status of any individual item. We can summarise the criteria we have used as in (129) below: criteria (a–c) serve to differentiate Auxiliaries from Nonauxiliary Verbs, and criteria (d–g) serve to differentiate Modal Auxiliaries from other Verbs:

(129) (a)   Auxiliaries can undergo inversion in direct questions, whereas Nonauxiliary Verbs cannot (and require *do*-periphrasis)

(b)   Auxiliaries can occur in tags, whereas Nonauxiliary Verbs cannot (and require *do*-tags)

(c)   Auxiliary Verbs can be negated by *not/n't*, whereas Nonauxiliary Verbs cannot, and require *do*-negatives

(d)   Only Modals take a 'bare' infinitive VP complement

(e)   Unlike other Verbs, Modals have no infinitive form, and hence cannot be used after the infinitive particle *to*, or after another Modal

(f)   Unlike other Verbs, Modals have no -*n* participle form, and hence cannot be used after perfective *have*

(g)   Unlike other Verbs, Modals have no -*ing* form

Using these criteria, we can establish the status of any individual verb. To see this, let's consider the status of *do* in its so-called *periphrastic* use.

In this connection, consider the following sentences from a fictitious spaghetti western:

(130) (a)   *Do* you like spaghetti?

(b)   You like spaghetti, *do* you?

(c)   I *do not/don't* like spaghetti

(d)   I really do *like/*liking/*liked* to eat spaghetti

(e)   *I want you to really *do* make an effort to eat your spaghetti

(f)   *Why have you *done* not eat your spaghetti?

(g)   *I want you really *doing* make an effort to eat your spaghetti

Examples (130) (a–c) show that periphrastic *do* must be an Auxiliary, because it can undergo Inversion in direct questions, occur in tags, and has a negative form in *not/n't*. But examples (130) (d–g) show that periphrastic *do* must be a Modal Auxiliary because it must be followed by a bare infinitival V (such as *like* in (130) (d), and lacks an infinitive form (cf. (130) (e)), a participle form (cf. (130) (f)), and a gerund form (cf. (130) (g)). Overall, then, our seven criteria set out in (129) above lead us to the conclusion that periphrastic *do* is syntactically a Modal Auxiliary Verb. And this is an assumption which we shall make throughout the rest of the book.

To summarise: we can distinguish three important subclasses of Verbs, e.g. in the manner represented schematically in (131):

(131)

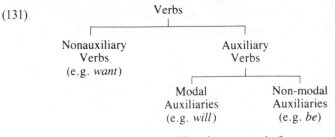

But what has all this got to do with using syntactic features to capture subcategorial generalisations? Well, within any theory which takes categories as *primitive* elements not decomposable into smaller units, it is hard to see any principled way of capturing the *similarities and differences* between these various subclasses of Verbs. Such a theory is forced to adopt one of two extreme positions. Either we say that all such items are Verbs and hence belong to the primitive category V (in which case it is not obvious how we handle the morphosyntactic differences between Nonauxiliary Verbs, Modal Auxiliary Verbs, and Non-modal Auxiliary Verbs); or, we posit that each subclass of Verb belongs to a different primitive category, so that Nonauxiliary Verbs belong to the category V, Modal Auxiliaries belong to the category M, and Non-modal Auxiliaries belong to the category AUX (but then it is far from obvious how we handle the similarities between the three types, e.g. the fact that they can all carry morphological Tense-marking).

The problems which beset the *primitive* Theory of Categories find a ready solution in the *componential* Theory of Categories which sees categories as composites of syntactic features. For within a feature-based analysis of categories, we can capture the similarities between Nonauxiliary Verbs, Modal Auxiliaries, and Non-modal Auxiliaries by saying that they all share the *major* categorial features [+ V, − N]. The class division between Auxiliary Verbs on the one hand, and Nonauxiliary Verbs on the other could then be handled in terms of a *minor* categorial feature [±AUX]. And the distinction between Modal and Non-modal Auxiliaries could be handled in terms of another *minor* categorial feature such as [± M]. The feature-complexes associated with each of these different types of Verb would then be as in (132) below:

(132)   Verbs (of any kind)   = [+ V, − N]
         Auxiliary Verbs   = [+ V, − N, + AUX]
         Nonauxiliary Verbs   = [+ V, − N, − AUX]
         Modal Auxiliary Verbs   = [+ V, − N, + AUX, + M]
         Non-modal Auxiliary Verbs = [+ V, − N, + AUX, − M]

We could then say (for instance) that the property of being able to be morphologically marked for Tense is associated with items which carry the major categorial features [+ V, − N]; the property of being able to undergo 'inversion' in direct questions is associated with items which carry the minor categorial feature [+ AUX]; and the property of lacking nonfinite forms is associated with items bearing the minor categorial feature [+ M]. Thus, a feature-based analysis of categories enables us to capture both the *similarities* and *differences* between related subcategories. Therefore, as we noted earlier, a feature analysis enables us to capture *subcategorial* as well as *supercategorial* generalisations.

A feature-based analysis might also help us resolve some of the problems which beset traditional analyses of *Simple Coordination*. In Chapter 2, we argued that only identical categories can be conjoined, idiomatically. However, apparent exceptions to this claim are not hard to find. For example, a variety of different phrase types can be coordinated when used *predicatively* – e.g. as the complement of a Verb like *be*: cf.

(133) (a)   John is *a banker* and *extremely rich* [NP and AP]
      (b)   John is *moody* and *under the weather* [AP and PP]
      (c)   John is *a superb athlete* and *in a class of his own* [NP and PP]

Such sentences are fully idiomatic, and yet involve what would seem to be coordination of two unlike categories, in apparent violation of our 'identical categories' condition. How can we overcome this obvious problem with our analysis of Ordinary Coordination? Syntactic Feature Theory offers us a possible answer: we might follow Sag *et al.* (1985) in assuming that constituents used predicatively (e.g. as the complement of a copula verb such as *be*) carry a supercategorial feature such as [+ PRD] (indicating that they are used predicatively); we might then assume that a *partial* identity in the feature composition of conjoined categories is sufficient to ensure grammaticality; in the case of (133), the fact that the conjuncts are all phrases headed by a category which carries the feature [+ PRD] will ensure grammaticality. Obviously, important questions of detail remain to be worked out (as Sag *et al.* attempt to do in their paper, though within a very different theoretical framework from that used here). But the important point to emphasise is that the feature analysis enables us to cope with apparent counterexamples to our earlier claims about Ordinary Coordination.

Of course, any reanalysis of word categories such as N, V, A, and P as composites of categorial features will have obvious ramifications throughout our grammar. For one thing, the corresponding *phrasal* categories will have to be modified accordingly, since phrases are expansions of their head categories (e.g. NP is an expansion of N). So, for example, if N is reanalysed as $[+N, -V]$, then NP will have to be reanalysed accordingly (e.g. as $[+NP, -VP]$). Similarly, if the categorial feature analysis is adopted, then traditional category labels (such as N, NP, etc.) in Phrase-markers will have to be replaced by the corresponding set of categorial features. And likewise, the category symbols used in Phrase Structure Rules will have to be replaced by feature complexes, so that a rule such as:

(134)   VP → V NP

will be replaced by its feature counterpart (135) below:

(135) $[+VP, -NP] \rightarrow [+V, -N]$ $[+NP, -VP]$

Before you begin to start thinking that maybe it's about time you gave up Syntax, let me hasten to add that I'm going to continue to use the conventional letter symbols N, NP, V, VP, P, PP, A, AP, etc. throughout the rest of the book to designate the appropriate categories, for typographical and expository convenience. It should be borne in mind, however, that my use of a single-letter symbol such as M to designate the subcategory of Modal Auxiliary Verbs is simply a typographically convenient shorthand form of the corresponding categorial feature complex $[-N, +V, +AUX, +M]$, and is used merely to make life easier for both of us! I shall only use categorial features to capture generalisations which would otherwise be lost without them.

You should now be able to tackle exercises VIII, IX, and X

3.9 Summary

This chapter has been concerned with examining some of the formal properties of Phrase-markers, the rules that generate them, and the nature of the categories used to label the nonterminal nodes of Phrase-markers. Section 3.2 identified the *dominance* and *precedence* relations holding between nodes within a P-marker, and showed how simple constituency relations could be defined in terms of *dominance*. Section 3.3 showed how *dominance* could be used to define the more complex *c-command* relation which plays an important role in the description of numerous syntactic and semantic phenomena (including *anaphora*). In 3.4 we argued that Phrase-markers should be constrained so as to disallow *crossing branches* (i.e. discontinuous constituents). In 3.5 we saw that a simple recursive set of Phrase Structure Rules can be devised which will generate an infinite set of sentence-structures.

We then went on to consider the range and nature of the syntactic categories used in Phrase-markers and Phrase Structure Rules. In 3.6 we argued against expanding our existing set of word categories to include *Particle* and *Conjunction*, and we saw that these could be satisfactorily analysed as Prepositions. In 3.7 we looked at the question of whether our existing inventory of categories could be reduced; and we found that although there was some compelling evidence to suggest that Adjectives and Adverbs are different manifestations of the same category (which we called *Advective*), there was no such evidence in favour of reanalysing Determiners as a subclass of Adjectives. Finally, in 3.8 we examined the nature of categories, suggesting that categories are not primitive elements, but rather are composites of major and minor categorial features.

EXERCISES

Exercise I
In relation to the Phrase-marker (8) below, specify (with appropriate explanation):

(1)   Which pairs of adjacent words do (and don't) form constituents?
(2)   Which sets of nodes are sisters?
(3)   What is the mother of each of the NPs?
(4)   What are the immediate constituents of VP?
(5)   What are the daughters of PP?
(6)   What are the Subject, Direct Object, and Prepositional Object in the sentence?
(7)   How would the same structure be represented as a set of labelled bracketings?

(8)

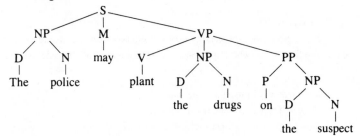

*Exercise II

Compare the following three different accounts of the distinction between *who* and *whom*. In traditional prescriptive grammar, we find the following two prescriptive rules:

(1) (a)   *Who* is used as the Subject of a Verb, and *whom* as the Object of a Verb or Preposition

    (b)   Never separate a Preposition from its object

In Quirk *et al.*'s descriptive grammar of contemporary English, we find (1985, pp. 366–70) a set of descriptive rules which amount to the following:

(2) (a)   *Who* is used as the Subject of a Verb (in any style)

    (b)   As the Object of a Verb or Preposition, *whom* is used in formal style, and *who* in informal style

    (c)   Prepositions can be stranded (i.e. separated from their object) in informal, but not formal style.

Emonds (1976, p. 198) proposes a generative account of the distinction, which involves the following assumptions:

(3) (a)   The form *who* is used when immediately dominated by S; the form *whom* is used elsewhere

    (b)   A clause-initial NP or PP containing a wh-word like *who(m)* is an immediate constituent of S

    (c)   *who(m)* is a (pronominal) NP

Decide for yourself which of the following examples are grammatical. Compare and contrast the predictions made by each of these analyses about the grammaticality of the examples, and how well these predictions correspond with your intuitive judgments. Suggest ways of modifying the proposed rules, if necessary.

(4)   *Who/whom* will come to the party?
(5)   *Who/whom* will you meet at the party?
(6)   You met *who/whom* at the party?
(7)   *Who/whom* will you write to?
(8)   To *who/whom* will your write?
(9)   You will write to *who/whom*?

*Exercise III

Show how the C-COMMAND CONDITION ON ANAPHORS would account for data such as the following (where any possible antecedent(s) of the reflexive are italicised):

(1)   *John* will buy himself another car
(2)   *John* will buy another car for himself
(3)   *John* might show *Harry* pictures of himself

(4)   *John* considers [himself to be the champion]

(5)   *John* wants [there to be pictures of himself on the wall]

Assume that the bracketed infinitives in examples (4) and (5) are S constituents which have the immediate constituents [NP I VP], where I represents the infinitive marker *to*; assume that *there* in (5) is an NP (more precisely, a pro-NP).

Exercise IV

The word *ever* in English cannot normally occur in positive sentences: cf. the ungrammaticality of:

(1)   *I will *ever* forgive you for that

But it can occur in negative sentences: cf.

(2) (a)   Nobody will *ever* forgive you for that

    (b)   I won't *ever* forgive you for that

However, there are restrictions on the use of *ever* in negative sentences: for example, it can't occur in the following negative sentences:

(3) (a)   *I will *ever* forgive nobody for that

    (b)   *Someone who didn't like you would *ever* forgive you for that

Now, we might assume that the restrictions on the use of *ever* in negative sentences can be characterised in structural terms along the following lines:

(4)   *Ever* is an Adverbial expression (ADVP) which occurs as an immediate constituent of S. In negative sentences, *ever* must be preceded and c-commanded by a negative constituent (e.g. by a negative Modal, or by a Noun Phrase containing the negative Determiner *no* as one of its immediate constituents)

Show how the condition imposed in (4) would account for the (un)grammaticality of the following sentences, assuming the well-formedness judgments given (draw tree-diagrams to illustrate your answer):

(5) (a)   No Frenchman *ever* would help an Englishman

   (b)   No Frenchman would *ever* help an Englishman

   (c)   No Frenchman would help an Englishman *ever*

(6) (a)   *Some Frenchmen *ever* wouldn't help an Englishman

   (b)   Some Frenchmen wouldn't *ever* help an Englishman

   (c)   Some Frenchmen wouldn't help an Englishman *ever*

(7) (a)   *Some Frenchmen *ever* would help no Englishman

   (b)   *Some Frenchmen would *ever* help no Englishman

   (c)   *Some Frenchmen would help no Englishman *ever*

(8) (a)   *Some Frenchmen who don't like English people *ever* would help an Englishman

(b)   *Some Frenchmen who don't like English people would *ever* help an Eng-lishman

(c)   *Some Frenchmen who don't like English people would help an English-man *ever*

Assume that *no, some,* and *an* are all Determiners, that *don't* is a negative Modal, that *who* is an NP, and that *ever* is an Adverbial Phrase comprising the single Adverb *ever*, and hence has the structure [$_{ADVP}$ [$_{ADV}$ *ever*]]. Assume also that the expression [*Some Frenchmen who don't like English people*] is a Noun Phrase which has the simpli-fied constituent structure (9) below:

(9)   [$_{NP}$ [$_{NP}$ some Frenchmen] [$_{S}$ [$_{NP}$ who] [$_{M}$ don't] [$_{VP}$ like English people]]]

Exercise V

List 10 well-formed sentences (without drawing the associated P-markers) which can be generated by the set of Phrase Structure Rules in (1) below, together with the associated Lexicon in (2). List a further 10 ill-formed sentences which can be gener-ated by the rules, and specify in what way(s) they are ill-formed.

In addition, draw Phrase-markers representing the structure of any five of your well-formed sentences. Take one of these Phrase-markers, and represent its structure instead by an equivalent set of labelled brackets.

(1) (a)   S → NP M VP   (d)   AP → (ADVP) A
    (b)   VP → V NP   (e)   ADVP → ADV
    (c)   NP → D (AP) N

(2)   *a(n)* = D; *absolutely* = ADV; *apple* = N; *arrest* = V; *buy* = V; *can* = M; *emotional* = A; *extremely* = ADV; *fairly* = ADV; *girl* = N; *handsome* = A; *highly* = ADV; *impeccable* = A; *may* = M; *nice* = A; *policeman* = N; *pretty* = A; *ripe* = A; *sparrow* = N; *tall* = A; *tasty* = A; *that* = D; *the* = D; *this* = D; *will* = M

*Exercise VI

Quirk *et al.* (1985, pp. 253–64) maintain that there are three distinct sub-classes of Determiner in English, with each class containing items such as those listed below:

PREDETERMINER	CENTRAL DETERMINER	POSTDETERMINER
all/half	the	one, two, three ...
double/treble	this/these	first, second ...
once/twice ...	that/those	much/few
	each	several
	some/any	additional/further
	either/neither	next/last/past
	whose/which	more/less
	whatever/whichever/whosever	

Their reasons for setting up these three different categories of Determiner are based on the *distributional* differences between them. More precisely, they maintain that items in one class can only be combined with items in another class in the order specified, so that we can have, for example:

> PREDET + CENDET + POSTDET: *all the five boys*
> PREDET + CENDET: *double the quantity*
> PREDET + POSTDET: *all three boys*
> CENDET + POSTDET: *the second occasion*

Other orders, they maintain, are not possible: cf.

> POSTDET + CENDET + PREDET: **five the all boys*
> CENDET + PREDET + POSTDET: **the all five boys*

Moreover, items belonging to the same class generally cannot be combined with each other: cf.

> CENDET + CENDET: **the this book*

though they note that Postdeterminers can sometimes be combined, as in *the last two pages*, or *the two last pages*, etc. Using these distributional criteria, and inventing your own examples, try and determine which subclass(es) of Determiner the following items belong to (supporting your arguments with relevant examples):

> (1) *a(n)*; (2) *no*; (3) *such*; (4) Possessives like *my*, *your*, *his*, etc.; (5) *every*; (6) *both*; (7) *what?/what!* (8) *little*; (9) *(an)other*; (10) *many*

Point out the problems associated with Quirk *et al.*'s classification: illustrate your answer by showing that there are (i) ungrammatical combinations generated by their schema; and (ii) grammatical combinations not generated by their schema.

Exercise VII

In the text, we suggested that Adjectives and Adverbs are in complementary distribution, and so are members of the same category. Discuss the status of the italicised items in the examples below with respect to this claim:

(1)   John can become *temperamental*
(2)   John can behave *temperamentally*

Exercise VIII

In the text, we presented seven criteria which help us differentiate between Nonauxiliary Verbs and Auxiliary Verbs, and (within the class of Auxiliaries) between Modal Auxiliary Verbs and Nonmodal Auxiliary Verbs. On the basis of these criteria, devise illustrative examples of your own to determine whether each of the italicised items below (in each of its uses) has the categorial status of a Verb, a Modal Auxiliary, or a Nonmodal Auxiliary (or more than one of these). Which items prove problematic to classify, and in what respect(s)? The italicised labels in parentheses are provided

161

Phrase-markers

purely as a way of helping you differentiate between different uses of a given item (e.g. the use of *is* in (1) (a) might be called the *copula* use, etc.).

(1) (a)   John *is* a nice guy/very tall/in Paris (*copula*)
  (b)   John *is* working hard (*progressive*)
  (c)   John *is* arrested every now and then (*passive*)
  (d)   John *is* to leave for Paris tomorrow (*infinitival*)

(2) (a)   John *has* no money (*possessive*)
  (b)   John *has* finished (*perfective*)
  (c)   John *has* to go there (*infinitival*)

(3) (a)   John *needs* a haircut (*nominal*)
  (b)   John *needs* to think about it (*to-infinitival*)
  (c)   I doubt if John *need* come (*bare infinitival*)

(4) (a)   John *got* a new car (*nominal*)
  (b)   John *got* arrested (*passive*)
  (c)   John *got* to be famous (*infinitival*)

(5)   John *used* to go there quite often

(6)   John *ought* to go back again

If you run out of ideas, you might find it useful to consult a good reference grammar, e.g. the section on Auxiliaries in Quirk *et al.* (1985, pp. 120–48): but don't be put off if you find that they use the relevant terminology rather differently from the way in which we do here: stick to our terminology for the purposes of the exercise!

Exercise IX
Consider the sentence:

(1)   He might have been writing a letter

In (2)–(6) below are a number of suggested analyses of the superficial syntactic structure of this sentence (adapted in minor ways so as to make them compatible with our present framework):

(2)   Chomsky, *Syntactic Structures* (1957)

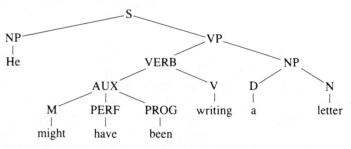

(AUX = Auxiliary; PERF/PROG = Perfective/Progressive Auxiliary)

162

(3)   Chomsky, *Logical Structure* (1955/1975)

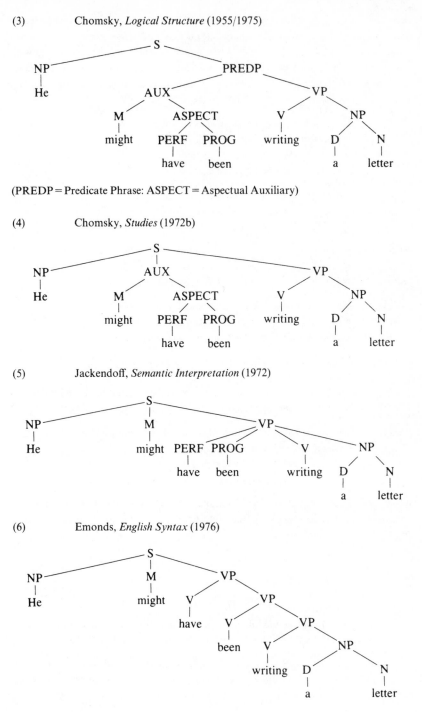

(PREDP = Predicate Phrase: ASPECT = Aspectual Auxiliary)

(4)   Chomsky, *Studies* (1972b)

(5)   Jackendoff, *Semantic Interpretation* (1972)

(6)   Emonds, *English Syntax* (1976)

Below are a set of sentences: for the purposes of the exercise, assume that they are all grammatical (though, for stylistic reasons, you may find some of them 'better' than others, e.g. on the grounds that they are less 'repetitive', etc.). Taking the relevant well-formedness judgments as given, use the constituent structure 'tests' discussed in the previous chapter to determine which of the five analyses is/are compatible with the data given, and which is/are not.

(7)   SPEAKER A: What might he have been doing?
        SPEAKER B: *Writing a letter*
                   Been writing a letter
                   Have been writing a letter

(8) (a)   He might have been *writing a letter* or *watching TV*
    (b)   He might have *been writing a letter* or *been watching TV*
    (c)   He might *have been writing a letter* or *have been watching TV*

(9) (a)   He might have been – or he might not have been – *writing a letter*
    (b)   He might have – or he might not have – *been writing a letter*
    (c)   He might – or he might not – *have been writing a letter*

(10) (a)   He might – *for example* – have been writing a letter
     (b)   He might have – *for example* – been writing a letter
     (c)   He might have been – *for example* – writing a letter

(11) (a)   Mary thinks he might have been writing a letter, and *so* he might have been
     (b)   Mary thinks he might have been writing a letter, and *so* he might have
     (c)   Mary thinks he might have been writing a letter, and *so* he might

(12)   SPEAKER A: Do you think he might have been writing a letter?
         SPEAKER B: Yes, he might have been
                    Yes, he might have
                    Yes, he might

Write a separate set of sentence-formation rules to generate each of the sentence structures in (2)–(6) above (i.e. one set of rules for (2), another for (3), another for (4), and so on).

**Exercise X

Show which of the following generalisations can and cannot be captured straightforwardly using the system of syntactic features developed in the text:

(1) In Dutch (according to Hoekstra (1984), p. 31) Prepositions and Nouns take following complements, whereas Adjectives and Verbs take preceding complements: cf. his examples:

(1) (a)   *voor* [de maaltijd]
               before the meal

(b)   een *verhaal* [over vogels]
               a story about birds

(c)   ... dat hij [dat gezeur] *moe* is
               ... that he that drivel weary is
               ... 'that he is weary of that drivel'

(d)   ... dat hij [een fout] *maakte*
               ... that he a mistake made
               ... 'that he made a mistake'

(2) In English (as noted in Stowell (1981), p. 57, fn. 17) only Adjectives and Verbs permit direct *un*-prefixation, not Nouns or Prepositions: cf.

(2) (a)   unafraid, unaware, unfit, unkind [Adjectives]

(b)   undo, untie, unfold, unpack, unravel [Verbs]

(c)   *unfear, *unconvention, *unafraid [Nouns]

(d)   *uninside, *unby, *unon, *unfrom [Prepositions]

Why are examples such as *unfriendliness* not counterexamples to this claim? Can you find genuine counterexamples?

(3)   In questions in English, an NP, PP, or AP containing a question-word like *who*, *what*, *which*, *how*, etc. can be positioned at the front of the sentence, but not a VP:

(3) (a)   [NP *Which girl*] does he seem most keen on?

(b)   [PP *In which town*] does he live?

(c)   [AP *How fond of you*] is he?

(d)   *[VP *Live in which town*] does he?

(4) In Russian (according to Stowell (1981, p. 142), only Adjectives and Nouns carry case-marking: cf. his Russian example:

(4)   Ivan   sčitaet   Masǔ   krasivoj
               Ivan [NOM] considers Masha [OBJ] pretty [INST]
               (NOM = Nominative; OBJ = Objective; INST = Instrumental)

(5) In English only NP and PP may be relativised (i.e. may contain a relative pronoun such as *which*, or *who*), as the following examples from Stuurman (1985, p. 132) illustrate:

(5) (a)   food [*which* he may appear fond of] (NP)

(b)   food [*of which* he may appear fond] (PP)

(c)   *food [*fond of which* he may appear] (AP)

(d)   *food [*appear fond of which* he may] (VP)

(6) In Italian, Nouns, Adjectives, and Verbs (but not Prepositions or Adverbs) are inflected for Number:

(6)   Due bell*e*   ragazz*e*   parl*ano* spesso con Gino
                  Two pretty girls   talk   often with Gino
                    PLURAL PLURAL   PLURAL   INV   INV   SING
                (INV = 'invariable'; SING = 'singular')

(7) In English, Adjectives, Nouns, and Prepositions can be modified by *all* (in the sense of 'completely'), but not Verbs:

(7) (a)   I'm [all wet] (AP)
    (b)   It's [all gold] (NP)
    (c)   I'm [all in] (PP)
    (d)   *I've [all finished] (VP)

4
Noun Phrases

4.1 Overview

Most of our discussion in the previous two chapters has been concerned with providing empirical substantiation for the claim that sentences are hierarchically structured out of constituents belonging to a restricted (perhaps universal) set of *categories*, and with considering the nature of categories. Implicitly, we postulated a *two-level* Theory of Categories: that is to say, we tacitly assumed that there are two *levels* of categories in natural language, namely

(1) (i)   *word-level categories*, e.g.
             N = Noun; V = Verb; A = Adjective; P = Preposition;
             ADV = Adverb; M = Modal; D = Determiner, etc.
     (ii)   *phrase-level categories*, e.g.
             NP = Noun Phrase; VP = Verb Phrase; AP = Adjectival Phrase;
             PP = Prepositional Phrase; ADVP = Adverbial Phrase, etc.

In this chapter and the next, however, we are going to argue that our existing Theory of Categories should be extended to include a third type of category intermediate between word-level and phrase-level categories. That is to say, we are going to argue in favour of positing that there are nominal constituents larger than the Noun but smaller than a full Noun Phrase, verbal constituents larger than the Verb but smaller than a full Verb Phrase, adjectival constituents larger than the Adjective but smaller than a full Adjectival Phrase . . . and so on. We'll begin our discussion in this chapter by looking at the internal structure of Noun Phrases: in the next chapter, we shall go on to look at the syntax of other types of Phrase.

4.2 Small nominal phrases

Let's begin our story by introducing the hero – namely, the fictional character designated in (2) below:

(2)   the king of England

There can surely be little doubt that the overall sequence in (2) is a Noun Phrase: for example, like other NPs, it can take the genitive *'s* inflection, as in:

(3)   *the king of England's* crown

Likewise, there seems to be plenty of evidence that the sequence [*of England*] is a PP constituent in (2). After all, it can be coordinated with another similar PP (= *of*-phrase), as in:

(4)   the king [pp *of England*] and [pp *of the Empire*]

It can also function as the 'shared constituent' in cases of *shared constituent coordination*, as in:

(5)   He is the king, and she is the queen, [pp *of England*]

And it can function as a *sentence fragment* in an appropriate context: cf.

(6)   SPEAKER A: Was he the king of France?
            SPEAKER B: No, [pp *of England*]

Moreover, it can be preposed, e.g. in questions:

(7)   [pp *Of which country*] was he the king?

And it can be replaced (in a somewhat archaic style) by the pro-PP *thereof*: cf.

(8)   He dwelled in England, and was the king *thereof* for many a year

The obvious conclusion to draw is thus that there is overwhelming evidence that [*of England*] is a PP constituent of the overall Noun Phrase [*the king of England*].

But what is the immediate constituent structure of the whole Noun Phrase? In his influential 'Immediate Constituents' article, Rulon Wells argued (1947 [1957, p. 188]):

> that the ICs [= immediate constituents] of *the king of England opened Parliament* are *the king of England* and *opened Parliament*, that those of the former are *the* and *king of England* and those of the latter are *opened* and *Parliament*, and that *king of England* is divided into *king* and *of England*.

What is of interest to us here is Wells' implicit claim that the phrase [*the king of England*] has the structure (9) below:

(9)

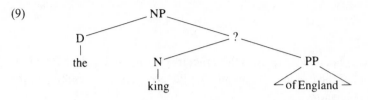

I have not attached any specific category label to the constituent [*king of England*] here, since Wells gives no label for it. But let's speculate on what our mystery constituent (designated by ? in (9) above) might be.

Well, since it's a phrase containing the Noun *king*, an obvious suggestion is that the sequence *king of England* is just another Noun Phrase. In other words, we might assume that [*the king of England*] has the skeletal structure (10) below:

(10)

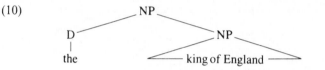

But this seems to be wrong, for several reasons. For one thing, the 'small' nominal phrase [*king of England*] does not have the same distribution as a 'full' Noun Phrase such as [*the king of England*], as we see from (11) below:

(11) (a)   {*The king of England*} opened Parliament
             {*King of England*}

(b)   They crowned {*the king of England*} yesterday
             {*king of England*}

(c)   Parliament grants little power to {*the king of England*}
             {*king of England*}

Secondly, if [*king of England*] were a Noun Phrase, then it would mean that Determiners like *the* would be analysed as premodifying full Noun Phrases: for, a structure such as (10) above would need to be generated by a Phrase Structure Rule such as (12) below:

(12)   NP → D NP

But rule (12) is *recursive* (in that the symbol 'NP' occurs on both the lefthand and the righthand side of the arrow). Now, this means that the rule will generate NPs containing *multiple Determiners* (in fact, NPs containing indefinitely many Determiners). To see this, consider what happens when we apply rule

169

(12): it will generate the structure (13) below:

(13)

But rule (12) can now re-apply to the structure (13), to expand the NP node at the bottom of the tree in (13) into another [D NP] sequence, resulting in the structure (14) below:

(14)

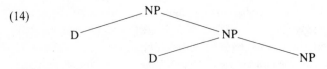

And (14) also contains an NP node at the bottom of the tree which can likewise be expanded into a [D NP] sequence by re-application of rule (12), thereby deriving the structure (15) below:

(15)

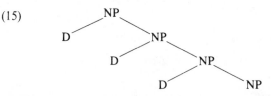

And it should be obvious to you by now that we can go on recursively (= repeatedly) re-applying the same rule to produce an NP structure containing not just three Determiners (as in (15) above), but four, five, six . . . in fact a potentially *infinite* number.

'Well, what's wrong with that?' you might ask. The problem is that multiple Determiner sequences are ill-formed in English, as we see from the impossibility of NPs such as those in (16) below (each of which contains a sequence of just two Determiners):

(16) (a) *[D *the*] [D *the*] king of England
   (b) *[D *the*] [D *this*] king of England
   (c) *[D *a*] [D *the*] king of England
   (d) *[D *our*] [D *your*] king of England
   (e) *[D *the*] [D *our*] king of England
   (f) *[D *an*] [D *our*] king of England
   (g) *[D *that*] [D *our*] king of England

Of course, it may well be true that part of the reason why some of the Phrases in (16) are ill-formed is *semantic* in nature. And indeed, this might be argued to be the case in (16) (a) – (d); for example (16) (c) might be said to be odd because *a* is indefinite and *the* is definite, so that we have a contradiction of some sort. And we might argue that if *multiple Determiner* sequences result in some form of semantic anomaly, then there's nothing *syntactically* wrong with them: i.e. we might argue that such sequences are grammatical, but semantically ill-formed. If this is so, then there's no reason to prevent *syntactic* rules like (12) from generating such sequences, since the task of syntactic rules is to generate *syntactically well-formed structures*.

But the question is whether it is plausible to claim that *all* multiple Determiner sequences in English can be ruled out as ill-formed on semantic grounds. As we have already suggested, this is plausible enough for examples such as (16) (a) – (d) above. But it could surely not be said that Phrases such as (16) (e) – (g) are semantically ill-formed. Why not?

Well, for one thing, ungrammatical *Determiner + Possessive* sequences such as those in (16) (e) – (g) have perfectly grammatical paraphrases in English, as we see from the following paradigm:

(17) (a)   **a my* book
     (b)   *a* book *of mine*

(18) (a)   **this your* tie
     (b)   *this* tie *of yours*

(19) (a)   **some your* friends
     (b)   *some* friends *of yours*
     (c)   *some of your* friends

Now, if multiple Determiner sequences are simply *meaningless*, then we wouldn't expect to find an alternative grammatical way of expressing the same meaning in English: and yet examples such as (17) – (19) show that we can indeed find grammatical ways of expressing the relevant concept. The fact that the ill-formed Noun Phrases in the (a) examples in (17)–(19) above have perfectly grammatical synonymous counterparts in the (b) sentences suggests that the nature of the ill-formedness in the (a) examples is *syntactic* rather than *semantic*.

A second argument for analysing the ill-formedness of multiple Determiner sequences in English as *syntactic* is that many such sequences which are ill-formed in English are well-formed in other languages. For example, *Determiner + Possessive* sequences have grammatical counterparts in languages such as Italian, Spanish, and Romanian – as the following examples show:

(20) (a)   *un mio* libro [Italian]
         a my book ('a book of mine')

(b)   *esas* ideas *tuyas* [Spanish]
       those ideas yours ('those ideas of yours')

(c)   cart*ea ta* [Romanian]
       book + the your (= book the your = 'your book')

Now, if multiple Determiner sequences were semantically anomalous, one would expect synonymous sequences to be equally anomalous in other languages: the fact that they are not suggests that the ill-formedness of multiple Determiner sequences in English is *syntactic* rather than *semantic* in nature (though in the case of NPs such as (16) (c) [*a the king of England*], the ill-formedness may be both syntactic and semantic). In other words, it seems likely that 'multiple Determiner' sequences are ruled out in English by some syntactic principle, not by semantic considerations alone. And the obvious principle to invoke is one to the effect that Determiners in English modify a type of nominal phrase which is smaller than a full Noun Phrase, though larger than a single Noun.

Overall, then, it would seem likely that our mystery constituent (indicated by '?') in (9) above is an 'intermediate' type of nominal phrase, larger than N, but smaller than NP. But what label can we attach to it? Well, I'm afraid that our existing inventory of categories summarised in (1) above simply doesn't provide us with enough category labels to go round. For, (1) recognises only two types of nominal constituent, namely N and NP: it has no label for a constituent 'intermediate' between the two. So, we need a rather more sophisticated set of category labels. But where can we find them?

Fortunately, Zellig Harris' (1951) *Structural Linguistics* provides us with a simple answer. Harris (ibid., p. 266) suggests a system of what he calls 'raised numbers' to label successively larger phrasal expansions of a given head constituent. Adapting his *numerical superscript* system in minor ways (e.g. Harris starts counting at '1', but we're going to start counting at '0'!), we might then resolve the problem posed by the phrase [*the king of England*] in the following way. We might argue that the Noun *king* is an N^0, that the 'small' nominal phrase [*king of England*] is a single phrasal expansion of *king* and hence an N^1, and that the full NP [*the king of England*] is a double phrasal expansion of the head Noun *king*, and hence an N^2. Given this notation, (2) would have the structure (21) below:

(21)

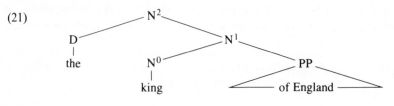

In the *numerical superscript* notation, N^0 corresponds to the simple category N of our earlier system in (1), N^2 corresponds to NP, and N^1 has no counterpart at all in our original system.

At this point, however, we should mention two rival (but entirely equivalent) notational alternatives to Harris' *number notation*. One is the *bar notation* introduced in Chomsky's (1970) 'Remarks on Nominalisation' paper; and the second is the *prime notation* used (for example) in an influential study of Phrase Structure by Jackendoff (1977a). The three systems are notational variants of each other (i.e. different ways of saying the same thing), and the correspondences between the three can be summarised as in (22) below:

(22)   NUMBER NOTATION   BAR NOTATION   PRIME NOTATION

      N^0 (N-zero)   N   N

      N^1 (N-one) $\overline{\text{N}}$ (N-bar)   N' (N-prime)

      N^2 (N-two) $\overline{\overline{\text{N}}}$ (N-double-bar) N'' (N-double-prime)

Thus, the skeletal structure of [*the king of England*] could be represented in exactly equivalent fashion in each of the three systems as in (23) below:

(23) (a)   [$_{N^2}$ the [$_{N^1}$ [$_{N^0}$ king] of England]]

    (b)   [$_{\overline{\overline{\text{N}}}}$ the [$_{\overline{\text{N}}}$ [$_{\text{N}}$ king] of England]]

    (c)   [$_{\text{N''}}$ the [$_{\text{N'}}$ [$_{\text{N}}$ king] of England]]

Given that these three notational systems are entirely equivalent, it is not surprising to find that they are used interchangeably: for example, Jackendoff's (1977a) book uses the bar notation in its title (it is called $\overline{X}$ *Syntax*), but uses the prime notation throughout the rest of the book!

For typographical reasons (if you use a typewriter or a word-processor, you'll understand what they are!), we'll henceforth use the prime-system [N, N', N''] in our tree diagrams, though (somewhat schizophrenically!) we'll refer to the relevant constituents as N, N-bar, and N-double-bar. Believe it or not, this is standard practice! Given these conventions, the constituent structure of our (in)famous phrase [*the king of England*] will now be represented in the manner outlined in (24) below:

(24)

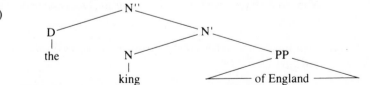

And we'll say that *king* is an N, [*king of England*] is an N-bar, and [*the king of England*] is an N-double-bar (hence also an NP, since we earlier said that N'' corresponds to the traditional category of NP).

4.3 Evidence for N-bar

Having managed to disentangle ourselves from the notational knots we were tied up in, we can now go on to ask ourselves what evidence there is that Wells was right to assume that an NP such as [*the king of England*] contains the 'small' nominal phrase (i.e. what we are calling an N-bar) [*king of England*] as one of its immediate constituents. In this connection, it is interesting to consider the arguments which Wells himself put forward in support of his own analysis (though it should be borne in mind that Wells was writing in a different era, and within a different theoretical framework). One such argument which he adduces (1957, p. 192) is a *distributional* one to the effect that [*king of England*] must be a constituent because it can occur as an independent unit in other types of sentence-structure, as in Wells' example:

(25)   He became [*king of England*]

A second argument which he puts forward (ibid., p. 191) is that such an analysis will enable us to capture the structural parallelism between the two phrases in (26) below:

(26) (a)   the [*English king*]
     (b)   the [*king of England*]

Wells assumes (though does not argue) that the bracketed sequence [*English king*] is a constituent in (26) (a), and argues that a parallel analysis of (26) (b) along the lines of (24) above would be 'the best analysis of that phrase' because 'it harmonizes with other analyses' (i.e. with his analysis of phrases like [*the English king*]). He is implicitly invoking a principle of maximising *structural symmetry* between related constructions.

While there are potential pitfalls in Wells' argumentation, other independent evidence can be adduced in support of his analysis. For example, a further argument in support of the key claim that the sequence [*king of England*] is a constituent concerns the fact that it can undergo *Ordinary Coordination* with another similar sequence, as in:

(27)   Who would have dared defy the [*king of England*] and [*ruler of the Empire*]?

Moreover, it can function as the 'shared constituent' in cases of *Shared Constituent Coordination*: cf.

(28)   He was the last (and some people say the best) [*king of England*]

Given our assumption that only a unitary constituent can undergo *Simple Coordination*, or can function as the 'shared constituent' in cases of *Shared Con-*

stituent Coordination, the obvious conclusion to draw is that the sequence [*king of England*] must indeed be a constituent. And this provides empirical support for the analysis in (24) above.

An additional type of argument in support of the N-bar analysis can be formulated in relation to *Pronominalisation* facts. Recall from our discussion in Chapter 2 that only a unitary constituent can be replaced by a proform – and indeed only a *phrasal* constituent of some sort. In the light of this observation, consider the use of the proform *one* in the following examples:

(29) (a)   The present [king of England] is more popular than the last *one*

   (b)   *The [king] of England defeated the *one* of Spain

How can we account for the contrast here? Well, if we posit that [*king of England*] is a 'small' nominal phrase of some sort (an N-bar, to be precise), then we could say that *one* in English is the kind of proform which can replace a 'small nominal phrase': in other words, we can say that *one* is a pro-N-bar. Thus, we could argue that [*king of England*] in (29) (a) can be replaced by *one* because it is an N-bar; whereas *king* in (29) (b) cannot be replaced by *one* because it is only an N and not an N-bar (and we already know that proforms replace phrasal constituents, not individual words). But any such analysis naturally presupposes that [*king of England*] is indeed a phrasal constituent of some sort, as in Wells' analysis (24).

So, both *Coordination* and *Pronominalisation* facts provide strong empirical support for the N-bar analysis. Accordingly, we shall henceforth assume that this analysis is correct, and that there is indeed an intermediate type of nominal constituent (namely N-bar) which is larger than N but smaller than NP. We thus posit that there are three types of nominal constituent in English, namely N, N' (= N-bar), and N'' (= N-double-bar = NP). This means that we no longer recognise only two categorial *levels* of nominal constituent (N and NP): on the contrary, we are now assuming that there are three categorial levels of nominal constituent, namely N, N-bar, and N-double-bar.

4.4   Complements and Adjuncts

What we have argued so far is that in an NP such as [*the king of England*], the postnominal PP [*of England*] expands the head Noun *king* into the N-bar [*king of England*], while the Determiner *the* expands the N-bar [*king of England*] into the N-double-bar [*the king of England*]. Now, we might seek to generalise our conclusions about the function of the PP [*of England*] in this phrase by suggesting that all postnominal PPs (and indeed perhaps all postnominal phrases of any kind) have essentially the same constituent structure status, and thus serve to expand N into N-bar.

Noun Phrases

However, any such hasty conclusion would ignore the traditional distinction between two different types of postnominal phrase – namely (i) those which function as *Complements*, and (ii) those which function as *Adjuncts*. We can illustrate the difference between these two types of postmodifier in terms of the contrast in (30) below:

(30) (a)   a student [*of Physics*] (= Complement)
    (b)   a student [*with long hair*] (= Adjunct)

In the case of (30) (a) [*a student of Physics*], the bracketed PP [*of Physics*] is (in an intuitively fairly obvious sense) the 'Complement' of *student*: the PP tells us what it is that the individual concerned studies. Hence the NP [*a student of Physics*] can be paraphrased by a clausal construction in which *Physics* functions as the Complement of the Verb *study*: cf.

(31) (a)   He is [*a student of Physics*]
    (b)   He is [*studying Physics*]

But this is not at all the case in (30) (b), [*a student with long hair*]. In this case, the bracketed PP [*with long hair*] doesn't in any sense function as the Complement of *student*, so that we don't have any corresponding paraphrase in which [*long hair*] is used as the Complement of the Verb *study*: cf.

(32) (a)   He is [*a student with long hair*]
    (b)   ≠ He is [*studying long hair*]

Thus, in (31) (a) [*a student of Physics*], the bracketed PP [*of Physics*] specifies what the student is studying: but in (32) (a) [*a student with long hair*] the bracketed PP doesn't tell us anything about what the student is studying; it merely serves to give us additional information about the student (i.e. that he happens to have long hair). In traditional terms, the kind of PP found in [*student of Physics*] (or indeed [*king of England*]) is said to be a *Complement*, whereas that found in [*student with long hair*] is said to be an *Adjunct*.

Of course, terms like *Complement* and *Adjunct* denote grammatical functions or relations, and thus have the same status as terms like 'Subject' and 'Object'. The obvious question to ask therefore is what is the *structural* correlate of the Complement–Adjunct distinction, and how do Complements and Adjuncts differ from the other class of nominal modifiers which we are already familiar with – namely Determiners. What we shall claim here is that the difference is essentially the following:

(33) (a)   Determiners expand N-bar into N-double-bar
    (b)   Adjuncts expand N-bar into N-bar
    (c)   Complements expand N into N-bar

Given the assumptions in (33), a Noun Phrase containing a Determiner, an Adjunct, and a Complement would have the schematic structure (34) below:

(34)

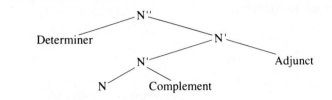

We can see from (34) that Determiners are sisters of N-bar and daughters of N-double-bar; Adjuncts are both sisters and daughters of N-bar; and Complements are sisters of N and daughters of N-bar. This means that Adjuncts resemble Complements in that both are daughters of N-bar; but they differ from Complements in that Adjuncts are sisters of N-bar, whereas Complements are sisters of N. Likewise, it means that Adjuncts resemble Determiners in that both are sisters of N-bar, but they differ from Determiners in that Adjuncts are daughters of N-bar, whereas Determiners are daughters of N-double-bar.

Perhaps we can bring out the relevant distinctions rather more clearly in terms of the respective Phrase Structure Rules needed to generate Determiners, Adjuncts, and Complements. Given the claims made in (33) above, Determiners will be introduced by the rule (35)(i) below, Adjuncts by rule (35)(ii), and Complements by rule (35)(iii):

(35) (i)   N'' → D N' [Determiner Rule]
   (ii)   N' → N' PP [Adjunct Rule]
   (iii)   N' → N PP [Complement Rule]

For ease of reference, we have called (35)(i) the Determiner Rule (since it introduces Determiners), (36)(ii) the Adjunct Rule, and (35)(iii) the Complement Rule.

Now, if you think about it, you'll realise that the rules in (35) make rather interesting predictions about the relative *ordering* of Adjuncts and Complements. More specifically, they predict that Complements will always be 'closer' to their head Noun than Adjuncts. In other words, our rules in (35) predict that if we modify *student* by an Adjunct PP such as [*with long hair*], and a Complement PP such as [*of Physics*], then the Complement phrase must precede the Adjunct phrase. And, (as Hornstein and Lightfoot 1981a, p. 22) note, this prediction is entirely correct – cf. their examples:

(36) (a)   the student [*of Physics*] [*with long hair*]
   (b)   *the student [*with long hair*] [*of Physics*]

Given the 'no crossing of branches' restriction, it follows that the rules in (35) will generate Adjunct PPs to the right of Complement PPs as in (37) (a) below, not to the left as in (37) (b):

(37) (a)

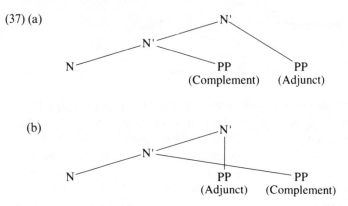

(b)

(38)

(37) (b) (which is the structure associated with the ungrammatical (36) (b)) is ruled out because it violates the 'no crossing of branches' restriction. But (37 (a) (which is the structure of the grammatical (36) (a)) contains no crossing branches, and thus is well-formed. So, it follows from (37) that Complements must occur closer to their head Nouns than Adjuncts. And this is precisely why the Complement phrase has to precede the Adjunct phrase in (36) – and why (more generally) postnominal Complements precede postnominal Adjuncts (as noted by Jackendoff 1977a, p. 58).

But I bet you're wondering whether the rules proposed in (35) above really work! So let's see whether they do. If we apply the Determiner Rule (35) (i) [N'' → D N'], we generate the substructure (38) below:

(38)

If we then apply the Adjunct Rule (35) (ii) [N' → N' PP] to expand the N-bar in (38), we derive:

(39)

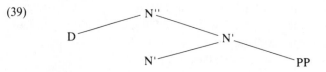

If we subsequently apply the Complement Rule (35) (iii) [N' → N PP] to the N' at the bottom of the tree in (39), we derive the structure (40) below (we have attached the relevant lexical items, to make the discussion less abstract):

(40)
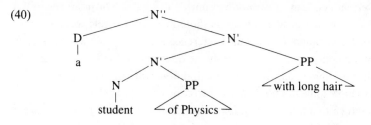

And this is precisely the constituent structure associated with a Noun Phrase such as [*a student of Physics with long hair*]. So, you see, the rules do actually work, after all!

4.5   Optional constituents of the Noun Phrase

Thus far, we have been looking at the internal structure of Noun Phrases of the schematic form (41) below:

(41)   Determiner + Noun + Complement PP + Adjunct PP

and we have argued that such NPs can be generated by a set of Phrase Structure Rules such as (35) above, repeated here for convenience as (42) below:

(42) (i)   N'' → D N' [Determiner Rule]
    (ii)   N' → N' PP [Adjunct Rule]
    (iii)   N' → N PP [Complement Rule]

However, one fairly obvious point which we have overlooked in our rules in (42) is that Determiners, Adjuncts, and Complements are all *optional* constituents of Noun Phrases. Let's consider first the optional use of Determiners.

One thing which it is important to get clear at the very outset of our discussion is exactly what we do and do not mean by claiming that 'Determiners are optional constituents of the Noun Phrase'. All we mean is that 'Some Noun Phrases are used without Determiners': what we emphatically do not mean is that 'Any Noun Phrase of any kind can optionally be used with or without a Determiner'. Of course, there are complex conditions which determine when Determiners can or cannot be omitted from a Noun Phrase: for example, in general, Noncount Nouns and Plural Count Nouns can be used without an overt Determiner, but Singular Count Nouns cannot: cf.

(43) (a)   *Childhood* can be traumatic (= Noncount Noun)
    (b)   *Children* can be traumatic (= Plural Count Noun)
    (c)   **Child* can be traumatic (= Singular Count Noun)

However, it is not our purpose here to deal with the complex conditions under which Determiners can or cannot be omitted in English (or more generally): the reader interested in such questions should consult the relevant section on the use of Determiners in a detailed reference grammar such as Quirk *et al.* (1985). What concerns us here is simply the question: 'What is the structure of Noun Phrases which lack Determiners, and how will our existing set of rules (42) above have to be modified in order to cope with such NPs?'

So, to return to a familiar example, what concerns us here is how we are to generate a simple Determiner-less nominal expression such as:

(44)   Students of Physics with long hair

The first question we should ask about (44) is: 'What is the constituent status of the overall phrase?' In other words, is (44) an N-bar, or an N-double-bar (i.e. full Noun Phrase)? The answer is that (44) is indeed a full Noun Phrase, as can be shown by a variety of familiar constituent structure tests. For example, it can occur in isolation as a 'sentence-fragment', as in (45) below:

(45)   SPEAKER A: What kind of students do you hate teaching?
            SPEAKER B: [*Students of Physics with long hair*]

Given our assumption that only full Phrases can occur as sentence fragments, it follows that the bracketed Phrase [*students of Physics with long hair*] uttered by Speaker B in (45) must be a full Noun Phrase.

And indeed this analysis is independently confirmed by other sets of facts. For example, such expressions can be coordinated with a full NP, and can also be pronominalised by a pro-NP such as *them*:

(46) (a)   [$_{NP}$ Students of Physics with long hair] and [$_{NP}$ *their professors*] often don't see eye to eye
     (b)   [$_{NP}$ Students of Physics with long hair] sometimes think the world owes *them* a living

But given that expressions such as [*students of Physics with long hair*] can function as NPs, how can we account for the fact that they lack Determiners?

Sadly, the answer is disappointingly unspectacular! We say the obvious, and specify that Determiners are *optional* constituents of NP. Or, more precisely, we replace our earlier Determiner Rule (42)(i) [N'' → D N'] by the revised rule (47) below:

(47)   N'' → (D) N' [new Determiner Rule]

The parentheses around D in (47) indicate that the Determiner is an optional constituent of N'' (recall that N'' = NP). If we replace our earlier Determiner

Rule (42) (i) by our new rule (47), our revised system of Phrase Structure Rules is now (48) below:

(48) (i)   N'' → (D) N' [Determiner Rule]

(ii)   N' → N' PP [Adjunct Rule]

(iii)   N' → N PP [Complement Rule]

Let's consider how our revised rule system works.

We start by applying the Determiner Rule (48) (i), which tells us that we can expand an N'' into an optional Determiner plus an N-bar: if we reject the option of having a Determiner, then our rule will generate the structure (49) below:

(49)

$$N''$$
$$|$$
$$N'$$

We now apply the Adjunct Rule (48) (ii): this tells us that we can expand N-bar into another N-bar plus a PP Adjunct; thus, if we apply the rule to (49) above, we derive the structure (50) below:

(50)

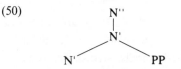

Now let's move on to the Complement Rule (48) (iii), which tells us that we can expand N-bar into a head Noun followed by a PP Complement; applying this rule to (50) above will yield the structure (51) below (we have inserted appropriate lexical items for concreteness):

(51)

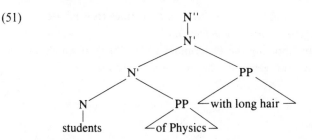

Thus, our revised rules in (48) above can indeed generate NPs which contain no Determiner.

But hold on a minute! It isn't just *Determiners* which are optional constituents of Noun Phrases: for, as we noted above, *Complements* and *Adjuncts* are also optional constituents of NP. For example, in the case we are discussing, both the Complement PP [*of Physics*] and the Adjunct PP [*with long hair*] are optional, as we see from the paradigm in (52) below:

(52) (a)　　a student [*of Physics*] [*with long hair*] (Complement and Adjunct)

　　(b)　　a student [*with long hair*] (Adjunct, no Complement)

　　(c)　　a student [*of Physics*] (Complement, no Adjunct)

　　(d)　　a student (no Adjunct, no Complement)

The obvious question to ask, therefore, is how we are to modify our existing Phrase Structure Rules (48) above so as to take into account the optionality of Complements and Adjuncts.

Let's consider first the question of how we generate NPs which contain an Adjunct but no Complement – i.e. NPs such as (52) (b) [*a student with long hair*]. The obvious suggestion is to deal with optional Complements in the same way that we dealt with optional Determiners – namely by specifying that a Complement PP is an optional constituent of N-bar. Thus, we might propose to replace our existing Complement Rule (48) (iii) [N' → N PP] by the revised rule (53) below:

(53)　　　N' → N (PP) [new Complement Rule]

where the parentheses round PP in (53) indicate that a Prepositional Phrase Complement is an optional constituent of N-bar. If we now replace our earlier Complement Rule by our new one, our revised overall system of Phrase Structure Rules becomes (54) below:

(54) (i)　　N'' → (D) N' [Determiner Rule]

　　(ii)　　N' → N' PP [Adjunct Rule]

　　(iii)　　N' → N (PP) [Complement Rule]

Let's see how we can apply our revised system of rules to generate a Noun Phrase such as (52) (b) [*a student with long hair*].

First, we start by applying the Determiner Rule (54) (i): if we choose the optional Determiner, this generates the structure (55) below:

(55)

We now go on to apply the Adjunct rule (54) (ii) to expand N-bar in (55) into the sequence [N' PP], as in (56) below:

(56)

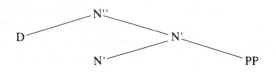

We now apply our new Complement Rule (54) (iii): this tells us that we can expand an N-bar into an N with or without an optional PP complement. Well, let's suppose that we decide not to choose the PP complement. In this case, N-bar will be expanded into N alone, as in (57) below (we have inserted relevant lexical items for the sake of making our discussion more concrete, and thus more intelligible):

(57)

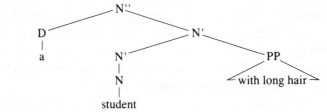

Hence, we see that a very simple modification of our earlier Complement Rule will suffice to enable us to generate NPs in which the head N has no Complement.

So, now we've seen how to deal with optional Determiners on the one hand, and optional Complements on the other. But what about optional *Adjuncts*? In other words, how are we going to generate a structure such as (52) (c) [*a student of Physics*], which contains a Complement PP [*of Physics*], but no Adjunct PP? Well, the obvious suggestion is to deal with optional Adjuncts in exactly the same way that we dealt with optional Determiners and Complements. That is to say, we might simply stipulate that Adjuncts are an optional constituent of N-bar. The natural way of doing this might seem to be simply to put parentheses round the Adjunct PP introduced by our existing Adjunct Rule (54) (ii) above, so that our earlier rules (54) would be revised along the lines of (58) below (where (58) (ii) is the new Adjunct Rule):

(58) (i)   N'' → (D) N' [Determiner Rule]
     (ii)   N' → N' (PP) [new Adjunct Rule]
     (iii)   N' → N (PP) [Complement Rule]

But if you think about it, you'll realise that (58) (ii) can't be right at all. After all, one of the possibilities allowed for in our new Adjunct Rule (58) (ii) is that of omitting the PP Adjunct, in which case the Adjunct Rule would amount to:

(59)   N' → N'

But rule (59) is *vacuous*, in a number of ways. For one thing, it's self-defining, and hence doesn't actually tell us anything about how to form an N-bar (it's a bit like a person who, when asked to define a *troglodyte* says 'Well, a troglodyte's a troglodyte, and that's all there is to say about it!'). More seriously, rule (59) does no more than chase its own tail (well, if you want the relevant technical jargon, the rule is *vacuously recursive!*). Why? Because its output (= N') is the same as its input (= N'), so that the rule allows you to stack a potentially infinite number of non-branching N-bar constituents on top of each other. This means that we (quite wrongly) predict that any Noun Phrase should be potentially infinitely structurally ambiguous, according to how many non-branching N-bars it has stacked on top of other N-bars. For, we assume that differences in structure will generally correlate with perceived differences of meaning: so, rule (59) implies that a simple NP like [*a boy*] should be infinitely ambiguous according to whether it contains one, two, three, four, five, ... etc. non-branching N-bar constituents. But this is an absurd claim, and one which we shall treat with the contempt it deserves!

The bottom line of our argumentation here is that we cannot deal with the optionality of Adjuncts in terms of a rule such as (58) (ii) saying that an N-bar can be expanded into another N-bar plus an optional Adjunct PP. So, assuming that we don't opt for the 'tail-chasing' (sorry, I mean *vacuous recursion!*) solution (59), how are we going to deal with the optionality of Adjuncts? Well, there's an even simpler solution than you might have expected: and that is to simply stipulate that our earlier Adjunct Rule (54) (ii) is *an optional rule*. That is to say, we can either choose to apply the rule, or not apply it, as we wish. In other words, we might revise our earlier rules (54) in the manner indicated in (60) below:

(60) (i)   N'' → (D) N' [Determiner Rule]
    (ii)   N' → N' PP [Adjunct Rule: *optional*]
    (iii)   N' → N (PP) [Complement Rule]

In the light of our claim that the Adjunct Rule (60) (ii) is *optional* (and hence can be 'skipped' if we wish to do so), let's go back to the question of how we generate a structure like (52) (c) [*a student of Physics*]. As before, we start by applying the Determiner Rule (60) (i) [N'' → (D) N']: this tells us that we can form an NP (= N-double-bar) out of an optional Determiner and an N-bar. If we take the Determiner option, then we generate the structure (61) below:

(61)

Now we come to the Adjunct Rule, (60) (ii). Since this rule is *optional*, we can choose to either apply it, or not apply it. We'll take the latter course, and choose to 'skip' the rule altogether. This means that we go on to apply the Complement Rule (60) (iii), which expands N-bar into a head N plus an optional PP Complement. Well let's suppose we take up the option of having a PP Complement: in this case, the result of applying the Complement Rule (60) (iii) to (61) will be the structure (62) below (as before, we have inserted appropriate lexical items, for the sake of clarity):

(62)

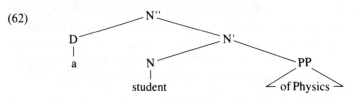

Since the PP [*of Physics*] in (62) is a Complement of the head of Noun *student*, we have now managed to achieve our goal of generating a Noun Phrase without an Adjunct.

So, we have managed to adapt our original rule system so as to cope with NPs which contain Adjuncts but not Complements, and conversely NPs which contain Complements but not Adjuncts. But what about NPs which contain neither Complements, nor Adjuncts – e.g. NPs such as (52) (d) [*a student*]. Can our revised system of Phrase Structure Rules (60) handle these? Well, let's see.

We'll begin by applying the Determiner Rule (60) (i) to generate the structure (61) above. We then 'skip' the optional Adjunct Rule (60) (ii): we go directly on to the Complement Rule (60) (iii), which tells us that we can expand an N-bar into a head N, plus an optional PP complement. But this time, let's take the option of not choosing to have a PP complement, so that we expand N-bar simply into an unmodified N: the result will be that by applying the Complement Rule (60) (iii) to (61) above we generate (63) below (as before, the relevant lexical items have been inserted):

(63)

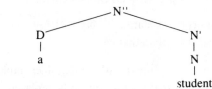

Since the NP in (63) above contains neither a Complement PP nor an Adjunct PP, it seems clear that our existing system of rules in (60) is perfectly adequate to deal with NPs which lack both Complements and Adjuncts.

We have now seen that the very simple set of rules we devised in (60) will generate a full range of NP structures, with or without Determiners, with or without Adjuncts, and with or without Complements, and will assign appropriate structures to the NPs concerned: for example, (52) (a) [*a student of*

Physics with long hair] will be assigned the structure (40) above; (52) (b) [*a student with long hair*] will be assigned the structure (57); (52) (c) [*a student of Physics*] will be assigned the structure (62); and (52) (d) [*a student*] will be assigned the structure (63). Now, if you look closely at these four structures (40), (57), (62) and (63), you'll see that the categorial status of the expression *student* changes from one example to another. More precisely, *student* has the status of a simple N in (40) and (62); whereas it has the status of an N-bar immediately dominating an N in (57) and (63). To underline this fact, we give the structure of the relevant examples in skeletal form in (64) and (65) below:

(64) (a)   [$_N$'' a [$_N$' [$_N$' [$_N$ *student*] of Physics] with long hair]]

    (b)   [$_N$'' a [$_N$' [$_N$ *student*] of Physics]]

(65) (a)   [$_N$'' a [$_N$' [$_N$' [$_N$ *student*]] with long hair]]

    (b)   [$_N$'' a [$_N$' [$_N$ *student*]]]

The difference is that when the Noun *student* has an overt Complement like [*of Physics*] (as in (64) above), then it functions only as an N (because the corresponding N-bar is the whole Noun + Complement structure [*student of Physics*]). But when the Noun *student* has no overt Complement (as in (65) above), then it is not only an N, but also an N-bar.

Now, the assumption that *student* is an N in (64) but an N-bar in (65) has far-reaching consequences. We can see this if we look at the predictions the two structures make about the use of the proform *one*. Recall that we argued earlier that *one* in English can function as a pro-N-bar, but not as a pro-N (because proforms do not replace word-level categories). Now, if it is true (as our analysis claims) that *student* is an N-bar in (65), then since *one* is a pro-N-bar, we should expect that *student* can be replaced by *one* in structures like (65): and as (66) below illustrates, this prediction is entirely correct:

(66) (a)   The [student] with short hair is dating the *one* with long hair

    (b)   This [student] works harder than that *one*

It therefore follows that *student* must have the status of N-bar in examples like (65) and (66). But by contrast, we find that *student* cannot be replaced by the proform *one* in examples such as (64) above, as (67) below illustrates:

(67) (a)   Which [student] were you referring to? *The *one* of Physics with long hair?

    (b)   *The [student] of chemistry was older than the *one* of Physics (Lightfoot (1982), p. 54)

Since *student* cannot be replaced by the pro-N-bar *one* here, it therefore follows that *student* cannot have the status of N-bar in phrases such as (64), but rather must have the simple status of N.

We can use our *one*-pronominalisation test to provide further confirmation of the constituent structure analyses we have posited in (64) and (65) above. For, our proposed analysis also specifies that the sequences [*student of Physics*] in (64) (a), [*student of Physics with long hair*] in (64) (a), [*student of Physics*] in (64) (b), and [*student with long hair*] in (65) (a) are all N-bar constituents; hence we should expect that all four phrases can be proformed by the pro-N-bar *one*. And as (68) below indicates, this prediction is entirely correct:

(68) (a)   Which [student of Physics]? The *one* with long hair?
     (b)   Which [student of Physics with long hair]? This *one*?
     (c)   Which [student of Physics]? That *one*?
     (d)   Which [student with long hair]? This *one*?

Thus, *one*-pronominalisation facts provide quite remarkable independent corroboration of our analysis. In particular, they lend strong support to our claim that *a Noun which has an overt Complement is simply an N, whereas a Noun which lacks a Complement has the status of N-bar* (*as well as N*).

4.6   More differences between Complements and Adjuncts

Hitherto, we have argued that Determiners, Adjunct PPs and Complement PPs should be generated by the following set of Phrase Structure Rules (cf. (60) above):

(69) (i)   N'' → (D) N' [Determiner Rule]
     (ii)   N' → N' PP [Adjunct Rule: *optional*]
     (iii)   N' → N (PP) [Complement Rule]

As we have already seen, these rules specify (amongst other things) that Determiners, Adjuncts, and Complements differ from each other in the following ways:

(70) (a)   Determiners are sisters of N' and daughters of N''
     (b)   Adjuncts are sisters and daughters of N'
     (d)   Complements are sisters of N and daughters of N'

In this section, we are going to look (rather more briefly) at a number of further arguments in support of the structural distinction between Complement PPs and Adjunct PPs drawn in (70) above.

One such argument is of a semantic nature. Hornstein and Lightfoot (1981a, p. 21) note that the structural differences between Complements and

Adjuncts in (70) correlate in an obvious way with an associated difference in semantic structure. In relation to the pair of sentences in (71) below:

(71) (a)   John is a [N' [N *student*] *of Physics*]
     (b)   John is a [N' [N' [N *student*]] *with long hair*]

they comment:

> We also assume that syntactic constituent structure will play a role in determining the semantics of Noun Phrases, and specifically that each N-bar specifies a 'semantic property'. Therefore, to attribute (71) (a) to John is to attribute one property to him, that he studies Physics; to attribute (71) (b) to John is to attribute two properties, that he studies, and that he has long hair. Hence it follows that *John is a student of Physics*, meaning what it does (i.e. denoting only one property), cannot be assigned a structure like (71) (b); conversely, *John is a student with long hair*, meaning what it does (i.e. denoting two properties) cannot have a structure like (71) (a).
>
> (Hornstein and Lightfoot, *Introduction to Explanation in Linguistics* (1981a), p. 21)

A related semantic argument can be formulated with regard to *disambiguation*. It should be obvious that the structural distinction we have drawn between Complement PPs (which modify N) and Adjunct PPs (which modify N-bar) will enable us to provide a principled account of the structural ambiguity of phrases such as:

(72)   a student [*of high moral principles*]

The NP in (72) is ambiguous as between the two interpretations:

(73) (i)   a person who studies high moral principles
     (ii)   a student who has high moral principles

And we might characterise this ambiguity in structural terms by saying that on interpretation (73) (i) the bracketed PP (72) is a Complement (hence a sister) of the head Noun *student*; whereas on interpretation (73) (ii), the bracketed PP in (72) is an Adjunct, hence a sister of the N-bar headed by the Noun *student*. This would mean that on the first interpretation, (72) would have the skeletal structure (74) (a) below, whereas on the second interpretation it would have the structure (74) (b):

(74) (a)   a [N' [N student] of high moral principles] (= 73(i))
     (b)   a [N' [N' [N student]] of high moral principles] (= 73(ii))

Thus, our structural distinction between Complements and Adjuncts enables us to characterise some fairly interesting cases of structural ambiguity.

But let's return to syntactic arguments in favour of our claim that Complement PPs expand N into N-bar, whereas Adjunct PPs expand N-bar into N-bar. An important difference between the Adjunct Rule (69) (ii) above (which introduces Adjunct PPs), and the Complement Rule (69) (iii) (which introduces Complement PPs) is that the Adjunct Rule is *recursive*, whereas the Complement Rule is not: for convenience, we have repeated our earlier rules (69) above as (75) below:

(75) (i)   N'' → (D) N' [Determiner Rule]

   (ii)   N' → N' PP [Adjunct Rule: *optional*]

  (iii)   N' → N (PP) [Complement Rule]

The Adjunct Rule (75) (ii) is recursive by virtue of the fact that the same symbol N' appears both on the left and on the right of the arrow, whereas the Complement Rule (75) (iii) is non-recursive. Since the rule generating Adjuncts is recursive, it predicts that indefinitely many Adjunct PPs can be 'stacked' on top of each other. But because the rule introducing Complements is not recursive, it does not allow PP Complements to be *stacked* in this way. And in fact, the prediction that PP Adjuncts can be 'stacked' but PP Complements cannot seems to be correct, as we see from the contrast in (76) below:

(76) (a)   the student [*with long hair*] [*with short arms*]

   (b)   *the student [*of Physics*] [*of Chemistry*]

Moreover, our analysis predicts that PP Adjuncts can be stacked on top of each other in any order: and this again seems to be true, as examples such as (77) below (where both italicised phrases are Adjunct PPs) illustrate:

(77) (a)   the [N' [N' [N' student] *with long hair*] *in the corner*]

   (b)   the [N' [N' [N' student] *in the corner*] *with long hair*]

Furthermore, under our proposed analysis of (77) (a) the sequences [*student*], [*student with long hair*], and [*student with long hair in the corner*] would all be N-bar constituents, so that we correctly predict that all three bracketed strings can be replaced by the pro-N-bar *one* in an appropriate context. And as we see from (78) below, the bracketed sequences can indeed be proformed by *one* in each case:

(78) (a)   Which [student]? The *one* with long hair in the corner?

   (b)   Which [student with long hair]? The *one* in the corner?

   (c)   Which [student with long hair in the corner]? That *one*?

Once again, our analysis turns out to make just the right predictions.

A further syntactic argument in favour of the structural distinction between Complements and Adjuncts which we are assuming here can be formulated in relation to facts about *Ordinary Coordination*. Note that we can coordinate two PPs which are both Complements: cf.

(79)   a student [*of Physics*] and [*of Chemistry*]

And likewise we can coordinate two PPs which are both Adjuncts: cf.

(80)   a student [*with long hair*] and [*with short arms*]

But we cannot coordinate a Complement PP with an Adjunct PP: cf.

(81) (a)   *a student [*of Physics*] and [*with long hair*]
    (b)   *a student [*with long hair*] and [*of Physics*]

Under the analysis proposed here, we can account for this in structural terms by assuming that Adjuncts and Complements are attached at different levels (Complements are sisters of N, and hence are attached at the N level; whereas Adjuncts are sisters of N-bar, and hence are attached at the N-bar level), and by positing that only constituents attached at the same level can be coordinated. It would then follow that the two Complement PPs in (79) can be coordinated (since both are attached at the N level), as can the two Adjunct PPs in (80) (since both are attached at the N-bar level): but it would also follow that an Adjunct cannot be coordinated with a Complement (as in (81)), since Complements are attached at the N level, whereas Adjuncts are attached at the N-bar level.

Incidentally, we might note in passing that our proposed analysis makes a number of further correct predictions about coordination. For example, since both Complements and Adjuncts are daughters of N-bar (i.e. both Noun + Complement and Noun + Adjunct sequences have the status of N-bar), our analysis correctly predicts that the Noun + Complement sequence [*student of Physics*] and the Noun + Adjunct sequence [*student with long hair*] have the same constituent status of N-bar, and so can be coordinated with themselves and each other in such a way that the whole conjoined sequence forms an N-bar, and thus can be modified by a Determiner such as *the*: and the fact that examples such as (82) below are grammatical shows that this prediction is correct:

(82) (a)   the [*students of Chemistry* and *professors of Physics*]
    (b)   the [*students with long hair* and *professors with short hair*]
    (c)   the [*students of Chemistry* and *professors with short hair*]

Each of the italicised conjuncts in (82) is thus an N-bar, as indeed is each of the bracketed coordinate structures.

An additional syntactic argument in favour of drawing a structural distinction between Complements and Adjuncts derives from *Extraposition* facts (we shall discuss this phenomenon more fully in Chapter 8). It appears that PP Adjuncts can be *extraposed* from their Heads (i.e. separated from their Heads and moved to the end of their Clause) more freely than PP Complements: cf.

(83) (a)   a student came to see me yesterday [*with long hair*]
   (b)   *a student came to see me yesterday [*of Physics*]

It would seem that in some sense PP Complements are more 'inseparable' from their Heads than PP Adjuncts. Once again, our analysis provides us with a principled way of accounting for these differences in purely *structural* terms. Thus, we might posit that the more closely related a PP is to its Head, the less freely it can be extraposed. And (to extend the genealogical terminology introduced in Chapter 3), we might say that Complements are *sisters* to their Heads, whereas Adjuncts are *aunts* (an *aunt* being a sister of the mother of a given node). To clarify the term *aunt*, consider a structure such as (84) below:

(84)

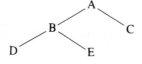

We might say that in an abstract tree structure such as (84), E is the sister of D, whereas C is the *aunt* of D. In these terms, a Complement would be a sister of its Head Noun, and hence more closely related to the Head than an Adjunct (which would be an *aunt* of the Head Noun): and we might suppose that it is because there is a greater structural affinity between Heads and Complements than between Heads and Adjuncts, that Complements are more resistant to being extraposed.

Given that Extraposition involves *Postposing*, the obvious question to ask is whether Complements and Adjuncts behave any differently with respect to *Preposing*. There is some evidence that this is indeed the case. It would seem that an NP which is the Object of a Preposition heading a *Complement* PP can be preposed more freely than an NP which is the Object of a Preposition heading an *Adjunct* PP: cf. the contrast below:

(85) (a)   [*What branch of Physics*] are you a student of?
   (b)   *[*What kind of hair*] are you a student with?

Thus, in (85) (a), the preposed bracketed NP is the Object of the Preposition *of*, and *of* introduces a Complement phrase, so that (85) (a) involves preposing an NP which is part of a Complement PP. But by contrast, the bracketed preposed NP in (85) (b) is the Object of the Preposition *with*, and *with* introduces an Adjunct, so that the ungrammaticality of (85) (b) suggests that an NP which is part of an Adjunct PP cannot be preposed. Thus, there is an obvious contrast insofar as the Object of a Complement Preposition can be preposed, but not the Object of an Adjunct Preposition.

Yet another syntactic argument in support of positing a structural distinction between Complement and Adjunct Phrases relates to *Co-occurrence Restrictions*. In the case of a PP Complement, there are severe restrictions on the choice of P heading the PP; particular Nouns require (or, in the terminology we shall introduce in Chapter 7, *subcategorise*) a PP introduced by a particular Preposition: for example, only some Nouns, not others permit an *of*-phrase Complement: cf.

(86) (a)   a *student* of Physics
   (b)   *a *boy* of Physics
   (c)   *a *girl* of Physics
   (d)   *a *teenager* of Physics
   (e)   *a *punk* of Physics

By contrast the type of PP which functions as an Adjunct can be used to modify *any* type of head Noun (subject to semantic and pragmatic restrictions), as we see from:

(87) (a)   a *student* with long hair
   (b)   a *boy* with long hair
   (c)   a *girl* with long hair
   (d)   a *teenager* with long hair
   (e)   a *punk* with long hair

Once again, it seems as if, in some informal sense, Complements are more closely linked to their head Nouns than Adjuncts. And we might argue that the N-bar analysis enables us to define 'closeness' in purely structural terms, in the manner outlined earlier: e.g. we might say that *sisters* are more closely linked to their Heads than *aunts*, and we could posit that subcategorisation restrictions hold only between a Head and its sisters, not between a Head and its more distant relatives (e.g. aunts). Thus, in the case of a structure such as (40) above, repeated as (88) below:

(88)

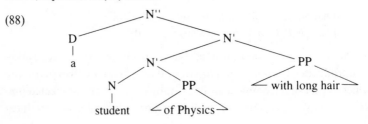

we find subcategorisation restrictions holding between the head Noun *student* and its sister Complement PP [*of Physics*], but not between *student* and its aunt Adjunct PP [*with long hair*]. But, naturally, any such account of *subcategorisation* restrictions presupposes a structural distinction such as that in (70) between *Complements* and *Adjuncts*.

At this point, it might be useful to summarise our discussion in this section. We have argued that there are a vast array of facts (some semantic, and some syntactic) which lend strong empirical support to the claim that Complements are attached at the N-level, and Adjuncts at the N-bar level. More precisely, the key claim we have made is that:

(89) (i)　　Complements expand N into N-bar

    (ii)　　Adjuncts recursively expand N-bar into N-bar

Thus, Complements and Adjuncts are similar in that they are both daughters of N-bar; but they differ in that Complements are sisters of (i.e. modify) N, whereas Adjuncts are sisters of (i.e. modify) N-bar.

Given the arguments we have presented here, PPs such as those italicised in (90) below would be *Complements*:

(90) (a)　　your reply [*to my letter*]

    (b)　　the attack [*on the Prime Minister*]

    (c)　　the loss [*of the ship*]

    (d)　　her disgust [*at his behaviour*]

    (e)　　his disillusionment [*with Linguistics*]

whereas PPs such as those italicised in (91) below would be *Adjuncts*:

(91) (a)　　the book [*on the table*]

    (b)　　the advertisement [*on the television*]

    (c)　　the fight [*after the match*]

    (d)　　his resignation [*because of the scandal*]

    (e)　　a cup [*with a broken handle*]

I leave you to verify this for yourself, applying the various 'tests' we have devised in this section, and previous sections (I bet you won't bother!)

Of course, our discussion here has been limited to postnominal Prepositional Phrases. But the Complement–Adjunct distinction can be shown to be valid for other types of postnominal phrase as well (though we lack the space to do this here). Generally speaking, only Prepositional Phrases and Clauses can function as the Complements of Nouns. For example, the italicised constituents in (90) above are Complement PPs; and the italicised in (92) below are *Complement Clauses* – i.e. the italicised Clause in each case functions as the Complement of the capitalised Noun:

(92) (a)   the SUGGESTION [*that we should abandon cruise missiles*]

(b)   the DEMAND [*for him to resign*]

(c)   the QUESTION [*whether euthanasia is ethical*]

By contrast, a much wider range of constituents can function as postnominal Adjuncts – not just PPs, but also temporal NPs, APs and Clauses (more precisely, Restrictive Relative Clauses). For example, in (93) below, each of the italicised constituents is an Adjunct of the N-bar containing the capitalised constituents:

(93) (a)   the [$_{N'}$ [$_{N'}$ ABOLITION OF TAXES] [$_{NP}$ *next year*]]

(b)   those [$_{N'}$ [$_{N'}$ STUDENTS OF PHYSICS] [$_{AP}$ *absent from class*]]

(c)   the [$_{N'}$ [$_{N'}$ KING OF ENGLAND] [$_{S}$ *who abdicated*]]

But I guess you've had just about enough of postnominal Phrases by now, so I'll spare you the relevant argumentation ... or rather, leave you to devise some of it for yourself in an appropriate exercise!

However, there's one additional complication which we'll touch upon briefly. So far, all the Noun Phrases we've looked at have been *simple* NPs comprising a head Noun with or without an optional Determiner, Complement, or Adjunct. What we have not considered is the structure of *complex* NPs such as those in (94) below:

(94) (a)   an *advocate* of the *abolition* of indirect taxation

(b)   a *woman* with an *umbrella* with a red handle

(c)   her *dislike* of *men* with big egos

(d)   a *girl* with a *dislike* of macho men

For reasons which should now be familiar, the *of*-phrases in these examples are all Complement PPs (hence sisters of N), whereas the *with*-phrases in each case are all Adjunct PPs (hence sisters of N-bar). But the crucial point that we want to make here is that although all the examples contain two PPs, the first PP in each case modifies the first italicised nominal, while the second PP modifies the second italicised nominal. To make matters clearer, let's briefly look in rather more detail at the internal structure of each of the NPs in (94) (omitting the relevant argumentation for the sake of brevity).

In (94) (a), both *of*-phrases are Complement PPs: but they are Complements of different head Nouns. More precisely, the first *of*-phrase is a Complement of the Noun *advocate*, whereas the second one is a Complement of the Noun *abolition*. Given our earlier arguments that Complements are sisters of N, then (94) (a) will have the structure (95) below:

(95)

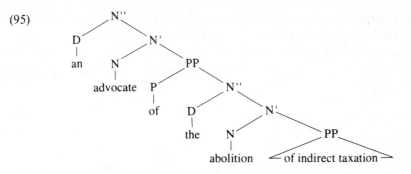

Conversely, in (94) (b) both *with*-phrases are Adjunct PPs, and hence (given our earlier arguments) both sisters of N-bar. But the crucial point is that they are Adjuncts of different N-bar constituents: the first *with*-phrase modifies the N-bar *woman* whereas the second modifies the N-bar *umbrella*, so that (94) (b) has the structure (96) below:

(96)

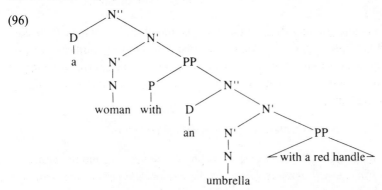

In (94) (c), the *of*-phrase is a Complement PP whereas the *with*-phrase is an Adjunct PP (recall that Complements are sisters of N, and Adjuncts are sisters of N-bar). However, whereas the *of*-phrase modifies the N *dislike*, the *with*-phrase modifies the N-bar *men*, so that (94) (c) has the structure (97) below:

(97)

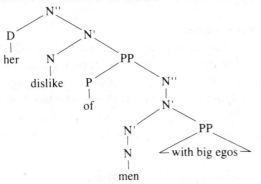

195

In (94) (d) we have a rather different situation: the first PP (= the *with*-phrase) is an Adjunct (hence a sister of N-bar), whereas the second PP (= the *of*-phrase) is a Complement (hence a sister of N). But whereas the *with*-phrase modifies *girl*, the *of*-phrase modifies *dislike*, so that (94) (d) has the structure (98) below:

(98)

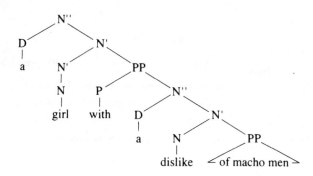

Thus, in more complex cases of postnominal modification we have to be concerned not only with the question of whether a given postmodifier is a Complement or an Adjunct, but also with the question of which particular nominal it modifies. Not surprisingly, therefore, we find cases of structural ambiguity such as the following:

(99)　　　　a woman with three children with ginger hair

where the Adjunct PP [*with ginger hair*] might be taken to modify either the N-bar [*woman with three children*], or the N-bar *children*: in other words, it might be either the woman or the children who have ginger hair. And on that colourful note, we'll conclude our discussion of postnominal modifiers!

You should now be able to tackle exercises I, II, III, IV, and V

4.7　Nominal premodifiers

So far, our discussion has been limited to the syntax of *postnominal* modifiers. But what about *prenominal* modifiers? We shall argue that there are three structurally distinct classes of nominal premodifier, namely (i) *Determiners*, (ii) *Complements*, and (iii) *Attributes* (this last term is borrowed from Bloomfield 1935, p. 195). We shall further argue that these three different classes of premodifier have the different structural properties described in (100) below:

(100) (i)　　*Determiners* expand N-bar into N-double-bar

(ii)   *Attributes* recursively expand N-bar into N-bar

(iii)   *Complements* expand N into N-bar

Since both *Attributes* and *Adjuncts* recursively expand N-bar into N-bar, it seems clear that the two have essentially the same function, so that *Attributes* are simply prenominal Adjuncts (though we shall continue to follow tradition and refer to attributive premodifiers as *Attributes* rather than *Adjuncts*). For the time being, we shall concentrate on the distinction between *Complements* and *Attributes*: and more specifically, we shall concentrate on the distinction between Complement NPs and Attribute NPs.

In this connection, consider the following Noun Phrase:

(101)   a [*Cambridge*] [*Physics*] student

Clearly, (101) is ambiguous, between the two interpretations which can be paraphrased as in (102) below:

(102) (i)   a student of Physics (*who is*) at Cambridge

(ii)   a student of Cambridge Physics (i.e. the particular brand of Physics taught at Cambridge, as opposed to *Oxford Physics*)

In our discussion here, we'll concern ourselves solely with the first and most natural interpretation, namely (102) (i): this is purely for didactic purposes, to make our exposition as simple and concise as possible (our analysis can be extended straightforwardly to deal with the second interpretation (102) (ii), in ways that I'll leave you to work out for yourself).

In analysing (101) (on interpretation (102) (i)), we might like to bear in mind the principle of 'structural symmetry' which Rulon Wells invoked in his analysis of *the king of England* (recall that he wanted to treat this as structurally parallel to *the English king*). What this means is that we'd like to make our analysis of (101) *a Cambridge Physics student* as close to our analysis of (102) (i) [*a student of Physics (who is) at Cambridge*] as possible. So, let's start by looking at the internal structure of (102) (i), ignoring the material in parentheses. Given all the arguments we put forward in the previous section, (102) (i) will have the structure (103) below:

(103)

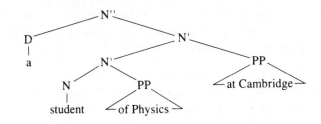

And it should (by now!) be obvious to you that the PP [*of Physics*] in (103) is a Complement (hence modifies N), whereas the PP [*at Cambridge*] is an Adjunct (hence modifies N-bar). We can provide some empirical support for the analysis in (103) by standard constituent structure 'tests': for example, (103) specifies that *student* is an N, [*student of Physics*] is an N-bar, and [*student of Physics at Cambridge*] is also an N-bar. Therefore, the analysis predicts that the latter two constituents (but not the former) can be replaced by the pro-N-bar *one*: and as (104) below illustrates, this is indeed the case:

(104) (a) Which [student of Physics]? The *one* at Cambridge?
  (b) Which [student of Physics at Cambridge]? This *one*?
  (c) Which [student]? *The *one* of Physics at Cambridge?

So, the analysis in (103) above seems to produce the right results.

  Now, if we want to attain maximal structural symmetry between (101) [*a Cambridge Physics student*] and (103) [*a student of Physics at Cambridge*], then the natural suggestion to make is that *Physics* in (101) should be analysed as a Complement, and *Cambridge* as an Attribute (recall that Attributes are the prenominal counterpart of Adjuncts). In other words, our *structural symmetry* principle would suggest that (101) should be assigned the structure (105) below:

(105)

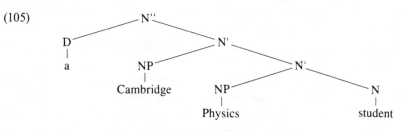

(For didactic reasons, we use the label NP for Noun Phrases whose internal structure is not the focus of our interest, and which we choose not to represent, and N'' for Noun Phrases whose structure we want the reader to concentrate on, and which we show in some detail: but recall that from a theoretical viewpoint, NP and N'' are equivalent terms.) Given the structure (105), then *Physics* would be a Complement because it is the sister of the N *student*, whereas *Cambridge* would be an Attribute, because it is the sister (and daughter) of an N-bar. A structure such as (105) could be generated by a set of Phrase Structure Rules such as (106) below:

(106) (i) N'' → (D) N' [Determiner Rule: cf. (75) (i)]
  (ii) N' → NP N' [Attribute Rule: *optional*]
  (iii) N' → (NP) N [Complement Rule]

We make the Attribute Rule (106) (ii) optional because not all Noun Phrases contain Attributes: and we make the NP Complement in (106) (iii) optional because not all head Nouns have NP Complements.

However, while it would obviously be extremely satisfying if we were to be able to establish structural symmetry between the prenominal and post-nominal Phrases in (103) and (105) above, clearly we need to base our analysis in (105) on some firmer foundation than a mere desire to find structural symmetry. So, what evidence is there that (105) is the right analysis for (101) [*a Cambridge Physics student*?] Well, part of the evidence comes from word-order facts. For, we have already argued that Complements must always come closer to their head Noun than Adjuncts (if we are to avoid 'crossing branches'). And if *Attributes* are the prenominal counterparts of Adjuncts, then we should expect that Complements must also come closer to their Head Noun than Attributes. And this does indeed turn out to be the case. For as we see from (107) below, the Complement NP *Physics* must come closer to the head Noun *student* than the Attribute NP *Cambridge*:

(107) (a)   a [*Cambridge*] [*Physics*] student
      (b)   *a [*Physics*] [*Cambridge*] student

Now, if we posit that Complement NPs are generated to the left of N (cf. the Complement Rule (106) (iii) above) whereas Attribute NPs are generated to the left of N-bar (cf. the Attribute Rule (106) (ii) above), then it should be obvious why (107) (b) is ungrammatical: for, the only way in which we can generate a structure like (107) (b) in which the Attribute NP is closer to the Head Noun than the Complement NP is to allow 'crossing branches' as in (108) below:

(108)

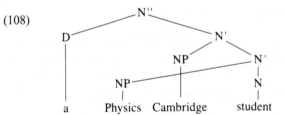

But a structure such as (108) is ill-formed because it violates our condition that branches should not be allowed to cross. By contrast, there is no violation of the 'crossing branches' condition in (105) above, so that we correctly predict that only the Attribute + Complement order found in (105) is possible, not the Complement + Attribute order found in (108).

A second argument in support of the analysis in (105) can be formulated in relation to *one*-pronominalisation facts. For note that our analysis in (105)

specifies that both [*Physics student*] and [*Cambridge Physics student*] are N-bar
constituents, whereas *student* is not (it is simply an N). Given our assumption
that *one* is a pro-N-bar, we therefore predict that the first two of these expressions can be proformed by *one*, but not the third. And as (109) below illustrates, this is indeed the case:

(109) (a)   Which [Physics student]? The Cambridge *one*?
      (b)   Which [Cambridge Physics student]? This *one*?
      (c)   Which [student]? *The Cambridge Physics *one*?

So, *one*-pronominalisation facts lend strong empirical support to our analysis.

A third argument in favour of (105) comes from facts about *Simple Coordination*. Given that both the sequences [*Physics student*] and [*Cambridge
Physics student*] in (105) are assigned the status of N-bar, then we should
expect that both can be coordinated with another N-bar such as [*hockey
player*]: and as (110) below shows, this is indeed the case:

(110) (a)   a Cambridge [*hockey player* and *Physics student*]
      (b)   a [*hockey player* and *Cambridge Physics student*]

Moreover, while we can coordinate two Complement NPs (as in (111) (a)
below) or two Attribute NPs (as in (111) (b)), we cannot coordinate a Complement NP with an Attribute NP (hence the ungrammaticality of (111) (c)), or
an Attribute NP with a Complement NP (cf. *(111) (d)):

(111) (a)   several [*Physics*] and [*Chemistry*] students
      (b)   several [*Oxford*] and [*Cambridge*] students
      (c)   *several [*Physics*] and [*Cambridge*] students
      (d)   *several [*Cambridge*] and [*Physics*] students

So, it seems that Coordination facts provide strong support for our analysis.

A fourth argument can be based on the different properties of the rules
introducing Complement NPs on the one hand, and Attribute NPs on the
other. The rules which we gave earlier in (106) above are repeated in (112)
below:

(112) (i)   N'' → (D) N' [Determiner Rule]
      (ii)   N' → NP N' [Attribute Rule: *optional*]
      (iii) N' → (NP) N [Complement Rule]

Note that the Attribute Rule (112) (ii) is recursive (since it has the symbol
N-bar both in its input and in its output): thus, the rule predicts that indefinitely many Attribute NPs can be stacked on top of each other. For

example, if we apply the Determiner Rule (112) (i), we generate the structure (113) below:

(113)

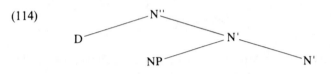

If we now apply the optional Attribute Rule (112) (ii) to expand the N-bar in (113), we derive:

(114)

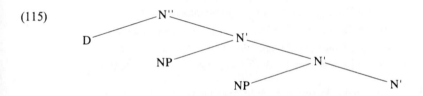

But we can now re-apply the same Attribute Rule (112) (ii) to expand the N-bar at the bottom of the tree in (114), yielding:

(115)

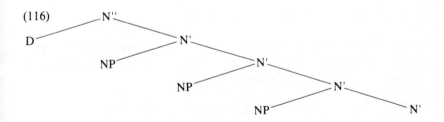

And we can even re-apply the same Attribute Rule once more, again expanding the lowest N-bar, thereby deriving:

(116)

However, let's assume that at this point we get tired of playing the game of repeatedly re-applying the same recursive rule, and instead choose to skip the Attribute Rule (112) (ii) this time and pass on to the Complement Rule (112) (iii). Now, if we choose to omit the optional NP Complement and instead choose to expand the lowest N-bar in (116) only as N, the resulting

201

structure will be (117) below (assuming insertion of appropriate items):

(117)

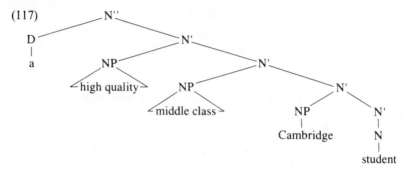

Each of the NPs in (117) is an Attribute: and we should expect that they can be freely stacked on top of each other in any order (subject to stylistic, etc. restrictions). And as (118) below shows, this is indeed the case:

(118) (a)   a [*Cambridge*] [*high quality*] [*middle class*] student
    (b)   a [*Cambridge*] [*middle class*] [*high quality*] student
    (c)   a [*high quality*] [*Cambridge*] [*middle class*] student
    (d)   a [*high quality*] [*middle class*] [*Cambridge*] student
    (e)   a [*middle class*] [*high quality*] [*Cambridge*] student
    (f)   a [*middle class*] [*Cambridge*] [*high quality*] student

So, our recursive Attribute Rule seems to make precisely the right predictions (I leave to you the task of working out in how many different ways the NPs in (118) above can be pronominalised by the pro-N-bar *one*!).

But now let's compare the Attribute Rule with the Complement Rule (112) (iii), repeated as (119) below:

(119)   N' → (NP) N [Complement Rule]

We see from (119) that the Complement Rule is not recursive, so that we predict that Complement NPs cannot be recursively stacked: and (120) below suggests that this is indeed the case:

(120)   *a [*Physics*] [*Economics*] [*Agriculture*] student

So, our analysis correctly predicts that Attributes can be recursively stacked (cf. (118) above), but not Complements (cf. (120) immediately above).

There seems little point in cataloguing more and more empirical evidence in support of our proposal that prenominal Complement NPs are sisters of N and daughters of N-bar, whereas prenominal Attribute NPs are both sisters and daughters of N-bar. If I haven't convinced you by now, I'm obviously not going to! Instead, let's comment briefly on some aspects of the rules in (112) which we have used to generate Complement and Attribute NPs: these rules are repeated in (121) below:

(121) (i)   N'' → (D)   N' [Determiner Rule]
     (ii)   N' → NP   N' [Attribute Rule: *optional*]
     (iii)   N' → (NP) N [Complement Rule]

The rules in (121) specify that Determiners, Attributes, and Complements are all optional constituents of a Noun Phrase: i.e. they tell us that the only constituent which an NP must contain is a head Noun. Let's see how we can use our rules in (121) to generate first an NP containing an Attribute but no Complement, and secondly an NP containing a Complement but no Attribute; and let's examine the different structures assigned by the rules in these two cases.

If we apply the Determiner Rule (121) (i) – selecting the optional Determiner – we generate the substructure (122) below:

(122)

If we now apply the optional Attribute Rule (121) (ii) to (122), we derive:

(123)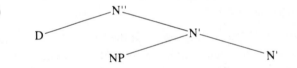

And if we subsequently apply the Complement Rule (121) (iii) – omitting the optional complement NP – we derive the structure (124) below (we have inserted appropriate lexical items for the sake of clarity):

(124)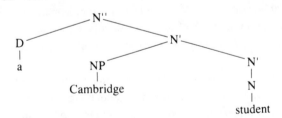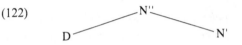

Given our earlier definition of an *Attribute* as a sister and daughter of N-bar, then it is clear that *Cambridge* in (124) functions as an Attribute. Note that both *Cambridge student* and *student* in (124) are assigned the status of N-bar, so that we correctly predict that both expressions can be proformed by the pro-N-bar *one*, as in:

(125) (a)   Which [Cambridge student]? This *one*?

(b)   Which [student]? The Cambridge *one*?

So, our analysis seems to have strong empirical support.

But now let's use our rules in (121) to generate a rather different type of structure. As before, we first apply the Determiner Rule (121)(i) to generate the substructure (122) above. But this time, we 'skip' the Attributive Rule (121)(ii), and go straight on to the Complement Rule (121)(iii): if we select the optional NP Complement, then from (122) by application of the Complement Rule we will derive the structure (126) below (assuming insertion of the relevant lexical items):

(126)

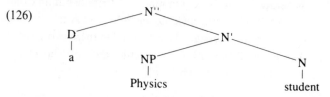

Note that the sequence [*Physics student*] in (126) has the status of N-bar, but not *student* (which is only an N). Hence, we correctly predict that only the former and not the latter can be proformed by the pro-NP *one*: cf.

(127) (a)   Which [Physics student]? This *one*?

(b)   Which [student]? *The Physics *one*?

Thus, our analyses in (124) and (126) show that the NPs [*a Cambridge student*] and [*a Physics student*] are similar insofar as both the sequences [*Cambridge student*] and [*Physics student*] have the status of N-bar; but they differ in that *student* in the case of [*a Physics student*] has the status of N, whereas *student* in the case of [*a Cambridge student*] has the status of N-bar. This follows from the observation we made earlier that an N which has an overt Complement has the status of N, whereas an N which lacks a Complement has the status of an N-bar dominating an N. And we have already seen that our analyses in (124) and (126) make precisely correct predictions about *one*-pronominalisation facts.

In this section, we have argued that just as some postnominal PPs function as Complements to Nouns, and others as Adjuncts, so too some prenominal NPs function as Complements to Nouns, and others as Attributes. In fact, the parallel between *postnominal PPs* and *prenominal NPs* is a very close one. For example, all the postnominal PP Complements in the (a) examples below have prenominal NP Complement counterparts in the corresponding (b) example:

(128) (a)   the ban [*on pornography*]

(b)   the [*pornography*] ban

(129) (a)   recruitment [*of personnel*]
     (b)   [*personnel*] recruitment

(130) (a)   the appeal [*for charity*]
     (b)   the [*charity*] appeal

(131) (a)   relief [*from famine*]
     (b)   [*famine*] relief

(132) (a)   damage [*to the brain*]
     (b)   [*brain*] damage

(133) (a)   the investigations [*into fraud*]
     (b)   the [*fraud*] investigations

(134) (a)   a fan [*of Debbie Harry*]
     (b)   a [*Debbie Harry*] fan

(135) (a)   the allegations [*of treachery*]
     (b)   the [*treachery*] allegations

And in much the same way, the postnominal PP Adjuncts in the (a) examples
below all have prenominal NP Attribute counterparts in the corresponding (b)
example:

(136) (a)   the shop [*on the corner*]
     (b)   the [*corner*] shop

(137) (a)   the strike [*in the shipyard*]
     (b)   the [*shipyard*] strike

(138) (a)   the lady [*of iron*]
     (b)   the [*iron*] lady

(139) (a)   the bridge [*over the river*]
     (b)   the [*river*] bridge

(140) (a)   a keyboard [*for a typewriter*]
     (b)   a [*typewriter*] keyboard

(141) (a)   a sauce [*with cream*]
     (b)   a [*cream*] sauce

(142) (a)   tea [*from China*]
     (b)   [*China*] tea

(143) (a)   the weather [*in winter*]
     (b)   the [*winter*] weather

Noun Phrases

It thus seems clear that prenominal NPs are the natural counterpart of postnominal PPs.

The two are not completely equivalent however. There are obvious syntactic differences between the two: premodifiers have the status of NP and precede the N-bar they modify, whereas postmodifiers have the status of PP and follow the N-bar they modify. Moreover, this syntactic difference is reflected in parallel semantic differences. To be more precise, the semantic relation between a prenominal NP and the N-bar it modifies is much more *vague* (and has to be inferred from pragmatic clues) than in the case of a postnominal PP. By way of example, consider a phrase such as the following:

(144)   the [*proportional representation*] campaign

The bracketed prenominal NP in (144) has two very different postnominal PP counterparts: cf.

(145) (a)   the campaign [*for proportional representation*]
      (b)   the campaign [*against proportional representation*]

The difference between (144) and (145) is that the postnominal modifier in (145) contains a Preposition whose semantics specifies the relation between the Head Noun and the NP [*proportional representation*]: but in (144) there is no Preposition, and hence no additional semantic information, so that the exact relationship between [*proportional representation*] and *campaign* has to be inferred on the basis of pragmatic clues (i.e. knowledge of the way the world is). Thus, the two bracketed NPs in (146) below are likely to be interpreted very differently:

(146) (a)   Nancy Reagan's [*drugs*] campaign
      (b)   Ronald Reagan's [*re-election*] campaign

Our knowledge of the views of the individuals concerned helps us interpret the N-bar [*drugs campaign*] as paraphraseable by 'campaign *against* drugs' in (146) (a), but 'campaign *for* re-election' (e.g. of his own party) in (146) (b). And *your* knowledge of Syntax should (by now) enable you to work out for yourself whether the bracketed Phrases in (144–6) above are Complements, Attributes, or Adjuncts!

There are also other important differences between nominal premodifiers and postmodifiers. For example, generally speaking it seems to be that an NP which is part of a postnominal PP can alternatively be positioned in front of the nominal which it modifies. Thus, the italicised NP contained within the bracketed PP Complement in (147) (a) below can alternatively be positioned prenominally, as in (147) (b):

(147) (a)   a lover [PP of [NP *classical music*]]

    (b)   a [NP *classical music*] lover

But let's see what happens if we try to do the same in the case of the italicised NP in (148) below:

(148)   a lover [PP of [NP *the opera*]]

What we'd expect to get is (149) below:

(149)   *a [NP the opera] lover

But, as you can see, we don't get this: instead, we have:

(150)   an [NP opera] lover

Why? What's going on here? Well, there seems to be some restriction to the effect that prenominal NP Complements cannot contain a Determiner. Moreover, examples such as (151) below suggest that the same restriction operates in the case of Adjuncts and Attributes:

(151) (a)   a/the/this strike [PP in [NP *the shipyard*]]

    (b)   *a/the/this [NP *the shipyard*] strike

    (c)   a/the/this [NP *shipyard*] strike

The exact nature of the restriction is anything but clear. It seems that only *some* kinds of Determiner are barred from occurring in Attribute NPs, and that *others* can indeed be used in this function. Thus, in the following examples:

(152) (a)   the [*All* India] radio station

    (b)   an [*all* points] bulletin

    (c)   a [*half* frame] camera

    (d)   the president's [*no* compromise] policy

    (e)   an [*each* way] bet

    (f)   an [*any* topic] discussion

    (g)   an [*every* weekend] girl

the italicised constituents might be argued to be Determiners, so discounting the possibility of a 'blanket restriction' against the use of Determiners in prenominal NPs. It would seem that Articles (*a, the*) and Demonstratives (*this/that/these/those*) are barred from occurring in attribute NPs, whereas Quantifiers like *every/each/all/both/half/any/some/no*, etc. are not. Quite why this should be is not a question which need concern us here (OK . . . I'll admit that I always say that when I don't know the answer to my own question!)

You should now be able to tackle exercise VI

4.8   Adjectival premodifiers

Thus far, all the examples of Attributes which we have considered have involved attributive NPs. But other categories can be used in an attributive function as well. The commonest class of Attributes are APs (Adjectival Phrases): for example, the bracketed expressions in (153) below are attributive APs:

(153) (a)   a [*really excellent*] film
      (b)   a [*most entertaining*] evening
      (c)   a [*delightfully mysterious*] stranger
      (d)   a [*patently obvious*] lie

In many cases, attributive APs alternate with attributive NPs: for example, each of the (a) examples below involves an NP attribute which has an AP attribute counterpart in the corresponding (b) example:

(154) (a)   the [*England*] football players
      (b)   the [*English*] football players

(155) (a)   a [*Paris*] nightclub
      (b)   a [*Parisian*] nightclub

(156) (a)   a [*metal*] finish
      (b)   a [*metallic*] finish

(157) (a)   a [*prestige*] project
      (b)   a [*prestigious*] project

(158) (a)   the [*winter*] weather
      (b)   the [*wintry*] weather

Moreover, the following example (taken from confidential University papers!) shows that an attributive AP can be conjoined with an attributive NP:

(159)   Any change is bound to have numerous [$_{AP}$ *academic*] and [$_{NP}$ *cost*] implications

So, there does seem to be an apparent parallelism between attributive NPs and attributive APs.

Now, if attributive NPs are generated by rule (121)(ii) above, repeated as (160) below:

(160)   N' → NP N' [Attribute Rule: *optional*]

and if attributive Adjectival Phrases seem to be structurally parallel to attributive Noun Phrases, then we might propose to generate Attributive APs by a parallel rule such as (161) below:

(161)   N' → AP N' [Attribute Rule: *optional*]

Moreover, it may well be that we can conflate our two Attribute Rules (160) and (161) above into a single rule. How? Well, recall that in Chapter 3 we argued that categories are analysable into matrices (= sets) of syntactic features, so that (e.g.):

(162)   Noun = [+ N, − V]   Adjective = [+ N, + V]

Thus, Noun and Adjective might be argued to form a supercategory of [+ N] elements. And in the same way, we might say that NP and AP form a corresponding phrasal supercategory which we might designate as [+ NP] (i.e. a phrasal constituent with a [+ N] head). Given these assumptions, then our two Attribute Rules (160) and (161) could be conflated as (163) below:

(163)   N' → [+ NP] N' [Attribute Rule: *optional*]

If we incorporate our generalised Attribute Rule (163) into our earlier system of rules in (121) above, our revised set of rules becomes (164) below:

(164) (i)   N" → (D) N' [Determiner Rule]
      (ii)   N' → [+ NP] N' [Attribute Rule: *optional*]
      (iii)   N' → (NP) N [Complement Rule]

Now, since our revised Attribute Rule (164) (ii) is recursive, it predicts (amongst other things) that Noun Phrases can contain indefinitely many stacked attributive APs: and this does indeed seem to be the case, as (165) below illustrates (where each of the bracketed constituents is an attributive AP):

(165) (a)   a [*handsome*] stranger
      (b)   a [*dark*] [*handsome*] stranger
      (c)   a [*tall*] [*dark*] [*handsome*] stranger
      (d)   an [*intelligent*] [*tall*] [*dark*] [*handsome*] stranger
      (e)   etc.

By way of illustration, let's see how our rules (164) would generate a Noun Phrase such as (165) (c) [*a tall dark handsome stranger*]. Applying the Determiner Rule (164) (i) and selecting the Determiner option would generate the structure (166) below:

(166)

209

Applying the Attribute Rule (164) (ii) to (166), and selecting AP as our [+ NP] category, will yield (167) below:

(167)

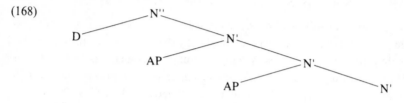

Reapplying the same rule in the same way to the lower N′ in (167) will then derive (168) below:

(168)

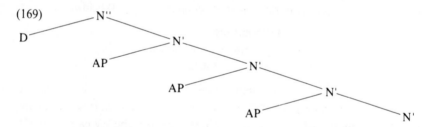

Applying the same Attribute Rule in the same fashion once more to expand the lowest N-bar in (168) will give us (169) below:

(169)

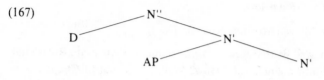

Finally, if we apply the Complement Rule (164) (iii) to expand the lowest N′ in (169) into N, the result will be (170) below (we have inserted the relevant words for illustrative purposes; of course, AP will have further internal structure, but this need not concern us for the time being):

(170)

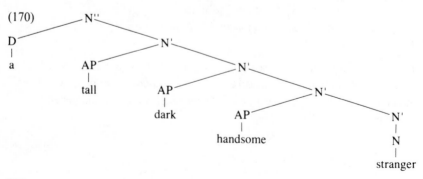

Now, the structure (170) predicts that the sequences *stranger*, [*handsome stranger*], [*dark handsome stranger*], and [*tall dark handsome stranger*] are all N-bar constituents. Among the predictions we therefore make is that each of these can be proformed by the pro-N-bar *one*: and (171) below shows us that this prediction is exactly correct:

(171) (a)   Which [stranger]? The tall dark handsome *one*?
    (b)   Which [handsome stranger]? The tall dark *one*?
    (c)   Which [dark handsome stranger]? The tall *one*?
    (d)   Which [tall dark handsome stranger]? This *one*?

So, it would appear that the structural parallels between attributive NPs and attributive APs are quite striking: both can be used to recursively expand N-bar into N-bar.

Now, if we are correct in positing that both NPs and APs can be used as Attributes (hence can recursively expand N-bar into another N-bar), then it follows that we should expect that two different kind of Attributes can be recursively stacked on top of each other in any order. We can demonstrate this by the free relative ordering of the NP and AP Attributes in (172) below:

(172) (a)   a [AP *Japanese*] [NP *toy*] [NP *plastic*] duck
    (b)   a [AP *Japanese*] [NP *plastic*] [NP *toy*] duck
    (c)   a [NP *toy*] [AP *Japanese*] [NP *plastic*] duck
    (d)   a [NP *toy*] [NP *plastic*] [AP *Japanese*] duck
    (e)   a [NP *plastic*] [AP *Japanese*] [NP *toy*] duck
    (f)   a [NP *plastic*] [NP *toy*] [AP *Japanese*] duck

Thus, word order facts provide striking support for our analysis: they are exactly as predicted. I leave you to verify for yourself how many different ways [*a Japanese toy plastic duck*] can be pronominalised by *one*: think about it, next time you play with your toy duck in the bath (if you don't have a toy duck, a toy boat etc. will do just as well).

We have argued in this section that APs can function as prenominal Attributes: but recall that we argued at the end of section 3.6 above that APs can also be used as postnominal Adjuncts. Indeed, in certain types of construction, APs of a given class can be positioned either pre- or post-nominally: cf. the following examples from Quirk *et al.* (1985, pp. 418–29):

(173) (a)   the best [*possible*] use
    (b)   the best use [*possible*]

(174) (a)   the greatest [*imaginable*] insult
    (b)   the greatest insult [*imaginable*]

(175) (a)   the best [*available*] person
   (b)   the best person [*available*]

(176) (a)   the only [*suitable*] actor
   (b)   the only actor [*suitable*]

But there are extremely complex restrictions on when APs can or cannot be used prenominally, and when they can or cannot be used postnominally: the examples below illustrate some of the restrictions concerned:

(177) (a)   He has a [*similar*] car
   (b)   *He has a car [*similar*]

(178) (a)   He has a [*similar though subtly different*] car
   (b)   He has a car [*similar though subtly different*]

(179) (a)   He has a [*similar enough*] car
   (b)   He has a car [*similar enough*]

(180) (a)   He has a [*fairly similar*] car
   (b)   He has a car [*fairly similar*]

(181) (a)   *He has a [*very similar indeed*] car
   (b)   He has a car [*very similar indeed*]

(182) (a)   *He has a [*similar to mine*] car
   (b)   He has a car [*similar to mine*]
   (c)   He has a [*similar*] car [*to mine*]

We are not here going to attempt to unravel the complex syntactic and stylistic factors which determine the position of APs used to modify N-bars: the interested reader should consult a good reference grammar such as Quirk *et al.* (1985).

Well, I know you'd want me to end the chapter on a high, so I'll conclude with an argument of your favourite type – relating to *structural ambiguity*. No, don't groan – this one is quite straightforward. Consider the Noun Phrase in (183) below:

(183)   an English teacher

This is ambiguous in a fairly obvious way between the two interpretations represented by the paraphrases in (178) below:

(184) (i)   someone who teaches English
   (ii)   someone who teaches, and who is English

Now, it seems plausible to assume that the source of the ambiguity of (183) is *structural* in nature, and that part of the ambiguity relates to the fact that

English has two different categorial functions in (183). On the first interpretation (= someone who teaches English), *English* functions as a Noun, and hence can be modified by an Adjective, as in (185) below:

(185) (a) an [NP *Old English*] teacher
    (b) a [NP *Middle English*] teacher
    (c) a [NP *New English*] teacher

On the second interpretation (= a teacher who is English), *English* functions as an Adjective, and hence can be modified by an Adverb, as in (186) below:

(186) (a) a [AP *typically English*] teacher
    (b) a [AP *very English*] teacher
    (c) a [AP *disappointingly English*] teacher

So, part of the ambiguity of [*an English teacher*] lies in the categorial status of *English*, which can either be a prenominal NP, or a prenominal AP: cf.

(187) (a) an [*NP English*] teacher (= someone who teaches English)
    (b) an [*AP English*] teacher (= a teacher who is English)

But this is only part of the story. I suppose you'd already guessed that the answer couldn't be that simple! But why not?

Well, what we're going to argue is that when [*an English teacher*] means 'someone who teaches English', then the prenominal NP *English* is a Complement; but when the NP means 'a teacher who is English', the prenominal AP *English* is an Attribute. Now, if I'm right (am I ever wrong?), then it follows that the NP [*an English teacher*] could have either of the two structures in (188) below:

(188) (a) [= a person who teaches English]

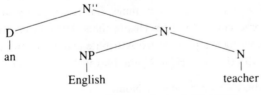

    (b) [= a person who teaches, and who is English]

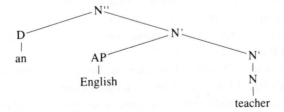

(I leave you to work out for yourself which of our rules in (164) apply to generate each of the structures in (188).) Now, the analysis in (188) has a certain amount of *semantic* plausibility. After all, if we accept the claim (cited earlier) by Hornstein and Lightfoot (1981a, p. 21) that 'each N-bar specifies a *semantic property*', then from the fact that (188) (a) contains only the single N-bar [*English teacher*], it follows that (188) (a) will attribute only one semantic property to the person concerned, namely that (s)he teaches English. But by the same token, the fact that (188) (b) contains two N-bar constituents, namely [*teacher*] and [*English teacher*], entails that (188) (b) will attribute two properties to the individual concerned, namely (i) that (s)he teaches, and (ii) that (s)he is English.

However, the proposed analysis also has independent *syntactic* support. Well, I won't bore you with a whole battery of syntactic arguments in support of our analysis. Let's just look at one such argument, relating to *word-order* facts. Consider a sentence such as the following:

(189)   I think it would be crazy to employ [*a French English teacher*]

Just think about what (189) means: does it mean (190) (i) below, or (190) (ii)?

(190) (i)   I think it would be crazy to employ a French person to teach English

(ii)   I think it would be crazy to employ an English person to teach French

Well, I think it's pretty clear that the NP [*a French English teacher*] can only be interpreted along the lines of (190) (i) as 'a French person who teaches English', and not along the lines of (190) (ii) as 'an English person who teaches French'. But if you think about it, that's exactly what our analysis in (188) predicts. For, as we have noted many times, our rules specify that Complements always come closer to their Heads than Attributes/Adjuncts. This means that when we have a prenominal Attribute and a prenominal Complement associated with the same Head Noun, they will occur in the order:

(191)   Attribute + Complement + Noun

Thus, in a sequence such as [*French English teacher*], since *English* is closer to the Head Noun *teacher*, it must be a Complement; and since *French* is further away from *teacher*, it must be an Attribute. Hence, we correctly predict that the only possible interpretation for [*a French English teacher*] is 'a person who teaches English who is French'. So our analysis not only has semantic plausibility; but in addition it has independent syntactic support.

But what is even more exciting is that there is also *phonological* evidence in support of the structural ambiguity represented in (188) above. For, just as differences of syntactic structure correlate with differences of semantic struc- ture (i.e. meaning), so too we might expect them to correlate with *phonological* differences. And this is precisely what we find. For if you think about it, you'll realise that the phrase [*an English teacher*] has two different stress patterns, namely those represented in (192) below (where the syllables receiving primary stress are CAPITALISED):

(192) (i)   an **EN**glish teacher
     (ii)   an **EN**glish **TEA**cher

And if you think even harder, you'll realise that the two different stress patterns correspond to the two different interpretations in (184) above: that is, (192) (i) means 'someone who teaches English', whereas (192) (ii) means 'a teacher who is English'.

Now, why should the two different stress patterns in (192) be associated with two different meanings? Well, let's assume that just as each N-bar in a sentence is a *semantic unit* (recall Hornstein and Lightfoot's (1981a, p. 21) ob- servation that 'each N-bar specifies a *semantic property*'), so too each N-bar is a *phonological unit*. More specifically, let's assume that the rule for primary stress assignment in English is along the lines given very informally in (193) below:

(193)   Assign a separate primary stress to each separate N-bar (i.e. to an appropriate syllable of an appropriate word in each N-bar)

If we look at the two structures assigned to [*an English teacher*] in (188) above, we see that the N-bar constituents which each contains are as in (194) below:

(194) (a)   an [$_{N'}$ *English* teacher] (= Complement = 'someone who teaches English')
     (b)   an [$_{N'}$ *English* [$_{N'}$ teacher]] (= Attribute = 'someone who teaches who is English')

And our Stress Rule (193) above will accordingly assign primary stress only to the (first syllable of the) word *English* in (194) (a), but to (the first syllable of) both the words *English* and *teacher* in (194) (b). Thus, it seems clear that phonological facts provide strong independent empirical support for our claim that [*an English teacher*] exhibits the structural ambiguity characterised in (188) above. So, it's nice to find that an analysis which has syntactic and semantic plausibility turns out to have independent phonological motivation.

You should now be able to tackle exercises VII – XVI

Noun Phrases

4.9 Summary

The general aim of this chapter has been to provide empirical support for the claim that there is a type of nominal constituent which is larger than the Noun but smaller than the Noun Phrase. In 4.2 we examined Rulon Wells' claim in 1947 that the NP [*the king of England*] has as one of its immediate constituents just such a 'small nominal phrase', [*king of England*]; and we proposed to adopt Chomsky's *bar-notation* for such cases, whereby *king* is an N, [*king of England*] is an N-bar, and [*the king of England*] is an N-double-bar. In 4.3 we produced empirical evidence in support of the proposed analysis, based on Coordination and *one*-pronominalisation facts. In 4.4, we argued that N-bar has a crucial role to play in differentiating two different classes of postnominal modifier – *Complement PPs* (which are sisters of N and daughters of N-bar), and *Adjunct PPs* (which are both sisters and daughters of N-bar). In 4.5 we looked at how to deal with the optionality of Determiners, Adjunct PPs, and Complement PPs in Noun Phrases. In 4.6 we presented further evidence in support of the structural distinction drawn between postnominal PP Complements and PP Adjuncts. In 4.7 we argued in favour of positing a parallel structural distinction for premodifiers between Complement NPs (which expand N into N-bar), and Attribute NPs (which recursively expand N-bar into N-bar). In 4.8 we argued that not only NPs, but also APs can function as Attributes, and accordingly we generalised our Attribute Rule to allow [+ NP] phrases (i.e. NPs and APs) to function as Attributes.

We have summarised the various rules we have posited in this chapter in (195) below, for your convenience:

(195) (i) N'' → (D) N' [Determiner Rule]
(ii) (a) N' → N' PP [Adjunct Rule: *optional*]
 (b) N' → [+ NP] N' [Attribute Rule: *optional*]
(iii) (a) N' → N (PP) [PP Complement Rule]
 (b) N' → (NP) N [NP Complement Rule]

As we have already seen, the Determiner Rule (195) (i) has to apply, if we want to generate a Noun Phrase; the Adjunct Rule (195) (ii) (a) and the Attribute Rule (195) (ii) (b) are optional; and one of the two Complement Rules (195) (iii) (a) or (b) must also apply if we are to generate a properly terminated subtree (i.e. an NP which terminates in an N-node).

216

EXERCISES

Exercise I

It might be argued that the bracketed Prepositional Phrase in (1) below is a *Complement*, whereas that in (2) below is an *Adjunct*:

(1)   the discussion [*of the riots*]
(2)   the discussion [*in the bar*]

Given this assumption, what structure would be assigned to each of the Noun Phrases in (1) and (2), and what rules would be necessary to generate the relevant structures (show each individual step in the derivation)?

Show how the assumption that the bracketed PP is a Complement in (1) but an Adjunct in (2) would account for the following contrasts (assuming the grammaticality judgments given):

(3) (a)   *The discussion of the match was more animated than the one of the riots
    (b)   The discussion at the match was more animated than the one in the bar

(4) (a)   The discussion of the riots and of their implications was full and frank
    (b)   The discussion at the match and in the bar was full and frank
    (c)   *The discussion of the riots and in the bar was full and frank

(5) (a)   The discussion of the riots in the bar was full and frank
    (b)   *The discussion in the bar of the riots was full and frank

(6) (a)   The discussion was rather misleading in the document
    (b)   *The discussion was rather misleading of the document

(7) (a)   Which document did they ban the discussion of?
    (b)   *Which document did they ban the discussion in?

Exercise II

Discuss the syntax of the bracketed Noun Phrases in the following sentences, presenting empirical arguments to support your analysis:

(1)   I met [*a specialist in fibreoptics from Paris*]
(2)   [*The girl on the stage in jeans*] is a friend of mine
(3)   [*The journey from Paris to Rome on Sunday*] was tiring
(4)   [*The ban on belts with studs in the school*] has caused a lot of resentment
(5)   [*The girl at the disco last week*] rang me up yesterday

Now discuss possible differences in structure between the bracketed NPs in (6) and (7) below:

(6)   She's [*another friend of Mary*]
(7)   She's [*another friend of Mary's*]

(For the purposes of this exercise, simply assume that *of Mary* and *of Mary's* are PPs, and don't concern yourself with the internal structure of these PPs.)

*Exercise III

In the text, we considered only one analysis of [*the king of England*]. Evaluate this analysis against the two alternative analyses given in (1) and (2) below:

(1)

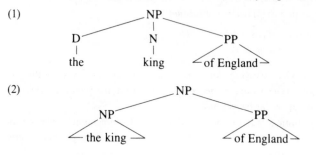

(2)

*Exercise IV

The discussion in the text ignored *clausal* postmodifiers. We might suppose that just as postnominal Prepositional Phrases can function either as Complements or as Adjuncts, so too can postnominal Clauses. For example, we might argue that the bracketed postmodifying Clause in (1) (a) below is a Complement of the head Noun *claim*, whereas that in (1) (b) is an Adjunct:

(1) (a)   the claim [that you made a mistake]
   (b)   the claim [that you made]

This correlates with the traditional distinction drawn between *Noun Complement Clauses* (NCC) such as that bracketed in (1) (a), and *Restrictive Relative Clauses* (RRC) such as that bracketed in (1) (b). The two different types of Clause have differing lexical properties: for example, the particle *that* can be replaced by an appropriate wh-pronoun such as *which* or omitted altogether in Relative Clauses like (1) (b), but not in Noun Complement Clauses such as (1) (a): cf.

(2) (a)   the claim [*that*/*which/*Ø you made a mistake]
          (Noun Complement Clause)
   (b)   the claim [*that*/*which*/Ø you made]
          (Restrictive Relative Clause)

More importantly, we might argue that the two types of Clause have different *structural* properties, in that NCCs are Complements, whereas RRCs are Adjuncts. Show how this difference might be represented in structural terms within the N-bar framework (assume that the bracketed Clauses in (1) have the status of S, but ignore their internal structure); and present empirical arguments in support of your analysis.

Why would examples such as the following prove problematic for such an analysis?

(3) (a)   The claim which Reagan made that no arms had been exchanged for hostages was greeted with scepticism
   (b)   The claim has been reiterated that no arms were exchanged for hostages

How would these problems be overcome if we assumed a general CLAUSAL EXTRAPOSI-
TION rule along the lines of:

(4)   Any postnominal Clause (i.e. NCC or RRC) can be extraposed to the end
           of the minimal Phrase or Clause containing it

*Exercise V

For the purposes of the exercise, assume that the Determiner *any* (in its
existential function, where it is similar in meaning to 'some') is subject to the following
restriction:

(1)   *Any* must be preceded and c-commanded by a negative

(Recall that in Exercise IV of Chapter 3, we suggested a similar restriction to the effect
that *ever* must be preceded and c-commanded by a negative.) Show how a restriction
such as (1) above would account for the (un)grammaticality of existential *any* in the
bracketed NPs in the following examples: concentrate only on the structure of the
bracketed NPs, ignoring the rest of the sentence for the purposes of the exercise. Assume that *no* and *lack* are 'negative' constituents in the requisite sense, and assume the
grammaticality judgments given.

(2) (a)   [*No king of any country*] abdicated
    (b)   [*No king of any importance*] abdicated
    (c)   [*No king of any country of any importance*] abdicated

(3) (a)   [The lack of any discipline in some schools] worried them
    (b)   *[The lack of discipline in any schools] worried them
    (c)   [The lack of teachers with any qualifications] worried them

Assume that *no*, *any*, and *some* all have the categorial status of Determiners (more precisely, they belong to the subset of Determiners called *Quantifiers*).

Show how facts such as these could be used as the basis for an argument supporting
the structural distinction we have drawn in the text between *Complements* and *Adjuncts*.

*Exercise VI

Discuss the ambiguity of the following NPs, and how it might be represented in structural terms, giving evidence in support of your analysis. What rules
would be required to generate the relevant structures?

(1)   the house in the wood near the park
(2)   a toy factory
(3)   a brass button holder
(4)   the king of England's people

Show how the rules in the text would assign two different structures to an NP such as:

(1)   the tall girl in jeans

corresponding to the two (very subtly different!) interpretations in (2) below:

(2) (i)   the girl in jeans who is tall
  (ii)   the tall girl who is wearing jeans

Discuss which rules would be needed to generate the relevant structures, and how they would apply. In addition, show how your analysis accounts for the *one*-pronominalisation facts in (3) below:

(3) (a)   Were you talking to the tall [girl in jeans], or the short *one*?
  (b)   Were you talking to the [tall girl] in jeans, or the *one* in a miniskirt?

Discuss the ambiguity of the following

(1)   an old French student
(2)   the nuclear test ban treaty

How might it be represented in structural terms? What evidence is there is favour of your proposed analysis? And what rules would need to apply (how?) to generate the relevant structures?

A Noun Phrase such as

(1)   the English king

might be argued to be open to the two interpretations paraphrased in (2) below:

(2) (i)   the king who is English
  (ii)   the king of England

Compare and contrast the two following accounts (A and B below) of this 'dual interpretation':

> *Analysis A: a structural ambiguity analysis*
> On interpretation (2) (i) *English* is an Attribute, whereas on interpretation (2) (ii) *English* is a Complement

> *Analysis B: a pragmatic analysis*
> On both interpretations, *English* is an Attribute: there is no structural ambiguity. The relationship between *English* and *king* is left vague, so that *English king* means more or less 'king connected in some unspecified way

with England' (so that the phrase could mean all sorts of things, including 'king born in England', 'king who rules over England', 'king who behaves in a typically English fashion' (as in 'King Hussein of Jordan is the most English king I've ever met'), etc.).

Discuss the structures assigned by each of these two accounts to (1).

What predictions would each of the two analyses (A and B) make about possible and impossible interpretations of *English* in the italicised phrases below, and why? Which set of predictions are correct, and what is the implication of this for each of the analyses proposed?

(3) (a) Why do philosophers always use examples involving a bald French king, rather than a bald *English one*?

(b) There's not much to choose between the present English and French kings, except that the French king is less bald that the *English one*

(4) (a) Henry VIII is the best known *English Protestant king*

(b) We've had relatively few *English septuagenarian kings*

(c) Boedicea was the most famous *English pagan queen*

(d) Henry IV was the last *English French king*

**Exercise X

Much of the justification for the analysis of Noun Phrases presented in the text rests on the assumption that (i) the antecedent of *one* is always a unitary constituent, and (ii) it is an N-bar. Given these (and other related) assumptions, a phrase like *a big black dog* will have the structure (1) below:

(1)

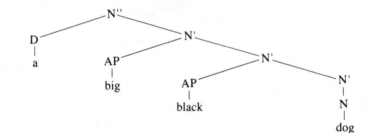

For speakers such as myself (and the late David Kilby, who first pointed out the problem to me), sentence (2) (a) below can have either of the interpretations (2) (b) or (2) (c), and sentence (3) (a) can have either of the interpretations (3) (b) or (3) (c):

(2) (a) Jane has a big black dog, and Jean has a small one

(b) . . . a small black dog

(c) . . . a small dog

(3) (a) Jane has a big black dog, and Jean has a brown one

(b) . . . a big brown dog

(c) . . . a brown dog

Which interpretation of which sentence proves problematic for the assumptions we are making about *one*, and why? Can you think of any way(s) in which we might defend the assumption that *one* is a pro-N-bar in the face of such apparent counterevidence?

HINT: You might like to explore pragmatic rather than purely syntactic solutions to the problem.

Now consider the following two dialogues:

(4)　　　SPEAKER A: Pass me that picture over there
　　　　　SPEAKER B: Which one? The one of a girl in a bikini?
(5)　　　SPEAKER A: Pass me that picture over there
　　　　　SPEAKER B: Which one? The one with a gold frame?

Which reply by Speaker B proves problematic for the analysis of *one* given in the text, and why?

**Exercise XI

In the text, we argued that multiple attributive APs are hierarchically, not linearly stacked. But consider the alternative possibility that APs can be stacked in either way onto an N-bar, giving rise to possible structural ambiguities such as the following:

(1)

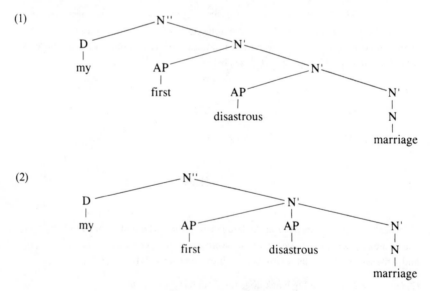

(2)

This structural difference might correlate with a semantic difference: thus, we might suppose that *disastrous* has a restrictive interpretation in (1), and an appositive interpretation in (2). On the restrictive interpretation (1), the phrase would be taken to imply that I had other disastrous marriages; whereas on the appositive interpretation (2), the phrase would be taken as implying that I had other marriages, though they were not necessarily disastrous. Note that English spelling marks the difference between the two interpretations: on the restrictive interpretation, there are no punctuation marks of any sort separating the two APs *first* and *disastrous*; but on the appositive interpretation, the two APs are separated by a comma, a hyphen, or a bracket: cf.

(3) (a)   my first disastrous marriage = (1) = restrictive
   (b)   my first, disastrous, marriage = (2) = appositive
   (c)   my first (disastrous) marriage = (2) = appositive
   (d)   my first – disastrous – marriage = (2) = appositive

Of course, the punctuation differences here reflect intonational differences. What kind of additional evidence might be adduced in support of (or against) such an analysis? And how would our PS rules have to be revised so as to allow for structures such as (2) as well as (1)?

**Exercise XII
Leonard Bloomfield in his classic work *Language* (1935, pp. 203–6) recognises the following classes of *Determiners*:

(1) (i)   Definite Article *the* and Indefinite Article *a*
   (ii)   Demonstratives *this/that/these/those*
   (iii)   Quantifiers such as *every/each/all/any/some/no/many/most/few*, etc.
   (iv)   Interrogatives such as *which/what*
   (v)   Genitive (= possessive) NPs like *the man next door's*, and the corresponding Possessive Pronouns *my/your/his/her*, etc.

In the text, we suggested that Determiners are non-recursive premodifiers which expand N-bar into N-double bar. Discuss the apparent problems posed for this claim by the bracketed Phrases in the examples below. To what extent can these problems be handled within our existing grammar, or do they require modifications to the grammar, and if so of what sort(s)?

(1)   [*His many faults*] can't be overlooked
(2)   Don't expect me to indulge [*your every whim*]
(3)   [*My few real friends*] would never desert me
(4)   [*All the African competitors*] have withdrawn
(5)   [*What a silly fool*] he is!
(6)   There's [*many a slip*] twixt cup and lip
(7)   You are [*such an insufferable bore*]
(8)   The hole has [*too narrow an aperture*]
(9)   I've never seen [*so pretty a picture*]

**Exercise XIII
It is generally assumed (cf. e.g. Bloomfield's classification cited in Exercise XII) that Genitive (= possessive) NPs function solely as (non-recursive) Determiners in

English. Show what problems appear to be posed for this assumption by the bracketed
NPs in examples such as those below:

(1)   %[*Your last week's letter*] was very interesting
(2)   [*My John Smith's best bitter*] has gone flat
(3)   It's no more than [*a silly old wives' tale*]
(4)   Look at [*those three quaint old Cornish fisherman's two-bedroomed ter-
        raced cottages*]
(5)   It was [*a typical old men's dreary fisherman's tale*]

How might these various problems be overcome? How will your analysis deal with the
ambiguity of phrases like:

(6)   an old man's bicycle

**Exercise XIV
Discuss the syntax of the following pairs of examples, pointing out the
similarities and differences between them. What complications (if any) do they pose for
the analysis in the text, and what modifications to that analysis (if any) do they entail?

(1) (a)   Salvador Dali's latest portrait
    (b)   the latest Salvador Dali portrait

(2) (a)   my family's income
    (b)   my family income

(3) (a)   the film about aparthied last week
    (b)   last week's apartheid film

(4) (a)   the presentation of the medals to the athletes
    (b)   the medal presentation to the athletes

(5) (a)   my Linguistics lecture to the Faculty
    (b)   my Faculty Linguistics lecture

*Exercise XV
Try and work out the nature of the restrictions illustrated in the examples
below (inventing further examples of your own as necessary to expand the paradigm
given below):

(1) (a)   this/that green one
    (b)   this/that one

(2) (a)   the tall one in the corner
    (b)   the one in the corner

(3) (a)   a yellow one
    (b)   *a one

(4) (a)   my/your gold one
  (b)   %my/your one

(5) (a)   many/all old ones
  (b)   *many/all ones

(Dialectally, 'He's a one' can mean 'He's a strange person')

**Exercise XVI

    In examples (1) and (2) below, the bracketed NPs might be argued to be structurally ambiguous in respect of which nominal is modified by the italicised Adjunct PP. Draw Phrase-markers to show how this ambiguity could be represented (limiting yourself to the structure of the bracketed NPs, and ignoring the rest of the sentences). Which interpretation of each sentence proves problematic for the assumption made about Adjunct PPs in the text (i.e. that they expand N-bar into N-bar), and why?

(1)   I like [that picture of him *in his pushchair*]
(2)   [The workers and the managers *in the factory*] just don't get on

Suppose we were to redefine a nominal Adjunct as an expression which expands a nominal of a given type into another nominal of the same type (hence, expands N into N, or N-bar into N-bar, or NP into NP). Would this help us deal with the problems posed by the italicised Adjunct phrases in (1) and (2) above?

5
Other Phrases

5.1 Overview

In the previous chapter, we argued that there are 'small' nominal phrases larger than the Noun but smaller than the Noun Phrase. And accordingly, we argued that there are three types of nominal category in English, namely N, N-bar, and N-double-bar. Under the analysis presented there, a Noun Phrase such as that bracketed in (1) below:

(1)   John is [*a student of Physics*]

would have the structure (2) below:

(2)

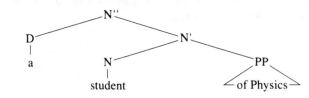

The overall sequence [*a student of Physics*] would thus have the status of a Noun Phrase (recall that N'' and NP are equivalent terms, and that the distinction we are drawing between them here is purely didactic: i.e. we use N'' for Phrases whose internal structure we show in detail, and NP for Phrases whose internal structure we omit in order to simplify exposition; we shall generalise this convention to other categories in the discussion which follows). In a structure such as (2), the Noun *student* is the *head* (i.e. key constituent) of the overall N'', in the sense that what makes an NP into a *Noun Phrase* (rather than a *Verb Phrase*) is the fact that it contains a head *Noun* (and not a head *Verb*). The head Noun *student* together with its Complement PP [*of Physics*] form a 'small nominal phrase' [*student of Physics*], called an N-bar. This N-bar together with the Determiner *a* form the N-double-bar (or full NP) constituent [*a student of Physics*].

Given that in an optimal theory of categories we should expect to find a broad structural symmetry across categories, we might hope that our conclusions about nominals in the previous chapter can be generalised to other types

226

of constituent as well. So, for example, we might expect to find that just as there are 'small nominal phrases' (= N-bar) larger than N but smaller than NP, so too there are 'small Adjectival Phrases' larger than A but smaller than AP; that there are 'small Adverbial Phrases' larger than ADV but smaller than ADVP; that there are 'small Prepositional Phrases' larger than P but smaller than PP; and that there are 'small Verb Phrases' larger than V but smaller than VP. And in fact, this is precisely what we are going to claim in this chapter. That is to say, we shall argue that all major word-level categories like Noun, Adjective, Adverb, Preposition and Verb have not just one, but rather *two* different types of phrasal expansion. More specifically, we shall argue that the internal structure of the bracketed NP in (1) – repeated as (3)(a) below – is paralleled by that of the bracketed AP in (3)(b) below, ADVP in (3)(c), PP in (3)(d), and VP in (3)(e):

(3) (a)   John is [NP a *student* of Physics]
    (b)   She is [AP very *proud* of her son]
    (c)   She discovered it [ADVP quite *independently* of me]
    (d)   The thief fell [PP right *out* of the window]
    (e)   You must [VP be *thinking* of her]

To prepare the way for our subsequent discussion, let's introduce some simple terminology. In each of the bracketed phrases in (3), the italicised constituent is the *Head* of the bracketed phrase, in an intuitively obvious sense. For example, the Noun *student* in (3)(a) is the Head of the bracketed Noun Phrase, precisely because what makes a Noun Phrase into a *Noun* Phrase (rather than e.g. a *Verb* Phrase) is the fact that it contains a *Noun*; in much the same way, the Adjective *proud* in (3)(b) is the Head of the bracketed Adjectival Phrase; the Adverb *independently* in (3)(c) is the Head of the bracketed Adverbial Phrase; the Preposition *out* in (3)(d) is the Head of the bracketed Prepositional Phrase; and the Verb *thinking* in (3)(e) is the Head of the bracketed Verb Phrase.

In addition, we shall say that the expression which follows the italicised item (= an *of*-phrase in all our examples in (3) above) functions as its *Complement*. So, for example, in (3)(a) the PP [*of Physics*] is the Complement of the head Noun *student*; in (3)(b) the PP [*of her son*] is the Complement of the Adjective *proud*; in (3)(c) the PP [*of me*] is the Complement of the Adverb *independently*; in (3)(d), the PP [*of the window*] is the Complement of the Preposition *out*; and in (3)(e) the PP [*of her*] is the Complement of the Verb *thinking*.

And finally, we shall also say that in each of the examples in (3) above, the item which precedes the italicised Head constituent functions as its *Specifier*:

thus, *a* is the *Specifier* of the Noun *student* in (3) (a); *very* is the Specifier of the Adjective *proud* in (3) (b); *quite* is the Specifier of the Adverb *independently* in (3) (c); *right* is the Specifier of the Preposition *out* in (3) (d); and *be* is the Specifier of the Verb *thinking* in (3) (e).

Given the terminology we have introduced here, we can say that all of the bracketed phrases in (3) above are of the schematic form (4) below:

(4)   Specifier + Head + Complement

Now, we have already argued in the case of Noun Phrases that a Head Noun together with its Complement form an N-bar; and that this N-bar together with its Specifier (= Determiner) forms an N-double-bar. Thus, if other types of Phrase have a parallel internal structure to Noun Phrases (as we shall argue in detail in this chapter), then we might extend our bar-analysis from Noun Phrases such as that bracketed in (3) (a) above to all the other bracketed Phrases in (3) above. For example, we might argue that in the case of (3) (b), *proud* is an A, *proud of her son* is a 'small' Adjectival Phrase which (by analogy with N') we might call an A' (= A-bar) constituent, and the overall phrase [*very proud of her son*] is an A'' (= A-double-bar) or 'full' Adjectival Phrase (= AP). And extending the parallel still further, we might go on to claim that in (3) (c) *independently* is an ADV, [*independently of me*] is an ADV' (= ADV-bar), and [*quite independently of me*] is an ADV'' (= ADV-double-bar); that in (3) (d) *out* is a P, [*out of the window*] is a P' (= P-bar), and [*right out of the window*] is a P'' (= P-double-bar); and finally, that in (3) (e) *thinking* is a V, [*thinking of her*] is a V' (V-bar), and [*be thinking of her*] is a V'' (= V-double-bar). Given these assumptions, the bracketed phrases in (3) above will have the skeletal constituent structure indicated in (5) below:

(5) (a)   [N'' a [N' [N student] of Physics]]
   (b)   [A'' very [A' [A proud] of her son]]
   (c)   [ADV'' quite [ADV' [ADV independently] of me]]
   (d)   [P'' right [P' [P out] of the window]]
   (e)   [V'' be [V' [V thinking] of her]]

The structural parallelism between the various different types of Phrase in (5) above is clearly so striking that we would like to be able to replace the *particular* statements we have made about the internal structure of specific types of Phrase (Noun Phrase, Adjectival Phrase, Verb Phrase, etc.) in (5) by a single more *general* statement about *all* types of Phrase. But how can we do this?

Well, what we need in order to generalise from the particular statements made in (5) about how categories can be built up into Phrases to a more general statement is some device which will enable us to talk not about *indi-*

vidual categories (e.g. Noun, Verb, Adjective, etc.), but rather about *all* categories in general. More technically, what we need is a *category variable* – that is, a symbol which can 'stand for' any category of a given type. So, let's introduce the symbol *X* as a category variable representing any word-level category: e.g. X stands for N, or A, or ADV, or P, or V, etc. We can then generalise the pattern in (5) above by saying that all Phrases have the schematic structure indicated in (6) below (note that we are simplifying our discussion for the time being by ignoring 'optional extras' such as Adjuncts and Attributes):

(6)
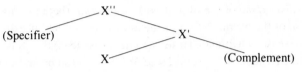

(Specifier)   X'

X   (Complement)

X here is a *category variable* which stands for any major word-level category like N(oun), V(erb), P(reposition), A(djective), ADV(erb) etc. 'Specifier' and 'Complement' are not categorial terms, but rather represent grammatical functions or relations; hence they have a similar status to terms such as 'Subject' and 'Object'. So, when we say that in a Noun Phrase such as [*a student of Physics*], the word *a* is a Determiner which functions as the Specifier of *student*, the word 'Specifier' is used to denote a grammatical function, whereas the word 'Determiner' is used to designate the category which *a* belongs to.

But why are there brackets round the Specifier and Complement in (6)? Well, these indicate that Specifier and Complement are *optional* constituents of a Phrase (recall from our discussion in the previous chapter that this means that they can be omitted from *some*, though not necessarily *all* Phrases, since there will obviously be complex conditions governing when they can and cannot be omitted). Phrases such as those bracketed in (7) below illustrate the optionality (in our sense) of Specifiers and Complements, since the bracketed Phrases contain a Head without either type of modifier:

(7) (a)   They are [N'' *students*]
    (b)   She is [A'' *proud*]
    (c)   She discovered it [ADV'' *independently*]
    (d)   The thief fell [P'' *out*]
    (e)   You must [V'' *think*]

Since the bracketed constituents in (7) above have the same distribution as their full-phrase counterparts in (3) above, they are assigned the same categorial status of full Phrases (i.e. of double-bar constituents), for reasons which should by now be boringly familiar to you (cf. section 2.7)!

In the generalised X-bar schema (6) above, the word-level category X is said to be the (*Immediate*) *Head* of the X-bar constituent containing X and its Complement. This X-bar is itself the (*Immediate*) *Head* of the X-double-bar constituent containing it and the Specifier Phrase. In addition, X may be said to be the *Ultimate Head* (or, less precisely, *Head*) of the overall X'' Phrase. Thus, perhaps rather irritatingly, the term 'Head' is used in two different senses, corresponding either to 'Immediate Head' or 'Ultimate Head'. So, for example, if you ask me: 'What is the Head of the Noun Phrase [*a student of Physics*], I could reply either 'The N-bar [*student of Physics*]' (because this is the *Immediate Head* of the overall NP), or '*student*' (because this is the *Ultimate Head* of the overall NP). For the most part, we shall use the term *Head* here in the sense of 'Ultimate Head', and hence say (e.g.) that N is the Head of N'', A is the Head of A'', V is the Head of V'' . . . and so on and so forth.

For reasons which should now be apparent, the overall Theory of Categories upon which our discussion in this chapter and the last is based is known as *X-bar Syntax*. Within this framework, any given simple word-level category X has two different types of phrasal expansion or *bar projection*, namely a single-bar projection into a 'small' X-bar Phrase, and a further double-bar projection into a 'large' X-double-bar Phrase. The terms X'' (= X-double-bar) and XP (= X-Phrase) are entirely equivalent from a theoretical viewpoint, and hence can be used interchangeably. However (as noted above), for expository convenience, we shall draw a simple didactic distinction between them here: in general, we shall use the label X'' for a constituent whose internal bar projection structure we show in some detail (and which we want to draw the reader's attention to), and the label XP for phrases whose internal structure we choose not to represent, and which we don't want the reader to pay undue attention to.

Well, by now I can tell from your fidgeting that you're beginning to suffer terminological traumas. What was that you wanted: 'Less of the theory, more of the facts'? OK, then: let's look at some of the facts which justify the claims made above. We'll begin by attempting to probe the internal structure of Verb Phrases: and we shall argue in some detail in support of positing a V-bar constituent larger than V but smaller than VP.

5.2   Verb Phrases

We'll begin our defence of the X-bar schema outlined in (6) above by looking at whether or not the schema in (6) is applicable to the analysis of Verb Phrases. In this connection, it is interesting to note that Ray Jackendoff – in what has become the classic work on X-bar Syntax, namely his (1977a) $\overline{X}$ *Syntax* book – argues that V and its Complements together form a V-bar con-

stituent, and that V-bar can be expanded by the addition of appropriate Specifiers (which he takes to be the Aspectual Auxiliaries *have/be*) into a V-double-
bar constituent. Given this assumption, the bracketed VP in (8) below:

(8)   John may [*be reading a book*]

might have a structure along the lines of (9) below (where ASP designates an
Aspectual Auxiliary):

(9)

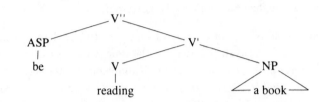

But what empirical evidence is there in favour of positing a V-bar constituent
larger than V, but smaller than VP?

Akmajian, Steele and Wasow (1979) point to a number of syntactic properties distinguishing V-bar from VP. For example, they note (p. 22) that only a
V-bar, not a whole VP can be fronted in the construction illustrated in (10)
below:

(10)   They swore that John might have been taking heroin, and

(a)   ... [V' *taking heroin*] he might have been!

(b)   *... [VP *been taking heroin*] he might have!

(c)   *... [VP *have been taking heroin*] he might!

Moreover, they argue (p. 40) that Verbs like *begin* and *see* subcategorise (i.e.
'take') a Complement containing a V-bar, not a full VP: cf.

(11) (a)   I saw John [V' *run down the road*]

(b)   *I saw him [VP *be running down the road*]

(c)   *I saw him [VP *have finished his work*]

Further empirical evidence in support of positing a category V-bar comes
from the fact that it turns out to have an important role to play in accounting
for the syntax of various types of verbal modifier. Consider first the question
of verbal postmodifiers. As in the case of NPs, we can draw an important distinction here between *Complements* (which expand X into X-bar) and
Adjuncts (which recursively expand X-bar into X-bar). The Complement/
Adjunct distinction is implicitly drawn (using rather different terminology) by
Chomsky in *Aspects* (1965, pp. 101–3), where he distinguishes between
'internal' postmodifiers (which show a strong degree of what he calls *cohesion*
to their governing Verb), and 'external' postmodifiers (which show less

cohesion to the Verb). For example, he argues that in sentences such as the (a) examples below, the bracketed PP is an 'internal' postmodifier, whereas in the corresponding (b) example it is an 'external' one:

(12) (a)   He will work [*at the job*] (= internal)
    (b)   He will work [*at the office*] (= external)

(13) (a)   He laughed [*at the clown*] (= internal)
    (b)   He laughed [*at ten o'clock*] (= external)

Within the X-bar framework we are using here (which had not yet been adopted in the Chomskyan paradigm at the time when *Aspects* was written) we can interpret *internal* as designating a Complement internal to the V-bar containing the head V, and *external* as designating an Adjunct external to the V-bar containing the head V. This would mean that (12) (a) and (b) above would have the respective structures (14) (a) and (b) below:

(14) (a)   [PP = internal = Complement]

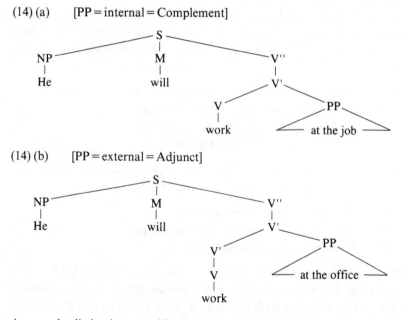

(14) (b)   [PP = external = Adjunct]

Any such distinction would presuppose that verbal Complements and Adjuncts are generated by two different Phrase Structure rules such as those in (15) below:

(15) (a)   V' → V' [Adjunct Rule]
    (b)   V' → V PP [Complement Rule]

Thus, Adjuncts would be sisters and daughters of V-bar, and Complements would be sisters of V, and daughters of V-bar. But what empirical evidence is there in support of the distinction between verbal *Complements* and *Adjuncts*?

One such argument can be formulated in relation to *structural ambiguity*: thus, consider the following examples (adapted from Chomsky (1965), p. 101, and Young (1984), p. 37):

(16) (a)   He may decide on the boat
    (b)   He couldn't explain last night

Within the X-bar framework, we can provide a principled account of the ambiguity in (16) in structural terms. Thus, in (16) (a) the PP *on the boat* may either be a Complement within the V-bar containing the head V (as in (17) (a) below), or an Adjunct outside the V-bar containing the head V (as in (17) (b) below):

(17) (a)

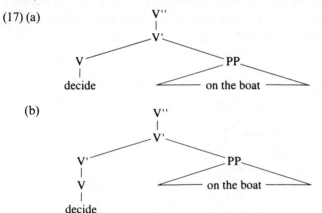

   (b)

Likewise, in (16) (b) the NP [*last night*] could either be a Complement NP expanding V into V-bar, or an Adjunct NP expanding V-bar into V-bar.

An interesting correlate of the *Complement/Adjunct* distinction is that an NP in a Complement PP can generally be passivised, whereas an NP in an Adjunct PP cannot: cf. the following contrasts:

(18) (a)   [*This job*] needs to be worked at by an expert
    (b)   *[*This office*] is worked at by a lot of people

(19) (a)   [*The clown*] was laughed at by everyone
    (b)   *[*Ten o'clock*] was laughed at by everyone

In this connection, it is interesting to note that in passive sentences such as (20) below:

(20) (a)   [*The boat*] was decided on after lengthy deliberation
    (b)   [*Last night*] couldn't be explained by anyone

the italicised NP can only correspond to an active *Complement*, not to an active *Adjunct*.

A further argument in support of drawing a structural distinction between verbal Complements and Adjuncts can be formulated in relation to *pro-nominalisation* facts. Jackendoff (1977a, p. 58) notes that the phrase *do so* appears to function as a pro-V-bar. In the light of this observation, consider the following contrast:

(21) (a)   John will buy [NP *the book*] [PP *on Tuesday*]
    (b)   John will put [NP *the book*] [PP *on the table*]

Superficially, both sentences seem to contain V-bar constituents of the schematic form [V NP PP]: and yet we might argue that whereas in the *put* example, both the NP and the PP are Complements, in the *buy* example by contrast the NP is a Complement but the PP is an Adjunct. This would mean that the two V-bars would have the respective structures:

(22) (a)

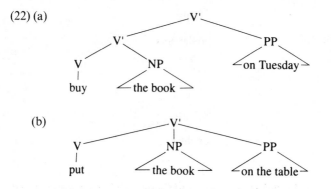

(b)

In the light of these structures, consider the following contrasts:

(23) (a)   John will [buy the book on Tuesday], and Paul will *do so* as well
    (b)   John will [buy the book] on Tuesday, and Paul will *do so* on Thursday

(24) (a)   John will [put the book on the table], and Paul will *do so* as well
    (b)   *John will [put the book] on the table, and Paul will *do so* on the chair

In (23), we see that the pro-V-bar *do so* can replace either [*buy the book on Tuesday*] or [*buy the book*], suggesting that both of these are V-bar constituents (precisely as we claim in (22) above); but in (24), *do so* can only replace the whole string [*put the book on the table*], not the substring [*put the book*], suggesting that the former and not the latter is a V-bar constituent (precisely as we claim in (22) above). Thus, the X-bar analysis makes exactly correct predictions about *do so* Pronominalisation facts.

A further argument in support of the distinction between verbal *Complements* and *Adjuncts* can be formulated in relation to *ordering* restrictions. As we have already seen in connection with our discussion of Complements and Adjuncts in Noun Phrases, the X-bar analysis predicts that Complements will always occur closer to their heads than Adjuncts. Our analysis thus predicts that in sentences such as (12) and (13) above, if the Complement Phrase and the Adjunct Phrase co-occur within the same VP, the Complement will precede the Adjunct. And as the examples below illustrate, this prediction is entirely correct:

(25) (a)   He worked [*at the job*] [*at the office*]
   (b)   *He worked [*at the office*] [*at the job*]

(26) (a)   He laughed [*at the clown*] [*at ten o'clock*]
   (b)   *He laughed [*at ten o'clock*] [*at the clown*]

You should be excruciatingly familiar with the logic of this type of argument by now, so I shall not elaborate further.

An additional argument in support of the distinction can be formulated in relation to *Co-occurrence Restrictions*. As we have already noted in our discussion of Noun Phrases in the previous chapter, Head categories impose *Subcategorisation* restrictions on the range of possible *Complements* they permit, but not on the range of *Adjuncts* with which they can occur. For example, only a restricted class of Verbs can be followed by an NP designating the person from whom some information is requested: cf.

(27) (a)   John asked [*the man next door*]
   (b)   *John inquired [*the man next door*]

This suggests that the italicised NP [*the man next door*] must be a Complement in cases like (27), since Subcategorisation restrictions hold between items and their Complements. By contrast, a temporal NP (i.e. time-phrase) such as [*yesterday afternoon*] can occur with an unrestricted choice of Verbs, as we see from (28) below:

(28)   John   died/sneezed/wept/exploded/apologised/laughed/escaped/
      defected/slept [*yesterday afternoon*]

The obvious conclusion to draw is that the NP [*yesterday afternoon*] must be an Adjunct in structures such as (28), since Verbs don't generally impose restrictions on Adjuncts.

Other Phrases

A related distinction is that (as noted by Jackendoff (1977a), p. 58) Complements tend to be (though are not always) *obligatory*, whereas Adjuncts are *always optional*: it follows from this that *obligatory* constituents must be Complements. In this connection, consider the following contrasts:

(29) (a) John treated [*Mary*] [*badly*] [LAST NIGHT]
 (b) John treated [*Mary*] [*badly*]
 (c) *John treated [*badly*] [LAST NIGHT]
 (d) *John treated [*Mary*] [LAST NIGHT]
 (e) *John treated [LAST NIGHT]

(NB: we are concerned here only with the Verb *treat* in the sense of 'behave towards', not in the sense of 'provide a treat for', or 'provide medical care for'.) The fact that the capitalised NP [LAST NIGHT] is optional here suggests (though doesn't prove) that it is an Adjunct; while conversely, the fact that an NP such as *Mary* and an ADVP such as *badly* are obligatory indicates that they are Complements.

Moreover, the distinction between the italicised Complements and the capitalised Adjunct in (29) above is supported by *ordering* facts: note that the capitalised Adjunct [LAST NIGHT] cannot be positioned between the two italicised Complements [*Mary*] and [*badly*] in (30) below:

(30) *John treated [*Mary*] [LAST NIGHT] [*badly*]

By now, you should be able to tell me why this is exactly what the X-bar analysis would predict! I'm crossing my fingers hoping that you can ... but *I'm not crossing my branches* (hint, hint!).

A further test distinguishing verbal Complements from Adjuncts can be formulated in relation to facts about Ellipsis. As Akmajian, Steele and Wasow (1979, p. 21) note, any phrasal expansion of V (i.e. V-bar, or VP) can undergo Ellipsis under appropriate discourse conditions, so that a V and all its Complements, with or without its Adjuncts can be ellipsed. So, for example, in (31) below.

(31) SPEAKER A: Who might be going to the cinema on Tuesday?
 SPEAKER B (i) : John might [b̶e̶ g̶o̶i̶n̶g̶ t̶o̶ t̶h̶e̶ c̶i̶n̶e̶m̶a̶ o̶n̶ T̶u̶e̶s̶d̶a̶y̶]
 SPEAKER B (ii): John might be [g̶o̶i̶n̶g̶ t̶o̶ t̶h̶e̶ c̶i̶n̶e̶m̶a̶ o̶n̶ T̶u̶e̶s̶d̶a̶y̶]

the whole VP [*be going to the cinema on Tuesday*] has been ellipsed in (31) (i), whereas only the V-bar [*going to the cinema on Tuesday*] has been ellipsed in (31) (ii). Now, in (31) (ii), the V has been ellipsed along with both the Complement PP [*to the cinema*], and the Adjunct PP [*on Tuesday*]. However, another

236

possibility, as (32) below shows, is for the Verb to be ellipsed along with its Complement but without its Adjunct:

(32)   SPEAKER A: Who might be going to the cinema when?
        SPEAKER B: John might be [g̸o̸i̸n̸g̸ ̸t̸o̸ ̸t̸h̸e̸ ̸c̸i̸n̸e̸m̸a̸] on Tuesday

Given the assumptions we are making here, we might argue that a VP such as [*be going to the cinema on Tuesday*] has the structure (33) below:

(33)

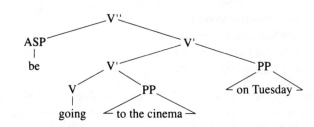

Thus, Speaker B's reply involves ellipsis of V'' in (31) (i), of the higher V' in (31) (ii), and of the lower V' in (32) (so showing that either V-bar or V-double-bar can undergo Ellipsis).

But now consider why Ellipsis is not possible in the following example (adapted from Culicover and Wilkins (1984), p. 27):

(34) (a)   Who will put the book where?
     (b)   *John will [p̸u̸t̸ ̸t̸h̸e̸ ̸b̸o̸o̸k̸] on the table

The answer becomes obvious if we look at the constituent structure of *John will put the book on the table*, namely

(35)

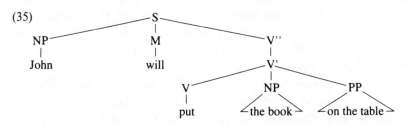

For, we see from (35) above that the sequence [*put the book*] which has been ellipsed in (34) is not even a constituent, let alone a V-bar or V-double-bar. So, what the contrast between (33) and (34) suggests is that [*on the table*] is a Complement of *put* in a sentence such as *John will put the book on the table*, whereas [*on Tuesday*] is an Adjunct in a sentence such as *John might be going to the cinema on Tuesday*.

A related (somewhat more subtle) argument in support of the *Complement/ Adjunct* distinction is formulated by Culicover and Wilkins (1984, pp. 29–30)

237

in relation to a type of Ellipsis known as GAPPING (so-called because it leaves a 'gap' in the middle of some Phrase or Clause). Quite frequently, the Verb of one Clause can be 'gapped' (= omitted) when it is identical to the Verb of another Clause. However, there are complex restrictions determining when GAPPING of the head of V of a VP is and is not permitted: for example, Culicover and Wilkins note that GAPPING is permitted in (36) (a) below, but not in (36) (b):

(36) (a)   John sells trucks on Thursdays,
            and Mary [s̶e̶l̶l̶s̶ cars] *on Fridays*
     (b)   *John put Fido in the doghouse,
            and Sam [p̶u̶t̶ Spot *in the yard*]

In both cases, GAPPING results in a VP with a 'missing' Verb followed by an NP PP sequence. And yet the result is grammatical in (36) (a), but ungrammatical in (36) (b). Why should this be? Culicover and Wilkins suggest that the answer is connected to the fact that the italicised PP in (36) (a) is an Adjunct which is external to the bracketed V-bar, whereas the italicised PP in (36) (b) is a Complement which is internal to the bracketed V-bar; and they suggest a restriction on GAPPING essentially along the following lines:

(37)   GAPPING of a V may not leave more than one Complement of V within the containing V-bar

(36) (a) does not violate this restriction, since only a single constituent (the NP *cars*) remains inside the bracketed V-bar after GAPPING; but (36) (b) violates the restriction, since two separate constituents (the NP *Spot* and the PP [*in the yard*]) remain within the bracketed V-bar after GAPPING. The significance of these observations for us is that they provide independent motivation for our assumption that the PP [*on Fridays*] is an Adjunct in (36) (a), whereas the PP [*in the yard*] is a Complement in (36) (b).

A further argument in support of the Complement/Adjunct distinction (adapted from Culicover and Wilkins (1984), pp. 27–8) can be formulated in relation to the distribution of *emphatic reflexives*. Consider the following contrast:

(38) (a)   John will bake [the cake] *himself* [for the party]
     (b)   *John will put [the candles] *himself* [on the cake]

In (38) (a), the emphatic reflexive *himself* can be positioned between the NP [*the cake*] and the PP [*for the party*]; but in (38) (b), it is not possible for *himself* to be positioned between the NP [*the candles*] and the PP [*on the cake*]. Why should this be? An obvious answer would be to suggest that this is because of structural differences between the two sentences: that is, we might suggest that the PP [*for the party*] in the (a) example is an Adjunct, whereas the PP [*on the cake*] in the (b) example is a Complement. This would mean that the two VPs [*bake the cake for the party*] and [*put the candles on the cake*] have the respective structures (39) (a) and (b) below:

(39) (a)

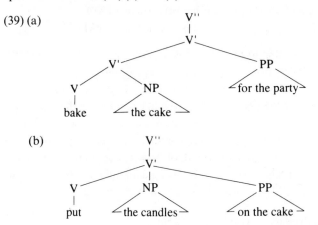

(b)

We might then suggest that a restriction to the effect that *emphatic reflexives* cannot occur as sisters to V (though can occur as sisters of V-bar). This would account for the contrast between (38) (a) and (b) in ways which should be apparent to you. Once again, the key spin-off of this argument is that it provides us with empirical evidence that [*for the party*] is a PP Adjunct in (38) (a), whereas [*on the cake*] is a PP Complement in (38) (b).

Since by now you are probably beginning to yawn (perhaps you've even reached the double-bar yawn stage!), I shall say no more about the various different types of verbal postmodifier. Instead, let me turn briefly to say a few words about verbal *premodifiers*. Since English generally lacks preverbal Complements, we might expect to find a distinction between *Attributes* and *Specifiers*. We defined Attributes in the previous chapter as 'Premodifiers which expand X-bar into X-bar'; so we might ask whether there are any verbal Attributes which expand V-bar into V-bar. It is interesting to note in this connection that attributive Adjectival Phrases used to premodify nominals have Adverbial counterparts used to premodify the corresponding verbal expressions: cf.

(40) (a)   his [*desperate*] search for her (AP)
     (b)   He [*desperately*] searched for her (ADVP)

(41) (a)   his [*complete*] adoration of her (AP)
     (b)   He [*completely*] adores her (ADVP)

Moreover, the *Selection Restrictions* holding between AP and N in such cases parallel those holding between ADVP and V: cf.

(42) (a) his [*utter*/**high*] rejection of the accusation (AP)
     (b) He [*utterly*/**highly*] rejected the accusation (ADVP)

(43) (a) their [*high*/**utter*] praise for her performance (AP)
     (b) They [*highly*/**utterly*] praised her performance (ADVP)

So, it would seem plausible to posit that just as AP can attributively modify N-bar, so too ADVP can attributively modify V-bar.

Moreover, if we follow Jackendoff (1977a, p. 54) in positing that the Aspectual Auxiliaries (progressive *be* and perfective *have*) are verbal Specifiers which expand V-bar into V-double-bar, then our analysis of attributive Adverbials (such as *completely, utterly*, etc.) predicts that such expressions can only be positioned to the immediate left of V-bar, not to the left of the Aspectual Specifiers of V-bar. And the following data (adapted from Jackendoff (1972), p. 76) provide empirical confirmation of this prediction:

(44) (a) George will have *completely* read the book
     (b) ?*George will *completely* have read the book
     (c) *George *completely* will have read the book

From (44), we see that *completely* can only idiomatically be positioned to the immediate left of the V-bar [*read the book*]. But these ordering restrictions would follow automatically from the twin assumptions that (i) Adverbials like *completely* are V-bar attributes which expand V-bar into V-bar, and (ii) that Aspectuals are verbal Specifiers. For, under this analysis, (44) (a) would have the structure (45) below:

(45)

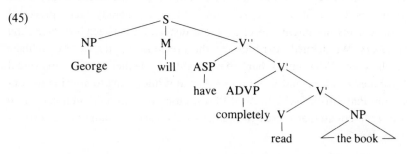

and the 'no crossing branches' restriction would determine that *completely* can only be positioned between *have* and *read*, given the assumptions we are making here. And this prediction is entirely correct, as we see from (44) above. Thus, Jackendoff's analysis of Aspectual Auxiliaries as Specifiers which expand V-bar into V-double-bar seems to have some empirical support (though we should point out that by no means all X-bar syntacticians are happy to treat *Aspectuals* as Specifiers which expand V-bar into V-double-bar: some prefer to treat them as Verbs which head their own VP, for reasons which you can work out for yourself when you come to Exercise VII).

Now, bearing in mind that, as we saw in the previous chapter, many Attributes can also function as Adjuncts (so that we have alternations such as 'the greatest *imaginable* insult'/'the greatest insult *imaginable*'), we might expect to find that Adverbials like *completely* can be adjoined not only to the left of V-bar (and hence function as Attributes), but also to the right of V-bar (and hence function as Adjuncts). And as (46) below shows, this is indeed the case:

(46) (a)   George will have read the book *completely*

    (b)   *George will have read *completely* the book

If *completely* is a V-bar adjunct in (46), then (46) (a) will have the structure (47) below:

(47)

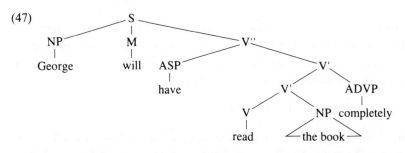

And in (47) – just as in (45) above – the Adverbial *completely* expands V-bar into V-bar. This shows up an inaccuracy of our earlier analysis of Adverbs like *completely* in Chapter 2, where we referred to them as *VP Adverbs*; within the more sophisticated X-bar Theory of Categories we have now developed, we can describe them more accurately as *V-bar Adverbs* – i.e. as Adverbs which function as Verbal Attributes or Adjuncts.

> **You should now be able to tackle exercise I**

5.3 Adjectival Phrases

Having looked at the structure of NPs in some detail in the previous chapter, and having attempted to unravel the internal complexities of VPs in some detail in section 5.2, let's turn briefly to look at the internal structure of APs (= Adjectival Phrases). Given the assumptions we are making about the structural symmetry between different Phrase types, we should expect to find that A can be expanded into A-bar by the addition of a set (possibly null) of Complements; that A-bar can be recursively expanded into A-bar by following Adjuncts or preceding Attributes; and that A-bar can be expanded into A-double-bar by the addition of appropriate Specifiers. We shall suggest that all of these assumptions are correct.

To get our discussion on a concrete footing, let's consider the structure of the bracketed AP in (48) below:

(48)   John isn't [*that fond of Mary*]

We shall suggest that this has the structure (49) below:

(49)

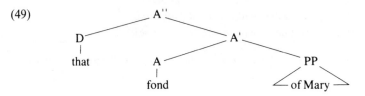

D here is our familiar category of Determiner. The range of Determiners which can modify an A-bar thus overlaps (in part, at least) with the range of Determiners which can modify an N-bar: not only *that*, but also *this* can be used to modify an A-bar as well as an N-bar: cf.

(50)   It was [$_{A''}$ *this* [$_{A'}$ [$_A$ big]]]

(Recall our arguments in the previous chapter that an X without a Complement has the status of an X-bar, so that *big* is not just A here, but also A-bar.) Likewise *more* and *less* can quantify both N-bar and A-bar, as (51) below illustrates:

(51) (a)   John shows [$_{N''}$ more/less [$_{N'}$ *indulgence to Mary*]] than he should do
     (b)   John is [$_{A''}$ more/less [$_{A'}$ *indulgent to Mary*]] than he should be

However, the overlap is only a partial one, since Adjectival and Nominal Determiners are often disjoint (i.e. different in distribution) in English: for example, *very* can be used to modify an A-bar, but not an N-bar: cf.

(52) (a)   He wasn't [$_{A''}$ very [$_{A'}$ *kind to Mary*]]
     (b)   *He didn't show [$_{N''}$ very [$_{N'}$ *kindness to Mary*]]

By contrast, *much* is the kind of Determiner which is used to modify an N-bar, but not an A-bar in English: cf.

(53) (a)   He didn't show [$_{N''}$ much [$_{N'}$ *kindness to Mary*]]
     (b)   *He wasn't [$_{A''}$ much [$_{A'}$ *kind to Mary*]]

Thus, we might say that *very* (and perhaps also *as, so, how, quite, too,* etc.) is an Adjectival Specifier in English (i.e. it is the kind of Determiner which can modify an A-bar), whereas *much* is a Nominal Specifier (i.e. it is the kind of Determiner which can modify an N-bar). It is interesting to note that in some languages, the same word can serve both functions (cf. e.g. Italian *molto,* which corresponds both to English *very* and to English *much*) – thus confirming the essential similarity of function (= that of Specifier of an X-bar) between the two types of Determiner. Of course, as we pointed out earlier, this is also true of some Determiners in English – for example, *more* and *less.*

But let's return to (49) above, and ask what evidence is there that the PP [*of Mary*] is a Complement of the Adjective *fond,* and hence that [*fond of Mary*] is an A-bar constituent in (49). Well, for one thing, note that the *of*-phrase in (49) is obligatory – hence the ungrammaticality of (54) below:

(54)   *John isn't [$_{AP}$ *that fond*]

Now, since it is a property of Complements (not Adjuncts) that they may be obligatory, then it seems clear that [*of Mary*] must be the Complement of *fond* in (49), and hence that [*fond of Mary*] must constitute an A-bar. Moreover, further evidence in support of this assumption comes from Coordination facts: cf.

(55)   John is [$_{A''}$ very [$_{A'}$ *fond of Mary*] and [$_{A'}$ *proud of her*]]

In (55) above the sequence [*fond of Mary*] has undergone Ordinary Coordination with the string [proud of her], thus suggesting that both are constituents of the same type – i.e. both are A-bar constituents.

Furthermore, the whole sequence [*fond of Mary*] can be replaced by the proform *so,* as in:

(56)   John used to be very [$_{A'}$ *fond of Mary*], but now he is much less *so*

On the assumption that only a unitary constituent can be replaced by a proform, then it seems clear that [*fond of Mary*] in (56) must be a 'Small Adjectival Phrase', viz. an A-bar. It also seems clear that *so* functions as a pro-A-bar in (56).

We suggested in our discussion of NPs and VPs that there are two types of Postmodifier, namely (i) *Complements* which expand X into X-bar, and (ii) *Adjuncts* which expand X-bar into X-bar. Now we might wonder whether the same distinction holds in the case of APs. We shall suggest here that it does, and that in an AP such as:

(57)   fond [pp *of Mary*] [pp *in some ways*]

the first PP [*of Mary*] functions as a Complement, whereas the second PP [*in some ways*] functions as an Adjunct, so that the overall AP has the structure (58) below:

(58)

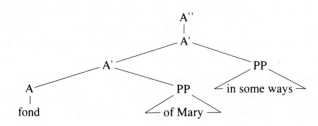

Evidence from PREPOSING in *though*-clauses suggests that the whole structure in (58) may function as a unitary AP constituent: cf.

(59)   [*Fond of Mary in some ways*] though he is, he doesn't really love her

But within this AP, what reason is there to suppose that the *of*-phrase is a Complement, and the *in*-phrase an Adjunct?

Well, for one thing, the *of*-phrase has the typical Complement property of being obligatory (as we have already seen), whereas the *in*-phrase has the typical Adjunct property of being optional:

(60) (a)   *fond [*in some ways*]
     (b)   fond [*of Mary*]

Moreover, note that the unmarked (i.e. normal) word-order is for the *of*-phrase to precede the *in*-phrase, in keeping with our earlier observation that Complements must occur closer to their heads than Adjuncts: cf.

(61) (a)   fond [*of Mary*] [*in some ways*]
     (b)   ??fond [*in some ways*] [*of Mary*]

Even more significant is the fact that both the A-bar constituents in (58) above – viz. [*fond of Mary*] and [*fond of Mary in some ways*] – can be proformed by the pro-A-bar *so*, as we see from the examples in (62) below:

(62) (a)   John is [A″ very [A′ [A′ *fond of Mary*] in some ways]], but is
            [A″ less [A′ [A′ *so*] in other ways]]
     (b)   John is [A″ very [A′ [A′ *fond of Mary*] *in some ways*]], but is
            [A″ less [A′ *so*]] than he used to be

Thus, there seems to be strong empirical support for the distinction we have drawn here between two different kinds of adjectival Postmodifier – viz. *Complements* (which are sisters of A and daughters of A-bar), and *Adjuncts* (which are both sisters and daughters of A-bar).

But what about adjectival *Premodifiers*? Now, since Adjectives in English do not permit preceding *Complements*, we should expect to find two types of adjectival Premodifier – *Attributes* and *Specifiers*. Given the obvious parallelism between APs such as those bracketed in (63) (a) below and their bracketed ADVP counterparts in (63) (b):

(63) (a)   [$_{AP}$ *complete/utter*] fools
     (b)   [$_{ADVP}$ *completely/utterly*] foolish

we might suggest that just as APs can be used as Attributes expanding N-bar into N-bar, so too the corresponding ADVPs can be used as Attributes expanding A-bar into A-bar. In other words, we might handle examples such as (63) (b) above in terms of an optional rule such as (64) below:

(64)   A' → ADVP A' [Adjectival Attribute Rule: *optional*]

Now, since rule (64) is recursive, it predicts that ADVPs of the appropriate class can be recursively stacked on top of A-bar constituents: and the grammaticality of sentences such as (65) below shows that this prediction is correct:

(65)   He was *severely directly personally* [$_{A'}$ critical of the President]

Thus our analysis of adjectival Attributes has strong empirical support.

Moreover, the analysis also makes an interesting prediction about *word-order* facts. Now, given that adjectival Determiners (like *that, this, very, too, so, quite, more*) expand A-bar into A-double-bar, but that adjectival Attributes expand A-bar into A-bar, we should expect that (as in the case of Noun Phrases) Attributes will always occur closer to their head Adjective than Determiners: and as (66) below illustrates, this is indeed so:

(66) (a)   [$_D$ *so*] [$_{ADVP}$ *utterly*] incompetent
     (b)   *[$_{ADVP}$ *utterly*] [$_D$ *so*] incompetent

So, once more, our analysis of Adjectival Phrases is vindicated!

Given the close relationship between Adjectives and Adverbs (recall that in section 3.6 we argued that Adverbs are positional variants of Adjectives), we should obviously expect that ADVPs will have a similar internal structure to the corresponding APs. Accordingly, we might argue that in the bracketed ADVP in (67) below:

(67)   He made up his mind [*quite independently of me*]

245

the Head of the Phrase is the ADV *independently*; this together with its PP complement [*of me*] forms an ADV-bar constituent, which in turn is expanded into an ADV-double-bar by the addition of the Determiner *quite*. Given these assumptions, the bracketed Phrase in (67) would have a structure along the lines of (68) below:

(68)

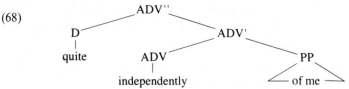

And if, as we argued in Chapter 3, Adverbs are reincarnations (or do I mean *mutations*?) of Adjectives, then we should expect that Adverbs will permit the same range of Determiners as Adjectives: and as (69) below illustrates, this is indeed the case:

(69) (a)   Her work is *very/quite/so/too/rather* careless
(b)   She works *very/quite/so/too/rather* carelessly

Bearing in mind that *so* can quantify both an A-bar and an ADV-bar, you should now be able to see for yourself that our earlier example (66) (a) *so utterly incompetent* is structurally ambiguous as between whether *so* quantifies the A-bar [*utterly incompetent*], or the ADV-bar *utterly*.

You should now be able to tackle exercise II

5.4 Prepositional Phrases

The final phrasal category we shall look at are PPs (Prepositional Phrases). Once more, these seem directly amenable to an X-bar analysis. For example, we might argue that the bracketed PP below:

(70)   Put it [*right on the top shelf*]

is headed by the P *on*, and that together with its NP complement [*the top shelf*] it forms a P-bar constituent; and this in turn is expanded into a P-double-bar by the addition of the Determiner *right*. If these assumptions are correct, then the bracketed PP in (70) would have the structure (71) below:

(71)

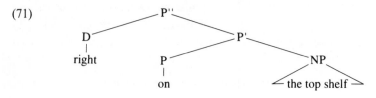

Support for the postulation of a P-bar constituent in (71) comes from *Pronominalisation* facts: thus, note that the P-bar [*on the top shelf*] can be replaced by the proform *there*, so that alongside (70) we have (72) below:

(72)   Put it [*right there*]

Thus, we might posit that *there* functions as a (locative) pro-P-bar constituent.

Further support for the postulation of a P-bar constituent comes from *Coordination* facts: for, note that in structures such as (73) below, the two italicised P-bar constituents can be conjoined in such a way that the resulting coordinate P-bar can be modified by *right*:

(73)   The vase fell [p'' right [p' *off the table*] and [p' *onto the floor*]]

Thus, our postulation of an 'intermediate' P-bar constituent larger than P but smaller than PP has some empirical support.

However, bearing in mind that (as we have already seen) single-bar constituents such as N-bar, V-bar, and A-bar can be expanded into another constituent of the same type by the addition of Adjuncts or Attributes, we might expect to find that P-bar constituents too can be expanded into another P-bar by the addition of an Adjunct or Attribute. And this does indeed seem to be the case. For, just as an Adverb such as *completely* can function as a V-bar or A-bar Attribute/Adjunct, so too it can also function as a P-bar Attribute/Adjunct, and thus modify a P-bar such as [*in the wrong*]: cf.

(74) (a)   He was [*completely* in the wrong]
     (b)   He was [in the wrong *completely*]

The P-bar status of [*in the wrong*] here is confirmed by the fact that it can be replaced by the proform *so*: cf.

(75)   He was [partly *in the wrong*], and perhaps completely *so*

Moreover, the analysis of *completely* as a P-bar Attribute/Adjunct expanding P-bar into P-bar correctly predicts that it will always be positioned closer to the head P than the type of Determiner which expands P-bar into P-double-bar – e.g. *so*: cf.

(76) (a)   He was [*so completely* in the wrong]
     (b)   *He was [*completely so* in the wrong]

Given the assumptions we are making here, then (76) (a) – on the relevant interpretation – will have the structure (77) below:

(77)

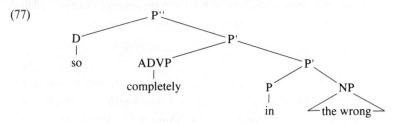

And the 'no crossing branches' restriction will determine that the Specifier *so* must precede the Attribute *completely*. (Of course, (76) (a) also has a second interpretation, on which *so* modifies *completely*, and the whole ADVP [*so completely*] functions as the Attribute of [*in the wrong*].)

Bearing in mind that (as we have seen in the last chapter and this) Prepositional Phrases can function as Adjuncts to N-bar, V-bar, and A-bar constituents, we might expect to find that PPs can also function as Adjuncts to P-bar constituents. And we might suppose that this is precisely the function which the italicised PP [*with his friends*] fulfils in (78) below – namely that of an Adjunct to the P-bar *at odds*:

(78)   He is [less at odds *with his friends*] now

If this is so, then the bracketed PP in (78) would have the structure (79) below:

(79)

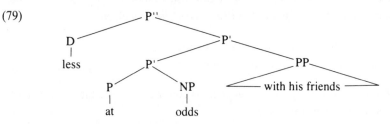

Some support for the structure posited in (79) comes from *Pronominalisation* facts: for, note that both the 'smaller' P-bar [*at odds*], and the 'larger' P-bar [*at odds with his friends*] can be replaced by the pro-P-bar *so*, in an appropriate discourse setting: cf.

(80) (a)   I know that he's [*at odds*] with his colleagues, but he's less *so* with his friends

     (b)   I know that he always used to be [*at odds with his friends*], but he's less *so* these days

Thus, our claim that PP can function as a P-bar Adjunct has strong empirical support.

Now, if we are right in claiming that Adverbials like *completely* can function as P-bar Attributes/Adjuncts, and that Prepositional Phrases can function as P-bar Adjuncts, then since both types of constituent expand P-bar into P-bar, we should expect that the two can be stacked on top of each other in either order. What this means in practical terms is that the bracketed PP in a sentence such as:

(81)   He is [*completely at odds with his friends*]

should be structurally ambiguous as between whether *completely* modifies the simple P-bar [*at odds*], or whether it modifies the complex P-bar [*at odds with his friends*]. In other words, we should expect the bracketed PP in (81) to have either of the structures in (82) below:

(82) (a)

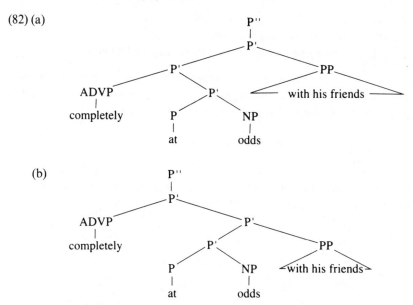

(b)

We can use *Pronominalisation* facts to support this claim: cf.

(83) (a)   He's slightly [*at odds*] with his colleagues, but completely *so* with his friends
     (b)   He used to be only slightly [*at odds with his friends*], but now he's completely *so*

The significance of examples such as (83) should by now be painfully obvious to you ... If not, take a break!

Interesting confirmation of our analysis comes from the fact that when *completely* is used as an Adjunct (and hence follows the P-bar it modifies), we find that it can be positioned either immediately after the simple P-bar [*at odds*], or after the complex P-bar [*at odds with his friends*]: cf.

(84) (a)   He is [at odds] *completely* with his friends
     (b)   He is [at odds with his friends] *completely*

And this is – of course – precisely what our analysis would have led us to expect.

It thus seems clear from our discussion above that PPs can function as prepositional Adjuncts (i.e. Adjuncts which expand P-bar into P-bar). However, you may recall (What! You mean you've forgotten already?) that we argued in Chapter 3 that some Prepositions subcategorise (i.e. take) PP complements: for example, in (85) below:

(85) (a)   He stayed at home *because* [of the strike]
     (b)   He fell *out* [of the window]
     (c)   Few people *outside* [of the immediate family] know

the italicised Preposition has a PP complement (= the bracketed *of*-phrase). This means that PPs can function both as prepositional Complements and as prepositional Adjuncts. For example, in a sentence such as:

(86)   He is [so out *of touch* IN SOME WAYS]

we might argue that the italicised PP is a Complement of the Preposition *out*, whereas the capitalised PP is an Adjunct. If this is so, then the bracketed PP in (86) would have the structure (87) below:

(87)

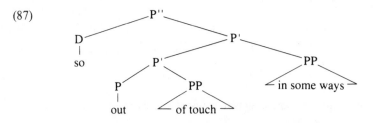

Now, bearing in mind that the 'no crossing branches' restriction requires Complements to be positioned closer to their heads than Adjuncts, an analysis such as (87) correctly predicts that the Complement PP [*of touch*] must be positioned before the Adjunct PP [*in some ways*]. And the grammaticality of (86) above taken together with the ungrammaticality of (88) below:

(88)   *He is [so out IN SOME WAYS *of touch*]

provides striking confirmation of our claim.

Thus far, we have said little about prepositional *Specifiers*. Van Riemsdijk (1978, pp. 45–8) claims that a wide range of different phrase types can function as Specifiers of PP: he would maintain that in examples such as (89–92) below, each of the bracketed NP, AP, ADVP, and PP constituents functions as the Specifier of the following (italicised) P + NP sequence:

(89) (a)   They found the dead miners [NP two miles] *under the surface*
   (b)   They held a reunion [NP twenty years] *after the war*

(90) (a)   The rabbit burrowed [AP quite deep] *under the surface*
   (b)   The bodyguards stood [AP really close] *behind him*

(91) (a)   He disappeared [ADVP immediately] *before the drugs raid*
   (b)   He died [ADVP very shortly] *after the operation*

(92) (a)   I found it [PP up] *in the attic*
   (b)   You must have left it [PP down] *in the cellar*

If indeed Prepositions can be used as Specifiers of P-bar (e.g. in examples such as (92) above), then (as Van Riemsdijk (1982), pp. 57–60 notes) in some 'multiple Preposition' sequences, it may not be immediately obvious whether a given Preposition functions as a Head or as a Specifier. In this connection, it is interesting to contrast the italicised PPs in the following pair of examples:

(93) (a)   The dispute dates *from before the war*
   (b)   I've put your books *over in the corner*

In both examples, it seems clear that the second Preposition (*before/in*) functions as a Head which takes an NP complement (*the war/the corner*), so that the sequences [*before the war*] and [*in the corner*] are P-bar constituents headed by the Prepositions they contain (*before/in*). But what is less clear is whether the first Preposition (*from/over*) functions as a Specifier which takes a P-bar complement, or as a Head which takes a PP complement. What we shall claim here is that the Preposition *from* in (93) (a) functions as a Head, whereas the Preposition *over* in (93) (b) functions as a Specifier. Let's examine this claim in rather more detail.

What we are claiming here about (93) (a) is that *from* is the Head of the overall italicised PP, and that it takes as its Complement another PP [*before the war*] (which is itself headed by the Preposition *before*), so that (93) (a) has the structure (94) overleaf:

(94)

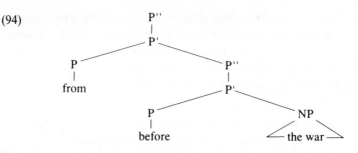

This seems right for several reasons. For one thing, note that *from* is not an optional constituent of the italicised PP in (93) (a), as we see from the ungrammaticality of (95) below:

(95)   *The dispute dates *before the war*

Now, bearing in mind that Specifiers are generally optional whereas Heads are not, the obvious conclusion to draw from (95) is that *from* is a Head, and not a Specifier. Moreover, analysing *from* as the Head of a complex PP would be consistent with known *subcategorisation* facts (i.e. facts about the range of complements which a given item permits), since we have independent evidence from examples like (96) below that the Verb *date* (in the relevant sense) subcategorises (i.e. 'takes') a PP complement headed by *from*:

(96)   The dispute dates [PP *from the time of World War I*]

So, *subcategorisation* facts argue in favour of treating *from* as a Head, not as a Specifier. Moreover, the *before*-phrase can take its own Specifier, as we see from the examples below, where the Specifier is italicised:

(97) (a)   The dispute dates from [*right* before the war]
     (b)   The dispute dates from [*several years* before the war]

If we assume that Phrases can generally have only one Specifier, it follows that if the italicised constituents in (97) above function as the Specifiers of the *before*-phrase, then the Preposition *from* cannot have the same Specifier function.

However, we claim here that the italicised PP in (93) (b) 'I've put your books *over in the corner*' has a very different structure. More precisely, the Preposition *over* functions as a Specifier of the following P-bar [*in the corner*], so that the italicised PP in (93) (b) has the structure (98) below:

(98)

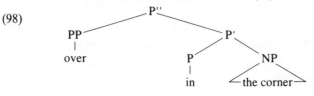

There are several facts which support our claim that *over* here functions as a Specifier of the following P-bar. For one thing, note that *over* is optional in this example, as typical Specifiers generally are: cf.

(99)   I've put your books *in the corner*

Furthermore, the presence of *over* excludes the presence of another prepositional Specifier such as *right*: cf.

(100)   *I've put your books *over right in the corner*

And in addition, *over* can take a Complement of its own, such as that italicised in (101) below:

(101)   I've put your books [over *there* in the corner]

– a fact which strongly suggests that [*in the corner*] is not the Complement of *over* in (101). Thus, we see that there is strong empirical support for our earlier claim that the first Preposition in the italicised PP is a Head in (93) (a), but a Specifier in (93) (b).

   To summarise this section: we have argued that like other word-level categories, Prepositions have two phrasal expansions. More precisely, a P together with its NP, PP, or Clause complement forms a P-bar constituent, which in turn can be expanded into a P-double-bar by the addition of a Specifier such as *right*, *so*, etc. We also argued that Adverbials like *completely* can function as P-bar Attributes or Adjuncts (which expand P-bar into P-bar), and that PPs can function as Complements, Adjuncts, or Specifiers of other prepositional constituents.

You should now be able to tackle exercise III

5.5   Cross-categorial structural symmetry

   We can summarise the overall claims made so far in this chapter and the last about the internal structure of Phrases in the following terms. We have argued that there is broad structural symmetry across categories insofar as all major lexical categories (e.g. N, V, P, A, ADV) permit two types of phrasal expansion. More particularly, any head lexical category X can be expanded into an X-bar by the addition of a set of Complements; and X-bar can be expanded into X-double-bar by the addition of a Specifier/Determiner. Thus, the 'basic' structure of Phrases (if we exclude 'optional extras' such as

Attributes and Adjuncts) is of the schematic form (102) below:

(102)

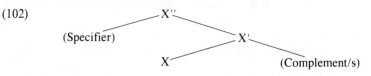

(Recall that *Specifier* and *Complement* are functional, not categorial terms). This cross-categorial structural symmetry can be demonstrated by two simple facts. Firstly, some types of Prepositional Phrase can function as Complements to any major lexical category: for example, we saw in relation to our earlier examples (3) above – repeated as (103) below – that a PP headed by *of* can function as the complement of an N, A, ADV, P, or V: cf.

(103) (a)   John is a *student* [of Physics] (N + PP)
   (b)   She is very *proud* [of her son] (A + PP)
   (c)   She discovered it quite *independently* [of me] (ADV + PP)
   (d)   The thief fell right *out* [of the window] (P + PP)
   (e)   You must be *thinking* [of her] (V + PP)

And secondly, some types of Determiner in English (e.g. Demonstratives such as *this/that*) can act as Specifiers for any major single-bar category. For example, *that* (in my idiolect) can be used to premodify an N', A', ADV', P', or V', as we see from (104) below:

(104) (a)   I don't like *that* [$_{N'}$ picture of you]
   (b)   I'm not *that* [$_{A'}$ fond of pasta]
   (c)   She doesn't act *that* [$_{ADV'}$ independently of you]
   (d)   She's not *that* [$_{P'}$ in demand]
   (e)   I don't *that* [$_{V'}$ dislike her]

Thus, the degree of symmetry between categories would appear to be quite striking.

However, the simplified picture painted in (102) above is complicated by the fact that in addition to Complements and Specifiers, we have to recognise a third type of modifier – namely *Attributes* and *Adjuncts*. Although (following tradition) we have distinguished between *Adjuncts* and *Attributes* here, the difference between the two seems to be largely terminological, since both have the same constituent function of recursively expanding X-bar into X-bar. Moreover, the only real distinction we drew between them was that Attributes precede and Adjuncts follow the X-bar constituents they modify. Yet even this distinction seems a tenuous one, for the simple reason that many types of modifier can occur in both positions. For example (as we pointed out in

Chapter 4) prenominal attributive APs have obvious postnominal counterparts, as we see from the italicised APs in (105) below:

(105) (a)   a *very pretty* [photographic model]
(b)   a [photographic model] *pretty as a picture*

And likewise (as we saw earlier in this chapter), postverbal Adjuncts often have preverbal counterparts: hence the italicised ADVP in (106) below can either precede or follow the bracketed V-bar:

(106) (a)   He doesn't [take her there] *very often*
(b)   He doesn't *very often* [take her there]

So, it seems likely that *Adjuncts* and *Attributes* are one and the same thing. I leave to you the task of devising a suitable cover term to subsume both functions. (I hope you'll come up with something less horrific than *Attrunct* or *Adjibute!*)

The essence of an *Adjunct/Attribute* is that it is an expression which expands a constituent of a given type into another constituent of the same type. Hitherto, we have been assuming that all Adjuncts/Attributes are single-bar modifiers (i.e. they recursively expand X-bar into X-bar). However, we leave open the possibility that there may be different types of Adjunct/Attribute which attach at different categorial levels (i.e. there may also be double-bar Adjuncts/Attributes which expand X-double-bar into X-double-bar, and perhaps even word-level Adjuncts/Attributes which expand X into X). These possibilities might be schematised as in (107) below:

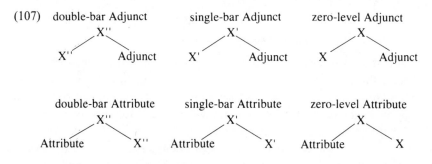

For example, we might suppose that the word *even* can function as a double-bar Attribute or Adjunct which can optionally expand NP into NP, PP into PP, AP into AP, ADVP into ADVP, and VP into VP: cf.

(108) (a)   [$_{NP}$ Even [$_{NP}$ the older residents]] were surprised
(b)   [$_{NP}$ [$_{NP}$ the older residents] even] were surprised

255

(109) (a)   [PP Even [PP right at the top]] life is hard
    (b)   [PP [PP right at the top] even] life is hard

(110) (a)   He was very fond of his sister, and [AP even [AP very fond of his brother]]
    (b)   He was very fond of his sister, and [AP [AP very fond of his brother] even]

(111) (a)   He defended her loyally, and [ADVP even [ADVP quite courageously]]
    (b)   He defended her loyally, and [ADVP [ADVP quite courageously] even]

(112) (a)   He might [VP even [VP have got lost]]
    (b)   He might [VP [VP have got lost] even]

So, the suggestion that there may be a class of double-bar Adjuncts and Attributes seems a plausible one.

But is it plausible to posit a class of word-level Adjuncts or Attributes which expand X into X? Perhaps it is. One possible candidate for membership of such a class would be the word *enough*. In one of its many functions, it can serve to postmodify adjectival constituents: cf.

(113)   He is [AP competent *enough*]

But what is the function of *enough* in this kind of structure? One obvious suggestion would be that *enough* is an A-bar Adjunct which expands A-bar into A-bar. However, word-order facts such as those in (114) below appear to contradict this assumption:

(114) (a)   He isn't [AP proud *enough* OF HIS COUNTRY]
    (b)   *He isn't [AP proud OF HIS COUNTRY *enough*]

For reasons which we gave in section 5.3, it is clear that the capitalised phrase here is the Complement of the Adjective *proud*. But since Complements are positioned closer to their Heads than Adjuncts, it should be obvious to you that if *enough* were an A-bar Adjunct, we should expect it to be positioned after the whole A-bar [*proud of his country*]. But as we see from (114) above, this is not the case: *enough* can only be positioned after the Adjective *proud*, not after the A-bar [*proud of his country*]. Thus, the A-bar Adjunct analysis seems implausible, since it wrongly predicts that (114) (a) is ungrammatical, and (114) (b) grammatical.

But if *enough* isn't an A-bar Adjunct, what is it? Well, an alternative possibility might be to analyse it as an A Adjunct which recursively expands A into A. Under the A Adjunct analysis, the bracketed AP in (114) (a) above would have the structure (115) (we have followed the traditional dictionary classification of *enough* as an Adverb here – though its precise status is far from clear):

(115)

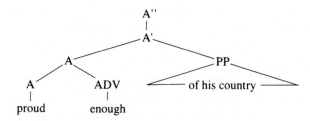

And we might even extend our word-level Adjunct analysis to nominal structures such as the bracketed NPs in (116) below:

(116) (a)   Surely we have [NP proof *enough* THAT HE IS A SPY]
      (b)   Surely we have [NP proof *enough* OF HIS GUILT]

where the word *enough* is positioned between the head Noun *proof* and its capitalised clausal or prepositional complement. This might suggest that *enough* in (116) functions as an adjectival N Adjunct which expands N into N.

Another possible candidate for the status of word-level Adjunct are the prepositional particles which form part of so-called 'Phrasal Verbs'. For example, in a sentence such as:

(117)   The weather may *turn out* rather frosty

it is traditionally claimed that the italicised sequence *turn out* forms a kind of 'complex verb'. One way of formalising this intuition would be to say that the Preposition *out* here functions as a V Adjunct, which expands V into V, e.g. in the manner indicated in (118) below:

(118)

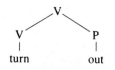

As we saw in section 2.8, a structure like (118) would account for why *out* cannot be premodified by a P-bar Specifier such as *right*, or be separated from its associated Verb by an Adverb such as *later*: cf.

(119) (a)   *The weather may [turn *right* out] rather frosty
      (b)   *The weather may [turn *later* out] rather frosty

We shall return to reconsider Phrasal Verbs in Chapter 8, so we shall have nothing further to say about them for the moment.

We can summarise this section in the following terms. We have suggested that there is a broad structural symmetry across all the major lexical categories (N, V, P, A, and ADV) insofar as any major lexical category X together with its Complements (if any) forms an X-bar constituent which is expanded into an X-double-bar by the addition of an optional Specifier. We have also suggested that any X-bar can be recursively expanded into another X-bar by the addition of an appropriate Adjunct or Attribute; and in this section we suggested that we may have to recognise two further types of Adjunct/Attribute, namely (i) double-bar Adjuncts/Attributes which expand XP into XP, and (ii) word-level Adjuncts/Attributes which expand a given word-category X into another word-level constituent of the same type. This means positing three different types of Adjunct/Attribute – namely (i) double-bar, (ii) single-bar, and (iii) word-level Adjuncts or Attributes. A further consequence would be that it would not be sufficient simply to specify that a given constituent functions, for example, as a nominal Adjunct: we should have to specify precisely whether the constituent in question functions as an N Adjunct, an N-bar Adjunct, or an N-double-bar Adjunct (or indeed has more than one of these functions).

You should now be able to tackle exercise IV

5.6   Constraining Categorial Rules

In the course of our discussions in this chapter and the two previous ones, we have posited numerous Categorial Rules (i.e. Phrase Structure Rules) specifying how Clauses and Phrases are built up out of lower-level constituents. Now, as we noted in Chapter 1, our ultimate goal is to develop a *maximally constrained* Theory of Language, in order to provide a principled account of the rapidity and uniformity of Language Acquisition. To achieve this goal, we have to impose severe restrictions on the expressive power of the technical devices which our theory makes available for natural language grammars. One such device is *Categorial Rules*: it therefore follows that any restrictive Theory of Grammar should attempt to maximally constrain the expressive power of Categorial Rules – i.e. put precise limits on what is and isn't a possible Categorial Rule in any natural language Grammar.

The need to impose constraints on the set of admissible Phrase Structure Rules was recognised even before the advent of X-bar Syntax by John Lyons, in the following passage (1968, p. 33):

> Phrase Structure Grammars fail to formalise the fact that NP and
> VP are not merely mnemonically convenient symbols, but stand

for sentence-constituents which are necessarily nominal and verbal respectively, because they have N and V as an obligatory major constituent. What is required, and what was assumed in traditional grammar, is some way of relating constituents of the form XP to X (where X is any major category: N, V, etc.). It would not only be perverse, but it should be theoretically impossible for any linguist to propose, for example, rules of the following form:

(120) $NP \rightarrow V \ VP$

(121) $VP \rightarrow D \ N$

To borrow a traditional term from Bloomfield (1935, p. 194), we might say that Lyons is implicitly arguing that Categorial Rules should be restricted to generating *endocentric* structures – i.e. structures where the category of a given Phrase matches that of its Head. But how can we incorporate this condition into our Theory of Grammar?

Jackendoff (1977a) argues that within an X-bar framework we can meet the *endocentricity* requirement (and hence rule out such 'perverse' rules as (120) and (121) above) by imposing a universal constraint on the form of PS rules such as (122) below (we might call this the ENDOCENTRICITY CONSTRAINT for obvious reasons):

(122)   ENDOCENTRICITY CONSTRAINT
         All possible Phrase Structure Rules are of the form
         $X^n \rightarrow \ldots X^{n-1} \ldots$ (Jackendoff (1977), p. 34)

X here is a *category variable* (i.e. stands for any category such as N, V, P, A, ADV, etc.); by convention, X is assumed to have the same value on the lefthand side of the arrow as on the righthand side, so that if we take X to be V(erb) on the lefthand side, then X must also be V on the righthand side. The superscript n is a *level variable* (or, more informally, *bar variable*) which stands for any level of bar projection of X; hence X^n stands for X^0, X' or X''. The dots represent other constituents which might be introduced by the rule. In simple terms, what (122) amounts to is the claim (123) below:

(123)   The output of a rule must contain a category of the same type as the input category, but one bar-level lower

Suppose that (for illustrative purposes) we let the variable X have the value P(reposition) in (122). Then if we take the superscript level variable n to have

259

the value 2, the constraint (122) specifies that a rule like (124) below is a possible rule:

(124)   P'' → D P'

(since the output of the rule contains a P-bar which is one bar-level lower than the P-double-bar category which serves as input to the rule); whereas rules such as (125) below:

(125) (i)   P'' → D AP
      (ii)   P'' → V' NP

would be ruled out as impermissible by virtue of the fact that their output contains no P-bar constituent. If we take X to be P and n to be 1, then (122) specifies that (126) below is a possible rule:

(126)   P' → P NP

(since P is the same kind of (prepositional) category as P-bar but is one bar-level lower); whereas (122) prohibits rules such as (127) below:

(127)   P' → A P''

since the output of the rule does not contain a P constituent. Of course, it also follows that a rule such as (128) below would also (unless blocked in some way) be allowed by schema (122):

(128)   P → P^{-1} N

However, we might posit that rules such as (128) would be prohibited by a universal constraint to the effect that:

(129)   Syntactic categories cannot have a negative level value

What (129) says is that the 'smallest' kind of syntactic category is a zero-level category; there are no syntactic categories of the form X^{-1}, X^{-2}, etc.

Of course, by substituting different values for X and n in (122), we can see that (122) stipulates (for example) that a rule with V'' as its input must have V' in its output; a rule with V' as its input must have V in its output; a rule with N'' as its input must have N' in its output; a rule with N' as its input must have N in its output; a rule with A'' as its input must have A' in its output; a rule with A' as its input must have A in its output ... and so on and so forth. Thus, a condition such as (122) seems to answer Lyons' appeal for severe constraints to be imposed on what are possible and impossible Constituent Structure Rules.

However, in some respects, Jackendoff's schema appears to be too restrictive. For one thing, it would disallow recursive expansion of one category into another identical category. And yet we earlier argued that Adjuncts/ Attributes have the function of expanding an X-bar into another X-bar; indeed, we even suggested in section 5.5 (cf. (107) above) that there might be other types of Adjunct/Attribute which recursively expand double-bar constituents, and a further type which recursively expand zero-level constituents. To allow for the possibility of rules adjoining one category of a given type to another category of the same type, we might revise (122) as (130) below:

(130)   ENDOCENTRICITY CONSTRAINT (revised)
        All Constituent Structure Rules are of the form:
        $X^n \rightarrow \ldots X^m \ldots$ (m = n or n − 1)

What (130) says is that the output of a rule must contain a category which is of the same type (nominal, prepositional, etc.) as the input category, and which is at the same bar-level or one bar-level lower.

However, even (130) will prove too restrictive if we accept Chomsky's claim (*Barriers* (1986b), p. 4) that an X-double-bar can either have an X-bar or an X as its Immediate Head, so that the structure of the NP *students* in a sentence such as (131):

(131)   Some people think *students* are parasites

could be either (132) (a) below, or (132) (b):

(132) (a)   N''   (b)   N''
               | |
               N'   N
               | |
               N   students
               |
            students

If structures such as (132) (b) are indeed well-formed, then we shall have to allow for rules of the schematic form:

(133) $X'' \rightarrow \ldots X \ldots$

This in turn would mean that (130) would have to be revised along the lines of (134) below:

(134)   ENDOCENTRICITY CONSTRAINT (revised)
        All Constituent Structure Rules are of the form:
        $X^n \rightarrow \ldots X^m \ldots$ (n ⩾ m)

261

What (134) says is that the output of a rule must contain a category which is of the same type (nominal, prepositional) etc. as the input category, and which is at the same or at a lower bar-level.

It might be argued, however, that the particular version of the ENDO-CENTRICITY CONSTRAINT proposed in (134) is still too weak and needs to be tightened up in many respects: for instance, it allows (potentially infinite) *vacuous recursion* of a given constituent. To see what we mean by this, consider a hypothetical rule such as (135) below:

(135)   N' → N'

We argued in section 4.5 against allowing any such rule in our Theory of Grammar: recall that we noted that any such rule would be *self-defining* and *vacuously recursive*, and would wrongly predict that any Noun Phrase should be potentially infinitely structurally ambiguous, according to how many non-branching N-bars it has stacked on top of other N-bars. So, clearly, we want to exclude rules such as (135) as being *impossible in principle*: but unfortunately, our existing ENDOCENTRICITY CONSTRAINT (134) doesn't do this, since it would allow for a rule like (135).

The bottom line of the argument here is that we need to tighten up our ENDOCENTRICITY CONSTRAINT (134) in such a way as to disallow rules which are *vacuously recursive*. One way of doing this would be to revise (134) along the lines of (136) below, adding the italicised condition:

(136)   ENDOCENTRICITY CONSTRAINT (final version!)
          All Constituent Structure Rules are of the form:
          $X^n \rightarrow \ldots X^m \ldots (n \geqslant m)$
          where $m \neq n$ *if* $\ldots$ *is null* (*i.e. if* X^n *is non-branching*)

There are numerous other ways in which we might seek to 'tighten up' the *endocentricity* requirement on rules (e.g. by incorporating Emonds' requirement (1976, p. 15) that Phrases should have a *unique* head, thereby banning multiple-headed structures), but we shall not pursue these questions of detail any further here. The essential point that I want to underline here is the need to constrain the class of Categorial Rules which our Theory of Grammar allows for.

However it is eventually formulated, the ENDOCENTRICITY CONSTRAINT amounts to a requirement that rules should generate structures which are *properly headed*. But the *endocentricity* condition imposes no constraints on sets of elements which may appear as Specifiers, Adjuncts, Attributes, or Complements. Jackendoff (1977a, p. 36) suggests that (with certain exceptions which need not concern us) these be limited to 'major phrasal categories'; and in the same vein, Chomsky (*Barriers* (1986a), p. 3) posits that only Maximal Projections can function as Specifiers, Complements, etc. What this amounts to is a claim that all *Modifiers* (viz. Specifiers, Adjuncts, Attributes, and Complements) must be Maximal Projections (i.e. full Phrases like NP, AP, PP, etc.). For obvious reasons, therefore, we might refer to this condition as the MODIFIER MAXIMALITY CONSTRAINT. Following Stowell (1981), we might formulate the relevant condition as in (137) below:

(137)   MODIFIER MAXIMALITY CONSTRAINT
'Every non-head term in the expansion of a rule must itself be a Maximal Projection of some category'
(Stowell, 'Origins of Phrase Structure' (1981), p. 70)

Of course, the constraint (137) could be incorporated directly into (136), e.g. by adding a condition to the effect that '... cannot contain any categories other than Maximal Projections': however, we shall keep the two constraints (136) and (137) separate here, partly for ease of exposition, and partly because the two impose rather different types of conditions on rules, (136) relating to *Heads*, and (137) relating to *Modifiers*.

Constraints such as those discussed above have far-reaching consequences for our analysis of sentence structure in all sorts of ways. By way of example, consider the implications of the MODIFIER MAXIMALITY CONSTRAINT (137) for the Categorial Rules introducing nominal Determiners such as *this*, *that*, *these*, and *those*. In Chapter 4, we proposed the following rule for generating Determiners within Noun Phrases:

(138)   N'' → (D) N'

However, the MODIFIER MAXIMALITY CONSTRAINT (137) would debar us from having a rule such as (138) in our Grammar. Why? Because rule (138) contains a non-head term (namely D) which is not a Maximal Projection, in violation of the MODIFIER MAXIMALITY CONSTRAINT. In order to satisfy the constraint (137), rule (138) would have to be revised along the lines of (139) below:

(139)   N'' → (DP) N'

where the word-level category D in (138) has been replaced by the phrase-level category (i.e. Maximal Projection) DP. But of course, any such modification would entail that the word-level category D can function as the head of a phrasal DP (Determiner Phrase, or D-double-bar) constituent (as Reuland (1986), p. 43 claims). But is there any empirical evidence that this is so? Well, perhaps there is: some support for the claim that Demonstrative Determiners permit phrasal expansions comes from examples such as (140) overleaf:

263

(140) (a)   He advocated an analysis along [*essentially these*] lines
    (b)   He made [*precisely that*] point

and also from nonstandard dialectal forms such as:

(141)   %[*This here*] book is better than [*that there*] one

And if 'Quantifiers' such as *all, many, few, some*, etc. are treated as Determiners, then it is interesting to note that they too permit phrasal expansions:

(142) (a)   [*Nearly all*] the chocolates have gone
    (b)   [*Rather too many*] students failed the exams
    (c)   [*So few*] people appreciate culture
    (d)   [*Quite some*] time has gone by since then

Accordingly, we shall henceforth assume that Determiners are in fact phrasal constituents, and have the status of DP (= D''), rather than just D. But note that this revision to our earlier assumptions about the nature of Determiners was forced upon us by the search for universal principles which forced us to call into question our earlier descriptive assumptions. This provides a nice illustration of the complex interplay between descriptive generalisations and theoretical principles: that is, on the basis of descriptive generalisations, we formulate theoretical principles which in turn lead us to call into question the empirical adequacy of earlier descriptive generalisations.

We can summarise the contents of this section in the following terms. We began by arguing on metatheoretical grounds that there is a need to constrain the sentence-formation rules used to generate syntactic structures. And we have proposed two simple constraints on Categorial Rules: the ENDOCENTRICITY CONSTRAINT (136) amounts to the requirement that rules should assign proper *Heads* to the Phrases they generate; while the MODIFIER MAXIMALITY CONSTRAINT (137) specifies that any non-head terms (i.e. Modifiers) mentioned in rules must be Maximal Projections.

> *You should now be able to tackle exercise V*

5.7   Generalising Categorial Rules

In the previous section, we discussed how we can *constrain* the set of Categorial Rules used to generate sentence-structures; in this section, we are going to look at ways of *generalising* the numerous individual Categorial Rules which we have proposed so far. We shall see that just as *category variables* play an important role in helping us formulate constraints on rules (hence the fact that the ENDOCENTRICITY CONDITION is formulated entirely in terms of category and level variables), so too they play an important part in helping us generalise Categorial Rules. Let's see how category variables can be used to achieve this end.

As we have already noted earlier, Prepositional Phrases can be used as Complements of all five major lexical categories: cf. examples such as those in (143) below:

(143) (a)   He must have [$_{V'}$ spoken *to Mary*] (V + PP)
  (b)   She is so [$_{A'}$ fond *of her son*] (A + PP)
  (c)   Yours works quite [$_{ADV'}$ differently *from mine*] (ADV + PP)
  (d)   His [$_{N'}$ reply *to Mary*] was ambivalent (N + PP)
  (e)   I'll wait right [$_{P'}$ until *after the wedding*] (P + PP)

Now, within the framework we have been using so far, each of the different bracketed constituents in (143) would have to be generated by a different rule, as we see from (144) below:

(144) (a)   V' → V   PP
  (b)   A' → A   PP
  (c)   ADV' → ADV   PP
  (d)   N' → N   PP
  (e)   P' → P   PP

Intuitively, it would seem that we are missing a fairly obvious generalisation by generating each of the bracketed constituents in (143) by a separate rule. What we'd like to be able to do is collapse all five rules in (144) into a single rule. But how can we do this? The answer is to make use of *category variables*. Thus, if we use the variable X to stand for any word-level category, and the variable X' to designate the corresponding single-bar category, we can conflate all five rules in (144) above into the single rule (145) below:

(145)   X' → X   PP (Prepositional Complement Rule)

By convention, we take X to have the same value on the lefthand and righthand sides of the arrow, so that (for example) if X-bar is N-bar, then X will be N. Given this convention, you can verify for yourself that (145) subsumes all the five different rules which we posited in (144) in terms of a single PP Complement Rule. If categories are sets of features (as we suggested in Chapter 3), then the category variable X is in effect an abbreviation for the corresponding matrix of categorial features [$\pm F_1 \ldots \pm F_n$].

While (145) is clearly more general than the five category-specific rules in (144), we might wonder whether it can be generalised still further. For although two of the terms in (145) are *category variables* (namely X-bar and

X), the third term (viz. PP) is not, but rather is a *category constant*. Obviously, we could achieve even greater generality if we were able to replace the category constant (= PP) in (145) by a category variable. What this amounts to is saying that we want to be able to generalise rule (145) from prepositional complements to other types of phrasal complement, in order to capture the obvious generalisation that not just PPs can function as Complements, but also other types of Phrase. For example, we see from (146) below that Verbs may take a wide variety of phrasal complements:

(146) (a)   He can't have [$_{V'}$ enjoyed *blue films*] (V + NP)
   (b)   She may be [$_{V'}$ suffering *from a throat infection*] (V + PP)
   (c)   It would have [$_{V'}$ been *quite convenient*] (V + AP)
   (d)   You shouldn't have [$_{V'}$ behaved *so badly*] (V + ADVP)

And other categories (e.g. Adjectives and Prepositions) also take a variety of different types of phrasal complement. Accordingly, we might seek to generalise rule (145) still further by replacing the category constant 'PP' by the category variable 'YP' (designating 'any type of double-bar constituent') along the lines indicated in (147) below:

(147)   X' → X YP (Revised Complement Rule)

As noted above, X must have the same value on the lefthand as on the righthand side of the arrow: but Y here may either have the same categorial value as X, or a different value from X. Thus, (147) subsumes (among many others) both rules in (148) below:

(148) (i)   P' → P PP
   (ii)   P' → P NP

Our revised rule (147) will subsume (and hence obviate the need for) the specific rule (148) (i) if X is taken to have the same categorial value as Y (i.e. if X = Y = P); but by the same token, the revised rule (147) will also subsume the specific rule (148) (ii) if X is taken to have a different value from Y (i.e. if X = P, and Y = N). Since rule (147) now makes use only of category variables, we might claim that it is maximally general.

   And yet, there are two different problems with rule (147). The first is that it fails to allow for the possibility that a given X-bar constituent may simply contain X without a Complement: i.e. it fails to allow for the fact that Complements are sometimes optional. The second problem posed by rule (147) is that it fails to recognise the fact that a given item may take more than one Complement Phrase: for example, a Verb such as *give* may take two NP Complements, or an NP Complement and a PP Complement: cf.

(149) (a)   John may have [$_{V'}$ given [$_{NP}$ *his sister*] [$_{NP}$ *the book*]]
    (b)   John may have [$_{V'}$ given [$_{NP}$ *the book*] [$_{PP}$ *to his sister*]]

Thus, we need to modify rule (147) above so as to allow for the possibility that X may have not just one Complement, but no Complements at all, or alternatively more than one Complement. This we might do by replacing (147) above by (150) below:

(150)   X' → X YP* (Generalised Complement rule)

(adapted from Chomsky, *Barriers* (1986b), p. 3) where the asterisk operator is used to indicate 'any number, possibly none', so that YP* means 'any number of Phrases of any type (not necessarily all of the same type)'. A rule such as (150) – formulated entirely in terms of category variables – thus conflates an infinite number of rules like (144) which make use of category constants, and thereby achieves maximum generality. Such a rule might be said to be *category-neutral* (to borrow a term from Stowell (1981)), in the sense that no term mentioned in the rule is a category constant (i.e. designates a specific category).

A rule such as (150) defines a new set of problems for the linguist. If we assume (in keeping with the arguments we have presented in the previous section) that there is broad structural symmetry across categories, then we should expect to find that all word-level categories permit the same range of phrasal Complements. And a Categorial Rule such as (150) above precisely embodies this claim, since it specifies that any word-level category X permits any phrase-level category YP as its Complement. The problem posed by rule (150) is that the rule *overgenerates*: that is to say, as well as generating many grammatical structures, it will also generate numerous ungrammatical structures. For example, rule (150) allows for not just Prepositions and Verbs to take NP Complements, but also Nouns, Adjectives and Adverbs: but as (151) below indicates, whereas P and V do take NP complements in English, N, A, and ADV generally do not:

(151) (a)   The rabbit was right [$_{P'}$ inside [$_{NP}$ *the burrow*]]
    (b)   He may have [$_{V'}$ finished [$_{NP}$ *the book*]]
    (c)   *He proposed a [$_{N'}$ ban [$_{NP}$ *cruise missiles*]]
    (d)   *I'm none too [$_{A'}$ fond [$_{NP}$ *Italian food*]]
    (e)   *She talks so [$_{ADV'}$ differently [$_{NP}$ *other people*]]

Since structures such as those bracketed in (151) (a) and (b) above are grammatical, they pose no problem for us, because they are accounted for by rule (150). The problem we face is that of explaining just why it is that Nouns, Adjectives, and Adverbs don't allow NP complements, when rule (150) wrongly predicts that they do. Thus, we have now shifted the burden of explanation away from *explaining grammaticality* to that of *explaining ungrammaticality*. The more general our Categorial Rules become, the more they overgenerate, and the more we are faced with the problem of explaining ungrammaticality. Much of the second volume of our book will be devoted to this problem of explaining ungrammaticality: we shall see that this can often be accounted for in terms of independent principles. Since Volume Two is concerned with developing such principles, we do no more than mention the methodological implications of positing ever more general Categorial Rules here.

Just as we can generalise numerous category-specific Complement Rules by the use of category variables, so we can generalise other types of rule by the same device. For example, we earlier noted Van Riemsdijk's claim (illustrated by examples such as (89–92) above) that any major phrasal category can function as the (optional) Specifier of a P-bar. If this is so, then we can capture the relevant generalisation in terms of a rule such as (152) below:

(152)   P'' → (YP) P' (Prepositional Specifier Rule)

Given the assumption of cross-categorial structural symmetry, we might posit that if any type of phrasal category can function as the Specifier of a P-bar constituent, then we should expect the same to be true in principle of other single-bar categories. Accordingly, rule (152) might be generalised along the lines of (153) below:

(153)   X'' → (YP) X' (Generalised Specifier Rule)

Rule (153) is clearly more general than rule (152), since the two category constants in (152) (namely the P'' and P' constituents) have been replaced by the corresponding category variables X'' and X' in (153). Thus, our Generalised Specifier Rule (153) – like our earlier Generalised Complement Rule (150) – is a *category-neutral* rule formulated entirely in terms of category variables. Once again, the rule vastly overgenerates, and in doing so defines an interesting problem for the linguist (viz. that of explaining why the ungrammatical structures generated by the rule are ill-formed).

Since we have generalised the rules introducing Complements and Specifiers, a natural question to ask is whether the rules introducing Attributes/Adjuncts can be generalised in much the same way. In the previous chapter on Noun Phrases, we argued that both APs and NPs can be used as N-bar Attributes, recursively expanding N-bar into N-bar. However, what we overlooked there was the fact that (a limited class of) *Prepositional Phrases* can be used as N-bar Attributes: for example, in (154) below the bracketed PP functions as an attributive premodifier of the italicised N-bar sequence:

(154) (a)   an [up to the minute] *news report*
   (b)   an [out of date] *moral code*
   (c)   an [under the counter] *illegal transaction*
   (d)   an [in] *political joke*

Moreover, (again, subject to severe restrictions), it seems that VPs can also be used as N-bar attributes: for example, in (155) below the bracketed expressions might be argued to be VPs functioning as attributive premodifiers of the italicised N-bar constituents:

(155) (a)   the [ban the bomb] *election campaign*
   (b)   the [spot the ball] *newspaper competition*
   (c)   his [beggar my neighbour] *attitude towards others*
   (d)   the [name that tune] *television game*

Thus, since NP, AP, VP, and PP constituents can all function as N-bar Attributes, we might propose to introduce nominal attributes by a rule such as (156) below:

(156)   N' → YP N' (Nominal Attribute Rule)

And we might assume a convention to the effect that all recursive rules are optional, so that (156) would then be an optional rule: this would amount to the claim that N-bar Attributes are optional constituents of NP.

Of course, we could generalise rule (156) still further by replacing the category constant N' by the corresponding category variable X'. If we were to do so, rule (156) would then be replaced by (157) below:

(157)   X' → YP X' (Generalised Attribute Rule)

And rule (157) would amount to the claim that any kind of phrasal constituent can be used as an attributive premodifier of any kind of single-bar constituent. Given our convention that recursive rules are optional, then rule (157) will specify that Attributes are optional modifiers of X-bar. Once again, rule (157) will vastly overgenerate in obvious ways, and in doing so will define for us an interesting set of problems (in particular, the problem of determining what kind of principles explain the ill-formedness of ungrammatical outputs of the rule).

Let's turn now to consider whether we can generalise the rules generating *Adjunct Phrases* in a parallel fashion. In Chapter 4, we argued that a variety of Phrases can function as nominal Adjuncts expanding N-bar into N-bar: for example, the capitalised PP, NP, and AP constituents in (158) overleaf function as Adjuncts to the italicised N-bar:

(158) (a) that [$_{N'}$ [$_{N'}$ *picture of Mary*] [$_{PP}$ OVER THERE]]
  (b) the [$_{N'}$ [$_{N'}$ *abolition of taxes*] [$_{NP}$ NEXT YEAR]]
  (c) those [$_{N'}$ [$_{N'}$ *Physics students*] [$_{AP}$ ABSENT FROM CLASS]]

In this chapter, we have seen that a wide variety of Phrases can function as Adjuncts to V-bar: for example, the capitalised PP, NP, and ADVP constituents in (159) below function as Adjuncts to the italicised V-bar:

(159) (a) John will [$_{V'}$ [$_{V'}$ *read it*] [$_{PP}$ AT HOME]]
  (b) John will [$_{V'}$ [$_{V'}$ *read it*] [$_{NP}$ TOMORROW EVENING]]
  (c) John will [$_{V'}$ [$_{V'}$ *read it*] [$_{ADVP}$ VERY CAREFULLY]]

And similarly, a number of different types of Phrase can be used as P-bar Adjuncts – e.g. Phrases such as those capitalised in (160) below:

(160) (a) John was [$_{P'}$ [$_{P'}$ *at odds*] [$_{PP}$ WITH HIS FRIENDS]]
  (b) I am [$_{P'}$ [$_{P'}$ *with you*] [$_{NP}$ ALL THE WAY]]
  (c) John is [$_{P'}$ [$_{P'}$ *in the wrong*] [$_{ADVP}$ COMPLETELY]]

And the same point could obviously be made in relation to other types of Adjunct as well.

Of course, one way of dealing with Adjuncts such as those capitalised in (158–60) would be to posit a different Adjunct Rule generating each Adjunct type, so that we might envisage a set of Adjunct Rules including the following:

(161) (i) N' → N' PP
  (ii) N' → N' NP
  (iii) N' → N' AP
  (iv) V' → V' PP
  (v) V' → V' NP
  (vi) V' → V' ADVP
  (vii) P' → P' PP
  (viii) P' → P' NP
  (ix) P' → P' ADVP

Well, by now you should know exactly what I'm going to say next! Rather than stand back and admire the intrinsic beauty and symmetry of the Categorial Rules we have devised in (161), we should instead be asking ourselves whether we can't generalise the rules. The answer is, of course, that we can if we make use of category variables: more specifically, the use of category variables enables us to conflate all nine separate rules in (161) above into the single *category-neutral* rule (162) below:

(162)   X' → X' YP (Generalised Adjunct Rule)

Rule (162) amounts to the claim that any kind of phrasal (i.e. double-bar) constituent can be used as an Adjunct recursively expanding a single-bar constituent into another single-bar constituent of the same categorial type. Given our convention that recursive rules are optional, (162) will be an optional rule. Of course, a general (i.e. category-neutral) rule such as (162) will overgenerate in obvious ways; it follows, therefore, that independent principles in other components of our grammar will have to deal with this overgeneration (in ways which we shall discuss in Volume Two).

5.8 Eliminating Categorial Rules

At this point, it's useful to take stock of the direction of our argumentation so far. What we argued in the last section was that by replacing *category constants* in rules by *category variables*, we can conflate sets of individual rules into a single *generalised* rule, and thus achieve a much higher level of generality in the formulation of Categorial Rules. By using category variables in this way, we have managed to subsume all our earlier *category-specific* rules under the four *category-neutral* rules summarised in (163) below:

(163) (i) $X'' \rightarrow (YP)$ X' (Generalised Specifier Rule)
  (ii) $X' \rightarrow YP$ X' (Generalised Attribute Rule)
  (iii) $X' \rightarrow X'$ YP (Generalised Adjunct Rule)
  (iv) $X' \rightarrow X$ YP* (Generalised Complement Rule)

Given our convention that recursive rules are optional, it follows that the Attribute and Adjunct Rules (163) (ii) and (iii) will be optional.

It is interesting to reflect on the nature of the generalised rules which we have arrived at in (163) above. Not one of the terms mentioned in any of the rules is a *category constant*; on the contrary, all terms specified in the rules are *category variables*. This suggests that (in order to achieve maximum generality in our formulation of Categorial Rules) we might impose a universal constraint on all sentence-formation rules to the effect that they must be formulated entirely in *category-neutral* terms – i.e. in terms of *category variables*. We might thus envisage a constraint along the lines of (164) below:

(164)   CATEGORY NEUTRALITY CONSTRAINT
  All Categorial Rules must be formulated entirely in terms of *category variables*

The constraint (164) encapsulates the spirit of Stowell's stipulation (1981, p. 85) that 'The Phrase Structure Rules of all languages are unable to refer to categorial features'.

Now, if you think about it carefully, you'll realise that (164) captures the very essence of *X-bar Syntax* – namely the assumption that there is *cross-categorial symmetry* in the way in which word-level categories can be expanded into phrase-level categories (so that, for example, Nouns permit exactly the same range of Modifiers and phrasal expansions as Adjectives, or Prepositions, etc.). This cross-categorial symmetry principle is embodied into our Theory of Grammar in terms of the CATEGORY NEUTRALITY CONSTRAINT (164) by virtue of the fact that (164) requires us to have a single set of category-neutral Categorial Rules like (163) to generate all types of constituent.

As Stowell notes (1981, p. 85), if we were to impose the constraint (164) that all sentence-formation rules must be formulated entirely in *category-neutral* terms, then 'Effectively, this would eliminate the Categorial Component in the traditional sense'. How so? Well, the very essence of traditional Categorial Rules such as those which we formulated in Chapter 3 was that they expanded *specific categories into specific sequences of categories*: in more technical terms, we might say that the rules were formulated entirely in terms of *category constants*, since the input of the rule in each case was a category constant, and the output was an ordered set of category constants. Since traditional Constituent Structure Rules were formulated entirely in terms of category constants, and since we have now replaced these by generalised rule-schemas formulated entirely in terms of category variables, we have effectively eliminated traditional category-specific Categorial Rules altogether from our Theory of Grammar. Thus, whereas the Categorial Component formerly comprised a vast set of individual category-specific rules, it now comprises instead a highly restricted set of maximally general category-neutral rule-schemas such as (163) above, together with a set of category-neutral rule-constraints such as the ENDO-CENTRICITY CONSTRAINT (136), the MODIFIER MAXIMALITY CONSTRAINT (137) and the CATEGORY NEUTRALITY CONSTRAINT (164). We have thus arrived at a model in which the Categorial Component comprises a mere handful of category-neutral principles (rule-schemas and rule-constraints).

However, there is an important difference between *rule-schemas* and *rule-constraints*. For, whereas rule-constraints like those mentioned above are putatively *universal* principles (hence, e.g. the *endocentricity requirement* holds for all constituents in all languages, and is not in any sense an idiosyncratic property of particular languages such as English), by contrast rule-schemas such as (163) above are clearly language-specific. Why? Well, for one thing, category-neutral rules such as (163) define a fixed linear ordering on constituents; and since word-order varies from one language to another, it follows that the corresponding rules-schemas will likewise vary from one language to another. For example, whereas the head Verbs, Adjectives, Nouns, and Prepositions italicised in (165) below typically precede their [bracketed] Complements in English: cf.

(165) (a) *Close* [the door] (V + Complement)
 (b) *fond* [of Mary] (A + Complement)
 (c) *desire* [for change] (N + Complement)
 (d) *in* [London] (P + Complement)

we find that the converse order holds in a language such as Korean, where Nouns, Prepositions, and Verbs (Korean makes no morphological distinction between Adjectives and Verbs) all *follow* their Heads, so that, for obvious reasons, Prepositions are called *Postpositions* in such languages): cf.

(166) (a) [Moon-ul] *dateo-ra*! (Complement + V)
  Door-OM close-IM ('Close the door')
  (OM = Objective Marker; IM = Imperative Marker)
 (b) [byunhwa-edaehan] *kalmang-ul* (Complement + N)
  change-for   desire-NM ('desire for change')
  (NM = Nominative marker)
 (c) [Seoul]-eseo (Complement + P)
  Seoul   -in ('in Seoul')

This means that the *Complement Rule* for languages like English will generate any head category X as the leftmost constituent of the minimal X-bar containing it (as in (167) (i) below), whereas the corresponding *Complement Rule* in Korean will generate Heads as the rightmost constituent of their containing X-bar constituent (as in (167) (ii) below):

(167) (i)   X' → X YP* (English Complement Rule)
 (ii) X' → YP* X (Korean Complement Rule)

Thus, we see that there will be *parametric variation* between languages according to whether they position Heads as the first or last constituent of the minimal X-bar constituent containing them. Hence, we could say that languages such as English are *head-first* languages, whereas those such as Korean are *head-last* languages. For obvious reasons, this is known as the *head-first/head-last parameter*. What both types of language have in common is (as Stowell (1981), p. 70 notes) that 'The Head always appears adjacent to one boundary of X-bar' – i.e. both types of language position any head category X at the *periphery* (viz. lefthand or righthand end) of the minimal X-bar constituent containing it. There will be similar parametric variation across languages in the linear ordering of constituents in at least two further respects: (i) some languages position Specifiers *before*, and some *after* the constituents they modify (so that we have *specifier-first* languages on the one hand, and *specifier-last* languages on the other; and (ii) some languages position Attributes/Adjuncts *before* and some *after* the expressions they modify (so that we can draw a distinction between *adjunct-first* and *adjunct-last* languages).

In more concrete terms, this means that whereas head-first languages have the Complement Rule (168) (i) below, head-last languages have the 'mirror image' rule (168) (ii):

(168) (i)   X' → X   YP* (Head-first Complement Rule)

(ii)   X' → YP*   X (Head-last Complement Rule)

And whereas specifier-first languages have the Specifier Rule (169) (i) below, specifier-last languages have the 'mirror image' rule (169) (ii):

(169) (i)   X'' → (YP)   X' (Specifier-first Rule)

(ii)   X'' → X'   (YP) (Specifier-last Rule)

And whereas adjunct-first languages have the Adjunct Rule (170) (i) below, adjunct-last languages have the 'mirror image' rule (170) (ii):

(170) (i)   X' → YP   X' (Adjunct-first Rule)

(ii)   X' → X'   YP (Adjunct-last Rule)

This will mean that the relevant typological variation between languages will be reduced to the question of whether the *Categorial Component* of the grammar of a given language contains rules (168) (i) or (ii), (169) (i) or (ii), and (170) (i) or (ii).

In terms of the typology developed above, it might seem simple enough to classify English as (for example) a head-first and specifier-first, language, on the basis of examples such as the following:

(171) (a)   *in* here (Head Preposition + Complement)

(b)   *both* John and Mary (Specifier + Nominal)

However, the reality is somewhat more complex (as I'm sure you've guessed by now). For, alongside examples such as (171) we find those such as (172) below:

(172) (a)   *herein* (Complement + Head Preposition)

(b)   John and Mary *both* (Nominal + Specifier)

How are we to deal with such apparently 'aberrant' cases?

One answer which we might explore to this question would be in terms of the *Theory of Markedness* which we touched upon in Chapter 1. That is, we might say that the *unmarked* word-order in English is *head-first* and *specifier-first*, and that the mirror image *head-last* and *specifier-last* orders represent a *marked* construction. We might expect to find that *marked* constructions are subject to heavy lexical and stylistic constraints. This certainly seems to be true of the *specifier-last* construction illustrated in (172) (b). For one thing, this construction is subject to heavy *lexical* restrictions (i.e. restrictions on the choice of words which can participate in the construction), since the vast majority of Determiners in English cannot follow the nominal which they modify: cf.

(173) (a)   *my* new car/*new car *my*
    (b)   *the* outgoing President/*outgoing President *the*
    (c)   *this* dirty war/*dirty war *this*
    (d)   *many* other people/*other people *many*
    (e)   *all* other factors/*other factors *all*

Moreover, the construction is also *stylistically marked* in the sense that (172) (b) is a colloquialism which would be frowned upon in literary style.

It seems equally clear that the 'Complement + Preposition' order illustrated in (172) (a) is likewise highly marked, and hence subject to heavy restrictions on its use. And sure enough, this does indeed seem to be the case: for one thing, forms such as *thereafter, herein, whereby* are stylistically highly marked (e.g. they are only used in particular registers such as legal language). For another thing, there are severe syntactic restrictions on the construction: only a locative Pronoun like *there, here,* and *where* can be used as a preceding Complement of a Preposition (hence the ungrammaticality of *London from, himfrom,* etc.). Furthermore, there are also *lexical* restrictions on the construction – i.e. restrictions on the choice of Prepositions which can take a preceding locative Complement: for example, we can have *thereby, therein, thereto, thereafter,* and *therefrom,* but less freely *??thereunder,* or *?thereover,* and not at all *thereinside, *therebehind* etc. In fact, the construction is so restricted in its use in Modern English that it is questionable whether it should be regarded as in any sense productive. Indeed the very fact that the English spelling system writes *in there* as two words but *therein* as one word might be taken as suggesting that only the former is a productive syntactic construction in Modern English, the latter being a now extinct construction which has left behind a few fossil remnants in the form of compound words such as *thereby*.

At this point, let's gather together various loose ends, and try and paint a simple picture of the overall model of grammar which we are moving towards. We might suppose that Universal Grammar makes available a set of category-neutral pairs of rule-schemas such as those numbered (i) and (ii) in (168–70) above. The members of each pair of rule-schemas differ only in respect of the relative ordering of constituents. The task of the child acquiring the grammar of a particular language is thus to determine which ordering options are selected in the language he is acquiring. For example, the child has to determine whether a given language is a *head-first* language incorporating rule-schema (168) (i), or a *head-last* language incorporating schema (168) (ii): in other words, the child has to 'set' the relevant word-order parameter for Complements, Specifiers, Adjuncts, and so forth. The picture is complicated by the fact that some languages permit more than one ordering option: for example, as we have already seen, English selects the head-first and specifier-first orders as the *unmarked* option, but also selects the 'mirror image' orders as a *marked* option.

We have several times commented on the 'mirror image' character of pairs of rule-schemas such as those in (168–70) above. Consider, for example, the pair in (168) above, repeated as (174) below:

(174) (i)   X' → X YP* (Head-first Complement Rule)
    (ii)   X' → YP* X (Head-last Complement Rule)

Let's just think about the kinds of structures which each rule generates. Suppose we take the category variable X in (174) to have the value of V(erb), and the category variable Y to have the value of N(oun); and let's further suppose that we limit ourselves to generating structures with a single Complement. Given these assumptions, then rule (174) (i) will generate structures such as (175) (a) below, while rule (174) (ii) will generate structures such as (175) (b):

(175) (a)   V'   (b)   V'
         V   NP   NP   V

Now, although the two structures in (175) differ in respect of the relative linear ordering of V and NP, they have the same *hierarchical structure* (in both cases, V-bar immediately dominates V and NP, so that V and NP are the two immediate constituents of V-bar). Thus, our two rules in (174) *define the same set of constituency/dominance relations* (though they obviously define different sets of linear ordering relations). And yet, by formulating (174) (i) and (ii) as two entirely separate rules, we are unable to capture the 'common core' which the two rules have. This has seemed to some linguists to be an unsatisfactory situation (the problem of 'mirror image' rules was first discussed in detail in Langacker (1969a, b)). Is there any way of extracting the 'common core' out of such related pairs of rules?

One way of achieving this aim (suggested by a variety of linguists from the 1960s onwards) would be to separate off the two different functions of Categorial Rules, namely (i) defining constituency relations, and (ii) defining linear ordering relations. One proposal along these lines (adapted from Lightfoot (1979)) would be as follows. We might suppose that Universal Grammar contains a set of universal *Constituency Rules* which generate unordered sets of constituents: such rules might include the following (where the notation 'X, Y' indicates an unordered set):

(176) (i) $X'' \rightarrow X', (YP)$ (Specifier Rule)

     (ii) $X' \rightarrow X', YP$ (Adjunct Rule)

    (iii) $X' \rightarrow X, YP^*$ (Complement Rule)

A rule such as (176) (i) can be regarded as saying 'The two immediate constituents of X-double-bar are X-bar and an optional Specifier Phrase': the rule imposes no linear ordering on constituents. The Constituency Rules in (176) are 'metagrammatical' (to use Lightfoot's term): that is, they are 'part of the Theory of Grammar and not of particular grammars' (Lightfoot (1979), p. 52). Particular Grammars will superimpose specific *linearisation* (i.e. word-order) conditions on unordered universal schemas such as those in (176), so that *universal* order-free rules such as those in (176) above will thereby be 'fleshed out' into *particular* order-specific rules such as those in (168–70) above. Numerous alternative versions of this type of proposal have been put forward in the past three decades: most amount to factoring Constituent Structure Rules into two separate subsystems, viz. (i) a set of *Constituency Rules* which define the *immediate dominance* relations between constituents, and (ii) a set of *Linearisation Rules* which define the *immediate precedence* (i.e. word-order) relations between constituents.

Whatever technical devices are developed to deal with the problem, it is clear that one of the parameters of variation across languages (and hence one of the parameters whose value has to be set by the language learner) is the *linear ordering* (i.e. word-order) parameter. However, recent research has suggested that there may also be parametric variation between languages with respect to the hierarchical complexity (or 'depth' of structure) of Phrases. For example, for languages such as English there are good reasons to suppose that the maximum value of the level-variable n is 2 (so that we have double-bar constituents but no treble-bar constituents in English). However, for languages such as Japanese (according to Farmer (1984)) it may be that the maximum value of n is 1, so that categories have single-bar projections, but no double-bar projections: this would mean that Japanese Phrases would have a much 'flatter' structure than in English. It would also entail other structural differences: for example, if Specifiers are universally immediate constituents of Maximal Projections, then if the maximal projection of X is X'' in English but X' in Japanese, it follows that Specifiers are daughters of X'' in English, but daughters of X' in Japanese. If we also take into account word-order differences between English and Japanese (e.g. English is a *head-first* language and so positions Heads before Complements, whereas Japanese is *head-final* and hence positions Heads after their Complements), then the canonical structure of simple Phrases containing a head X, a Specifier and a Complement will be (177) (a) in English, and (177) (b) in Japanese:

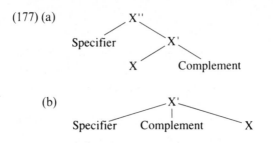

(177) (a)

(b)

Moreover, if we assume that Specifiers are universally daughters of maximal projections, and that Complements are universally daughters of single-bar constituents, then it follows that we will be able to differentiate Specifiers from Complements in configurational terms (i.e. in terms of *dominance* relations) only in 'hierarchical' languages like English, not in 'flat' languages like Japanese. Why so? Well, in English, Specifiers are sisters of X-bar and daughters of X-double-bar, whereas Complements are sisters of X and daughters of X-bar, so that it is possible to differentiate the two in purely *configurational* terms. But in Japanese, both Specifiers and Complements are sisters of X and daughters of X-bar, so that it is not possible to define them in purely *configurational* terms. Extending the relevant terminology in an obvious sense, we might say that English-type languages are *configurational*, whereas Japanese-type languages are *nonconfigurational*. If future research provides firm empirical substantiation for this claim, then a further parameter of variation between languages will be the *configurationality parameter* – i.e. the question of whether languages have a *configurational* structure such as (177) (a) above, or a 'flat' *nonconfigurational* structure such as (177) (b). We shall return to a detailed discussion of this issue in Volume Two, but for the time being, we shall put the question to one side.

You should now be able to tackle exercises VI–X

5.9   Summary

We began this chapter by suggesting that the internal structure of Noun Phrases (discussed in the previous chapter) might be reflected in the constituent structure of other Phrases. In 5.2 we argued that the X-bar analysis we had proposed in the previous chapter for NPs was directly applicable to Verb Phrases, in that a Verb and its Complements (if any) form a V-bar, which in turn can be recursively expanded into another V-bar by the addition of, for example, a prepositional or adverbial Adjunct/Attribute; and we suggested that the Aspectual Auxiliaries *have* and *be* may function as verbal Specifiers which expand V-bar into V-double-bar (i.e. into VP). We extended the analysis of Phrases as double-bar projections of word categories to Adjectival and Adverbial Phrases in 5.3, and to Prepositional Phrases in 5.4. In 5.5 we went on to suggest that there is uniformity across lexical categories with respect to the internal constituent structure of Phrases: more specifically, we suggested that any given head category X can be expanded into an X-bar by the addition of a set (possibly null) of Complements; X-bar can in turn be recursively expanded into another X-bar by the addition of a preceding Attribute or following Adjunct; and X-bar can be expanded into an X-double-bar by the addition of a Specifier phrase. We also suggested that as well as single-bar Adjuncts/Attributes (which expand X-bar into X-bar), there may also be double-bar Adjuncts/Attributes (which expand X-double-bar into X-double-bar), and zero-level Adjuncts/Attributes (which expand X into X).

In 5.6 we argued that the attempt to develop a maximally constrained Theory of Grammar requires us to impose severe constraints on rules of the Categorial Component of our grammar. We argued that our theory should exclude *vacuously recursive* rules in principle. We also argued that rules should be constrained in such a way as to generate only *endocentric* (i.e. properly headed) structures, and that only Maximal Projections can function as non-head terms in a rule. We suggested that all three constraints should be maximally generalised by formulating them uniquely in terms of *category variables* and *level variables*. In 5.7 we argued that we can also use category variables to generalise the Categorial Rules which generate sentence structures. Thus, in place of specific Categorial Rules expanding specific categories into specific sequences of categories, we have a set of *category-neutral* rule-schemas formulated entirely in terms of category variables. In 5.8 we argued that the move to replace category-specific rules by generalised category-neutral rule-schemas amounts to the virtual elimination of Categorial Rules in the traditional sense. We noted that there would be parametric variation across languages with respect to the particular rule-schemas which particular grammars incorporate. And we suggested that rule-schemas for different languages might vary along two different parameters, namely (i) the *linear ordering parameter* (e.g. some languages are head-first, others are head-last), and (ii) the *configurationality parameter*, so that some languages are configurational and have a 'hierarchical' structure, whereas others are nonconfigurational and have a 'flat' structure.

You should now be able to tackle exercises VI–X

EXERCISES

Exercise I
Discuss (with arguments) the structure of the bracketed VPs in the sentences below:

(1)   He may [*have turned against his wife*]
(2)   I don't [*completely agree with you over this*]
(3)   I'll [*send some flowers to Mary for you*]
(4)   He might [*run after Mary*]

Exercise II
Provide an empirically substantiated analysis of the structure of the bracketed Adjectival Phrases in the following sentences:

(1)   She is [*extremely good at chess*]
(2)   Madonna makes me go [*all weak at the knees*]
(3)   We're [*short of funds for the disco*]
(4)   The affair could end [*disastrously for you*]
(5)   I got [*so cross with her about the key*]

Exercise III
Discuss the analysis of the bracketed Phrases in the sentences below:

(1)   I'm saving the cognac [*for after dinner*]
(2)   I'll meet you [*round by the bank*]
(3)   Few CIA agents escape [*from behind the Iron Curtain*]
(4)   She is [*outside in the garden*]
(5)   You looked pretty rough [*the morning after the party*]
(6)   [*Out from under the bed*] crawled a naked man
(7)   People are much the same [*the whole world over*]
(8)   He left home [*several weeks ago*]

**Exercise IV

What problems (apparent or real) might seem to be posed for the analysis in this chapter and the last by the bracketed Phrases in the following sentences? Can you think of parallel problems which arise in relation to other Phrase types, or ways in which the problems might be resolved?

(1)   He's [*extremely fond and rightfully proud of his mother*]
(2)   [*Extremely fond*] though he is [*of his mother*], he wouldn't want to live with her
(3)   I'm [*sick to death of your blabbering*]
(4)   [*The boy and the girl in the corner*] are behaving disgracefully
(5)   Hey, [*you over there*]! What are you up to?
(6)   He is [*a close friend and loyal supporter of the Prime Minister*]

Exercise V

Discuss the way(s) in which each of the following rules violate the rule constraints discussed in this chapter:

(1) $N' \rightarrow (A) \begin{cases} N' \\ N \end{cases}$

(adapted from Hornstein and Lightfoot (1981a), p. 18)

(2) $S' \rightarrow COMP \begin{cases} S'' \\ S \end{cases}$ (Chomsky (1977b), p. 91)

(3) $N'' \rightarrow D \ N'$

(4) $V'' \rightarrow$ (have) (be) V' (adapted from Jackendoff (1977a), p. 54)

(5) $N'' \rightarrow$ ing V'' (Jackendoff (1977a), p. 52)

(6) $N' \rightarrow NP$ (Selkirk (1977), p. 312)

Exercise VI

Discuss the linear ordering of constituents in each of the following examples, saying whether it is or is not consistent with the principles developed in the text, and why.

(1)   a possible missile attack on our bases
(2)   a generous property bequest to charity
(3)   a spy exchange with the Russians
(4)   my Thermodynamics lecture to the Faculty
(5)   the bribery allegations in the press

**Exercise VII

Under the classical analysis of Aspectual Auxiliaries as Specifiers of VP, the bracketed VP in a sentence such as:

(1)   He might [*have been writing a letter*]

might be supposed to have a structure along the lines of either (2) below (adapted in minor ways from Jackendoff (1977a)), or (3) below (adapted from Jacobsen (1986)):

(2)

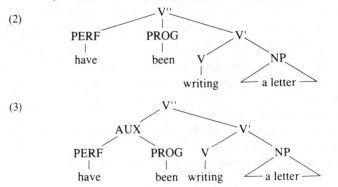

(3)

What rules would be necessary to generate each of these structures, and what would the status of each set of rules be with respect to the various rule-constraints outlined in the chapter (e.g. the ENDOCENTRICITY CONSTRAINT, etc.)?

Now turn back to Exercise IX in Chapter 3, and look at sentences (7–12). Which of those sentences would prove problematic for which of these two analyses, and why?

On the assumption that the constituents which appear in the bracketed focus position in *pseudo-cleft* sentences such as (4) (a) below and *equative* sentences such as (4) (b) must be Maximal Projections (i.e. double-bar phrases), and that the same is true of *sentence-fragments* such as that in (4) (c):

(4) (a)   What I need is [*a new car*/*new car*/*car*]
   (b)   There's one thing you'll never be able to afford: [*A new car*/*new car*/*car*]
   (c)   What did you buy? [*A new car?*/*new car*/*car*]?

discuss whether the Specifier analyses in (2) and (3) could account for the grammaticality of the following sentences:

(5) (a)   What he might have been doing is [*writing a letter*]
   (b)   There's one thing he might have been doing: [*writing a letter*]
   (c)   What might he have been doing? [*Writing a letter*]?

Now consider an alternative analysis of Aspectual Auxiliaries as head Vs of VPs, under which the bracketed VP in (1) above would have the structure:

(6)

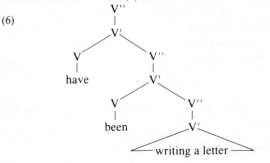

Exercises

Discuss how this 'Head' analysis of Aspectuals fares in comparison with the Specifier
analysis, in relation to the issues raised above, and in the text.

Exercise VIII

In the text, we made the following assumptions:

(A) (i)   Verbal adjuncts recursively expand V-bar into V-bar
    (ii)   *do so* is a pro-V-bar
    (iii)   Ellipsis can affect either V-bar or VP

Now consider two alternative sets of assumptions:

(B) (i)   Verbal adjuncts expand V-bar into VP
    (ii)   *do so* is a pro-V-bar
    (iii)   Ellipsis can affect either V-bar or VP

(C) (i)   Verbal adjuncts may occur either as constituents of VP as in (A) (i), or as
        immediate constituents of S
    (ii)   *do so* is a pro-VP (not a pro-V-bar)
    (iii)   Ellipsis can affect VP (not V-bar)

Compare and contrast these three analyses in respect of data such as that discussed in
the text, and any other data you deem relevant. What problems arise with analyses B
and C, and how (if at all) might they be overcome? What implications (if any) would
analyses (B) or (C) have for the analysis of Aspectual Auxiliaries presented in the text?

Exercise IX

In this chapter, we argued that Phrases in English have a hierarchical internal structure, not a flat structure. More particularly, we assumed a hierarchical
three-level theory, which has the properties in (A) below:

A: *hierarchical three-level theory*
    Complements expand an X into an X-bar, Adjuncts/Attributes expand
    X-bar into another X-bar, and Specifiers expand X-bar into X-double-bar

But now consider two alternative hierarchical analyses:

B: *hierarchical two-level theory*
    Complements expand X into X-bar; an X-bar can be expanded into
    another X-bar by the addition of either an Adjunct/Attribute or a Speci-
    fier

C: *hierarchical one-level theory*
    X can be expanded into another X by the addition of either a Comple-
    ment, or an Adjunct/Attribute, or a Specifier

283

What structure would be assigned by each of these analyses to a Noun Phrase such as (1) below?

(1)   [*a student of Physics with long hair*]

Could each of these analyses deal equally successfully with the various differences between Complements, Adjuncts/Attributes, and Determiners which we highlighted in the text?

What would be the implications of analyses B and C for Phrases such as those bracketed below:

(2)   He fell [right into the mud]
(3)   I didn't realise he was [that fond of his mother]
(4)   He may [have been writing a letter]

**Exercise X

One of the 'standard' assumptions of the type of constituent structure analysis we have presented here is what we might call the MAXIMAL STRUCTURE HYPO-THESIS. This principle specifies that any unmodified X which has the same distribution as XP is to be regarded as an XP, and likewise that any specifier-less X' which has the same distribution as a full XP is likewise to be analysed as a full XP. Given the assumptions of the MAXIMAL STRUCTURE HYPOTHESIS, a sentence such as:

(1)   Presidents can lie

would not be assigned a structure such as (2) below:

(2)

```
              S
        _____|_____
      N       M       V
      |       |       |
  Presidents can     lie
```

Rather, it would be argued that *presidents* must be an NP as well as an N, and that *lie* must be a VP as well as a V, so that (2) would have the structure (3) below:

(3)

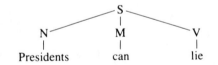

```
              S
        _____|_____
      NP      M      VP
      |       |       |
      N'      can     V'
      |               |
      N               V
      |               |
  Presidents         lie
```

Among the arguments conventionally used in support of analysis (3) are the following. First, *presidents* has the same distribution as (and can be replaced by) a full NP such as [*the officials in the White House*], and likewise *lie* has the same distribution as (and can be replaced by) a full VP such as [*carefully conceal the truth from the media*]: cf.

(4)   [*The officials in the White House*] can [*carefully conceal the truth from the media*]

Secondly, *presidents* can be replaced/referred to by a pro-NP such as *they*, just as *lie* can be replaced/referred to by a pro-VP such as *so*:

(5)   *So they* can

Thirdly, both can undergo 'emphatic preposing' (which is normally restricted to Phrases): cf.

(6) (a)   *Presidents*, we all know can lie
   (b)   *Lie*, they certainly can

Fourthly, both *presidents* and *lie* can serve as sentence-fragments (a property of full Phrases):

(7) (a)   SPEAKER A: Who can lie?
          SPEAKER B: *Presidents*
   (b)   SPEAKER A: What can presidents do best?
          SPEAKER B: *Lie*

And fifthly, *lie* can undergo *Ellipsis*, a process which normally applies only to VP or V-bar:

(8)   They certainly can l̷i̷e̷

Hence, given traditional assumptions, analysis (3) is clearly to be preferred over analysis (2); for, a number of phenomena which apply only to *maximal projections* (= full Phrases) can apply to *presidents* and *lie*.

But now consider an alternative hypothesis, which we might term the MINIMAL STRUCTURE HYPOTHESIS: under this alternative set of assumptions, an unmodified X is assigned the status of X alone, and not that of X' or XP; and an X' which lacks a specifier is assigned the status of X-bar only, not that of XP. Given the MINIMAL STRUCTURE HYPOTHESIS, sentence (1) above would have the structure (2), and *not* the structure (3). For the purposes of this alternative analysis, we should have to assume the following revised definition of Maximal Projection:

(9)   The maximal projection of a given head constituent X is the largest projection of that X in the P-marker in which the X occurs

Thus, given (9), the Noun *presidents* in (2) would be the Maximal Projection (and also the minimal projection) of the head Noun *presidents*, and hence would be eligible to undergo rules which apply to maximal projections: likewise, the Verb *lie* would be the maximal (and also the minimal) projection of the head Verb *lie*, and thus could function either as a minimal or a maximal projection.

How would our revised analysis handle the facts of (4)–(8) above? What structure might we posit for a sentence such as (10) overleaf, under the MINIMAL STRUCTURE HYPOTHESIS?

Other Phrases

(10)   Presidents of America can distort truth

Which of the following Noun Phrases would prove problematic for the proposed analysis, on the assumption that only identical categories can be conjoined by Ordinary Coordination?

(11) (a)   Presidents and [their advisers in the White House]
   (b)   Some [presidents and senior politicians]

(Brackets are added to indicate the intended reading.) Can you think of any way of overcoming the problem concerned, while still maintaining that *presidents* here is only an N, and not also an N-bar or NP?

Are there any other problems which the MINIMAL STRUCTURE HYPOTHESIS would run into?

6
Clauses

6.1 Overview

In the previous chapter, we took a detailed look at the internal structure of various different types of *Phrases* (Noun Phrases, Verb Phrases, Adjectival Phrases, Adverbial Phrases, and Prepositional Phrases). Now, by contrast, we shall turn to look in some detail at the internal structure of *Clauses*. Since much of our subsequent discussion will focus on similarities and differences between *finite* and *nonfinite* Clauses, we shall begin with a brief characterisation of the essential differences between these two Clause types.

6.2 Finite and nonfinite Clauses

The distinction between *finite* and *nonfinite* Clauses is based partly (though not wholly) on morphological criteria: thus, a Clause is *finite* if it contains a *finite* Verb (i.e. a Verb inflected for Tense/Agreement), and *nonfinite* if it lacks a finite Verb (e.g. if it is a verbless Clause, or if it is a Clause containing a *nonfinite* tenseless and agreementless Verb). Let's look briefly at the relevant Tense and Agreement properties which characterise finite Verbs.

From a morphological point of view, English can be said to have a binary (i.e. two-way) Tense contrast between *present* and *past* tense forms (in finite Clauses, obviously). The relevant set of inflections for finite regular Verbs are listed in (1) below:

(1)   PAST TENSE: -(*e*)*d* for all persons and numbers
        PRESENT TENSE: -(*e*)*s* for 3rd person singular forms
        -*Ø* for all other forms

(Note that *Ø* represents a 'zero inflectional morpheme', and hence indicates that no overt ending is added to mark Tense in the relevant forms.) Hence we find paradigms such as the following:

(2)   PRESENT TENSE: I/you/we/they *hate* Syntax
        He/she/it *hates* Syntax
        PAST TENSE: I/you/he/she/it/we/they *hated* Syntax

The inflections in (1) mark not only *Tense* but also *Agreement*: for example, the Present Tense -*(e)s* inflection is only used with a Third Person Singular Subject, so that -*(e)s* marks not only Tense (= Present), but also Agreement (with a Third Person Singular Subject). At first sight, it might seem as if Agreement isn't marked in Past Tense forms at all: but Agreement is overtly marked in the Past Tense forms of the irregular Verb *be*, as we see from:

(3) (a)　　I/he/she/it *was* late

　　(b)　　You/we/they *were* late

where the *was*-form is used to mark Agreement with a First or Third Person Singular Subject, and the *were* form is used to mark Agreement with other Subjects. Hence, rather than say that Agreement is a property only of irregu- past tense forms in English, we shall say that all Past Tense forms are marked for Agreement, but that this Agreement is *overtly* marked in the case of irregu- lar Verbs, and *covertly* marked in the case of regular Verbs (in much the same way as we might say that the plural morpheme is *overtly* marked in the Noun *lambs* in an expression such as 'two lambs', but *covertly* marked on the Noun *sheep* in an expression such as 'two sheep').

In contrast to finite Clauses, *nonfinite* Clauses are those which contain no Verb inflected for Tense or Agreement: so, for example, a Clause which con- tains only *nonfinite* Verbs – i.e. Verbs which are uninflected for Tense/ Agreement – is a nonfinite Clause. There are three types of *nonfinite* verb-form in English: viz. (i) uninflected *infinitive* forms which comprise simply the *base* or *stem* of the Verb with no added inflection (such forms are frequently used after the so-called 'infinitive particle' *to*); (ii) *gerund* forms which comprise the base plus the -*ing* suffix; and (*perfect/passive*) *participle* forms which generally comprise the base plus the -*(e)n* inflection (though there are numerous irregu- lar participle forms in English). Thus, the bracketed Clauses in (4) below are all nonfinite, because they contain only nonfinite verb-forms: for example, the italicised Verb in (4) (a) is an *infinitive*, that in (4) (b) is a *gerund*, and that in (4) (c) is a (passive) *participle*:

(4) (a)　　I've never known [John (to) *be* so rude to anyone]

　　(b)　　We don't want [it *raining* on your birthday]

　　(c)　　I had [my car *stolen* from the car-park]

Nonfinite verb-forms are intrinsically tenseless and agreementless; they re- main invariable in form whatever the context, and cannot carry finite Tense/ Agreement inflections such as Present Tense -*(e)s* or Past Tense -*(e)d*: hence, the italicised *infinitive* Verb *hate* in (5) (a) below cannot be replaced by a finite form such as *hates* or *hated*, as we see from the ungrammaticality of (5) (b) and (c) below:

(5) (a)   It would be silly [for me/you/him/her/us/them to *hate* Syntax]
    (b)   *It would be silly [for him/her to *hates* Syntax]
    (c)   *It would have been silly [for you/them to *hated* Syntax]

Of course, since the present tense inflection is -Ø for first and second person singular forms, and for all plural forms of regular finite Verbs, it is often not immediately apparent from the morphology of a given verb-form which carries no overt inflection whether it is finite or nonfinite. For example, consider the Verb *hate* in the bracketed Clauses below:

(6) (a)   I know [that you *hate* Syntax]
    (b)   I'd never known [you *hate* anything as much as Syntax]

Is *hate* finite in either or both of these examples? We cannot (in this case) tell by looking at the morphology of the Verb *hate*, since although it carries no overt inflection, second person forms (i.e. *you*-forms) of present tense regular Verbs carry a 'zero' inflection and hence appear to be inflectionless. So how can we tell? There are a number of 'tests' we can apply here. Firstly, we can change the Subject of the Clause from *you* to a third person singular Subject like *John*, and then see whether the Verb remains invariable, or adds the present tense -(*e*)*s* inflection: the results are as in (7) below:

(7) (a)   I know [that John *hates*/*hate* Syntax]
    (b)   I've never known [him *hate*/*hates* anything as much as Syntax]

So, this 'test' suggests that *hate* is finite in (6) (a), but nonfinite in (6) (b).

A second 'test' we can apply is to see whether the relevant verb-form can be replaced by a past tense verb-form carrying the overt past tense inflection -(*e*)*d*. Applying this test to our two sentences in (7) yields the results in (8) below:

(8) (a)   I knew [that John *hated*/*hate* Syntax]
    (b)   I'd never known [him *hate*/*hated* anything as much as Syntax]

So once again, we reach the same conclusion that the Verb is finite in the (a) examples, and nonfinite in the (b) examples.

A third test we can apply is to take advantage of an idiosyncratic morphological property of Modal Auxiliaries (which we discussed in Chapter 3), namely the fact that they lack nonfinite forms, and hence are *intrinsically finite*. So, it follows that any Clause which can contain a Modal Auxiliary is finite, while any Clause which cannot contain a Modal is nonfinite. Applying this criterion to our examples in (6) above gives the results in (9) below:

(9) (a)   I know [that you *will/might/could/should* hate Syntax]

(b)   *I've never known [you *will/might/could/should* hate anything as much as Syntax]

The fact that we can have a Modal in (9) (a) but not (9) (b) confirms our earlier findings that the Verb in the (a) sentence in (6) is finite, while the Verb in the corresponding (b) sentence is nonfinite.

We can summarise our discussion so far in the following terms. We have seen that finite Clauses are those which contain a finite Verb (overtly or covertly) marked for Tense/Agreement, and that nonfinite Clauses are those which lack a finite Verb, e.g. verbless Clauses, or Clauses containing an invariable tenseless/agreementless verb-form such as an infinitive, gerund, or perfective/passive participle).

The distinction between *finite* and *nonfinite* Clauses (as noted above) is based 'partly (though not wholly) on morphological criteria'. What we meant by this is that any Clause which does or can contain an inflected Verb or Auxiliary is indeed a finite Clause; but the converse is not necessarily true: that is, a Clause containing an apparently uninflected (or invariable) Verb is not necessarily nonfinite. The reason for saying this is that some verb-forms which it is convenient to treat for syntactic purposes as *finite* lack the typical morphological characteristics of finite Verbs. For example, in traditional grammars it is usual to draw a distinction between two different types of finite Clause: namely, *indicative* Clauses like that bracketed in (10) (a) below, and *subjunctive* Clauses like that bracketed in (10) (b):

(10) (a)   I know [that you *leave* for Hawaii tomorrow]

(b)   I demand [that you *leave* for Hawaii tomorrow]

Both of them are introduced by the particle *that*; and both types of *that*-Clause are generally classified as *finite*. But there are clear morphological differences between the two; the Verb in the (a) example can take the present tense -(*e*)*s* and past tense -(*e*)*d* inflections (in an appropriate context), whereas the Verb in the (b) example cannot but rather must remain invariable: cf.

(11) (a)   I know [that John *leaves/*leave* for Hawaii tomorrow]

(b)   I know [that John *left/*leave* for Hawaii last week]

(12) (a)   I demand [that John *leave/*leaves* for Hawaii tomorrow]

(b)   I demanded [that John *leave/*left* for Hawaii the following day]

So, it follows from this that Verbs in indicative Clauses like those italicised in (11) are variable, whereas those in subjunctive Clauses like that in (12) are invariable. But if subjunctive Clauses do not contain any overt Tense/ Agreement marking, why are they considered *finite*?

The claim that subjunctive Clauses are finite can be defended on both *universalist* and *particularist* grounds. On universalist grounds, we can argue that in languages which have a richer inflectional system than English, subjunctive Clauses do indeed turn out to be inflected. For example, the Spanish counterparts of the bracketed Clauses in (12) contain a verb-form overtly inflected for Tense and Agreement: cf.

(13) (a) Exigo [que Juan *parta* para Hawaii mañana]
         I-demand that Juan leave (*3rd Person Singular Present Subjunctive*) for Hawaii tomorrow

   (b) Exigí [que Juan *partiese* para Hawaii el día siguiente]
         I-demanded that Juan left (*3rd Person Singular Past Subjunctive*) for Hawaii the following day

And the same point could be made in relation to countless other languages with rich inflectional systems (Italian, Romanian, etc.). Since subjunctive Clauses are clearly *finite* in such languages, we might argue that on universalist grounds it is plausible to consider them finite in English also.

The second (obviously more compelling) reason for treating subjunctive Clauses in English as *finite* is that they share certain morphosyntactic properties in common with indicative Clauses which differentiate them from nonfinite Clauses. For example, neither indicative nor subjunctive Clauses can be *subjectless*, whereas nonfinite Clauses can indeed be subjectless: cf.

(14) (a) *I know [*that leaves for Hawaii tomorrow*] (indicative)
   (b) *I demand [*that leave for Hawaii tomorrow*] (subjunctive)
   (c) I intend [*to leave for Hawaii tomorrow*] (infinitive)
   (d) I intend [*leaving for Hawaii tomorrow*] (gerund)

Secondly, subjunctive Clauses pattern like indicative Clauses (and unlike nonfinite Clauses) with respect to the *case-marking* of any overt Subject which the Clause contains. Personal Pronouns like *I, you, he* etc. in English have three different *case-forms*, illustrated by the partial paradigm below:

(15)   NOMINATIVE   I   he   we   they
        OBJECTIVE   me   him   us   them
        GENITIVE   my   his   our   their

291

Now, the Subject of either an indicative or a subjunctive Clause is always assigned *Nominative* case, as we see from:

(16) (a)   I know [that *they/*them/*their* leave for Hawaii tomorrow]
     (b)   I demand [that *they/*them/*their* leave for Hawaii tomorrow]

By contrast, the Subject of an infinitive Clause is assigned *Objective* case, as we see from:

(17)   I want [*them/*they/*their* to leave for Hawaii tomorrow]

And the Subject of a *gerund* Clause is assigned either *Objective* or *Genitive* case: cf.

(18)   I don't like the idea of [*them/their/*they* leaving for Hawaii tomorrow]

Thus, both in respect of never being subjectless, and in respect of requiring *Nominative* case-marking for their Subjects, subjunctive Clauses pattern like indicative Clauses (and unlike nonfinite Clauses), and for this reason are considered to be 'finite'. Thus, we have two major types of finite Clause (indicative and subjunctive), and three major types of untensed Clause (infinitival, gerundive, and participial).

6.3   Constituent structure of Clauses

After this brief terminological excursion, we now return to consider the problem of more immediate concern to us here – namely the question of the internal constituent structure of Clauses. Most of our discussion will revolve around indicative Clauses on the one hand, and infinitive Clauses on the other. We shall begin by looking at the internal structure of indicative Clauses.

In all of our discussion so far, we have been assuming that the basic Phrase Structure Rule expanding indicative Clauses is (19) below:

(19)   S → NP M VP

(where NP is the maximal phrasal expansion of N, and VP is likewise the maximal phrasal expansion of V). But note that a rule like (19) makes no provision for Clauses in which the Subject NP is preceded by a clause-introducing particle like *that, for*, or *whether* – as in the bracketed Clauses below:

(20) (a)   We know for certain [*that* the President will approve the project]
     (b)   We would obviously all prefer [*for* the matter to be resolved amicably]
     (c)   I couldn't really say [*whether* it will rain]

Since such particles are typically used to introduce *Complement Clauses* (i.e. Clauses which function as the *Complement* of a Verb, Noun, Adjective, etc.), they are known as *Complementisers*, which is generally abbreviated as COMP, or (in more recent work) simply C. But what exactly is the constituent structure of Clauses which contain a C constituent ? One possibility (suggested by Emonds (1976), p. 142, and Soames and Perlmutter (1979), p. 63) would be that C is generated within S as a sister to the subject NP of the Clause, by a rule such as:

(21)   S → C NP M VP

However, Bresnan (1970) puts forward an alternative analysis: she suggests that C and S together form a larger clausal unit which she calls S-bar (= S'). Her analysis incorporates the following two Phrase Structure Rules:

(22) (i)   S' → C S
    (ii)   S → NP M VP

For convenience, we'll refer to Emonds' analysis as the S analysis, and to Bresnan's as the S-bar analysis.

Under the S analysis (21), the *that*-clause in (20) (a) – [*that the President will approve the project*] – might have the structure (23) (a) below, whereas on the alternative S-bar analysis (22), it would have the structure (23) (b):

(23) (a)

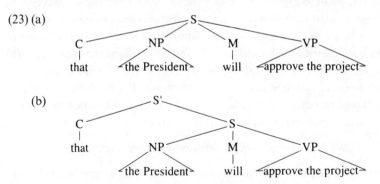

(b)

Which analysis is the correct one ? There are a number of arguments which seem to favour the S-bar analysis (23) (b).

One such argument can be formulated in relation to *Shared Constituent Coordination*. Consider the following example:

(24)   I've been wondering whether (but am not entirely sure that) *the President will approve the project*

Recall that in this type of structure, the 'shared sequence' must be a constituent: it follows, therefore, that the italicised string in (24) must be a constituent.

But this would be true only under an S-bar analysis like (23) (b), not under an S analysis like (23) (a).

A further argument in support of the S-bar analysis comes from facts relating to a type of Ellipsis known as *Gapping* – so called because there is an apparent 'gap' in the middle of one or more of the conjuncts. This type of Ellipsis is subject to an interesting restriction, illustrated by the contrast in (25):

(25) (a)   I wonder whether [s John likes fish]
           and [s *Mary meat*]
     (b)   *I wonder [s' whether John likes fish]
           and [s' whether *Mary meat*]

Observe that the Verb *likes* can be omitted from the italicised second conjunct (leaving a 'gap' where we would otherwise expect the Verb to be) in (25) (a), but not in (25) (b). How can we account for this puzzling contrast? One possible answer would be to posit that *Gapping* can only take place when S constituents are conjoined, not when S-bar constituents are conjoined. But, of course, any such solution presupposes the existence of S and S-bar as separate categories, and hence is consistent only with the S-bar analysis (23) (b), not with the S analysis (23) (a).

Thus far, we have argued that *Complement Clauses* like those bracketed in (20) form an S-bar constituent whose immediate constituents are C and S: in other words, we have assumed that the constituent structure of Complement Clauses is generated by rules such as (22), and is thus along the lines of (23) (b) above. But one problem posed by this analysis is that not all Complement Clauses do in fact contain overt Complementisers. For example, in place of the bracketed *that*-clause in (20) (a) we could have had the same Clause without any overt Complementiser (i.e. without *that*): cf.

(26)   We know for certain [*the President will approve the project*]

How are we to analyse the italicised complementiserless Clause in (26)? There are two obvious possibilities. One is to say that it is an S constituent (and *not* an S-bar), and therefore does not contain a Complementiser. The second is to say that it is an S-bar of the usual [C S] structure, except that the Complementiser position has been left '*empty*'. The two different analyses for the bracketed string in (28) can be represented schematically as in (27) below:

(27) (a)   [s the President will approve the project]
     (b)   [s' [c e] [s the President will approve the project]]

(*e* = 'empty', so [c e] means that the Complementiser position has been left empty.) Which analysis is better? This is clearly not an issue which can be resolved by any appeal to 'intuitions about structure'; rather, it must be resolved on the basis of empirical evidence. And, as we shall see, the balance of the evidence available favours the second (empty Complementiser) solution.

One piece of evidence in support of the 'empty C' analysis comes from *Coordination* facts. Thus, we find that a complementiserless Clause can be conjoined with one containing an overt Complementiser: cf.

(28)   We know [*the President will approve the project*], and [*that Congress will ratify his decision*]

There is no doubt that the second bracketed Complement Clause in (28) is an S-bar, since it contains an overt Complementiser, *that*. But given the constraint that *only constituents belonging to the same category can be conjoined*, it follows that the first italicised Clause must also be an S-bar; and since it has no overt Complementiser, a natural conclusion is that the C position has been left *empty*.

6.4   Structure of Main Clauses

So far, we have looked only at *Complement Clauses*, and concluded that – irrespective of whether they contain an overt Complementiser or not – they have the status of S-bar. But what about *non-embedded Clauses* (i.e. 'main', 'principal', 'root', or 'independent' Clauses)? Is it plausible to claim that these too are S-bar constituents containing a C (= Complementiser)? At first sight, this might not seem plausible; for whereas Complement Clauses either can or must contain an overt Complementiser, main Clauses by contrast can never contain an overt Complementiser in English: hence the ungrammaticality of:

(29) (a)   *That the government may change its decision
     (b)   *Whether the Prime Minister will resign?

Obviously, one way of accounting for why Main Clauses cannot contain overt Complementisers would be to say that they have the status of S constituents, and *not* of S-bar. However, we shall reject this analysis here, and argue instead in favour of an alternative analysis in which Main Clauses are indeed S-bar constituents, though (in languages like English) subject to a language-particular restriction that the C position in a Main Clause must obligatorily be left empty of overt Complementisers like *that/for/whether*.

This analysis can be defended on both *universalist* and *particularist* grounds. On universalist grounds, we might argue that the 'Complementiser' analysis is rendered more plausible by the fact that many languages do use overt Complementisers to introduce main Clauses. For example, there are countless languages which use an overt interrogative Complementiser (usually called a *question particle* in traditional grammars) to introduce interrogative main Clauses (i.e. they say '*Whether* you are leaving?' instead of 'Are you leaving?'): cf. e.g.

(30) (a) *Vai* māte mājā? (Latvian)
          Whether mother home? ('Is mother at home?')

     (b) *Kas* suitsetate? (Estonian)
          Whether you-smoke? ('Do you smoke?')

     (c) *Aya* Ali ketab darad? (Persian)
          Whether Ali books has? ('Does Ali have any books?')

     (d) *Waš* hdarti mᶜah? (Colloquial Moroccan Arabic)
          Whether you-spoke with-him? ('Did you speak to him?')

     (e) *Nga* nin ndut-am e mɛnndɛ bɔ (Duala)
          Whether this sorrow-my it will end? ('Will this sorrow of mine (ever) end?')

     (f) *Czy* zamykacie okna? (Polish)
          Whether you-close windows? ('Are you closing the windows?')

     (g) *Walay* sarai khaza khuwakhae? (Pashto)
          Whether man woman likes? ('Does the man like the woman?')

     (h) *Razve* on ne prixodil? (Russian)
          Whether he not came ('Hasn't he come?') [Comrie (1984), p. 22]

     (i) *An* bpósfaidh tú mé? (Irish)
          Whether will-marry you me ('Will you marry me?')
          [McKloskey (1979), p. 79]

     (j) *Is* idda hmad s tmazirt (Berber)
          Whether went Ahmed to country
          'Did Ahmed go to the country?' [Sadiqi (1986), p. 9]

     (k) *Tsi* hot er geleient dos bux? (Yiddish)
          Whether has he read the book?
          'Has he read the book?'
          [den Besten and Moed-van Walraven (1986), p. 114]

     (l) *Ob* Johanna den Wagen verkauft hat? (German)
          Whether Joan the car sold has
          'Has Joan sold the car?'
          [Clahsen and Smolka (1986), p. 156]

A similar construction was found in Old English: cf.

(31)   *Hwæðer* ge nu secan gold on treowum?

296

Whether you now seek gold in trees?
'Do you now seek gold in trees?' [Traugott (1972), p. 73]

And it is interesting to note that young children learning English may mis-
analyse preposed Auxiliaries in questions as invariable 'question particles':
thus (as we noted in Chapter 1), Akmajian and Heny (1975, p. 17) report one
three-year-old girl producing questions of the form:

(32) (a)   *Is* I can do that?
     (b)   *Is* you should eat the apple?
     (c)   *Is* Ben did go there?
     (d)   *Is* the apple juice won't spill?

One possible interpretation of these facts is that the child uses *is* as an invariable interrogative Complementiser, and thus has Complementisers introducing main Clauses.

   Nor is the occurrence of overt Complementisers in main Clauses restricted
to interrogative sentences: for example, exclamative main Clauses in many
languages can be introduced by an overt Complementiser: cf.

(33) (a)   *At* du junne gøre det! (Danish)
           That you could do it
           How could you do such a thing! [Jacobsen (1986), p. 37]
     (b)   *Daß* mir das nicht früher aufgefallen ist! (German)
           That me that no earlier struck is
           'To think that it didn't strike me earlier!'
           [Haider (1986), p. 50]
     (c)   *Qu'*elle est bavarde! (French)
           That she is talkative
           'What a chatterbox she is!' [Gérard (1980), p. 24]
     (d)   *Að* María skuli elska Jón (Icelandic)
           That Mary shall-SUB love John [SUB = subjunctive]
           'That Mary should love John!' [Thráinsson (1986), p. 188]

And the same is also true of certain imperative constructions in many
languages: cf.

(34) (a)   *Qu'*il aille se faire foutre! (French)
           That he go-SUB himself make do
           'Let him go and get stuffed'
     (b)   *Daß* du ja die Füße vom Tisch läßt! (German)
           That you yes the feet off table keep
           Keep your feet off the table! [Clahsen and Smolka (1986), p. 156]

(c)   *Que* vengan todos! (Spanish)
        That come all
        'Let them all come' [Harmer and Norton (1945), p. 179]

And Ross (1970, pp. 245 and 270) cites the following examples to show that independent declarative Clauses in Classical Arabic and Spanish can be introduced by a declarative Complementiser (italicised):

(35) (a)   *?inna* lwalada qad taraka lbayta (Arabic)
            That the-boy did leave the-house
            'The boy left the house'
     (b)   *Que* mi gato se enratonó
            That my cat itself enmoused
            'My cat got sick from eating too many mice'

Given that main Clauses can contain overt Complementisers in many different languages, it seems plausible enough (on universalist grounds) to argue that main Clauses in English contain a *covert* Complementiser (= C) constituent.

However, a more compelling set of arguments in favour of the 'empty Complementiser' analysis for English can be formulated in *particularist* terms (i.e. in relation to internal facts about English). Central to the argumentation here are interrogative structures (i.e. questions) which contain an 'inverted' Auxiliary. To see what we mean by the term *inverted Auxiliary*, consider the following contrast:

(36) (a)   Your sister *could* go to College
     (b)   *Could* your sister go to College?

In the statement (36) (a), the Modal Auxiliary Verb *could* occupies its 'normal' position following the Subject NP [*your sister*] and preceding the VP [*go to College*]; but in the corresponding question (36) (b), the Auxiliary *could* has (in some intuitive sense which we shall make precise in Chapter 8) been 'inverted' with the subject NP [*your sister*], and occupies pre-subject position. Now, pre-subject position is the position typically occupied by *Complementisers*, as we see from examples such as (20) above. Hence, an obvious suggestion to make is that inverted Auxiliaries occupy the pre-subject Complementiser position. Now, if this is the case, then we should expect that Complementisers and inverted Auxiliaries are mutually exclusive, since both occupy the C position in a Clause. In other words, we should expect that Clauses introduced by Complementisers cannot contain inverted Auxiliaries, and conversely. And we shall present two pieces of evidence that this is indeed the case in English.

Our first piece of evidence comes from a type of construction known traditionally as 'semi-indirect speech'. The following paradigm will serve to illustrate what we mean by this term:

(37) (a)   '*Will I get a degree?*' John wondered
     (b)   John wondered *whether he would get a degree*
     (c)   John wondered *would he get a degree*

The italicised sequence in (37) (a) is said to be an instance of *direct speech*: John's exact words are recorded verbatim, and are bounded in the spelling by a question mark and inverted commas; points to note here include the use of the present tense Auxiliary *will*, the inversion of the Auxiliary, and the use of the first person pronoun *I* to represent the speaker. The italicised sequence in (37) (b) is said to be an example of *indirect speech* or *reported speech*; note that the present tense Auxiliary *will* used in the direct speech has been transposed to the Past Tense form *would*, there is no inversion of the Auxiliary, and the Pronoun *I* used to designate the speaker in the direct speech has been transposed to its third person counterpart *he*. The italicised sequence in (37) (c) is said to be an instance of *semi-indirect speech*, because it shares some of the features of indirect speech (viz. Tense Transposition and Pronoun Transposition), while retaining other characteristics of direct speech (in this case, the use of Auxiliary Inversion). However, what is of particular interest to us here is the fact that the presence of the Complementiser *whether* in (37) (b) above excludes the possibility of having an inverted Auxiliary in pre-subject position, as we see from the ungrammaticality of (38) below:

(38)   *John wondered *whether would he get a degree*

Why should this be? The answer we propose here is that this is because both Complementisers and inverted Auxiliaries occupy the pre-subject C position: hence, when (as in (38) above) the C position is already filled by the Complementiser *whether*, inversion of the Auxiliary is not possible, on the assumption that once a given position is filled by one constituent, it cannot be filled by another (i.e. we can only have one constituent occupying any given position). More generally, we might conclude that the ungrammaticality of sentences such as (38) provides us with strong empirical evidence in support of our assumption that inverted Auxiliaries occupy the pre-subject C position.

Further evidence in support of this conclusion comes from the rather more archaic subjunctive construction illustrated in (39) below:

(39) (a)   One must be vigilant, [*whether* it be at home or abroad]
     (b)   One must be vigilant, [*be* it at home or abroad]
     (c)   *One must be vigilant, [*whether be* it at home or abroad]

In each case, the bracketed Clause in (39) is a subjunctive Clause (= S-bar) containing the subjunctive Auxiliary Verb *be*. In example (39) (a), the subjunctive Clause is introduced by the italicised Complementiser *whether*, which occupies the pre-subject C position. In (39) (b), the bracketed Clause is introduced by the subjunctive Auxiliary *be*, which is likewise positioned immediately before the Subject NP *it*, and so might be assumed to occupy the pre-subject C position. In (39) (c), we see that it is not possible for both the Complementiser *whether* and the Auxiliary *be* to be positioned in front of the Subject NP *it*. Why should this be? Well, if (as we claim here) both Complementisers and inverted Auxiliaries are positioned in C, then the presence of the Complementiser *whether* in C in (39) excludes the possibility of the Auxiliary *be* being inverted with the subject NP *it*. What is of more general interest to us here is that paradigms such as (39) provide further empirical support for our claim that inverted Auxiliaries in English are positioned in C.

Thus, we have two pieces of language-particular evidence that inverted Auxiliaries in English are positioned in C. Now, this means that an interrogative main Clause such as:

(40)   Would she get a degree?

must have the status of an S-bar constituent containing the Modal Auxiliary *would* in C, and thus will have the simplified structure (41) below:

(41)

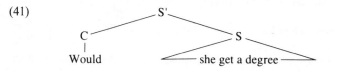

So, the general conclusion to emerge from our discussion is that not just interrogative *Complement Clauses* but also interrogative *main Clauses* have the status of S-bar constituents.

However, we might object that while it is plausible to analyse interrogative main Clauses which contain an inverted Auxiliary as S-bar constituents, it is not plausible to claim S-bar status for noninterrogative main Clauses lacking an inverted Auxiliary – e.g. for simple declarative Clauses (i.e. statements) such as (36) (a) above, repeated as (42) below:

(42)   Your sister could go to College

However, Coordination facts seem to undermine this hasty conclusion: thus, consider the following:

(43)   [Your sister could go to College], but [*would she get a degree?*]

The second (italicised) conjunct is a Clause containing an inverted Auxiliary, *would*. Given our earlier assumptions that inverted Auxiliaries are in C, and that C is a constituent of S-bar, it follows that the italicised Clause in (43) must be an S-bar. But our familiar constraint on Coordination tells us that only constituents belonging to *the same Category* can be conjoined. Since the second Clause in (43) is clearly an S-bar, then it follows that the first Clause must also be an S-bar – one in which the C(omplementiser) position has been left empty.

The specific conclusions which we have reached in our discussion can be summarised as follows:

(44) (i)   Embedded Clauses containing an overt Complementiser are S-bar constituents

   (ii)   Embedded Clauses lacking an overt Complementiser also have the status of S-bar (with an empty C)

   (iii)   Main Clauses containing an overt Complementiser or inverted Auxiliary are S-bar constituents

   (iv)   Main Clauses lacking an overt Complementiser or inverted Auxiliary are S-bar constituents (with an empty C)

The obvious generalisation to extract from (44) is that:

(45)   All *Ordinary Clauses* have the status of S-bar constituents of the schematic form [C   S], and thus contain a C constituent which may either be *filled* (e.g. by an overt Complementiser or an inverted Auxiliary) or left *empty*

What precisely we mean by the term *Ordinary Clause* here is something which will become clearer as our discussion proceeds.

Given that both Complement Clauses and main Clauses have the status of S-bar constituents, it follows that a *complex sentence* (i.e. sentence containing more than one Clause) such as:

(46)   Mary might think [that he will resign]

will contain two S-bar constituents, one containing the Modal *might*, and the other containing the Modal *will*: thus, (46) will have the structure indicated in (47) below:

(47)

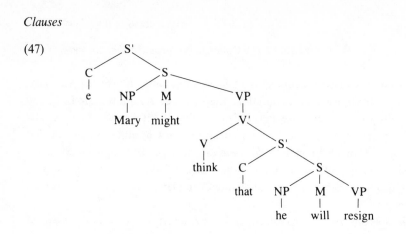

The only difference between the two Clauses in that the main Clause contains an *empty* Complementiser constituent, whereas the Complementiser position in the Complement Clause is *filled* by the overt Complementiser *that*: but both Clauses are finite indicative S-bar constituents.

We already know (cf. rule (22)(i)) that the two immediate constituents of S-bar are C and S: C can either be filled by a Complementiser (*that/for/ whether/if*), or by an inverted Auxiliary (*will/would/can/could/has/have/is/was/ were*, etc); or it can be left empty. Complementisers can be classified into types on the basis of two different criteria: (i) syntactic (whether they are used in interrogative or noninterrogative Clauses), and (ii) morphological (whether they serve to introduce finite or nonfinite Clauses). So, for example, we might classify *that* as a noninterrogative finite Complementiser, since it only introduces finite Clauses, not infinitives: cf.

(48) (a) I am anxious [*that* you should arrive on time]
  (b) *I am anxious [*that* you to arrive on time]

Conversely, we might classify *for* as a noninterrogative infinitive Complementiser, since it can introduce infinitive Clauses, but not finite Clauses – cf. e.g.

(49) (a) I am anxious [*for* you to arrive on time]
  (b) *I am anxious [*for* you should arrive on time]

By contrast, *whether* is an interrogative Complementiser which can introduce finite and nonfinite Clauses alike; whereas *if* by is an interrogative Complementiser which can only introduce finite Complement Clauses: cf.

(50) (a) I don't know [*whether/if* I should agree]
  (b) I don't know [*whether/*if* to agree]

If we were to use the feature [± WH] to indicate whether a Complementiser is interrogative or not, and the feature [± FINITE] to indicate whether a Complementiser can introduce a finite or nonfinite Clause (or both), then we could analyse each of the four Complementisers discussed above as having the feature structure (51) below:

(51)   *that*   = [− WH, + FINITE]
         for   = [− WH, − FINITE]
         whether = [+ WH, ± FINITE]
         if   = [+ WH, + FINITE]

We might further assume that the constituent C can be expanded into a feature complex by a feature rule such as (52) below:

(52)   C → [± WH, ± FINITE]

and this rule would then generate the feature complexes specified in (53) below:

(53)   [+ WH, + FINITE] (can be filled by *whether/if*)
         [+ WH, − FINITE] (can be filled by *whether*)
         [− WH, + FINITE] (can be filled by *that*)
         [− WH, − FINITE] (can be filled by *for*)

6.5   Internal structure of S

As we see from rule (22) (i), the two immediate constituents of S-bar are [C S]. Having looked at the range of Complementisers which can occur in C, we now turn instead to examine in some detail the internal structure of S. Recall that we have assumed that in finite indicative Clauses, S has three immediate constituents: [NP M VP] (cf. rule (22) (ii) above). But what about the internal structure of S in *nonfinite* Clauses – and more especially, infinitival Clauses? Observe that there is an apparent parallelism of structure between indicative Clauses like that italicised in (54) (a) below, and its (italicised) infinitival counterpart in (54) (b):

(54) (a)   I am anxious *that* [*John should finish by Friday*]
     (b)   I am anxious *for* [*John to finish by Friday*]

In each case, the italicised Clause is an S-bar containing an overt Complementiser (= *that/for*) and an S (bracketed). In the (a) example, the bracketed S contains an NP Subject *John*, an M *should*, and a VP [*finish by Friday*]; in the

(b) example, the bracketed S contains an NP Subject *John*, an Infinitival Particle *to*, and a VP [*finish by Friday*]. Thus, the bracketed finite S in (a) is of the form [NP M VP], whereas the bracketed nonfinite S in (b) is of the form [NP *to* VP]. The obvious structural parallelism here would suggest that *to* fulfils the same role in infinitive Clauses that M fulfils in indicative Clauses. But how can we capture this parallellism? The obvious answer is to assume that M and *to* are different members of the same Category. Since this category contains both *inflected* Modals like *should* (which carries the past tense suffix *-d* and is thus overtly inflected for Tense and covertly inflected for Agreement), and the *uninflected* infinitive particle *to*, we might follow Chomsky (*Lectures* (1981d), p. 18) in terming the appropriate category INFLECTION, abbreviated to INFL, or (in more recent work) simply I. This would then mean that all Ordinary Clauses contain 'an element (call it 'INFL', suggesting 'inflection') indicating in particular whether the Clause is finite or infinitival' (Chomsky, ibid.). Given this proposal, the basic structure of Ordinary Clauses will be as specified in the two rules below:

(55) (i)   S' → C S

   (ii)   S → NP I VP

This will mean that all Ordinary Clauses are of the schematic form (56) below:

(56)

The plausibility of conflating Modals with infinitive *to* into the category I is supported by a variety of syntactic arguments. For example, Chomsky notes (in *Essays* (1977a), p. 87) that Modals and *to* cannot co-occur (cf. **can to/*to can*), and that this simple fact can be accounted for by assigning them to the same category (here called I). In much the same vein, Bresnan (1976, p. 17) notes that VP ELLIPSIS is possible after Modals, but not after Lexical Verbs: cf.

(57)   First people began pouring out of the building, and then
        smoke {*did Ø*
             {**began Ø*

However, she notes, VP ELLIPSIS is also possible after infinitival *to*: cf.

(58)   First people began to pour out of the building, and then smoke
        began *to Ø*

The obvious conclusion is thus that Modals and the infinitive particle *to* are members of the same category.

Since I(nflection) is an unfamiliar category which we did not make use of in earlier chapters, it may be useful to look briefly at the nature and role of I. We have already suggested that I is the position which may be filled by the infinitival particle *to* in infinitive Clauses, and by a Modal Auxiliary in finite Clauses. Hence, we might say that I can be either finite, or nonfinite. A finite I may contain a Modal Auxiliary which is (overtly or covertly) inflected for both Tense and Agreement. The relevant Tense properties specify whether I is present or past: for example, the italicised Modal Auxiliaries in (59)(a) below are (morphologically) present-tense forms, whereas those in (59)(b) are morphologically past-tense forms (and hence carry the past-tense suffix *-d*):

(59) (a)   John *can/will/shall* do it
    (b)   John *could/would/should* do it

It is, of course, important to draw a fundamental distinction here between *Tense* (a morphosyntactic property) and *Time Reference* (a semantic property). So, for example, in (60) below:

(60)   If I *went* there tomorrow, would you come with me?

went is morphologically a past-tense form, and yet is used in a future timeframe.

In addition to being inflected for Tense, a finite I(nflection) constituent is also inflected for Agreement. The relevant Agreement properties are Person and Number features which must match those of the Subject of the Clause. Recall (from our brief discusion in section 1.5) that English has a binary Number and ternary Person system. *Number* is the traditional term for the contrast between *singular* forms like *student* and *plural* forms like *students*. *Person* is a grammatical property which is overtly manifested in so-called Personal Pronouns: forms which include the speaker (*I/we*) are said to be 'first person' Pronouns; forms which include the addressee (*you*) and not the speaker are said to be 'second person' Pronouns; while forms which exclude both speaker and addressee (*he/she/it/they*) are 'third person' Pronouns. Thus, the system of (Nominative) Personal Pronouns in English can be represented as in (61) below:

(61)

Person	Singular	Plural
	Number	
1	I	we
2	you	you
3	he/she/it	they

Nonpronominal NPs (e.g. *Harry, the man next door, ripe bananas*, etc.) are grammatically third person forms.

Having clarified what we mean by 'Person' and 'Number', we can now return to our earlier observation that a finite I is inflected not only for Tense, but also for *Agreement*. More particularly, I inflects for Person and Number, and must 'agree' with its Subject, in the sense that the Person/Number features of I must match those of the Subject. So, for example, the capitalised Auxiliary *do* contained within the finite I constituent in (62)(a) below takes the third person singular present-tense inflection *-es* in (62)(a) but not in (62)(b) below, because only in (62)(a) is the italicised Subject NP third person singular (recall that nonpronominal NPs like *John* are third person forms):

(62) (a)   *John/he* really DOES like Syntax

    (b)   *I/we/you/they* really DO like Syntax

Although AGREEMENT is *overtly* marked in (62) by the presence of the *-es* inflection in (62)(a), so impoverished is English inflectional morphology that Agreement is only *covertly* marked in present-tense Modals other than *do*, and in all past-tense Verbs other than *be*: what we mean by saying that Agreement is *covert* in such cases is that no overt inflection is added to mark the Agreement (so that, for example, there is no present-tense *-s* inflection added to the third person singular form of Modal Auxiliaries like *may, can, will*, etc.). As we noted earlier, the only exception in English to the claim that Agreement is *covert* in all past-tense forms is the verb *be*, where Agreement determines the *was/were* choice (i.e. *was* is used in agreement with a first or third person singular Subject, and *were* with any other kind of Subject).

Although a finite I (= INFL = INFLECTION) constituent is (overtly or covertly) inflected for TENSE and AGREEMENT properties, it should be obvious that a nonfinite I in English lacks these properties. Hence, the infinitival particle *to* which occurs in a nonfinite I is by its very nature *tenseless* and *agreementless* (i.e. it carries no Tense or Agreement properties, and is thus an entirely uninflected form). The difference between a *finite* and a *nonfinite* Clause can thus be seen to lie in the nature of I: a finite Clause is one which contains a finite I (carrying Tense and Agreement properties); a nonfinite Clause is one which contains a nonfinite I which is tenseless and agreementless.

We claimed earlier in (55) and (56) that all Clauses are S-bar constituents of the form [C S], and that all S-constituents are of the form [NP I VP]. One of the assumptions incorporated into these claims is that all Clauses contain an I constituent. At first sight, however, there might seem to be obvious counter-examples to this claim: for example, although the bracketed indicative Complement Clause in (63) (a) below has a finite I containing the Modal *should*, its bracketed subjunctive counterpart in (63) (b) lacks a Modal:

(63) (a)   The committee may insist [that he *should* resign]

    (b)   The committee may insist [that he resign]

Are we to conclude that because the bracketed subjunctive Clause in (63) (b) lacks a Modal, it follows that it does not contain an I constituent?

Before we jump to this hasty conclusion, we should remember that in our earlier discussion of the C(omplementiser) constituent, we argued that Clauses which lack an overt C constituent in fact have an *empty* C node introducing them. So, an alternative interpretation of the structure of the bracketed Complement Clause in (63) (b) would be to say that it contains an *empty* (finite) I. And it is this alternative 'empty I' analysis which we shall choose to adopt here. Let's consider why.

One argument in favour of the 'empty I' analysis can be formulated in relation to complex interconnection between I and C. This interconnection is illustrated by the fact that a kind of 'Agreement' relation holds between I and C, in the sense that a Clause containing a finite C requires a finite I (as we see from examples like (48) above), whereas a Clause containing a nonfinite C requires a nonfinite I (cf. example (49) above). This 'Agreement' relation between C and I is even more overtly marked in some other languages: for example, in Irish, not only a finite I but also a finite C is marked for Tense (cf. McCloskey (1979), p. 12); and in West Flemish, not only a finite I but also a finite Complementiser like *dat* ('that') is marked for Agreement in Person and Number with the Subject of the Clause it introduces (cf. Haegman (1983), p. 87); a similar phenomenon is found in Lower Bavarian German (cf. Bayer 1984). Such facts suggest that there is a complex interdependency between C and I.

What particularly interests us about this interdependency between C and I here, however, is the fact that the following generalisation seems to hold:

(64)   Any Clause which contains C contains a compatible I

so that a Clause introduced by a finite C will contain a finite I, whereas a Clause introduced by a nonfinite C will contain a nonfinite I. Some support for the generalisation embodied in (64) above comes from the fact that an infinitive Complement introduced by an overt Complementiser like *for* must include an I constituent containing the infinitive particle *to*: cf.

(65) (a)   They are anxious [*for* you *to* make up your mind]

    (b)   *They are anxious [*for* you make up your mind]

The same restriction holds in the case of interrogative infinitive Complements introduced by *whether*: once again, the presence of *whether* in C requires the presence of *to* in I: cf.

(66) (a)   I don't know [*whether to* go there on my own]
   (b)   *I don't know [*whether* go there on my own]

Examples such as (65) and (66) above provide empirical support for our claim in (64) that all Clauses which have a C constituent must also have an I constituent.

But what has all this got to do with our claim that subjunctive Clauses like (63) (b) contain an empty finite I constituent? Well, it is interesting to note that (except in 'liberal' dialects of English) subjunctive Clauses require an overt Complementiser: hence, we can't readily miss out the *that* Complementiser in (63) (b) above: cf.

(67) (a)   The committee may insist [*that* he resign]
   (b)   *The committee may insist [he resign]

Now, given that subjunctive Complement Clauses are introduced by an overt Complementiser, and given our generalisation in (64) that any Clause which contains a C constituent also contains an I constituent, then it follows that subjunctive Clauses must contain an I constituent. And since the I constituent does not appear *overtly*, then the obvious conclusion to draw is that subjunctive Clauses have an *empty* I constituent.

We might extend our 'empty I' analysis of subjunctive Clauses to indicative Clauses which lack an overt Modal in I. That is to say, we might posit that the two bracketed indicative Complement Clauses in (68) below have essentially the same [C NP I VP] constituent structure, and differ only in that I is filled by the Modal *does* in (68) (a), but is left empty in (68) (b):

(68) (a)   I really think [that John *does* like you]
   (b)   I really think [that John likes you]

Indeed, the 'empty I' analysis will be forced upon us if we are to maintain our earlier generalisation in (64) that all Clauses containing C also contain I. Moreover, we can generalise our conclusion to all *Ordinary Clauses*: for if (as we concluded in (45) above) all Ordinary Clauses contain an overt or covert C, then it follows from (64) that all Ordinary Clauses must also contain an overt or covert I. In other words, all Ordinary Clauses which appear to lack an I constituent in fact have an empty I constituent. The bottom line of our argument is thus the conclusion that:

(69)   All Ordinary Clauses contain an I constituent, which may be

either filled (e.g. by a Modal if I is finite, or by infinitival *to* if I is nonfinite), or left empty

The 'empty I' analysis also offers some additional advantages which are less immediately apparent. For example, it makes it possible for us to achieve a very simple structural account of Nominative case-marking. We saw in relation to our earlier examples (16–18) above that an NP which is the subject of a finite Clause is assigned Nominative case. Under the empty I analysis, we could handle Nominative case assignment by a simple structural condition, e.g. to the effect that:

(70)   An NP which is a *sister* of a finite I is assigned Nominative case

It should be clear enough how a rule like (70) would work in the case of a finite Clause containing a Modal in I. For example, the bracketed finite Complement Clause in (68) (a) above would have the simplified structure (71) below:

(71)

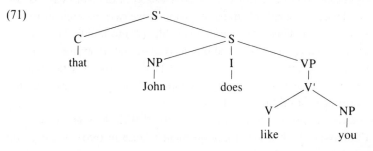

and since the NP *John* here is a sister of the finite I constituent containing the Modal *does*, it is clear that rule (70) will assign Nominative case to *John*. This is obviously the correct result, as we see from the fact that if we replace *John* by a Personal pronoun which is overtly marked for case, we require the Nominative form *he*, not the Objective form *him*: cf.

(72)   I really think [that *he/*him* does like you]

But now consider the case-marking of *John* in a finite Clause such as that bracketed in (68) (b) above: here again, it is clear that the NP *John* must be assigned Nominative case, since it is replaceable only by a Nominative Pronoun: cf.

(73)   I really think [that *he/*him* likes you]

But how will Nominative case assignment work in such examples? Well, if (contrary to what we are arguing here) we suppose that finite Clauses which don't contain an overt Modal simply lack an I constituent altogether, then the bracketed Complement Clause in (68) (b) above will have the structure (74) below:

(74)

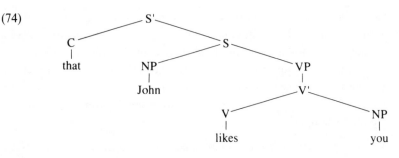

However, the problem which a structure like (74) confronts us with is that it's not at all clear how we are going to handle the Nominative case-marking of *John*. After all, our earlier rule (70) is clearly not applicable here, since *John* is not the sister of a finite I constituent (nor even a sister of the finite V *likes*). So, we need to devise some entirely different Nominative case assignment rule in order to handle (74). Thus, we need one rule like (70) to handle Nominative case-marking in finite Clauses containing a Modal, and an entirely separate Nominative rule to handle finite Clauses which lack a Modal. The fact that we don't seem able to achieve a unitary account of Nominative case-marking clearly counts against the 'no I' analysis.

But does the 'empty I' analysis fare any better? Well, let's see! Under the 'empty I' analysis, the bracketed Complement Clause in (68) (b) above will have the structure (75) below:

(75)

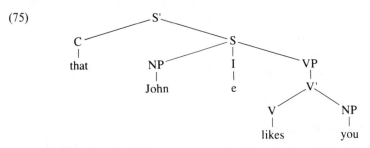

Since the NP Subject *John* in (75) is a sister of the empty finite I constituent, our case-marking rule (70) will correctly assign Nominative case to *John*. Thus, an obvious advantage of the 'empty I' analysis is that it enables us to provide a unitary account of the case-marking of the subjects of finite Clauses: irrespective of whether they contain a Modal or not, finite Clauses will have Nominative case assigned to their subjects by rule (70). More generally still, the 'empty I' analysis provides us with a uniform way of characterising the structural differences between finite and nonfinite Clauses: for, we can say that finite Clauses are Clauses which contain a finite I constituent (whether filled or empty), and nonfinite Clauses are those which contain a nonfinite I constituent.

The 'empty I' analysis does leave one minor problem in its wake, however. After all, why should it be that the -(e)s inflection carrying the relevant Tense and Agreement properties ends up suffixed to the Modal *do* in a structure such as (71) above, but on the head V *like* of the VP in a structure such as (75)? Fortunately, the 'empty I' analysis provides us with a very simple answer to this question. We simply say that if a finite I is filled (by a Modal), the relevant Tense/Agreement properties of I are realised on the item in I; but that if I is empty (i.e. contains no Modal), then the relevant Tense/Agreement properties are realised on the leftmost V of VP. Thus, since the finite Clause [*that John does like you*] in (71) has I filled by the *do* Auxiliary, the third person singular present tense inflection -(e)s is realised on the Auxiliary (cf. *does*); but since the bracketed finite Clause [*that John likes you*] in (75) contains an empty finite I, the -(e)s inflection carrying the relevant Tense/Agreement properties is realised on the Verb (cf. *likes*). How this generalisation can be formalised is a technical question which we put aside for the moment, and return to discuss in Chapter 8.

For these and a variety of other more technical reasons which it would not be appropriate to go into at this point, we shall henceforth assume that all Ordinary Clauses do in fact contain an I constituent, and that I can either be *filled*, or left *empty* (just like C). Thus, where an Ordinary Clause appears to lack I, we shall analyse it as containing an *empty* I, which we shall designate as [$_I$ e], where 'e' stands for 'empty'.

But what of the internal structure of I? We assume that I can either be finite or nonfinite, and that a finite I carries Tense and Agreement properties, whereas a nonfinite I is tenseless and agreementless; we also assume that a finite I can be either Past or Present tense. We might formalise the different properties of a finite and a nonfinite I in terms of a set of rules such as the following, expanding I into a Feature Complex:

(76) (i) $\quad\quad\quad$ I → [αTNS, αAGR]

(ii) $\quad$ [+ TNS] → [± PAST]

(iii) $\quad$ [+ AGR] → [βNUMBER, γPERSON]

[α] in rule (76) (i) is a Feature Variable which must either be positive in both its occurrences, or negative in both its occurrences: hence, rule (76) (i) specifies that I can either be [+ TNS, + AGR] (i.e. marked for Tense and Agreement, and so finite) or else [− TNS, − AGR] (i.e. tenseless and agreementless, and therefore nonfinite). Rule (76) (ii) tells us that a tensed I can either be [+ PAST], or [− PAST] (= Present). In rule (76) (iii), [*β*] is a binary Number feature, with the values 'Singular' or 'Plural'; while [*γ*] is a ternary Person feature with the values 'first/second/third' (Person). Obviously, the values for [*β*] and [*γ*] in AGR must be compatible with those of the Clause Subject, to satisfy the Agreement requirement.

From our discussion so far it has emerged that the finite Tense/Agreement inflections -(*e*)*s* (third person singular present tense) and -(*e*)*d* past tense) are I-inflections – that is inflections which are the overt morphological realisation of the Tense/Agreement properties of I. But since English also has two *nonfinite* inflections, namely -*ing* and -(*e*)*n*, an obvious question to ask is what is the source of these. The -*ing* ('gerund') suffix is used mainly after the Aspectual Auxiliary *be* in so-called 'progressive' forms (indicating an 'action in progress'): cf.

(77)   John may be *working*

The -(*e*)*n* particle has two main functions: first, it is used with the Aspectual Auxiliary *have* in so-called 'perfective' forms, as in:

(78)   They may have *thrown* it away

And secondly, it is used in passive structures as the Complement of Verbs like *be*, *get*, etc.: cf.

(79)   It may be/get *thrown* away

Could -*ing* and -(*e*)*n* be I-inflections like -(*e*)*s* and -(*e*)*d*?

The simple answer is 'No!'. On the contrary, there is abundant empirical evidence that the nonfinite inflections -*ing* and -(*e*)*n* cannot possibly be I-inflections. For one thing, items which occur in I (viz. the Modals and infinitive *to*) never take either inflection, as we see from the ungrammaticality of:

(80) (a)   *maying/*mighting/*canning/*coulding/*musting/*shalling/
            *shoulding/*toing, etc.
     (b)   *mayen/*mighten/*cannen/*coulden/*musten/*shallen/
            *shoulden/*toen, etc.

Secondly, -*ing* and -(*e*)*n* forms occur in Clauses which already have I filled, as with the bracketed Clauses in the following:

(81) (a)   It would be a pity [for you [ɪ to] be *working*]
     (b)   It would have been wrong [for you [ɪ to] have *thrown* it away]
     (c)   [He [ɪ may] be *working*]
     (d)   [He [ɪ may] have *thrown* it away]

Thus, *-ing* and *-(e)n* cannot originate in I in such cases, since I is filled by *to* in (72) (a) and (b), and by *may* in (81) (c) and (d).

But if *-ing* and *-(e)n* are not I-inflections, what kind of inflections are they? The obvious answer is that they are V-inflections, i.e. inflections which attach only to a V generated under VP (i.e. to a non-modal Verb). If indeed they are V-inflections, then this accounts for why they are not used with Modals (since Modals are generated under I and not under V), so that the pattern in (80) is immediately accounted for. Conversely, if they are V-inflections, there is no reason why they should not occur on a Verb contained in a Clause with an item such as *to* or *may* in I, as in (81) above. So it seems that the natural conclusion for us to draw is that the finite verbal inflections present *-(e)s* and past *-(e)d* are I-inflections whereas their nonfinite counterparts *-ing* and *-(e)n* are V-inflections. The converse of the argument also holds: that is, items (such as Modals) which lack *-ing* and *-en* forms must be generated under I, whereas items which have *-ing* and *-en* forms must be generated within VP (e.g. Aspectual Auxiliaries and Nonauxiliary Verbs).

6.6   Clauses with empty Subjects

At this point, we leave aside our discussion of I, and turn instead to consider another aspect of the internal structure of S. Recall that in addition to specifying that I is an obligatory constituent of all Clauses, our earlier Categorial Rules (22) also specified that all Clauses have an NP Subject. However, at first sight this claim would seem to be falsified by the fact that some Clauses appear to be *subjectless*: compare, for example, the bracketed Complement Clause in (82) (a) below with that in (82) (b):

(82)   The President isn't sure
              (a) [*whether he should approve the project*]
              (b) [*whether to approve the project*]

The bracketed Clause has an overt Subject (*he*) in (82) (a) but not in (82) (b). Are we therefore to say that the infinitive is *subjectless* in (82) (b), and accordingly revise rule (22) (ii) so as to make NP an *optional* immediate constituent of S (by enclosing it in parentheses)? We shall argue that this is not an appropriate analysis, and will instead maintain that the infinitive in (82) (b) has an *empty* subject: the difference between (82) (a) and (b) is then that the embedded Clause has an *overt* Pronoun Subject in (82) (a), but a *covert* (i.e. 'empty' or 'invisible') Pronoun Subject in (82) (b). This 'empty Pronoun Subject' we might designate as PRO, following the usual convention in the relevant linguistic literature. Given this assumption, the embedded Clauses in (82) (a) and (b) would have the following respective structures:

(83) (a)

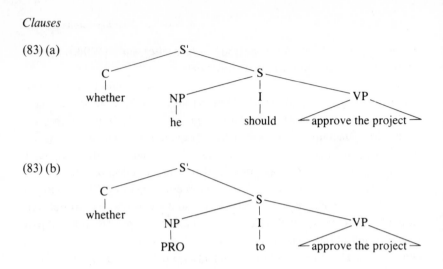

(83) (b)

Part of the evidence in support of the PRO analysis comes from *Agreement* facts. Consider a sentence such as the following:

(84)   They are not sure [whether he should be *a candidate*/*candidates*]

Note that the italicised *Predicate Nominal* (i.e. nominal expression used as the complement of a so-called 'copula' Verb like *be*) in (84) must be singular, and cannot be plural. Why? The traditional answer is that (in this type of construction) a Predicate Nominal agrees with the *Subject of its own Clause*. Since the Predicate Nominal is contained within the bracketed *whether*-clause, and the Subject of that Clause is the singular Pronoun *he*, then we require the singular form [*a candidate*]. Note in particular that the Predicate Nominal cannot be made to agree with the plural Subject of the main Clause (*they*) since we cannot have **candidates*. In the light of this generalisation about Agreement, consider:

(85)   The President is not sure [whether to be *a candidate*/*candidates*]

Once again, the Predicate Nominal is contained within the *whether*-clause, and is apparently agreeing with some constituent, since it has to be singular, and cannot be plural. But what is it agreeing with? It cannot be agreeing with [*the President*], since that belongs to a different Clause, and we already know that Predicate Nominals agree with the Subject of *their own Clause*. But if [*a candidate*] does not agree with [*the President*], what does it agree with? Under the analysis proposed here, the bracketed infinitive complement would have an empty PRO subject, so that (85) would have the S-structure:

(86)   The President is not sure ...

        ... [whether PRO to be *a candidate*/*candidates*]

The antecedent of PRO (i.e. the expression that PRO is understood as referring to) would be [*the President*], and we might assume that PRO inherits the
Number, Gender, and Person of its Antecedent, and is thus third Person Masculine Singular. Given this assumption, we can say that the Predicate Nominal
in (86) is singular because it is agreeing with its singular Subject, PRO. Thus,
Agreement facts lend some empirical support to the claim that apparently
subjectless Clauses have an empty Pronoun Subject.

Further support for this conclusion comes from facts about *Reflexives* (i.e.
forms ending in -*self*/-*selves*). In a sentence like:

(87)   Bill thinks [that John might kill *himself*]

the Reflexive *himself* can be understood as referring back to *John*, but not to
Bill. Why so? A traditional answer (simplified in ways which need not concern
us here) is that Reflexives require a *clausemate antecedent*, i.e. an antecedent
within their own Clause. Since *John* is in the same (bracketed) Clause as *himself* in (87) but *Bill* is not, then it follows that only *John* can be the antecedent
of *himself*. In the light of this generalisation about Reflexives, consider a sentence such as:

(88)   The President is not sure [whether to vote for *himself*]

What is the antecedent of *himself* here? It cannot be [*the President*], since Reflexives require a clausemate antecedent, and *himself* is in a different Clause
from [*the President*]. But if we assume that the apparently subjectless bracketed Complement Clause in (88) has an empty PRO subject understood as
referring back to *the President*, then (88) will have the structure:

(89)   The President is not sure [*whether PRO to vote for himself*]

We can then say that PRO is the antecedent of *himself*, thereby satisfying the
clausemate condition on Reflexives. The more general conclusion to be drawn
from our discussion is that apparently subjectless Clauses have an 'empty
Pronoun' (PRO) subject.

As our discussion has developed, we have made increasing use of *empty
categories*. We have suggested that C is sometimes empty, that I may be
empty, and that NP can also be empty (so that, for example, apparently subjectless infinitive Clauses contain an empty pronominal NP subject designated
by PRO). A general question of principle which arises from the use of empty
categories is:

(90)   What kinds of categories can be left empty, and in what sentence-
            positions?

Clauses

We have already suggested that C, I, and NP can be empty, in an appropriate context. But might not the same be true of other categories as well? For example, we might argue that VP can be left empty under appropriate discourse conditions, so that we might suppose that the Modal *will* has an empty VP Complement in a sentence like:

(91)   She may come to the party, and in fact she probably will [$_{VP}$ e]

Likewise, Adjectival Phrases can sometimes be left empty – cf.

(92)   They say she's very rich, but I don't think that she is [$_{AP}$ e]

We might even argue that whole Clauses can be left empty, e.g. in cases such as:

(93)   She was very ill, though nobody knew [$_{S'}$ e]

Thus, we might allow for the possibility envisaged in Emonds (1976, p. 67) that *any category* can in principle be left empty, under appropriate conditions. If this is so, we could capture the relevant generalisation within the X-bar framework by a rule such as:

(94) $X^n \rightarrow e$ (= 'Any category can be left empty')

What (94) says is that any bar projection of any category can be left empty (optionally). For any given category, we have the option either of applying rule (94) and leaving the category *empty*, or of not applying (94) – in which case the category will be *filled*. In other words, we should expect that:

(95)   In the unmarked case, any category can be either *empty* or *filled*.

Henceforth, we shall adopt (95) as a working hypothesis. This then defines a set of problems of special interest to the linguist; sentences which are consistent with principle (95) are of little theoretical interest, since they are accounted for by (95). Of much greater interest are apparent 'exceptions' to our working hypothesis (95); and much of our subsequent discussion in the second volume will be concerned with providing principled explanations for apparent 'exceptions' to the putatively universal principle (95).

We can summarise our discussion of the syntax of Ordinary Clauses in the following terms. We have argued at length that (indicative and infinitive) Clauses are not simply S constituents, but rather that S has a phrasal expansion into S-bar by the addition of a C(omplementiser) constituent. We have further argued that in the unmarked case, all Clauses have the status of S-bar, with the immediate constituents of S-bar being C and S; and we have claimed that the immediate constituents of S are [NP I VP]. Thus, it follows that

316

Ordinary Clauses have four obligatory constituents, namely [C NP I VP]. And we have argued that each of these constituents may be either *filled* or *empty* (subject to complex restrictions to be discussed in Volume Two). Thus, it follows that Ordinary Clauses which appear to lack one or more of these four obligatory constituents do in fact have an *empty* constituent occupying the relevant sentence-position (so that, for example, apparently subjectless Clauses have an empty PRO subject).

You should now be able to tackle exercises I, II, III, and IV

6.7 Exceptional Clauses

We have remarked several times that *Ordinary Clauses* are S-bar constituents of the canonical form [C NP I VP]. But this raises the obvious question of whether there are other types of Clause which do not have the status of S-bar. A number of linguists have suggested that there are two unusual types of Complement Clause which do not have S-bar status: we shall refer to these as *Exceptional Clauses* on the one hand, and *Small Clauses* on the other. We'll look at Exceptional Clauses in this section, and Small Clauses in the next.

Exceptional Clauses occur as the Complements of a specific subset of Verbs (especially 'cognitive' Verbs, i.e. Verbs of saying or thinking): for example, the bracketed infinitive Complements in (96) below are Exceptional Clauses:

(96) (a)   I believe [*the President to be right*]

(b)   I've never known [*the Prime Minister to lie*]

(c)   They reported [*the patient to be in great pain*]

(d)   I consider [*my students to be conscientious*]

Such Exceptional Complement Clauses are typically of the form [NP to VP]. They are 'exceptional' in several respects. Firstly, they cannot be introduced by an overt Complementiser such as infinitival *for*: cf.

(97) (a)   *I believe [*for* the President to be right]

(b)   *I've never known [*for* the Prime Minister to lie]

(c)   *They reported [*for* the patient to be in great pain]

(d)   *I consider [*for* my students to be conscientious]

One way of accounting for this property would be to maintain that Exceptional Clauses have the status of S, not S-bar; since Complementisers are constituents of S-bar (cf. rule (22) (i) above), it would follow that if Exceptional Clauses are S constituents, they cannot in principle contain Complementisers.

317

A second idiosyncratic property of Exceptional Clauses concerns the fact that their Subjects in some respects behave more like Objects of the preceding Verb than Subjects of the following Verb. For example, just like the Object of a typical Verb, Exceptional Clause Subjects are assigned Objective case: cf

(98) (a)   I believe [*him* to be right]
    (b)   I've never known [*her* to lie]
    (c)   They reported [*him* to be in great pain]
    (d)   I consider [*them* to be conscientious]

Moreover, just like the Object of a typical verb, they can undergo passivisation: cf

(99) (a)   *He* is believed [— to be right]
    (b)   *She* has never been known [— to lie]
    (c)   *He* was reported [— to be in great pain]
    (d)   *They* are considered [— to be conscientious]

And in addition, they can surface as a Reflexive whose antecedent is the main Clause Subject: cf.

(100) (a)   The President believes [*himself* to be right]
    (b)   I've never known [*myself* to lie]
    (c)   They reported [*themselves* to be in great pain]
    (d)   My students consider [*themselves* to be conscientious]

Such data as (98–100) are all the more puzzling in view of the fact that case-marking, passivisation, and reflexivisation do not normally apply 'across' clause-boundaries. But if we were to posit that Exceptional Clauses are S complements, then we could say that passivisation etc. can apply 'across' S, but not across S-bar. We might then handle the contrast between (101) and (102) below:

(101) (a)   We never intended [*that* to happen]
    (b)   *That* was never intended [— to happen]

(102) (a)   We never intended [for that to happen]
    (b)   **That* was never intended [for — to happen]

by positing that the bracketed Complement in (101) is an Exceptional Clause and thus an S, whereas the bracketed Complement in (102) is an Ordinary Clause, and thus an S-bar; if passivisation can apply 'across' an S but not across an S-bar, the contrast between (101) and (102) is then accounted for in simple terms. We shall return to provide a rather more adequate account of various aspects of the syntax of Exceptional Clauses in the second volume: but the observations we have made above will suffice for present purposes.

At this point you might be wondering whether we couldn't find a rather simpler account of the 'object-like' behaviour of subjects of Exceptional Clauses. Perhaps, after all, the relevant NPs are main Clause Objects, rather than subordinate Clause Subjects? Nice try ... but *wrong*! Why? Well, English has a class of expressions which have the curious property that they are restricted to occurring as the *Subjects* of Clauses: for obvious reasons, we'll refer to them as *Subject Expressions*. One such class of Subject Expressions are so-called *Subject Idiom Chunks*, like those italicised below:

(103) (a)   *The chips* are down
   (b)   *The cat* is out of the bag
   (c)   *The shit* hit the fan (quaint American idiom)
   (d)   *The fur* will fly

In such sentences, the italicised expression is an *Idiom Chunk* in the sense that it has no independent (idiomatic) meaning, but rather only assumes its idiomatic meaning as part of the overall idiom. Since the italicised expressions in (103) can be used (in their idiomatic sense) only as Subjects of the idioms of which they form part, they are *Subject Expressions*.

A second class of *Subject Expressions* in English are so-called *pleonastic pronouns* such as *it* and *there* in sentences like:

(104) (a)   *It* is raining/*It* is a long way to Dallas/*It*'s time to leave/*It* is obvious that you're right
   (b)   *There* must have been some mistake/*There* walked into the room the most beautiful woman I had ever encountered

These Pronouns are called 'pleonastic' (which means 'redundant') in traditional grammar because (in their 'pleonastic' use, but not in other uses) they are felt to be (in some vague intuitive sense) 'semantically empty', and thus cannot have their reference questioned (cf. **What is raining? *Where must have been some mistake?*). But what is of more direct concern to us here is the fact that Pleonastic Pronouns can generally only occur in Subject position, and hence are *Subject Expressions*.

Returning now to Exceptional Clauses, consider the significance of data such as the following:

(105) (a)   I believe [*the chips* to be down]
   (b)   I've never known [*the fur* to fly so quickly]
   (c)   They reported [*the cat* to be out of the bag]
   (d)   I consider [*the shit* to have hit the fan]

(106) (a)   I believe [*it* to be unlikely that he'll come]

     (b)   I've never known [*it* to snow in summer]

     (c)   They reported [*it* to be likely that he'd resign]

     (d)   I consider [*it* to be time to leave]

(107) (a)   I believe [*there* to be no alternative]

           I've never known [*there* to be such poverty]

     (c)   They reported [*there* to be considerable dissent among the peasants]

     (d)   I consider [*there* to be no good reason not to]

The fact that the italicised NP in each case is a *Subject Expression* (viz. a Subject Idiom Chunk in (105), and a Pleonastic Subject Pronoun in (106) and (107)) provides strong empirical support for our claim that the italicised NP is the Subject of the bracketed Complement Clause, not the Object of the main Clause. Thus, our analysis of the bracketed sequences as S Complements (= Exceptional Clauses) of the canonical form [NP to VP] has a certain plausibility and attractiveness.

It is interesting to contrast Exceptional Clause structures like those discussed above with sentences such as (108) below:

(108)   John persuaded Mary to resign

At first sight, it might seem as if (108) has the same structure as sentences such as (96) above, viz.

(109)   John persuaded [*Mary to resign*]

where the bracketed Complement is an Exceptional Clause (hence an S, not an S-bar). However, there are a variety of reasons for thinking that (109) is not an appropriate analysis for (108). For one thing, we cannot replace *Mary* in (108) by an appropriate *Subject Expression:*

(110) (a)   *We persuaded [*the shit* to hit the fan]

     (b)   *We persuaded [*the fur* to fly]

     (c)   *We persuaded [*there* to be a strike]

     (d)   *We persuaded [*it* to rain]

This strongly suggests that *Mary* isn't the subordinate Clause Subject in (108), but rather the main Clause Object. In other words, it suggests that the structure of (108) is not (109) above, but rather (111) below:

(111)   We persuaded Mary [*PRO to resign*]

Moreover, it seems likely that the bracketed complement in (111) has the status of S-bar, not of S. This follows from two observations. First, PRO cannot occur as the Subject of an infinitival S complement such as the Exceptional Clauses bracketed in (96) above: cf.

(112) (a) *The President believes [*PRO to be right*]
    (b) *I've never known [*PRO to lie*]
    (c) *They reported [*PRO to be in great pain*]
    (d) *I consider [*PRO to be conscientious*]

And secondly, PRO can occur as the Subject of an infinitival S-bar such as that bracketed in (113) below (where the S-bar Complement is introduced by the interrogative Complementiser *whether*):

(113)   I wonder [*whether PRO to stay at home*]

In the next volume, we shall provide a principled explanation for why PRO can function as the Subject of an infinitival S-bar Complement, but not as the Subject of an S Complement. For the time being, however, we shall be content to merely observe the contrast between (112) and (113), and to remark that it suggests that the bracketed infinitive Complement in (111) must be an S-bar of the canonical structure [C NP *to* VP]. In other words, the superficially similar sentences (114) (a) and (b) below:

(114) (a) John persuaded Mary to resign
    (b) John believed Mary to be innocent

would be assigned the very different structures in (115) below:

(115) (a) John persuaded Mary [$_{S'}$ [$_C$ e] [$_S$ PRO to resign]]
    (b) John believed [$_S$ Mary to be innocent]

So, it seems that we must draw a clear distinction between [*believe NP to VP*] structures on the one hand, and [*persuade NP to VP*] structures on the other. There are a number of further syntactic and semantic properties which help us differentiate between the two types of structure. For example, as Chomsky (*Lectures* (1981d), p. 100) notes, the two constructions differ with respect to the positioning of verbal Adjuncts: cf.

(116) (a) John persuaded Mary *firmly* [$_{S'}$ C PRO to resign]
    (b) *John believed [$_S$ Mary *firmly* to be innocent]

Thus, the italicised Adjunct of *persuaded* in (116) (a) can be positioned after *Mary*, but the italicised Adjunct of *believed* in (116) (b) cannot. If we assume that the sentences in (116) have the structures indicated, then we might suppose that an Adjunct must be contained within the same S as the V it modifies, and that this condition is satisfied in (116) (a), but not in (116) (b).

A parallel argument (from Chomsky, *Lectures* (1981), p. 99) can be formulated in relation to so-called 'floating emphatic reflexives' (i.e. emphatic reflexives which don't immediately follow their antecedent). Note the following contrast:

(117) (a)   John persuaded Mary *himself* [$_{S'}$ C PRO to resign]
   (b)   *John believed [$_S$ Mary *himself* to be innocent]

How can we account for this contrast? If we posit that Reflexives generally require a *clausemate* antecedent (i.e. an antecedent within the S containing the Reflexive), and if we assume that the two sentences in (117) have the structures indicated, then the contrast follows directly from the fact that *himself* and its antecedent *John* are clausemates in (117) (a), but not in (117) (b).

A further argument (cited in Chomsky *Lectures* (1981d), p. 146, fn. 93) comes from *Preposing* facts in Concessive Clauses introduced by *though*. As Chomsky notes, the *persuade NP* sequence can be preposed in this type of structure, though not the *believe NP* sequence: cf.

(118) (a)   Though I may persuade her [to resign], I can't imagine I'll persuade her to leave town
   (b)   *Persuade her* though I may to resign, I can't imagine I'll persuade her to leave town

(119) (a)   Though I believe [her to be innocent], I can't prove it
   (b)   **Believe her* though I may to be innocent, I can't prove it

It would seem plausible to suppose that this contrast is related to the fact that *her* is the Object of *persuade* in (118), but not the Object of *believe* in (119).

In view of the obvious *syntactic* differences between *persuade*-class Verbs on the one hand and *believe*-class Verbs on the other, it is perhaps not surprising to find that there are also significant *semantic* differences between the two classes of Verb. For example, note that the two infinitive structures in (114) above, repeated as (120) below:

(120) (a)   John persuaded Mary to resign
   (b)   John believed Mary to be innocent

have very different finite Clause paraphrases: cf.

(121) (a)   John persuaded *Mary* [$_{S'}$ that *she* should resign]
   (b)   John believed [$_{S'}$ that *Mary* was innocent]

Thus, in (121) (a) *persuade* is clearly a *three-place Predicate* — that is, a Predicate which takes three Arguments: the first of these Arguments is the Subject NP *John*, the second is the Primary Object NP *Mary*, and the third is the Secondary Object S-bar [*that she should resign*]. By contrast, *believe* in (121) (b) is clearly a *two-place Predicate* (i.e. a Predicate which has two Arguments): its first Argument is the Subject NP *John*, and its second Argument is the Object S-bar [*that Mary was innocent*]. This difference in *Argument Structure* between the three-place Predicate *persuade* and the two-place Predicate *believe* is reflected in the two different analyses we have assumed for their infinitive Complements: thus, we analysed *persuade* in (120) (a) [*John persuaded Mary to resign*] as a three-place Predicate in (115) (a) above, while we analysed *believe* in (120) (b) [*John believed Mary to be innocent*] as a two-place Predicate in (115) (b). Note incidentally that PRO in the infinitive structure (115) (a) corresponds to *she* in its finite Clause counterpart (121) (a).

So, somewhat inaccurately, we might say that the NP which follows *persuade* in infinitive structures has two semantic roles to play: it functions directly as the Object of *persuade*, and indirectly (through PRO) as the Subject of the following infinitive. By contrast, the NP which follows *believe* in infinitive structures has only one semantic role to play, namely that of Subject of the following infinitive Complement. As Chomsky (*Aspects* (1965), pp. 22–3) notes, the different semantic roles played by the postverbal NP in the two infinitive constructions accounts for the fact that while active and passive Complements of *believe* are 'cognitively synonymous': cf.

(122) (a)   I believed *a specialist to have examined John*
     (b)   = I believed *John to have been examined by a specialist*

by contrast, active and passive Complements of *persuade* show a very obvious meaning difference: cf.

(123) (a)   I persuaded *a specialist to examine John*
     (b)   ≠ I persuaded *John to be examined by a specialist*

In short, then, there are numerous syntactic and semantic arguments in support of claiming that Verbs like *believe* are two-place Predicates which take an infinitival S Complement, whereas Verbs like *persuade* are three-place Predicates which take a Primary NP Object and a Secondary infinitival S-bar Object: cf. the different structures assigned to the two in (115) above.

Verbs like *persuade* take an infinitive complement with a PRO Subject whose reference is *controlled* by the Direct Object of *persuade*: thus, in:

(124)   John persuaded Mary [$_{S'}$ C PRO to resign]

PRO (i.e. the 'understood Subject' of the infinitive) has to be interpreted as referring back to the matrix (i.e. containing) Clause Object, not to the matrix Clause Subject, so that (124) can be paraphrased as in (121) (a) above. Predicates which take an infinitival complement with a PRO subject whose reference is controlled by some NP in the matrix Clause are known as *Control Predicates*: items like *persuade* which require PRO to refer back to the matrix Clause Object are (for obvious reasons) known as *Object-control Predicates*. They are to be contrasted with items like *promise* which take an infinitival S-bar complement with a PRO subject which is controlled by the *Subject* of *promise*; thus, in:

(125)   John promised Mary [$_S$' C PRO to resign]

PRO is interpreted as referring back to the matrix Subject *John*, so that (125) can be paraphrased as in (126) below:

(126)   *John* promised Mary [$_S$' that *he* would resign]

For this reason *promise* (and items with similar control properties) are known as *Subject-control Predicates*.

You should now be able to tackle exercises V and VI

6.8   Small Clauses

In section 6.6 we claimed that all *Ordinary Clauses* are S-bar constituents of the form [C NP I VP]; but we then went on to suggest in section 6.7 that *Exceptional Clauses* lack C altogether and are simple S constituents of the canonical form [NP I VP]. We are now going to suggest that there may be a third type of Clause whose defining characteristic is that it lacks both C and I: this type of Clause is generally known in the relevant literature as a *Small Clause* (abbreviated to SC). Since they lack both C and I, Small Clauses have the canonical structure [NP   XP], where XP = AP, NP, PP, etc.

The bracketed sequences in (127) below might all be argued to be Small Clause Complements of the immediately preceding Verb:

(127) (a)   I believe [*the President* incapable of deception]
      (b)   I consider [*John* extremely intelligent]
      (c)   They want [*Zola* out of the team]
      (d)   Could you let [*the cat* into the house]?
      (e)   Most people find [*Syntax* a real drag]
      (f)   Why not let [*everyone* go home]?

Note that the italicised NP in such cases can be replaced by an appropriate *Subject Expression:* cf.

(128) (a)   I believe [*it* inevitable that war will break out]
  (b)   I consider [*it* time to leave]
  (c)   Why did you let [*the cat* out of the bag]?
  (d)   I find [*it* inconceivable that he should have gone]
  (e)   Let [*there* be light]

This strongly suggests that the bracketed Complements in (127) are Subject + Predicate structures, and hence Clauses of some sort.

There are a variety of further sets of facts which seem to support the conclusion that the postverbal NP in structures of the schematic form *V* [*NP XP*] is a clausal Subject. One such argument can be based on the syntax of *floating emphatic reflexives*. Napoli (1987, chapter 6, p. 54) provides us with the following examples of how floating emphatic reflexives can (and can't) be used:

(129) (a)   *The president* is coming **himself**
  (b)   *We put *the president* in our car **himself**
  (c)   *I looked behind *the president* for guards **himself**

On the basis of examples such as these, she concludes (ibid.) that 'Floated emphatic reflexives can find an antecedent only in GF Subject position' (GF = Grammatical Function).

Now, if indeed floated emphatic reflexives require a Subject antecedent, then it seems clear that in structures such as:

(130)   I consider [*the president* entirely responsible **himself**]

the italicised antecedent [*the president*] must be a Subject NP. If this is so, then it seems plausible to claim that the bracketed structure in (130) must be a Small Clause whose Subject is the NP [*the president*].

A second *Reflexive* argument in support of the Small Clause analysis can be formulated in relation to examples such as the following:

(131)   I don't want [you near *me/*myself*]

Why should *myself* be ungrammatical here? The Small Clause analysis provides us with a simple answer, given our (simplified) assumption that Reflexives requires a clausemate antecedent. For, under the analysis proposed here, *myself* would be a constituent of the bracketed Small Clause in (131): but since the antecedent of *myself* (namely the main Clause subject *I*) lies outside this bracketed Small Clause, then it follows that (131) violates the *clausemate* restriction, and thus is ill-formed.

In fact, we can use a number of other traditional tests of *subjecthood* to support the Small Clause analysis. For example, on the basis of examples such as:

(132) (a)   *Not many gorillas* have learned to tapdance
      (b)   I would prefer for *not much* to be said about this
      (c)   *Joe kissed *not many models*
      (d)   *Jane earns *not much money*
      (e)   *Sally talked to Bob about *not many problems*
      (f)   *I bought kangaroos from *not many Australians*

Postal (1974, p. 95) concludes that *not*-initial NPs occur only in superficial Subject position. If this generalisation is correct, then it would seem that the italicised *not*-initial NP in structures such as:

(133)   I consider [*not many people* suitable for the post]

must be a Subject NP; if so, then it seems clear that the bracketed structure in (133) must be a Small Clause.

Another test of *subjecthood* devised by Postal concerns the distribution of *alone*-final NPs (i.e. NPs which end in *alone* used in the sense of *only*). On the basis of examples such as the following:

(134) (a)   *Gronzmeyer alone* can help you
      (b)   It would be strange for *you alone* to be nominated on the first
            ballot
      (c)   *Call *Bob alone*
      (d)   *I believe *that alone*
      (e)   *I talked to *Smith alone* about the wombat question
      (f)   *I refuse to work with *her alone*

Postal (1974, pp. 99–100) concludes that *alone*-final NPs can occur only in superficial Subject position. Now, if this is so, then the grammaticality of sentences such as:

(135)   I consider [*Gronzmeyer alone* responsible for the collapse of Arc
            Pair Grammar]

would suggest that the italicised expression is a subject NP, and hence that the bracketed structure is a Small Clause. Of course, the *not*-initial and *alone*-final arguments are only as strong as the (somewhat subtle) grammaticality judgments on which they are based. (It should perhaps be noted that Postal's (1974) book was devoted to a vigorous but notoriously unsuccessful attack on the 'standard' analysis of Small and Exceptional Clauses, so it is somewhat ironic that we should use Postal's own 'tests' to support the Small Clause analysis!)

Thus far, we have argued that Small Clauses are simple Subject + Predicate Structures of the schematic form [NP XP]. Implicit in this assumption is the claim that Small Clauses lack a C constituent, and hence cannot have S-bar status. There are two reasons for suggesting this. First, they cannot be introduced by overt Complementisers, as the ungrammaticality of (136) below illustrates:

(136)   *I didn't consider [*that/if/whether/for* it suitable]

And secondly, Small Clauses cannot contain an inverted Auxiliary in presubject position, unlike their finite Clause counterparts – hence the ungrammaticality of:

(137)   *Let [*be* there light]

Given our earlier suggestion that both Complementisers and inverted Auxiliaries are positioned in C, then the ungrammaticality of (136) and (137) would follow from the assumption that Small Clauses are not S-bar constituents, and therefore contain no C constituent.

Moreover (as noted above), Small Clauses seem to have no I constituent either. For example, they cannot contain the infinitive particle *to*, or a Modal – hence the ungrammaticality of:

(138) (a)   *I consider [your attitude *to/can* deeply offensive]
   (b)   *Let [there *to/can* be light]

Thus, since Small Clauses are 'smaller' than Ordinary Clauses by virtue of lacking both C and I, they are aptly named!

Subjects of Small Clauses share many of the properties of subjects of Exceptional Clauses. For example, they are assigned Objective case, they permit main Clause passivisation and reflexivisation, and they do not permit PRO subjects: cf.

(139) (a)   I consider [*him* intelligent]
   (b)   *He* is considered [— intelligent]
   (c)   I consider [*myself* intelligent]
   (d)   *I consider [*PRO* intelligent]

The fact that a Small Clause Subject (or indeed an Exceptional Clause Subject – cf. (100) (b) above) can be a Reflexive with an antecedent which lies outside the Clause immediately containing the Reflexive obviously calls into question the generality of the traditional *clausemate* condition on Reflexives. The search for a more adequate characterisation of the complex conditions determining the use of Reflexives will occupy a large part of one of the chapters of Volume Two, so we shall not pursue the matter any further here. For the purposes of the argumentation developed here, it is sufficient to note that the *clausemate* condition works well enough for *Non-subject Reflexives*, though it raises complex problems in the case of *Subject Reflexives* (i.e. Reflexives which function as the Subject of a Clause, or which are contained within an NP which functions as the Subject of a Clause).

So far, we have implicitly assumed that Small Clauses occur only as the Complements of *Verbs*. However, Beukema and Hoekstra (1984) argue that so-called *Absolute Prepositional Phrases* (typically introduced by *with/without*) such as those italicised below involve a bracketed Small Clause complement of the canonical [NP XP] form:

(140) (a) *With [Dick Cavett on television]*, what's the point in going out?
   (b) I don't want you preparing food *with [your hands dirty]*
   (c) *With [the kitchen a mess]*, how can I possibly cook anything?

Some support for the Small Clause analysis comes from the fact that *Subject Expressions* can typically occur immediately after the Preposition in the absolute construction: cf.

(141) (a) *With [the cat out of the bag]*, there's not much point in trying to hide the truth anymore
   (b) *What with [it raining all day long]*, I didn't get a chance to hang the washing out

Such facts suggest that the NP immediately following the Preposition is not in fact the Object of the Preposition, but rather the Subject of a Small Clause Complement.

Beukema and Hoekstra offer an argument from Dutch in support of the Small Clause analysis, based on the phenomenon of R SUPPLETION in Dutch. For those of you unfamiliar with Dutch, it will perhaps be useful to point out that this phenomenon has an unproductive and somewhat archaic counterpart in English, whereby the Pronouns *it* and *them* (provided that *them* designates nonhuman entities) can be replaced by the suppletive variant *there* when used as the object of a specific class of Prepositions: hence alternations such as the following:

(142)   One principle that the law insists on in relation to crime/criminal acts is that criminals should not be allowed to profit *by it/by them/ thereby*

Likewise, the Pronoun *this* has the suppletive variant *here*: cf.

(143)   I'm enclosing a facsimile of the original document *with this/herewith*

Much the same is true of relative *which*, which has the suppletive variant *where*:

(144)   I'd rather not discuss the means *by which/whereby* he attained his end

Since *there*, *here* and *where* contain an *r*, and since they appear to function as suppletive variants of *it/them/this/which*, it seems appropriate to refer to this phenomenon as R SUPPLETION. One of the many curious aspects of this phenomenon is that when the R-form of the pronoun is used, the Pronoun must be positioned *after* the Preposition (cf. *thereby/*by there; whereby/*by where*).

In Dutch, the phenomenon of R SUPPLETION is more widespread and fully productive, so that in place of the ungrammatical *op het 'on it' or '*op dat 'on that', we find the obligatory suppletive R-variant *er op* 'there on'; likewise, in place of the *op wat 'on what', we find the R-form *waar op* 'where on' (cf. Koster (1975), p. 121; den Besten (1978b), p. 645; Vat (1978), pp. 699–700). What Beukema and Hoekstra observe is that although R SUPPLETION is obligatory for nonhuman prepositional Objects in Dutch, it is blocked from applying in Absolute Prepositional Phrases such as their example (145) below:

(145) (a)   *Met dat* nog allemaal voor de boeg, wilde Jan niet weggaan
             With that still all ahead of him, wanted Jan not leave
             'With all that still ahead of him, Jan did not want to leave'
      (b)   *Daarmee nog allemaal voor de boeg, wilde Jan niet weggaan
             Therewith (i.e. 'with that') still all ahead of him, wanted Jan not leave

Since R SUPPLETION is obligatory for nonhuman pronouns used as the Object of a Preposition in Dutch, they conclude that the impossibility of R SUPPLETION in absolute constructions such as (145) demonstrates that the NP following the Preposition is the Subject of a Small Clause complement, and not the Object of the Preposition. The argument can be adapted to archaic registers of English in ways which I leave you to work out for yourselves. (Haven't you begun to think like a linguist yet?!)

So far, all examples of the Small Clause construction which we have looked at involve Small Clauses being used as *Complements* – either the Complement of a Verb, or the Complement of a Preposition. This obviously raises the question of whether Small Clauses can only function as Complement Clauses, or whether they can also function as independent sentences. One possible source of Small Clauses functioning as independent sentences in English is the Clause type given the somewhat perplexing label of *Mad Magazine Sentences* by Akmajian (1984). These are semi-echoic independent sentences such as those italicised in Akmajian's examples below:

(146)   SPEAKER A: I don't know how to tell you this, but I think Mary's taking valium . . .
SPEAKER B: Oh my God – *Mary take valium*? Please say it isn't true [NP VP]

(147)   SPEAKER A: I think Bronsky is such a clever author
SPEAKER B: What! *Bronsky clever?!* Ha! [NP AP]

(148)   SPEAKER A: Do you suppose Larry is a doctor by now?
SPEAKER B: *Larry a doctor?!* What a laugh! [NP NP]

(149)   SPEAKER A: I'm furious that Mary joined the army
SPEAKER B: What! *Mary in the army?!* It can't be [NP PP]

Since *Mad Magazine Sentences* seem to lack both C and I constituents, and to be of the schematic form [NP XP], they bear an obvious resemblance to Small Clauses, and hence might be analysed as such. However, this is clearly a *marked* construction in a fairly obvious sense: thus, *Mad Magazine Sentences* seem to be limited to 'echo contexts', and cannot e.g. be used to initiate a conversation (you can't walk into a room and address a complete stranger with a *Mad Magazine Sentence*).

So far, we haven't addressed ourselves to the question of the categorial status of Small Clauses. Since they lack C, Small Clauses cannot have the status of S-bar; moreover, if it is a defining property of S constituents that they contain I, then since Small Clauses don't contain I they cannot have the status of S either. For the time being, we shall therefore use the symbol SC to denote Small Clauses. We shall take up the question of the precise categorial status of Small Clauses (and indeed of other Clauses) in Chapter 9.

We have thus seen that there are three major Clause types in languages like English, namely those represented schematically in (150) below:

(150) (a)   Ordinary Clauses

(b)   Exceptional Clauses

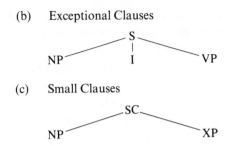

(c)   Small Clauses

The three Clause types differ principally in that Ordinary Clauses contain both I and C, Exceptional Clauses contain I (= infinitival *to*) but not C, and Small Clauses contain neither C nor I. Moreover, both Exceptional Clauses and Small Clauses are highly restricted in their distribution: for example, Exceptional Clauses typically occur only as the Complements of certain specific types of Verb; and Small Clauses occur mainly as the Complements of a subset of Verbs and Prepositions (though it may well be that *Mad Magazine Sentences* should be analysed as Small Clauses functioning as independent sentences).

You should now be able to tackle exercises VII and VIII

6.9   Summary

We began our discussion of Clauses in section 6.2 with an outline of the traditional division of Clauses into *finite* (i.e. indicative or subjunctive) Clauses and *nonfinite* (e.g. gerund, infinitive, or participial) Clauses. In 6.3 we discussed the constituent structure of Ordinary Clauses, outlining Bresnan's analysis of them as S-bar constituents comprising a Complementiser constituent C and a Proposition constituent S; and we argued that finite Complement Clauses which lack an overt Complementiser should be analysed as S-bar constituents in which the C position has been left empty. In 6.4 we extended the S-bar analysis to main Clauses: we argued that main Clauses which contain an inverted Auxiliary have the Auxiliary positioned in C, and hence are S-bar constituents; and we went on to argue that other main Clauses have an empty C constituent, and hence are also S-bar constituents. Our overall conclusion at this stage was thus that all Ordinary Clauses are S-bar constituents. In 6.5 we looked at the internal structure of the Proposition (= S) component of Clauses, arguing that its three immediate constituents are [NP I VP], where I is an Inflection constituent which can either be finite or nonfinite. We noted that a finite I carries Tense/Agreement features, and can either be filled by a Modal such as *can/could/will/would* etc., or be left empty; if I is left empty, its

Tense/Agreement features are then realised on the leftmost Verb of the Verb Phrase. A nonfinite I carries no Tense/Agreement properties, and can contain the tenseless agreementless infinitival particle *to*. In 6.6 we argued that Clauses which lack overt subjects have an 'understood' empty pronominal subject designated as PRO; and we went on to suggest that not only subject NPs, Complementisers, and Inflection constituents can be left empty, but in principle *any* constituent can be left empty (under appropriate conditions).

In 6.7 we argued that although all Ordinary Clauses have the status of S-bar, there is a special type of infinitive complement Clauses (known as *Exceptional Clauses*) which have a number of idiosyncratic characteristics, including the fact that they can never be introduced by an overt Complementiser: and we argued that these defining characteristics could be accounted for in a principled way if we posited that *Exceptional Clauses* have the status of S (and not S-bar) constituents. In 6.8 we went on to argue that there are a further class of Clauses known as Small Clauses (= SC), which are simple Subject + Predicate structures of the schematic form [NP XP]; and we argued that it was a defining characteristic of Small Clauses that they have no Complementiser or Inflection constituent. Thus, in this chapter, we have distinguished between three different types of Clauses: *Ordinary Clauses* which contain both C and I constituents (whether filled or empty); *Exceptional Clauses* which lack C but contain I (whether filled or empty); and *Small Clauses* which lack both C and I.

EXERCISES

Exercise I

Discuss the internal constituent structure which would be assigned to the italicised Clauses in the examples below within the S-bar framework, presenting empirical evidence in support of your analysis.

(1)   I wonder *if she can speak Spanish*
(2)   They're anxious *for you to help them*
(3)   I'm almost sure *nobody will do the assignment*
(4)   I wonder *whether to go to the party*
(5)   *Could you pass me the salt?*
(6)   *John hates Linguistics*

*Exercise II

Given the assumption that all categories can be either filled or empty, we should expect that the C position in all types of Clauses (including *that*-clauses like those below) can always be either filled or empty. Some of the sentences below are consistent with this claim, whereas others prove more problematic. See if you can clarify the problems, and suggest possible generalisations about when C in a *that*-clause can and cannot be left empty in English. The notation *e* here is used to designate an empty C. Assume that the bracketed Clause in each case has the status of S-bar.

(1)   I said [*that/e* I would assume full responsibility]
(2)   I protested to the Police [*that/*e* I was innocent]
(3)   Mike grunted [*that/*e* he was tired]
(4)   The Press demanded [*that/*e* he be given a retrial]
(5)   [*That/*e* the world is round] is obvious
(6)   [*That/*e* the President was guilty], I refuse to believe
(7)   I like the theory [*that/*e* all categories can be empty]
(8)   The guy [*that/e* you are going out with] is a drongo
(9)   The guy [*that/*e* is going out with you] is a drongo
(10)   I admit [*that/e* I was tired], but not [*that/*e* I was asleep]

Exercise III

In the text, we made no mention of *Imperative Clauses* (i.e. Clauses used to issue a command). In English, Imperatives can have overt (usually second person) subjects such as those italicised in (1) below:

(1) (a)   *You* be quiet, John!
    (b)   Don't *you* answer me back!

But more often, they are apparently subjectless, as in (2) below:

(2) (a)   Do be careful!
    (b)   Mind the dog!

Imperative Clauses are traditionally said to be *finite*: why should this be, and what apparent problems does such a classification raise?

Subjectless Imperative Clauses have traditionally been assumed to have an 'understood' second person subject (i.e. what in our terms might be analysed as an empty second person pronominal singular or plural subject which we might designate as YOU). Discuss how sentences such as the following might be used to provide empirical justification for such a claim:

(3) (a)   Don't hurt yourself/yourselves/*ourselves/*themselves!
    (b)   Do be careful, won't you/*he/*we/*they/*I?
    (c)   Don't lose your/*his/*their/*my/*our temper!
    (d)   Use your/*his/*her/*their own pen!

What differences can you see between YOU (= the empty second person pronominal subject found in Imperatives) and PRO?

**Exercise IV

In the text, we posited that C expands S into S-bar. However, Jackendoff (1977, p. 47) suggests the alternative possibility that C may expand S into S, so that a Clause such as that bracketed in (1) below:

(1)   John thinks [*that you may lose the election*]

would have a structure along the lines of:

(2)

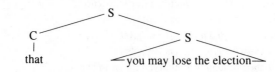

Compare and contrast the S-analysis of Clauses introduced by overt Complementisers (outlined in (2) above) with Bresnan's S-bar analysis, e.g. in respect of data such as those discussed in the text.

Exercise V

Discuss the structure of the bracketed VPs in the following examples, presenting empirical evidence to substantiate your conclusions, and noting any problematic cases:

(1)   I don't [*expect you to win*]
(2)   I can't [*force you to help me*]
(3)   Why don't you [*get Mary to cook the food*]?
(4)   The courts may [*declare Syntax to be unconstitutional*]
(5)   Nobody will [*tell you to work harder*]
(6)   I can't [*imagine Mary to be entirely blameless*]
(7)   They may [*ask (for) the chairman to resign*]

*Exercise VI

The examples below all involve (bracketed) noninterrogative infinitive Complements used after particular Verbs. However, as these examples illustrate, different types of Verb take different types of infinitive Complement (in the dialect in question). Try and identify the similarities and differences between the various types, the restrictions which operate, and the internal structure of the infinitive complement in each case.

(1) (a)   I would very much prefer [*for John to stay*]
    (b)   I would prefer very much [*for John to stay*]
    (c)   *I would very much prefer [*for to stay*]
    (d)   *I would prefer very much [*for to stay*]
    (e)   I would very much prefer [*John to stay*]
    (f)   *I would prefer very much [*John to stay*]
    (g)   I would very much prefer [*to stay*]
    (h)   I would prefer very much [*to stay*]

(2) (a)   *I very much want [*for John to stay*]

   (b)   I want very much [*for John to stay*]

   (c)   I very much want [*for to stay*]

   (d)   *I want very much [*for to stay*]

   (e)   I very much want [*John to stay*]

   (f)   *I want very much [*John to stay*]

   (g)   I very much want [*to stay*]

   (h)   I want very much [*to stay*]

(3) (a)   *I sincerely believe [*for John to be wrong*]

   (b)   *I believe sincerely [*for John to be wrong*]

   (c)   *I sincerely believe [*for to be wrong*]

   (d)   *I believe sincerely [*for to be wrong*]

   (e)   I sincerely believe [*John to be wrong*]

   (f)   *I believe sincerely [*John to be wrong*]

   (g)   *I sincerely believe [*to be wrong*]

   (h)   *I believe sincerely [*to be wrong*]

(4) (a)   *I desperately tried [*for John to win*]

   (b)   *I tried desperately [*for John to win*]

   (c)   *I desperately tried [*for to win*]

   (d)   *I tried desperately [*for to win*]

   (e)   *I desperately tried [*John to win*]

   (f)   *I tried desperately [*John to win*]

   (g)   I desperately tried [*to win*]

   (h)   I tried desperately [*to win*]

*Exercise VII

Discuss the structure of the bracketed VPs in the following examples, pointing out why it might (or might not) be appropriate to analyse the head V as taking a Small Clause complement.

(1)   The jury will probably [*find the defendant guilty*]

(2)   Nobody can [*call John a liar*]

(3)   Overwork can [*give you a heart attack*]

(4)   I could [*hear a noise inside the house*]

(5)   I won't let you [*put your feet on the table*]

(6)   I might [*have my coffee black*]

(7)   I might [*have my coffee in the kitchen*]

(8)   You might [*get me into trouble*]

(9)   There seems to [*be a fly in my soup*]

(10)   John may [*regard Bill as his best friend*]

(11)   Nobody could [*take John for a fool*]

(12)   John was kind enough to [*help an old lady (to) cross the street*]

Exercise VIII

Discuss the structure of the italicised Clauses in the examples below within the SC/S/S-bar framework, presenting empirical arguments in support of your analysis, and highlighting any problems which you encounter.

(1)   I hope *you can help me*

(2)   *Can you help me?*

(3)   I'd very much prefer (*for*) *you to be with me*

(4)   I'm not sure *whether to give her this one*

(5)   She attempted *to beat the world record*

(6)   *He may consider John (to be) utterly incompetent*

(7)   *I think I can compel John to tell the truth*

(8)   What! *John resign his post!* Impossible!

(9)   I'm hopeless *without you by my side*

In addition, say how you would account for the structural ambiguity of the italicised sequence in (10) below, giving empirical arguments in support of your analysis:

(10)   I don't like *women in jeans*

7
The Lexicon

7.1 Overview

Thus far, we have been assuming that the syntactic component of a Grammar contains three main subcomponents, namely:

(1)(i)   a *Categorial Component* comprising a set of X-bar principles (e.g. category-neutral rule-schemas and rule-constraints)

(ii)   a *Lexicon* (or dictionary) containing a list of all the words in a language, together with a specification of their idiosyncratic syntactic, semantic, phonological, and morphological properties

(iii)   a *Lexicalisation Principle*, attaching lexical items (= words) under appropriate word-level category nodes (e.g. inserting *man* under N)

Let us say that the three components listed in (1) together constitute the *Base Component* of our grammar. In earlier chapters, we have looked in some detail at the role and form of the *Categorial Component* (1) (i) in a Grammar; in this chapter, we turn instead to consider the kind of information contained in the *Lexicon* (1) (ii). We also take a closer look at the Lexicalisation Principle (1) (iii), suggesting that it should be revised, and that perhaps it can ultimately be subsumed under a more general principle, and hence eliminated.

7.2 Categorial information

So far, we have considered only one kind of syntactic information which the Lexicon must provide us with – namely *categorial* information. That is, we have assumed that for each item listed in the Lexicon, our grammar must specify which syntactic category (or categories) it belongs to. For example, our Lexicon will have to tell us that *cat* is a Noun, that *dog* can be either a Noun or a Verb, that *need* can function as a Verb, a Modal, or a Noun ... and so on and so forth. Assuming that simple categories can be decomposed into sets of categorial features (as we argued in Chapter 3), this information will be given in the form of feature complexes (= feature sets), so that (e.g.) the Lexical Entry for *cat* will specify (*inter alia*):

(2)   *cat*: [+ N, − V], . . .

However, it seems clear that the *categorial* information which dictionary entries contain must be rather more detailed than is assumed by the simple partition of words into major classes like 'Noun', 'Verb', 'Adjective', and so on. In particular, it seems necessary to posit that the members of a given category may belong to a variety of different categorial subclasses. By way of illustration, consider the category *Noun*. Both traditional grammarians like Quirk *et al.* (1985, pp. 245–52) and generative grammarians like Chomsky (*Aspects* (1965), pp. 79–86) assume that Nouns must be divided into a number of distinct subclasses. One important distinction is that between *Proper* and *Common* Nouns. Proper Nouns are generally names of people (e.g. *Debbie*), places (e.g. *London*), months (e.g. *April*), events (e.g. *Christmas*), etc.; they differ from Common Nouns in that they are not usually premodified by Determiners like *a* and *the* (cf. **a/*the London*), whereas Common Nouns are not so restricted (cf. *a/the cinema*). The class of Common Nouns can in turn be subdivided into two distinct sets – *Count* and *Noncount* Nouns. Nouns which can be used with a singular Determiner like *a/one*, or a plural Determiner like *two/ three/four* are known as Count Nouns (hence *chair* is a Count Noun, since we can say both *a chair* and *two chairs*); but Nouns which cannot be so used are known as Noncount (or Mass) Nouns (hence *furniture* is a Noncount/Mass Noun, since we do not say **a furniture* or **two furnitures*). Likewise, a singular Mass Noun can be used without a Determiner, whereas a singular Count Noun cannot (cf. *We need furniture/*chair*); and a Mass Noun can be premodified by *much* but not *many*, whereas a Count Noun can be premodified by *many* but not *much* (cf. *We don't have much furniture/*chair. We don't have many chairs/*furniture(s)*). It may well be that distinctions such as those between Common and Proper Nouns on the one hand, and Count and Mass Nouns on the other can be handled in terms of sets of *minor* categorial features such as [±Common] and [±Count] (as suggested by Chomsky in *Aspects* (1965), p. 82). If this is so, then our entry for *cat* in (2) above will have to contain not just the *major* categorial features [+ N, − V], but also the *minor* categorial features [+ Common, + Count]. Thus, our entry for *cat* will have to be revised along the lines indicated in (3) below:

(3)   *cat*: [+ N, − V, + Common, + Count], . . .

You should now be able to tackle exercise I

7.3   Subcategorisation

What we have argued so far is that part of the syntactic information contained in the Lexical Entry for any item is a specification of the categorial status of the item concerned, in the form of a matrix of major and minor
categorial features such as that illustrated in (3) above. But what other kind(s)
of syntactic information should be included in Lexical Entries? Traditional
dictionaries such as Hornby's (1974) *Oxford Advanced Learner's Dictionary of
Current English* include not only *categorial* information in their entries, but
also information about the range of *Complements* which a given item permits
(this information is represented by the use of a number/letter code). In traditional terms, a given item is said to *take* a particular type of Complement; in
more recent terminology, we say that an item *subcategorises* a particular range
of Complements. Using this terminology, we can refer to information about
the range of Complements which a given item takes as *subcategorisation* information. The tacit assumption embodied in traditional dictionaries such as
Hornby's is thus that dictionary entries should contain not only *categorial* information, but also *subcategorisation* information. But why should this be so?

Let's try and answer this question in concrete terms by considering the
range of items which can appear in the empty V-position marked by '?' in a
sentence-structure such as (4) below (here and elsewhere, we are concerned
only with the structure of S, and hence we omit all mention of S-bar in the
ensuing discussion, except where it is of immediate relevance to the discussion
at hand):

(4)

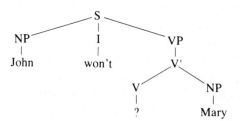

The Lexicalisation Principle (1) (iii) allows us to insert any word specified as a
V in its Lexical Entry in any V-position in any sentence-structure. But this
fails to take into account the fact that only a specific subset of Verbs can be
used in structures like (4), as we see from the contrast below:

(5) (a)   John won't *defy/invite/hit/harm/like/kill/help* Mary
    (b)   *John won't *come/go/wait/fall* Mary

And yet, our existing grammar fails to account for the contrast in (5), since it
allows us to insert any Verb under any V-node.

Why has our grammar broken down at this point? It is not difficult to see why. For, we have failed to make any provision for the fact that only *some* Verbs in English (i.e. Verbs like those italicised in (5) (a), traditionally called *Transitive Verbs*) subcategorise (= 'take') an immediately following NP Complement, whereas others (such as those italicised in (5) (b), traditionally referred to as *Intransitive Verbs*) do not. There doesn't seem to be any general way in which we can predict which Verbs do or do not take a following NP complement: it doesn't seem to depend on the meaning of the Verb, since pairs like *await/wait* seem to have much the same meaning, yet only the former, not the latter can be used with an NP Complement: cf.

(6) (a)   I shall await *your instructions*
    (b)   *I shall wait *your instructions*

Since there doesn't seem to be any way in which we can predict whether a given Verb does or does not permit a following NP Complement, it seems that this is the kind of idiosyncratic syntactic information which we shall have to include in the Lexical Entry for each particular Verb. But how can we do this – i.e. how can we incorporate into our Lexical Entries the subcategorisation information that Verbs like *defy* take an NP Complement, whereas Verbs like *come* do not?

Somehow or other, we need to specify in our Lexical Entries that Verbs like *defy* can occur as the head of a V-bar in which they are immediately followed by an NP, whereas Verbs like *come* cannot be used in this way. One way of doing this (essentially following proposals made by Chomsky in *Aspects* (1965)) would be to incorporate into our Lexical Entries *subcategorisation features* which specify whether or not a given Verb can occur in a V-bar containing an immediately following NP complement. Our lexical entries would then contain not only *categorial features* (telling us, for example, that both *defy* and *come* can function as Verbs), but also *subcategorisation features* telling us that only *defy* can be inserted into a V-bar in which it has an immediately following NP complement, not *come*. Given these assumptions, our lexical entries for these two items might be along the following lines:

(7) (a)   *defy*: CATEGORIAL FEATURES: $[+V, -N]$
                 SUBCATEGORISATION FEATURES: $+[_{V'} - NP]$
    (b)   *come*: CATEGORIAL FEATURES: $[+V, -N]$
                 SUBCATEGORISATION FEATURES: $-[_{V'} - NP]$

The first line of each entry in (7) provides a specification of the *categorial features* of the items concerned (i.e. they tell us that the items in question are Verbs); the second line gives us a specification of the *subcategorisation features* of the relevant items. What these subcategorisation features tell us is that *defy* can (= +) occupy, and *come* cannot (= −) occupy the position indicated by the elongated dash (—), as the leftmost constituent of a V-bar in which it is immediately followed by an NP. What appears on the second line of the entry in (7) (a) is a *positive subcategorisation feature* which tells us the kind of Complement a given Verb *can* take; whereas what appears on the second line of the entry in (7) (b) is a *negative subcategorisation feature* which tells us the kind of Complement the Verb in question *cannot* take.

Thus, by the use of positive and negative subcategorisation features, we can account for the difference between Verbs like *defy* which can occur in a V-bar with an NP complement, and those like *come* which cannot. However, we can simplify our specification of *subcategorisation features* in two respects. First, the information incorporated into (7) that Verbs like *defy* and *come* occur as the leftmost constituent of a V-bar, and not (e.g.) as the leftmost constituent of an N-bar, or A-bar etc. is surely redundant, since it follows from the *endocentricity* requirement imposed within the framework of X-Bar Syntax that a V can function only as the head of a V-bar not as the immediate head of any other type of constituent. Given that the relevant *categorial features* in the entry for *defy* and *come* say that they are Verbs, it follows from the ENDOCENTRICITY CONSTRAINT that they can only be used to head a V-bar, not any other type of Phrase. Hence, we can eliminate the V-bar label attached to the bracketed Phrase in (7), since it is entirely redundant. This means that we can simplify our entries in (7) along the lines of (8) below:

(8) (a)   *defy*: CATEGORIAL FEATURES: [+V, −N]
                     SUBCATEGORISATION FEATURES: +[— NP]
    (b)   *come*: CATEGORIAL FEATURES: [+V, −N]
                     SUBCATEGORISATION FEATURES: −[— NP]

A second way in which we can simplify our specification of subcategorisation features is to include only *positive* subcategorisation features in lexical entries, and eliminate any specification of *negative* subcategorisation features. What this means in simple terms is that we follow the traditional dictionary practice of specifying what types of Complement a given item *does* permit, and omit any specification of the range of Complements which it *doesn't* permit. We can assume by convention that unless an item is positively subcategorised as permitting a certain Complement type, then it will be negatively subcategorised in respect of the Complement concerned (i.e. if the dictionary doesn't say that a particular item takes a particular type of Complement, then we can assume that it doesn't). This revision would enable us to simplify our lexical entries in (8) by eliminating the negative subcategorisation features which appear in our entry for *come* in (8) (b). Our revised, simplified set of subcategorisation conventions essentially follow those introduced by Chomsky in *Aspects* (1965, p. 93). Since we shall henceforth only be including *positive* subcategorisation features in lexical entries, it becomes redundant to mark each such subcategorisation property as being positively specified: therefore, we shall in future simply specify the range of structures which a given item can occur in, without attaching any positive 'feature' to this specification. And we shall refer to this specification of the range of complement types which a given item permits as the *subcategorisation frame* of the item concerned.

So far, we have considered only the question of the range of Verbs which can occur in *transitive* structures like (4) above. But what about the range of Verbs which can appear in the empty V-position marked by '?' in *intransitive* structures such as (9) below?

(9)

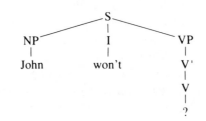

Once again, we find that only a restricted class of Verbs can be used without any Complement in this type of structure: cf.

(10) (a)   John won't *come/go/rest/stay/play/help*

  (b)   *John won't *await/hit/defy/put/award*

How can we account for the fact that Verbs like those in (10) (a) can be used without any overt Complement, but Verbs like those in (10) (b) cannot be so used? Subcategorisation provides us with one obvious mechanism for handling this distinction; we could argue that Verbs like those in (10) (a) subcategorise *zero Complements* (that is to say, they can be used without any Complement). There are a variety of ways of formalising the claim that a given item may take zero Complements; two different (but equivalent) notational devices for expressing this are suggested in (11) (a) and (b) below:

(11) (a)   *come*: CATEGORIAL FEATURES: $[+V, -N]$
       SUBCATEGORISATION FRAME: $[— \emptyset]$

  (b)   *come*: CATEGORIAL FEATURES: $[+V, -N]$
       SUBCATEGORISATION FRAME: $[—]$

(11) (a) tells us that *come* can occur with zero Complements (zero being sym-

bolised by $\emptyset$ here); while (11) (b) tells us that *come* can be used on its own in a V-bar, without any Complement of any kind. Both statements amount to saying that *come* can be used intransitively without a Complement. By contrast, Verbs like *defy* cannot occur 'alone' in a V-bar, and hence are not marked as having the subcategorisation frame [— $\emptyset$] (or [—]): this means that they cannot be used intransitively as in (10).

Thus, we have seen that Verbs which permit an NP complement are assigned the subcategorisation frame [— NP], whereas those which can occur without any Complement whatever are assigned the subcategorisation frame [— $\emptyset$]. But what of Verbs which can be used in both types of structure – i.e. in transitive structures like (4) as well as intransitive structures like (9)? There are quite a number of Verbs of this type, as we see from (12) below:

(12) (a)   John won't *help/watch/understand* Mary
(b)   John won't *help/watch/understand*

Such Verbs will have to be doubly subcategorised as both transitive and intransitive. One way of doing this would be as in (13) below:

(13)   *help*: CATEGORIAL FEATURES: [+ V, − N]
SUBCATEGORISATION FRAME: [— NP], [— $\emptyset$]

Our entry for *help* in (13) specifies that *help* can be used with an NP Complement, and also without any Complement at all. Another way would be as in (14) below:

(14)   *help*: CATEGORIAL FEATURES: [+ V, − N],
SUBCATEGORISATION FRAME: [— (NP)]

where the brackets round NP indicate that *help* takes an *optional* NP Complement. So, we have seen that some Verbs subcategorise an NP Complement, some subcategorise no Complement whatever, and some occur in both types of structure.

To summarise: under the revised model present here, lexical entries contain not only *categorial features* (which tell us whether some item functions as a Verb, or Noun, etc.), but also a *subcategorisation frame* giving us information about the kind of Complements which a given lexical item allows. It follows that we will now have to revise our earlier Lexicalisation Principle (1) (iii), perhaps along the lines indicated informally in (15) below:

(15)   LEXICALISATION PRINCIPLE
Insert under any terminal category any item from the Lexicon which (i) can have the relevant categorial status, and (ii) is subcategorised as permitting the relevant type of Complement(s)

To see how our revised principle (15) works, let's return to the problem of choosing some item from the Lexicon which can be inserted under the empty V-node in the P-markers (4) and (9) above. Note that the empty V in (4) has an immediately following NP Complement; hence, our Lexicalisation Principle (15) will only allow us to insert into the empty V-position in (4) a Verb whose lexical entry assigns it a subcategorisation frame [— NP] which specifies that it permits an NP Complement. Since the entries for *defy* in (8) (a) and *help* in (13/14) satisfy this condition, but not the entry for *come* in (11), it follows that *defy* and *help* can be inserted in (4), but not *come*. Conversely, in (9) there is no Complement for V within V-bar; hence, our Lexicalisation Principle (15) will only allow us to insert under the V-node a Verb which can occur without any Complement, and thus is subcategorised as [— ∅]. Since the entries for *come* in (11) and *help* in (13/14) contain this subcategorisation frame, but not the entry for *defy* in (8) (a), we can insert *come* or *help* in (9), but not *defy*.

So far, we have considered only transitive Verbs which take a single NP Complement. However, there are a subset of transitive Verbs (known as *ditransitive Verbs*) which can take two NP Complements, as illustrated in (16) below (where the NP Complements are bracketed):

(16) (a)   John gave [*Mary*] [*a present*]
    (b)   The postman handed [*me*] [*a parcel*]
    (c)   He showed [*her*] [*his credentials*]
    (d)   He sent [*his mother*] [*some flowers*]
    (e)   Never promise [*anyone*] [*anything*]

The relevant subcategorisation frame for Verbs used in this construction will be [— NP NP], indicating that they can take two NP Complements.

7.4 Prepositional Complements

Although we have concentrated on Verbs which take either NP Complements, or no Complement at all (or both), it should be obvious that Verbs will have to be subcategorised with respect to the full range of Complements which they permit. For example, some Verbs permit one or more PP Complements: as we see from (17) below, different Verbs take different PP Complements headed by different Prepositions:

(17) (a)   I defer [*to/*at/*on/*by/*with* your suggestion]
    (b)   John waited [*for/*to/*after/*from* the taxi]
    (c)   I can rely [*on/*by/*with/*from/*to* you]
    (d)   Nothing can detract [*from/*by/*on/*at* her merit]
    (e)   He declaimed [*against/*at/*for/*after* Syntax]

(f)   You must abide [*by/*at/*on/*to/*from* my decision]

(g)   He jibs [*at/*against/*for/*with* hard work]

Clearly, therefore, it is little use subcategorising such Verbs as simply taking PP complements, and assigning them the subcategorisation frame [— PP], since this would (wrongly) allow any of the Verbs to take a PP Complement headed by any Preposition. Instead, it seems that the choice of Preposition used to introduce the PP Complement in each case will have to be specified in the relevant lexical entry, so that, for example, the entry for *rely* might be along the following (informal) lines:

(18)   *rely*: CATEGORIAL FEATURES: [+ V, − N]

SUBCATEGORISATION FRAME: [— [pp *on* NP]]

There is an important complication which arises with Verbs which occur in V-bar structures of the schematic form [V P NP], however; and this concerns the potential structural ambiguity of [V P NP] structures. Consider, for example, the following contrast (familiar from our discussion in Chapter 2):

(19) (a)   John ran up the hill

(b)   John rang up his sister

In Chapter 2, we argued that *up* in sentences like (19) (a) 'goes with' the following NP *the hill* to form a PP [*up the hill*]; but that in (19) (b) *up* 'goes with' the preceding verb *rang* to form a 'Phrasal Verb' [*rang up*]. As part of the evidence for this, we saw that *up the hill* could be preposed as a unit in (19) (a), whereas *up his sister* could not in (19) (b): cf.

(20) (a)   *Up the hill* John ran/ran John

(b)   *Up his sister John rang/rang John

In more traditional terms, *run up* (in the sense of 'ascend') is a *Prepositional Verb*, whereas *ring up* is a *Phrasal Verb*. Clearly, it's no use assigning both *ran* and *rang* the subcategorisation frame [— *up* NP], since this would fail to reflect the important structural differences between structures like (19) (a) on the one hand, and those like (19) (b) on the other. Hence, the relevant lexical entries need to contain more structural information – enough to differentiate Phrasal Verbs like *ring up* from Prepositional Verbs like *run up*. There are numerous ways in which we might handle this structural difference between these two types of Verb. One possibility is as in (21) below:

(21) (a)   *run*: CATEGORIAL FEATURES: [+ V, − N]

SUBCATEGORISATION FRAME: [— [pp *up* NP]]

(b)   *ring*: CATEGORIAL FEATURES: [+ V, − N]

SUBCATEGORISATION FRAME: [[v — *up*] NP]

The entry in (21) (a) clearly indicates that *up* forms part of a PP Complement when used with *run*, whereas the entry in (21) (b) shows that *up* forms part of the Phrasal Verb [*ring up*] when used with *ring*. Of course, our discussion is somewhat oversimplified for expository purposes: in reality, *run up* can be used as a Phrasal Verb when it has the sense of 'incur', as in:

(22)   He *ran up* huge debts

So, there are important structural differences between *running up a hill*, and *running up a bill*!

For the time being, however, let's concentrate on running up hills, rather than running up bills. Thus far, we have proposed to deal with Prepositional Verbs by subcategorising them as taking PP complements headed by a specific Preposition: for example, *run* is subcategorised in (21) as taking a Complement of the schematic form [pp *up* NP]. However, we might object to any such subcategorisation on two grounds: first, some of the information contained in it is inaccurate; and secondly, other information it contains is redundant. Consider first two ways in which the subcategorisation frame in (21) (a) is inaccurate. For one thing, the entry in (21) (a) specifies that *up* must occur as the leftmost constituent of the PP it heads: but this ignores the possibility of having a Specifier preceding the head Preposition, as with the italicised expression in:

(23)   He ran [pp *all the way* up the hill]

In (23), the italicised Phrase is an NP which functions as the Specifier of the P-bar *up the hill*. But our entry in (21) (a) made no provision for possible Specifiers. Moreover, (21) (a) specifies that *up* requires an NP Complement: and yet this is not true, as we see from the grammaticality of (24) below:

(24)   He ran [pp all the way up]

Hence, we need to amend (21) (a) in such a way as to allow for the optional occurrence of a Specifier in front of *up* on the one hand, and the optional occurrence of an NP Complement after *up* on the other.

Now, we might propose to achieve both ends by revising our entry for *run* in the following way:

(25)   *run*: CATEGORIAL FEATURES: $[+V, -N]$
          SUBCATEGORISATION FRAME: $[— [pp (XP) \; up \; (NP)]]$

where (XP) indicates an optional Specifier phrase, and (NP) indicates an optional NP Complement. But the problem with our revised entry (25) is that it now contains a vast amount of redundant information: and we assume that the most fundamental requirement of all for lexical entries is that we should *minimise redundancy* (i.e. lexical entries should contain only such information as is not otherwise predictable). Hence, as Chomsky notes (*Aspects* (1965), p. 87), only 'properties of a formative that are essentially idiosyncratic will be specified in the Lexicon' (N.B. 'formative' = 'lexical item'). There are two types of redundancy in (25), which we might term (i) lexical, and (ii) structural. The lexical redundancy comes from the fact that our Lexicon will contain a separate entry for *up*, specifying that it is a Preposition which can either be used transitively (taking an NP Complement), or intransitively (taking no Complement at all): thus, (25) duplicates information already contained in the lexical entry for *up*. The structural redundancy in (25) lies in the fact that the major structural properties of the *up*-phrase used as the complement of *run* follow from more general principles of X-Bar Theory. For example, the fact that the *up*-phrase has the status of a full Phrase (i.e. a double-bar rather than a single-bar constituent) follows from the MODIFIER MAXIMALITY CONSTRAINT discussed in Chapter 5, which specifies that only maximal projections may appear as non-head terms within a Phrase. Likewise, the fact that the overall *up*-phrase has the status of a PP follows from the fact that *up* is a Preposition (as its lexical entry tells us), given that the ENDOCENTRICITY CONSTRAINT specifies that Phrases must have the same categorial features (though not the same level features) as their Heads. And the fact that the *up*-phrase Complement after *run* can have an optional Specifier follows from a category-neutral X-bar rule-schema which specifies that any X-bar constituent can be expanded into an X-double-bar constituent by the addition of an optional Specifier Phrase.

How can we eliminate all this redundancy from our lexical entry for *run*? The answer is to revise our entry (21)(a) so as to stipulate no more than that *run* takes a Complement headed by *up*. This we might do along the following lines:

(26)   *run*: CATEGORIAL FEATURES: [+ V, − N]
             SUBCATEGORISATION FRAME: [— [. . . *up* . . .]]

The fact that *up* is a Preposition which takes an optional NP Complement will be stipulated in the corresponding lexical entry for *up*; the fact that the bracketed Complement [. . . *up* . . .] has the status of PP and permits an optional Specifier will follow from other principles of X-Bar Theory, as we have seen. What we have done in (26) is strip our lexical entry of all redundant information, in keeping with our overall aim of *minimising redundancy in lexical entries*.

However, let's leave aside the general methodological issue of eliminating redundancy from lexical entries, and return to consider some of the subcategorisation problems specific to Verbs which subcategorise PP complements. We have already seen that one such problem relates to the distinction between Prepositional and Phrasal Verbs. A second such problem which arises concerns the fundamental distinction between *Complement PPs* on the one hand, and *Adjunct PPs* on the other. Recall that in Chapters 4 and 5, we presented a number of criteria for distinguishing between Complements and Adjuncts. For example, we saw that Complements occur closer to their heads than Adjuncts, that Complements may be obligatory whereas Adjuncts are always optional, that items impose restrictions on the choice of Complements (but not the choice of Adjuncts) they permit, and so forth. In the light of the *Complement/Adjunct* distinction, consider a sentence such as the following:

(27)   John abided [pp by my wishes] [pp through fear]

It would seem that the *by*-phrase here is a Complement PP, whereas the *through*-phrase is an Adjunct PP. One reason for positing this is that the *by*-phrase is obligatory (a property of the Complements of many items), whereas the *through*-phrase is optional (a property of all Adjuncts): cf.

(28) (a)   *John abided [through fear]
     (b)   John abided [by my wishes]
     (c)   *John abided

A second reason is that the unmarked (i.e. 'normal') word-order in (27) is for the *by*-phrase to precede the *through*-phrase (in accordance with the generalisation that Complements normally occur closer to their Heads than Adjuncts):

(29) (a)   John abided [by my wishes] [through fear]
     (b)   *John abided [through fear] [by my wishes]

A third reason is that the Verb *abide* imposes restrictions on the choice of Preposition which can head the *by*-phrase, but not on the choice of Preposition which can head the *through*-phrase: cf.

(30) (a)   John abided [*by*/*with*/*from*/*to*/*at* my wishes]
     (b)   John abided by my wishes [*through/out of/because of/owing to/thanks to/by reason of/by dint of*/(etc.) fear]

Since Verbs impose restrictions on their choice of Complements but not on their choice of Adjuncts, (30) lends strong empirical support to our claim that the *by*-phrase is a Complement, whereas the *through*-phrase is an Adjunct. More generally still, we can conclude from examples like these that items should be subcategorised only with respect to the range of *Complements* they permit, not with respect to the optional *Adjuncts* which can accompany them.

So far, we have looked at two types of Complement: NP Complements, and PP Complements. Some Verbs take both types of Complement, as the following examples illustrate:

(31) (a)   John gave [the letter] [*to/*by/*with* the police]
     (b)   John blamed [the incident] [*on/*to/*at* Mary]
     (c)   Television can distract [you] [*from/*by/*out of* your work]
     (d)   John's friends dissuaded [him] [*from/*by/*at/*into* retaliatory action]

In each of the examples (31) above, the first bracketed Complement is an NP, while the second is a PP. As we see from these examples, the Verb imposes restrictions on the choice of Preposition which it permits to head its PP Complement in each case: for example, *give* takes a *to*-phrase Complement, but not a *by*-phrase or *with*-phrase Complement. And we have already seen that such restrictions are typical of subcategorised PP Complements. Accordingly, we might argue that a Verb such as *give* (when used in structures such as (31) (a)) should have a lexical entry along the following lines:

(32)   *give*: CATEGORIAL FEATURES: [+ V, − N]

          SUBCATEGORISATION FRAME: [— NP [PP ... *to* ...]]

(We add the information that the *to*-phrase must be a PP here in order to avoid confusion with the infinitive particle *to* which functions as an I constituent.)

7.5   Complement order

Thus far, we have looked at a variety of types of redundancy in lexical entries, and proposed various ways of eliminating them. The revised subcategorisation frames which we have proposed are thus much simpler in form than we originally envisaged. However, we might argue that there is yet further redundant information included in our existing entries which should be eliminated – namely information about the relative linear ordering (= word-order) of Complements. If (as we shall suggest here) *Complement order* is predictable from general structural principles, then any specification of it in lexical entries is redundant, and should be eliminated.

To make our discussion more concrete, let's look at our existing entry for *give* in (32) above. Among the information contained in the entry (32) is information about the relative *linear ordering* of the Verb *give* and its Complements: thus, (32) specifies that *give* can take both an NP and a PP

Complement, and that when it does, *give* occurs first, the NP Complement occurs after *give*, and the PP Complement occurs last. But word-order facts such as these might be argued to follow from more general linearisation principles which are in part universal, and in part language-particular. For example, the fact that *give* must occur as the leftmost constituent of the V-bar containing it follows from two conditions. The first is a putatively universal linearisation (i.e. word-order) principle proposed by Stowell (1981, p. 68) which we might call the PERIPHERY PRINCIPLE: this can be outlined informally as in (33) below:

(33)   PERIPHERY PRINCIPLE
          The head term of a Phrase appears at the periphery of X-bar

What (33) says is that the Head must be the leftmost or rightmost immediate constituent of X-bar. The second is a language-particular linearisation principle which we mentioned briefly in chapter 5, and which we repeat in (34) below:

(34)   HEAD FIRST PRINCIPLE
          In English-type languages, Heads precede Complements

These two principles together determine that in *head-first* languages like English, the head V of VP will always occur as the leftmost constituent of the V-bar containing it, and hence will always precede any Complements of V: and this principle applies to *all* Verbs in English, not just to *give*. Since this ordering is not an idiosyncratic lexical property of the Verb *give*, it should not be listed in the entry for *give*. The lexical entry for any given item should contain all and only such information as is idiosyncratic to the item concerned.

Moreover, the stipulation in (32) that the NP Complement of *give* precedes its PP Complement is also redundant, since this follows from independent facts about word-order in languages such as English. Recall that in Chapter 2, we said that Keyser (1968, p. 371) had noted a 'general tendency to prevent anything from intervening between a Verb and the following Noun Phrase': and we suggested that this principle might be formulated as follows:

(35)   STRICT ADJACENCY PRINCIPLE
          An NP complement of a V must be strictly adjacent to V

(We shall attempt to explain why this should be so in Volume Two.) Given that the HEAD FIRST PRINCIPLE tells us that V must be the leftmost constituent of V-bar, it follows that (35) entails in English that an NP complement of V should immediately follow its governing V. Given the STRICT ADJACENCY PRINCIPLE, it follows that when a Verb subcategorises both an NP and a PP

Complement, the NP Complement must come immediately after the Verb, and hence must precede the PP Complement. Accordingly, this ordering information should not be included in lexical entries, since it is the automatic consequence of an independent restriction on English word-order. This means that the subcategorisation frame of a lexical item should simply specify the range of different categories which the item subcategorises, without imposing any ordering of Complements. So, for example, in the case of *give*, the only subcategorisation information which the relevant dictionary entry need contain is that *give* can take both an NP Complement and a PP Complement headed by *to*. Accordingly, we might revise our entry for *give* along the following lines:

(36)   *give*: CATEGORIAL FEATURES: [+ V, − N]
         SUBCATEGORISATION FRAME: [NP, PP]
         (where [NP, PP] indicates an unordered set, and where PP is
         headed by *to*)

And (36) differs from earlier entry (32) in that it specifies no ordering of the two Complements.

The same STRICT ADJACENCY PRINCIPLE (35) will also predict that when a Verb subcategorises both an NP and an S-bar Complement, the NP Complement must precede the S-bar Complement: and as we see from the examples below, this is indeed the case:

(37) (a)   John persuaded [NP Mary] [S' that he was right]
     (b)   *John persuaded [S' that he was right] [NP Mary]

(38) (a)   John promised [NP Mary] [S' that he would resign]
     (b)   *John promised [S' that he would resign] [NP Mary]

Indeed, there may be a second word-order principle operating here which conspires to ensure [V NP S'] order. For, it would appear from the examples below that S-bar Complements follow not only NP Complements, but also PP Complements:

(39) (a)   He admitted [PP to me] [S' that you are right]
     (b)   *He admitted [S' that you are right] [PP to me]

(40) (a)   They asked [PP of him] [S' what they should do]
     (b)   *They asked [S' what they should do] [PP of him]

(41) (a)   They appealed [PP to the judge] [S' that he be freed]
     (b)   *They appealed [S' that he be freed] [to the judge]

This suggests the following general word-order principle:

(42)   CLAUSE-LAST PRINCIPLE
An S-bar Complement must occur at the rightmost periphery
[= righthand end] of its containing X-bar, in languages like
English

We might argue that the language-particular principle (42) in turn follows
from a universal principle to the effect that S-bar Complements are positioned
at the opposite periphery of X-bar from the Head: since the HEAD FIRST PRIN-
CIPLE (34) determines that the head X must be the leftmost constituent of X-
bar in English, the 'opposite periphery' principle would amount to (42) in
head-first languages. In Volume Two, we shall provide a principled explanation of the ordering condition imposed in (42).

None of the ordering principles we have formulated so far determine the
relative ordering of two PP Complements. It may well be that in such cases,
the relative ordering of the two Complements is free: this, at any rate, would
seem to be suggested by examples such as the following (where the bracketed
expressions are PPs):

(43) (a)   I never argue [with anyone] [about anything]
     (b)   I never argue [about anything] [with anyone]

(44) (a)   I talked [about the problem] [to my doctor]
     (b)   I talked [to my doctor] [about the problem]

(45) (a)   He climbed [into the house] [through the window]
     (b)   He climbed [through the window] [into the house]

More generally still, it may be that we can assume that the relative ordering of
Complements is free, except in those cases where independent linearisation
principles impose a fixed order.

Our discussion of the principles determining Complement ordering have
obvious implications for the format of subcategorisation frames in lexical
entries. Clearly, if Complement ordering is determined by independent principles, then it should not be specified in lexical entries, since this ordering is
not an idiosyncratic property of particular lexical items (e.g. there is no Verb
in English which is exactly like *give* except that its PP Complement precedes its
NP Complement). Given this assumption, subcategorisation frames will no
longer specify the relative position of the V with respect to its Complements,
or of the Complements with respect to each other, since such word-order facts
are predictable from more general principles. Instead, subcategorisation
frames simply present an *unordered list* of the set of categories which can occur

as Complements to a given V. Where a Verb like *come* can occur without any Complements at all, its subcategorisation frame will contain the entry [∅], specifying that it can be used with zero Complements (in accordance with the convention in (11) (a) above).

> ***You should now be able to tackle exercise II***

7.6   Clausal Complements

Our discussion of Complement order in the previous section touched briefly on the question of the position occupied by Ordinary Clause Complements. This raises the more general question of how we are to subcategorise items with respect to the range of *clausal* Complements which they permit. Now, we argued in Chapter 6 that there are three major structural types of clausal Complement, namely (i) Ordinary Clauses (= S-bar), (ii) Exceptional Clauses (= S), and (iii) Small Clauses (= SC). These three types of Clause differ in that Ordinary Clauses contain both C and I constituents, Exceptional Clauses contain I but not C, and Small Clauses contain neither C nor I. Cutting across this purely syntactic classification of Complement Clauses is an alternative typology of Clauses based on their communicative function. For example, Complement Clauses can be declarative (as with the bracketed Complement Clause in (46) (a) below), imperative (cf. (46) (b)), interrogative (cf. (46) (c)), or exclamative (cf. (46) (d)):

(46) (a)   I knew [*that you'd turn up*] (declarative)
    (b)   The judge ordered [*that the sentence be carried out*] (imperative)
    (c)   He asked me [*whether I was leaving*] (interrogative)
    (d)   I noticed [*what a pretty dress she was wearing*] (exclamative)

Now, it may well be that the question of the type(s) of clausal Complement which a given item permits is in large measure predictable from its semantic properties. This is an assumption which underpins a lot of work in both traditional and generative grammars. To take an example from a traditional grammar, Quirk *et al.* (1985, pp. 155–7) note that only what they call MANDATIVE Predicates (e.g. 'insist', 'demand', 'request', 'propose', 'recommend', 'order', 'prefer', etc.) take subjunctive Complements: cf. their examples:

(47) (a)   I insist [*that the Council's decision be reconsidered*]
    (b)   The committee proposed [*that Mr Day be elected*]
    (c)   They recommend [*that this tax be abolished*]
    (d)   The employees have demanded [*that the manager resign*]

353

(It should be noted, however, that subjunctive Complements are a literary construction, and in more casual speech they tend to be replaced by indicative Complements headed by a Modal such as *should*.) If this is so, then we shall not have to specify in the lexical entries for each of the particular Verbs in question that they permit subjunctive Complements, since this will be predictable from their semantic properties by a general principle.

And much the same underlying idea – namely that the range of clausal Complements which a given item permits is determined in large measure by its semantic properties – is found in generative studies of complementation, such as Bresnan (1979). Thus, Bresnan claims (1979, p. 67) that interrogative Complements 'occur with intrinsically INTERROGATIVE and DUBITATIVE Predicates', such as those italicised in her examples (48) below:

(48) (a)   I'll *ask* [whether Linda is coming]
   (b)   She *inquired* [who was coming]
   (c)   They *wonder* [when they'll be allowed to leave]
   (d)   We *doubt* [whether you're capable]
   (e)   They *debated* [whether conclusive evidence had been presented]

In much the same vein, she claims (1979, pp. 82–3) that infinitive Complements introduced by *for* typically occur after DESIDERATIVE and EMOTIVE Predicates, such as those italicised in (49) below:

(49) (a)   I'd *prefer* [for you not to be there]
   (b)   I'm *aiming* [for my team to win] (Bresnan (1979), p. 81)
   (c)   I'm *dying* [for you to tell me]
   (d)   It would *astound* me [for a man to act that way] (Bresnan (1979), p. 84)

And in the same way, we might claim that the question of which Predicates select declarative (indicative) Complements can be determined – in part at least – from their semantic properties: e.g. COGNITIVE Verbs (like 'know', 'feel', 'think', 'realise', 'imagine', etc.), and ASSERTIVE Verbs (like 'say', 'assert', 'declare', 'announce') generally take indicative Complements, as we see from (50) below:

(50) (a)   I *know* [that I am right]
   (b)   You must *realise* [that you are mistaken]
   (c)   I *imagine* [that you must be tired]
   (d)   He *claimed* [that he was innocent]

Overall, then, there seems to be some basis for claiming that the range of clausal Complements which Predicates permit may be in large measure determined from their semantic properties by a set of general principles.

But what exactly is the nature of these 'general principles', and what role do they play in our overall grammar? What we mean by 'general principle' in this context is a type of rule which is conventionally termed a *Lexical Redundancy Rule*. In our present case, we are tacitly assuming a set of redundancy rules which we can outline in an informal, simplified fashion as in (51) below:

(51) (i)   MANDATIVE Predicates take subjunctive Complements (in formal registers of English)

(ii)   INTERROGATIVE and DUBITATIVE Predicates take interrogative Complements

(iii)   DESIDERATIVE and EMOTIVE Predicates take infinitival Complements with *for*

(iv)   COGNITIVE and ASSERTIVE Predicates take declarative (indicative) Complements

These particular rules link semantic properties of items (viz. whether they are 'MANDATIVE', 'INTERROGATIVE', 'DUBITATIVE', 'DESIDERATIVE', 'EMOTIVE', 'COGNITIVE', or 'ASSERTIVE' in sense or not) to their syntactic properties (viz. whether they take a subjunctive, interrogative, infinitival, or declarative Complement). Such rules vastly simplify our lexical entries, since they make it unnecessary to list separately in the lexical entry for each individual Verb the specific type(s) of clausal Complement which it permits, insofar as this is determined by a set of general principles. Of course, such rules linking semantic to syntactic properties are problematic to the extent that terms such as 'MANDATIVE', 'DESIDERATIVE', 'ASSERTIVE' etc. remain essentially intuitive notions whose precise formal definition remains to be worked out.

As our discussion progresses, we shall make more and more use of *Lexical Redundancy Rules* of various types. The general aim of such rules is to minimise the information that needs to be included in the dictionary entries for particular items – or, more generally still, to eliminate lexical redundancy (since information which is predictable from a general rule or principle is clearly not idiosyncratic to specific lexical items, and hence should not be included in particular lexical entries). Of course, our use of Lexical Redundancy Rules entails some modifications to our existing model of grammar. In particular, our Lexicon will now contain not only a set of lexical entries and a Lexicalisation Principle, but also a set of Redundancy Rules. Hence, we now envisage a Lexicon comprising the following three components:

(52) (i)   a set of *Lexical Entries* comprising a list of all the words in a language, together with a specification of their idiosyncratic properties, e.g. their categorial status, their idiosyncratic subcategorisation properties, etc.

355

(ii)   A set of *Lexical Redundancy Rules* which determine those properties of lexical items which are predictable from general principles

(iii)   a *Lexicalisation Principle*, attaching lexical items (= words) under
appropriate word-level category nodes (e.g. inserting *man* under N)

But let's leave general questions about the overall organisation of the Lexicon
aside for the moment, and return to our discussion of clausal Complements.

As we have already seen, the type(s) of clausal Complement which a given
item permits (whether interrogative, declarative, etc.) may be largely predictable from its inherent semantic properties. However, we can go beyond this,
and claim that in many cases the internal structural properties of Complement
Clauses may also be predictable from more general grammatical principles.
Consider, for example, the internal structure of interrogative Complements. If
a Verb selects an interrogative Complement, then its Complement will be an
'Ordinary Clause' (= S-bar), which may either be finite (more precisely, indicative) and have an overt subject, or be infinitival and have a covert (i.e. empty
PRO) subject: cf.

(53) (a)   I don't know [*what I should do*]
     (b)   I don't know [*what PRO to do*]

(54) (a)   I wonder [*how I can help him*]
     (b)   I wonder [*how PRO to help him*]

(55) (a)   He didn't tell me [*whether I should wear a tie*]
     (b)   He didn't tell me [*whether PRO to wear a tie*]

(56) (a)   He asked me [*what he should do*]
     (b)   He asked me [*what PRO to do*]

It follows from this that there are no interrogative 'Exceptional Clauses' or
'Small Clauses': this restriction might be argued to be a consequence of other
more general principles (though discussion of the relevant theoretical principles would be premature at this stage). What is more important for our
present purposes is that the fact that Verbs which select interrogative Complements always take an S-bar Complement need not be stipulated in the relevant
lexical entries, since it will follow from more general principles which apply to
all interrogative Complements, irrespective of the Predicate which selects
them. And in Volume Two, we shall see that the requirement that finite interrogative Clauses must have overt (not covert, i.e. PRO) Subjects whereas infinitival interrogative Clauses must have covert (= PRO) not overt Subjects
also follows from more general structural principles.

The ultimate goal which we seek to attain is not to have to stipulate anything whatsoever about interrogative Complements in our lexical entries. That is, we hope that the question of whether an item does or does not select an interrogative Complement will be predictable from redundancy rules making reference to its meaning, and that the major structural properties of interrogative Complement Clauses (e.g. the fact that they always have the status of S-bar, and that they can be either indicative with an overt subject, or infinitival with a covert subject) will again follow from general structural principles whose precise nature we shall discuss in Volume Two. This is the optimal solution: that is, we minimise redundancy to the point where nothing at all has to be stipulated in lexical entries about interrogative Complements.

Naturally, we hope that the same will be true of other types of Complement, for example noninterrogative infinitive Complements. We have already seen that the class of Predicates which take an infinitival S-bar Complement introduced by *for* (what Bresnan terms DESIDERATIVE and EMOTIVE Predicates) is largely predictable from their semantic properties. In much the same way, the internal structural properties of such infinitive Complements also seem to be predictable. For example, for reasons which we shall probe in Volume Two, when the Clause has an overt Subject, it requires an overt Complementiser; when it has a covert Subject (= PRO), it requires a covert (= empty = e) Complementiser: cf.

(57) (a)   I'm dying [$_C$ *for*/*e] *you* to do it
    (b)   I'm dying [$_C$ *e*/*for*] *PRO* to do it

Given this principle, it follows that all items which take an infinitival S-bar Complement with an overt Subject introduced by *for* also take an infinitive S-bar Complement with an empty PRO Subject and an empty Complementiser.

However, the converse does not appear to be true: that is, there are Verbs which permit infinitive Complements with an empty Subject and an empty Complementiser, and yet do not permit a *for* infinitive counterpart with an overt Subject and an overt Complementiser: cf.

(58) (a)   He attempted [[$_C$ *e*] *PRO* to break into the house]
    (b)   *He attempted [[$_C$ *for*] *me* to break into the house]

(59) (a)   He didn't dare [[$_C$ *e*] *PRO* to answer back]
    (b)   *He didn't dare [[$_C$ *for*] *me* to answer back]

It may well be that such restrictions are explicable in terms of more general semantic/pragmatic principles: for example, the oddity of (59) (b) may be purely pragmatic (hence not syntactic) in nature, in that it doesn't make sense to talk about feeling courageous in respect of an action performed by someone else (hence the parallel anomaly of '*!He didn't have the courage for me to answer back*').

If our assumptions here are correct, then the distribution and structure of noninterrogative infinitival S-bar Complements will be in large measure predictable either from the semantic properties of the matrix Predicate (i.e. the Predicate which takes the Complement), or from independent grammatical principles (e.g. the principle that noninterrogative infinitive Complements have an overt C when they have an overt Subject, and a covert C when they have a covert Subject). If this (admittedly ambitious) goal can be attained, then once again we find that nothing need be stipulated about noninterrogative infinitival S-bar Complements in lexical entries, since their distribution and structure are determined by independent principles.

One class of infinitive complement which we have not yet dealt with are 'Exceptional Clauses' – i.e. S complements which have an I constituent, but no C constituent. It may well be that the distribution and structure of these Complements, too, is in the main predictable from more general principles. Thus, Exceptional Clause Complements typically occur immediately following a subset of transitive Verbs, particularly 'COGNITIVE' and 'ASSERTIVE' Verbs such as those italicised below:

(60) (a)   I *knew* [there to be no escape]
  (b)   I *believe* [you to be innocent]
  (c)   I'd never *imagined* [anyone to be so beautiful]
  (d)   The doctors *declared* [the president to be fit]
  (e)   The police *reported* [the traffic to be heavy]

Such Exceptional Clause Complements cannot have a covert (PRO) Subject, as we saw in Chapter 6: however, this is not an idiosyncratic property of particular Predicates, but rather a general property of all Exceptional Clause Complements, which in turn follows from a more general principle governing the distribution of PRO which we shall look at in Volume Two.

Finally, we shall return briefly to 'Small Clause' Complements. These have much the same distribution (viz. occurring only immediately following a subset of transitive Verbs) and structural properties (viz. not allowing a PRO subject) as Exceptional Clauses, so we might imagine that their syntactic properties are also predictable from the same kind of principles which account for the distribution and structure of Exceptional Clauses. Now, given that Small Clauses are of the canonical form [NP XP], we expect to find four major types of Small Clause structures – viz. SCs with AP Predicates (let's call these *Adjectival Small Clauses*), SCs with PP Predicates (= *Prepositional Small Clauses*), SCs with NP Predicates (= *Nominal Small Clauses*), and SCs with

VP Predicates (= *Verbal Small Clauses*): we could further subdivide *Verbal Small Clauses* into *Infinitival, Gerundive,* and *Participial* Small Clauses, according to the morphological properties of the head V of the Predicate VP. Now, all things being equal, we might expect that any Predicate which takes a Small Clause Complement will take the full range of such Complements – viz. an AC (= Adjectival Small Clause), PC (= Prepositional SC), NC (= Nominal Small Clause), or VC (= Verbal Small Clause) Complement headed either by a gerund (V-ing) form, or by a participial form (V-en), or by an uninflected infinitive form (V–∅). And we might argue that this is indeed the case with a Verb like *have*, as the examples below suggest:

(61) (a) I won't have [$_{AC}$ you moody all the time]
  (b) I'd like to have [$_{PC}$ you with me]
  (c) We'll soon have [$_{NC}$ you a new man]
  (d) I won't have [$_{VC}$ there being any noise after dark]
  (e) I won't have [$_{VC}$ unfair advantage taken of the weak]
  (f) I'll have [$_{VC}$ you know that I'm not that kind of person]

But the behaviour of *have* is by no means typical of Verbs which take an SC Complement. As Stowell (1981, p. 259) notes, most such Verbs permit only a limited range of SC Complement types: for example, *imagine* doesn't seem to allow an NC Complement, or an infinitival VC Complement:

(62) (a) I can't imagine [$_{AC}$ you content with your lot]
  (b) I can't imagine [$_{PC}$ you in kinky boots]
  (c) I can't imagine [$_{VC}$ there being any trouble]
  (d) I can't imagine [$_{VC}$ you dominated by anyone]
  (e) *I can't imagine [$_{NC}$ you a policeman]
  (f) *I can't imagine [$_{VC}$ you be nice to anyone]

Even more restricted in its choice of SC complement is *let*; this seems to permit only a PC or an infinitival VC complement:

(63) (a) I won't let [$_{PC}$ you out of the house]
  (b) I won't let [$_{VC}$ you go to the disco]
  (c) *I won't let [$_{AC}$ you unhappy]
  (d) *I won't let [$_{NC}$ you a complete fool]
  (e) *I won't let [$_{VC}$ unfair advantage (being) taken of the unemployed]

Unless these puzzling restrictions can be accounted for in terms of general principles, then it seems that we have no choice but to follow Stowell's (1981) suggestion, and include in the subcategorisation frame for the items concerned a specification of the range of different types of SC complement which they permit (viz. AC, or PC, or NC, or VC-ing, or VC-en, or VC-∅).

As we have emphasised time and again in our discussion, we want to avoid simply having to stipulate in lexical entries the type(s) of clausal Complement which a Verb subcategorises. For example, we want to be able to stipulate in the lexical entry for *persuade* simply that it takes NP and a clausal Complement (and indeed we might hope that ultimately even this minimal stipulation can be seen to be a consequence of the meaning of *persuade*, and hence will be redundant). From the meaning of *persuade*, it will follow that the clausal Complement cannot be interrogative or exclamative. From independent word-order restrictions (an NP Complement must be positioned immediately adjacent to its sister V), it will follow that the NP Complement must precede the clausal Complement. Given that both Exceptional Clauses and Small Clauses must immediately follow a transitive Verb, it will follow that the clausal Complement of *persuade* cannot be an S or an SC, but rather must be an S-bar. Given that S-bar can be either finite or infinitival, we should expect to find that in the unmarked case, either type of clausal Complement is possible with *persuade*: and examples such as the following suggest that this is correct:

(64) (a)   Mary persuaded John [$_{S'}$ [$_C$ that] he should resign]
(b)   Mary persuaded John [$_{S'}$ [$_C$ e] PRO to resign]

In either case, *persuade* takes both an NP Complement *John* and a (bracketed) S-bar Complement. Moreover, the structure of the Complement Clause is essentially the same in the two cases: thus, the empty C in the infinitive corresponds to the *that* Complementiser in the tensed Clause; the 'empty Pronoun' (PRO) Subject of the infinitive corresponds to the 'overt Pronoun' (*he*) Subject of the tensed Clause; and the *to* in I in the infinitive corresponds to the Modal *should* in I in the tensed Clause.

The fact that *persuade NP to* ... sentences have essentially the same structure as *persuade NP that* ... sentences is arguably not a coincidence. As Chomsky remarks:

> We expect to find that infinitival and tensed Clauses appear in approximately the same positions. In the unmarked case, we expect to find pairs such as ... 'I persuaded him that he should leave', 'I persuaded him to leave'; etc. If a Verb (similarly, a Noun or Adjective) takes a clausal Complement as a lexical property, then in the unmarked case it should take either type of clausal Complement.
>
> (Chomsky, *Lectures* (1981d), p. 79)

We might refer to the principle tacitly embodied in this quotation as the LEXICAL UNIFORMITY PRINCIPLE: that is, the principle that we want to achieve maximum uniformity and symmetry in lexical entries (so that we assume, for example, that in the unmarked case untensed Complements occupy the same structural positions as the corresponding tensed Complements).

You should now be able to tackle exercise III

7.7 Subcategorising Adjectives, Nouns, and Prepositions

From our lengthy discussion of Verb complementation (i.e. the set of Complements which Verbs take) above, we get some idea of the nature of the subcategorisation information that will have to be included in the Lexicon. The essential principle of subcategorisation is that items are subcategorised with respect to any idiosyncratic (i.e. not predictable from general rules or principles) Complements which they permit. So far, we have of course only considered the problem of subcategorising *Verbs* with respect to the types of V-bar that they occur in. But similar problems arise with other categories: for example, Adjectives, Nouns, Prepositions, etc. will have to be subcategorised with respect to the types of idiosyncratic Complement which they permit within the A-bar, N-bar, or P-bar containing them. Some of the subcategorisation properties of items belonging to these categories will follow from more general principles, and hence need not be stipulated in lexical entries. For example (for reasons which we shall discuss in Volume Two) Adjectives and Nouns (i.e. [+ N] categories) do not take NP complements, or S complements, or SC complements: hence the ungrammaticality of:

(65) (a) *anxious [NP success]
   (b) *anxious [S John to be successful]
   (c) *anxious [SC John successful]

(66) (a) *his belief [NP the President]
   (b) *his belief [S the President to be incompetent]
   (c) *his belief [SC the President incompetent]

In fact, the only types of Complement which Adjectives and Nouns permit are clausal or prepositional Complements. Since we have already seen that [+ N] categories do not permit S or SC Complements, it follows that the only Complements they permit are S-bar complements. Given the Lexical Uniformity Principle, we should expect that (in the unmarked case) an Adjective or Noun which permits an S-bar Complement will permit either a finite Complement, or an infinitival Complement. Semantic properties of the Noun or Adjective should determine whether its clausal Complement is interrogative or not. Semantic properties will also determine whether the item permits a subjunctive Complement or not (recall that only MANDATIVE Predicates permits subjunctive Complements). In the case of a noninterrogative infinitival Complement, we should expect (bearing in mind our earlier observation that noninterrogative infinitives with overt Subjects require an overt C, whereas if they have a covert Subject they require a covert C) to find either an infinitive introduced by the overt C *for* with an overt Subject, or a Complement with both an empty C and an empty (PRO) Subject. And sure enough, this is exactly what we find with typical Adjectives or Nouns which take an infinitive Complement: cf. the following examples (where 'e' designates an empty C):

(67) (a)   keen [that Mary should do it] (indicative)
     (b)   keen [that Mary do it] (subjunctive)
     (c)   keen [for Mary to do it] (infinitive with subject)
     (d)   keen [e PRO to do it] (subjectless infinitive)

(68) (a)   desire [that Mary should do it] (indicative)
     (b)   desire [that Mary do it] (subjunctive)
     (c)   desire [for Mary to do it] (infinitive with subject)
     (d)   desire [e PRO to do it] (subjectless infinitive)

Thus, all our lexical entry for Adjectives like *keen* and Nouns like *desire* need stipulate is that they take a clausal Complement: everything else about the nature of the Complement (e.g. that it is a noninterrogative S-bar which may be indicative, subjunctive, or infinitival, and so forth) will be predictable from general redundancy rules.

In the case of prepositional Complements of Adjectives and Nouns we find much less predictability, however. As in the case of Verbs, it is not enough simply to subcategorise an Adjective or Noun as taking a PP Complement, since different items take PP Complements headed by different Prepositions. For example, *fond* requires an obligatory *of*-phrase Complement when used predicatively, as we see from:

(69) (a)   Mary is fond [*of*/*by/*with/*to John]
     (b)   *Mary is fond

Hence, our entry for the predicative use of *fond* might be along the following lines:

(70)   *fond*: CATEGORIAL FEATURES: [+ V, + N]
                SUBCATEGORISATION FRAME: [[. . . *of* . . .]]

In much the same way, the Noun *reliance* requires an obligatory *on*-phrase Complement: cf.

(71) (a)   his reliance [*on*/**at*/**with*/**by* her help]
     (b)   *his reliance

Accordingly, part of our entry for *reliance* might be as follows:

(72)   *reliance*: CATEGORIAL FEATURES: [− V, + N]
                    SUBCATEGORISATION FRAME: [[... *on* ...]]

In the same way that Adjectives and Nouns have to be subcategorised with
respect to the particular range of categories they permit as their Complements,
so too do Prepositions. Recall that in Chapter 3, we argued (following
Emonds (1976), pp. 172–6) that Prepositions play a much more extensive role
in Syntax than is assumed in traditional grammars. Given the assumptions we
made there, we might say that in a paradigm such as:

(73) (a)   I haven't seen him [*since the party*]
     (b)   I haven't seen him [*since the party began*]
     (c)   I haven't seen him [*since*]

since is a Preposition which subcategorises an NP Complement [*the party*] in
(73) (a), a clausal (arguably S-bar) Complement [*the party began*] in (73) (b),
and a null Complement in (73) (c). If this is so, then our lexical entry for *since*
will be along the lines of (74) below:

(74)   *since*: CATEGORIAL FEATURES: [− V, − N];
                 SUBCATEGORISATION FRAME: [NP], [S'], [∅]

Other Prepositions, however, would subcategorise a narrower range of Complements: for example, *until* can take an NP or S' Complement, but not a null
Complement (i.e. it cannot be used intransitively): cf.

(75) (a)   He waited [*until her departure*]
     (b)   He waited [*until she left*]
     (c)   *He waited [*until*]

During can subcategorise only an NP Complement: cf.

(76) (a)   He left [*during the party*]
     (b)   *He left [*during the party was still going on*]
     (c)   *He left [*during*]

And *while* subcategorises only a clausal Complement:

(77) (a)   *He collapsed [*while the party*]
     (b)   He collapsed [*while the party was in full swing*]
     (c)   *He collapsed [*while*]

In general, the clausal Complements used after those Prepositions which permit clausal Complements are finite Complements. However, we saw in Chapter 6 that Prepositions such as *with(out)* might be argued to permit Small Clause complements. And indeed, it may be that the analysis can be extended to other Prepositions, such as those italicised below:

(78) (a)   The prospect *of* [SC Reagan in the White House for another term] gives heart to out of work actors

(b)   Mary isn't very keen *on* [SC Bill as her coach]

(c)   I'm very partial *to* [SC cream on my apple pie]

(d)   The campaign *against* [SC Noddy for mayor of Toytown] is gathering momentum

(e)   *After* [SC Rambo as a lover], she was exhausted

(f)   John's turned on *by* [SC Mary in tight trousers]

(g)   She's fond *of* [SC John naked]

And it may well be that comparative *than* should also be analysed as a Preposition permitting a Small Clause Complement, in structures such as:

(79)   Rather than [VC you do/doing it], I'd prefer to do it myself

However, we shall not pursue the matter any further here, since it raises similar problems to those we have already discussed in relation to the Small Clause complements of transitive Verbs.

Although we have concentrated on Prepositions which take zero Complements, NP Complements, or clausal Complements in our discussion above, there seems no reason in principle to exclude the possibility of Prepositions taking prepositional Complements. And it may well be that items such as those italicised below are Prepositions which subcategorise a PP Complement headed by *of*:

(80) (a)   He stayed at home *because* [of the strike]

(b)   He fell *out* [of the window]

(c)   Few people *outside* [of the immediate family] know

(d)   %It fell *off* [of the table] (dialectal)

Hitherto, we have discussed the subcategorisation of Verbs in some detail, and touched briefly on some issues which arise in relation to the subcategorisation of Adjectives, Nouns, and Prepositions. Since we have now looked at a wide range of categories and the types of Complements they subcategorise, this may be a convenient point to summarise our discussion of subcategorisation. What we have suggested so far is that:

(81) (a) Verbs are subcategorised with respect to the range of idiosyncratic Complements they permit within the V-bar containing them

(b) Adjectives are subcategorised with respect to the range of idiosyncratic Complements they permit within the A-bar containing them

(c) Nouns are subcategorised with respect to the range of idiosyncratic Complements they permit within the N-bar containing them

(d) Prepositions are subcategorised with respect to the range of idiosyncratic Complements they permit within the P-bar containing them

It seems a simple enough matter to extract a general principle of subcategorisation out of (81), along the lines of:

(82) SUBCATEGORISATION PRINCIPLE
Any lexical item of category X will be subcategorised with respect to the range of idiosyncratic Complements (i.e. sister constituents) which it permits within the (minimal) X-bar containing it

The subcategorisation frame for X will simply be an unordered list of the sets of categories which X permits as its Complements: we assume that the relative ordering of X and its Complements will be determined by independent principles (e.g. the HEAD FIRST PRINCIPLE).

The SUBCATEGORISATION PRINCIPLE (82) has a number of interesting consequences. For example, in the case of a sentence such as:

(83) I wonder whether he might have been [ᵥ' *playing* tennis]

it tells us that the Verb *playing* will have to be subcategorised with respect to the NP *tennis*, since that NP is a *sister* of the V *playing*, and is contained within the (bracketed) V-bar immediately dominating the head V *playing*. But our SUBCATEGORISATION PRINCIPLE (82) also tells us that the V *playing* will not have to be subcategorised with respect to any of the constituents which lie *outside* the bracketed V-bar, since none of these are sisters of the V in question. More generally, it tells us that Verbs are not subcategorised with respect to any Auxiliaries which precede them, or their Subjects, or the Complementisers introducing their Clauses, and so on. And this prediction is exactly right, since (e.g.) although there are Verbs which cannot co-occur with an NP (Object) Complement, there are none which cannot co-occur with an Auxiliary, a Subject, or a Complementiser. What the principle predicts is that although Verbs like *eat* and *devour* may differ with respect to the range of Complements they permit or require (*devour* requires an obligatory NP Complement, whereas *eat* does not), there will never be (in English or any

365

other language) any related pair of Verbs which differ solely in the fact that one always requires a Subject, whereas the other is always used without a Subject. And although there may be Verbs like *give* which permit two NP Complements (cf. *give someone something*), there will never be Verbs which permit two NP Subjects.

> ### *You should now be able to tackle exercises IV, V, and VI*

7.8 Eliminating redundancy

Throughout our discussion of subcategorisation, we have stressed the importance of eliminating redundancy in lexical entries: and we have suggested various ways of achieving this goal. For example, we have eliminated redundant categorial and ordering information in subcategorisation frames; and we have eliminated a great deal of subcategorisation information by the use of *Lexical Redundancy Rules*. An obvious question to ask, however, is whether there are other devices which we can exploit in our quest for paring down the information contained in lexical entries to a minimum? In one sense, we have already encountered one technical device which enables us to eliminate a great deal of redundancy from lexical entries – namely the reanalysis of simple categories as sets of Categorial Features. For example, consider the fact that the item *claim* may take a clausal Complement when used either as a Verb (as in (84) (a) below), or as a Noun (as in (84) (b)):

(84) (a)   John *claimed* [that Mary was innocent]

    (b)   John's *claim* [that Mary was innocent]

Within the framework of Syntactic Feature Theory, instead of listing two separate items *claim* in our Lexicon, one a Verb subcategorising an S-bar Complement, and the other a Noun also subcategorising an S-bar complement, we can have a single entry for *claim*, assigned a single subcategorisation frame [S'], and a single set of Categorial Features [αN, $-\alpha$V], as in the partial entry (85) below:

(85)   *claim:* CATEGORIAL FEATURES: [αV, $-\alpha$N]

                SUBCATEGORISATION FRAME: [S']

α here is a feature-value variable which may either be positive or negative. The notational convention used in (85) – a convention borrowed from work in Phonology – is that the value of α for V must be different from the value of α

for N. In other words, (85) tells us that *claim* can either be [+ V, − N] and hence a Verb, or [− V, + N] and hence a Noun; but in either case, the item has the same Subcategorisation Frame. Thus, Syntactic Feature Theory in effect enables us to conflate the entries for two different (but related) items into one entry, with a single set of Categorial Features, and a single subcategorisation frame.

Thus far, we have explored a variety of ways of eliminating redundancy from lexical entries (e.g. paring down subcategorisation frames so that they don't contain redundant categorial or ordering information, making use of redundancy rules, exploiting categorial features, etc.). However, while efforts to eliminate redundancy from within the Lexicon are laudable, we also need to explore simplicity and redundancy in a broader context, and consider whether or not there is yet further redundancy in our *overall Grammar* which we might eliminate.

In Chapter 6, we suggested that traditional *category-specific* Phrase Structure Rules might be eliminated from the Categorial Component of our grammar in favour of a set of *category-neutral* rule-schemas. We shall now reinforce the argument in favour of eliminating PS rules by suggesting that much of the information contained in traditional PS rules is redundant, because it duplicates information already contained in the subcategorisation frames of lexical entries.

Let's put our discussion on a firm empirical footing by taking a concrete example of this 'overlap' between Phrase Structure Rules and subcategorisation frames. The relevant entries in our Lexicon will tell us that Verbs like *give* subcategorise either an [NP NP] (= *give someone something*) structure, or an [NP PP] (= *give something to someone*) structure; that Verbs like *persuade* subcategorise an [NP S'] structure (= *persuade someone that ...*); that Verbs like *complain* subcategorise a [PP S'] structure (= *complain to someone that ...*), and so on and so forth. And yet at the same time, traditional PS rules expanding V-bar also tell us that a V-bar comprises a V and a variety of NP, PP, S-bar, etc. Complements, and thus generate V-bar constituents of the schematic form [V NP NP], [V NP PP], [V NP S'], [V PP S'], and so on. Surely the PS rules generating these structures are redundant, since the relevant structural information about the range of Complements which a V can take within V-bar is contained in the subcategorisation entry for each V listed in the Lexicon? Thus, syntactic information which simply mirrors lexical properties of particular items (e.g. information about the range of Complements an item belonging to a given category permits or requires) could and should be eliminated from Phrase Structure Rules. So, PS rules specifying the range of complements which Major Categories like V, N, A, and P take, i.e. rules such as:

(86) (a)   V' → V NP NP
    (b)   A' → A PP
    (c)   P' → P NP
    (d)   N' → N S'

can be eliminated from our overall grammar, given that such information is already contained in the Subcategorisation Frames associated with the Lexical Entries for items belonging to the associated head categories. As Chomsky (*Knowledge* (1986a), p. 82) notes: 'Since these facts are expressed in the Lexicon, they need not be duplicated in the Syntax by Phrase Structure Rules'. Moreover, since (as Chomsky, ibid. notes) the relative ordering of Head and Complements 'can in large part be determined by other general principles' (e.g. universal principles such as the PERIPHERY PRINCIPLE, and language-specific principles such as the HEAD FIRST PRINCIPLE), PS rules are not even needed to stipulate the relative ordering of Complements within X-bar. As Chomsky (*Knowledge* (1986a), pp. 82–3) comments, this opens up the possibility that:

> the Phrase Structure Component can be entirely eliminated, apart from certain parameters of X-bar theory: e.g. does the Head precede its Complements, as in English-like languages, so that we have the constructions N-Complement, V-Complement, A-Complement, P-Complement; or does it follow them, as in Japanese-like languages, so that we have the corresponding constructions Complement-N, Complement-V, Complement-A, Complement-P?

The obvious conclusion to reach about PS rules is thus that 'There are no rules of this type in language' (Chomsky, *Knowledge* (1986a), p. 83).

Chomsky's statement here echoes the conclusion we reached in the previous chapter, where we argued in favour of replacing PS rules by a set of category-neutral rule-schemas. Within this revised view of the Categorial Component, subcategorisation frames can be seen as performing a *filtering* function: that is, they throw out certain structures as ill-formed. To see what we mean by this, consider the Generalised Complement Rule (87) (a) below which we proposed in Chapter 6, and the P-marker (87) (b) which is one of the (infinite) set of structures generated by that rule:

(87) (a)   X' → X YP* (* = 'indefinitely many')

    (b)

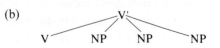

The category-neutral rule-schema (87) (a) will generate structures such as (87) (b), if we take the value of the variable X in (87) (a) to be V, and the value of Y to be N. And yet, while there are Verbs in English which take two NP Complements (e.g. *give* in structures such as *give someone something*), there are none which subcategorise *three* NP Complements. So, (87) simply isn't a structure which can be *lexicalised*. Thus, our category-neutral rule-schemas such as (87) (a) will *overgenerate* in an obvious fashion. How are we going to block this kind of overgeneration? Well, it seems natural to propose a constraint on what counts as a 'possible syntactic structure' in a language to the effect that only structures which can be *lexicalised* are well-formed. This we might do in terms of the following principle (adapted from Chomsky, *Lectures* (1981d), p. 29):

(88)   PROJECTION PRINCIPLE
        Syntactic representations [i.e. syntactic structures] must be projected from the Lexicon, in that they observe the subcategorisation properties of lexical items

It will then follow that 'Where improper structures are generated, they will be excluded by properties of the Lexicon' (Chomsky (1981c), p. 14) – i.e. structures such as (87) will be ill-formed because they can't be lexicalised.

7.9   Selection Restrictions

Thus far, our discussion of lexical entries has focused almost entirely on the *subcategorisation* information contained in dictionary entries. We might refer to subcategorisation information more generally as *contextual* information, since it specifies the linguistic context in which a given item can be used. An obvious question to ask is whether there is any further *contextual* information which should be included in lexical entries. In much early work on the Lexicon (dating back to Chomsky's *Aspects* (1965)), it was argued that dictionary entries should contain not only *subcategorisation* information, but also *selectional* information. Let's briefly consider the difference between the two types of contextual information.

As we have already seen, *subcategorisation restrictions* are restrictions on the range of *categories* which a given item permits or requires as its Complements. For example, *devour* takes an obligatory NP Complement, *rely* takes an obligatory PP Complement headed by *on*, and so on. However, when an item subcategorises a Complement belonging to a particular category, it is not usually the case that *any expression whatever* belonging to the relevant category can function as a Complement of the item concerned; on the contrary, there are generally clear restrictions on the choice of Complement. For

The Lexicon

example, the Verb *convince* subcategorises an NP Complement; and yet there
are severe restrictions on the class of NPs which can function as its Object: cf.

(89) (a)　　You have convinced [*my mother*]
　　(b)　　You have convinced [*my cat*]
　　(c)　　?You have convinced [*my goldfish*]
　　(d)　　??You have convinced [*my computer*]
　　(e)　　?!You have convinced [*my frying-pan*]
　　(f)　　!You have convinced [*my theory*]
　　(g)　　!!You have convinced [*my birth*]

The relevant restrictions are not *subcategorisation restrictions*, since in each of
the examples above *convince* subcategorises a (bracketed) NP Complement.
Rather, they are *selection restrictions* – i.e. semantic/pragmatic restrictions on
the choice of expressions within a given category which can occupy a given
sentence-position. In example (89) above, the relevant restriction seems to be
that the NP Complement has to denote some RATIONAL (i.e. mind-possessing)
entity. We can draw a terminological distinction between the two types of restriction by saying that *convince* (and other similar verbs) *subcategorise* an NP
Complement, but *select* a RATIONAL Complement. The two notions of *subcategorisation* and *selection* are clearly distinct: subcategorisation restrictions
are purely syntactic (more precisely *categorial*) in nature, whereas selection
restrictions are semantic/pragmatic in nature. But what does it mean to say
that selection restrictions are *semantic/pragmatic* in nature? Well, what we are
saying (in the case of (89) above) is that it is a *semantic* property of the Verb
convince (i.e. part of the meaning of the Verb) that its Object is presupposed to
be a RATIONAL being. But the degree to which a particular individual accepts a
sentence such as (89) (d) *You have convinced my computer* as well-formed
depends on pragmatic factors – in this case, the individual's beliefs about the
degree to which computers are RATIONAL entities or not.

The difference between (syntactic) *subcategorisation* and (semantic/
pragmatic) *selection* is highlighted by the fact that although items (e.g. Verbs)
do not subcategorise their Subjects, they do nonetheless *select* (i.e. impose
selection restrictions on) their choice of Subject. For example, there are
obvious restrictions on the class of NPs which can serve as the Subject of a
Verb like *faint*: cf.

(90) (a)　　*My mother* fainted
　　(b)　　*My giraffe* fainted
　　(c)　　?!*My frying-pan* fainted
　　(d)　　!*My theory* fainted

370

If we use the term *Argument* to subsume 'Subject' and 'Complement', then we can say that selection restrictions hold between a given item and its Arguments; or, equivalently, we can say that items *select* (= impose selection restrictions on) their Arguments.

In the light of our observation that selection restrictions hold between a given item and its Arguments, we can now return to our discussion in Chapter 6 of *NP to VP* complements of Verbs like *persuade* on the one hand, and *consider* on the other. Recall that we argued that *persuade-* and *consider-*sentences have the respective structures indicated below:

(91) (a) John persuaded Mary [to tell the truth]
    (b) John considers [Mary to dislike him]

so that *Mary* is the main Clause Object in (91) (a), but the Complement Clause Subject in (91) (b). This being so, then it follows that *Mary* is an Argument of *persuaded* in (91) (a), but not an Argument of *considers* in (91) (b). Now, if selection restrictions hold between items and their Arguments, then we should expect to find that there are clear selection restrictions holding between *persuaded* and *Mary* in (91) (a), but none holding between *considers* and *Mary* in (91) (b). The fact that this is indeed the case is suggested by the examples below:

(92) (a) *John persuaded his *frying-pan* [to burn the chops]
    (b) John considers [*his frying-pan* to be indispensable]

(93) (a) *John persuaded *his birth* [to startle the world]
    (b) John considers [*his birth* to have been a momentous event in the history of civilisation]

So it seems that evidence from *selection restrictions* provides independent confirmation of the conclusions we arrived at earlier about the structural difference between [*persuade NP to VP*] and [*consider NP to VP*] constructions. And we might use similar evidence to differentiate between *phrasal* and *clausal* Complement structures – e.g. to 'disambiguate' [V NP PP] structures: where NP and PP are Complements of V, then V will impose selection restrictions on NP. But where NP and PP are the Subject and Predicate of a Small Clause complement of V and we have the structure [V [$_{SC}$ NP PP], then we should expect no such selection restrictions to hold between V and NP.

If we follow the assumption made in Chomsky's *Aspects* (1965) that Selection Restrictions are idiosyncratic properties of lexical items, then it follows that the selectional properties of items should be specified in their lexical entries. For example, in order to account for the contrast in:

(94) (a)   Sincerity may frighten the boy (Chomsky (1965), p. 63)

(b)   !The boy may frighten sincerity

we might want to include in our lexical entry for *frighten* the fact that it 'allows Abstract Subjects (as distinct from *eat, admire*) and Human Objects (as distinct from *read, wear*)' (Chomsky, *Aspects* (1965), p. 64). Since selection restrictions hold only between a Predicate and its Arguments (not e.g. its Adjuncts), then our lexical entry for a given Predicate will have to specify what Selection Restrictions it imposes on each of its Arguments. For example, if *murder* requires that both its first Argument (= its Subject) and its second Argument (= its Object) be HUMAN, then we might incorporate this information into the corresponding lexical entry along the following lines:

(95)   *murder*: CATEGORIAL FEATURES: $[+V, -N]$

SUBCATEGORISATION FRAME: [NP]

SELECTION RESTRICTIONS: ⟨HUMAN — HUMAN⟩

The third line of the entry in (95) simply tells us that both the NP preceding *murder* (= its Subject) and that following it (= its Object) denote a human being. Perhaps the best way of interpreting selection restrictions such as those in (95) is as telling us that both the Subject and the Object of *murder* are interpreted as being (more technically, *presupposed* to be) human beings. Hence, when we come across a sentence containing *murder* used with novel (= previously unencountered) expressions as its Subject and Object, as in:

(96)   *Kambomambo* murdered *Zombaluma*

we infer that the italicised expressions are the names of human beings: this inference is based in large part upon our knowledge of the *selectional* properties of *murder*.

You should now be able to tackle exercises VII and VIII

7.10   Thematic relations

Thus far, we have suggested that lexical entries should contain at least three different types of idiosyncratic information, relating to the *categorial, subcategorisation*, and *selectional* properties of items. However, we might argue that there is yet a fourth type of information which lexical entries should contain, namely *thematic* information. In numerous works over the past two decades, beginning with the pioneering work of Gruber (1965), Fillmore (1968a), and Jackendoff (1972), it has been argued that each Argument (i.e. Subject or Complement) of a Predicate bears a particular *thematic role* (alias *theta-role*, or *θ-role* to its Predicate), and that the set of *thematic functions* which Arguments can fulfil are drawn from a highly restricted, finite, universal set. The precise set of thematic functions assumed to constitute primitive elements of the associated THEORY OF THEMATIC STRUCTURE (or THETA THEORY) varies somewhat from author to author: but in (97) below, we list some of the commonly assumed theta-roles, and for each such role provide an informal gloss, together with an illustrative example (in which the italicised Argument is assumed to have the thematic function specified):

(97) (a) THEME (or PATIENT) = Entity undergoing the effect of some action
          (*Mary* fell over)

     (b) AGENT (or ACTOR) = Instigator of some action
          (*John* killed Harry)

     (c) EXPERIENCER = Entity experiencing some psychological state
          (*John* was happy)

     (d) BENEFACTIVE = Entity benefitting from some action
          (John bought some flowers *for Mary*)

     (e) INSTRUMENT = Means by which something comes about
          (John wounded Harry *with a knife*)

     (f) LOCATIVE = Place in which something is situated or takes place
          (John hid the letter *under the bed*)

     (g) GOAL = Entity towards which something moves
          (John passed the book *to Mary*)

     (h) SOURCE = Entity from which something moves
          (John returned *from Paris*)

Thus, in a sentence such as:

(98)   John gave Mary the book

John bears the θ-role AGENT to the verbal Predicate *gave*, *Mary* bears the role GOAL, and *the book* bears the role THEME.

The obvious question to ask at this point is: 'Why posit the existence of a set of Thematic Relations (THEME, AGENT, INSTRUMENT, etc.) distinct from constituent structure relations?' The answer given to this question in the relevant literature is that a variety of linguistic phenomena can be accounted for in a more principled way in terms of Thematic Functions than in terms of constituent structure relations. We shall look briefly at a number of arguments adduced in support of this claim.

One such argument is that incorporating Thematic Functions into our model of Syntax allows us to capture the similarity between different (but related) uses of the same lexical item. For example, a Verb such as *roll* can be used both in *transitive* structures like (99) (a) below, and in so-called *ergative* structures such as (99) (b) (an *ergative* structure is one in which an expression which normally functions as the Object of a given transitive Verb is used intransitively as the Subject of the Verb):

(99) (a)   John rolled *the ball* down the hill

    (b)   *The ball* rolled down the hill

The italicised expression clearly has a different constituent structure status in the (a) and (b) sentences: more precisely, *the ball* is the Object of the Verb *rolled* in (99) (a), but its Subject in (99) (b). And yet, in another sense, the italicised expression seems intuitively to play the *same* role in the (a) sentence as in the corresponding (b) sentence: thus, *the ball* is the entity undergoing motion in both (99) (a) and (b). We can capture this role-identity by saying that the italicised expression has the same *thematic role* in the (a) sentence as in the corresponding (b) sentence, in spite of the fact that it has a different constituent structure status in the two cases. To be precise, *the ball* has the θ-role THEME in both (99) (a) and (b), since in both cases it is the entity undergoing motion.

But on what evidence do we say that *the ball* has the same thematic role in (99) (a) as in (99) (b)? Surely *intuition* alone isn't sufficient (since we have already argued that informants frequently do not have reliable intuitions)? Quite right! Fortunately, however, there is substantial empirical evidence in support of the crucial role-identity claim; and part of this evidence comes from *Selection Restrictions*. For, it turns out that selection restrictions seem to correlate with thematic structure, in the sense that expressions which bear the same thematic relation to some item will be subject to the same selection restrictions; whereas those which bear different thematic roles to a given item will be subject to different selection restrictions. In the light of this observation, it is interesting to note that the NP which is the Object of *roll* in (99) (a) seems to obey the same selection restrictions as the NP which is its Subject in (99) (b): cf.

(100) (a)   John rolled *the ball/the rock/!the theory/!sincerity* down the hill

    (b)   *The ball/the rock/!the theory/!sincerity* rolled down the hill

Thus, the fact that the Object of *roll* when used transitively obeys the same selection restrictions as its Subject when used ergatively provides interesting independent confirmation of our initial assumption that the two NPs play the same *thematic role*, even though they have different *constituent structure status*.

Thus far, we have argued that Thematic Functions enable us to capture the similarity between different but related uses of the same item. However, the converse is also true: namely, that by assuming that Arguments play a thematic role in sentences independent of their constituent structure status, we can account for the differences between apparently similar (but unrelated) uses of the same item. For example, consider the following pair of sentences:

(101) (a)   *The vase* shattered the glass
  (b)   *The vase* shattered

In both sentences, the NP, *the vase*, fulfils the same grammatical role – that of the Subject of *shattered*. However, intuitively it seems as if *the vase* plays two quite distinct thematic roles in the two different sentences. Thus, in (101) (a) *the vase* is the cause of the shattering, whereas in (101) (b) it is the entity which undergoes the effects of the shattering, Accordingly, we might posit that *the vase* plays the thematic role of INSTRUMENT in (101) (a), but the role of THEME in (101) (b). This difference of thematic status is reflected in a difference of selection restrictions: cf.

(102) (a)   *The vase/the noise/a hidden flaw* shattered the glass
  (b)   *The vase/!the noise/!a hidden flaw* shattered

And this provides independent confirmation of our initial suspicions (given our postulate that similarities or differences in thematic structure are reflected in similarities or differences in selection restrictions).

Thus far, we have argued that Thematic Functions enable us to reveal similarities and differences between related construction types which are not reflected in their constituent structure. However, a number of linguists have argued that the thematic structure of a sentence plays a much more pervasive role in Syntax. For example, it has been argued that the distribution of certain types of Adverbial and Prepositional Phrases is thematically determined: thus, Gruber (1976) argues that Adverbs like *deliberately* can co-occur only with AGENT phrases: cf.

(103) (a)   *John* (= AGENT) deliberately rolled the ball down the hill
  (b)   **The ball* (= THEME) deliberately rolled down the hill

Likewise, Fillmore (1972, p. 10) argues that the Adverb *personally* can only co-occur with EXPERIENCER arguments: cf.

(104) (a)   Personally, *I* (= EXPERIENCER) don't like roses
  (b)   Personally, your proposal doesn't interest *me* (= EXPERIENCER)
  (c)   *Personally, *I* (= AGENT) hit you
  (d)   *Personally, you hit *me* (= THEME)

The Lexicon

And in much the same vein, Anderson (1977, pp. 267–71) argues that only Verbs with AGENT subjects permit *by*-phrase nominal counterparts:

(105) (a) *The mayor* (= AGENT) protested
      (b) the protest *by the mayor*

(106) (a) *The mayor* (= THEME) died
      (b) *the death *by the mayor*

Many other areas of Syntax have also been argued to be subject to thematic constraints. For example, Fillmore (1968a, p. 22) argues that only constituents with the same Thematic Function can be conjoined. So, for example, since the two subject NPs *John* and *a hammer* play different thematic roles in the following sentences:

(107) (a) *John* (= AGENT) broke the window
      (b) *A hammer* (= INSTRUMENT) broke the window

the two subject NPs cannot be idiomatically conjoined – hence the oddity of:

(108)   ??*John* and *a hammer* broke the window

And Jackendoff (1972) argues at length that a number of constraints on Passive and Reflexive structures can best be accounted for in thematic rather than grammatical terms. For example, he argues (1972, p. 44) that the ill-formedness of passive sentences like:

(109) (a) *Five dollars are cost by this book
      (b) *Two hundred pounds are weighed by Bill

is attributable to violation of the following condition (formulated in terms of Thematic Structure):

(110)   PASSIVE THEMATIC HIERARCHY CONDITION
          The passive *by*-phrase must be higher on the Thematic Hierarchy than the superficial Subject

The hierarchy referred to in (110) is that in (111) below:

(111)   THEMATIC HIERARCHY

$$\text{AGENT} > \left\{ \begin{array}{l} \text{LOCATIVE} \\ \text{SOURCE} \\ \text{GOAL} \end{array} \right\} > \text{THEME}$$

Jackendoff maintains that the *by*-phrase in both examples in (109) fulfils the THEME role, whereas the superficial subject is a LOCATIVE phrase; since THEME is lower than LOCATIVE on the hierarchy (111), the Passive Thematic Hierarchy

Condition (110) is thereby violated – hence the ill-formedness of both sentences in (109).

Elsewhere (1972, p. 148), Jackendoff posits that the distribution of *Reflexives* is also determined by thematic structure, in the following manner:

(112)   REFLEXIVE THEMATIC HIERARCHY CONDITION
    A Reflexive may not be higher on the Thematic Hierarchy (111) than its antecedent

He argues that the condition (112) provides a principled account of the ill-formedness of sentences such as (113) below (where the italicised pairs of expressions are coreferential):

(113) (a)   *John* was shaved by *himself*
    (b)   *I talked about *Thmug* to *himself*

This is because in (113) (a) the Reflexive *himself* is an AGENT, and thus higher on the Thematic Hierarchy (111) than its THEME antecedent *John*; and in (113) (b), the Reflexive *himself* is a GOAL argument, and therefore higher on the Thematic Hierarchy (111) than its THEME antecedent *Thmug*.

The evidence we have given so far primarily relates to facts about English Syntax/Semantics. However, some *universalist* support for positing a primitive set of theta roles comes from *morphological* facts. Travis and Williams (1982) argue that verbal morphology in Malayo-Polynesian languages may directly reflect thematic structure: they remark (p. 57):

> Certain Malayo-Polynesian languages have a complex verbal system which adds morphology to the Verb and thereby marks one of the Arguments of the Verb as Topic. This Topic NP is specified in two ways. First, its theta-role is marked by the morphology of the Verb, and secondly, either it is preceded by a Topic marking particle (*ang* in Tagalog and Cebuano), or it is placed in Topic position (sentence final in Malagasy). Depending on the theta-role of the NP, the verbal morphology may be a prefix, infix, or suffix.

Among the examples they adduce in support of this claim are the following:

(114) (a)   *Mag*luto [ang babaye] [ug bugas] [sa   lata]
    AT cook TOP woman O rice   OBL can
    'The woman will cook rice in the pan' (Cebuano)

    (b)   Luto' *an* [sa   babaye] [ang lata] [ug bugas]
    Cook LT GEN woman TOP can O rice
    'The can will be cooked rice in by the woman' (Cebuano)

(c)   *I*bili   [ang bata] [ng   babaye] [ng bigas]
BT-buy TOP child GEN woman O rice
'The children were bought rice for by the woman' (Tagalog)

[AT = Actor Topic verbal affix; LT = Locative Topic verbal affix; BT = Benefactive Topic verbal suffix; TOP = Topic particle; O = Object Particle; OBL = Oblique Particle; GEN = Genitive Particle.] In each case, the italicised verbal affix encodes the theta-function of the Topic NP, so that verbal morphology directly reflects thematic structure.

From our brief discussion above, it seems that we have abundant empirical evidence in support of positing that thematic functions have an important role to play in any adequate description of certain areas of natural language Syntax, Semantics, and Morphology. Indeed, Thematic Structure plays such a central role in more recent work in Syntax that we shall devote the whole of a chapter in Volume Two to considering it in more detail. For the time being, however, it is sufficient to note the fundamental assumption that sentences have a thematic structure which is in large measure independent of their categorial constituent structure.

You should now be able to tackle exercises IX and X

7.11   Correlating Thematic and Syntactic Structure

Although we have argued that Thematic Structure plays an important role in the proper description of a variety of linguistic phenomena, we have not yet addressed ourselves to the question of how we can correlate the thematic structure of a sentence with its syntactic constituent structure. An important point to bear in mind about Thematic Structure is that there is no obvious way of predicting the theta-role that a given Argument of a given item will play from its constituent structure function. For example, the Subject of *murder* is an AGENT, the Subject of *collapse* is a THEME, the Subject of *receive* is a GOAL, the Subject of *contain* is a LOCATIVE, and so on. Since θ-roles are unpredictable and idiosyncratic to particular items, it seems that the obvious place to represent information about the particular theta-role which a particular Argument of a particular item plays is in the Lexicon, as part of the lexical entry for the item concerned. This means that in addition to *categorial* information (about whether a given item functions as an V, A, N, P, etc.), *subcategorisation* information (about the range of categories which a given item allows or requires as its Complements), and *selectional* information (about the choice of expressions which can fill a particular Argument function) lexical entries will also have to contain *thematic* information (about the theta-role assumed by each of the Arguments of a given item). Following terminology introduced by Stowell (1981), let's refer to this abstract specification of the thematic function fulfilled by each of the Arguments which a given Predicate permits as the *theta-grid* of the item concerned.

But how can this type of thematic information be incorporated into lexical entries? Jackendoff (1972, p. 35) suggests that 'The lexical entry of a Verb must correlate grammatical and thematic relations'. To make our discussion more concrete, let's consider how the lexical entry for the Verb *murder* would look in Jackendoff's Lexicon. Given the general schema for lexical entries suggested by Jackendoff (1972, p. 38), it is clear that the entry for *murder* would be along the following lines:

(115) (i)   *murder*

    (ii) $[+V, -N]$

    (iii) $[NP \quad - \quad NP]$

              | |

    (iv)   AGENT   THEME

           | |

    (v)   ⟨HUMAN⟩ ⟨HUMAN⟩

The first line of the entry in (115) (i) would be a specification of the phonological properties of the word (e.g. in terms of a matrix of phonological distinctive features). The second line (115) (ii) is a specification of the categorial properties of the word, and tells us that *murder* can be used as a Verb (for simplicity of exposition, we ignore its use as a Noun). The third line of the entry (115) (iii) is a specification of the 'grammatical properties' of *murder*: it tells us that *murder* can be preceded and followed by an NP (in other words, *murder* takes an NP Subject, and an NP Complement). The fourth line (115) (iv) is a specification of the thematic properties of *murder*: it tells us that the NP which precedes *murder* (= its Subject) has the thematic function of AGENT, whereas the NP which follows *murder* plays the θ-role of THEME: the function of the solid line linking (iii) and (iv) is to 'correlate grammatical and thematic relations' (i.e. it is to make sure we know that it is the Subject of *murder* rather than the Object which plays the role of AGENT). Although Jackendoff does not include *selectional* information in his lexical entries, we have indicated in (115) (v) how this might be done within a typical Jackendoff lexical entry.

While the schema for lexical entries in (115) might seem to be a paragon of simplicity, there are numerous objections which we might raise. For example, the way in which Jackendoff seeks to 'correlate grammatical and thematic relations' is by arbitrary *stipulation*. For example, lines (iii) and (iv) of the entry in (115) simply *stipulate* that both the AGENT and THEME Arguments of *murder* are assigned the categorial status of NP (rather than e.g. PP), and like-wise *stipulate* that the AGENT rather than the THEME is selected as the Subject of *murder*. To stipulate this kind of information in lexical entries is to imply that there are no general principles which correlate the thematic role of an Argument with its categorial or grammatical status, and that the correlation is an idiosyncratic property which varies from one lexical item to another. But is this so?

In work two decades ago, Fillmore suggested the contrary: he argued that there are a set of general principles (some universal, some language-particular) which correlate the thematic function of Arguments with their categorial status and grammatical function. Before we look at the kinds of principles involved, however, it will be useful to draw a distinction between two different kinds of Argument: those which are *internal* to VP (= Complements), and those which are *external* to VP (= Subjects). For example, in sentences such as (116) below:

(116) (a)   *John* will [give the book to Mary]
     (b)   *John* will [give Mary the book]

the italicised NP *John* is the *external Argument* of the verbal Predicate *give* in each case (since it lies outside the bracketed VP), whereas the expressions *the book* and (*to*) *Mary* are *internal Arguments* of *give* (because they are contained within the bracketed VP).

For the time being, we'll concentrate on *internal arguments* (i.e. on Complements). Fillmore posits a set of general principles of *Complement Selection* (some universal, others language-particular) which determine which internal Arguments of a Verb are assigned the categorial status of NP, and which are realised as PP. In this connection, consider the following examples (all taken from various works by Fillmore):

(117) (a)   Harry sprayed *paint* [on the wall]
     (b)   Harry sprayed [the wall] *with paint* (1968b, p. 391)

(118) (a)   John planted *peas and corn* [in his garden]
     (b)   John planted [his garden] *with peas and corn* (1968a, p. 48)

(119) (a)   I loaded *hay* [onto the truck]
     (b)   I loaded [the truck] *with hay* (1977, p. 79)

(120) (a)   I smeared *mud* [on the wall]
     (b)   I smeared [the wall] *with mud* (1977, p. 79)

Fillmore supposes that in each case the italicised expression is an INSTRUMENT, and the bracketed expression is a LOCATIVE. The Complement Selection prin-

ciples which apply to Verbs such as those above will specify that either the
INSTRUMENT or the LOCATIVE Argument of the Verb can be selected as an NP
Complement (whichever is regarded as more 'salient' is selected as NP), and
that the other member of the pair is then realised as a PP (i.e. if INSTRUMENT is
NP, then LOCATIVE will be PP, as in the (a) examples above; but if LOCATIVE is
chosen as NP, then INSTRUMENT will be PP, as in the (b) examples above). The
choice of P which heads the PP concerned will be determined by the semantic
properties of individual Prepositions: we might assume that the lexical entry
for Prepositions includes a specification of the kind of thematic functions that
they are used to encode, as indicated informally in (121) below:

(121)	PREPOSITION	θ-FUNCTION	PREPOSITION	θ-FUNCTION
	in	LOCATIVE	*on*	LOCATIVE
	onto	LOCATIVE	*to*	GOAL
	by	AGENT	*with*	INSTRUMENT
	from	SOURCE	*for*	BENEFACTIVE

We might interpret this as meaning that a 'locative' Preposition such as *on*
assigns the theta-role LOCATIVE to its NP Complement, so that in a phrase
such as 'on the table', both the overall PP [*on the table*], and the NP [*the table*]
have a LOCATIVE function. Independent word-order principles (viz. the STRICT
ADJACENCY CONDITION) will determine that the NP Complement of the Verb
concerned must precede its PP Complement.

We can illustrate how these Complement Selection principles might work in
relation to (117) above, repeated as (122) below (we have specified the thematic
function of each of the two Complements, for the reader's convenience):

(122) (a)   Harry sprayed *paint*   [on the wall]
                        INSTRUMENT   LOCATIVE

      (b)   Harry sprayed [the wall]   *with paint*
                        LOCATIVE   INSTRUMENT

The relative 'salience' of the two internal arguments determines which is
selected as NP. If the INSTRUMENT Argument is regarded as the more salient,
then it will be realised as the NP *paint*, as in (122) (a): it therefore follows that
the LOCATIVE Complement will be realised as a PP headed by a LOCATIVE Preposition. Since the dictionary entry for *on* in (121) specifies that it can be used
to encode LOCATIVE function, the LOCATIVE Complement surfaces as the PP
[*on the wall*] in (122) (a). However, if the LOCATIVE Argument is selected as the
NP Complement, then *the wall* will be realised as a 'bare' (i.e. prepositionless)
NP, as in (122) (b): it then follows that the INSTRUMENT Argument must be
realised as PP. Since *with* is listed in the Lexicon (cf. (121) above) as encoding

an INSTRUMENT θ-function (but *on* is not), then the INSTRUMENT Complement is realised as a PP headed by *with*. Thus, the choice of NP and PP Complements in such cases is determined by Lexical Redundancy Rules of Complement Selection which correlate thematic function with categorial status. But these 'Complement Selection' rules do not themselves determine the relative ordering of the NP and PP complements. Rather, this ordering is determined by independent linearisation principles, such as the STRICT ADJACENCY PRINCIPLE, which requires that an NP Complement always appear immediately adjacent to its governing Verb: moreover, the HEAD FIRST PRINCIPLE determines that V will appear at the left-periphery of V-bar, so that the resultant order of constituents within V-bar is [V NP PP].

A rather more recent attempt to develop a set of principles which correlate thematic and syntactic structure is found in the work of Edwin Williams. Williams (1981) argues that lexical entries will contain (*inter alia*) a specification of the *Argument Structure* of items. This will comprise an unordered list of the thematic role played by each Argument of a Predicate: the External Argument of a Predicate will be notationally differentiated from its Internal Argument(s) by being *underlined*. Thus, given Williams' analysis, the entry for *give* might be along the following lines:

(123)   *give*: CATEGORIAL FEATURES: $[+V, -N]$
              ARGUMENT STRUCTURE: [Actor, Theme, Goal]

(NB. *Actor* = AGENT). The syntactic realisation of the internal THEME and GOAL Arguments will be determined by a set of REALISATION RULES which include the following (Williams 1981, p. 88):

(124) (i)   Theme: (NP)
      (ii)   Goal: (NP, PP_{to})
      (iii) Goal: (NP_2)

Rule (124) (i) tells us that a THEME Argument of a Predicate is always realised as a bare NP; (124) (ii) says that a GOAL Argument can be realised as an NP which is the Object of a PP headed by *to*; while (124) (iii) tells us that a GOAL Argument can also be realised as the first NP in a [V NP NP...] structure: as Williams notes (1981, p. 89) 'The subscript "2" on NP in the realisation rule for Goal is simply a shorthand for whatever the appropriate distinction is between the first and second NP of the double object construction in English'; presumably, '2' serves to indicate that the GOAL NP will be the second NP in the Clause, the first being the Subject.

It should be clear that Williams' REALISATION RULES in (124) will correctly predict that (125) (a) and (b) are grammatical, but (125) (c) is ungrammatical:

(125) (a)   John will give *the book* [to Mary]
                  THEME   GOAL

    (b)   John will give [Mary] *the book*
                  GOAL   THEME

    (c)   *John will give *the book* [Mary]
                  THEME   GOAL

As specified in (124) (i), the THEME Complement [*the book*] is in each case realised as a bare NP. In (125) (a) the GOAL Complement has been realised as the *to*-headed PP [*to Mary*], in accordance with rule (124) (ii). And in (125) (b), the GOAL Complement has instead been realised as a bare NP which occurs as the second NP in the sentence (the Subject NP being the first) by rule (124) (iii). But in (125) (c), the GOAL Complement has been positioned as the third NP in the sentence, in violation of the 'second NP' requirement imposed by rule (124) (iii).

In spite of some mechanical differences between the proposals of Fillmore and Williams, there are obvious similarities of approach. For, both assume that a set of general Lexical Redundancy Rules (variously termed COMPLEMENT SELECTION RULES, or REALISATION RULES) will determine (at least, in the unmarked case) the categorial status of the Internal Arguments of a Predicate (viz. whether they surface as NP, or PP headed by *to*, etc.). But if indeed the categorial status of Arguments can be predicted from their thematic function, then this has fundamental implications for the overall organisation of the Lexicon. For, it means that the *subcategorisation* properties of items are predictable (in the unmarked case, at least) from their *thematic* properties. Or, in other words, it means that we can eliminate subcategorisation frames from lexical entries, since the information they contain is predictable from the theta-grids of the items concerned, given an appropriate set of redundancy rules (i.e. Complement Selection Rules). For example, our entry for *give* will no longer have to include a subcategorisation frame specifying that *give* subcategorises either two bare NP complements, or an NP complement and a PP complement headed by *to*: rather, we can eliminate this subcategorisation information entirely from our entry for *give*. Instead, our entry for *give* will comprise a theta-grid which includes an unordered list of the theta-roles which *give* assigns to its internal arguments, in the manner indicated in (123) above, repeated (in a slightly adapted form) as (126) below:

(126)   *give*: CATEGORIAL FEATURES: [+ V, − N]
        THETA-GRID: [<u>Actor</u>, Theme, Goal]

We assume that independent principles such as those discussed above will determine the categorial status and relative ordering of the two Internal Arguments.

If the above discussion is along the right lines, then we face the welcome prospect that *subcategorisation* information (which Chomsky refers to in *Knowledge* (1986a), p. 86 as involving *categorial selection*, or *c-selection*) is predictable from *thematic* information (which Chomsky (ibid.) refers to as involving *semantic selection* or *s-selection*), so that the former can be eliminated from lexical entries in favour of the latter. As Chomsky (ibid.) tentatively suggests, 'if c-selection is redundant, in general, then the Lexicon can be restricted to s-selection'. This is a welcome prospect in that it eliminates a further source of redundancy from lexical entries, in keeping with our guiding principle of minimising redundancy. Of course, this simplification of lexical entries by the elimination of subcategorisation frames will only be possible for items whose subcategorisation properties are predictable from general principles: for items which are 'exceptions' to these principles, we shall have to list in the Lexicon the specific range of Complements they subcategorise, and the θ-function associated with each such Complement. It hardly needs to be pointed out that our conclusions here are somewhat speculative in nature, and that our present knowledge of the relevant principles is extremely rudimentary: it remains to be seen in the light of future research whether the goal we have set ourselves (eliminating subcategorisation information in favour of thematic information) will prove to be attainable.

7.12 Theta-marking of Subjects

So far, we have considered only possible correlations between theta-roles and categorial status in the case of *Internal Arguments*. But what of *External Arguments* – i.e. Subjects? Generally speaking, Subject expressions have NP rather than PP status as we can see from examples such as (127) below:

(127) (a)   You could loosen them *with a torque wrench*
      (b)   *A torque wrench* would loosen them

Thus, if the instrument phrase remains inside VP (as in (127) (a)), it is realised as a PP headed by *with*; but if it is selected as the Subject (i.e. External Argument), then it is realised as NP. Thus, we might propose a Redundancy Rule to the effect that (in the unmarked case) Subjects are realised as NP.

A more interesting question, however, is how the theta-role assigned to an External Argument (i.e. a Subject) is determined. Now, we have already seen that the Internal Arguments (i.e. Complements) of a verbal Predicate are assigned their theta-role by the head V of the VP containing them. It might seem natural, therefore, to suppose that External Arguments (i.e. Subjects) are also assigned their theta-role by V. And indeed, this was an assumption explicitly made by Fillmore in the 1960s: he assumed that the theta-grid for a given Predicate would simply be an unordered list of the theta-roles assigned to the Arguments of the Predicate (whether internal or external). For example, the theta-grid for *give* might simply comprise an unordered list of theta-roles, as in (126) above. Fillmore suggested that general redundancy rules of *Subject Selection* would determine which theta-role was assigned to the External Argument (i.e. Subject) of *give*: one such (putatively universal) Subject Selection principle would be that in simple active structures, whenever a Verb has an AGENT argument, it is the AGENT which becomes the subject. As Fillmore observes:

> Some of the Subject Selection Principles seem to be language-universal ... One candidate for a universal Subject Selection Principle is this: If there is an AGENT which is brought into perspective, the nominal which represents it must be its (deep) Subject.
>
> (Fillmore, 'The Case for Case Reopened' (1977), p. 52)

This proposal seems to be echoed by Williams' (1981, p. 87) suggested rule that 'If there is an Actor, it must be external for V' (recall that ACTOR = AGENT, and External Argument = Subject).

However, Fillmore (ibid.) notes that some other Subject Selection principles are more idiosyncratic:

> Other Subject Selection principles appear to be language-specific. Japanese, according to Kuno (1973, p. 31), and German, according to Rohdenburg (1970), do not allow certain kinds of enabling or occasioning causes to be chosen as Subjects of their sentences, whereas English does tolerate such choices, as in sentences like those in (128):

(128) (a)   *Fifty dollars* will buy you a second-hand car
     (b)   *The smell* sickened me
     (c)   *The accident* killed the woman

Still other Subject Selection principles appear to be word-specific. This appears to be true, for example, of (at least) one member of the pair *regard* and *strike*, as in Chomsky's examples (1965, p. 162) given here in (129):

(129) (a)   *I* regard John as pompous
     (b)   John strikes *me* as pompous

What is idiosyncratic about Subject Selection in (129) is simply that in (129) (a) the italicised EXPERIENCER Argument of a cognitive Predicate is selected as its Subject, whereas in (129) (b) it is not (but rather is selected as a Complement).

Thus, the fundamental assumption underlying Fillmore's work is that it is the Verb which assigns a theta-role to *all* its Arguments, and that independent Subject Selection principles will determine the choice of External Argument (i.e. Subject). However, this assumption has been called into question in more recent work by Chomsky. Chomsky argues that although a Verb assigns a theta-role to its *Internal Arguments*, it is not the Verb but rather the whole Verb Phrase which assigns a theta-role to its *External Argument* (i.e. Subject). In this connection, it is interesting to note the following remarks made by Chomsky:

> In NP-V-NP sequences it is not uncommon for the V-NP string to function as a semantic unit with a compositionally determined meaning, as in the following examples:
>
> (130) (a)   John threw a party (threw a fit, threw the ball)
>   (b)   John broke his arm (broke the window)
>
> In (130) (a), semantic rules determine the meaning of *threw*-NP, and the semantic role of the Subject may vary depending on the meaning assigned to this unit: thus, *John* is the AGENT in 'John threw the ball', but not in 'John threw a fit'. Similarly in (130) (b), *John* is the AGENT with the Object *the window* and also in one interpretation of *John broke his arm* (e.g. 'John broke Bill's arm'). But there is a second interpretation of the latter with the sense 'John's arm broke', in which case *John* is not the AGENT. Again, the V–NP string is assigned its meaning as a unit, and the semantic role of the Subject is determined compositionally, depending on the meaning of the unit V-NP ... This makes sense on the assumption that the Verb-Object string is a Phrase, a VP, which is given a meaning and the capacity to assign a semantic role as a unit (in most cases, as determined solely by the verbal Head).
>
> (Chomsky, *Knowledge* (1986a), pp. 59–60)

(N.B. Chomsky uses 'semantic role' here in the sense of 'thematic role'.) In a nutshell, what Chomsky is claiming is that V assigns a theta-role *directly* to its Internal Arguments (i.e. Complements), but only *indirectly* (= compositionally, i.e. as a compositional function of the semantic properties of the overall VP) to its External Argument (= Subject).

So far, we have implicitly assumed that all Subjects are assigned a theta-role by their Predicates. But this is something of an oversimplification. For while most Predicates do indeed assign a theta-role to their Subjects, there are a small subset of Predicates (whose syntax we shall discuss in detail in the next chapter) which have *nonthematic* Subjects (i.e. Subjects not assigned any theta-role at all by their Predicate). Thus, while *try* has a thematic Subject (which is assigned the theta-role AGENT), *seem* on the other hand has a non-thematic Subject. But how can we prove this? Well, we can take advantage of our earlier observation that Arguments which are theta-marked (i.e. assigned a theta-role) by a given Predicate will also be *selectionally constrained* by that Predicate. It seems reasonable to suppose that the converse also holds – i.e. that if an expression is not theta-marked by a given Predicate, then it will not be selectionally constrained by that Predicate. In the light of these assumptions, consider the contrast between (131) and (132) below:

(131) (a) *John* tried to understand the problem
    (b) *My goldfish* tried to escape
    (c) ??*The amoeba* is trying to reproduce
    (d) ?!*Your kettle* is trying to boil over
    (e) !*Your theory* is trying to be foolproof
    (f) !!*The jig* is trying to be up
    (g) !!*There* is trying to be a misunderstanding
    (h) !!*It* is trying to be likely that he will come

(132) (a) *John* seemed to understand the problem
    (b) *The goldfish* seems to have escaped
    (c) *My pet amoeba* seems to be reproducing
    (d) *My kettle* seems to be boiling over
    (e) *Your theory* seems to be foolproof
    (f) *The jig* seems to be up
    (g) *There* seems to be a misunderstanding
    (h) *It* seems to be likely that he will come

In (131), strong selection restrictions hold between *try* and its (italicised) Subject: the Subject of *try* has to be RATIONAL (i.e. mind-possessing), hence capable of having intentions. Given our assumption that selection restrictions hold only between a Predicate and expressions which it theta-marks, then it follows that the italicised subject NPs in (131) must be theta-marked by *try*: i.e. it follows that *try* has a thematic Subject to which it assigns an appropriate theta-role (e.g. AGENT). But by contrast, in (132) there are no selection restrictions holding between *seem* and its Subject. Why should this be? Given the assumptions we made earlier, a natural answer would be that this is because *seem* takes a nonthematic Subject (i.e. a subject to which it assigns no theta-role). If this is so, then it follows that whereas some Predicates (e.g. *try*) theta-mark their Subjects, others (e.g. *seem*) do not. We shall explore some of the syntactic consequences of the distinction between Predicates with thematic Subjects and those with nonthematic Subjects in the next chapter.

One final point which we might make is the following. Suppose that we define an *Argument* of a Predicate as an expression which is theta-marked (i.e. assigned a theta-role) by the Predicate concerned. It then follows that if a Predicate like *seem* has a nonthematic Subject, then that Subject is not an Argument of *seem* in the relevant technical sense. This is a point which need not concern us for the moment, but which we shall return to in Volume Two when we come to consider the Logical Form of sentences.

> *You should now be able to tackle exercise XI*

7.13 Selection Restrictions and Thematic Structure

Our discussion of thematic and nonthematic Subjects in the previous section was predicated on the assumption that there is a strong tie-up between thematic structure and selection restrictions. Now, if this is so, then we might well wonder whether or not the *selectional* information contained in dictionary entries in works such as Chomsky's *Aspects* (1965) is redundant. And it does indeed seem plausible to assume this. More precisely, we might posit that the selection restrictions which hold between a given Predicate P and a given Argument A will be determined jointly by (i) the meaning of the Predicate (P), and (ii) the theta-role played by the Argument (A). To take a simple example, we might suppose that an EXPERIENCER Argument of a COGNITIVE predicate must be (or perhaps is presupposed to be) an expression denoting a RATIONAL (i.e. mind-possessing) entity. Such a principle would account for the obvious parallelism in the selection restrictions operating in sentences such as the following:

(133) (a) *Mary/?my goldfish/!my birth* thinks that John is very clever
 (b) *Mary/?my goldfish/!my birth* knows that John is very clever

(134) (a) It strikes *Mary/?my goldfish/!my birth* that John is very clever
 (b) John impressed *Mary/?my goldfish/!my birth* as being very clever

(135) (a) John seems to *Mary/?my goldfish/!my birth* to be very clever
 (b) John appears to *Mary/?my goldfish/!my birth* to be very clever

Note that the italicised expressions are subject to the same selection restrictions in each case: and yet, the NP concerned has the constituent structure status of a Subject in (133), a Verbal Object in (134), and a Prepositional Object in (135). Given that the italicised expression fulfils different grammatical functions in each set of sentences, what determines that it is subject to the same set of selection restrictions in each case? The answer is twofold: namely that (i) in each case it is an Argument of a COGNITIVE predicate; and (ii) in each case it fulfils the theta-role of an EXPERIENCER Argument. Thus, semantic properties (viz. the fact that *think/impress/appear* are COGNITIVE predicates in the use in question) together with thematic properties (viz. the fact that the italicised expression in each case functions as an EXPERIENCER Argument of the Predicate) together determine that the italicised constituent in each case is required (i.e. presupposed) to be a RATIONAL entity. Of course, the degree to which a given speaker accepts sentences like those above as well-formed will depend on his own personal beliefs – e.g. on the degree to which he believes that goldfish are RATIONAL beings.

Given our assumption that selection restrictions are jointly determined by the *semantic* and *thematic* properties of Predicates, then it follows that we can eliminate *selection restrictions* from our lexical entries. This is again a welcome result, since it eliminates redundancy, and correspondingly simplifies lexical entries. Moreover, it ties in with our earlier suggestion in section 7.11 that it might be possible to eliminate *subcategorisation* information in favour of thematic information. Now, if indeed it does turn out to be the case that both *subcategorisation* and *selectional* information are redundant (because they are predictable from *thematic* information), then we face the welcome prospect that instead of including three different types of *contextual* information in lexical entries (viz. information about subcategorisation, selection, and theta-marking), we need only include one such type of information – namely, information about the theta-marking properties of Predicates. Under this view, the only contextual information contained in lexical entries will be a theta-grid specifying what theta-role a given Predicate assigns to its Internal Arguments (i.e. Complements), and what theta-role (if any) it assigns compositionally to its Subject. This is admittedly a somewhat utopian goal in the present fragmentary state of our knowledge: but it is surely the kind of ambitious goal which any serious Theory of Language should set itself. For, as we saw in Chapter 1, the ultimate goal of any Theory of Language must be to attain *explanatory adequacy*. And clearly, we come much nearer to attaining that goal if we are able to inter-relate three fundamental properties of lexical items (viz. their subcategorisation, selectional, and thematic properties) in a principled way, without the need to simply *stipulate* all three properties separately in lexical entries.

389

7.14 Constraints on Theta-marking

As our discussion of lexical entries has proceeded in this chapter, theta-roles have come to play an ever-increasing part: and indeed discussion of the syntactic importance of theta-roles will pervade much of Volume Two as well. It is therefore appropriate that we should end this chapter with a few remarks about the general principles which determine how theta-roles are assigned to the categories which express them.

An obvious question to ask is how many theta-roles can be assigned to a given category in a given sentence-position. It seems intuitively implausible to imagine that a given NP could bear two (or more) theta-roles to the same Predicate. For example, a sentence such as:

(136)   Deranged people can kill

cannot receive the interpretation (137) below:

(137)   *Deranged people* can kill
       [AGENT]
       [THEME]

on which [*deranged people*] is both AGENT and THEME of *kill*. On the contrary, the meaning we are trying to convey in (137) can only be properly expressed by a structure in which *kill* has two different coreferential NPs as its Arguments, each of which is assigned a distinct theta-role, as in (138) below:

(138)   *Deranged people* can kill *themselves*
       [AGENT]   [THEME]

Nor does it seem any more plausible to imagine that a given Predicate could assign a given theta-role to more than one Argument: in other words, it doesn't seem plausible that a Verb could have two AGENT Arguments, or two THEME Arguments, etc. Such a condition would rule out a structure such as (139) below:

(139)   *John* killed *Harry*
       [AGENT]   [AGENT]

in which both *John* and *Harry* bear the same AGENT role to the Predicate *kill*.

Thus, we clearly want to build into our Grammar some constraint on theta-marking which rules out inadmissible structures such as (137) and (139). The relevant constraint will have to rule out the twin possibilities of (i) assignment of more than one theta-role to a given Argument, and (ii) assignment of a given theta-role to more than one Argument. We might rule out these twin possibilities by imposing the following constraint on theta-marking:

(140)   THETA CRITERION
        'Each Argument bears one and only one θ-role, and each θ-role is
        assigned to one and only one Argument'
                                        (Chomsky, *Lectures* (1981d), p. 36)

Moreover, it seems plausible to assume that (140) is a *universal* rather than a
language-particular condition, since it doesn't simply seem to be an accidental
fact about English that it doesn't allow structures like (137) or (139).

   Now that we have extended lexical entries to include *thematic* information
in addition to (or perhaps *in place of*) subcategorisation information, it might
seem sensible to revise our earlier PROJECTION PRINCIPLE (88), repeated as (141)
below:

(141)   PROJECTION PRINCIPLE
        Syntactic representations [i.e. syntactic structures] must be pro-
        jected from the Lexicon, in that they observe the subcategorisa-
        tion properties of lexical items

We might now revise (141) so as to include not just the c-selection (i.e. subcategorisation) properties of items, but also their s-selection (i.e. thematic)
properties as well. Thus, we might replace (141) by (142) below:

(142)   PROJECTION PRINCIPLE (generalised)
        Syntactic representations must be projected from the Lexicon, in
        that they observe the lexical properties of the items they contain

We might assume that the term *lexical properties* in (142) subsumes all relevant contextual properties, including subcategorisation and thematic properties. (142) would then tell us, for example, that a Verb such as *murder* which is
specified in the Lexicon as permitting only an AGENT Subject cannot be
inserted into a structure in which it has a THEME or GOAL (etc.) Subject; and
that, for example, a Verb like *seem* which is specified as having a nonthematic
Subject cannot be inserted into a structure in which its Subject has been
assigned a theta-role of some sort. Indeed, we might construe the term *lexical
properties* even more widely to cover the *categorial* properties of lexical items
as well. This would then mean that the PROJECTION PRINCIPLE (142) would
account for why it is not possible to insert an item specified as a V in the Lexicon under a node labelled N. We might then assume that lexical insertion
applies in a random fashion (inserting any item from the Lexicon under any
terminal node), but that structures in which, for example, a Verb is inserted

under an N-node will be filtered out by our generalised PROJECTION PRINCIPLE. In other words, we might argue that our earlier LEXICALISATION PRINCIPLE (15) is in fact subsumed under the PROJECTION PRINCIPLE, and hence is redundant.

In Volume Two, we shall see that thematic constraints such as the THETA CRITERION and the PROJECTION PRINCIPLE have a fundamental role to play in the description of the Syntax of a variety of constructions. For the time being, however, we merely note the existence of these principles.

You should now be able to tackle exercises XII and XIII

7.15 Summary

In this chapter, we have taken a look at the internal organisation of the Lexicon. We started off in 7.1 with the assumption that the Lexicon should comprise a set of lexical entries (= a list of the lexical items in the language), with each such entry specifying the idiosyncratic properties of the item concerned. In 7.2 we argued that among the information contained in lexical entries will be a specification of the categorial status of the item concerned, in terms of a matrix of categorial features such as [± V, ± N]. In 7.3 we suggested that if we are to differentiate between *transitive, ditransitive* and *intransitive* Verbs, lexical entries will have to contain information about whether an item permits one or two NP Complements, or can be used without any Complements at all: and we suggested that this information could be incorporated into dictionary entries in the form of a *subcategorisation frame*. In 7.4 we showed that Verbs also have to be subcategorised with respect to the range of PP complements which they permit, and with respect to the choice of Preposition heading the PP: however, we argued that in order to avoid redundancy, we should simply stipulate that a given V takes a Complement headed by a specific item (e.g. *on, up, in*, etc.), since the categorial status and internal structure of the PP Complement would be predictable from general X-bar structural principles, and from the lexical properties of the subcategorised Preposition. In 7.5 we argued that it is redundant to specify Complement order in lexical entries, since the relative ordering of Heads and Complements follows from independent linearisation principles (e.g. the HEAD FIRST PRINCIPLE, the STRICT ADJACENCY PRINCIPLE, the CLAUSE LAST PRINCIPLE, etc.): subcategorisation information should thus be limited to an unordered list of the range of categories which a given item permits as its Complements. In 7.6 we looked at various types of clausal Complement, and suggested that their distribution might be predictable from general LEXICAL REDUNDANCY RULES which (in this case) link semantic properties of Predicates to the types of clausal Complement which they permit (so that e.g. only MANDATIVE Predicates permit subjunctive Complements). We also suggested that independent syntactic principles (to be discussed in detail in Volume Two) might account for the internal structure of clausal Complements, so that, for example, infinitival Clauses with an overt Complementiser require overt Subjects, whereas those with a covert Complementiser require a covert (PRO) Subject. In 7.7 we argued that Adjectives, Nouns, and Prepositions have to be subcategorised in much the same way as Verbs; and we suggested a general SUBCATEGORISATION PRINCIPLE to the effect that any item of category X must be subcategorised with respect to the range of idiosyncratic sister constituents which it permits within the minimal X-bar containing it. In 7.8 we argued that the subcategorisation information contained in lexical entries duplicates much of the information contained in traditional Phrase Structure Rules, thus reinforcing the conclusion we reached in the previous chapter that PS rules are redundant, and so can be eliminated from the Categorial Component of our grammar.

In 7.9 we turned to consider Chomsky's suggestion in his early works (e.g. *Aspects* (1965)) that lexical entries should contain not only *subcategorisation* information, but also information about the *selection restrictions* which items impose on their choice of Subjects and Complements (so that, for example, *convince* requires a RATIONAL Object NP).

In 7.10, we turned to look at a third type of contextual information which dictionary entries contain – namely thematic information about the *theta-role* which a Predicate assigns to each of its Arguments (i.e. to its Subject and Complements). We showed that thematic information plays an important role in the proper description of a variety of syntactic and semantic phenomena. In 7.11 we suggested that thematic information should be incorporated into lexical entries in the form of a *theta-grid* which specifies the theta-role which a Predicate assigns to each of its Arguments. We went on to make the tentative suggestion that there might be general *Complement Selection Principles* which determine which of the theta-marked Arguments of a Predicate is realised as an NP Complement, which as a PP Complement, etc. And we argued that if that were so, then it might be possible to eliminate *subcategorisation* (= *c-selection*) information from lexical entries entirely, in favour of *thematic* (= *s-selection*) information, so that lexical entries would then contain theta-grids but no subcategorisation frames. In 7.12 we argued that *Subjects* differ from *Complements* with respect to theta-marking in two ways. Firstly, whereas Complements are *directly* assigned a theta-role by their Heads, Subjects on the other hand are only *indirectly* theta-marked by their Heads, as a compositional function of the semantic properties of the overall [*Head + Complement*] structure. And we suggested that this difference might correlate with an obvious structural difference between Subjects and Complements – e.g. the Complement of a V is *internal* to VP, whereas the Subject of a VP is *external* to VP. We therefore suggested that *Internal Arguments* (Complements) are directly theta-marked by their Predicates, whereas *External Arguments* (i.e. Complements) are indirectly theta-marked. A second difference which we highlighted between Complements and Subjects is that whereas all Complements are theta-marked by their Predicates, this is not true of Subjects: although most Predicates assign a theta-role to their superficial Subjects, there are some Predicates (e.g. *seem*) which assign no theta-role at all to their superficial Subjects, and thus have *nonthematic* Subjects. In 7.13 we suggested that since Selection Restrictions are entirely determined by the *semantic* and *thematic* properties of Predicates (interacting with *pragmatic* factors such as the personal beliefs of the speaker), they are redundant and hence can be eliminated from lexical entries. If indeed it were the case that information about both *subcategorisation* and *selection restrictions* could be eliminated from lexical entries, then it would follow that the only contextual information which dictionary entries would need to contain would be *thematic* information. In 7.14 we argued that any attempt to develop a proper theory of thematic structure (viz. THETA THEORY) would require us to impose severe constraints on the set of admissible thematic structures. And accordingly, we proposed the following two putatively universal constraints on theta-marking:

(140)   THETA CRITERION
         'Each Argument bears one and only one θ-role, and each θ-role is assigned to one and only one Argument'

         (Chomsky *Lectures* (1981d), p. 36)

(142)   PROJECTION PRINCIPLE
         Syntactic Representations must be projected from the Lexicon, in that they observe the lexical properties of the items they contain

    Given the assumptions we have made in this chapter, the Lexicon (as we now envisage it) will comprise:

(143) (i)   a set of *Lexical Entries* comprising a list of all the words in a language, together with a specification of their idiosyncratic properties, e.g. their categorial status, their idiosyncratic contextual properties, etc.

     (ii)   A set of *Lexical Redundancy Rules* which determine those properties of lexical items which are predictable from general principles

We assume that the PROJECTION PRINCIPLE will guarantee that lexical items can only be inserted into P-markers at appropriate points (e.g. a Verb can only be inserted under a V-node). If this is so, then our earlier LEXICALISATION PRINCIPLE can be dispensed with.

EXERCISES

Exercise I

In the text, we distinguished between Count and Noncount Nouns, arguing that only Count Nouns have singular and plural forms. This means that we find three types of Common Noun in English, viz.

(i)   Singular Noncount Nouns
(ii)   Singular Count Nouns
(iii)   Plural Count Nouns

(Of course, Count Nouns generally have both a singular and a plural form.)

Determine which class(es) the following Nouns belong to:

(1)   (a) coffee (b) criteria (c) oats (d) syntax (e) sadness (f) poem (g) poetry
          (h) scissors (i) data (j) advice (k) barley (l) biceps

In addition, determine which of the three Noun types above the following Nominal premodifiers can co-occur with (one, two, or all three?):

(2)   (a) several (b) much (c) every (d) any (e) all (f) both (g) most (h) many
          (i) my (j) this (k) some (l) few (m) these (n) enough (o) no (p) each (q) the
          (r) a (s) either (t) which (u) more

A well-known study of the development of NPs in young children points out that at around the age of 27 months children typically produce Determiner + Noun combinations such as the following:

(3)   (a) a coat; (b) a celery; (c) a Becky; (d) a hands; (e) the top; (f) my mummy;
          (g) my stool; (h) more coffee; (i) more nut; (j) two sock; (k) two shoe;
          (l) two tinker-toy;

Discuss the possible nature of the errors that the children are making at this stage.

Exercise II

Discuss the nature of the ill-formedness of each of the following examples:

(1)   *John can't go his office
(2)   *The Prime Minister dismissed from the cabinet
(3)   *You can depend by my support
(4)   *John explained Mary the problem
(5)   *John met last night Mary

(6)   *He will stand over the incident by her
(7)   *John said to Mary nothing
(8)   *They demanded that the arms shipments to Iran cease immediately of the
         government

Exercise III
Provide a principled account of the ill-formedness of the following
examples:

(1)   *The jury found reluctantly the defendant guilty
(2)   *I realise that he resign
(3)   *Aren't you sure whether you to go there?
(4)   *I'm longing for to see you again
(5)   *She attempted for me to win the race
(6)   *He confessed his wife to be guilty
(7)   *I know you innocent
(8)   *He won't let you near himself

Exercise IV
Account for the ill-formedness of the following examples:

(1)   *We're really keen John to take part
(2)   *They accepted his proof the defendant guilty
(3)   *He was late because of his car wouldn't start
(4)   *I wasn't sure if to come or not
(5)   *John forced the kettle to boil over
(6)   *The garden weeded John

Exercise V
On the basis of the grammaticality judgments below, discuss how items
such as *anxious, quarrel,* and *ask* should be subcategorised with respect to the range of
Complements they permit in these sentences (inventing further examples of your own,
as necessary). Can you suggest any ways of eliminating unnecessary redundancy in
your entries?

(1) (a)   He is anxious about her behaviour
    (b)   He is anxious about whether she will behave herself
    (c)   *He is anxious about that she (should) behave herself
    (d)   *He is anxious her behaviour
    (e)   He is anxious whether she will behave herself
    (f)   He is anxious that she (should) behave herself

(2) (a)   He asked about her behaviour
    (b)   He asked about whether she behaved herself
    (c)   *He asked about that she (should) behave herself

(d)	*He asked her behaviour
(e)	He asked whether she behaved herself
(f)	He asked that she (should) behave herself
(3) (a)	They quarrelled about her behaviour
(b)	They quarrelled about whether she should be sacked
(c)	*They quarrelled about that she (should) be sacked
(d)	*They quarrelled her behaviour
(e)	*They quarrelled whether she should be sacked
(f)	*They quarrelled that she (should) be sacked

*Exercise VI

Discuss the nature of the restriction which appears to operate in examples such as (1–3) below, adding further examples of your own as necessary. Can you suggest a *Redundancy Rule* which will deal with the relevant restriction?

(1) (a)	I can't bear to think (of) [what a terrible ordeal she had to endure]
(b)	I can't bear to think (of) [why she abandoned him]
(c)	I can't bear to think (*of) [that she may be dead]
(2) (a)	I was surprised (at) [what a brave face she put on the affair]
(b)	I was surprised (at) [which one she chose]
(c)	I was surprised (*at) [that she was so brave]
(3) (a)	I'm perfectly sure (about) [what a huge success the show will be]
(b)	I'm not sure (about) [why he loves her]
(c)	I'm sure (*about) [that he loves her]

What apparent problem is posed for the Redundancy Rule you propose by sentences such as the following, and how can it be overcome?

(4) (a)	She cried out [that she was innocent]
(b)	He wrote down [that he missed her]
(c)	She owned up [that she hadn't taken the pill]
(d)	He mumbled on [that she'd let him down]

*Exercise VII

Discuss the nature of the ill-formedness of the following sentences (from Chomsky's *Aspects* (1965), pp. 75–6), and the nature of the restrictions which appear to have been violated. Invent further examples of your own as necessary, to exemplify your answer.

(1)	The boy may frighten sincerity
(2)	Sincerity may admire the boy
(3)	John amazed the injustice of that decision
(4)	The boy elapsed

(5)   The boy was abundant
(6)   The harvest was clever to agree
(7)   John is owning a house
(8)   The dog looks barking
(9)   John solved the pipe
(10)   The book dispersed

*Exercise VIII

English has a wide variety of Adverbs which can be used to modify adjectival expressions, including *very, highly, extremely, so, really, quite, fairly, rather, pretty, somewhat, absolutely, terribly, deadly*, and so on. However, there are interesting restrictions in that some Adverbs can only be used to modify some types of Adjective, and not others; for example, *big* can be modified by *very* (cf. 'very big'), but not by *highly* (cf. *'highly big'). Try and establish the nature of these restrictions by taking 100 or so Adjectives at random from a dictionary, and seeing which Adverbs can and cannot combine with which Adjectives – and try to establish the nature of the restrictions (syntactic? semantic?).

Exercise IX

What role might thematic structure play in a principled account of the grammar of the following examples?

(1) (a)   John handed Mary the microfilm
    (b)   John handed the microfilm to Mary

(2) (a)   John smashed the window with a brick
    (b)   A brick smashed the window
    (c)   The window smashed

(3) (a)   You can get an invitation from Mary
    (b)   Mary can get you an invitation

(4) (a)   The police deliberately killed the prisoner
    (b)   *The prisoner deliberately died

(5) (a)   Personally, inflatable dolls bore me
    (b)   *Personally, my wife beats me

(6) (a)   The attack on the airport by the terrorists was scandalous
    (b)   *The disappearance from the airport by the terrorists was scandalous

(7) (a)   Mary brought John a lot of happiness
    (b)   Last summer brought John a lot of happiness
    (c)   ??Mary and last summer brought John a lot of happiness

**Exercise X

Discuss the problems (apparent or real) posed for any claim that Thematic Relations provide a more principled account of Selection Restrictions, Adverb Distribution, Coordination, etc. by sentences such as the following:

(1) (a)   John broke the window/his promise/his silence

   (b)   The window/!his promise/?his silence broke

(2) (a)   !John and a tin of paint fell off the ladder

   (b)   !I hit John and the ground with my stick

   (c)   !I saw John and a daffodil in the park

(3) (a)   Personally, I've never sent a Xmas card to Maggie

   (b)   Personally, I've never been sent a Xmas card by Maggie

   (c)   Personally, I've never been sent to see Maggie

(4) (a)   The gradual economic decline by Great Britain in the last few years has led to worsening unemployment

   (b)   Even a fall of a few points by stocks and shares can wipe millions off their value

Exercise XI

In the examples below, discuss whether or not the italicised NP is a theta-marked Argument of the capitalised Predicate, and how you can establish this empirically.

(1)   *The government* MANAGED to avoid defeat

(2)   *You* NEED to be more careful

(3)   *The terrorists* WANT to overthrow the government

(4)   We consider *Mary* UNLIKELY to succeed

(5)   Nobody EXPECTS *the government* to back down

(6)   You can't FORCE *anyone* to do anything

Exercise XII

Discuss the contextual information which needs to be included in the lexical entry for *say*, as used in the constructions below, assuming the judgments given. How much of this information is predictable from general principles, and what principles are involved? Invent further examples of your own, as necessary.

(1)   He said a few words to the Press

(2)   *He said to the Press a few words

(3)   *He said the Press a few words

(4)   *He said a few words the Press

(5)   He said a few words

(6)   *He said to the Press

(7)   He said to the Press that he was resigning
(8)   *He said that he was resigning to the Press
(9)   *He said the Press that he was resigning
(10)   He said that he was resigning
(11)   He won't say whether he's resigning
(12)   He won't say whether to leave
(13)   *He won't say whether you to help me
(14)   He said for me to find someone else
(15)   *He said for to find someone else
(16)   He said to find someone else
(17)   *He said me to be incompetent
(18)   *He said me incompetent
(19)   He said that I should find someone else
(20)   *They said that he resign

Now invent parallel examples of your own with *tell* (in its use as a Verb of saying), and discuss the similarities and differences between *say* and *tell*.

Exercise XIII

Discuss the contextual information which might be included in dictionary entries for the Verbs used in the constructions below, and the extent to which it is predictable, and therefore redundant.

(1) (a)   She handed a parcel to the postman
    (b)   She handed the postman a parcel

(2) (a)   I gave a parcel/!a clip round the ear/!a kick in the pants to him
    (b)   I gave him a parcel/a clip round the ear/a kick in the pants

(3) (a)   The postman delivered the parcel to him
    (b)   *The postman delivered him the parcel

(4) (a)   I explained my theory to her
    (b)   *I explained her my theory

(5) (a)   I revealed the awful truth to her
    (b)   *I revealed her the awful truth

(6) (a)   They presented a medal to her
    (b)   They presented her with a medal

8
Transformations

8.1 Overview

So far, we have been assuming that there is only one level of structure in syntax – that is, the level of S-structure which represents the superficial syntactic structure of sentences. And we have been assuming that the task of any adequate syntax of a language is to characterise (= generate) all the well-formed S-structures of the language. We have assumed that the class of well-formed S-structures in a given language will be determined by the *Base* of the Grammar, which comprises (i) a Categorial Component, and (ii) a Lexicon. The Categorial Component comprises a set of category-neutral X-bar rule-schemas; the Lexicon specifies the categorial status and contextual restrictions associated with individual lexical items in a given language (e.g. the fact that an inherently transitive Verb such as *devour* cannot be used in an intransitive V-bar in which it lacks an NP complement).

In this chapter, however, we are going to argue that our existing model of Syntax is not adequate to handle certain characteristic constructions in natural languages, and that in order to provide a principled account of the syntax of these constructions, we need to posit an additional level of structure known as *D-structure* (corresponding to the level of *Deep Structure* in earlier models). We shall argue that the two levels of structure (*S-structure* and *D-structure*) are inter-related by a set of movement rules known technically as *Transformations*; and we shall look at the arguments in favour of positing a number of transformational rules, including V MOVEMENT, I MOVEMENT, NP MOVEMENT, and EXTRAPOSITION. We shall see later that the incorporation of movement transformations into our model requires radical revisions to our overall Theory of Grammar. We'll begin our discussion by looking at one such transformation – the rule of V MOVEMENT.

8.2 V MOVEMENT

Hitherto, the finite Clauses we have been looking at have generally contained a Modal Auxiliary such as *will/would, can/could, shall/should, may/might*, etc. We have assumed that Modals are generated under a finite I, and that a finite I carries Tense (Past/Present) and Agreement (Person, Number) features. Because these features are an intrinsic property of I, and because Modals are generated under I, the relevant Tense and Agreement features are realised on the Modal. Thus, in a sentence such as:

(1)   John [$_I$ *does*] [$_{VP}$ annoy me]

it is the Modal *does* in I which is inflected and carries the relevant Tense/ Agreement features (viz. 3SG PRESENT) which are realised as the present tense suffix -*es*, while the V in VP is uninflected and hence assumes the tenseless agreementless base (infinitive) form *annoy*.

However, since not all finite Clauses contain Modal Auxiliaries, the obvious question is what structure we assign to a finite clause which lacks a Modal. In such a case, I will still carry the relevant Tense/Agreement features, but will be empty of any lexical item (a possibility which the Theory of Empty Categories allows for by virtue of permitting any category to be left empty). Leaving I empty will give rise to structures such as:

(2)   John [$_I$ e] [$_{VP}$ annoy me]

I here will contain Tense and Agreement features which are normally realised as a suffix on the Modal in I. However (as we suggested in Chapter 6), when there is no Modal in I, these features are realised on the leftmost V of VP, which is then inflected for the relevant Tense/Agreement features, as we see from examples such as:

(3)   John *annoys* me

where *annoys* carries the -*s* inflection which characterises a third person singular present tense Verb.

But how can Tense/Agreement inflections associated with I end up on a Verb which originates as the head V of VP? Two rather different answers to this problem are suggested in the relevant literature. The solution proposed in Chomsky's *Lectures* (1981d, p. 256) is to suppose that 'there is a rule – call it R – which assigns the elements of INFL to the initial verbal element of VP. Assume R to be, in effect, a rule of AFFIX MOVEMENT'. The rule involves 'affix movement' in the sense that Tense/Agreement affixes which would normally be suffixed to the Modal in I (e.g. the third person singular suffix -*s*) end up suffixed to the leftmost V of VP. If, as Chomsky suggests (ibid., p. 257), the rule of AFFIX MOVEMENT in fact involves attachment of an empty finite I to the right of V to form an inflected Verb, then the way in which it would apply to a structure such as (2) above can be outlined in simplified schematic terms as in (4) below:

(4) (a)   John   [ɪ e]   [ᵥ P   [ᵥ annoy]   me]
                 └─ AFFIX MOVEMENT ─┐
                                          ↓
    (b)   John   [ᵥ P   [ᵥ *annoys*]   me]

The result of AFFIX MOVEMENT is that the V *annoy* acquires the relevant Tense/ Agreement features normally associated with I, and the resultant inflected verb-form *annoys* remains as the head V of VP.

However, a very different solution to this problem is suggested in Koopman (1984): here it is proposed that in finite Clauses where I does not contain a Modal and hence is empty, the head V of VP moves into the empty I position by a rule of V MOVEMENT (more specifically, V-to-I Movement), and thereby comes to acquire the Tense/Agreement properties associated with I, so becoming an inflected verb-form. The way in which V MOVEMENT would apply to a structure such as (2) above can be represented in simplified schematic terms as in (5) below:

(5) (a)   John   [ɪ e]   [ᵥ P   [ᵥ *annoy*]   me]
                                                      │
                 ┌── V MOVEMENT ──┘
                 ↓
    (b)   John   [ɪ *annoys*]   [ᵥ P   me]

The essential difference between the two analyses (4) and (5) is that under the AFFIX MOVEMENT analysis (4) the resultant inflected Verb *annoys* remains within VP, whereas under the V MOVEMENT analysis (5) the inflected V *annoys* ends up as a constituent of I.

But which analysis is the right one? Well, as in any serious field of research, the consequences of making different assumptions about a particular pheno- menon are often so complex and far-reaching that the full implications of the decision to adopt one analysis rather than another are not always immediately apparent. That's a rather long-winded way of saying that it's not always obvious what the right answer is! The reason why it is difficult to choose between a rule which attaches I to V on the one hand, and a rule which attaches V to I on the other is that in English I and V are adjacent constitu- ents, so that in either case the rule applies *vacuously*. What's meant by saying that a rule applies *vacuously* is that it applies in such a way as to change con- stituent structure without producing any observable change of word-order. So, for example, irrespective of whether we adopt the AFFIX MOVEMENT ana- lysis (4), or the V MOVEMENT analysis (5), we end up with the same overall

NP V NP word-order *John annoys me* in the resultant sentence. For this reason, Koopman (1984) suggests that if we are to choose between the two analyses, we must look at languages where I and V are not adjacent constituents, and where the two rules will not apply vacuously, but rather will produce an observable change of word order. In this connection, she notes (1984, p. 42) that in Vata (a language of the Kru family, spoken in the Ivory Coast) the normal word-order is [NP I [VP XP* V]], where XP* represents one or more Complements of the head V of VP, and where V is positioned at the right periphery of V-bar. She notes that in Vata, a finite Clause containing an Auxiliary will have the AUX positioned in I between the subject NP and the VP, with the V positioned at the end of VP, as in (6) below:

(6)   [NP a]   [I la] [VP saka *li*]
        We   have   rice *eat* (= 'We have eaten rice')

But if I contains no Auxiliary (i.e. is empty), the Verb of the VP will move from V into I, and hence no longer be positioned at the end of VP, but rather in the characteristic I position between NP and VP: cf.

(7)   [NP a]   [I *li*] [VP saka —]
        We   ate   rice   (= 'We ate rice')

Here, the movement of the Verb out of VP-final position (marked by —) into I produces an obvious change in the linear ordering of constituents, thus lending clear empirical support to the V MOVEMENT analysis. And Koopman goes on to suggest that given that we have clear empirical motivation for positing a rule of V MOVEMENT for languages such as Vata, universalist considerations argue in favour of adopting the V MOVEMENT analysis rather than the AFFIX MOVEMENT analysis for English, in default of any evidence to the contrary.

However, it is one thing to claim that Vata has a rule of V MOVEMENT, and quite another to claim that the same is also true of English: Koopman's evidence is suggestive, but not conclusive (in respect of English). What we need to ask is whether there is any *particularist* evidence in support of positing a V MOVEMENT rule in English (i.e. any evidence based on facts of English). Well, it seems that there may be some evidence in support of such a rule in English, based on the behaviour of finite forms of the Verbs *have* and *be*. Recall that we argued in section 5.2 that in all their uses, *have* and *be* originate within VP, either as Specifiers of V (in their use as Aspectual Auxiliaries), or as the head V of VP (in their other uses). However, what a number of linguists have suggested is that there is empirical evidence that although finite forms of *have* and *be* originate within VP, they get moved out of VP and into I by a rule akin to Koopman's V MOVEMENT rule (a rule known in the earlier literature as HAVE-BE

RAISING). What the V MOVEMENT analysis entails is that in a finite Clause with an empty I, the leftmost occurrence of *have* or *be* moves out of VP into the empty I constituent, thereby acquiring all the relevant Tense/Agreement inflections associated with I. Under this analysis, *have* and *be* would originate in VP in sentences such as the following:

(8) (a)   He *has* no money
   (b)   He *has* finished
   (c)   He *is* a fool
   (d)   He *is* working
   (e)   He *was* arrested

and would then be 'raised' out of VP into I (provided that I is finite and empty) by the rule which we are here calling V MOVEMENT: in the case of a sentence such as (8) (a) above, the rule would apply in the fashion indicated schematically in (9) below (we omit S-bar for the sake of simplicity):

(9)

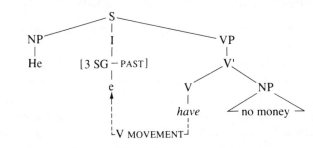

Thus, *have* would originate as the head V of VP, and would then be moved by the rule of V MOVEMENT into the empty I, where it would acquire the relevant Tense/Agreement features, and so surface as the third person singular present tense form *has*.

But what evidence is there that finite forms of *have* and *be* end up in I (even though they clearly originate within VP)? We'll look at three arguments in support of this claim. One such piece of evidence in support of the analysis is offered by Jackendoff (1972, p. 78) in relation to *negation* facts. In sentences such as (10) below:

(10) (a)   He [I may] *not* [VP have finished]
    (b)   He [I may] *not* [VP be working]

we see that the negative particle *not* is positioned after the Modal *may* in I but before the Aspectual Auxiliaries *have* and *be* in VP. But in sentences such as (11) below:

(11) (a)   He has *not* finished
    (b)   He is *not* working

we see that *not* is positioned *after* the Aspectual Auxiliaries *has* and *is*. How can this be, since we have already seen that *not* is positioned after I and before VP, and since we argued in Chapter 5 that Aspectual Auxiliaries originate within VP? The V MOVEMENT analysis provides us with a simple answer: we posit that *have* and *be* originate within VP, but that the leftmost occurrence of *have/be* gets moved out of VP into I by V MOVEMENT, if I is finite and empty. Thus, after application of V MOVEMENT, *have* and *be* in (11) will come to be positioned in I (where they acquire the relevant Tense/Agreement features and surface as *has/is*), and so precede the negative particle *not* (which is positioned after I and before VP). The operation of the rule in a case such as (11)(a) above can be schematised as in (12) below:

(12) (a)   He   [₁ e]   not   [ᵥₚ *have* finished]

       ┌─ V MOVEMENT ──┘

  (b)   He   [₁ *has*]   not   [ᵥₚ — finished]

Thus, *negation* facts seem to provide some support for the V MOVEMENT analysis of *have* and *be*.

A second argument (adapted from Jackendoff (1972), pp. 75–6) supporting the claim that finite forms of *have* and *be* end up in I (even though they originate within VP) can be formulated in relation to *Adverb distribution*. In section 2.5 we argued that English has a class of S-Adverbials (including *certainly*, *probably*, *definitely*, etc.), so called because they are restricted to occurring as immediate constituents of S. The assumption that *probably* is an S-Adverb accounts for contrasts such as the following:

(13) (a)   George will *probably* have been working
  (b)   *George will have *probably* been working
  (c)   *George will have been *probably* working

For, if we posit that *George will have been working* has the structure (14) below (simplified by omission of S-bar, etc.):

(14)

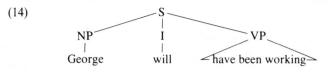

then it is apparent that the only internal positions which an S-Adverbial like *probably* can occupy are between NP and I, or between I and VP – but not any position internally within VP.

However, the distributional facts are rather different in sentences such as the following:

(15) (a)   George has *probably* been working
 (b)   *George has been *probably* working

Why should it be that the S-Adverb *probably* can be positioned after the Aspectual Auxiliary *have* in (15), but not in (13)?

The V MOVEMENT analysis provides us with a very straightforward answer. We might suppose that although *have* originates as an Aspectual Auxiliary within VP in both (13) and (15), what happens in the case of (15) is that because the I constituent is finite and empty, the leftmost occurrence of *have/be* within VP moves into the empty I (so acquiring the relevant Tense/Agreement features, and surfacing in the form *has*) in the manner indicated schematically in (16) below:

(16) (a)   George   [₁ e]   [vp *have* been working]
                        |
                  ┌─ V MOVEMENT ─┘
                  ▼
 (b)   George   [₁ *has*]   [vp — been working]

Thus, after the application of V MOVEMENT, the resultant superficial structure will be as in (17) below:

(17)

George has been working structure tree — S branching to NP (George), I (has), VP (been working).

Given the S-structure in (17), it is simple enough to account for the Adverb distribution facts in (15) above: for, the only internal positions which we should expect an S Adverbial to be able to occupy are between NP and I, and between I and VP. And this prediction is precisely correct (as I leave you to verify for yourself), so lending further empirical support to the claim that (the leftmost occurrence of) *have/be* undergoes V MOVEMENT into an empty finite I. Why isn't V MOVEMENT of *have* also possible in structures like (14)? The obvious answer is that V MOVEMENT is only possible into an empty finite I, and so is blocked in (14) because I is already filled by the Modal *will*.

Our third argument in support of claiming that finite forms of *have* and *be* end up in I (even though they originate within VP) is based on a phenomenon which I shall refer to as HAVE CONTRACTION. The word *have* has the stressed form /hav/, and two unstressed (or 'weak') vocalic (i.e. vowel-containing) forms /həv/ and /əv/. But after a Pronoun ending in a vowel or a diphthong, unstressed *have* can lose its vowel and be contracted down to the *nonvocalic* (i.e. vowel-less) form /v/, which is written as *'ve* in the spelling: cf.

(18) (a)　　*I've/You've/We've/They've* finished
　　(b)　　*Who've* you seen?

This vocalic contraction (i.e. vowel loss) seems to take place only after Pronouns terminating in a vowel or diphthong, since it is not possible (in my dialect) after nominal NPs ending in a vowel or diphthong, or after Pronouns ending in a consonant, or after Modals ending in a diphthong, etc.: cf.

(19) (a)　　**The Masai've* lost their traditional homelands
　　(b)　　**Whom've* you seen?
　　(c)　　*They *may've* left already

Only the weak vocalic form /əv/ is possible in (19), not the nonvocalic weak form /v/. So, it would appear that one condition on vocalic HAVE CONTRACTION is that it takes place only after a Pronoun terminating in a vowel or diphthong.

A second condition on vocalic HAVE CONTRACTION can be illustrated by the following paradigm:

(20) (a)　　I could have been playing tennis, and *you could have* been playing football
　　(b)　　= I could have been playing tennis and *you Ø have* been playing football
　　(c)　　≠ I could have been playing tennis, and *you've* been playing football

As we can see, the second instance of *could* in (20) (b) can undergo a kind of Ellipsis known as GAPPING, leaving a 'gap' in the sentence (marked by Ø) where *could* would otherwise have occurred. But note that the resultant sequence of *you have* cannot then undergo vocalic contraction to *you've*, so that sentence (20) (c) is ungrammatical as an elliptical form of (20) (a). Why should this be? One possible explanation is that the presence of the elliptical 'gap' Ø between *you* and *have* in (20) (b) blocks the application of vocalic HAVE CONTRACTION. Thus, we might propose that it is a general condition on vocalic contraction that *have* must immediately follow a Pronoun terminating in a vowel or diphthong, and that there should be no 'gap' between them. In (18) above, there is no 'gap' between the Pronoun and *have*, so vocalic contraction is possible. But in (20) (b), there is a Ø gap between the Pronoun and *have*, so that contraction is blocked.

In the light of the claim that the presence of a 'gap' between the Pronoun and *have* blocks vocalic contraction, consider the following example:

(21)　　　*They've* completed the project

Why should it be possible for *have* to be contracted down to the nonvocalic form /v/ here? Given our assumptions in section 5.2, *have* will originate here as an Aspectual Auxiliary within a VP which is the complement of an empty I – as represented in schematic terms in (22) below:

(22)   They [I e] [VP *have* completed the project]

However, the fact that vocalic contraction is possible in (21) strongly suggests that *have* cannot remain within VP. For, if *have* were positioned in VP at S-structure, then there would be an empty I constituent separating the Pronoun *they* from the Aspectual Auxiliary *have*; and we have already seen from examples like (20) (c) above that vocalic contraction is blocked by the presence of an empty I constituent 'gap' between the Pronoun and *have*. However, under the V MOVEMENT analysis, no such problems arise. For, *have* will move out of the VP in (22), into the empty finite I, resulting in the S-structure (23) below:

(23)   They [I *have*] [VP — completed the project]

(— marks the position in VP out of which *have* was moved by the rule of V MOVEMENT). Once *have* has been moved into I (as in (23) above), there is no longer any 'gap' separating *they* from *have*, with the result that vocalic contraction can apply freely.

So, it seems that we have three independent pieces of evidence supporting the postulation of a rule of V MOVEMENT in English, at least applying to items such as *have* and *be*. Given that the corresponding rule in Vata applies to *all* Verbs, we might generalise the rule in English from *have* and *be* to all non-modal Verbs: and this is precisely the analysis assumed by Chomsky in *Barriers* (1986b). That is, we might argue that all non-modal Verbs in English originate within VP, but move out of VP into I in a finite Clause containing an empty I. As we illustrated in (5) above, such an analysis would provide a simple, unified account of verbal morphology in English. Thus, in a finite Clause containing an I filled by a Modal, the Tense/Agreement inflections associated with I are realised on the Modal in I. But in a finite Clause containing an empty I, the leftmost V of VP moves out of VP and into I, and there comes to acquire the relevant Tense/Agreement inflections associated with I. Moreover, as we shall see in Chapter 10, the V MOVEMENT analysis schematised in (5) above offers certain theoretical advantages over the converse AFFIX MOVEMENT analysis sketched out in (4): for whereas V MOVEMENT 'raises' a V into I, the AFFIX MOVEMENT analysis 'lowers' an I onto V; and in Chapter 10, we shall propose a constraint prohibiting *lowering* operations. It should be noted, however, that the assumption that V MOVEMENT in English can be generalised from *have* and *be* to *all* non-modal Verbs is far from being unproblematic (cf. *Exercise II* at the end of this chapter).

In spite of the many uncertainties surrounding the rule, for expository purposes we shall henceforth follow Chomsky in his 1986b *Barriers* monograph in adopting the V MOVEMENT analysis. We shall thus assume that all finite non-modal Verbs originate in VP, but are moved into an empty I by application of V MOVEMENT, and thereby acquire the Tense and Agreement properties associated with I. Two general points should be made about the operation of the rule, however. The first is that (as already noted) V MOVEMENT is blocked from applying if I is filled – e.g. if it contains a Modal: cf.

(24)   John [ɪ does] [ᵥₚ *have/*has* some bad habits]

Thus, the verb *have* cannot move into I in (24) because I is already filled by *does*: hence, *have* cannot acquire the Tense and Agreement properties of I, and so remains in the uninflected infinitive form *have*. The second point to note is that where the conditions of application of the rule are met, V MOVEMENT is obligatory. This is arguably because non-application of the rule in contexts where its conditions of application are met would result in a verbal Tense/Agreement suffix (e.g. present tense *-s* or past tense *-d*) being stranded in I with no Verb stem to attach to, so resulting in ill-formed structures such as:

(25)   *John [ɪ *-s*] [ᵥₚ have some bad habits]

And we might in turn argue that structures containing unattached affixes are ruled out by a putatively universal principle proposed by Lasnik (1981, p. 162) to the effect that 'A morphologically realised affix must be realised as a syntactic dependent at surface structure' (i.e. it is in the very nature of an *affix* that it has to be *affixed* to something). We assume that the affix *-s* cannot attach to the Noun *John* in (25), because *-s* is a *verbal* affix and hence must attach to a verbal host. Given these assumptions, it follows that movement of V into an empty finite I is in effect *forced* by morphological considerations.

The incorporation of a rule of V MOVEMENT into our description of English Syntax turns out to have fundamental theoretical implications for our overall Theory of Grammar: it means that we are no longer able to posit that the syntactic structure of a sentence can be described in terms of a single Phrase-marker representing its S-structure. For, the postulation of a rule of V-MOVEMENT means that we must recognise at least two different levels of structure in our Theory of Grammar – namely, a level of *D-structure* (formerly known as 'Deep Structure') which serves as input to the rule, and a separate level of *S-structure* which is formed by application of the rule. For example, in the case of a sentence such as *They have completed the project*, the D-structure will be of the schematic form (22) above, while the corresponding S-structure will have the simplified form (23). We shall return to explore the theoretical consequences of this move in more detail in a later section, after we have looked at the operation of a number of other movement rules.

You should now be able to tackle exercises I and II

8.3   I MOVEMENT

Having looked briefly at the operation of one movement rule (V MOVEMENT), we now turn to look at the operation of a second movement rule which we mentioned earlier, namely the rule of I MOVEMENT. This rule is responsible (*inter alia*) for the phenomenon generally known as 'Subject–Auxiliary Inversion', which has a central role to play in the syntax of Direct Questions in English. Thus, the most obvious syntactic difference between a statement like (26)(a) below and the corresponding direct question (26)(b):

(26) (a)   [$_S$ He *will* tell the truth]

   (b)   *Will* [$_S$ he tell the truth]?

is that the Modal *will* is positioned within S after the Subject NP *he* in the declarative (26)(a), but is positioned outside S before the Subject NP *he* in the interrogative counterpart (26)(b). What we shall argue here is that in such cases, the italicised Modal originates in the I position within S, and is subsequently moved into an empty C position outside S by a rule which we might appropriately call I MOVEMENT (or more precisely, I-to-C Movement). The operation of this rule in the case of (26) can be outlined schematically as in (27) below:

(27) (a)   [$_C$ e]   [$_S$ he   [$_I$ *will*]   [$_{VP}$ tell the truth]]

               ┌── I MOVEMENT ──┘

   (b)   [$_C$ *Will*]   [$_S$ he   [$_I$ —]   [$_{VP}$ tell the truth]]?

In the terminology introduced at the end of the previous section, we might say that (27)(a) is the *D-structure* of the sentence, and (27)(b) is the corresponding *S-structure*. Obviously, the I MOVEMENT analysis is based on two key assumptions: (i) inverted Modals like *will* originate in I, and (ii) they end up in C. Let's consider separately the motivation for each of these two assumptions.

We'll look first at four arguments supporting the claim that inverted Modals originate within I. Our first argument is of a type which is generally referred to as the '*gap* argument'. Let us suppose that (contrary to what we claim here) inverted Modals do not originate within S, but rather originate outside S in C. This would mean that a sentence such as (26) (b) above *Will he tell the truth?* would lack an overt I constituent within S. But since I is one of the three obligatory immediate constituents of S, we should then expect to be able to have an I constituent within the bracketed S in (26) (b), containing either a Modal Auxiliary like *can*, or the infinitival particle *to*: however, neither of these is possible, as we see from the ungrammaticality of (28) below:

(28) (a) *Will [S he [I *can*] tell the truth]?
  (b) *Will [S he [I *to*] tell the truth]?

Why should it not be possible to have an overt (italicised) I constituent within S in sentences like (28)? We can find a simple answer to this question if we assume that in (26) (b) the Modal Auxiliary *will* originates within I, and is subsequently preposed (by the rule of I MOVEMENT) from its normal position between NP and VP within S to the empty C position outside S in the manner indicated schematically in (27) above. The reason why we cannot have *can* or *to* in I within S in (28) should now be obvious – namely that the I position was originally filled by the Modal *will*. When the rule of I MOVEMENT applies to move *will* into C, a 'gap' is left behind in the original I position: but if we assume a convention that such gaps cannot be refilled (i.e. that once a given position has been filled it cannot be refilled, even if subsequently vacated), then we have a natural explanation for the ungrammaticality of sentences such as (28). What's wrong with (28) is that the I position was originally filled by the Modal *will*; and after *will* is moved into C by the rule of I MOVEMENT, the original I position has subsequently been refilled by *can/to*, in violation of our 'no refilling' condition.

A second argument in support of the assumption that 'inverted' Modals originate inside S can be formulated in relation to *subcategorisation* facts. Modal Auxiliaries like *can* subcategorise an infinitival VP Complement (i.e. take a VP Complement headed by a Verb in the 'base' or 'infinitive' form): in particular, they do not allow VP complements headed by a gerundive or perfective verb-form, or by a finite Verb, as we see from (29) below:

(29) John can *go/*going/*gone/*goes/*went* to the party

Interestingly, precisely the same set of restrictions hold for 'inverted' Modals in direct questions; cf.

(30) Can [S John *go/*going/*gone/*goes/*went* to the party]?

Now, on the assumption that subcategorisation restrictions hold between a Head and its *sister* constituents at D-structure, then *can* and its VP complement must be sister constituents at D-structure. But this clearly would not be the case if *can* originates outside S in C, as represented schematically in (31) below:

(31)

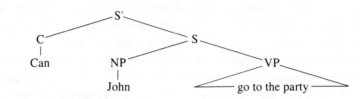

since only S is a sister of C in (31), not VP. But by contrast, if *can* originates within I as in (32) below:

(32)

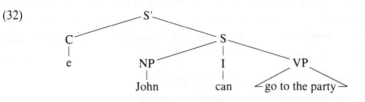

then VP would be the sister of the I containing *can*. Since (as our discussion in Chapter 5 showed) subcategorisation restrictions hold between a Head constituent and its sister Complements, the subcategorisation restrictions found in (30) would then simply follow from the normal restrictions which Heads impose on their sisters. Note that we cannot get around the subcategorisation argument by saying that *can* in (30) subcategorises a 'bare' (i.e. *to*-less) infinitival S complement with an overt Subject, because this would lead us to expect that when *can* occurs within I it can also take a 'bare' infinitival S Complement with an overt Subject; however, this is false, as the ungrammaticality of (33) below illustrates:

(33)   *John can [ₛ *Mary go there*]

Thus, subcategorisation facts provide strong support for our assumption that inverted Modals which are positioned in C at S-structure originate in I.

A third argument in support of the claim that inverted Modals in direct questions originate within S concerns the fact that these Modals do in fact show up within S in the relevant indirect speech counterparts. For example, a direct question such as:

(34)   *Can* [ₛ we do anything for Mary]?

has the following indirect question counterpart:

(35)   I don't know whether [ₛ we *can* do anything for Mary]

In (35), the Modal Auxiliary *can* occupies the characteristic I position between the Subject NP [*we*] and its VP Complement [*do anything for Mary*]. Thus, a natural way of capturing the structural similarities and differences between direct and indirect questions like (34) and (35) would be to say the two sentences are similar in that in both cases the Modal *can* originates in I within S, but that they differ in that only in direct questions is I preposed to the immediate left of the overall S into C, by operation of the rule of I MOVEMENT.

A fourth argument in favour of the I MOVEMENT analysis comes the phenomenon of vocalic HAVE CONTRACTION which we discussed in the previous section. Recall that we established that vocalic contraction of *have* down to /v/ is subject to two conditions. The first is that it takes place only after a Pronoun ending in a vowel or diphthong; and the second is that it is blocked by the presence of a 'gap' between the Pronoun and *have*. In the light of these two conditions, consider why vocalic contraction should be blocked in examples such as the following:

(36) (a)   Should *I have/*I've* called the Police?
　　 (b)   Will *we have/*we've* finished by 4 o'clock?
　　 (c)   Would *you have/*you've* wanted to come with me?
　　 (d)   Could *they have/*they've* done something to help?

In each case, vocalic contraction of the sequences *I've/we've/you've/they've* is blocked. But why? The I MOVEMENT analysis provides us with a ready answer. For, under this analysis, the initial Modals *should/will/would/could* originate at D-structure between the Pronoun *I/we/you/they* and the Auxiliary *have*, in the typical I position between NP and VP, as in the corresponding declaratives:

(37) (a)   I *should* have called the Police
　　 (b)   We *will* have finished by 4 o'clock
　　 (c)   You *would* have wanted to come with me
　　 (d)   They *could* have done something to help

They subsequently undergo 'inversion' (= I MOVEMENT) in direct questions, and are moved out of their position between the Pronouns *I/we/you/they* and *have*, into pre-subject position in front of the Pronoun. This movement would have the effect of leaving a 'gap' in the original position out of which the Modal has been moved, between the Subject Pronoun and *have*. If we symbolise this gap by Ø, we could say that after 'inversion' the sentences in (36) would have the respective structures:

(38) (a)   Should *I Ø have* called the Police?
　　 (b)   Will *we Ø have* finished by 4 o'clock?

(c) Would *you Ø have* wanted to come with me?

(d) Could *they Ø have* done something to help?

The presence of the 'gap' Ø here between the Pronoun and *have* would then suffice to block HAVE CONTRACTION. But note that this account of contraction rests heavily on the assumption that Modals originate in post-subject position, and get moved into pre-subject position by a rule of 'inversion' (= I MOVE-MENT), thereby leaving a 'gap' in their original post-subject position which blocks HAVE CONTRACTION. What precisely is meant by a 'gap' is a matter which we shall discuss in section 10.5.

Having argued that 'inverted' Modals in direct questions originate within I, let's now turn to consider where exactly they get moved to when they are pre-posed (or, in more technical terms, what is the *landing-site* for inverted Modals). In (27) above, we assumed that Modals in I are moved into an empty C, in the manner indicated schematically in (39) below:

(39)

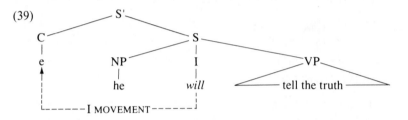

There are a number of reasons for positing that C is the landing-site for pre-posed Modals, as we noted in our discussion of 'inverted Auxiliaries' in Chapter 6. Perhaps the most important of these is that the I-to-C MOVEMENT analysis correctly predicts that 'inversion' will be blocked by the presence of an overt Complementiser. As Emonds (1976, p. 25) notes, inversion can take place not only in main Clauses but also in embedded Clauses (in so-called 'semi-indirect speech'), as in:

(40) She wondered [*would he* come back again]

But (as noted by Goldsmith (1981), p. 546), inversion is blocked when the embedded Complement Clause is introduced by an overt Complementiser: cf.

(41) (a) *She wondered [*whether/if* would he come back again]

(b) She wondered [*whether/if* he would come back again]

Now, in an analysis which claims that 'Auxiliary Inversion' involves move-ment from I into an empty C, we correctly predict that Inversion can only take place in Clauses not introduced by an overt Complementiser (i.e. we predict that where there is Inversion there will be no Complementiser, and where there is a Complementiser there will be no inversion). And examples such as (41) above provide obvious empirical substantiation of this claim.

Further empirical support for the claim that inverted Auxiliaries are positioned in C comes from the literary construction illustrated in (42) below (as we again noted in Chapter 6):

(42)   I shall avenge myself of this craven cur
    (a)   [whether] it *be* in this kingdom or the next
    (b)   [*be*] it in this kingdom or the next
    (c)   *[whether *be*] it in this kingdom or the next

For here we see that preposing of the italicised subjunctive Verb *be* into the bracketed C position is possible only where C is not already filled by the Complementiser *whether*.We might also follow Rizzi (1984, p. 123) in assuming that something similar is going on in conditional sentences such as (43) below, if we assume that *if* is a Complementiser:

(43)   Please look after my dog
    (a)   [if] I *should* die
    (b)   [*should*] I die
    (c)   *[if *should*] I die

Thus, the fact that Complementisers and preposed Auxiliaries are mutually exclusive provides strong empirical support for the claim that 'inversion' involves movement from I into C by the rule of I MOVEMENT. Similar support comes from universalist considerations. Thus, Rizzi (1984, pp. 110–24) notes that 'Inversion' in standard Italian and in Italian dialects such as Romagnolo is blocked by the presence of an overt Complementiser: Taraldsen (1986, p. 11) argues that I MOVEMENT is blocked in Norwegian by the presence of an overt Complementiser; and Platzack (1986, p. 32) reports that the same is true of Swedish.

Before we leave our discussion of the I MOVEMENT rule, let's look a little more closely at its operation. One thing we might ask is what set of elements undergo I MOVEMENT. The examples we looked at in (36) all involved the preposing of a Modal I. But the rule doesn't just apply to Modals: as we see from the examples in (42) above and (44) below, the rule can also apply to *have* or *be*, in a variety of different uses:

(44) (a)   *Has* [S he a car]?
    (b)   *Have* [S I to keep my promise]?
    (c)   *Have* [S you finished your assignment]?
    (d)   *Is* [S John unhappy]?

(e)   *Am* [s I to believe what you tell me]?

(f)   *Are* [s you washing your hair again tonight]?

(g)   *Was* [s she harassed by the police]?

It is clear that in all such cases, *have* and *be* originate within VP, either as the Head or as the Specifier of VP. Moreover, given the arguments presented above, it is equally clear that they end up in C. Accordingly, it might at first sight seem plausible to suppose that they move directly from their position in VP into C. But closer reflection tells us that this cannot be so. Why? Because inverted forms of *have/be* are inflected for Tense and Agreement properties, as we see from (44) above, where, for example, *has* in (44) (a) is a third person singular present tense form (hence contains the relevant inflectional suffix -*s*). Now, bearing in mind that (as we argued in the previous section) non-modal Verbs originate within VP and only become inflected for Tense and Agreement by virtue of being moved out of their position in VP into I by the rule of V MOVEMENT (since it is I which contains the relevant Tense/Agreement features), then it seems clear that *have* and *be* must move first from VP into I by V MOVEMENT, and then subsequently from I into C by I MOVEMENT. Given this 'dual movement' analysis, a sentence like (44) (a) *Has he a car?* would be derived in the manner indicated schematically in (45) below:

(45)   [c e] [s he [ι e] [vp [v′ *have* a car]]]
              └─I MOVEMENT─┘ └─V MOVEMENT─┘

That is, the Verb *have* would originate as an uninflected V heading the bracketed V-bar, and would first be moved into I (where it would acquire the relevant Tense/Agreement features which surface in the form *has*), and then subsequently move from I into C. So, two different movement rules would be involved in the derivation of the resulting sentence (44) (a) *Has he a car?*.

A second conclusion which we can draw from our discussion is that the rule of I MOVEMENT applies not just to Modals in I, but also to forms of *have* and *be* which have undergone prior movement into I. There are, however, some verbal uses of *have* which do not permit I MOVEMENT (i.e. 'inversion'): for example, the sentences in (46) below:

(46) (a)   He *has* his sister go shopping for him

     (b)   He *has* his car repaired at the garage

lack a direct question counterpart with inversion of *have*: cf.

(47) (a)   *Has* he his sister go shopping for him?

     (b)   *Has* he his car repaired at the garage?

Transformations

Given the assumption made at the end of the previous section that Non-modal Verbs acquire finite inflections by being moved out of VP into I by V MOVE-MENT, it seems clear that *have* must have moved out of VP into I in (46) in order to surface as the inflected form *has*. But if *has* is in I in (46), and if *have* generally permits 'Auxiliary Inversion' (as in examples (44)(a–c) above), why can't *has* be moved out of I into C in (47)? The answer is not at all obvious: it would seem clear that there are some rather puzzling lexical restrictions on the class of items within I which can undergo I MOVEMENT; the rule applies to Modals, to *be*, and to some uses of *have*. But it does not apply to any Verbs other than these, as we see from the ungrammaticality of:

(48) (a)   *Wants* [ₛ he to leave]?
     (b)   *Knew* [ₛ you the answer]?

In terms of the feature analysis of categories introduced at the end of Chapter 3, we might claim that the I MOVEMENT rule applies only to [+AUX] elements contained in I: this would imply that *have* in its uses in (44) above is [+AUX], whereas the 'causative' use of *have* illustrated in (46) above in [−AUX].

Independent empirical support for this claim comes from the criteria which we established in 3.8 for differentiating Auxiliaries from full Verbs. For example, Auxiliary *have* in (44) can be copied in tags, and can be directly negated without *do*, as we see from the examples in (44) below:

(49) (a)   He *hasn't* any money, *has* he?
     (b)   He *hasn't* to say anything, *has* he?
     (c)   He *hasn't* finished his assignment, *has* he?

By contrast, nonauxiliary *have* in (46) requires *do*-tags and *do*-negatives, as we see from (50) below:

(50) (a)   He has his sister go shopping for him, *does* he?
     (b)   He has his car repaired at the garage, *does* he?
     (c)   He *doesn't have*/*hasn't* his sister go shopping for him
     (d)   He *doesn't have*/*hasn't* his car repaired at the garage

Thus, there is independent support for our analysis of *have* as an Auxiliary in (44), but a nonauxiliary Verb in (46).

At this point, it may be useful to summarise what we have claimed so far. We have argued in favour of positing two movement rules: a rule of V MOVE-MENT moving V out of VP into an empty finite I; and a rule of I MOVEMENT moving a [+AUX] constituent in I out of S and into C. We remarked earlier that the postulation of movement rules has important consequences for the overall organisation of the model of grammar we are developing here. The

418

reason is that the incorporation of syntactic movement rules into a grammar presupposes that there are two different levels of syntactic structure in grammars: (i) the level of *D-structure* which serves as *input* to the movement rules, and (ii) the level of *S-structure* which serves as the *output* of the movement rules. Clearly, S-structures are generated from D-structures by the application of movement rules: but how are D-structures generated? Well, let's assume that the *Categorial Component* (or *Base Component*) of our grammar directly generates *D-structures* (or *Base Structures*), and that these then serve as input to a set of *Movement Rules* which convert (or, to use the relevant technical term, *map*) them into the corresponding *S-structures*. In schematic terms, our revised model of the syntactic component of a grammar might be represented as in (51) below:

(51)   BASE

⇓

D-structures

‖

MOVEMENT TRANSFORMATIONS

⇓

S-structures

To use the appropriate technical terminology, we might say that the Categorial Component of the Base generates abstract prelexical structures which are lexicalised by the insertion of items from the Lexicon: these lexicalised structures are known as *D-structures* (or *Base structures*). By the subsequent application of Movement Transformations like V MOVEMENT and I MOVEMENT, these D-structures are then *mapped* or *transformed* into the corresponding *S-structures*.

Although the terminology used here is 'standard', a variety of other terms are frequently found in the relevant literature. For example, a bewildering variety of other terms are also used for *D-structure*, including not only 'Base Structure', but also 'Deep Structure', 'Remote Structure', and 'Initial Structure'. In earlier works, what is here called S-structure was frequently referred to as 'Surface Structure'; but in more recent work a crucial terminological distinction has been drawn between *S-structure* (= the output of the Syntactic Component of our Grammar) and *Surface Structure* (= the output of the Phonological Component).

We have tacitly assumed in our discussion above that more than one Movement Transformation may apply in the derivation of a given sentence, and that when this happens the rules concerned may apply *consecutively* (i.e. one after the other). For example, the derivation proposed for sentence (44) (d) *Is John unhappy?* could be represented in schematic terms as in (52) below:

(52) (a)   [C e]   [S John   [VP *be* unhappy]]

                        ┌ V MOVEMENT ┘
                        ↓

   (b)   [C e]   [S John [I *is*]   [VP — unhappy]]

              ┌ I MOVEMENT ┘
              ↓

   (c)   [C *Is*]   [S John [I —]   [VP — unhappy]]?

(52) (a) is the D-structure (= Base Structure) generated by the Base Component of the grammar. The output of one or more Movement Transformations is known as a *derived structure*. Hence, applying V MOVEMENT to the D-structure (52) (a) results in the derived structure (52) (b). This in turn is mapped into the derived structure (52) (c) by application of I MOVEMENT. If we define the S-structure of a sentence as the *final derived (syntactic) structure* of the sentence, then it follows that (52) (c) is the S-structure of sentence (44) (d) *Is John unhappy?* Conversely, (52) (b) is said to be the (immediate) *underlying structure* of (52) (c), and likewise (52) (a) is the (immediate) *underlying structure* of (52) (b), and the *ultimate* underlying structure of (52) (c). The *ultimate underlying structure* of any sentence is its D-structure (or Base Structure). OK, so you've had enough terminological traumas for the time being!

You should now be able to tackle exercise III

8.4   NP MOVEMENT in passive structures

So far, we have only looked at two Movement Rules in English, namely V MOVEMENT and I MOVEMENT. Now, by contrast, we're going to turn to look at a further Movement Transformation known in the linguistic literature as NP MOVEMENT. This rule has been argued to play a central role in the syntax of four important construction types in English, namely the 'passive', 'raising', 'ergative' and 'middle' constructions. We'll look first at the role of NP MOVEMENT in *passive* sentences like:

(53)   *The car* will be put — in the garage

Here, we shall argue that the italicised NP [*the car*] originates in the postverbal object NP position marked —, and is subsequently moved out of there into the italicised preverbal subject NP position, in the manner indicated schematically in (54) below:

(54)   [$_S$[$_{NP}$ e] will be [$_{V'}$ put [$_{NP}$ *the car*] in the garage]]

         └── NP MOVEMENT ──┘

Informally, you can think of (54) as being rather like the kind of impersonal passive structures we find in languages like Latin ('Will be put the car in the garage'): [$_{NP}$ e] here represents an 'empty' subject NP (there is no evidence for assuming that there is an overt underlying subject in (54), since there is no trace of any such expression in the corresponding S-structure (53)). NP MOVEMENT here is the transformational counterpart of the traditional grammarian's rule of 'passivisation' by which the Object of a sentence is 'passivised' and thereby moves into Subject position.

But what evidence is there that the preverbal NP italicised in (53) originates in the postverbal position marked by —? One such piece of evidence comes from *subcategorisation* facts. As we see from the examples in (55):

(55) (a)   John will put [$_{NP}$ *the car*] [$_{PP}$ *in the garage*]
   (b)   *John will put [$_{NP}$ *the car*]
   (c)   *John will put [$_{PP}$ *in the garage*]
   (d)   *John will put

the Verb *put* subcategorises (i.e. 'takes') obligatory NP and PP complements (to simplify exposition here, we ignore the fact that the subcategorisation properties of *put* may be predictable from its thematic properties, and from general word-order principles such as the STRICT ADJACENCY CONDITION). But in passive sentences such as (53), it would appear that *put* has been inserted into a V-bar containing only a following PP, but no following NP. If this is so, then our grammar will wrongly predict that sentences such as (53) are ungrammatical, since they (apparently) violate the subcategorisation restrictions on *put*. But of course that would be absurd, since (53) is in fact perfectly well-formed. How can we account for this? One possible answer is to posit that the preverbal italicised Subject NP in passive sentences like (53) originates at D-structure in the postverbal Object NP position, as represented in (54) above. Note that in (54), the Verb *put* occurs in a V-bar where it is followed both by an NP [*the car*], and by a PP [*in the garage*]. In other words, a sentence like (53) behaves for subcategorisation purposes as if it is derived from a D-structure like (54).

A second argument which can be adduced in support of the NP MOVEMENT analysis of passive sentences is our earlier 'gap' argument. If there is indeed a rule of NP MOVEMENT moving the Object of a passive Verb into Subject position, then we should expect (given our earlier assumptions) that movement of the Object would leave behind a 'gap' in Object position which cannot be refilled by another lexical NP: and sure enough, this is indeed the case, as we see from the ungrammaticality of (56) below:

(56)   *[The car] will be put *the bike* in the garage

(56) shows us that the 'gap' left behind by the movement of the bracketed NP [*the car*] from Object into Subject position cannot be re-filled by another lexical NP such as [*the bike*]. Why should this be so? The answer is that if we assume the transformational analysis of passives proposed here, then [*the car*] in (56) will originate as a postverbal NP Complement of *put*, so that (56) will derive from the D-structure (57) below:

(57)   — will be put [NP the car] [NP the bike] [pp in the garage]

But a Base Structure such as (57) will fail to satisfy the subcategorisation frame for *put*, since *put* in (57) has two NP Complements and a PP Complement, whereas we saw earlier in relation to (55) above that *put* subcategorises only a single NP and a PP Complement. So, (57) is ill-formed as a D-structure by virtue of a subcategorisation violation. If we further assume that any sentence which is ill-formed at any syntactic level (e.g. D-structure or S-structure) is ungrammatical, then it follows that the corresponding sentence (56) will be ungrammatical.

A third argument in support of our proposed transformational analysis of passives can be formulated in relation to a class of expressions known as *idiom chunks*. English has a class of Noun Phrases which are highly restricted in their distribution, in that (in their *idiomatic* use) they generally occur only in conjunction with some specific Verb: for example, each of the italicised expressions in (58) below generally occurs only immediately following the capitalised Verb in its idiomatic use:

(58) (a)   The government KEEPS *tabs* on his operations
     (b)   I want you to PAY *heed* to what I say
     (c)   The Chief of Staff PAYS *lip service* to the President
     (d)   The Prime Minister PAID *homage* to the dead
     (e)   You'll have to GRASP *the nettle* and BITE *the bullet*
     (f)   She TOOK *note* of what I said
     (g)   Let's TAKE *advantage* of the warm weather

For this reason, NPs like those italicised in (58) above are known as *idiom chunk NPs* (more particularly, as *Object idiom chunks*). They do not have the same syntactic freedom of distribution as other NPs – for example, they cannot occur in typical NP positions like those italicised in (59) below:

(59) (a)   *Tabs* won't affect me

(b)   *Everyone needs *tabs*

(c)   *I don't like talking about *tabs*

The relevant restrictions don't appear to be *semantic* in any obvious sense, since close synonyms of the items concerned are not subject to the same restrictions, as we can see by comparing *heed* with its close synonym *attention* (cf. *pay heed to = pay attention to*):

(60) (a)   You can't expect to have my *attention/*heed* all the time

(b)   He's always trying to attract my *attention/*heed*

(c)   He's a child who needs a lot of *attention/*heed*

(d)   I try to give him all the *attention/*heed* he wants

Nor indeed are these restrictions *pragmatic* in nature: i.e. the ill-formedness of the *heed*-sentences in (60) is entirely different in kind from the oddity of sentences like:

(61)   !That man will eat any car which thinks he's stupid

which is purely *pragmatic* (i.e. lies in the fact that (61) describes the kind of bizarre situation which just doesn't happen in the world we are familiar with, where cars don't think, and people don't eat cars). Hence it seems implausible to analyse sentences like (59) and (60) as involving violations of selection restrictions (the latter being typically pragmatic in nature, i.e. relating to our ideas about the world). Instead, it seems that the restrictions in (58), (59), and (60) are essentially lexical-syntactic: i.e. it just happens to be an arbitrary syntactic fact about the distribution of the item *heed* that in contemporary English it is virtually never used in any position save immediately following the verb *pay* (and perhaps *take*).

In the light of the claim that Object idiom chunk NPs such as *advantage*, *tabs*, *heed*, *note* and *homage* have an extremely restricted distribution (i.e. are generally restricted to occurring immediately *after* specific verbs like *take*, *keep* and *pay*), consider how we are to account for the grammaticality of sentences like:

(62) (a)   *Little heed* was paid — to her proposal

(b)   *Close tabs* were kept — on all Thatcherites

(c)   *Little note* was taken — of what I said

(d)   *Due homage* was paid — to the dead

(e)   *Little advantage* was taken — of the situation

For in (62), the idiom chunk NPs *precede* their associated Verbs, not *follow* them as we earlier stipulated that they must do. How can we account for this apparent contradiction? Once again, if we posit that the italicised idiom chunk NPs originate in the position marked — and are only subsequently moved into the italicised preverbal position by NP MOVEMENT, then we eliminate an apparent inconsistency in our grammar, and retain a simple generalisation about idiom chunk NPs – namely that they are restricted to occurring immediately after specific Verbs *at D-structure* (though of course they can subsequently be moved out of their underlying position by movement rules like NP MOVEMENT).

A fourth argument can be formulated in relation to *thematic relations*. It is interesting to note that *active Objects* (i.e. Objects of active sentences) play the same thematic role as the corresponding *passive Subjects*. For example, in the active sentence (63) (a) below the italicised Object NP fulfils the same thematic role (= THEME, or PATIENT) as its italicised Subject NP counterpart in the corresponding passive (63) (b):

(63) (a)   They rolled [*the ball*] down the hill
  (b)   [*The ball*] was rolled down the hill

Likewise, in the active sentence (64) (a) below, the italicised Primary Object NP *Mary* has the same θ-role (= GOAL) as its italicised Subject counterpart in the corresponding passive (64) (b):

(64) (a)   They will give [*Mary*] nothing
  (b)   [*Mary*] will be given nothing

In other words, passive Subjects play the same theta-role as the corresponding active Objects. How can we account for this? If we posit that the superficial Subject NP in a passive sentence originates at D-structure as the Object of the passive participle, then the identity of theta-roles can be accounted for in a straightforward fashion. For example, let's suppose that the D-structure of the passive (64) (b) *Mary will be given nothing* is along the lines indicated in (65) below:

(65)   [NP e] will be [V' given *Mary* nothing]

If we further assume that the lexical entry for *give* specifies that the NP immediately following *give* in [V NP NP] structures is assigned the theta-role of GOAL, then it follows that the italicised NP *Mary* in (65) will be assigned the role of GOAL at D-structure; and we might assume that theta-roles are 'preserved' under movement, so that when NP MOVEMENT applies to 'passivise' *Mary* (i.e. move *Mary* from Object to Subject NP position), *Mary* retains the theta-role of GOAL (we will consider the exact mechanism for theta-role assignment to moved NPs in section 10.5). The more general conclusion to be drawn from our discussion is that if we assume the transformational analysis of passives, then the identity of thematic function between active Objects and passive Subjects follows from the fact that both occupy the same postverbal position at D-structure.

Given that (as we suggested in Chapter 7) theta-roles play a part in determining *selection restrictions*, it is scarcely surprising that a fifth argument in favour of a transformational analysis of passives can be formulated in relation to *selection restrictions*. Recall that these are restrictions on the precise set of expressions belonging to a given category which can function as an Argument of a given Predicate. So, for example, in a sentence such as:

(66)   Mary will wear *a revealing dress/!a revealing theory*

both italicised expressions are NPs, and yet only the first 'makes sense' as the Object of *wear*. But observe that precisely the same restrictions are found in passive sentences like:

(67)   *Not many revealing dresses/!theories* will be worn — at the conference

How can we account for the apparently coincidental fact that passive Subjects exhibit the same selection restrictions as active Objects? An obvious answer would be to say that passive Subjects originate as underlying (postverbal) Objects – i.e. the italicised NP in sentences such as (67) originates in the postverbal position marked by — (i.e. the position characteristic of Direct Objects, in general), and is only subsequently moved into the italicised (preverbal, or Subject) position by application of NP MOVEMENT. We could then say that the restriction concerned holds between *wear* and the NP which immediately follows it at the level of D-structure.

Given the arguments outlined above, it seems that we have abundant empirical evidence in support of positing an NP MOVEMENT rule which (in the case of 'passive' structures) has the effect of preposing a postverbal NP into preverbal Subject position. The operation of the rule can be illustrated in relation to our earlier sentence (64) (b) *Mary will be given nothing* in the manner outlined schematically in (68) below (we omit S-bar for the sake of simplicity):

(68)

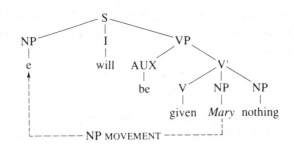

(We assume here for expository convenience that the Passive Auxiliary *be* is a Specifier of V-bar, though this is not of any importance to the issue at hand, concerning the operation of NP MOVEMENT: we shall look at an alternative analysis of passive *be* shortly.) There is no evidence that the empty subject NP ('e') contains any actual lexical item ('real word') in the underlying structure (68), since only the words *will, be, given, Mary* and *nothing* appear in the corresponding S-structure. Application of NP MOVEMENT to (68) results in the italicised NP *Mary* moving into the empty Subject NP position to the immediate left of *will*, thereby deriving the S-structure associated with the resulting sentence (64) (b) *Mary will be given nothing*.

So far, we have implicitly thought of NP MOVEMENT (as it applies in passive structures) as a rule moving Object NPs into Subject NP position within the same Clause. However, the rule can apply across S-boundaries, as we see from the fact that the active sentence (69) (a) below has the passive counterpart (69) (b):

(69) (a)   They consider [*John* to be incompetent]

(b)   *John* is considered [— to be incompetent]

Recall that we argued in Chapter 6 that infinitive Complements of Predicates such as *consider* are 'Exceptional Clauses' which have the status of S, not of S-bar (e.g. because they can never be introduced by an overt Complementiser). The significance of this is that (69) (b) therefore involves moving the *Subject NP* of a subordinate Clause into main Clause Subject NP position, in the manner indicated schematically in (70) below:

(70)   [$_{NP}$ e] is considered [$_S$ *John* to be incompetent]

            └— NP MOVEMENT —┘

Moreover, as (71) below indicates, the Subject of a Small Clause Complement can also undergo passivisation via NP MOVEMENT:

(71) (a)   They found [$_{SC}$ *the prisoner* guilty of the charges]

(b)   The *prisoner* was found [$_{SC}$ — guilty of the charges]

But while passivisation can apply to the Subject of an Exceptional Clause or Small Clause, it cannot apply to the subject of an Ordinary Clause, as (72) and (73) below illustrate:

(72) (a)   It was alleged [$_{S'}$ that *Burgess* was a spy]

(b)   **Burgess* was alleged [$_{S'}$ that — was a spy]

(73) (a)   It is forbidden [$_{S'}$ for *you* to smoke in here]

(b)   **You* are forbidden [$_{S'}$ for — to smoke in here]

In Volume Two, we shall look at various attempts to explain the restrictions in (72) and (73): for the time being, we merely note that passivisation cannot apply 'across' an S-bar boundary.

All the cases which we have looked at so far involve passivisation of an NP which is immediately adjacent to a Verb. But is adjacency to a Verb a necessary condition for passivisation to take place? There is some evidence to suggest that this is the case. For example, a sentence such as:

(74)   John gave *Mary* [the job]

has only one passive counterpart, not two: cf.

(75) (a)   *Mary* was given the job
     (b)   *[The job] was given Mary

Now, if we assume that only an NP immediately adjacent to a Verb can passivise, then the contrast in (75) is easily accounted for: *Mary* is adjacent to the V *gave* in (74) and hence can passivise: whereas [*the job*] in (74) is not adjacent to the Verb, and so cannot passivise. Of course, in (e.g. Northern British English) dialects which allow the converse Complement order in (74), the second passive form is indeed possible: cf.

(76) (a)   %John gave *the job* Mary
     (b)   %*The job* was given Mary

But this is because [*the job*] is adjacent to the Verb *gave* in (76) (a).

However, our general assumption that only an NP which is immediately adjacent to a Verb can passivise might at first sight seem to be called into question by so-called *prepositional passives* (or *pseudopassives*) such as (77) below:

(77) (a)   *Nothing* was agreed ON — by the committee
     (b)   *The information* was asked FOR — by the Dean
     (c)   *He* can be depended ON — for sound advice
     (d)   *John* was shouted AT — by his mother
     (e)   *He* must be talked TO — by someone

In (77), the passivised Subject seems to have been moved out of its underlying position (marked by —) as a Prepositional Object, in apparent violation of the condition that an NP can only be passivised if adjacent to a Verb. It seems likely that the Verbs in (77) are indeed Prepositional (rather than Phrasal), since the Preposition can be separated from the Verb, e.g. in Relative Clause structures such as (78) below:

(78) (a)   There was nothing *on which* the committee could agree
     (b)   The information *for which* you are asking is classified

(c)   He is someone *on whom* you can depend for sound advice

(d)   John is someone *at whom* you have to shout every now and then

(e)   He is someone *to whom* you can talk freely

So, it might appear as if our claim that only an NP immediately adjacent to a Verb can passivise is counterexemplified by data such as (77).

And yet, there are severe restrictions on passivisation of Prepositional Objects. For example, although Prepositional Verbs allow V and P to be separated by other material in their active form (as in the (a) examples below), they do not do so in their passive form (as in the (b) examples below):

(79) (a)   The committee agreed *unanimously* on the resolution

(b)   *The resolution was agreed *unanimously* on by the committee

(80) (a)   The Dean asked *the committee* for the information

(b)   *The information was asked *the committee* for

(81) (a)   You can depend *entirely* on his integrity

(b)   *His integrity can be depended *entirely* on

(82) (a)   Mary shouted *angrily* at John

(b)   *John was shouted *angrily* at by Mary

(83) (a)   He talked *about disarmament* to the President

(b)   *The President was talked *about disarmament* to

Likewise, although in their active form Prepositional Verbs permit the Preposition to be modified by a preceding Specifier such as *right* or *straight*, this type of premodification is not permitted in the passive: cf.

(84) (a)   Many people turned (*right*) against her

(b)   She was turned (*right) against by many people

(85) (a)   Everybody stared (*straight*) at her:

(b)   She was stared (*straight) at by everybody

What these two sets of facts suggest is that in prepositional passives, somehow the V and P must together form a single cohesive unit, a kind of Complex Verb which cannot be 'broken up' by intervening constituents. But how can this be? After all, the fact that the whole Prepositional Phrase can be separated from the Verb with which it is associated and 'fronted' as in (78) above suggests that the V and the following P do not together form a constituent.

So, we are faced with two conflicting sets of evidence. On the one hand, sentences such as (78) suggest that V and the following P belong to separate constituents; while on the other hand, sentences such as (79–85) suggest that V and P together form a single constituent. How can we resolve the obvious paradox? A traditional solution is to suppose that in a sentence such as:

(86)   People shouldn't [$_{V'}$ stare at Mary]

the bracketed V-bar underlyingly has the structure:

(87)

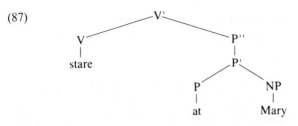

but that the head P *at* of the PP undergoes optional REANALYSIS whereby it is adjoined to the head V of the V-bar to derive a structure such as:

(88)

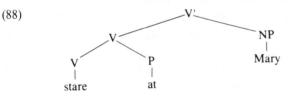

The result of this REANALYSIS is twofold. Firstly, the Preposition *at* is incorporated with the Verb *stare* into a 'complex', or 'compound' Verb [$_V$ *stare at*]: and secondly, loss of the head P *at* from the PP [*at Mary*] by REANALYSIS causes the *pruning* of the P' and PP'' nodes, so that *Mary* in (88) has the status of a verbal Object, not a prepositional Object.

Now, if we assume that Prepositional Verbs such as *stare at* optionally allow REANALYSIS into a Compound Verb provided that V and P are immediately adjacent, then we can continue to maintain that only an NP immediately adjacent to a Verb can passivise. For, as we see from (88) above, REANALYSIS results in the formation of a structure in which the NP *Mary* is adjacent to the derived Compound Verb [$_V$ *stare at*], so that passivisation is permitted just in case optional REANALYSIS has applied. By contrast, if we take the option of not applying REANALYSIS, then the PP Complement of the V will remain a separate constituent, and hence can be fronted as a unit, as in sentences such as (78) above. On the assumption that REANALYSIS is only permitted where V and P are immediately adjacent, and that prepositional passives are only possible where REANALYSIS has applied, then we can attribute the ungrammaticality of the (b) examples in (79–85) to the fact that the presence of intervening material between V and P blocks REANALYSIS, and hence blocks passivisation.

Although the REANALYSIS hypothesis seems initially attractive, it raises the question of why some types of Prepositional structures do not appear to allow REANALYSIS, and hence do not allow passivisation: cf.

(89) (a)   *The third round was lost in — by Rocky (Van Riemsdijk (1978), p. 220)

(b)   *His mother is travelled with — by John (ibid.)

(c)   *Many hours were argued for — (Van Riemsdijk and Williams (1986), p. 147)

The answer suggested by Chomsky in *Aspects* (1965, pp. 105–6) is that only an NP which is part of a *subcategorised PP* can undergo passivisation: in our terms, what this amounts to is the claim that only the head P of a *Complement PP* can undergo REANALYSIS, not the head P of an *Adjunct PP*. Thus, in (89) the Prepositions *in*, *with* and *for* are all head Adjunct PPs, and so cannot undergo REANALYSIS, with the result that passivisation is blocked.

A rather different proposal is offered in Chomsky's *Essays* (1977a, p. 87). Here, Chomsky suggests that prepositional passives are only possible where the Verb and the Preposition together form what he calls a 'semantic unit' (and what Van Riemsdijk and Williams (1986, p. 118) term a 'natural Predicate'). For example, Chomsky implies that the contrast between:

(90) (a)   England was lived in by many people

(b)   *England was died in by many people

can be accounted for by positing that '*live in*' forms a semantic unit, whereas '*die in*' does not. And in the same spirit, Van Riemsdijk (1978, p. 221) argues that the ill-formedness of (89) (a) and (b) above is attributable to the fact that *lose in* and *travel with* do not 'constitute semantic units'; while Van Riemsdijk and Williams (1986, p. 147) argue that the ill-formedness of (89) (c) lies in the fact that expressions like *argue for* 'cannot reasonably be interpreted as natural predicates'. As Van Riemsdijk (1978, p. 221) notes, 'what we are loosely calling semantic units might correspond to possible words': so, for example, *live in* is a possible semantic unit in (90) (a) because it can be paraphrased by *inhabit*; but *lose in* is not a possible 'semantic unit' in (89) (a), because it cannot be paraphrased by a single word.

No less interesting than prepositional passives are 'double passive' structures such as the following (from Radford (1981), p 137):

(91) (a)   Advantage was taken of John

(b)   John was taken advantage of

(92) (a)   Care was taken of her
     (b)   She was taken care of

(93) (a)   No notice was taken of her
     (b)   She was taken no notice of

(94) (a)   Account was taken of his claim
     (b)   His claim was taken account of

(95) (a)   Note was taken of his credentials
     (b)   His credentials were taken note of

How can we account for the fact that expressions such as *take advantage of* have two passive forms? It may well be that REANALYSIS once more provides us with the answer. That is, we might suggest that in cases like (91), the whole expression *take advantage of* can optionally be treated as some kind of Complex Verb, and that the NP immediately adjacent to this Verb can then passivise just like any other postverbal Complement NP. More specifically, we might assume that an expression like *take advantage of someone* underlyingly has the structure (96)(a) below, but that by optional application of REANALYSIS, it can be converted into the 'Complex Verb' structure (96)(b):

(96) (a)   [$_V$ *take* [$_{NP}$ *advantage*] [$_{PP}$ *of* [$_{NP}$ someone]]]

                === REANALYSIS ===⟹

     (b)   [$_V$ *take advantage of*] [$_{NP}$ someone]

Thus, if REANALYSIS does not apply, the NP *advantage* will be adjacent to the Verb *take*, and hence be eligible to undergo passivisation. But if REANALYSIS does apply, then the NP *someone* will be adjacent to the complex Verb [*take advantage of*], and hence will satisfy the 'adjacency' condition for the application of passivisation. Far from being radically new, the REANALYSIS proposal seems to have been envisaged half a century ago by Jespersen who writes:

> In *I was taken notice of* it will evidently not do to say that I is the Subject of *was taken*, and *notice* the Object of *taken*; but in reality nothing hinders us from saying that *take notice of* is a verbal phrase governing an Object (*me*), which can be made into the Subject if the whole phrase is turned into the passive.
>
> (Jespersen, *Modern English Grammar*, vol. III (1937), **19.7**4)

However, if we argue that expressions such as *take notice of* can undergo optional REANALYSIS (thereby permitting the whole expression to be passivised subsequently), the obvious question to ask is why the REANALYSIS rule can't apply to allow subsequent passivisation in cases such as the following (from Van Riemsdijk and Williams (1986), pp. 147–8):

(97) (a)   *Dinner is [*drunk brandy after*] by Bill

   (b)   *The problem was [*talked to Bill about*] by no-one

   (c)   *President de Gaulle was [*read a book about*]

We might offer the same two answers to this question as we earlier gave in the case of impossible prepositional passives. Thus, if we take the case of (97) (a), we might argue on the one hand that the PP [*after dinner*] is an Adjunct, and we have already suggested that only Complements of a V can undergo REANALYSIS; and on the other hand, we might also maintain that *drink brandy after* does not form a 'natural Predicate' or 'semantic unit', unlike *take advantage of* (so that, for example, English has a single-word Verb *exploit* which means more or less the same as *take advantage of*, but has no single-word counterpart of *drink brandy after*).

An obvious question to ask is: 'At what point in the grammar does REANALYSIS apply?' Although we cannot go into this question in detail at this stage, there are a number of important points to bear in mind. Clearly, if the rule is sensitive to the 'semantic content' of items (only 'semantic units' can be restructured), then it must apply after LEXICALISATION takes place in the Base (i.e. after the insertion of lexical items with semantic content into trees). But since the rule generates structures which serve as input to transformations like NP MOVEMENT (i.e. passivisation), then it must apply *before* transformations such as NP MOVEMENT. Moreover, if (as seems to be the case) the REANALYSIS rule itself never applies to the output of any transformations, then we can go further and claim that REANALYSIS must apply before *any* transformation. One way to ensure this would be to posit that REANALYSIS is a rule which applies in the *Base*, after lexicalisation. At any rate, this is the assumption which we shall make in our subsequent exposition.

Hitherto, we have assumed (for reasons which need not concern us at present) that passivisation is limited to applying to an NP which is immediately adjacent to a (simple or complex) Verb. However, not all NPs which are adjacent to Verbs can be passivised, as we see from the ungrammaticality of the (b) examples below:

(98) (a)   Few children play *football*/[all afternoon]

   (b)   *Football*/[*All afternoon] is played by few children

(99) (a)   Mary performed *the wrong piece*/[the wrong way]

   (b)   *The wrong piece*/[*The wrong way] was performed by Mary

Why can the italicised NP be passivised in such cases, but not the bracketed NP? The obvious answer is that the italicised NP in each case is a Complement, whereas the bracketed NP is an Adjunct: and we might accordingly suppose that passivisation is precluded from applying to Adjunct NPs.

From our discussion in this section, it is tempting to draw the conclusion that all passive structures (i.e. structures containing passive participles) involve NP MOVEMENT. However, traditional grammarians often distinguish two different types of passives: *verbal* and *adjectival*. The structures we have looked at so far in this section have all been instances of *verbal* passives, and all (as we have seen) involve NP MOVEMENT. So what of *adjectival* passives?

These are structures in which a passive participle is used in much the same way as an Adjective would be. For example, the italicised passive participles in (100) below might be argued to be adjectival rather than verbal in character:

(100) (a)   We were *unimpressed* by his efforts
  (b)   John is a *frightened* man
  (c)   He had *sunken* cheek bones
  (d)   He is *depraved* and uncouth
  (e)   I am very *interested* in what you say
  (f)   John seemed *annoyed*

But what tells us that the italicised passive participles in (100) are adjectival rather than verbal in nature? To answer this question, let's look at each example in turn.

Consider first the status of *unimpressed* in (100) (a). What is interesting to note here is that *un-* is a prefix which can be attached to Adjectives, but not generally to Verbs, as we see from (101) below:

(101) (a)   His efforts were *impressive/unimpressive*
  (b)   His efforts *impressed/*unimpressed* us

Hence, it seems plausible to conclude that *unimpressed* must be adjectival rather than verbal in character. In the case of the phrase *a frightened man* in (100) (b), what suggests that *frightened* here is quasi-adjectival in function is the fact that it occupies the typical Adjective position of a prenominal modifier, so that *a frightened man* seems to be structurally parallel to *an unlucky man*. And in (100) (c), the passive participle *sunken* seems restricted to adjectival use, since in purely *verbal* passives we find the alternative form *sunk*: cf.

(102)   An Argentian destroyer has just been *sunk/*sunken* by a British submarine

This underlines the fact that in the case of some irregular Verbs, adjectival and verbal passive participles may be morphologically distinct. Moreover, in (100) (d), the passive participle *depraved* has been coordinated with the Adjective *uncouth*, thus reinforcing our suspicions about the adjectival nature of the passive participle in such cases. And in (100) (e), we find that the passive participle is premodified by the kind of expression (*very*) which can be used to premodify an Adjective, but not a Verb: cf.

(103) (a)   What you say is *very relevant*
     (b)   *What you say *very interests* me

Finally, we see that in (100) (f), the participle *annoyed* occurs as the Complement of a 'copula' Verb (*become, seem, appear, look, sound, remain, stay*, etc.), in a position in which we typically find Adjectival Phrases, but not 'verbal' passive phrases: cf.

(104) (a)   John seems *very angry/very cross*
     (b)   *John seems *given a nasty shock*

Thus, it seems clear that we have abundant empirical evidence for differentiating between *adjectival* and *verbal* passives.

We have already argued in some detail that *verbal passives* involve application of NP MOVEMENT. However, there are equally cogent reasons for supposing that *adjectival passives* by contrast involve no application of any movement rule. In this respect, it is interesting to note the following contrasts:

(105) (a)   *There* is known [$_S$ — to be opposition in Congress to the arms deal]
     (b)   *There* is unknown [$_S$ — to be opposition in Congress to the arms deal]

(106) (a)   *There* was expected [$_S$ — to be a strike]
     (b)   *There* was unexpected [$_S$ — to be a strike]

In the (a) examples in (105) and (106), it is clear (from familiar arguments) that existential *there* originates in the position marked by the elongated dash as the Subject of the existential Predicate *be*, and subsequently undergoes 'long' NP MOVEMENT out of subordinate Clause Subject position into the italicised main Clause Subject position (by 'long' movement we mean movement out of one Clause into another). But in the (b) examples, the same movement is not possible. Why should this be? Well, we've already argued that *un-* is an adjectival (non-verbal) prefix, so that it seems clear that passive participles like *unknown* and *unexpected* must be adjectival in nature. Moreover, since neither of these adjectival passive participles can trigger 'long' NP MOVEMENT, it seems reasonable to conclude that this must be because adjectival passive participles never trigger NP MOVEMENT (although verbal passive participles do). In other words, it seems plausible to conclude from contrasts like those found in (105) and (106) above that only *verbal passives* involve NP MOVEMENT in their derivation (not *adjectival passives*). What this means in more concrete terms is that in an adjectival passive such as:

(107)   *Her reply* was unexpected

the NP [*her reply*] is the sentence Subject at all stages of derivation, and does not originate in postverbal Object position. Thus, (107) is treated in the same way as a purely adjectival structure such as:

(108)   *Her reply* was unusual

and hence does not involve application of NP MOVEMENT.

The bottom line of our discussion is thus that it is important to distinguish between *transformational* passives on the one hand (i.e. *verbal* passives which involve application of NP MOVEMENT), and *non-transformational* (or *lexical* or *base-generated*) passives on the other (i.e. *adjectival* passives which don't involve NP MOVEMENT). For a detailed defence of the distinction between *transformational* and *lexical* passives, see Wasow (1977).

You should now be able to tackle exercises IV and V

8.5   NP MOVEMENT in Raising structures

Thus far, we have argued that the rule of NP MOVEMENT is involved in the derivation of verbal 'passive' sentences. But recall that at the beginning of the chapter, we claimed that NP MOVEMENT also had a role to play in three other types of construction. One of these is the so-called '(Subject) Raising' construction illustrated by sentences such as:

(109)   *John* seems to me [— to be unhappy]

Here we will argue that the italicised NP originates not as the main Clause Subject, but rather as the subordinate Clause Subject, in the position marked —, whence it is subsequently 'raised' to become the main Clause Subject (by a rule earlier known as SUBJECT RAISING, but here called simply NP MOVEMENT). If this analysis is correct, it would mean that the underlying structure of (109) is *similar* (though not identical) to that of:

(110)   It seems to me [that *John* is unhappy]

The two underlying structures are not identical, since the subordinate Clause is nonfinite (or *untensed*) in (109), but finite (or *tensed*) in (110): moreover, whereas the bracketed finite Complement in (110) has the status of an S-bar (since it can be introduced by the Complementiser *that*), the bracketed infinitive Complement in (109) has the status of a 'plain' S (i.e. of an Exceptional Clause), since infinitive Complements of *seem* cannot be introduced by an overt Complementiser, as we see from the ungrammaticality of:

(111) (a) *It seems to me [*for* John to be unhappy]

     (b) *John seems to me [*for* to be unhappy]

Given these assumptions, then (109) *John seems to me to be unhappy* will have the derivation outlined schematically in (112) below:

(112)   [NP e] seems to me [S *John* to be unhappy]

              NP MOVEMENT

More precisely, the 'Subject Raising' analysis presupposes that *John* in (112) originates as the Subject of the bracketed embedded S Complement, and is subsequently 'raised' by application of NP MOVEMENT to become the superficial Subject of the main Clause. An analysis along essentially these lines is rooted in the traditions of descriptive grammar: thus, Poutsma (1928, pp. 150–60) uses the term 'Shifting of Subject' to label the appropriate construction, while Jespersen (1927, pp. 211–14, 1937, pp. 55–7, and 1940, pp. 315–20) refers to it as the 'Split Subject' construction.

One of the claims embodied in the 'Raising' analysis (112) is that *John* is underlyingly the Subject of the infinitive phrase *to be happy*. Let's look first at two arguments which support this claim. We'll begin by looking at one which relates to facts about the interpretation of *Reflexives*. Simplifying somewhat in ways which do not prejudice our conclusions here, we might say that a (non-subject) Reflexive requires a compatible clausemate antecedent. Thus, in a sentence such as:

(113)   John considers [S *Fred* to be too sure of *himself*]

the italicised Reflexive *himself* can only be construed with *Fred*, not with *John*: this follows from our assumption that non-subject Reflexives must have an antecedent within their own S. Notice, however, that in a sentence such as:

(114)   *John* seems to me [S — to have perjured *himself*]

himself must be construed with *John*. But how can we reconcile this with our earlier generalisation that Reflexives require a clausemate antecedent, given that *himself* and *John* are not contained in the same S in (114)?

A 'Subject Raising' analysis of sentences such as (114) gets us out of our dilemma: for, under a 'Raising' analysis in which we posit that *John* originates as the underlying Subject of the *perjured*-clause, Reflexive interpretation facts would present no real problems for us. We might then posit that the relevant condition on non-subject Reflexives is that:

(115)   A Reflexive can be construed with a compatible sometime clause-mate NP (i.e. with an NP which is contained in the same S as the Reflexive at some stage of derivation, and which is compatible with it in Person, Number, Gender, etc.)

Under the 'Subject Raising' analysis, (114) would have derived from a D-structure along the lines of:

(116)   [$_{NP}$ e] seems to me [$_S$ *John* to have perjured *himself*]

and since *John* is contained within the same S as the Reflexive *himself* in the D-structure (116), the 'sometime clausemate' condition in (115) would correctly predict that *John* can be interpreted as the antecedent of the Reflexive *himself* in (114) *John seems to me to have perjured himself*. Moreover, the 'sometime clausemate' condition also correctly predicts that *himself* can be construed with *John* in sentences such as:

(117)   *John* seems to *himself* [$_S$ — to be invincible]

since although *John* and *himself* are not clausemates at D-structure (where *John* occupies the position marked by — and hence functions as Subject of the embedded S Complement), they become clausemates at S-structure, as a result of the application of NP MOVEMENT (moving *John* from subordinate Clause Subject to main Clause Subject position).

There is, however, one way in which we might seek to subvert the Reflexive argument, and hence reject the 'Raising' analysis. Suppose we argue instead that sentence (114) *John seems to me to have perjured himself* doesn't actually contain two Clauses at all, but rather consists of a single-clause structure in which *seems* functions as some kind of *quasi-auxiliary*, which doesn't take an S Complement, but rather some kind of non-clausal Complement comprising the infinitive particle *to* and the VP [*have perjured himself*]. We could then argue that *John* is in the same S as *himself* at S-structure, so we don't need any abstract underlying structure to explain the facts about Reflexive interpretation in such sentences.

However, the 'single-clause' analysis turns out to be fatally flawed. For, if (114) does indeed really contain only one S, then not only are *John* and the Reflexive in the same Clause, but so too are *me* and the Reflexive; in which case, we'd expect to find that *me* could serve as the antecedent for an appropriate Reflexive within the embedded VP, in a sentence such as:

(118)   *John seems to *me* [to have deceived *myself*]

But this is not the case at all: *myself* cannot be construed with *me* here, and since there is no alternative antecedent for *myself* in the sentence, *myself* is uninterpretable, as is the sentence containing it. Why cannot *myself* be construed with *me* in (118)? The most obvious answer is that *myself* and *me* are in different Clauses: i.e. *me* is part of the *seems*-clause and *myself* is part of the *deceived*-clause. But if this is so, then sentences like (114) must have a two-clause structure – i.e. *John* cannot be in the same Clause as *himself* in the S-structure of (114). But if *John* is not in the same Clause as *himself* in (114), how can it be that *himself* is construed with *John*, bearing in mind that Reflexives generally require a *sometime clausemate antecedent*? The NP MOVEMENT analysis offers a simple answer to this question, as we have already seen.

Having looked at the *Reflexive* argument in some detail, let's look more briefly at a second argument which supports the claim that the superficial Subject of the *seem-to-VP* construction represents the underlying Subject of the infinitive (*to-VP*) Complement. This argument relates to *Agreement* facts. Generally speaking, a *Predicate Nominal* (that is, an NP used as the Complement of a *copula* verb like *be*) agrees in number with the Subject of its own Clause. Thus in:

(119)   They consider [$_S$ *John* to be *a fool/*fools*]

the Predicate Nominal (*a fool/fools*) agrees with the Subject *John* of its own S (the *be*-clause), not with the Subject *they* of the main Clause. In the light of this observation, consider Number Agreement in a sentence like:

(120)   *They* seem to me [$_S$ — to be *fools/*a fool*]

Here, the Predicate Nominal *fools* agrees with the italicised NP *they*, in spite of the fact that (as we argued earlier) the two are contained in different Clauses at S-structure. How can this be? Under the NP MOVEMENT analysis of *seem* structures, sentences like (120) pose no problem; if we suppose that *they* originates in the — position as the subordinate Clause Subject, then we can say that the Predicate Nominal agrees with the *underlying* Subject of its Clause. How does *they* get from its underlying position as subordinate Clause Subject to its superficial position as main Clause Subject? By NP MOVEMENT, of course!

So far, what we have argued is that sentences such a (109) *John seems to me to be unhappy*, involve a two-clause structure in which *seem* takes an

S-complement whose D-structure Subject is *John*. This might at first sight seem to provide conclusive evidence in support of a 'Subject Raising' analysis of *seem* structures. But if you think about it carefully, the arguments we have put forward so far would be equally compatible with an alternative analysis of such sentences as involving embedded infinitival S-bar complements with a PRO subject which is coreferential to the main Clause subject. In this connection, recall that we argued in previous chapters that sentences such as:

(121)   I am anxious to finish the assignment

have an S-structure along the lines of (122) below:

(122)   I am anxious [C PRO to finish the assignment]

where C is an empty Complementiser, and PRO is an empty pronominal NP Subject which is *controlled by* (i.e. which refers back to) the main Clause Subject *I*, so that (122) has much the same interpretation as:

(123)   I am anxious that I should finish the assignment

Predicates like *anxious* which take an infinitival Complement with a PRO subject controlled by some NP in the containing Clause are referred to as *Control Predicates*. The obvious question to ask, therefore, is why we couldn't analyse *seem* as a *Control Predicate*, and hence maintain that a sentence such as:

(124)   John seems to me to be a traitor to himself

has a D-structure along the lines of:

(125)   John seems to me [C PRO to be a traitor to himself]

where PRO is controlled by *John*. For notice that a 'Control' analysis of sentences such as (124) would account just as well as a 'Raising' analysis for the fact that the Predicate Nominal *traitor* is singular (because it agrees with PRO), or the fact that *himself* can be interpreted as referring back to *John* (because *himself* refers back to PRO, which is controlled by *John*, so that indirectly *himself* refers back to *John*). So why analyse *seem* as a 'Raising' Predicate rather than a 'Control' Predicate?

A very simple theory-internal argument against a 'Control' analysis can be formulated as follows. We argued in Chapter 6 that PRO can occur only as the Subject of an S-bar Complement (as in (122) above), not as the Subject of an S Complement – hence the ill-formedness of:

(126)   *John considers [S PRO to be intelligent]

Given that we have already argued in relation to sentences like (109) above that the infinitival Complement of *seem* has the status of S (*not* S-bar), it would follow from this that since PRO can only occur as the Subject of S-bar and not as the Subject of S, the infinitival Complement of *seem* cannot contain a PRO Subject. An obvious question to ask is whether we can find any independent empirical evidence corroborating our theory-internal reasons for supporting the 'Raising' analysis of *seem* structures over the 'Control' analysis. One such piece of evidence comes from *Pleonastic Pronouns*, such as existential *there*. An inherent characteristic of pleonastic *there* is that it has no reference, and so cannot have its reference questioned – hence the oddity of Speaker B's question in (127) below:

(127) SPEAKER A: There's someone at the door
       SPEAKER B: *Where's someone at the door?

Because it has no reference, pleonastic *there* cannot serve as the controller of PRO, whereas referential Pronouns like *you* can indeed serve as proper antecedents for PRO: cf. the contrast in:

(128) (a) *You* can't be kind without [PRO being cruel first]
      (b) **There* can't be peace without [PRO being war first]

A second relevant property of existential *there* is that it can only occur as the Subject of a class of 'existential' Predicates such as *exist, be, occur, arise, take place*, etc., as in:

(129) There *was/arose/occurred* an unfortunate incident

and not as a Subject or Complement of other Predicates: cf.

(130) (a) *I don't want to talk about *there*
      (b) **There* hurt me
      (c) *John gave *there* to Mary

In the light of these twin observations that pleonastic *there* is non-referential, and occurs only as the Subject of 'existential' Predicates, consider sentences such as the following:

(131) *There* seems to have been/*seen an accident

Under a 'Control' analysis, (131) would have the structure:

(132) *There* seems [PRO to have been/*seen an accident]

But a 'Control' structure such as (132) seems wrong, for three reasons. First, we have already seen in relation to (127) and (128) above that existential *there* is non-referential and cannot therefore function as the controller of PRO.

Secondly, the structure (132) violates the condition that pleonastic *there* can only function as the Subject of an *existential* Predicate, since it functions as the Subject of *seem* in (132), and we can hardly claim that *seem* is a 'Verb of existence'. Thirdly, (132) provides us with no basis for accounting for the fact that (131) is grammatical if the head V of the embedded VP is *been*, but not if it is *seen*. So, all in all, a 'Control' analysis of sentences such as (131) is thoroughly unsatisfactory.

But what about a 'Subject Raising' analysis? Under such an analysis, (131) would derive from an underlying structure in which *there* originates as the Subject of the embedded S, and is subsequently 'raised' to become the main Clause Subject by application of NP MOVEMENT, in the manner schematised in (133) below:

(133)   [NP e] seems [S *there* to have been/*seen an accident]

           NP MOVEMENT

(cf. '*It seems that there has been/*seen an accident.*') The 'Raising' analysis solves all three problems that beset the 'Control' analysis. There is no problem about having to posit that *there* controls PRO, since (133) is not a Control structure. Secondly, *there* satisfies the condition that it occurs as the Subject of an existence Predicate (*been*) in the underlying structure (though not in the S-structure, so that we might suppose that the relevant restriction must be met at some level of structure, though not necessarily S-structure). And thirdly, the contrast between *been* and *seen* in (131) can be accounted for by the fact that *been* is a Verb of existence, whereas *seen* is not (and recall that pleonastic *there* must occur as the Subject of an existential Predicate). So, on all three counts, the 'Raising' analysis proves vastly superior to the 'Control' analysis. Moreover, further empirical support for the proposed analysis comes from the fact that typical 'Control' Predicates like *anxious* simply don't allow pleonastic *there* as their subject: cf.

(134)   *There* is anxious to be an accident

Yet another argument which supports a 'Raising' analysis of *seem* structures over a 'Control' analysis is our familiar 'idiom chunk' argument. Recall that in Chapter 6, we noted that English has a class of *Subject Idiom Chunks*: cat-lovers will be pleased to note that many of these are feline: cf.

(135) (a)   *The cat* is out of the bag
    (b)   *The cat* has got his tongue
    (c)   *The fur* will fly

Transformations

These are *Subject Idiom Chunks* in the sense that *the cat* in its idiomatic sense of 'the secret' is restricted to occurring as the Subject of *be out of the bag*. In the light of this restriction, consider:

(136)   *The cat* seems [$_S$ — to be out of the bag]

Given that *the cat* has its idiomatic sense of 'the secret' here, and given that in this sense it can occur only as the Subject of *be out of the bag*, then it seems plausible to argue that *the cat* in (136) must originate as the underlying Subject of *to be out of the bag* and subsequently be raised up to become the main Clause Subject, in the manner indicated schematically in (137) below:

(137)   [$_{NP}$ e]   seems   [$_S$ *the cat* to be out of the bag]
           └─NP MOVEMENT ─┘

(cf. '*It seems that the cat is out of the bag.*') Additional support for the 'Raising' analysis comes from the fact that typical 'Control' predicates like *anxious* do not allow *Idiom Chunk Subjects*: cf.

(138)   **The cat* is anxious [C PRO to be out of the bag]

(C here is an empty Complementiser, and PRO an empty NP subject.) This is scarcely surprising since a Control structure such as (138) would require [*the cat*] to originate as the Subject of *anxious*, in violation of the restriction that (in its idiomatic sense) [*the cat*] occurs only as the subject of *be out of the bag* (cf. the ill-formedness of *'*The cat is anxious that it should be out of the bag*' on the idiomatic reading). Of course, in a non-idiomatic use, the NP [*the cat*] can indeed function as the Subject of anxious: cf.

(139)   *The cat* is anxious [C PRO to go outside]

Although the arguments given above are *syntactic* in nature, there are also a number of *semantic* properties which differentiate 'Raising' from 'Control' Predicates. For example, 'Raising' Predicates preserve truth-functional equivalence under passivisation, so that (140) (a) below is cognitively synonymous with (140) (b):

(140) (a)   The doctor *seems* to have examined John
      (b) = John *seems* to have been examined by the doctor

By contrast, 'Control' predicates do not preserve truth-functional equivalence under passivisation, so that (141) (a) below is not synonymous with (141) (b):

(141) (a)   The doctor is *anxious* to examine John
      (b) ≠ John is *anxious* to be examined by the doctor

Conversely, 'Control' Predicates assign a theta-role to and hence impose selection restrictions on their superficial Subjects: thus in (142) below, *anxious* assigns the theta-role EXPERIENCER to its Subject (designating the entity that experiences anxiety), and selectionally constrains the choice of Subject, allowing a *rational* (i.e. mind-possessing) NP such as *John*, but not an inanimate NP such as *the weather*:

(142)   *John/!the weather* is anxious to change

By contrast, a typical 'Raising' predicate like *seem* assigns no theta-role to its Subject (as we argued in Chapter 7), and hence does not selectionally constrain the choice of Subject either: cf.

(143)   *John/the weather* seems to have changed

Hence, 'Raising' and 'Control' Predicates are both syntactically and semantically distinct.

A variety of other arguments might be given in support of the distinction drawn here between 'Raising' and 'Control' Predicates (cf., for example, Postal (1974), pp. 33–9). But instead of cataloguing further arguments in support of a 'Raising' analysis for subjectless infinitive Complements of Predicates like *seem*, let's turn instead to consider some of the general properties of NP MOVEMENT as it operates in 'Raising' structures. One point to note is that there are only a relatively small class of 'Raising' Predicates: the following examples (from Postal (1974), p. 293) are representative:

(144) (a)   There is *about* to be a fight in the kitchen
      (b)   There is *apt* to be cholera in Turkey
      (c)   There is *bound* to be a riot in Dacca
      (d)   There is *liable* to be some trouble
      (e)   There is *going* to be trouble in Indiana
      (f)   There is (all) *set* to be a meeting at Bob's house
      (g)   There *chanced* to be a deathray in his pocket
      (h)   There *grew* to be opposition to the foam programme
      (i)   There *proved* to be toxins in the soap
      (j)   There *threatens* to be a famine in Bulgaria
      (k)   There *had better* not be any flaws in your argument

The fact that the italicised Predicates in (144) permit a non-referential Subject like existential *there* points to their status as 'Raising' rather that 'Control' predicates.

Recall that we noted earlier in relation to 'passive' structures that NP MOVEMENT can move not only the Subject of an S Complement, but also the Subject

443

of an SC (= Small Clause) Complement. Hence, we might ask whether there are any cases of 'Raising' out of Small Clause Complements. Bearing in mind that *seem* is a 'Raising' Predicate, it seems plausible to analyse sentences such as:

(145)   *Mary* seems [$_{SC}$ — keen on Bill]

as involving a 'Raising' derivation in which *Mary* originates in the position marked — as the Subject of the bracketed Small Clause Complement, and subsequently gets moved into main Clause Subject position by NP MOVEMENT. The grammaticality of sentences such as:

(146) (a)   *There* seems [$_{SC}$ — likely [$_S$ — to be a strike]]
    (b)   *The fur* seems [$_{SC}$ — likely [$_S$ — to fly]]

further supports the claim that 'Raising' is possible both out of S and SC complements. Thus, given our earlier arguments, existential *there* must originate as the Subject of *be* in (146) (a), and then be raised out of its containing S by NP MOVEMENT to become Subject of *likely*, whence it is raised out of its containing SC by NP MOVEMENT once more to become Subject of *seems*. And likewise, since *the fur* in its idiomatic sense is used only as the Subject of *fly*, it follows that it must originate as the underlying Subject of *fly* in (146) (b), and then be raised up to become first the Subject of the Small Clause headed by *likely*, and then the Subject of the *seems* Clause. But while the Subject of an S or SC Complement can be 'raised' by NP MOVEMENT, the rule cannot apply to 'raise' the Subject of an S-bar Complement, as the following example from Bresnan (1979, p. 123) illustrates:

(147) (a)   It is impossible [$_{S'}$ for *John* to have done that]
    (b)   **John* is impossible [$_{S'}$ for — to have done that]

The fact that exactly parallel restrictions hold in the case of 'passivisation' (as shown by our earlier examples (69–73)) strengthens the claim made here that 'Raising' and 'Passivisation' are two different manifestations of one and the same rule — namely the rule of NP MOVEMENT.

The interconnection between 'Passive' and 'Raising' becomes even more intimate if we accept the claim by Stowell (1981) and Burzio (1986) that both 'Passive' and 'Raising' are involved in the derivation of typical *be* passives. The fundamental assumption behind this analysis is that *be* is a 'Raising' Predicate. Thus, Burzio claims that in a sentence such as:

(148)   There is [$_{SC}$ *someone* at the door]

be takes a (bracketed) Small Clause Complement; he further claims that in the related structure:

(149)   *Someone* is [$_{SC}$ — at the door]

the italicised subject of the bracketed Small Clause Complement has undergone 'Raising' out of subordinate Clause Subject position into main Clause Subject position. If the 'Raising' analysis of *be* is extended to 'passive' uses of *be* (as Burzio proposes), then a typical *be* passive such as:

(150)   Nobody will be arrested

would have the simplified derivation outlined in (151) below:

(151) (a)   [$_{NP}$ e] will be [$_{SC}$ [$_{NP}$ e] arrested *nobody*]

                                           ┌NP MOVEMENT┘

(b)   [$_{NP}$ e] will be [$_{SC}$ [$_{NP}$ *nobody*] arrested —]

                         ┌—NP MOVEMENT┘

(c)   [$_{NP}$ *Nobody*] will be [$_{SC}$ — arrested —]

Thus, *nobody* would originate as the D-structure Object of *arrested* in (151) (a), and would then be 'passivised' so as to become the Subject of the bracketed Small Clause in (151) (b), whence it would subsequently be 'raised' to become the Main Clause Subject in the resultant S-structure (151) (c). Thus, under Burzio's analysis, *be* passives involve both 'Passive' and 'Raising' (i.e. involve a double application of NP MOVEMENT).

Some support for this analysis comes from the fact that 'Passive' can apply alone without subsequent application of 'Raising', resulting in structures such as:

(152)   There will be [$_{SC}$ *nobody* arrested —]

Moreover, 'Passive' can operate independently of *be*, as is shown by examples such as the following, where 'passivisation' takes place within the bracketed Complement in each case, in the absence of *be*:

(153) (a)   They got [*John* thrown into jail]

(b)   I need [*my toe* looking at by an experienced chiropodist] (Radford (1978), p. 45)

(c)   We could do with [*our burglar-alarm* checking over by someone] (Radford (1978), p. 46)

In each of these examples, the italicised 'passivised' subordinate Clause Subject can undergo subsequent 'Raising' if the main Clause Subject position is left empty, thereby deriving:

(154) (a)   *John* got [— thrown into jail]

    (b)   *My toe* needs [— looking at by an experienced chiropodist]

    (c)   *Our burglar-alarm* could do with [— checking over by someone]

While the analysis of passive *be* as a full Verb triggering 'Raising' seems preferable to an analysis of *be* as a 'Specifier' of VP, for the sake of simplicity of exposition, we shall largely ignore the role of *be* in passives in subsequent discussion.

8.6   NP MOVEMENT in ergative and middle structures

We remarked at the beginning of this chapter that NP MOVEMENT has been claimed to be involved in the derivation not only of 'Passive' and 'Raising' structures, but also of 'Ergative' structures. To illustrate what is meant by an 'Ergative' structure, consider the following set of examples:

(155) (a)   John broke *the door*

    (b)   *The door* broke

(156) (a)   John might drown *the kittens*

    (b)   *The kittens* might drown

(157) (a)   The artillery will sink *the ship*

    (b)   *The ship* will sink

(158) (a)   John rolled *the ball* down the hill

    (b)   *The ball* rolled down the hill

Following the terminology adopted in Chapter 7 (after Burzio (1986), p. 30), we might say that the (a) member of each of these pairs is a *transitive* structure, and the (b) member an *ergative* structure. In Burzio's use of the term, an *ergative* Clause is an intransitive Clause which has a transitive counterpart in which the transitive Object corresponds to the ergative Subject.

One way in which we might handle the relationship between transitive Objects and ergative Subjects is to follow Burzio (1986) in positing that the superficial Subject in ergative structures originates as the underlying Object of a transitive structure with an empty NP Subject, and that the underlying Object is moved into superficial Subject position by NP MOVEMENT. Given such an analysis, a sentence such as (156) (b) *The kittens might drown* would have the following schematic derivation:

(159)   [NP e] might drown *the kittens*

            └— NP MOVEMENT —┘

Such an analysis would provide a natural way of accounting for the fact that (inter alia) transitive Objects and their ergative Subject counterparts are assigned the same theta-roles, and hence are subject to the same Selection Restrictions. For example, in (160) below:

(160) (a)   John might drown *the kittens/his wife/??his goldfish/?!his frying-pan/!his birth*

(b)   *The kittens/his wife/??his goldfish/?!his frying-pan/!his birth* might drown

the italicised transitive Object in (160) (a) has the same theta role (= that of THEME or PATIENT (i.e. victim!) of *drown*) as the italicised ergative Subject in (160) (b), and accordingly is subject to the same Selection Restrictions. We might suppose that this is because in both cases the italicised NP originates in postverbal position as the Direct Object of *drown* (in accordance with our generalisation in Chapter 7 that THEME Arguments of Verbs are generally assigned Object NP status). Thus, it may well be that NP MOVEMENT is involved in the derivation of 'Ergative' structures, as well as in 'Passive' and 'Raising' structures.

A final construction type which may involve NP MOVEMENT is the so-called MIDDLE construction illustrated by sentences such as the following (from Keyser and Roeper (1984), p. 383):

(161) (a)   *Greek* translates easily
(b)   *The baggage* transfers efficiently
(c)   *Messages* transmit rapidly by satellite
(d)   *The letters* transpose easily
(e)   *The boxes* will not transport easily

In each case, it might be argued that the italicised NP originates in postverbal Object position and is subsequently preposed into preverbal Subject position by NP MOVEMENT. For a detailed discussion of the syntax of the middle construction (and how it differs from the ergative construction), see Keyser and Roeper (1984).

It should perhaps be noted, however, that the arguments in favour of an NP MOVEMENT analysis of *Ergative* and *Middle* structures are not as compelling as in the case of *Passive* and *Raising* structures: for example, although we find instances of 'long' NP MOVEMENT (i.e. movement of an NP out of one Clause into another) in 'Passive' and 'Raising' structures, there are no such instances of 'long' movement in 'Ergative' or 'Middle' structures – a fact which casts some doubt on the claim that they involve NP MOVEMENT.

You should now be able to tackle exercises VI and VII

8.7 EXTRAPOSITION

At this point, it may be useful to remind ourselves of the three Movement Transformations we have posited so far, and how they operate: this information is summarised in (162) below:

(162) (i)   V MOVEMENT (moves V out of VP into an empty finite I)

    (ii)   I MOVEMENT (moves an I containing an Auxiliary into an empty C)

    (iii)   NP MOVEMENT (moves an NP into an empty NP position)

All three rules have in common the fact that they move a constituent from one position into an existing empty position elsewhere in the sentence: such rules are known as *substitution* rules, because they substitute an empty constituent by a filled one. The obvious question to ask is whether all Movement Transformations are *substitutions*, or whether there are also other kinds of movement rules.

In most recent work, it is assumed that in addition to *substitution*, there is a second kind of movement known as *adjunction*. We shall illustrate this by looking briefly at just one *adjunction rule*, known in the relevant literature as EXTRAPOSITION (FROM NP). Although this rule is subject to certain restrictions of a poorly understood nature, we can say that in general it applies to move a PP or S-bar contained within an NP (i.e. an *adnominal* PP or S-bar) to the end of the S containing it. For example, it can move a PP Complement such as that italicised in (163) below out of the bracketed containing NP to the end of the whole S:

(163) (a)   [A review *of my latest book*] has just appeared

    (b)   [A review —] has just appeared *of my latest book*

Likewise, it can move a PP Adjunct such as that italicised in (164) out of the containing bracketed NP to the end of the S:

(164) (a)   [A gruesome figure *with jowelled cheeks*] answered the door

    (b)   [A gruesome figure —] answered the door *with jowelled cheeks*

The same rule can also 'extrapose' an S-bar Complement such as that italicised in (165) below, moving it out of the containing bracketed NP, to the end of the whole S:

(165) (a)   [A rumour *that he is ill*] has been circulating

     (b)   [A rumour —] has been circulating *that he is ill*

Moreover a clausal Adjunct (e.g. a Restrictive Relative Clause) can be extraposed out of its containing NP in a similar fashion, as we see from:

(166) (a)   [A snag *that I hadn't foreseen*] emerged later

     (b)   [A snag —] emerged later *that I hadn't foreseen*

The operation of our proposed EXTRAPOSITION rule in a case like (163) can be represented in simplified form as in (167) below:

(167)   [$_S$ [$_{NP}$ A review [$_{PP}$ *of my latest book*]] has just appeared]

                              └───── EXTRAPOSITION ─────┘

It seems clear that extraposed constituents are moved to the end of S rather than S-bar because EXTRAPOSITION is possible within an 'Exceptional Clause' (which has the status of S) such as that bracketed in (168) below:

(168) (a)   The Press reported [several attacks *on the besieged city* to have been mounted], in a recent despatch

     (b)   The Press reported [several attacks — to have been mounted *on the besieged city*], in a recent despatch

The obvious question to ask is what evidence there is in support of the EXTRAPOSITION analysis: and in particular, what evidence there is that the extraposed italicised PP or S' in the (b) sentences in (163–66) above originate within the bracketed NP in the position they occupy in the corresponding (a) sentences. One such piece of evidence can be formulated in relation to *subcategorisation* facts. As (169) below illustrates, different nominals require (i.e. subcategorise) PP complements headed by different Prepositions:

(169) (a)   A mass ESCAPE *from/*by/*with Alcatraz* has taken place

     (b)   An unprecedented ATTACK *on/*against/*at/*to the Press* was launched by the President

     (c)   A BAN *on/*at/*to foreign imports* has just been announced

     (d)   Numerous CHANGES *to/*at/*by the fuselage* will be required

Significantly, exactly the same restrictions hold for the corresponding extraposed counterparts: cf.

(170) (a)   A mass ESCAPE has taken place *from/*by/*with Alcatraz*

     (b)   An unprecedented ATTACK was launched by the President *on/ *against/*at/*to the Press*

(c)   A BAN has just been announced *on/*at/*to foreign imports*

(d)   *Numerous* CHANGES will be required *to/*at/*by the fuselage*

Given the postulate (defended in Chapter 7) that subcategorisation restrictions hold between a Head and its sister constituents, it is clear that the italicised PP must in each case originate as a sister Complement of the capitalised NOUN, within an NP headed by the Noun in question.

A second argument in support of the EXTRAPOSITION analysis is the familiar 'gap' argument. If (as we claim here) the italicised PP in sentences like (170) has indeed been moved out its underlying containing Subject NP, then we should expect to find a 'gap' after the capitalised head Noun of the NP, which cannot be filled by another PP. And sure enough, this is indeed the case, as we see from the ungrammaticality of sentences such as:

(171) (a)   *A REVIEW *of my latest book* has just appeared [of a new manual on Practical Pornolexicography]

(b)   *An unprecedented ATTACK *on the Press* was launched by the President [on the civil rights campaign]

(c)   *A BAN *on foreign imports* has just been announced [on Japanese cars]

(d)   *Numerous CHANGES *to the plane* will be required [to our marketing policy]

Under the EXTRAPOSITION analysis, the ungrammaticality of these sentences is simple to account for, since both the italicised PP and the bracketed PP would have originated as sister Complements of the capitalised head Noun, in violation of the subcategorisation restriction that the Nouns in question permit only one PP Complement of the relevant type.

Numerous other arguments parallel to those given earlier could be developed in support of positing the proposed EXTRAPOSITION rule. What is of more immediate interest to us here, however, is the operation of the rule – and more particularly, its *landing-site* (i.e. the question of where exactly extraposed constituents get moved to). It seems implausible to claim that EXTRAPOSITION could be a *substitution* rule which moves an adnominal PP or S-bar into a position normally occupied by some other constituent (e.g. in the way that I MOVEMENT moves an Auxiliary into a C position which would normally be held by a Complementiser). This is because there seems to be no obvious Clause-final constituent in English which could serve as a convenient landing-site for extraposed constituents. Hence, it seems more plausible to claim that EXTRAPOSITION is an adjunction rule. But what exactly is an *adjunction rule*? The effect of adjoining one constituent A to another constituent B can be represented schematically as in (172) below:

(172) (a)

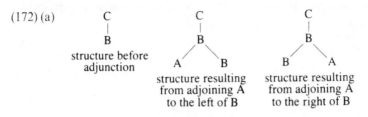

But if EXTRAPOSITION involves adjunction, then what is the constituent to which the extraposed phrase is adjoined?

Sentences such as the following (to be read without pauses):

(173) (a)   A review will appear in the *TLS* shortly *of my latest book*

(b)   *A review will appear *of my latest book* in the *TLS* shortly

(c)   *A review will appear in the *TLS* *of my latest book* shortly

suggest that the extraposed constituent must follow all the constituents of VP (including Adjunct Phrases). Thus, it would seem likely that extraposed constituents are adjoined either to VP, or to S. But to which? Adapting slightly a proposal made in Baltin (1981), let us suppose that a constituent extraposed from an Object NP contained within a VP is attached to the containing VP, whereas a constituent extraposed from a subject NP is attached to the containing S. Since VP is the first 'major constituent' dominating an Object NP, and since S is the first 'major constituent' dominating a Subject NP, this amounts to the principle that:

(174)   An extraposed PP or S-bar is adjoined to the first major (i.e. phrasal or clausal, XP or S) constituent containing the NP out of which it is extraposed

But what evidence is there in favour of this proposal?

Let's consider first the case of EXTRAPOSITION out of an Object NP: this is illustrated by the following examples (adapted from Baltin (1981), p. 267):

(175) (a)   John will call [people *who are from Boston*] up

(b)   John will call [people —] up *who are from Boston*

(176) (a)   John will call [people *from Boston*] up

(b)   John will call [people —] up *from Boston*

(example (176) (b) here is to be understood on the interpretation on which it is synonymous with (175) (b) and hence *from Boston* is an Adjunct of the Noun *people*, and not on the alternative interpretation where it is an Adjunct of the

451

Verb *calls*). On the assumption that material extraposed from an Object NP will be adjoined to VP, then (175)(b) will have the derived structure (177) below (suppressing S-bar, for ease of exposition):

(177)
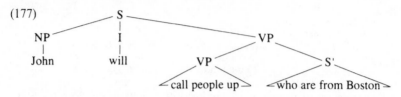

Such an analysis correctly predicts that the whole sequence [*call people up who are from Boston*] is a VP, and hence can undergo Preposing in an appropriate discourse setting: cf. Baltin's examples (1981, p. 269):

(178) (a)   John said that he would call people up who are from Boston, and [*call people up who are from Boston*] he will —

(b)   [*Call people up who are from Boston*] though he may —, he's generally pretty cheap about long-distance calls

By contrast, Extraposition off a Subject NP, as in:

(179) (a)   [Nobody *who knew him*] would ride with Fred

(b)   [Nobody —] would ride with Fred *who knew him*

will result in a derived structure for (179) (b) in which the italicised extraposed Relative Clause is adjoined to S, as in (180) below:

(180)
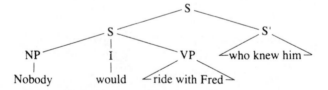

This analysis specifies that the sequence [*ride with Fred*] is a VP constituent, whereas the sequence [*ride with Fred who knew him*] is not a constituent at all. This prediction appears to be correct, since the VP [*ride with Fred*] can be preposed, but not the sequence [*ride with Fred who knew him*]: cf.

(181) (a)   [*Ride with Fred*] nobody would — who knew him

(b)   *[*Ride with Fred who knew him*] nobody would —

Likewise, the analysis correctly predicts that the VP [*ride with Fred*] can undergo VP Ellipsis: cf.

(182)   Although lots of people want to ride with Fred, nobody would [VP e] who knew him

A further prediction which the proposed analysis makes is that if EXTRA-
POSITION applies to move material both out of a Subject NP and out of an
Object NP in the same S, then (because material extraposed from an Object is
adjoined to VP whereas material extraposed from a Subject is adjoined to S,
and because VP is contained within S) the Object-extraposed phrase will precede the Subject-extraposed phrase. And as (183) below indicates, this prediction is indeed correct:

(183) (a)   [Nobody *who had any sense*] would call [a girl from Boston] up
      (b)   = [Nobody —] would call [a girl —] up *from Boston who had any
            sense*
      (c)   ≠ [Nobody —] would call [a girl —] up *who had any sense from Bos-
            ton*

(These sentences are to be understood on the interpretation on which *who had
any sense* modifies *nobody*, and *from Boston* modifies *girl*.) So, it seems that
there is considerable empirical support for the claim that material extraposed
off a Subject NP is adjoined to S, whereas material extraposed off an Object
NP is adjoined to VP.

Before leaving our EXTRAPOSITION rule, we will comment on three factors
relating to its operation. One point worthy of note is that the rule is *recursive*:
this is so because adjunction by its very nature is a recursive operation, i.e. one
which can be repeated indefinitely. That is, a rule adjoining A to B will create a
new B node to which another A can be adjoined by reapplication of the same
rule. Hence, we might expect to find that more than one constituent contained
within an NP can be extraposed. And (184) below suggests that this is indeed
possible:

(184) (a)   A snag [*with the plan*] [*which I didn't anticipate*] has emerged
      (b)   A snag [*with the plan*] has emerged [*which I didn't anticipate*]
      (c)   A snag has emerged [*with the plan*] [*which I didn't anticipate*]

Thus, in (184) both the bracketed PP and the bracketed S-bar can be extraposed, by two separate applications of our EXTRAPOSITION rule.

A second remark which we shall make about the rule is that although all the
examples we have looked at here involve Extraposition of a PP or S-bar out of
a containing NP, it may be that the rule is not restricted to extraposing material out of NPs, but can also remove material out of other types of phrasal constituent. For example, Baltin (1981, p. 262) cites the following examples in
support of his claim that the rule can extrapose an S-bar or PP from a containing Adjectival Phrase:

(185) (a)   [$_{AP}$ How certain *that the Mets will win*] are you?

(b)   [$_{AP}$ How certain —] are you *that the Mets will win*?

(186) (a)   [$_{AP}$ How fond *of Sally*] are you?

(b)   [$_{AP}$ How fond —] are you *of Sally*?

Moreover Baltin (1981, p. 263) adduces the following examples to show that EXTRAPOSITION can also remove material from Verb Phrases:

(187) (a)   [$_{VP}$ Suspect *that Fred killed his mother*] though I may, I'll never be able to prove it

(b)   [$_{VP}$ Suspect —] though I may *that Fred killed his mother*, I'll never be able to prove it

(188) (a)   [$_{VP}$ Talk to Fred *about Sally*] though I may, he is still blind about her

(b)   [$_{VP}$ Talk to Fred —] though I may *about Sally*, he is still blind about her

Moreover, what makes the similarities even more striking is the fact that the rule operating to remove the PP [*about Sally*] in (188) can apply recursively to remove the second PP [*to Fred*] as well, as we see from the grammaticality of (189) below:

(189)   [$_{VP}$ Talk — —] though I may [*to Fred*] [*about Sally*], he is still blind about her

If these observations are correct, then it would appear that EXTRAPOSITION can move a PP or S-bar out of any containing constituent, and not just out of NP. Baltin refers to his proposed generalised Extraposition rule as DETACHMENT (though we shall continue to refer to it by the traditional name of EXTRAPOSITION).

One final remark which we shall make about EXTRAPOSITION is the following. Although all the EXTRAPOSITION examples which we have looked at above involve movement of the extraposed constituent out of its containing Phrase with subsequent adjunction to VP or S, it seems plausible to suppose that EXTRAPOSITION may also apply in a more strictly 'local' fashion, and simply adjoin the extraposed constituent to the righthand end of the Phrase containing it. Thus, consider sentences such as the following:

(190) (a)   [The unsympathetic treatment IN THE PRESS LAST WEEK *of the Irangate scandal*] was predictable

(b)   [The allegations IN THE PRESS LAST WEEK *that the President had engineered a cover-up*] were predictable

Given standard arguments, it is clear that the italicised Phrase in (190) (a) is a Complement of the head Noun *treatment*, and that the italicised Clause in (190) (b) is the Complement of the head Noun *allegations*; likewise, it is equally clear that the capitalised Phrases in both examples are Adjuncts. But given the 'no crossing branches' constraint, we would surely expect that the Complement will come closer to its head Noun than the Adjunct Phrase, wouldn't we? Quite right! (And to think I thought you were falling asleep . . .) So what's gone wrong with our grammar here?

Well, nothing at all. Now, suppose we posit that just as EXTRAPOSITION can adjoin Complement PP or S-bar constituents to VP or S, so too it can also adjoin them to the NP immediately containing them. If this is so, then the bracketed NP in (190) (a) above would have the simplified derived structure indicated in (191) below:

(191)

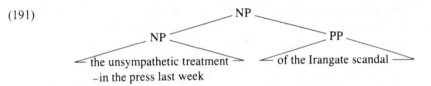

Thus, the PP [*of the Irangate scandal*] would have been moved out of the normal 'Complement' position marked — in (191) and adjoined to the right of the lower NP, thereby 'reversing' the normal 'Complement + Adjunct' order. So, it seems as if EXTRAPOSITION provides us with a very simple way of handling apparent counterexamples to the 'no crossing branches' constraint. Moreover, the assumption that an extraposed PP (etc.) can be adjoined to its containing NP opens up the possibility that EXTRAPOSITION of a PP out of a containing NP to be adjoined to a VP or S may apply in two 'steps', with adjunction first to the containing NP, and then to the VP or S containing the NP out of which the extraposed Phrase is being moved. This 'two step' analysis seems plausible in cases such as the following:

(192) (a)   [S [NP The arrest *of a former mayor of Toytown* ON DRUGS CHARGES] was announced this morning]

    (b)   [S [NP The arrest — ON DRUGS CHARGES *of a former mayor of Toytown*] was announced this morning]

    (c)   [S [NP The arrest — ON DRUGS CHARGES —] was announced this morning] *of a former mayor of Toytown*

Thus, we might suppose that the italicised Complement PP in (192) (a) is first extraposed to the end of the containing NP as in (192) (b), and then moved from there to the end of the containing S as in (192) (c). In Chapter 10, we shall show that a number of other rules apply in 'successive steps' in this way, thereby increasing the plausibility of the analysis sketched in (192).

You should now be able to tackle exercise VIII

8.8 Summary

In this chapter, we have argued that our Theory of Grammar must be enriched so as to include not just a *Base Component*, but also a *Transformational Component*, comprising a set of Movement Rules. The Categorial Component of the Base generates a set of abstract prelexical structures which are lexicalised by the insertion of items from the Lexicon. These lexicalised structures may be restructured by application of REANALYSIS rules in the Base. The output structures generated by the Base are known as *D-structures* (or *Base-structures*). They serve as input to the *Transformational Component*, where successive application of a variety of Movement rules transforms the D-structures generated by the Base into the corresponding *S-structures*. Thus, our revised model of grammar can be represented in simplified schematic terms in (193) below:

(193)

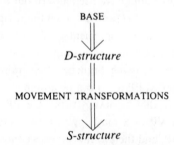

Movement Transformations are of two types. On the one hand, there are *substitution rules* which move constituents into an empty category position which would normally be occupied by some other constituent of the same type: and on the other hand, there are *adjunction rules* which adjoin a moved constituent X to a landing-site category Y, thereby creating a new Y node whose immediate constituents are X and the original Y.

In the early sections of the chapter, we looked at the operation of a number of *substitution rules*. In 8.2 we posited a rule of V MOVEMENT moving the leftmost verbal element in VP into an empty finite I, thereby accounting for the fact that the Tense/Agreement properties normally associated with I surface on the leftmost V of the VP if I is finite and does not contain a Modal: we noted that this rule has considerable empirical motivation for Verbs like *have* and *be*; and (not without reservations!) we followed Koopman and Chomsky in supposing that the rule could be extended from *have/be* to all non-Modal Verbs in English. In 8.3 we argued that the phenomenon known as 'Subject–Auxiliary Inversion' should be handled in terms of a rule of I MOVEMENT moving an Auxiliary out of I into an empty C. In 8.4 we posited that 'Passive' structures involve application of an NP MOVEMENT rule which moves a post-verbal NP into an empty preverbal 'Subject' position: we argued that 'prepositional passives' like *He can be relied on* and 'phrasal passives' like *She was taken notice of* involve prior application of a REANALYSIS rule in the Base which forms Compound Verbs out of sequences like *rely on* and *take notice of*; but we also argued that so-called *lexical* passives are not transformationally derived. In 8.5 we argued that NP MOVEMENT is also involved in the derivation of the 'Raising' construction found with Verbs like *seem*, whereby the Subject of a subordinate S or SC Complement is raised up to become the Subject of the matrix Verb *seem*. In 8.6 we noted (without much enthusiasm!) the claims made in the relevant literature that 'Ergative' structures (e.g. *It broke*) and 'Middle' structures (e.g. *This book reads easily*) also involve application of NP MOVEMENT. In 8.7 we turned from *substitution rules* to consider the *adjunction rule* of EXTRAPOSITION. We argued that the rule detaches a PP or S-bar from its underlying position within a containing host NP (and perhaps within other types of containing host Phrases) and adjoins it either to the host NP itself, or to the minimal phrasal or clausal category containing the host NP. Thus, EXTRAPOSITION of a constituent out of a Subject NP contained in an S will result in adjunction to S; whereas EXTRAPOSITION of a constituent out of an Object NP contained in VP will result in adjunction to VP.

EXERCISES

Exercise I

In the text, we assumed that V MOVEMENT applies in a Clause containing an empty *finite I*. However, all the examples we gave in the text involved *indicative* Clauses; and this raises the obvious question of whether V MOVEMENT also applies in *subjunctive* Clauses in English. On the basis of the examples below (assuming the judgments given), try and determine whether there is any motivation for claiming that V MOVEMENT applies in subjunctive Clauses in English.

(1) (a)   I demand [that the chairman not be reinstated]
   (b)   *I demand [that the chairman be not reinstated]

(2) (a)   I insist [that he definitely have finished by tomorrow]
   (b)   *I insist [that he have definitely finished by tomorrow]

(3) (a)   I demand [that he have a second chance]

  (b)   *I demand [that he've a second chance]

(4) (a)   I demand [that he be/*is expelled from the club]

  (b)   I demanded [that he be/*was expelled from the club]

Note: (1) (b) is an obsolete form which now survives only in archaic legal documents and university statutes. (4) is intended to show that subjunctive Verbs in English don't carry overt Tense or Agreement inflections (though in informal style, many speakers systematically replace subjunctive forms by indicative forms, and so will find the asterisked forms acceptable: but then, for them the bracketed Clauses will be *indicative* not subjunctive, and so not relevant to the discussion here).

**Exercise II

In the text, we argued that V MOVEMENT applies to finite forms of *have* and *be*, and we noted Chomsky's claim in *Barriers* (1986b) that the analysis can be extended to all finite non-modal Verbs in English. Discuss the apparent problems posed for this 'extended' analysis of V MOVEMENT by sentences such as the following (assuming the judgments given):

(1) (a)   The bombs may *completely* destroy it

  (b)   *The bombs *completely* may destroy it

(2) (a)   The bombs *completely* destroyed it

  (b)   *The bombs destroyed *completely* it

(You may find it useful to turn back to our discussion of Adverbs such as *completely* in sections 2.5 and 5.2.)

Consider also the problems posed for this 'generalised' V MOVEMENT analysis by contrasts such as the following:

(3) (a)   The bombs may *not* have destroyed it

  (b)   The bombs have *not* destroyed it

  (c)   *The bombs destroyed *not* it

Can you think of any ways of overcoming the problems posed for the 'extended' V MOVEMENT analysis by paradigms such as (1–3) above?

Exercise III

Discuss the derivation of the following sentences, giving arguments in support of your analysis:

(1)   John may sell his car

(2)   John has sold his car

(3)   John sold his car

(4)   Will John write a book?

(5)   Has John written a book?

(6)   Is John a writer?

Now, discuss the derivation of the following sentences, and account for why they are ill-formed:

(7)   *John love Mary

(8)   *John don't knows the answer

(9)   *Love you Mary?

(10)   *Can I helping you?

(11)   *Can John will do it?

(12)   *I don't know whether will he come

(13)   *Could they've finished work?

(14)   *Had John his secretary type the letter?

(15)   *Be you keen on sport?

Exercise IV

Discuss the derivation of the following passive sentences, giving empirical arguments in support of the derivation you propose:

(1)   Will John be arrested?

(2)   Was John betrayed?

(3)   Is John believed to be considered suitable for the post?

(4)   Will John be laughed at?

(5)   The patient was said to have been taken care of

In addition, account for why the following passives are ill-formed:

(6)   *John is believed will be resigning

(7)   *Dinner was argued during

(8)   *Mary's behaviour was disapproved thoroughly of

(9)   *Mary was given a book to by John

(10)   *The parcel was handed Mary

And say why the active sentences (a) below are ambiguous, whereas their passive counterparts (b) are not:

(11) (a)   Nobody could explain last night

     (b)   Last night couldn't be explained

(12) (a)   They decided on the boat

     (b)   The boat was decided on

*Exercise V

Consider the possibility that 'Phrasal Verbs' may be formed by optional REANALYSIS of a V P sequence, so that the bracketed V-bar in a sentence such as:

(1)   He might [$_{V'}$ tear off the label]

459

derives from a structure such as (2) (a) below, which is then restructured into (2) (b) by
REANALYSIS.

(2) (a)

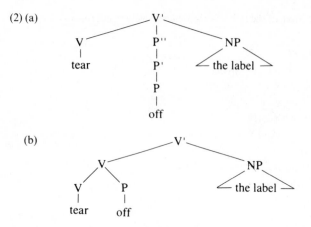

(b)

Why is it unlikely that the derived constituent structure of the bracketed V-bar in (1)
could be (2) (a)?

Now discuss how the following sentences might be derived or blocked in a REANALY-
SIS account, assuming the judgments given:

(3) (a)   He might tear the label off
  (b)   He might tear the label off the packet
  (c)   He might tear the label right off
  (d)   He might tear the label right off the packet

(4) (a)   He might tear off the label
  (b)   *He might tear off the packet the label
  (c)   *He might tear right off the label
  (d)   *He might tear right off the packet the label

(5) (a)   The label might be torn off
  (b)   The label might be torn off the packet
  (c)   The label might be torn right off
  (d)   The label might be torn right off the packet

Exercise VI

Discuss the derivation of the following sentences, giving empirical arguments in support of the analysis you propose:

(1)   John appears to admire Mary
(2)   John got treated very badly
(3)   John seems likely to be arrested

(4)   Is there likely to be anyone sent to jail?

(5)   The ball seems to have rolled down the hill

Secondly, account for why the following are ungrammatical:

(6)   *John would be unlikely for to quit his job

(7)   *John seems to many people to mistrust themselves

(8)   *John seems will give up his job

Thirdly, account for the structural ambiguity of the following sentence:

(9)   John promises to be a good student

Exercise VII

Discuss whether the italicised items when used in the construction illustrated in the sentences below are 'Raising' or 'Control' Predicates, and give empirical arguments to substantiate your analysis:

(1)   John *decided* to answer the letter

(2)   John *came* to know her quite well

(3)   Power *tends* to corrupt people

(4)   They *managed* to open the door

(5)   They *failed* to achieve their objectives

Exercise VIII

Discuss the derivation of the following sentences, saying why those which are ill-formed are ungrammatical:

(1)   A ban seems likely to be announced in the press on Japanese imports

(2)   Nobody would turn a friend away who needed help

(3)   *A review seems imminent of government policy to me

(4)   *Resign over the defeat who support the government, few people will

9

WH MOVEMENT

9.1 Overview

In this chapter, we focus on one particular transformation which we have not looked at hitherto – namely the rule of WH MOVEMENT. Our aim is partly methodological (to show the depth of argumentation which can be used to provide empirical support for the postulation of a single transformation), and partly theoretical (to show how detailed analysis of the operation of one rule can cause us to radically rethink our ideas about rules and structures). Since the rule of WH MOVEMENT plays a key role in the syntax of so-called *wh-questions*, we'll begin by establishing what exactly a wh-question is. Later, we'll look at the role played by WH MOVEMENT in Relative Clauses, and in other wh-constructions (Exclamatives, etc.). Finally, we'll turn to consider in some detail the question of the landing-site for moved wh-phrases, and see that this question forces us into a critical reappraisal and radical revision of our earlier assumptions about the constituent structure of Clauses.

9.2 Question types

Questions in natural languages can be classified into a number of types. One major typological division, for example, is between *yes-no questions* and *wh-questions*. *Yes–no questions* are so called because they permit 'Yes' and 'No' (or their counterparts in other languages) as appropriate replies – as in the following dialogue:

(1)   SPEAKER A: Are you going out tonight?
        SPEAKER B: Yes/No

Of course, speaker B does not have to reply *yes* or *no* to such a question: he might instead reply 'Maybe', 'I don't think so', 'That's right', 'Why do you ask?', 'Mind your own business', and so forth – but at least he has the option of answering 'Yes' or 'No'. *Wh-questions*, by contrast, are so-called because (in English) they typically involve the use of an interrogative word beginning with *wh-* (e.g. *why, what, when, where, which* – but note that *how* is also classified as a wh-word because it exhibits the same syntactic behaviour as other members of this class). In wh-questions, the speaker is requesting information about the identity of some entity in the sentence – for example, a *who*-question asks for information about the identity of a particular person, and an appropriate reply would therefore be a word, phrase, or sentence containing the requisite information: cf.

(2)   SPEAKER A: Who won the big fight?

         SPEAKER B: The Boston Bruiser

Similarly, a *why*-question asks for the specification of a reason, a *where*-question asks for the specification of a place, and so forth.

A second typological division of questions (which is independent of the *yes–no/wh* distinction) is that between *echo questions* and *nonecho questions*. Echo questions are so-called because they involve one person echoing the speech of another, as in the following dialogue:

(3)   SPEAKER A: I bought a car

         SPEAKER B: You bought a car?

Here, Speaker B is echoing a statement made by Speaker A by using a yes–no echo question. He might instead have used a wh-echo question, as in:

(4)   SPEAKER A: I bought a car

         SPEAKER B: You bought (a) what?

In both (3) and (4), Speaker B is echoing a *statement* made by Speaker A; but it is also possible to use an echo question to echo a *question* asked by another speaker, as for example in (5) below:

(5)   SPEAKER A: Did you buy a car?

         SPEAKER B: Did I buy a car? (Why do you ask?)

In (5), a yes–no nonecho question by Speaker A is echoed by a yes–no echo question from Speaker B; Speaker B might alternatively have used a wh-echo question, as in:

(6)   SPEAKER A: Did you buy a car?

         SPEAKER B: Did I what?

In both (5) and (6), Speaker B echoes a yes–no question by Speaker A. But we can echo not only questions and statements, but also other sentence-types – e.g. imperatives: cf.

(7)   SPEAKER A: Don't touch my projectile

         SPEAKER B: Don't touch your what?

463

Morphologically and syntactically, echo questions seem to have more in common with the sentence-types they are used to echo than with the corresponding nonecho questions.

In contrast to echo questions, *nonecho questions* are questions which do not echo the speech of others, but which can be used, for example, to initiate a conversation on some topic. So, for example, if a friend walks into a room, I can initiate a conversation with a nonecho question such as:

(8)   Where have you been?

but not with an echo question such as:

(9)   You have been where?

since echo questions by their very nature can only be used to echo a previous sentence.

A third typological distinction which it is useful to make in discussing the syntax of questions is the traditional one between *direct questions* and *indirect questions*. Direct questions are questions in which the interrogative structure is an independent sentence – as, for example, in:

(10)   When did you get back?

Indirect questions, by contrast, are questions in which the interrogative structure is a dependent (i.e. embedded or subordinate) clause which is the Complement of a Verb like *ask, wonder* etc., as with the italicised clause in:

(11)   He asked me *who I had talked to*

Note in particular the contrast between the italicised indirect question in (11) above, and the corresponding italicised direct question in (12):

(12)   He asked me: '*Who did you talk to?*'

Notice also from (11) and (12) that English spelling differentiates direct from indirect questions by enclosing direct – but not indirect – questions in quotation marks.

Having distinguished various different types of questions, let's now concentrate simply on *direct nonecho wh-questions* (for convenience, we'll use the term *wh-question* to mean *direct nonecho wh-question* unless otherwise specified, in what follows). For the sake of concreteness, let's start off by considering how we might generate a sentence like:

(13)   Which car will your father put in the garage?

On the assumption that V is the leftmost constituent of VP, and that the subject NP is the leftmost constituent of S, then (13) would appear to have the simplified structure (14) below:

(14) $[_{S'}$ Which car will $[_S$ your father $[_{VP}$ put in the garage]]]?

in which the V *put* is the leftmost constituent of the bracketed VP, and the subject NP [*your father*] is the leftmost constituent of the bracketed S. This in turn would mean that the wh-NP [*which car*] and the Modal Auxiliary *will* are both positioned outside S (but within the containing S-bar) in the superficial structure (S-structure) of the sentence: this ties up with our earlier arguments in section 8.3 that 'inverted' Modals are positioned outside S in C. What we shall argue here, however, is that underlying the S-structure (14) is a more abstract level of D-structure in which the wh-NP [*which car*] originates within VP as the Object of *put;* we shall also assume (for reasons given in section 8.3) that the Modal *will* originates within I immediately following the NP subject [*your father*]. In other words, we shall argue that (14) derives from a more abstract D-structure of the schematic form (15) below (where C is an empty Complementiser):

(15) $[_{S'}$ C $[_S$ Your father $[_I$ will] $[_{VP}$ put which car in the garage]]]

and that the S-structure (14) is derived from the D-structure (15) by the operation of two movement rules. One of these is the now familiar rule of I MOVE-MENT which moves the Modal *will* immediately in front of the bracketed S into C; and the second movement rule (WH MOVEMENT) moves the wh-NP [*which car*] to a position within S-bar in front of the preposed Modal *will*, as the leftmost constituent of S-bar. The operation of these two movement rules can be represented in a simplified schematic form as in (16) below:

(16) $[_{S'}$ C $[_S$ your father $[_I$ *will*] put $[_{NP}$ *which car*] in the garage]]
               └─ I MOVEMENT ─┘
          └─────── WH MOVEMENT ───────┘

It seems clear that movement of the Modal *will* and movement of the wh-NP [*which car*] must involve two separate movement rules, for two reasons. First, direct yes–no questions show preposing of Modals without preposing of wh-phrases: cf.

(17) $[_{S'}$ *Will* $[_S$ your father put the car in the garage]]?

And secondly, indirect wh-questions show preposing of wh-phrases without preposing of Modals, as in:

(18)   I don't know $[_{S'}$ *which car* $[_S$ your father will put in the garage]]

465

The key claim that we are making is thus that in sentences like (14) *Which car will your father put in the garage?* both the wh-NP [*which car*] and the Modal *will* originate inside S at D-structure, but get moved into a position outside S but within S-bar by the operation of two independent movement rules (WH MOVEMENT and I MOVEMENT) and thus both end up in pre-S positions within S-bar at S-structure.

Since we have already argued that 'Auxiliary Inversion' should be handled in terms of a rule of I MOVEMENT, we shall leave aside the syntax of Auxiliaries, and concentrate simply on the syntax of clause-initial wh-phrases. The essential claim that we are making is that although these end up in a clause-initial position outside S in S-structure, at the more abstract level of D-structure they originate internally within S. Their superficial pre-S position is then accounted for by positing that a rule of WH MOVEMENT applies in the course of the derivation of such sentences to move a wh-phrase which is inside S at D-structure to a position where it is the initial (i.e. leftmost) constituent within S-bar at the level of S-structure (the exact landing-site of preposed wh-phrases is a question which we shall gloss over for the time being, but return to at the end of this chapter). The operation of the rule can be represented in a simplified schematic form as in (19) below:

(19)   D-structure $[_{S'}.........[_S.......wh\text{-}XP........]\ ]$

WH MOVEMENT

S-structure $[_{S'}\ wh\text{-}XP...[_S....................]\ ]$

(wh-XP here stands for any wh-phrase: a *wh-phrase* in turn is a phrase which contains a wh-word, hence e.g. a wh-NP like *which car*, a wh-AP like *how pretty*, a wh-PP like *in which town*, a wh-ADVP such as *how slowly*, etc.)

The most controversial part of this analysis is obviously the claim that clause-initial wh-phrases which wind up outside S actually originate inside S. In the sections which follow, we shall present a substantial body of empirical evidence in support of the claim that wh-phrases cannot originate in their superficial position as the leftmost constituent of S-bar, but rather must originate inside S.

9.3 Syntactic arguments

Our first piece of evidence that wh-phrases originate within S comes from *subcategorisation* facts. On the basis of familiar examples such as (20) below:

(20) (a)   John put [$_{NP}$ *the car*] [$_{PP}$ *in the garage*]

(b)   *John put [$_{NP}$ *the car*]

(c)   *John put [pp *in the garage*]

(d)   *John put

we might subcategorise *put* as:

(21)   *put*: CATEGORIAL FEATURES: [+ V, − N]
           SUBCATEGORISATION FRAME: [NP   PP]

(We ignore for expository purposes the possibility that the subcategorisation properties of *put* may be predictable from its thematic properties, and from general word-order principles.) (21) says that *put* can only be inserted into a V-bar where it is immediately followed by both an NP and a PP. Now if (contrary to what we claim) initial wh-phrases originate as the leftmost constituent of S-bar, then we should wrongly predict that a structure such as (14) (repeated as (22) below) is ungrammatical:

(22)   [S' Which car will [S your father [V' put in the garage]]]?

The reason is that *put* in (22) has only the PP Complement [*in the garage*], and no NP complement, in violation of the subcategorisation frame in (21) which requires *put* to have both an NP and a PP Complement (since sentences like (20) (c) in which *put* takes only a PP Complement are ungrammatical). So, if we assume that wh-phrases originate in their S-structure position outside S, we wrongly predict that structures like (22) are ungrammatical (by virtue of a subcategorisation violation).

What's going on here is that although the wh-NP [*which car*] is the leftmost constituent of S-bar at S-structure, for subcategorisation purposes it behaves as if it were actually positioned after the Verb, as the NP Object of *put*. Notice that if indeed the *wh*-phrase [*which car*] had been positioned after the Verb *put* (in the 'normal' position characteristic of Direct Objects of Verbs), the subcategorisation problems that we faced in relation to sentence (22) would never have arisen in the first place. Now if instead of looking at *wh-nonecho questions* we had been looking at *wh-echo questions*, it would indeed have been the case that an Object phrase like [*which car*] would have occurred in typical Object position after its Verb, as we see from Speaker B's echo questions in the examples below:

(23)   SPEAKER A: My father will put the Mercedes in the garage
           SPEAKER B: Your father will put [*which car*] in the garage?

(24)   SPEAKER A: Will my father put the Mercedes in the garage?
           SPEAKER B: Will your father put [*which car*] in the garage?

And, interestingly, echo questions like those asked by Speaker B would not have posed any problems for our existing grammar. To see this, consider the kind of Verb that we might have been able to insert in the V-position marked by '—' in an echo-question structure like (25) below:

(25)   [$_S$ Your father will [$_{V'}$ — *which car* in the garage]]

Suppose we ask whether or not *put* can be inserted in the V-position in (25). The answer would of course be 'Yes', since we see from (21) that *put* subcategorises following NP and PP Complements, and in (25) the V *put* is followed by the NP [*which car*] and the PP [*in the garage*]. In other words, if only [*which car*] had occurred inside S as the Object of the Verb (as in (25)) rather than outside S (as in (22)), we would never have run into the subcategorisation problems that we faced in respect of (22); and hence our grammar would not wrongly have predicted that (13) *Which car will your father put in the garage?* was ungrammatical.

Thus, subcategorisation facts require us to posit that a sentence such as (13) *Which car will your father put in the garage?* derives from a D-structure such as (15) *Your father will put which car in the garage* via application of two movement rules – I MOVEMENT (which moves the Modal *will* from I into C), and WH MOVEMENT (which moves an appropriate wh-phrase within S to the left of C, hence to the left of the preposed Modal): cf. the schematic derivation in (16) above.

A variant of the subcategorisation argument is the familiar *idiom chunk argument*. As we saw earlier, English has a class of Noun Phrases which are highly restricted in their distribution, in the sense that they generally occur only in conjunction with some specific Verb: for example, the italicised Object Idiom Chunk NPs in (26) generally occur only immediately following the capitalised Verb:

(26) (a)   Nobody PAID *heed* to his warnings
     (b)   I want you to TAKE *note* of what I say
     (c)   The government KEEP *tabs* on his operations
     (d)   We must TAKE *advantage* of this opportunity

In the light of this restriction, consider how we are to handle sentences such as the following:

(27) (a)   *How much heed* do you think the committee will pay — to my proposals?
     (b)   *How much note* did you say you think she will take — of what I said?
     (c)   *How close tabs* do you think the FBI will keep — on the CIA?

(d)   *How much advantage* does the President think he can take — of his opponents' misfortunes?

If we say – as we did earlier – that idiom chunk NPs such as those above can only be used immediately following certain specific Verbs, how are we to account for the grammaticality of sentences such as (27) above, in which the *idiom chunk NP* actually occurs sentence-initially? Once again, one way out of this dilemma is to posit that the idiom chunk NPs in sentences like (27) originate in the — position in underlying structure, and are subsequently moved from there into sentence-initial pre-S position by WH MOVEMENT. We can then say that the sentences in (27) are grammatical precisely because the *idiom chunk wh-phrase* originated at D-structure to the immediate right of the Verb of which it is a Complement. But any such analysis presupposes both an abstract level of *underlying syntactic structure* (*D-structure*), and a transformation of WH MOVEMENT *mapping* (or *transforming*) that underlying structure into the corresponding superficial syntactic structure (*S-structure*).

A third argument which we can adduce in support of the claim that wh-phrases which are positioned outside S at S-structure originate inside S at D-structure is the familiar 'gap' argument (which is also essentially a variant of the *subcategorisation* argument). If we are correct in our assumption that there is a rule of WH MOVEMENT which moves wh-phrases from their original position within S to an appropriate landing-site outside S, then we should expect to find a 'gap' at the extraction site (i.e. in the position out of which the wh-phrase has been moved). For example, assuming the WH MOVEMENT analysis of sentence (13) outlined schematically in (16) above, we should expect to find an NP 'gap' in the position marked by the dash — in (28) below:

(28)   [$_{S'}$ Which car will [$_S$ your father put — in the garage]]?

This would lead us to expect that it would be impossible to insert an overt NP in this gap (given our convention that 'gaps' cannot be refilled): and sure enough, we find that we can't insert an appropriate NP such as *the bike* in the gap in (28), as we see from the ungrammaticality of (29) below:

(29)   *Which car will your father put *the bike* in the garage?

Why can't we insert the italicised NP in (29) into the gap in (28)? Our WH MOVEMENT analysis provides us with an obvious answer; for if we assume that the initial wh-NP [*which car*] in (29) originates as the D-structure Complement of *put*, then (29) will derive from the D-structure (30) below:

(30)   Your father will put [$_{NP}$ which car] [$_{NP}$ the bike] [$_{PP}$ in the garage]

And (30) would obviously be ill-formed since it does not satisfy the sub-categorisation frame of *put* given in (21) above, which requires the Verb *put* to occur in a V-bar of the schematic form [V NP PP], whereas in (30) *put* occurs in a V-bar of the form [V NP NP PP]. Thus, the 'gap' argument too provides strong support for the claim that wh-phrases originate inside S, but are subsequently moved outside S and repositioned as the leftmost constituent of S-bar by the rule of WH MOVEMENT.

A fourth argument for positing a rule of WH MOVEMENT can be based on facts about the syntax of Quantifiers and Adverbs discussed in Sag (1978). Sag notes that Quantifiers like *all* and Adverbs like *ever* can be positioned either before or after the Verb *be* in sentences such as:

(31) (a)   They *all* were Socialists
     (b)   They were *all* Socialists

(32) (a)   I don't know if they *ever* were happy
     (b)   I don't know if they were *ever* happy

However, when the Complement of the Verb *be* has undergone Ellipsis, the Quantifier/Adverb can only be positioned before (not after) *be*: cf.

(33) (a)   Most of them were Socialists, and perhaps they *all* were Ø
     (b)   *Most of them were Socialists, and perhaps they were *all* Ø

(34) (a)   They may have been happy, though I doubt if they *ever* were Ø
     (b)   *They may have been happy, though I doubt if they were *ever* Ø

(Ø here marks the constituent which has undergone Ellipsis.) It would seem that the relevant generalisation is that a Quantifier like *all* or Adverb like *ever* cannot be positioned immediately before a 'gap' in a sentence.

In the light of this restriction, consider how we can account for sentences such as (35) and (36) below:

(35) (a)   I'm not sure [S' *how happy* they all are —]
     (b)   *I'm not sure [S' *how happy* they are all —]

(36) (a)   I'm not sure [S' *how happy* they ever were —]
     (b)   *I'm not sure [S' *how happy* they were ever —]

How can we account for the ungrammaticality of the (b) counterparts in (35) and (36) above? Given our earlier restriction that Quantifiers/Adverbs of the appropriate class cannot be positioned immediately before a 'gap', the obvious answer to suggest is that there must be a 'gap' in the (b) sentences immediately following *all/ever*, in the position marked by the elongated dash —.

But how could there be a 'gap' in the sentence? The answer we are suggesting here is that the wh-AP [*how happy*] originates in the position marked by the dash, and is subsequently preposed into the italicised position by application of WH MOVEMENT: a 'gap' is then left behind in the position which the wh-phrase used to occupy, and the presence of this 'gap' suffices to block positioning of the Quantifier or Adverb immediately in front of this 'gap'. What precisely we mean by 'gap' is a question we take up in the next chapter.

9.4 Morphological arguments

Thus far, the three arguments we have presented in support of positing a rule of WH MOVEMENT (viz. the *subcategorisation, gap* and *idiom chunk* arguments) have all been syntactic in nature. But there are many other kinds of argument (morphological, phonological, and semantic) which we might develop, lending support to the postulation of such a rule. Let's look at two morphological arguments to begin with.

Our first such morphological argument is based on *case-marking* facts. In Personal Pronouns in English we find a morphological distinction between so-called *Nominative* forms like *I/he/we/they*, and so-called *Objective* forms like *me/him/us/them*. Although the exact conditions determining the assignment of these two cases are quite complex (and will form the subject matter of a chapter of Volume Two), for present purposes we can assume the following (simplified) case-marking rules:

(37) (i)   Nominative case is assigned to an NP which is a sister of a finite I
    (ii)   Objective case is assigned to an NP which immediately follows a transitive V or P

More informally, this amounts to saying that the Subject of a finite Clause is assigned Nominative case, whereas the Object of a transitive Verb or Preposition (as well as the Subject of a Small or Exceptional Clause Complement of a transitive Verb or Preposition) is assigned Objective case. The rules in (37) make correct predictions about the assignment of case to the italicised NPs in a sentence such as:

(38)   *I* will tell *her* about *him*

Let's assume that (38) has the following (simplified) structure:

(39)   [S I [I will] [VP tell her [PP about him]]]

Given this assumption, then the Subject NP *I* will correctly be assigned Nominative case by rule (37) (i), since it is a sister of the finite I filled by the Modal *will*; moreover, rule (37) (ii) will correctly assign Objective case to the NP *her*, because it immediately follows the transitive Verb *tell*; and likewise, the same rule will also correctly assign Objective case to the NP *him*, because it immediately follows the transitive Preposition *about*. Thus, our (simplified) case-rules correctly handle the facts of (38). Moreover, they also make exactly the right predictions about contrasts such as the following:

(40) (a)   *I/*me* might faint
   (b)   John can't see *me/*I*
   (c)   Mary won't speak to *me/*I*

for reasons which you should be able to work out for yourself!

A rather similar case-alternation is found with the (interrogative and relative) *wh*-pronoun *who*, which (in formal style) has the variant *whom*. In colloquial English, *who* is used as Nominative and Objective alike, whereas in formal English *who* is Nominative and *whom* Objective. So, for example, in echo questions we find alternations such as the following:

(41)   SPEAKER A: I'm sure [Nim Chimpsky would admire Noam Chomsky]
   SPEAKER B: You're sure [*who/*whom* would admire Noam Chomsky]?

(42)   SPEAKER A: I'm sure [Nim Chimpsky would admire Noam Chomsky]
   SPEAKER B: You're sure [Nim Chimpsky would admire *who/whom*]?

Our earlier case-marking rules (37) would handle the relevant facts in (41) and (42) quite straightforwardly. Thus, since the wh-pronoun is the sister of the finite I containing *would* in (41), the Nominative form *who* is required, by rule (37) (i). But in (42), since the wh-pronoun immediately follows the transitive Verb *admire*, the Objective form (colloquial *who*, literary *whom*) is required in accordance with rule (37) (ii). But now consider the corresponding nonecho wh-questions:

(43) (a)   *Who/*Whom* are [you sure — would admire Noam Chomsky]?
   (b)   *Who/Whom* are [you sure Nim Chimpsky would admire —]?

How can we account for the fact that the italicised wh-pronoun must be Nominative in (43) (a), but Objective in (43) (b)? Our case-marking rules (37) appear to break down at this point. The reason is that at S-structure the wh-pronoun is positioned outside the bracketed S, and thus is neither a sister of a finite I, nor a constituent which immediately follows a transitive V or P. Since

472

the wh-pronoun doesn't satisfy the conditions for either rule (37) (i) to apply, or rule (37) (ii) to apply, our case-rules simply break down in the sense that they fail to assign any case at all. So, we have no means to account for the facts in (43).

By contrast, in a transformational grammar incorporating a rule of WH MOVEMENT, no such problems arise: (43) (a) and (b) will derive from the respective D-structures:

(44) (a)   You are sure [*who*/*whom would admire Noam Chomsky]?

(b)   You are sure [Nim Chimpsky would admire *who*/*whom*]?

And in (44) (a) the wh-pronoun will be assigned the Nominative form *who* by virtue of being a sister of the finite I filled by *would*: while in (44) (b) the Pronoun will be assigned Objective case (formal *whom*, informal *who*) by virtue of being the Complement of the transitive Verb *admire*. Thus, provided that our case-marking rules have access to information about the position occupied by the Pronoun prior to the application of WH MOVEMENT (how to ensure this is a question we shall take up in the next chapter), sentences like (44) no longer pose any problem. But note that an essential part of the solution to the case-marking problem proposed here is the postulation of an abstract level of D-structure, linked to (the technical expression is *mapped into*) the corresponding S-structure by a transformation of WH MOVEMENT.

A second morphological argument in support of positing a rule of WH MOVEMENT comes from *Agreement* (= Concord) facts. As we saw in Chapter 6, English has a rule of *Person–Number Agreement* whose operation we might outline provisionally as:

(45)   An NP which is the sister of a finite I must agree with I in Person and Number

A finite I will contain either a base-generated Modal, or a V moved into an empty finite I by the rule of V MOVEMENT which we discussed in Chapter 8. Thus, in more informal terms, rule (45) says that a finite Verb must agree with its Subject. The agreement rule outlined in (45) is responsible for alternations such as:

(46) (a)   He might say [$_S$ THIS BOY [$_I$ *doesn't*/**don't*] like Mary]

(b)   He might say [$_S$ THOSE BOYS [$_I$ *don't*/**doesn't*] like Mary]

For, in (46) (a), the italicised Auxiliary in I must be in the third person singular form, to agree with the capitalised third person singular NP [*this boy*] which is a sister of the finite I; and conversely, in (46) (b) the italicised Auxiliary must be plural to agree with its capitalised plural subject NP *those boys*.

The same agreement phenomenon is found in wh-echo questions like:

(47) (a) He might say [s WHICH BOY [I *doesn't/*don't*] like Mary]?
(b) He might say [s WHICH BOYS [I *don't/*doesn't*] like Mary]?

Of course, sentences like (47) pose no problem for our rule (45) which specifies that a finite Verb in I agrees with a sister NP (i.e. with its Subject). But now consider nonecho wh-questions like:

(48) (a) WHICH BOY might he say [s — [I *doesn't/*don't*] like Mary]?
(b) WHICH BOYS might he say [s — [I *don't/*doesn't*] like Mary]?

Our existing rule (45) simply can't handle Agreement in such cases, since the bracketed S containing the italicised finite Auxiliary appears to be subjectless, and thus to have no sister NP to agree with. So, how can we get out of this dilemma?

What we want to be able to say in order to handle cases like (48) is that the italicised Auxiliary in I agrees with the capitalised NP that *used to* be its sister immediately prior to the application of WH MOVEMENT. But this commits us to recognising that sentences like (48) derive from an underlying structure like (47) in which the wh-phrase *which boy(s)* occupies the position indicated by — as a sister constituent of the Auxiliary *do(es)n't*. In other words, it commits us to recognising the existence of an abstract level of D-structure underlying the superficial syntactic structure (i.e. S-structure) of sentences, with a transformation of WH MOVEMENT *mapping* the D-structure into the corresponding S-structure.

9.5 Phonological arguments

Hitherto, we have argued that we need to appeal to an abstract D-structure underlying wh-questions in order to provide a principled account of certain syntactic and morphological facts. Now we shall go on and argue that there are certain *phonological* facts which cannot be accounted for in any principled way without invoking both an abstract level of *underlying structure* in syntax, and a transformation of WH MOVEMENT mapping that underlying structure into the associated *S-structure*.

Under certain conditions, Auxiliaries permit contracted forms such as those in (49) below:

(49)

Full form	*Contracted form*
is ⎫ has ⎭	's
had ⎫ would ⎭	'd

474

have	've
will	'll
am	'm
are	're

In sentences like (50) below, we find that we can freely have either the full form or the contracted form of the italicised item:

(50) (a) Mary is good at hockey, and Jean *is* good at volleyball

   (b) Mary is good at hockey, and Jean'*s* good at volleyball

Notice, however, that if we omit the second occurrence of *good* in (50), AUXILIARY CONTRACTION is no longer possible:

(51) (a) Mary is good at hockey, and Jean is Ø at volleyball

   (b) ≠ Mary is good at hockey, and Jean's Ø at volleyball

(where Ø is used simply to mark the fact that *good* has been omitted). Why should contraction be possible in (50), but not in (51)? The answer seems to have something to do with the fact that *good* has been omitted in (51), but not in (50). Informally, we might suggest some rule along the lines of:

(52)   Contracted forms cannot be used when there is a 'missing' constituent immediately following

Thus, in (51), the Adjective *good* is 'missing' from the position marked — immediately following *is*, and hence contraction is not possible here.

But now notice that contraction is also blocked in cases like:

(53) (a) *How good* do you think Mary is — at Linguistics?

   (b) *How good do you think Mary's — at Linguistics?

How can we account for the impossibility of contraction in (53)? Notice that if we postulate that the italicised wh-phrase originates in the position marked — and is subsequently moved out of that position by WH MOVEMENT to the front of the sentence, then there is an obvious sense in which we can say that there is a 'missing' constituent after *be* in (53). What is the missing constituent? Clearly, it is the preposed *wh*-phrase [*How good*].

Having looked at one phonological argument from AUXILIARY CONTRACTION, let's now turn to look at a second argument to do with WANNA CONTRACTION. In colloquial English, *want to* can contract to *wanna* in sentences like:

(54) (a) I *want to* win

   (b) I *wanna* win

In 'standard' varieties of English, WANNA CONTRACTION can apply in sentences such as:

(55) (a) Who do you *want to* beat —?
(b) Who do you *wanna* beat?

but not in sentences like:

(56) (a) Who do you *want* — *to* win?
(b) *Who do you *wanna* win?

How can we account for the fact that contraction is possible in (55), but not in (56)? Once again, the notion *underlying structure* seems to be central to any account of what is going on here. Let us assume that in underlyng structure *who* originates in each case in the position marked —, and is subsequently moved into sentence-initial position by WH MOVEMENT, leaving a 'gap' behind. And let's further suppose that WANNA CONTRACTION is blocked when there is a 'gap' between *want* and *to*. Given these assumptions, then the fact that there is a 'gap' (marked by —) between *want* and *to* in (56) (a) but not in (55) (a) correctly predicts that WANNA CONTRACTION will be blocked in (56), but will be possible in (55). But of course for this account to be workable, we have to posit an abstract structure underlying sentences such as (55) (b) and (56) (b), and a rule of WH MOVEMENT relating this underlying structure (i.e. D-structure) to the corresponding superficial syntactic structure (i.e. S-structure). Of course, we also have to suppose that when WH MOVEMENT applies, it leaves behind a 'gap' of some sort at the *extraction site* (i.e. in the position out of which the wh-phrase has been extracted): what exactly we mean by a 'gap' is a question we take up in the next chapter.

9.6 Semantic arguments

Having looked at a variety of morphological, syntactic, and phonological arguments in support of positing a rule of WH MOVEMENT, we now turn to look at *semantic* arguments in favour of the same assumption. One such argument relates to the interpretation of *Reflexives* (i.e. *self-* forms). Recall that in the previous chapter we suggested that (non-subject) Reflexives generally require a *sometime clausemate* antecedent. In the light of this generalisation, consider the apparent problem posed by wh-questions such as the following:

(57) WHICH WITNESS did you say you thought [— perjured *himself*]?

Clearly, the italicised Reflexive *himself* must be construed with the capitalised wh-NP [*which witness*] in (57); but this is in apparent violation of our *sometime clausemate* condition on Reflexives, because [*which witness*] is not contained in the same (bracketed) S as *himself* at S-structure: more precisely, [*which witness*] is positioned at the front of the *say* Clause, whereas *himself* is contained in the *perjured*-clause. How can we deal with this apparent counterexample to our *sometime clausemate* condition on Reflexives? One simple answer would be to posit that the wh-NP *which witness* in (57) originates at D-structure in the position marked by —, as the Subject of the bracketed Complement Clause. If this is so, then the capitalised wh-phrase and the italicised Reflexive would be clausemates at D-structure, so satisfying our *sometime clausemate* condition: our grammar would then correctly specify that sentences like (57) are grammatical. Naturally, any such solution would commit us to the twin assumptions of (i) an abstract level of underlying structure, and (ii) a rule of WH MOVEMENT mapping this abstract underlying structure into the associated superficial syntactic structure.

A second semantic argument in support of positing a transformation of WH MOVEMENT can be formulated in relation to the *structural ambiguity* of sentences such as the following:

(58)   To whom did you say that Mary was talking?

The ambiguity in (58) lies in whether the wh-PP [*to whom*] is taken as a Complement of the Verb *say*, or as a Complement of the Verb *talking*. The ambiguity is reflected in the fact that there are two different wh-echo questions corresponding to these two different interpretations, namely:

(59) (a)   You said [*to whom*] that Mary was talking?
   (b)   You said that Mary was talking [*to whom*]?

However, note that the structural ambiguity of (58) doesn't appear to be overtly reflected in its superficial syntactic structure (S-structure), in the sense that the sentence (58) seems to contain the same overt set of constituents occupying the same set of positions on either of its interpretations. So how can we provide a principled account of the structural ambiguity of sentences like (58)? The answer is to assume that sentence (58) derives from the two different D-structures represented informally in (60) below, each corresponding to a different interpretation of the sentence:

(60) (a)   You did say *to whom* [that Mary was talking]?
   (b)   You did say [that Mary was talking *to whom*]?

The structural ambiguity of sentence (58) would then be directly represented at D-structure, where the two interpretations of (58) correspond to two different D-structures. But how is it that the two different D-structures result in a single S-structure (58)? The answer is that in both cases I MOVEMENT applies to move the Auxiliary *did* in front of the main S, and WH MOVEMENT applies to move the italicised interrogative PP *to whom* in front of the preposed Auxiliary *did*. Thus, in both cases we derive the S-structure (58), resulting in an apparent obliteration of the structural differences between (60) (a) and (b).

A third semantic argument can be formulated in relation to *thematic structure*. Our lexical entry for a Verb such as *wear* will have to include a *theta-grid* which specifies that (in its active use) *wear* takes an obligatory preceding AGENT subject and an obligatory following THEME object: cf.

(61) (a)   [Mary] wore a [a new dress]
           [AGENT]   [THEME]
     (b)   *[Mary] wore
           [AGENT]
     (c)   *[A new dress] wore
              [THEME]

Thus, the theta-grid for *wear* might take the form:

(62)   [AGENT] — [THEME]

(We are simplifying the discussion here by ignoring the possibility that the choice of AGENT as Subject of *wear* is determined by independent Subject Selection principles.) In the light of this, consider the thematic structure of a sentence such as the following:

(63)   *Which dress* do you think Mary will wear?

A sentence such as (63) poses two problems with respect to theta-role assignment. First, the structure (63) appears not to satisfy the theta-grid for *wear* in (62), since although *wear* in (63) has a preceding AGENT *Mary*, it lacks a following THEME Complement. And secondly, the NP [*which dress*] fails to be assigned any theta-role by the theta-grid (62), in violation of the THETA CRITERION (which requires all Arguments to have a theta-role): note that [*which dress*] cannot be assigned the theta-role THEME since this is assigned by the theta-grid (62) only to an NP which *immediately follows* the Verb *wear*. Thus, as presently constituted, our grammar would wrongly predict that sentences such as (63) are ill-formed in respect of their thematic structure.

However, the WH MOVEMENT analysis again gets us out of this problem. For, if we posit that (63) derives from a D-structure which we can represent simplistically as:

(64)   You do think Mary will wear *which dress*?

and if we assume that THETA-ROLE ASSIGNMENT takes place at D-structure, then *Mary* will be assigned the role AGENT by virtue of being the NP preceding *wear*, and *which dress* will be assigned the role THEME by virtue of being the NP immediately following *wear* (and we might assume that NPs preserve their theta-roles under movement: the precise mechanism which ensures this need not concern us for the present). Thus, both the theta-grid (62), and the THETA CRITERION will be satisfied, and our grammar will thus correctly predict that there are no theta-violations in a sentence such as (63). The surface ordering of constituents in (63) is accounted for by positing that the rules of I MOVEMENT and WH MOVEMENT both apply to map the D-structure (64) into the corresponding S-structure (63). Of course, the *theta-role* argument outlined above is closely related to the *subcategorisation* argument given earlier, as we should expect if our earlier observation in Chapter 7 is correct about the mutual interdependence of subcategorisation and thematic structure.

A related semantic (but also partly pragmatic) argument supporting the postulating of a WH MOVEMENT transformation mapping D-structures into S-structures can be formulated in relation to facts about *Selection Restrictions*. Recall that these are restrictions which Predicates impose on the choice of Arguments (= Subjects/Complements) which they select, and are determined by the semantic and thematic properties of the Predicate (as well as by pragmatic factors relating, for example, to personal beliefs about the world, etc.); so, for example, it sounds OK to use an NP like [*a new dress*] as the Object of a Verb like *wear*, but not an NP like [*a new theory*]: cf.

(65)   She was wearing *a new dress*/!*a new theory*

The same type of semantic/pragmatic restrictions are found in echo questions such as:

(66)   He might think she was wearing *which dress*/!*which theory*?

and, more interestingly, in nonecho questions such as:

(67)   *Which dress*/!*which theory* might he think she was wearing —?

How can we account for the fact that sentence (67) is subject to exactly the same selection restrictions as (65)? If we posited that the italicised *wh*-phrase in (67) actually originates in the — position in underlying structure, then the wh-phrase would be an Argument of the Predicate *wearing* (more particularly, the THEME Complement, or Direct Object of *wearing*) at D-structure in both (66) and (67). If we were further to assume that selection restrictions hold between a Predicate and its D-structure Arguments, then we could achieve a unitary account of the selection restrictions in cases like (66) and (67).

| You should now be able to tackle exercise I |

9.7 WH MOVEMENT in Relative Clauses

Thus far, we have confined our discussion of WH MOVEMENT almost entirely to interrogative structures. However, there are reasons to suppose that there are many other types of *wh-construction* (i.e. constructions in which WH MOVEMENT operates either overtly or covertly) in natural language. One such type of wh-construction is *Relative Clauses*. Before we proceed any further with our discussion, it will be useful to draw a distinction between three rather different types of Relative Clause construction in English, namely:

(68) (a)   Restrictive Relative Clauses
     (b)   Appositive Relative Clauses
     (c)   Free Relative Clauses

Restrictive Relative Clauses include the bracketed Clauses in:

(69) (a)   I met the man [*who lives next door*] in town
     (b)   The book [*that you lent me*] was interesting
     (c)   I enjoyed the meal [*you made us*]

They are so called because in a Noun Phrase such as [*the man who lives next door*], the Relative Clause [*who lives next door*] restricts the class of men referred to to the one who lives next door. As we see from (69), Restrictive Relative Clauses can be introduced by a wh-pronoun (more precisely, a pronominal wh-XP) like *who*, a Complementiser like *that*, or they may contain *no* overt wh-pronoun or Complementiser (following a term suggested by Quirk *et al.* (1985), we might refer to this third type as *Zero Relatives*, though they are sometimes referred to as 'Contact Relative Clauses' in traditional grammars). As we see from (70) below, Restrictive Relative Clauses can sometimes be extraposed and separated from their *antecedent* (= the expression they modify):

(70)   SOMEONE came to see me [*who said he was from the bank*]

Thus in (70) above, the bracketed Restrictive Relative Clause is separated from its capitalised antecedent (i.e. the Nominal that it modifies).

Appositive Relative Clauses are those such as the italicised in:

(71) (a)   John (*who was at Cambridge with me*) is a good friend of mine
     (b)   Yesterday I met your bank manager, *who was in a filthy mood*
     (c)   Mary has left home – *which must be very upsetting for her parents*

480

They generally serve as 'parenthetical comments' or afterthoughts' set off in a separate intonation group from the rest of the sentence (this being marked by a comma, or hyphen, or brackets in writing); unlike Restrictives, they can be used to qualify unmodified Proper Nouns (i.e. Proper Nouns not introduced by a Determiner like *the*, as with *John* (in (71) (a)). They are always introduced by an overt wh-phrase (i.e. neither *that-relatives*, nor 'zero relatives' can be used appositively), as we see from (72) below:

(72) (a)   John – *whom you saw in town* – is a good friend of mine
     (b)   *John – *that you saw in town* – is a good friend of mine
     (c)   *John – *you saw in town* – is a good friend of mine

And, generally speaking, they cannot be extraposed (i.e. separated) from their antecedent: cf.

(73) (a)   *John came to see me – *who you met last week*
     (b)   *Mary is living at home – *who is very nice*

Free Relative Clauses are those such as the italicised in:

(74) (a)   *What(ever) he says* is generally true
     (b)   You can have *whichever one you want*
     (c)   I will go *where(ver) you go*
     (d)   *Whatever happens*, I'll stand by you

They are characterised by the fact that they are apparently antecedentless – i.e. the *wh*-expressions they contain don't appear to refer back to any other constituent in the sentence containing them. As in the case of Appositives, they are always introduced by an overt wh-phrase (i.e. neither *that* relatives nor 'zero relatives' can function as Free Relative Clauses).

For present purposes, we shall confine our discussion to *Restrictive Relative Clauses*: and we'll begin by looking at Restrictives which are introduced by an overt wh-pronoun (for convenience, let's refer to them as *wh-relatives*), i.e. structures such as:

(75) (a)   someone [*whom* I met —]
     (b)   the book [*which* I read —]
     (c)   the day [*when* we went to Paris —]
     (d)   the place [*where* we stayed —]
     (e)   the reason [*why* I went there —]

In each case, the superficial structure of these 'wh-relatives' seems fairly clear: an expression like (75) (a) [*someone whom I met*] is clearly an NP which comprises a nominal *someone* modified by a (bracketed) Restrictive Relative

Clause (= S-bar) [*whom I met*]. This S-bar in turn contains an initial wh-pronoun *whom*, followed by an S [*I met*]. That is, the structure of an expression like *someone whom I met* would be along the lines of:

(76)   [$_{NP}$ someone [$_{S'}$ *whom* [$_S$ I met —]]]

Given arguments of the type we developed in sections 9.3–9.6 above, it should be clear that the italicised wh-pronoun in each case must originate within S in the position marked — in (75) above. But if the relative wh-pronouns in such cases originate within S, and wind up outside S as the leftmost constituent of S-bar, then it seems clear that WH MOVEMENT must have applied to move them from their underlying to their superficial position.

Although it may appear obvious that restrictive wh-relatives such as those in (75) above involve overt WH MOVEMENT, what of their *that* relative counterparts in (77) below?

(77) (a)   someone [*that* I met —]
    (b)   the book [*that* I read —]
    (c)   the day [*that* we went to Paris —]
    (d)   the place [*that* we stayed —]
    (e)   the reason [*that* I went there —]

The traditional analysis of relative *that* (cf. Quirk *et al.* (1985), p. 366) is as a Relative Pronoun (just like *who*, or *which*). In our terms, this would mean analysing *that* as a pronominal wh-NP which originates at D-structure in the position marked — in (77), and is subsequently preposed by WH MOVEMENT into the italicised position as the leftmost constituent of S-bar.

However, an obvious alternative which suggests itself is that the word *that* in Restrictive Relative Clauses has precisely the same function which it has in Complement Clauses such as:

(78)   I think [$_{S'}$ [$_C$ *that*] [$_S$ you are wrong]]

In other words, relative *that* might be simply an invariable clause-introducing *Complementiser*. So, the question we are faced with is whether relative *that* is a Pronoun, or a Complementiser.

In actual fact, there are a number of reasons for supposing that relative *that* cannot be a pronominal wh-NP, and must be a Complementiser. For one thing, typical Pronouns (e.g. relative *who* or *which*) can function as the immediately following Complement of a Preposition, whereas *that* cannot: cf.

(79) (a)   the book [$_{PP}$ *about which*] they were arguing
    (b)   the man [$_{PP}$ *to whom*] he was talking

(80) (a)   *the book [pp *about that*] they were arguing
   (b)   *the man [pp *to that*] he was talking

Secondly, typical NPs have a Genitive case-form (cf. *John's, the man next door's*), and the same is true of pronominal NPs (cf. *his*): but whereas the relative wh-NPs *who* and *which* have the genitive form *whose*, the relative particle *that* has no genitive counterpart **that's* in standard varieties of English:

(81) (a)   the man *whose/*that's* mother died
   (b)   the book *whose/*that's* cover was torn

Thirdly, typical wh-pronouns tend (though this is not always the case) to carry specific syntactic or semantic properties (e.g. be marked for gender or animacy), whereas typical Complementisers do not. This criterion suggests that *who* and *which* should be analysed as Pronouns, since *who* implies a human antecedent, and *which* a non-human antecedent: but by contrast, *that* in English has the typical Complementiser property of being semantically 'neutral' or 'inert' (more precisely, though somewhat vaguely, we might say that Complementisers carry grammatical rather than lexical meaning), and hence can be used with any type of antecedent; cf. the contrasts in:

(82) (a)   the man *that/who/!which* we saw in the pub
   (b)   the film *that/which/!who* we saw on the telly

Fourthly, typical wh-NPs can occur freely in finite or infinitival Clauses (e.g. interrogative *what* in 'I don't know *what* I should say/I don't know *what* to say'), whereas typical Complementisers *may* be restricted to occurring only in a given type of Clause (for example *for* can only introduce infinitive Clauses, whereas *that* and *if* can only introduce finite Clauses). In the light of this, it is interesting to note that (subject to complex restrictions which need not concern us here), Relative Pronouns can be used not only in finite Clauses like (75) above, but also in infinitival Relative Clauses, as the following examples from Quirk *et al.* (1985, p. 1267) illustrate:

(83) (a)   She is not a person [pp *on whom*] to rely
   (b)   This is a good instrument [pp *with which*] to measure vibration

By contrast, *that* can only introduce finite Relative Clauses, not infinitival Relatives: cf.

(84) (a)   She is not a person [*that* you can rely on]
   (b)   *She is not a person [*that* to rely on]

Since it is a property of Complementisers but not wh-constituents that they are typically restricted to occurring e.g. in finite Clauses, this provides strong empirical support for the analysis of relative *that* as a (finite Clause) Complementiser.

A fifth argument which increases the plausibility of the Complementiser analysis is that Restrictive Relatives can indeed be introduced by an overt Complementiser: for example, infinitival relatives can be introduced by the infinitival Complementiser *for*, as the following examples (from Quirk *et al.* (1985), p. 1266) show:

(85) (a)   The man [*for* you to see] is Mr Johnson
     (b)   The thing [*for* you to be these days] is a systems analyst
     (c)   The time [*for* you to go] is July
     (d)   The place [*for* you to stay] is the university guest house

Thus, if there are infinitival Relative Clauses such as (85) above introduced by an overt Complementiser, then we should also expect to find finite Relative Clauses introduced by an overt Complementiser: and since the finite non-interrogative Clause Complementiser is *that*, then we should expect to find finite Relatives introduced by the Complementiser *that*. But this will only be the case if relative *that* is analysed as a Complementiser.

A sixth argument against the wh-pronoun analysis can be formulated in the following terms. We have already seen in section 9.3 that one of the key properties of WH MOVEMENT is that a moved wh-phrase leaves a 'gap' at its original *extraction site* (i.e. the original place out of which it moves). In the light of this restriction, consider nonstandard Relative Clauses such as that bracketed in (86) below:

(86)   %He is someone [*that* you never know whether to trust *him* or not]

Now, if *that* is a Relative Pronoun here, then it must have originated as the Object of *trust*, and should therefore leave a 'gap' which cannot be refilled when it is preposed by WH MOVEMENT. But, self-evidently, there is no 'gap' in (86), since the Pronoun *him* occupies the postverbal position of the Direct Object of *trust*. But if there is no 'gap', then there cannot have been movement of a wh-constituent out of the gap: or, in other words, *that* cannot be a preposed relative wh-NP in structures such as (86), but rather must be a Complementiser. But if relative *that* is a Complementiser in structures such as (86), it would seem sensible to conclude that it is also a Complementiser in other relative constructions. The ungrammaticality of the wh-pronoun counterpart of (86), namely

(87)   *He is someone [*whom* you never know whether to trust *him* or not]

would seem to provide further evidence against analysing *that* as a wh-pronoun, since if it were a wh-pronoun, we'd expect (86) to be as ungrammatical as (87).

We can summarise our discussion so far by saying that there is overwhelming evidence that relative *that* is a Complementiser, not a wh-NP (i.e. not a Relative Pronoun). But this poses something of a problem for us. To see this, consider a Restrictive Relative Clause such as that bracketed in (88) below:

(88)   the book [*that* I put on the table]

Now, we have already seen from examples like (20) above that *put* subcategorises both an obligatory NP Complement, and an obligatory PP Complement. But although *put* has a PP Complement [*on the table*] in (88), it appears to have no NP Complement at all (if we accept that relative *that* is a Complementiser, and not a wh-NP). But if there is no NP Complement at all for *put* in (88), there will be an obvious violation of the subcategorisation frame for *put*, so that our grammar will wrongly predict that Relative Clauses such as that bracketed in (88) above are ungrammatical. How can we get out of this dilemma?

One possible solution is the following. Let's suppose that in addition to *overt* relative pronouns like *who, which, where, when, why*, etc. English also has a corresponding set of *covert* (i.e. *empty*) relative pronouns. Extending somewhat Quirk *et al.*'s (1985) terminology, we might refer to these as *zero* relative pronouns; or, in the more recent terminology of Chomsky (1981d), we might refer to such 'covert' relative pronouns as *empty wh-operators*. Since the symbol 'O' is a convenient abbreviation both for the term 'zero pronoun', and for the term 'operator', we shall henceforth adopt the convention of using this symbol to denote a covert relative wh-proform.

What we are suggesting is the following. Let us suppose that underlying (88) is a D-structure along the lines of (89) below:

(89)   the book [$_{S'}$ [$_C$ that] [$_S$ I put O on the table]]

where 'O' designates an empty (i.e. 'zero') relative wh-NP operator (i.e. a kind of inaudible and invisible Pronoun). Note that a structure such as (89) would satisfy the subcategorisation frame for *put*, since *put* in (89) is followed by both an NP complement (= O), and a PP complement [*on the table*]. Let us further suppose that the empty wh-pronoun operator 'O' in (89) undergoes WH MOVEMENT in the same way as overt wh-phrases do, and moves out of its containing S to become the leftmost constituent of S-bar, in the manner indicated schematically in (90) overleaf:

(90) (a)   the book [$_{S'}$ [$_C$ that] [$_S$ I put O on the table]]

  ┌── WH MOVEMENT ──┘

(b)   the book [$_{S'}$ O [$_C$ that] [$_S$ I put —— on the table]]

The corresponding derived structure thus contains an empty wh-pronoun 'O' as the leftmost constituent of S-bar to the immediate left of the Complementiser *that*. The resulting sequence of *covert wh-pronoun + Complementiser* has an overt counterpart in nonstandard varieties of English, as the following example (recorded from a BBC radio programme) illustrates:

(91)   England put themselves in a position [*whereby that* they took a lot of credit for tonight's game] (Ron Greenwood, BBC radio 4)

Moreover, Relative Clauses containing sequences of *overt wh-pronoun + Complementiser* were found in earlier stages of English, as the following examples illustrate:

(92) (a)   rod *on ðaere ðe* Crist wolde ðrowian
       cross on which that Christ would suffer
       [Old English] (Bresnan (1976b), p. 359)

(b)   this book *of which that* I make mencioun
       [Middle English] (Bresnan (1976b), p. 357)

(c)   He hathe seyd that he woold lyfte them *whom that* hym plese
       (= 'them whom [that] it may please him')
       [Middle English] (Traugott (1972), p. 156)

(d)   a doghter *which that* called was Sophie
       [Middle English] (Traugott (1972), p. 156)

(cf. Maling (1978) for further examples). And parallel Relative Clause structures are found in other languages: e.g.

(93) (a)   la fille *avec qui que je parle* [Canadian French]
       the girl with who that I speak
       'the girl with whom I'm speaking' (Lefebvre (1979), p. 80)

(b)   de jongen *aan wie dat* Jan het probleem had voorgelegd
       the boy to whom that Jan the problem had presented
       'the boy that Jan had presented the problem to'
       [Dutch] (den Besten (1978b), p. 647)

Thus, the claim that relative wh-pronouns are moved to the left of C seems plausible, on universalist grounds. Moreover, we have already argued that in the case of direct questions such as (94) below:

(94)   [$_{S'}$ *What* [$_C$ will] [$_S$ he do —]]?

the preposed wh-pronoun ends up as the leftmost constituent of S-bar, to the left of the C constituent containing the inverted Modal Auxiliary *will*. Thus, since WH MOVEMENT involves movement of an interrogative wh-phrase to the left of C in interrogatives, it seems plausible to claim that it involves movement of a relative wh-phrase to the left of C in the case of relatives.

But while there may be strong empirical evidence (which I leave you to find for yourself – cf. *Exercise II* at the end of this chapter!) in support of positing an empty underlying Object NP 'O' in structures such as (89) [*the book that I put O on the table*], we might wonder what evidence there is that this empty operator gets preposed by WH MOVEMENT into initial (pre-C) position within S-bar (rather than simply remaining in its underlying position as the post-verbal Object of *put*). One argument in support of the *movement* analysis can be formulated in relation to a range of constructions that have the interesting property of being *islands* (to use a metaphor coined in Ross 1967). The general idea behind this picturesque metaphor is that once you're marooned on an island, you're stuck there, and can't be got off the island by any movement rule at all. By way of a concrete illustration of the phenomenon of *islandhood*, consider the following contrasts:

(95) (a)   *Who* did he engineer [the downfall of —]?
    (b)   *Who did [the downfall of —] cause consternation?
    (c)   *Who did the government collapse [after the downfall of —]?

In (95) (a), *who* has been extracted out of a bracketed NP which functions as the *Complement* of the Verb *engineer*; in (95) (b), *who* has been (illicitly) extracted out of a bracketed NP which functions as the *Subject* of the Verb *cause*; and in (95) (c), *who* has been (illicitly) extracted out of a bracketed PP which functions as an *Adjunct* of the Verb *collapse*. It would seem from (95) that movement rules can extract constituents out of containing *Complement Phrases*, but not out of containing *Subject Phrases* or *Adjunct Phrases*. Using Ross's colourful metaphor, we might express the relevant generalisation in terms of a condition on movement rules such as the following:

(96)   ISLAND CONDITION (on Movement Rules)
      Subjects and Adjuncts are islands; Complements are not

What this means is that constituents can be extracted out of Complement Phrases, but not out of Subject/Adjunct Phrases.

In the light of the claim we are making here that Relative Clauses containing overt wh-pronouns involve WH MOVEMENT, it is not surprising to find paradigms such as (97) below:

(97) (a)   someone *who* he engineered [the downfall of —]

(b)   *someone *who* [the downfall of —] caused consternation]

(c)   *someone *who* the government collapsed [after the downfall of —]

How can we account for the contrast between the grammaticality of (97) (a) and the ungrammaticality of (97) (b) and (c)? An obvious answer is that in (97) (a) the wh-relative pronoun *who* has been extracted out of a (bracketed) Complement Phrase, whereas in (97) (b) it has been extracted out of a Subject Phrase, and in (97) (c) out of an Adjunct Phrase. Now, since our ISLAND CONDITION (96) prohibits movement out of Subjects and Adjuncts (though not out of Complements), the contrast in grammaticality can be accounted for in a straightforward fashion.

However, what is of more immediate interest to us here is the fact that we find exactly the same pattern of grammaticality contrasts with the corresponding *that* relatives: cf.

(98) (a)   someone *that* he engineered [the downfall of —]

(b)   *someone *that* [the downfall of —] caused consternation]

(c)   *someone *that* the government collapsed [after the downfall of —]

How can we account for the fact that relatives introduced by *that* seem to show the same island-sensitivity as relatives introduced by moved wh-phrases like *who*, when *islandhood* is a property of movement rules? The obvious answer is that *that*-relatives involve movement of a covert wh-pronoun 'O', and that movement of covert constituents is subject to exactly the same *islandhood* restrictions as movement of overt constituents. (An even stronger *island* argument in support of the movement analysis of *that* relatives can be formulated in relation to the ungrammaticality of sentences such as: *He is someone that I don't know what Mary said to*: but since discussion of the evidence presupposes knowledge of constructs dealt with in the next chapter, it would not be appropriate to discuss the relevant construction any further at this point.)

Thus, there seems to be some empirical evidence from English in support of claiming that *that*-relatives contain a zero Relative Pronoun Operator 'O' which undergoes WH MOVEMENT. Further universalist support for the claim that the empty Relative Operator 'O' undergoes WH MOVEMENT can be adduced from facts about the corresponding construction in French. Now, French has a rule referred to in Kayne (1972) as STYLISTIC INVERSION, by which subject NPs can optionally be postposed in wh-clauses (i.e. Clauses which contain a wh-phrase): so, for example the italicised NP subject [*ton ami*] 'your

friend' in (99) (a) below can optionally be postposed into the position it occupies in (99) (b):

(99) (a)   Je me demande [$_{S'}$ quand [$_S$ *ton   ami*   partira]]
            I   me ask   when   your friend will-leave
            'I wonder when your friend will leave'

   (b)   Je me demande [$_{S'}$ quand [$_S$ partira   *ton   ami*]]
            I   me ask   when   will-leave your friend
            'I wonder when your friend will leave'

However, preposing of interrogative wh-phrases is optional in Direct
Questions in French, and as Kayne and Pollock (1978, p. 597) note, STYLISTIC
INVERSION (= Subject Postposing) is only possible in a Clause which contains a
preposed wh-phrase: hence, in their examples (100) below, postposing of the
Subject NP [*ton ami*] 'your friend' is permitted in (a) because the wh-phrase
quand 'when' has been preposed, but not in (b) or (c), where the wh-phrase
quand has not undergone WH MOVEMENT:

(100) (a)   Quand partira   *ton ami*?
             When   will-leave your friend?
             'When will your friend leave?'

    (b)   *Partira *ton ami* quand?

    (c)   *Partira quand *ton ami*?

Moreoever, STYLISTIC INVERSION is not generally permitted in a Clause introduced by the indicative Complementiser *que* 'that': hence the impossibility of
postposing the Subject NP [*ton ami*] in examples such as the following:

(101) (a)   Je crois [$_{S'}$ que *ton   ami*   partira]
             I   think   that your friend will-leave

    (b)   *Je crois [$_{S'}$ que partira   *ton   ami*]
             I   think   that will-leave your friend

So, the obvious conclusion to draw is that STYLISTIC INVERSION is possible in an
indicative Clause only when the Clause contains a preposed wh-phrase.

French has a class of Restrictive Relative Clause structures which appear to
resemble *that*-relatives, in that they are introduced by the indicative Complementiser *que* 'that': e.g.

(102)   l'homme [$_{S'}$ *que* Jean a   vu]
         the man   that John has seen
         'the man that John saw'

Kayne (1976) argues in considerable detail that French relative *que* is a Complementiser, and not a Relative Pronoun (using arguments similar to those we

developed above in relation to English *that*). But if *que* in (102) is a Complementiser and not a wh-pronoun, then how do we explain the fact that the subject NP *Jean* in (102) can undergo STYLISTIC INVERSION (= Postposing), as we see from the grammaticality of (103) below?

(103)   l'homme [$_{S'}$ qu'a vu *Jean*]
         the man that has seen John]
         'the man that John saw'

The answer we shall suggest here is that structures such as (102) and (103) involve preposing of a 'Zero Relative Pronoun' or 'empty wh-operator' out of its underlying position in (104) (a) below as the postverbal Complement of *vu* into its superficial position in (104) (b) to the left of the Complementiser *que*:

(104) (a)   l'homme [$_{S'}$ que [$_S$ Jean a vu O]
                                            |
                 WH MOVEMENT
                      ↑
      (b)   l'homme [$_{S'}$ O que [$_S$ Jean a vu —]

Given that the bracketed Relative Clause (S-bar) in (104) (b) contains a preposed wh-phrase (viz. the empty pronominal wh-NP symbolised as 'O'), the conditions for the application of STYLISTIC INVERSION (namely that the rule applies only in a Clause containing a preposed wh-phrase) are met, so that we correctly predict that STYLISTIC INVERSION can apply in (104) (b): and as the grammaticality of (103) above shows, this prediction is entirely correct. But note that this account of the way in which STYLISTIC INVERSION applies in *que*-relatives in French rests crucially on the assumption that the empty wh-operator 'O' *undergoes WH MOVEMENT*.

We might generalise our conclusions along the following lines. We have seen that there are Restrictive Relative Clause constructions in English (and also French) which are introduced by an overt Complementiser like *that* (= French *que*) or *for*, but which contain no overt wh-phrase: we might refer to such structures collectively as *Complementiser Relatives*. We have argued here that such Complementiser Relatives involve WH MOVEMENT of a 'Zero Relative Pronoun' or 'empty wh-operator' (which we have symbolised as 'O') out of its underlying position within S into its superficial position within S-bar to the immediate left of the Complementiser position.

Indeed, we might go further than this, and extend our 'empty operator' analysis from Complementiser Relatives (i.e. those which contain an overt Complementiser but no overt wh-phrase), to what are traditionally called 'Contact Relatives' (i.e. Relative Clauses which contain neither an overt Complementiser, nor an overt wh-phrase). For, recall that alongside wh-relatives like (75) above, and *that*-relatives such as (77), we also find 'Contact Relative' counterparts such as (105) below:

(105) (a)   someone [I met]
 (b)   the book [I read]
 (c)   the day [we went to Paris]
 (d)   the place [we stayed]
 (e)   the reason [I went there]

If we were to extend our 'empty operator' analysis to this type of relative structure, we might argue that Contact Relatives involve both an empty Complementiser, and an empty preposed wh-pronoun.

   Given this assumption, let's see how we might account for the similarities and differences between the three different types of (bracketed) Relative Clauses in (106) below:

(106) (a)   the book [$_{S'}$ *which I put on the table*]
 (b)   the book [$_{S'}$ *that I put on the table*]
 (c)   the book [$_{S'}$ *I put on the table*]

In (106) (a), we might argue that the bracketed Relative Clause contains an empty C, and that the wh-NP *which* originates as the immediately following NP Complement of *put*, and is moved out of S to occupy the leftmost position within S-bar, to the immediate left of the empty C, in the manner indicated schematically in (107) below:

(107)   the book [$_{S'}$ [$_C$ e] [$_S$ I put *which* on the table]]
         ⌊WH MOVEMENT ⌋

In (106) (b), the bracketed Clause contains the overt Complementiser *that*; and (given the arguments above), we might suppose that there is an empty pronominal wh-NP operator 'O' which originates as the postverbal Complement of *put*, and is subsequently preposed by WH MOVEMENT into pre-C position within S-bar in the manner indicated schematically in (108) below:

(108)   the book [$_{S'}$ [$_C$ that] [$_S$ I put O on the table]]
         ⌊WH MOVEMENT⌋

And we might likewise posit that in (106) (c), the Relative Clause contains an empty Complementiser, and an empty relative wh-NP 'O' which is similarly moved by WH MOVEMENT from its underlying position as the Object of *put* to its superficial pre-C position, in the manner represented informally in (109) below:

(109)   the book [$_{S'}$ [$_C$ e] [$_S$ I put O on the table]]
                          └─WH MOVEMENT─┘

Thus, given the analysis suggested here, all three types of Relative Clause in (106) involve application of WH MOVEMENT: the three structures vary along two parameters – namely (i) whether they contain an empty or a filled Complementiser, and (ii) whether they involve movement of an overt or a covert wh-pronoun.

Our discussion in this section has focussed on the internal structure of *Restrictive Relative Clauses*. Readers interested in the structure of Appositive Relatives and Free Relatives should refer to the relevant reading material listed in the **Bibliographical Background** section at the end of the book (though it should be noted that much of the relevant literature is likely to prove too advanced for the beginner).

> *You should now be able to tackle exercises II and III*

9.8   Other Wh-constructions

Thus far, we have argued that wh-interrogatives involve preposing of overt wh-phrases by WH MOVEMENT, and that wh-relatives likewise involve preposing of either overt or covert wh-phrases by WH MOVEMENT. However, there are a number of other structures which might be argued to involve overt or covert WH MOVEMENT. For example, we might argue that overt WH MOVEMENT is involved in direct wh-exclamatives such as:

(110) (a)   *What a nice pear* Mary's got —!
      (b)   *How charming* he can be —!

and in indirect (embedded) wh-exclamatives such as:

(111) (a)   He remarked on [*what a nice pear* Mary had —]
      (b)   It never ceases to amaze me [*how charming* he can be —]

We might claim that in each case the italicised wh-phrase originates at D-structure in the position marked —, and is subsequently preposed by WH MOVEMENT into the italicised position as the leftmost constituent of the exclamative S-bar. *Exercise I* at the end of this chapter is designed to help you devise a set of arguments for yourself which support this assumption, so we shan't go into the evidence in favour of a WH MOVEMENT analysis of wh-exclamatives here. Note that it is clear that structures like (111) (a) must be embedded exclamatives and not embedded interrogatives, since the expression *what a+ Count Noun* is never used in interrogatives: cf. the ungrammaticality of:

(112)   **What a nice dress* was she wearing?

A second construction which arguably involves WH MOVEMENT are so-called 'cleft sentences' of the schematic form [*it be XP S'*], such as the following:

(113) (a)   It is JOHN [*who* she really loves]
    (b)   It is JOHN [*that* she really loves]
    (c)   It is JOHN [she really loves]

In such cases, the capitalised constituent is said to be in *focus* position. The bracketed constituent here appears to be a Relative Clause which can be a *wh*-relative, or a *that*-relative, or a *zero*-relative: and we might assume that these three types of relative all involve WH MOVEMENT of an overt or covert wh-phrase (cf. our discussion of Restrictive Relatives in the previous section).

The precise internal structure of 'Cleft sentences' is far from clear. Superficially, they resemble Restrictive Relatives. But there are obvious differences between Clefts and Restrictive Relatives. For one thing, an unmodified Proper Noun like *John* cannot serve as the antecedent of a Restrictive (as we noted at the beginning of the previous section), though no such restriction is found in Clefts, as we see from (113) above. For another thing, whereas the whole *Antecedent + Relative* structure forms a unitary constituent in Restrictives, this is obviously not true of Clefts, since the focussed NP can freely be preposed without (and indeed cannot be preposed with) the following Clause, as we see from the examples below:

(114) (a)   *John* it is [who she really loves]
    (b)   **John* [*who she really loves*] it is

We shall not speculate further on the internal structure of Clefts here, since this would take us too far astray. It is important to point out, however, that *Cleft* sentences such as those above are distinct from so-called *pseudo-cleft* sentences such as (115) below:

(115) (a)   What I bought was a car
    (b)   What I feel is that we should all try harder

The exact syntax of *pseudo-clefts* is also shrouded in mystery; they seem to be related in a fairly obvious way to *Free Relatives*, in the sense that the expressions [*what I bought*] and [*what I feel*] might well be analysed as Free Relative NPs.

However, rather than get bogged down in abstract discussions about the syntax of poorly understood constructions, let's turn instead to look at further potential sources of wh-constructions. Chomsky in 'On Wh-movement' (1977b, p. 87) argues that overt WH MOVEMENT is also involved in the derivation of nonstandard wh-comparatives such as (116) below, found in some dialects of English:

(116) (a) %John is taller than [*what* Mary is —]
     (b) %Mary isn't the same as [*what* she was — five years ago]

More specifically, he posits that *what* in such cases is a wh-pronoun which originates in the position marked — as the Complement of *is/was*, and is subsequently preposed into the italicised position at the front of the bracketed containing comparative Clause. Moreover, he also maintains that the 'standard' counterparts of structures such as (116) (= without *what*) involve covert WH MOVEMENT. In terms of the framework we are using here, this could be interpreted as saying that 'standard' comparatives such as (117) below:

(117)   John is taller than Mary is

involve WH MOVEMENT of a 'Zero Relative Pronoun', in the manner indicated schematically in (118) below:

(118)   John is taller than [$_{S'}$ [$_C$ e] [$_S$ Mary is O]]
                     └─WH MOVEMENT─┘

Chomsky also argues in the same paper that structures such as:

(119) (a)   The job is prestigious enough [*for* us to offer — to John]
     (b)   The job is too prestigious [*for* us to offer — to John]
     (c)   John is easy [*for* us to please —]

involve covert movement of a wh-phrase (in our terms, this would be a 'zero' Relative Pronoun, 'O') from the position marked — to initial position in the bracketed S-bar in front of the italicised Complementiser. Thus, *if* Chomsky is right, many other constructions in English may also involve covert WH MOVEMENT.

     You should now be able to tackle exercise IV

9.9   Targets for WH MOVEMENT
     Having now given extensive syntactic, morphological, phonological, and semantic arguments in support of postulating a rule of WH MOVE-

MENT, and having argued that the rule applies in a variety of wh-constructions (wh-interrogatives, wh-relatives, wh-exclamatives, etc.), let's look a little more closely at the operation of the rule. An obvious question to ask is: 'What kind of constituents can be the *target* for (i.e. undergo) WH MOVEMENT?' The simple answer appears to be that *wh-phrases* undergo the rule: by *wh-phrase*, we mean simply 'a phrase which contains a wh-word like *who, what, when, why, where, which* or *how*' (although *how* does not begin with the sequence *wh-*, it is classified as a wh-word by virtue of the fact that it has the same syntactic properties as 'true' wh-words). We see from (120) below that a (bracketed) Noun Phrase containing a wh-word can be moved out of the position marked — into the italicised position by WH MOVEMENT:

(120) (a) [*What*] has he given — to Mary?
  (b) [*How many parcels*] will he send — to London?
  (c) [*Which witch*] might they burn — at the stake?

And in (121) below, we see that when a wh-NP is used as the Object of a Preposition, the whole Prepositional Phrase can undergo WH MOVEMENT:

(121) (a) [*To whom*] can I send this letter —?
  (b) [*About what*] are they quarrelling —?
  (c) [*In which book*] did you read about it —?

In (122) below, a (bracketed) Adjectival Phrase has undergone WH MOVEMENT:

(122) (a) [*How successful*] will Mary be —?
  (b) [*How famous*] has Nim Chimpsky become —?
  (c) [*How attractive*] do you find my proposal —?

And in (123) below, a (bracketed) Adverbial Phrase has undergone WH MOVEMENT:

(123) (a) [*How quickly*] will he drink the beer —?
  (b) [*How carefully*] did he plan his campaign —?
  (c) [*How well*] did he treat her —?

Thus, the obvious conclusion to draw is that WH MOVEMENT applies to phrases which contain a wh-word: i.e. the target of the rule is a wh-XP constituent (where a wh-XP is a Phrase containing a wh-word).

However, not all XP constituents containing a wh-word can undergo WH MOVEMENT. For example, WH MOVEMENT yields (at best) marginal results in interrogatives with VPs: cf.

(124) (a) ??[*Working how hard*] has he been?

   (b) ?*[*Do what*] did he ask you to?

And it seems not to be permitted at all in interrogatives with clausal constituents such as S-bar, S, or SC: cf.

(125) (a) *[$_{S'}$ *Where she was going*] do you know —?

   (b) *[$_S$ *John to be how foolish*] does he consider —?

   (c) *[$_{SC}$ *John how foolish*] does he consider —?

So, it seems that only *phrasal* constituents (NP, PP, AP, ADVP, and – albeit marginally – VP) can undergo WH MOVEMENT in interrogatives in English, not clausal constituents such as S-bar, S, or SC.

   However, the picture is complicated somewhat by the fact that in Appositive Relatives, subjectless infinitives containing a Relative Pronoun can be fronted by WH MOVEMENT, though not infinitive structures containing an overt Subject and an overt Complementiser, or finite Clauses: cf. the following examples (from Nanni and Stillings (1978), p. 311):

(126) (a) The elegant parties, [*to be admitted to one of which* was a privilege], had usually been held at Delmonico's

   (b) *The elegant parties, [*for us to be admitted to one of which* was a privilege], had usually been held at Delmonico's

   (c) *They bought a car, [*that their son might drive which* was a surprise to them]

Since it is not clear what the nature of the relevant restrictions operating here is, we shall do no more than mention the problem.

   Given that WH MOVEMENT can apply to both wh-NP and wh-PP constituents, it is perhaps not surprising to find that in PPs of the schematic form [P wh-NP], the rule can apply 'ambiguously', to prepose either the whole wh-PP (as in the (a) examples below), or just the wh-NP, so 'stranding' the Preposition (as in the (b) examples below):

(127) (a) [$_{PP}$ *To* [$_{NP}$ *whom*]] did you turn — for help?

   (b) [$_{NP}$ *Who*] did you turn [$_{PP}$ to —] for help?

(128) (a) [$_{PP}$ *Against* [$_{NP}$ *whom*]] are you fighting —?

   (b) [$_{NP}$ *Who*] are you fighting [$_{PP}$ against —]?

(129) (a) [$_{PP}$ *About* [$_{NP}$ *what*]] are you complaining —?

   (b) [$_{NP}$ *What*] are you complaining [$_{PP}$ about —]?

(130) (a) [$_{PP}$ *For* [$_{NP}$ *whom*]] did you buy those flowers —?

   (b) [$_{NP}$ *Who*] did you buy those flowers [$_{PP}$ for —]?

Thus, it would seem that when a wh-NP is used as the Object of a Preposition, the Preposition can optionally be moved along to the front of the Clause along with the wh-NP. In the picturesque terminology of Ross (1967), we might say that in such cases the Preposition has undergone PIED PIPING (the general idea behind this metaphor being that Prepositions can follow their wh-NP Objects to the front of Clauses in much the same way that the rats followed the Pied Piper out of Hamlin). And similarly, we might say that where the wh-NP Object of a Preposition has been fronted on its own (without the Preposition), then the Preposition has been *stranded* (or *orphaned*). Using this terminology, we might say that the Preposition has been *pied-piped* in the (a) examples in (127–30) above, but *stranded* or *orphaned* in the corresponding (b) examples. Rather more precisely, however, we should say that the (a) examples involve fronting of a wh-PP, whereas the (b) examples involve fronting of a wh-NP. Of course, given our assumption that any (non-clausal) wh-XP can undergo WH MOVEMENT, then we should precisely expect that either NP or PP could be preposed in such cases.

The (b) examples (involving *stranded* or *orphaned* Prepositions) are reminiscent of similar 'stranded Preposition' structures we encountered with passive structures involving NP MOVEMENT in the previous chapter – i.e. structures such as:

(131) (a) *Nothing* was agreed ON — by the committee
    (b) *The information* was asked FOR — by the Dean
    (c) *He* can be depended ON — for sound advice
    (d) *John* was shouted AT — by his mother
    (e) *He* must be talked TO — by someone

And recall that we argued that 'prepositional passives' such as (131) involve application of a REANALYSIS rule which combines the capitalised Preposition with the immediately preceding Verb to form a derived 'Complex Verb', such as [*agree on*], [*ask for*], [*depend on*], [*shout at*], [*talk to*], etc. Now, the obvious question to ask is whether preposition-stranding in wh-structures like the (b) examples in (127–30) above should be treated in the same way as in passives, viz. as the result of the prior application of REANALYSIS. In other words, what we are asking is whether a sentence such as (127) (b) *Who did you turn to for help?* has an initial base structure such as (132) (a) below, which is then restructured as (132) (b) by REANALYSIS, prior to the application of WH MOVEMENT:

(132) (a) You did [$_V$ *turn*] [$_{PP}$ *to* [$_{NP}$ who]]?
                   ||
            REANALYSIS
               ⇓
    (b) You did [$_V$ *turn to*] [$_{NP}$ who]?

More generally still, we are asking whether *all* cases of preposition-stranding in wh-structures should be treated as involving REANALYSIS.

The answer to this question appears to be negative. Although there is plenty of solid evidence to suggest that preposition stranding in passives is the result of REANALYSIS, the opposite is the case with stranded prepositions in wh-constructions. To see this, let's highlight some of the differences between preposition stranding in passives on the one hand, and preposition stranding in wh-questions on the other.

Recall that in Chapter 8, we saw that REANALYSIS in prepositional passives is blocked when another constituent intervenes between the Verb and the Preposition concerned. But this is not the case at all with preposition-stranding in wh-questions, as the following contrasts illustrate:

(133) (a) *The candidate was shouted *angrily* at
      (b) Which candidate did they shout *angrily* at?

(134) (a) *The information was asked *the committee* for
      (b) What information did they ask *the committee* for?

(135) (a) *The President was talked *about disarmament* to
      (b) Who did they talk *about disarmament* to?

Moreover, we also saw in Chapter 8 that REANALYSIS is possible only between a V and elements contained in its *Complements*, not between a V and elements contained in *Adjuncts*. But while we can never passivise an NP in an Adjunct Phrase, we can sometimes (though not always – cf. (95) (c) above) wh-prepose such an NP:

(136) (a) *The third round* was lost *in* by Rocky
      (b) *Which round* did Rocky lose *in*?

(137) (a) *Many hours* were argued *for*
      (b) *How many hours* did they argue *for*?

(138) (a) *The last scene of the play* was died *in* by the hero
      (b) *Which scene of the play* did the hero die *in*?

And finally, while an NP can only passivise 'across' a *Natural Predicate*, no such restriction seems to hold in the case of wh-questions: cf.

(139) (a) *President de Gaulle was *read a book about*
      (b) Who did you *read a book about*?

Given the obvious asymmetry between preposition-stranding in passives on the one hand, and in wh-structures on the other, it seems plausible to conclude that whereas Prepositions cannot be stranded in passive structures unless REANALYSIS has applied, no such restriction operates in the case of wh-structures: more precisely, WH MOVEMENT may apply to structures which have not undergone REANALYSIS (though, of course, it may also apply to structures which have, given that the REANALYSIS rule is optional when its conditions of application are met). This means that WH MOVEMENT may either apply to structures like (132) (a) which have not undergone REANALYSIS, or to those like (132) (b) which have undergone the rule.

You should now be able to tackle exercise V

9.10   The landing-site for moved Wh-phrases

In the previous section, we asked what kind of wh-phrases can (and cannot) undergo WH MOVEMENT. In this section, we're going to ask the related question: 'When a wh-phrase undergoes WH MOVEMENT, where exactly does it get moved to?' To use the relevant technical terminology, this amounts to asking what the ultimate *landing-site* for preposed wh-phrases is. We shall see that the eventual answer to this question which we come up with will require us to radically revise our earlier assumptions about the internal constituent structure of Clauses.

As a starting point for our quest to find the ultimate *landing-site* of moved wh-phrases, let's look at the position occupied by the preposed wh-NP *what* in a wh-question such as:

(140)   *What* will he do next?

Recall that in Chapter 8 we argued in some detail that 'inverted' Auxiliaries in direct questions are moved out of I into C by our familiar rule of I MOVEMENT. If this is so, then it is apparent that the wh-NP *what* in (140) must be positioned to the left of C, in the manner represented in a simplified fashion in (141) below:

(141)   *What* [c will] [s he do next]?

Thus, direct questions such as (140) would suggest that preposed wh-phrases occupy a pre-Complementiser position in English.

However, at first sight there would seem to be an obvious complication with any such claim, in the case of embedded questions (i.e. structures in which the question Clause is the Complement of some interrogative Predicate). For, given that Complement Clauses can (and in some cases must) be introduced by an overt Complementiser like *that*, then our 'pre-C' analysis of the landing-site of preposed wh-phrases would lead us to expect to find that wh-phrases can be positioned in front of Complementisers like *that*. But surely such *wh-phrase + that* interrogative structures never occur in English ... do they? Well, it may surprise you to learn that people *do* say things like that in spontaneous speech. I recorded the following examples of interrogative complement Clauses containing the sequence *wh-XP that* ... from a variety of BBC radio and television broadcasts:

(142) (a)   I'm not sure *what kind of ban that* FIFA has in mind (Bert Milli-chip, BBC radio 4)

(b)   We'll see *what sort of pace that* Daley Thompson's running at (Ron Pickering, BBC 1 TV)

(c)   It'll probably be evident from the field *which of the players that* are feeling the heat most (Jimmy Hill, BBC 1 TV)

(d)   ... no matter *what choice that* the committee makes ([Sir?] Bob Geldof, BBC 1 TV)

And at a Linguistics conference recently, I heard a speaker say:

(143)   We can look at our statistics and see *what sort of pattern that* we get (Bob Morris Jones)

Moreover, a similar situation obtained in Middle English and Old English, as the example below (from Bresnan (1970), p. 312, fn. 14) illustrates:

(144)   ... they stoden for to see *who that* ther com (Chaucer)

(cf. Grimshaw 1975, Bresnan 1976b and Traugott 1972 for further examples). So, perhaps the (in)famous individuals cited (or indicted?) in (142) and (143) above are just a little behind the times!

Moreover, the proposal that preposed wh-phrases occupy a pre-C position seems to have a certain amount of universalist support. For example, there are a number of languages which have wh-phrases positioned in front of overt Complementisers in indirect questions: cf.

(145) (a)   I woaß ned *wann daß* da Xavea kummt (Bavarian)
I know not *when that* the Xavier comes
'I don't know when Xavier will come'
[Bayer (1984), p. 24]

(b)   Jeg forfalte Jan *hvem som* var kommet (Norwegian)
I asked Jan who that had come
'I asked Jan who had come'
[Taraldsen (1978), p. 631, fn. 14]

(c)   Ik weten niet *wien dat* Jan gezeen heet (Flemish)
      I know not *whom that* John seen has
      'I don't know whom John has seen'
      [Haegeman (1983), p. 83]

Even more striking support for the 'pre-C' analysis comes from the fact that many languages which allow Complementisers in main Clauses also allow pre-posed wh-phrases to be positioned in front of overt Complementisers in direct questions, resulting in structures such as (146) below:

(146) (a)   *Où que* tu vas? (Popular French)
            Where that you go? (= 'Where are you going?')
      (b)   *Mᶜamn lli* hdarti? (Colloquial Moroccan Arabic)
            With-whom that you spoke (= 'Who did you speak to?')
      (c)   *Wat oft* ik drinke woe? (Frisian)
            What whether I drink would?
            'What would I drink?' [DeHaan and Weerman (1986), p. 98]
      (d)   *Cén bhean a* phósfadh sé? (Irish)
            Which woman that would-marry he?
            'Which woman would he marry?' [McCloskey (1979), p. 31]

Thus, we might tentatively suggest that pre-C position is *universally* the landing-site for preposed wh-phrases.

Further support for this proposal comes from the fact that (as we have already seen in relation to examples such as (91–3) above, there are languages (and even varieties of English) which have Relative Clause structures containing an overt wh-pronoun immediately preceding an overt Complementiser. And this is also true of wh-exclamatives, as the following examples illustrate:

(147) (a)   *What a mine of useless information that* I am!
            (Terry Wogan, recorded on BBC Radio 2)
      (b)   *Che belle gambe che* hai! [Italian]
            What beautiful legs that you-have
            'What beautiful legs you have!'

Thus, we have abundant empirical evidence in support of claiming that WH MOVEMENT in Interrogatives, Relatives, and Exclamatives alike involves movement of a wh-phrase out of S into pre-C position in S-bar.

It would seem as if WH MOVEMENT somehow involves 'attraction' of a wh-phrase to a clause-initial Complementiser. If this is indeed the case, then we might expect that only languages which have clause-initial Complementisers will have WH MOVEMENT: and Bresnan (1970, p. 317) claims that this is indeed the case. So, (as the following data from Li and Thompson (1984), pp. 51–4 illustrate), since Chinese has clause-final Complementisers and thus forms yes–no questions by using the clause-final interrogative Complementiser *ma* 'whether': cf.

(148)   Zhan-sang chang kan dianying *ma*
          Zhan-sang often see movie   *whether*
          'Does Zhang-sang often see movies?'

it does not have a syntactic rule of WH MOVEMENT moving wh-phrases to clause-initial position, but rather leaves them *in situ* (i.e. places them in the same position as their non-wh counterparts would occupy): cf.

(149)   Women *zai nar*   chi yecan?
          We   at where eat picnic
          'Where shall we have our picnic?'

Thus, it would seem as if the claim that WH MOVEMENT universally involves 'attraction' of a wh-phrase to a clause-initial Complementiser constituent has substantial empirical support.

Not surprisingly, therefore, a number of analyses of the landing-site of WH MOVEMENT have sought to incorporate this 'attraction to C' condition. For the sake of brevity, we shall mention only one such analysis here, namely the *C-adjunction* analysis proposed in Chomsky's 'On Binding' paper (1980, p. 5), and slightly modified in Chomsky's *Lectures* (1981d, p. 53). Chomsky suggests that WH MOVEMENT is an adjunction rule which adjoins wh-phrases to C. He further assumes a universal condition on Adjunction Rules to the effect that leftward movement rules adjoin moved phrases to the left of the constituent they attach to, whereas rightward movement rules adjoin moved phrases to the right of the constituent they attach to. It would thus follow from this universal property of movement rules that since WH MOVEMENT is a leftward movement rule, it will adjoin wh-phrases to the left of C. If we also assume that 'inverted' Auxiliaries are positioned in C, then it would follow that the derived structure of a direct wh-question such as:

(150)   What will he do?

would be along the lines of (151) below:

(151)

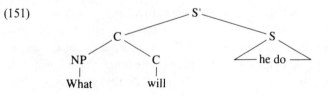

The *C-adjunction* analysis thus provides an obvious way of capturing the intuition that preposed wh-phrases are 'attracted' to Complementisers.

However, the C-adjunction analysis turns out to be fatally flawed. For one thing, there are numerous theoretical objections to any such rule (though these are of a highly technical nature, and it would not be appropriate for us to go into them here). Perhaps even more importantly, more recent research has questioned the empirical validity of the fundamental assumption on which the C-adjunction analysis was based – namely that only languages with clause-initial Complementisers have WH MOVEMENT. More specifically, the claim that WH MOVEMENT universally involves movement to the immediate left of C is called into question by the fact that there are a number of languages which have clause-initial preposed wh-phrases, but do not have clause-initial Complementisers: among these languages are Sharanahua (see Frantz 1973), Cuzco Quechua (see Lefebvre and Muysken 1979), Navajo (see Kaufman 1975), and Kamaiurá (see Brandon and Seki 1981).

By way of illustration of the problem, we might consider Koopman's analysis of WH MOVEMENT in Vata (a language of the Kru family spoken in the Ivory Coast). As we see from (152) below (from Koopman (1984), p. 45), Vata positions Complementisers like *ka* clause-finally:

(152) ń nÍkā [yÓ-Ó sàká nyÈ *kā*] mlÌ
       I will [child rice give *that*] go
       'I will go and [literally 'that'] give rice to the child'

But at the same time, Vata also has a WH MOVEMENT rule moving wh-phrases into clause-initial position, as we see from (153) (from Koopman (1984), p. 86):

(153) *yÍ* ń nÙ là?
       What you do PRT (= Particle)
       'What did you do?'

Thus, the obvious conclusion is that WH MOVEMENT cannot involve adjunction to C either in Vata, or universally.

Instead, let's consider an alternative, more recent analysis which turns out to have radical (though theoretically desirable) implications for the S-bar analysis of Ordinary Clauses which we proposed in Chapter 6. Recall that under the S-bar analysis, S-bar is a single bar-projection of S. But let's suppose that we reject the assumption that S is the head of S-bar, and instead analyse C as the head of S-bar (following Stowell 1981; Koopman 1984; and Chomsky's *Barriers* 1986b). More specifically, let us suppose that the S constituent introduced by C should be analysed as the Complement of C, and hence that C and its S Complement together form a C-bar constituent. Let us further assume that like other X-bar constituents, C-bar can be expanded by the addition of an *optional* Specifier phrase into a C-double-bar (= CP = Complementiser Phrase) constituent, corresponding to the traditional S-bar constituent (so that S' = CP = C''). Let's also assume that the Specifier of C-bar is a base-generated empty XP constituent (i.e. an empty NP, or PP, or AP, or ADVP, etc.) into which an appropriate wh-phrase can be preposed by WH MOVEMENT. Given these assumptions, and given independent evidence that English is a *head-initial* and *specifier-initial* language whereas Vata is a *head-final* and *specifier-initial* language, then it follows that WH MOVEMENT will operate in the two languages in the manner schematised below:

(154) (a)   English

(b)   Vata

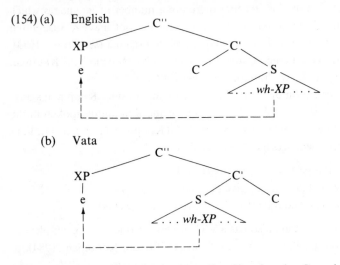

XP here is a base-generated empty Specifier for the Complementiser, and *wh-XP* is a wh-phrase. If the category of the wh-phrase matches that of the C-Specifier, then the wh-phrase can be moved (by a *substitution* operation) into the empty C-specifier position. Thus, in English-type languages (with initial Complementisers and initial wh-phrases), WH MOVEMENT will involve movement of a wh-phrase into an empty Specifier position to the left of C-bar, as in (154) (a) above: but in Vata-type languages (with final Complementisers and initial wh-phrases), WH MOVEMENT will again involve substitution of a wh-phrase into an empty Specifier position to the left of C-bar, as in (154) (b). Under this analysis, the universal aspect of WH MOVEMENT is not (as was originally thought) that it positions wh-phrases to the immediate left of C, but rather that it moves wh-phrases to the immediate left of C-bar, into an empty C-specifier position (in languages which are *specifier-initial*). For obvious reasons, therefore, we might refer to this as the *C-specifier* analysis.

Earlier, we saw that a direct wh-question such as (150) *What will he do?*

would be assigned the derived structure (151) above on the *C-adjunction* analysis. But how would (150) be analysed under the *C-Specifier* analysis? The answer is that (150) would be derived in the manner represented schematically in (155) below:

(155)

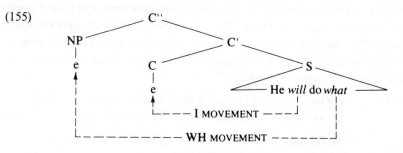

The Modal *will* in I will be moved into the empty C position by I MOVEMENT, and the wh-NP *what* will be moved into the empty NP C-specifier position by WH MOVEMENT. The resulting S-structure will thus be (156) below:

(156)

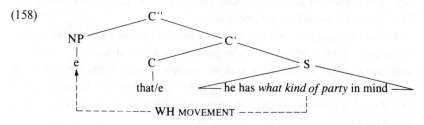

In the case of indirect questions such as that italicised in (157) below:

(157)   I wonder [*what kind of party* (% *that*) *he has in mind*]

WH MOVEMENT operates in precisely the same way, as indicated schematically in (158) below:

(158)

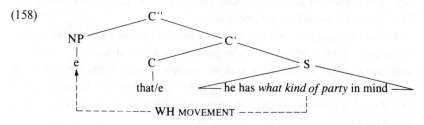

More specifically, WH MOVEMENT again moves the affected wh-phrase into the empty C-specifier position to the left of a C constituent which is obligatorily 'empty' in the majority dialect of English, but which can be filled by the Complementiser *that* in some minority dialects (and by the counterpart of *that* in many other languages).

The *C-specifier* analysis of preposed wh-phrases offers a number of descriptive and theoretical advantages over the earlier *C-adjunction* analysis. For example, a key prediction of the C-specifier analysis (though not of the C-adjunction analysis) is that the [C S] sequence following the preposed wh-phrase forms a constituent – a C-bar, in fact. And some empirical support for this claim comes from the fact that in Swedish this [C S] sequence can function as the 'shared constituent' in cases of *shared constituent coordination*, as the following example (from Engdahl (1986), p. 89) illustrates (where the shared [C S] sequence is italicised):

(159)   Jag minns   hur många pojkar, men har   glömt
          I   remember how many boys,   but have forgotten

          hur många flickor [*som   skulle   komma*]
          how many girls   [(that) should come]

The same point can be made by English examples like those below:

(160) (a)   I myself am wondering why – and I know that all my friends are also wondering why – [*didn't he come to the party*] (semi-indirect speech)
      (b)   What [*can I do*] or [*can anyone do*]?

Thus, if we assume that inverted Auxiliaries are preposed into C, then it would appear that the bracketed [C S] sequences in (159) and (160) (a) must be constituents because they can function as the 'shared constituent' in cases of *Shared Constituent Coordination*, and that likewise the bracketed [C S] sequences in (160) (b) must also be constituents, since they have undergone *Ordinary Coordination*. (It should be noted, however, that the precise derivation of complex coordinate structures such as those in (159) and (160) is somewhat problematic in ways which need not concern us here, so that this blunts the edge of this particular argument somewhat.)

A second descriptive advantage which the C-Specifier analysis offers over the C-adjunction analysis is that it provides a more natural account of an interesting restriction on the syntax of multiple wh-questions (i.e. questions containing more than one wh-phrase). Baker (1970, pp. 207–8) notes that in multiple wh-questions, no more than one wh-phrase can be preposed – as the following examples illustrate:

(161) (a)   He has left *what where*?
      (b)   *What* has he left *where*?
      (c)   *Where* has he left *what*?
      (d)   **What where* has he left?
      (e)   **Where what* has he left?

Under the C-Specifier analysis, we have a fairly straightforward way of accounting for this restriction: we simply posit that (in languages subject to this restriction) C permits only a single Specifier. This might (for example) be stipulated by a Base rule-schema such as the Specifier Rule which we posited in Chapter 5, namely

(162)   X'' → YP X' (Generalised Specifier Rule)

and this rule-schema would have as one of its specific instantiations the rule [C'' → YP C'], where YP is the (single) Specifier of C-bar. By contrast, it is much less obvious how we would block multiple preposed wh-phrases under the C-adjunction analysis, since adjunction is by nature a *recursive* operation.

Thus, it would seem that the C-specifier analysis offers apparent descriptive advantages over the C-adjunction analysis (i.e. the former attains a higher level of *observational adequacy* than the latter). But hand-in-hand with the descriptive advantages come some very considerable *theoretical* advantages. Not the least of these is the fact that analysing Ordinary Clauses as double-bar projections of C (into C'') rather than as single-bar projections of S (into S') enables us to get rid of some glaring anomalies inherent in the traditional S-bar analysis of Ordinary Clauses.

What's wrong with the traditional S-bar analysis of Ordinary Clauses? Well, the straight answer is that it simply doesn't fit in with the general X-bar schema which we outlined in Chapter 5. Recall that we argued there that (in the unmarked case), all Maximal Projections in English (NP, VP, PP, AP, ADVP, etc.) are of the canonical structure:

(163)

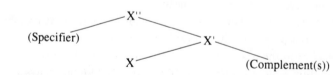

(Specifier)

X''

X'

X   (Complement(s))

But the S-bar analysis just doesn't square with the schema in (163). For one thing, S-bar is clearly a Maximal Projection (for example, it can function as the Complement of a Verb, Noun, or Adjective, and the MODIFIER MAXIMALITY CONSTRAINT we formulated in Chapter 5 tells us that only Maximal Projections can function as Complements); and yet, unlike other Maximal Projections, S-bar is only a single-bar projection of its head category (= S), not a double-bar projection (whereas NP is a double-bar projection of N, PP a double-bar projection of P, etc.). Moreover, a single-bar category in English typically comprises a Head plus a *postmodifying* Complement; but S-bar comprises a Head S plus a *premodifying* Complementiser constituent. And to make matters worse, the premodifying Complementiser constituent is a minimal projection (i.e. a word-level category), in violation of the MODIFIER MAX-IMALITY CONSTRAINT (which specifies that modifiers are Maximal Projections). Moreover, the S-bar analysis would make C itself an anomalous category, since unlike other word categories, it would have no single-bar or double-bar phrasal expansions (since under the S-bar analysis, there would be no C-bar or C-double-bar constituents). Finally, the S-bar analysis would also make S an anomalous category, since analysing S as the Head of S-bar would violate the obvious principle that the ultimate Head of any constituent larger than the word is a word-level category (so that N is the ultimate Head of NP, P of PP, etc.). Thus, the traditional S-bar analysis of Ordinary Clauses succeeds in making not only S-bar an anomalous category, but also S, and C.

But what of the alternative analysis of Ordinary Clauses as double-bar projections of a head Complementiser constituent? It should be immediately obvious that this alternative CP analysis of Ordinary Clauses is directly consonant with the general schema (163) above, and thus enables us to achieve maximal uniformity across categories in respect of the set of bar-projections which the various different categories allow. For, just as N can be projected into N-bar and NP, P into P-bar and PP, V into V-bar and VP, A into A-bar and AP, ADV into ADV-bar and ADVP, so too C has two phrasal projections into C-bar and CP. Moreover, as with other categories in English, the Complement follows, and the Specifier precedes the head category C (the Complement of C being S; and the Specifier of C being a preposed wh-phrase), so that we can achieve a very simple category-neutral statement of canonical word-order in Phrases and Clauses in English, to the effect that Complements follow, and Specifiers precede their heads.

Thus, it seems clear that the CP analysis of Ordinary Clauses offers considerable descriptive and theoretical advantages over the traditional S-bar analysis. And in the next two sections, we argue that the very same type of argumentation which has led us to reject the traditional analysis of S-bar should also lead us to question (and ultimately reject) the S analysis of Exceptional Clauses and the SC analysis of Small Clauses which was proposed in Chapter 6.

You should now be able to tackle exercise VI

9.11 Re-examining the status of S

Let's consider first the status of S. Within the framework we presented in Chapter 6, S serves two functions: it can be the complement of C (in 'Ordinary Clauses'), and it can be the complement of V (in the 'Exceptional

Clause' construction). But since (by the MODIFIER MAXIMALITY CONSTRAINT discussed in Chapter 5) Complements must be Maximal Projections, then it follows that S cannot itself be a 'primitive' category, but rather must be a projection of some other category. And if we assume that only word-level categories can serve as the ultimate heads of categories larger than the word (so that N is the ultimate head of NP, for example), then since S is a category larger than the word, it must be that S is itself a projection of some simple word category. But a projection of what category?

In order to try and answer this fundamental question, consider the structure of the bracketed S in the following pair of sentences:

(164) (a)   They are anxious that [*the President should go there*]
      (b)   They are anxious for [*the President to go there*]

What is it that makes the bracketed Clause finite in (164) (a), but nonfinite in (164) (b)? Clearly, it is not the nature of the subject NP, since both S constituents contain the same subject NP [*the President*]. By the same token, it cannot either be the Predicate VP, since both bracketed constituents contain the same VP [*go there*]. Hence, by a process of elimination, what determines that the bracketed S is finite in (164) (a) but infinitival in (164) (b) must be the contents of the I constituent. More precisely, the bracketed S is finite in (164) (a) because it contains a finite I containing the finite Modal Auxiliary *should*; whereas the bracketed S is infinitival in (164) (b) because it contains a nonfinite I containing the infinitival particle *to*. In other words, the (non)finiteness of I determines the (non)finiteness of S. For this reason, then, it seems plausible to analyse I as the ultimate head of S.

Now, since we have already argued that S functions as a Maximal Projection (e.g. in respect of the fact that it can serve as the Complement of a Verb or a Complementiser), and since we are assuming here a symmetrical theory of categories in which Maximal Projections are double-bar expansions of their heads, then it follows that if I is the ultimate Head of S, then S is a double-bar projection of I: i.e. S has the status of I'' (= Inflection-double-bar) or IP (= Inflection Phrase). Now, recall that within the X-bar schema (163), any zero-level category X is expanded into X-bar by the addition of a set (possibly null) of Complements, and expanded into an X-double-bar by the addition of a Specifier. Thus, if S is a double-bar projection of I, then it would seem plausible to claim that I together with its VP complement forms an I' (I-bar) constituent, which in turn is expanded into an I'' (= I-double-bar) constituent by the addition of an NP subject.

To make our discussion more concrete, compare the different structures assigned to the bracketed S constituents in (164) above under the classical analysis (165) below on the one hand, and under the I-double-bar analysis (166) on the other:

(165)

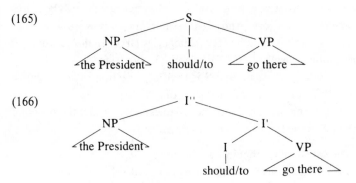

(166)

The I-double-bar analysis offers two obvious theoretical advantages over the S analysis. On the one hand, it eliminates the need to posit that S is a zero-level category (which, as we argued above, cannot be the case if only word-categories can be zero-level categories). And on the other hand, it eliminates what would otherwise be an unwelcome asymmetry in our Theory of Categories. For, under the S analysis (165), I is a word-level category which entirely lacks phrasal expansions (in violation of the basic tenet of X-bar theory that any word-level category X permits two phrasal expansions, into X-bar and X-double-bar). But this problem is resolved in (166), by virtue of the fact that I (just like other word-level categories such as N, A, V, and P) permits two phrasal expansions, into I-bar and I-double-bar.

However, while the I-double-bar analysis may offer apparent *theoretical* advantages over the classical S analysis, the obvious question we should ask ourselves is whether there is any *empirical* evidence favouring one analysis over the other. In this connection, it is interesting to note that the two analyses assign a rather different constituent structure to the 'Proposition' (i.e. Subject + Predicate) component of Clauses. Under the classical S analysis, Propositions are assumed to have a *ternary* immediate constituent structure, in the obvious sense that S is assumed to have the three Immediate Constituents [NP I VP]. But under the I-double-bar analysis, Propositions are assumed to have a *binary* immediate constituent structure, since their two immediate constituents are [NP I-bar]. So, in principle, we can make use of familiar constituent structure tests to help us decide between the ternary S analysis, and the binary I-double-bar analysis. Both analyses have been widely adopted in the relevant literature. For example, a binary analysis has been adopted in Katz and Postal (1964, p. 18); Chomsky, *Aspects* (1965, p. 106); Dougherty (1970); Emonds (1976, p. 61, fn. 20); Bresnan (1976a, p. 20); and Akmajian,

Steele and Wasow (1979); though all these are somewhat different in detail from the analysis in (165). Conversely, a ternary analysis is found in Chomsky, *Language and Mind* (1972a, p. 145); Jackendoff (1972, p. 76); Chomsky, *Lectures* (1981d, p. 25); Culicover (1982, p. 78), etc.

The main differences between the two analyses is that the binary analysis (166) claims that I and its VP complement together form an I-bar constituent which has no counterpart in the ternary analysis (165). An obvious question to ask therefore is: 'Is there any empirical evidence in favour of positing such a constituent?'

One type of evidence which we can appeal to in support of the binary analysis is *phonological* in nature. Thus, as Chomsky (*Logical Structure* (1955) 1975, p. 229) notes, the major intonation break in sentences comes immediately after the NP subject. For example, in a sentence such as:

(167)   The man next door * may be moving house soon

the major internal tone-group boundary comes in the position marked by the asterisk; this position corresponds to the constituent break between the NP Subject and the following I-bar. On the assumption that major intonation breaks occur at major constituent boundaries, then the binary analysis (which posits a major constituent break between NP and I-bar) proves superior to the ternary analysis (which posits major constituent breaks between NP and I, and between I and VP, and therefore wrongly predicts two major tone-group boundaries in (167)).

A second piece of evidence in support of positing an I-bar constituent of the form [I VP] comes from *Coordination* facts. Note, for example, that an [I VP] sequence can be coordinated with another similar sequence, as in:

(168)   I'm anxious for you [*to enter the race*] and [*to win it*]

Likewise, an [I VP] sequence can serve as the 'shared constituent' in examples of *Shared Constituent Coordination* such as:

(169)   Jean wants Paul – and Mary wants Jim – [*to enter the race*]

So it would seem as if the binary analysis has strong empirical support.

Given that both theoretical and empirical considerations favour the I-double-bar analysis, it would seem reasonable to adopt the claim made in Chomsky's (1986b) *Barriers* monograph that S is not a zero-level category, but rather is a double-bar projection of I, so that S = I'' = IP. Taken together with our claim in the previous section that Ordinary Clauses are not S-bar constituents, but rather CP constituents (i.e. double-bar projections of a head Complementiser constituent), this means that Ordinary Clauses will no longer have the canonical structure (170) below:

(170)

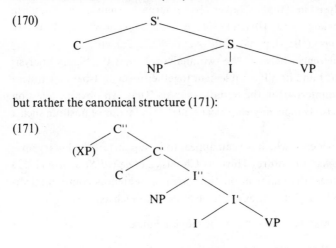

but rather the canonical structure (171):

(171)

C''
┌─────┴─────┐
(XP)   C'
       ┌────┴────┐
       C   I''
             ┌───┴───┐
            NP   I'
                 ┌───┴───┐
                 I   VP

(where XP is an optional Specifier constituent which serves as the landing-site for a matching preposed wh-phrase, and where NP is the Clause subject).

Since not all Ordinary Clauses contain overt wh-phrases or overt Complementiser constituents, an obvious question to ask at this point is how we deal with Ordinary Clauses which have no overt Complementiser, or which have no wh-phrase Specifier, or which have neither. Let's start by considering the first of these three possibilities: in this connection, consider the superficial structure of the bracketed Ordinary Clauses in the following pair of examples:

(172) (a)   I wonder [*which one will she give him*] (semi-indirect speech)

(b)   I wonder [*which one she will give him*] (indirect speech)

Given the assumptions we are making here, the inverted Modal *will* in (171) (a) will occupy the C position (and the I position normally occupied by Modals like *will* will correspondingly be empty), and the wh-NP [*which one*] will function as the Specifier of C, so that the bracketed Ordinary Clause complement (172) (a) will have the structure (173) below:

(173)

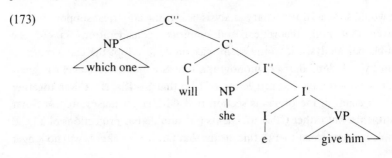

By contrast, in (172) (b), the Modal *will* occupies the I position, with the result
that the C position is left empty, as in (174) below:

(174)

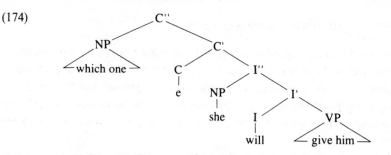

Now consider the structure of the two bracketed Clauses in (175) below:

(175) (a)   I knew [*that he would resign from his post*]
    (b)   I knew [*he would resign from his post*]

Since neither bracketed Clause contains a C-specifier, we might assume that
Specifiers are optional constituents of C-double-bar (just as Specifiers are optional constituents of NP, PP, AP, VP, etc.). If this is so, then the bracketed
complement Clause in (175) (a) will have the simplified structure (176) below:

(176)

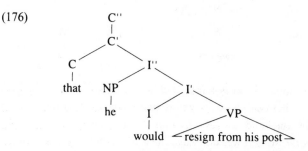

And we might further suppose that the bracketed Clause in (175) (b) differs
from that in (175) (a) only by virtue of the fact that the C position has been left
empty, so that (175) (b) has the structure (177) below:

(177)

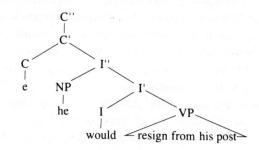

513

Of course, (177) would also be the structure of a main (or independent) Clause such as:

(178)   He would resign from his post

For, recall that we argued in section 6.5 that main Clauses have the status of S-bar; and we have argued in this section that S-bar should be reanalysed as C-double-bar. We assume here that Specifiers are optional, but that Heads are obligatory (given the *endocentricity* constraint) and hence any C-double-bar constituent (i.e. Ordinary Clause) lacking an overt C head must have an empty one.

Let's end our discussion in this section by pointing out two descriptive advantages which accrue from the analysis of S as IP. The first is that it permits us to achieve a unitary formulation of *Agreement* in sentence structures such as (179) below (recall that IP = I''):

(179)

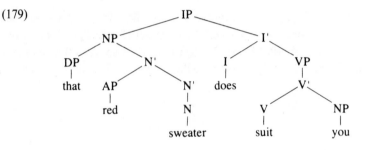

(Recall that *sweater* must be an N-bar as well as an N, since it can be pro-formed by the pro-N-bar *one*.) Now, there are two Agreement patterns which hold in (179): on the one hand, the DP *that* must be singular to agree with the singular Noun *sweater*, so that we can't have the plural form *those*; and on the other hand, the Modal *do* has to be in the third person singular form *does* to agree with the third person singular Subject NP [*That red sweater*] (hence the impossibility of *do*). Under the traditional S analysis, we need to posit two different Agreement Rules to handle sentences like (179), one controlling Agreement between DP and N, and a separate rule controlling Agreement between NP and I: the two rules have to be distinct, since NP and I are sisters, whereas DP and N are not. But under the alternative IP analysis, both Agreement patterns illustrated in (179) turn out to be particular instances of a more general phenomenon of *Specifier–Head Agreement*. Since N is the head of NP, and Determiners function as Specifiers of NP, it follows that Agreement between Determiners and Nouns will be a case of Specifier–Head Agreement; but under the IP analysis of Clauses, I will be the head of IP, and the NP Subject will be the Specifier of IP, so again we have the same phenomenon of Specifier–Head Agreement. Overall, then, it seems clear that the IP analysis of S simplifies and unifies our treatment of *Agreement*.

A second descriptive advantage which the IP analysis offers over the S analysis concerns our formulation of EXTRAPOSITION. Recall from Chapter 8 that a Phrase extraposed out of an Object NP is adjoined to VP, whereas a Phrase extraposed out of a Subject NP is adjoined to S. In this S/S-bar framework, this seemed a rather odd stipulation to have to make, since although VP was a Maximal Projection, S was not (on the contrary, S was the Head of S-bar). But under the IP analysis, this anomaly is resolved. For, IP is the Maximal Projection of I, in the same way as VP is the Maximal Projection of V. Thus, we can achieve a unitary formulation of EXTRAPOSITION by saying that an extraposed constituent moved out of its host Phrase is attached to the minimal XP (viz. VP or IP) containing the host Phrase: since IP is the minimal XP containing a Subject NP, and since VP is the minimal XP containing an Object NP, we precisely predict that Phrases extraposed off Subjects attach to IP (= S), whereas those extraposed off Objects attach to VP. Eureka!

You should now be able to tackle exercise VII

9.12   Re-examining the status of Small Clauses

Just as the kind of argumentation presented above led us to reanalyse S-bar as CP, and S as IP, so too it leads us to call into question our acronymic SC analysis of Small Clauses. It's important to realise that we can't dismiss the earlier 'SC' status we accorded to Small Clauses by saying 'It's only a *label*', and 'What's in a label?' The point is that within a formal grammar, labels make precise claims about the categorial status of constituents. For example, to claim that a Small Clause such as that bracketed in (180) below:

(180)   I consider [*the issue extremely important*]

has a structure such as (181) below:

(181)

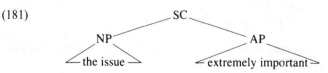

is to claim that the overall Small Clause has an entirely different categorial status from that of either its Subject NP, or its Predicate AP. To use the relevant technical jargon, an analysis such as (181) amounts to the claim that

515

Small Clauses are *exocentric* constructions (i.e. constituents whose categorial status is different from that of any of their immediate constituents), and that *Small Clause* is a primitive category (i.e. a category which is not itself a projection of any other category or categories). Now while it is true that more than half a century ago, Bloomfield (1935, p. 194) classified all Clauses as exocentric, it is clear that such an analysis is incompatible with the restrictive *endocentric* X-bar framework we are adopting here. Within the framework we have developed here, it should be clear from the discussion above that 'Small Clause' cannot be a primitive zero-level category, since it is not a word-level category. Moreover, since Small Clauses function as the Complements of certain Verbs and Prepositions, and since the MODIFIER MAXIMALITY CONSTRAINT tells us that only Maximal Projections can function as Complements, then it follows that Small Clauses must be Maximal Projections. And if we assume that only word-level categories can function as Ultimate Heads, then Small Clauses must be projections of some head word-level category. But projections of what head category?

Stowell (1981) argues that Small Clauses must be projections of the head category of the constituent functioning as the Predicate of the Small Clause. He adduces (1981, p. 259) an argument from *subcategorisation* facts (already partly familiar from our earlier discussion in Chapter 7) in support of this assumption. He notes that Verbs which permit Small Clause Complements differ in respect of the kind of SC complement they subcategorise. For example, a Verb like *consider* takes an SC Complement with an Adjectival Predicate, but not one with a Passive Participle Predicate, or a Prepositional Predicate: cf. Stowell's own examples:

(182) (a)   I consider [John *very stupid*]
     (b)   *I consider [John *killed by the enemy*]
     (c)   *I consider [John *off the ship*]

By contrast, *fear* permits an SC complement with a Participial Predicate, but not an Adjectival or Prepositional Predicate: cf. Stowell's examples:

(183) (a)   We feared [John *killed by the enemy*]
     (b)   *We feared [John *very stupid*]
     (c)   *We feared [John *off the ship* already]

And *expect* subcategorises an SC Complement with a Prepositional Predicate, but not an Adjectival or Participial Predicate: cf.

(184) (a)   I expect [that sailor *off the ship* (by midnight)]
     (b)   *I expect [that sailor *very stupid*]
     (c)   *I expect [that sailor *killed by the enemy*]

So, it seems as if different Verbs subcategorise different SCs of different types (e.g. *consider* takes an adjectival SC, *fear* takes a participial SC, and *expect* takes a prepositional SC), and that the type of an SC is determined by the type of Predicate it contains (i.e. whether the Predicate Phrase is headed by an Adjective, a Participle, or a Preposition). A natural way of capturing this generalisation would be to say that in Small Clauses of the schematic form [NP XP], X is the *head* of the overall SC; or in other words, a Small Clause is a phrasal expansion of the Predicate it contains.

Stowell (1981) assumes that the Predicate Phrases contained within a Small Clause are single-bar projections of their Heads, and that the overall Small Clause itself is a double-bar projection of the Head, so that the immediate constituent structure of Small Clauses is as in (185) below:

(185)

This would mean (for example) that a sentence such as (182) (a) above would be assigned the structure (186) below:

(186)   I consider [AP John [A' *very stupid*]]

But such an analysis seems to be wrong for a number of reasons. For one thing, Stowell's analysis claims that the Predicate Phrases in SCs are not Maximal Projections. However, this seems highly unlikely, in the light of examples such as (187) below:

(187) (a)   I've always considered [SC John [NP *THE best player in the team*]]
　　　(b)   I've never considered [SC John [NP *MY best friend*]]
　　　(c)   I'd never considered [SC John [AP *THAT fond of his mother*]]

For in each example in (187), the italicised Predicate Phrase contains a capitalised Determiner, and since the function of Determiners is to expand an X-bar into an X-double-bar (i.e. into a Maximal Projection), then it seems clear that the Predicate Phrase must be a Maximal Projection.

Moreover, Stowell's analysis makes entirely the wrong predictions about PREPOSING in Small Clauses. For, under his analysis, the Subject of a Small Clause would be the *Specifier* of the overall structure. Now, generally speaking, the Specifier of an NP, AP, PP, etc. cannot be preposed separately from the rest of its containing Phrase, as we see from the ungrammaticality of the (b) examples below:

(188) (a)   He is [*so* fond of Mary] that he won't leave her
　　　(b)   *So* is he [— fond of Mary] that he won't leave her

(189) (a)   I quite fancy [*John's* new girlfriend]

    (b)   **John's* I quite fancy [— new girlfriend]

(190) (a)   It spilled [*right* over the carpet]

    (b)   *Right it spilled [— over the carpet]

And yet the Subject of a Small Clause can freely be preposed in this way, as we see from Stowell's own examples (1981, p. 262)

(191) (a)   *John* I consider [— very stupid]

    (b)   *Who* do you expect [— off your ship by midnight]?

Thus, Stowell's analysis is untenable. It seems more likely that both the Subject Phrase and the Predicate Phrase of a Small Clause must be Maximal Projections: in other words, Small Clauses are indeed of the form [NP XP] as we originally claimed. But in turn, since Small Clauses function as Complements of Verbs like *consider*, and if only Maximal Projections can function as Complements, then Small Clauses too must be Maximal Projections.

We might therefore consider a rather different analysis of Small Clauses put forward by Chomsky in *Barriers* (1986b, p. 16), under which SCs are analysed as base-generated adjunction structures of the schematic form (192) below:

(192)

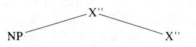

Under the analysis in (192), both the Predicate and the overall Small Clause have the same categorial status of XP (= X''). However, this analysis is not without posing problems either, since if we say that Verbs such as *consider* subcategorise (for example) an Adjectival Small Clause Complement which has the categorial status of an AP of the form [NP AP], then alongside structures such as (193) (a) below, we will also generate the ungrammatical (193) (b):

(193) (a)   I consider [$_{AP}$ John [$_{AP}$ highly intelligent]]

    (b)   *I consider [$_{AP}$ highly intelligent]

In both cases, the condition that *consider* subcategorises an AP Complement would be met. Moreover, if Adjectival Small Clauses have the status of AP, then since AP can function as an attributive modifier of N-bar, alongside grammatical structures such as (194) (a) below, we'd generate the ungrammatical (194) (b):

(194) (a)   a [$_{AP}$ highly intelligent] student of Physics

    (b)   *a [$_{AP}$ John highly intelligent] student of Physics

Moreover, since *adjunction* is a recursive operation, Chomsky's adjunction analysis would generate ill-formed Small Clause structures with more than one (indefinitely many) Subject NPs. Thus, assigning Small Clauses exactly the same categorial status as the Predicate Phrases they contain is going to lead to massive problems of *overgeneration* (i.e. the generation of lots of structures which are in fact ungrammatical): now, it may be that the 'overgenerated' structures can be filtered out by independent principles (e.g. Clauses with multiple Subjects might violate the THETA CRITERION because only one Subject Argument will be assigned a theta-role); but this remains to be seen.

If the [$_{XP}$ NP XP] analysis of Small Clauses proves unworkable, then we might look for ways of distinguishing between Small Clauses and the Predicate Phrases they contain. There are a variety of mechanical ways in which this could be done (though each has its own drawbacks). One would be to argue that the overall Small Clause is a treble-bar projection of the head category X of the Predicate Phrase, whereas the Predicate Phrase itself is only a double-bar projection of its Head. Another way would be to argue that the Small Clause and its Predicate Phrase differ by some feature such as Borsley's (1983) [± SUBJECT] feature, so that (for example) an Adjectival Small Clause (which has a Subject) would carry the categorial features [+ V, + N, + SUBJECT] and the level specification '2' (meaning that it is a double-bar projection), whereas the Adjectival Predicate Phrase it contains (which is itself subjectless) would carry the categorial features [+ V, + N, − SUBJECT], and the same level specification '2'. A third possibility would be to follow Williams (1980, 1982) and Taraldsen (1984) in suggesting that Clauses are double-headed, and thus are projections *both* of their Subject *and* of their Predicate.

We shall not pursue these problematic questions any further here. For expository purposes, we shall continue to use the label SC to denote Small Clauses in general, and the more specific labels AC, PC, VC, and NC to denote 'Adjectival Small Clause', 'Prepositional Small Clause', 'Verbal Small Clause', 'Nominal Small Clause' respectively. This is not intended in any way to prejudge their categorial status (e.g. to imply that they are primitive categories), but rather is merely a notational convenience (yes, I mean a cop-out!). Needless to say, much research remains to be done concerning the internal structure of Small Clauses, and how they fit into the X-bar framework. Moreover, the relationship between *Small Clauses* and *Exceptional Clauses* is problematic. Thus, as Chomsky notes (*Lectures* (1981d), p. 141, fn. 36), it is far from clear whether the bracketed Complement in a sentence such as:

(195)   John had [*Bill leave*]

should be analysed as a Small Clause lacking an I constituent, or as an Exceptional Clause with an empty I constituent. Indeed, we might go as far as to suggest that all Small Clauses could be analysed as projections of an abstract empty head I constituent, so that Small Clauses would have the same I-double-bar status as Exceptional Clauses (though this analysis too brings complex problems in its wake).

It may seem unsatisfactory to conclude our chapter on such an indecisive note. But we should take heart from the fact that it is always a major step forward in research when you finally come to understand the nature of the problem that you face (just as it is a major step forward in medicine when you isolate the virus responsible for a disease – even if, for the time being, the disease cannot be cured). In our present case, the 'break-through' we have achieved has been the realisation that within a restrictive endocentric framework, there can be no clausal categories such as 'S-bar', 'S', or 'SC'. Moreover, we have managed to arrive at a satisfactory endocentric reanalysis of two major Clause types (Ordinary Clauses and Exceptional Clauses): hence, the fact that present research has not yet provided a definitive answer to the question of the precise categorial status of Small Clauses (though it has suggested a variety of possibilities) should not be seen in too pessimistic a light.

> *You should now be able to tackle exercises VIII and IX*

9.13   Summary

In this chapter, we have focussed almost entirely on WH MOVE-MENT. In 9.2 we gave a brief characteristation of wh-questions. In sections 9.3–9.6, we presented a wide range of syntactic, morphological, phonological, and semantic arguments in favour of assuming that preposed wh-phrases originate in some position internal to S and are then preposed by WH MOVEMENT into initial position within S-bar, to the left of C. In 9.7 we argued that WH MOVE-MENT is involved in the derivation of wh-relatives; and we also suggested that non-wh-relatives (i.e. *that*-relatives and contact relatives) might involve WH MOVEMENT of a covert 'zero' relative pronoun operator, 'O'. In 9.8 we suggested that a variety of other constructions (including exclamatives, cleft sentences, comparatives, etc.) might involve overt or covert WH MOVEMENT. In 9.9 we looked at the types of constituent which can undergo the rule, and concluded that phrasal (not clausal) constituents such as NP, PP, AP, ADVP and (albeit marginally) VP are the primary targets for WH MOVEMENT, though we noted that subjectless infinitives can undergo WH MOVEMENT in Appositive Relatives. In 9.10 we discussed the problem of establishing the landing-site of the rule (i.e. just where it is that preposed wh-phrases get moved to). We argued that Ordinary Clauses are double-bar projections of a head Complementiser constituent, and that preposed wh-phrases are moved (by *substitution*) into an empty C-specifier position to the immediate left of C-bar. In 9.11 we saw that the same kind of arguments which led us to reanalyse S-bar as C-double-bar also lead us to reanalyse S as a double-bar projection of a head Inflection constituent, so that just as S-bar = CP, so too S = IP. In 9.12 we noted that within a restrictive endocentric framework, Small Clauses must be projections of some word-level category, and we investigated the possibility that they may be projections of the head category of the Predicate Phrase which they contain.

EXERCISES

Exercise I

For the purposes of this exercise, assume that the italicised *wh*-phrase in *wh*-exclamations like:

(1) (a)   *What a pretty dress* Mary is wearing —!
   (b)   *How tired* he looks —!

originates in the position marked —, i.e. in the position occupied by the corresponding *such/so*-phrase in sentences like:

(2) (a)   Mary is wearing *such a pretty dress*!
   (b)   He looks *so tired*!

Assume also that the *wh*-phrase in (1) is moved out of the — position into initial position within S-bar by WH MOVEMENT, as represented schematically in (3) below:

(3)   [S' [S Mary is wearing [*what a pretty dress*]]]
          └────── WH MOVEMENT ──────┘

Discuss how data such as (4) below might be used to justify the underlying structure assumed here:

(4) (a)   *What a lot of things she puts her comb in her handbag!
   (b)   How little note he took of what I said!
   (c)   How many girls he said were/*was coming to the party!
   (d)   *How happy they all are/*are all!
   (e)   *How good Mary's at Linguistics!
   (f)   *What a lot of people they wanna come to their party!
   (g)   How conceited about herself everyone thinks Mary is!
   (i)   How often Mary says that people dislike her!
   (j)   What a nice dress/!theory Mary is wearing!

Exercise II

In the text, we argue that in Restrictive Relative Clauses such as those bracketed in (1) below:

(1) (a)   the present [*which* he gave — to Mary]
    (b)   the man [*who* she talked to — in the bar]
    (c)   the place [*where* they met —]
    (d)   the time [*when* we first made love —]
    (e)   the reason [*why* she did it —]

the italicised wh-pronoun originates in the position marked —, and is subsequently moved to initial position in the bracketed clause by WH MOVEMENT. Devise a set of arguments parallel to those developed in sections 9.3–9.6 of the text in support of the postulated underlying structure (i.e. in support of the claim that the wh-pronoun originates internally within S), inventing examples of your own to illustrate each of the arguments you put forward.

We also claimed in the text that the corresponding 'zero relatives' illustrated in (2) below:

(2) (a)   the present [O he gave — to Mary]
    (b)   the man [O she talked to — in the pub]
    (c)   the place [O they met —]
    (d)   the time [O we first made love —]
    (e)   the reason [O she did it —]

contain a 'zero' wh-pronoun which originates in the position marked —, and is similarly preposed to clause-initial position by WH MOVEMENT. Which of the arguments you put forward to justify the underlying structure assumed for (1) can (and can't) be put forward to justify the underlying structure assumed in (2) (i.e. to justify the claim that the zero pronoun 'O' originates internally within S)? Are there some arguments which you used in relation to (1) which cannot be used in relation to (2)? Why?

Exercise III

Discuss the status of relative *what* in non-standard dialects of English which show the pattern illustrated below (viz. whether it is a Relative Pronoun or a Complementiser): the gloss is provided purely for the sake of intelligibility, and should not influence your analysis in any way.

(1)   the geezer *what* done him in
        'the man who murdered him'
(2)   the geezer *what* we met down the pub
        'the man who we met in the bar'
(3)   the motor *what* her old man bought
        'the car which her father bought'
(4)   the caf *what* they was rabbiting about
        'the café which they were talking about'

(5)   *the caf *about what* they was rabbiting
           'the café about which they were talking'
(6)   *the caf *what's roof* got blown off
           'the café whose roof was blown off'

Now consider the status of Spanish relative *que* (which, like English *that* can be used as
a finite Complementiser introducing indicative or subjunctive Complement Clauses) in
the examples below (the gloss is provided for convenience, not to (mis)lead you):

(7)   el chico *que* vino ayer
           the boy who came yesterday
(8)   un coche *que* va muy rápido
           a car which goes very fast
(9)   el chico *que* vimos ayer
           the boy who we-saw yesterday
(10)   el pueblo *a que* vamos ahora
           the town to which we-go now ('... we are now going')
(11)   Tengo mucho *que* hacer
           I-have much which do (infinitive)
           'I have a lot to do'

(Examples (7–11) are taken from Ramsden (1959), pp. 268–71.)

Exercise IV
           The sentences below illustrate some rather puzzling restrictions on *Cleft
Sentences* in English:

(1)   It was John *who/that/O* we talked to
(2)   It was John *to whom* we talked
(3)   It was to John [*that/??O/*who* we talked]
(4)   *It was to John [*that/O/who* we talked to]
(5)   *It was to John [*to whom* we talked]

See if you can try and work out what these restrictions are, and what's puzzling about
them. (In case you are thinking of invoking 'universals', it might be of interest to you to
note that the Spanish counterpart of sentences such as (5) is grammatical!)

Exercise V
           Discuss how the following data might be accounted for under a WH
MOVEMENT analysis. Which sentences prove problematic, and why?

(1) (a)   Which points did you agree on?
    (b)   On which points did you agree?

(2) (a)   Which cinema did you see the film in?
    (b)   In which cinema did you see the film?

(3) (a)   Which offer did you turn down?

(b)   *Down which offer did you turn?

(4) (a)   What did you put up with?

(b)   *With what did you put up?

(c)   *Up with what did you put?

(5) (a)   What did you say that for?

(b)   *For what did you say that?

(6) (a)   Where are you going to?

(b)   *To where are you going?

**Exercise VI

In the text, we considered two different analyses of WH MOVEMENT (viz. the C-adjunction and C-specifier analyses). Below, we sketch two further published analyses of WH MOVEMENT. Attempt to evaluate these, and discuss how each analysis copes with each of the problems raised in the text in section 9.10.

Analysis A: Chomsky's 'complex COMP' analysis

Chomsky in his 'Conditions' paper (1973) posits that the ultimate landing-site for preposed wh-phrases is a constituent which he terms COMP ($= C$, $=$ Complementiser). More specifically, he posits that COMP has a complex internal structure, and that wh-phrases move into a base-generated empty XP position within COMP to the immediate left of the Complementiser position itself (which he designates as [± WH]), so that in effect he assumes the following analysis of WH MOVEMENT in questions:

(1)

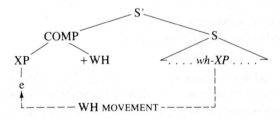

(where [+ WH] represents an interrogative Complementiser, and where XP will be AP, NP, or PP as appropriate). For obvious reasons, we might call this the 'complex COMP' analysis.

Analysis B: Bresnan's S-bar adjunction analysis

Joan Bresnan (1976b, p. 364) suggests that WH MOVEMENT might involve adjunction of a wh-XP to S-bar. Given this assumption, together with the assumption made in the text that C is the landing-site for preposed Auxiliaries in direct questions, then it follows that a wh-question such as:

(2)   What did he say to her?

would have an S-structure along the lines of (3) below:

(3)

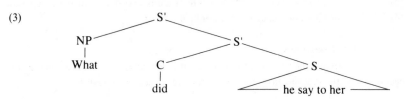

Exercise VII

Discuss the superficial structure which would be assigned to the italicised Clauses in the sentences below (i) in the traditional S/S-bar framework, and (ii) in the alternative IP/CP framework outlined in sections 9.10 and 9.11.

(1)   I hope *you can help me*
(2)   *Can you help me?*
(3)   I'd very much prefer (*for*) *you to be with me*
(4)   I don't know *whether to give her this one*
(5)   I don't know *which one to give her*
(6)   He is anxious *to win the race*
(7)   *He may consider John to be completely incompetent*
(8)   *I think I can persuade John to tell the truth*

*Exercise VIII

On the basis of examples such as the following (and any others of your own which you care to devise), discuss (and attempt to explain) the various differences between interrogative Complementisers like *whether/if* on the one hand, and interrogative wh-phrases like *where, when, how*, etc. on the other.

(1)   (a) *When* did it rain? (b) **Whether/*if* it rained?
(2)   I wonder *when/*whether/*if* will he go?
(3)   I think that John left, but I'm not really sure *when/*whether/*if*
(4)   SPEAKER A: I've decided to leave
           SPEAKER B: *When/*whether/*if*?
(5)   I don't really know *where/whether/*if* to go
(6)   He went *where/*whether/*if*?
(7)   I very much doubt *whether/if/*when* he'll go

In addition, on the basis of examples such as those below, try and work out some of the differences between *whether* and *if*:

(8)   I don't know *whether/if* he's coming
(9)   I'm not sure *whether/if* he's coming
(10)   The decision *whether/*if* he should be fired rests with the committee

(11)   *There's some doubt about *whether/*if* he's coming
(12)   *Whether/*if* he has won isn't clear
(13)   The prisoner begged *if/*whether* he could be transferred to an open prison
(14)   I don't know *whether/*if* or not he'll turn up

**Exercise IX

Discuss the various problems and puzzles raised by sentences such as the following, and their implications for the analyses proposed in the text:

(1)   %He's the man that's mother died last week
(2)   %What could've I done about it?
(3)   ... to know yf that any planete be directe or retrograde [Middle English: Astrolab] (*yf* = *if*)
(4)   Whether had you rather lead mine eyes, or eye your master's heels? [Middle English: Shakespeare]
(5)   Ik vroeg me af wie of dat Jan gezien had [Dutch]
        I asked me about who if that John seen had
        'I wondered who John had seen'
(6) (a) Hun spurði hvort að hann hefði farið [Icelandic]
         She asked whether that he had gone
         'She asked whether he had gone'
    (b) Hun spurði hvar (*að) hann hefði verið
         She asked where (that) he had been
(7)   the fellow who you don't know his name (Jespersen (1927), p. 111)
(8)   That's the problem that I asked you to find out from Fred about it (Van der Auwera (1985), p. 156)
(9)   That's the guy who I think's sister is the lead singer in a new band (disc jockey overheard in a well-known London superstore: his name is withheld to protect his job!)

10

ALPHA MOVEMENT

10.1 Overview

In the previous two chapters, we discussed in some detail the motivation for (and operation of) the five transformations listed in (1) below:

(1) (i)   V MOVEMENT (moves V out of VP into an empty finite I)

   (ii)   I MOVEMENT (moves an I containing an Auxiliary into an empty C)

  (iii)   NP MOVEMENT (moves an NP into an empty NP position)

  (iv)   EXTRAPOSITION (adjoins a PP or CP (S-bar) to the minimal XP containing the Phrase out of which it moves)

   (v)   WH MOVEMENT (moves a wh-phrase into an empty C-specifier position to the left of C-bar)

In this chapter, we begin by looking at a number of other transformations. We then go on to argue that there are many important similarities between the various different transformations we have looked at, and we explore the possibility of conflating all the various different transformations together into a single rule of ALPHA MOVEMENT. We also suggest that there are a number of general principles which determine the operations that movement rules can and cannot perform in natural language grammars, the ways in which they apply, how they interact, etc., and we take a look at some of the relevant principles involved.

10.2 Other movement rules

After reading the previous chapter, you're probably convinced that transformational grammarians are obsessive wh-paranoiacs (who see the ghosts of wh-phrases lurking in the inner recesses of even the most un-wh-like structures)! So, let me redress the balance somewhat by looking briefly at a few structures which appear to involve movement rules other than WH MOVEMENT. However, even in this section the ghost of WH MOVEMENT will still haunt us, since we shall suggest that each of the rules discussed below may have the same landing-site (viz. the C-specifier position) as WH MOVEMENT.

We'll begin by looking at a rule which I shall call NEGATIVE PREPOSING: we can illustrate its operation with the following examples:

(2) (a)   [NP *Few people*] WOULD [IP I trust — with such a mission]

  (b)   [PP *Under no circumstances*] MAY [IP candidates leave the room —]

  (c)   [ADVP *Very rarely*] DO [IP you find the ideal partner —]

In each case, we might argue that the italicised 'negative phrase' originates within IP (recall that IP = S) in the position marked —, and is subsequently moved outside IP, into the italicised position. We see from (2) that the construction also involves preposing of a (capitalised) Auxiliary from its underlying position in I within IP (= S), to some position outside IP. Since preposed Auxiliaries are moved from I into C by the rule of I MOVEMENT which we discussed in Chapter 8, it seems clear that the capitalised Auxiliaries here are in C at S-structure. If this is so, then bearing in mind that the preposed negative phrases in (2) are positioned in front of the preposed Auxiliaries, it seems likely that they occupy the same C-specifier position that preposed wh-phrases occupy in wh-constructions. Given these assumptions, a sentence such as (2) (a) would have the schematic derivation outlined in (3) below:

(3)   [CP [NP e] [C e] [IP I *would* trust *few people* with such a mission]]

                    I MOVEMENT

                ── NEGATIVE PREPOSING ──

(Recall that CP = S-bar, and IP = S.)

A further movement rule which we might argue for is the rule which Emonds (1976, p. 31) terms VP PREPOSING. He argues that it operates in sentences such as (4) below, to move the bracketed VP out of the position marked — into the italicised position at the front of the second Clause: cf. his examples:

(4) (a)   John hoped that Mary would find his hat, but [VP *find it*] she could not —

  (b)   John intends to make a table, and [VP *make one*] he will —

It would seem that the rule can also apply to move a VP in front of a preposed Auxiliary in a direct question, e.g. in cases such as:

(5)   [VP Working late] DO [IP you really think he was —]?

If this is so, then it suggests that preposed VPs are also moved into the

C-specifier position in front of a C containing a preposed (capitalised) Auxiliary.

A third construction which may also involve movement is so-called 'resultative' or 'consecutive' Clauses such as:

(6) (a)   [AP *So grave*] [C WOULD] the consequences have been —, that he would have had to resign

   (b)   [NP *Such gallantry*] [C DID] he show —, that he was awarded the Victoria Cross

Once again, traditional arguments of the type developed in sections 9.3–9.6 would lead us to conclude that the italicised Phrase in each case originates in the position marked —. Since the preposed constituent ends up to the immediate left of C, it seems plausible to suppose that some movement rule (which we might call RESULTATIVE PREPOSING) applies to move the italicised Phrase into the C-specifier position.

To summarise: we have suggested that the three rules of NEGATIVE PREPOSING, VP PREPOSING, and RESULTATIVE PREPOSING all resemble WH MOVEMENT in that they move a constituent out of IP into the C-specifier position within CP. Now if it is indeed the case (as we argued in the previous chapter) that Clauses in English contain a single C-specifier position, and if it is also the case that preposed negative phrases, VPs, consecutive phrases and wh-phrases all end up in the C-specifier position, then we should expect that all four types of preposed constituent are mutually exclusive. In other words, if the (single) C-specifier position is occupied by one type of preposed constituent, it cannot be filled by another: what this amounts to is the claim that no Clause can contain more than one preposed constituent of the relevant type. And the ungrammaticality of examples such as those in (7) below (with more than one preposed italicised Phrase in front of the capitalised Modal in C) suggests that this is so:

(7) (a)   *[ADVP *Never ever*] [NP *who*] [C WOULD] he trust with such a mission?

   (b)   *[NP *How many people*] [VP *work late*] [C DO] you really think would?

   (c)   *[PP *In which battle*] [NP *such gallantry*] [C DID] the soldiers show that they were all awarded medals?

   (d)   *[VP *Surrender*] [NP *so many soldiers*] [C DID] the enemy persuade to that our army was routed

Thus, our claim that all four rules involve preposing of the target constituent into an empty C-specifier seems to have some empirical support.

We turn now to look briefly at a further movement rule known generally as TOPICALISATION. Emonds (1976, p. 31) argues that in sentences such as (8) below (his examples):

(8) (a)   [NP *These steps*] I used to sweep — with a broom
    (b)   [NP *Each part*] John examined — carefully
    (c)   [NP *Our daughters*] we are proud of —
    (d)   [NP *Poetry*] we try not to memorise —

the bracketed NP originates in the position marked —, and is preposed into the italicised position by a rule of TOPICALISATION. Now, it seems from examples such as (9) below:

(9)   [NP *That kind of antisocial behaviour*] [C can] [IP we really tolerate — in a civilised society]?

that TOPICALISATION can move a Phrase in front of a preposed Auxiliary in C: so, once again, it seems likely that the landing-site for the rule is the C-specifier position. And indeed, such an assumption would correctly predict that preposed Topic Phrases exclude preposed wh-phrases – hence the ungrammaticality of the (c), (d), (e) and (f) examples below:

(10) (a)   *That kind of pen* you can use for what? (echo question)
    (b)   *What* can you use that kind of pen for?
    (c)   **What that kind of pen* can you use for?
    (d)   **That kind of pen what* can you use for?
    (e)   **For what that kind of pen* can you use?
    (f)   **That kind of pen for what* can you use?

So, it would seem that TOPICALISATION, like WH MOVEMENT, involves movement of Phrases into the C-specifier position.

It is interesting and instructive to contrast the TOPICALISATION construction discussed immediately above with the superficially similar DISLOCATION construction illustrated in (11) below:

(11) (a)   [NP John], I think *he*'s the pits
    (b)   I think *he*'s the pits, [NP John]

In each case, the bracketed Phrase is said to be the *dislocated* constituent: where this occurs to the left of the rest of the sentence, the construction is called LEFT DISLOCATION; where the dislocated constituent occurs to the right of the rest of the sentence, the construction is referred to as RIGHT DIS-LOCATION.

At first sight, DISLOCATION might seem to be parallel to TOPICALISATION; and we might therefore propose to handle it in terms of a movement rule preposing (or postposing) the dislocated Phrase. But there are numerous arguments as to why it would be appropriate to handle TOPICALISATION by a movement rule, but not DISLOCATION. For one thing, TOPICALISATION exhibits the typical 'movement' property of leaving a *gap* at the extraction-site of the rule (i.e. in the position out of which the moved constituent has been extracted): this gap is marked by — in (8) above. But by contrast, DISLOCATION involves no *gap* at all within IP: on the contrary, the Clause linked with the dislocated constituent contains some expression referring back (or forwards) to the dislocated Phrase. In (11) above, the expression is the italicised Pronoun *he*: since this Pronoun 'picks up' the dislocated Phrase, it is often called a *resumptive* pronoun. But as examples such as (12) below show, a full NP (italicised) can be used to serve the same resumptive function:

(12)   [NP John], I can't stand *the arrogant bastard/the creep/the jerk*

Thus, given that TOPICALISATION leaves a *gap* within IP whereas DISLOCATION does not, it seems that only the former can involve movement, not the latter.

Numerous other arguments could also be advanced in support of our claim that DISLOCATION does not involve movement. One such argument could be formulated in relation to *case-marking* facts. As we saw in section 9.4 in relation to examples such as:

(13) (a)   *Who/*Whom* are you sure — would admire Noam Chomsky?
     (b)   *Who/Whom* are you sure Nim Chimpsky would admire —?

a moved NP is assigned the case appropriate to the position it occupied prior to the application of the relevant movement rule. But examples such as (14) below make it clear that a dislocated NP does not assume the case of the resumptive Pronoun within IP:

(14) (a)   [NP *Me/*I*], everyone knows *I* can't stand weirdos
     (b)   Everyone knows *I* can't stand weirdos, [NP *me/*I*]

On the contrary, dislocated constituents seem to be assigned Objective case, irrespective of the case assigned to the resumptive NP (which is Nominative in the case of (14)). Since movement in some sense 'preserves' case-marking, it is therefore evident that DISLOCATION cannot involve movement.

Given the arguments here that dislocated constituents have not undergone movement, then the obvious conclusion is that dislocated constituents are *base-generated* in the position they occupy at S-structure (i.e. directly generated in that position by the Base Rules, and not generated elsewhere by the Base and then moved into the relevant position by a transformation). But what is the position they occupy at S-structure? On the basis of interrogatives such as:

(15) [NP *That kind of pen*] [C can] [IP you use it for anything special]?

where the italicised dislocated constituent is positioned to the immediate left of a C containing a preposed Auxiliary, we might suppose that dislocated constituents are positioned in the C-specifier position to the immediate left of C. However, examples such as the following seem to discount this possibility:

(16) [NP *That kind of pen*] [CP [NP what] [C can] [IP you use it for]]?

For, in (16), we see that the C-specifier position within the bracketed CP (alias S-bar) is filled by the wh-NP specifier *what*. It seems more likely, therefore, that dislocated constituents are adjoined to CP (or, for the traditionalists among you, to S-bar), perhaps by a Base Rule of the form:

(17) CP → XP CP

(where XP is the dislocated constituent: of course, given our arguments in Chapter 5, (17) would be a specific instantiation of a generalised category-neutral rule-schema formulated entirely in terms of category variables). Such an analysis would entail that Dislocation Clauses (i.e. Clauses containing dislocated constituents) have the same categorial status (viz. that of CP, alias S-bar) as Ordinary Clauses: hence, we should expect that Clauses containing dislocated constituents can freely be conjoined with Ordinary Clauses lacking dislocated constituents: and as (18) below shows, this is indeed the case:

(18) *I don't like insolence*, and [that kind of insolent behaviour, I simply won't stand for it]

For, in (18) we have conjoined an (italicised) Ordinary Clause with a (bracketed) Dislocation Clause.

Of course, since our rule generating Dislocation Clauses (17) is a recursive rule, it predicts that we can recursively stack dislocated constituents on top of each other. Now, while 'recursive dislocation' structures such as (19) below have a somewhat odd flavour:

(19) ?[NP *That kind of car*], [PP *in this kind of parking-lot*], you'd be crazy to want to leave it there

they are fully idiomatic in some varieties of English (e.g. Yiddish English), and the corresponding structures are also grammatical in some other languages. For example, French allows multiple dislocation, as the following examples from Larsson (1979), p. 15 illustrate:

(20) (a)   [NP *Mes parents*], [NP *la liberté sexuelle et tout*
         My parents   the liberty sexual and all
ça], ils en ont horreur
that, they of-it have horror
'*My parents, sexual freedom and all that*, they are horrified by it'

(b)   [NP *Les occasionelles*], [NP *leur prostitution*],
        The part-timers   their prostitution
elles la cachent à leur famille
they it hide   to their family
'*Part-timers, their prostitution*, they hide it from their families'

Hence, a recursive rule such as (17) is by no means implausible, on universalist grounds.

Some evidence confirming our suspicions that topicalised and dislocated constituents occupy different sentence positions comes from Greenberg (1984). He notes that in colloquial speech the interjection *man* can occur after dislocated constituents, but not after topicalised constituents: cf.

(21) (a)   *Bill*, man, I really hate him (dislocated NP)
(b)   **Bill*, man, I really hate (topicalised NP)

If we were to assume that Interjections like *man* and Dislocated constituents are CP adjuncts, but that Topicalised Phrases occupy the C-specifier position, such facts would automatically be accounted for, since (21)(b) would then violate the 'no crossing branches' constraint, but (21)(a) would not. Moreover, such an analysis would also predict that Interjections like *man* can precede both topicalised and dislocated constituents: and as the examples in (22) below show, this prediction is entirely correct:

(22) (a)   Man, *Bill*, I really hate him (dislocated NP)
(b)   Man, *Bill*, I really hate (topicalised NP)

By now, you should be able to draw your own tree diagrams to illustrate the argument relating to (21) and (22)!

However, before we get side-tracked too far, let's summarise the main thrust of this section. What we have been arguing here is that there are numerous movement rules (e.g. NEGATIVE PREPOSING, VP PREPOSING, RESULTATIVE PREPOSING, and TOPICALISATION) which seem to resemble WH-MOVEMENT insofar as they appear to move a Phrase from some position within IP (alias S) to the C-specifier position within CP (alias S-bar). We also pointed out, however, that it is important to distinguish between structures that involve *movement* (e.g. Topic Clauses), and those which are *base-generated* and hence do not involve movement (e.g. Dislocation Clauses).

> *You should now be able to tackle exercises I, II, and III*

10.3 ALPHA MOVEMENT

In the previous chapter, we discussed the rule of WH MOVEMENT; and in this chapter, we've looked at a variety of different movement rules in English, including NEGATIVE PREPOSING, VP PREPOSING, RESULTATIVE PREPOSING, and TOPICALISATION.However, we notice that all of these rules have certain properties in common. For example, they all have Maximal Projections (= full Phrases) as their *targets*, they all involve *substitution*, and they all appear to have the C-specifier position as their ultimate *landing-site*. This obviously raises the question of whether or not these five different rules are in reality different manifestations of the same rule: a rule which moves a target XP (= full Phrase = Maximal Projection) out of its underlying position within IP into a matching empty XP 'slot' (of the same category) in the C-specifier position to the immediate left of C. Since this rule moves an XP into a matching empty XP position, let's call this generalised rule XP MOVEMENT.

But perhaps there are wider parallels which we should explore. After all, as we saw in the last chapter and in the previous section of this chapter, WH MOVEMENT (and similar rules) may involve movement of a target NP into an empty NP which functions as the Specifier of C. And in Chapter 8, we argued that NP MOVEMENT involves movement of a target NP into an empty NP which functions as the Specifier of I (= into Subject NP position). Perhaps, then, NP MOVEMENT is no more than a particular manifestation of our more general XP MOVEMENT rule?

Now, at first sight, this might seem implausible. For, as we have seen, WH MOVEMENT can move not only NPs, but also APs, PPs, ADVPs, etc.; whereas NP MOVEMENT can have only NPs as its target. Surely, this asymmetry counts against any attempt to conflate the two rules into one more general rule? Not necessarily. There are two ways in which we might seek to counter this objection.

The first way is the following. Let's suppose (for the sake of argument) that it is indeed the case that NP MOVEMENT can only apply to NP CONSTITUENTS. Now, if we can show that this apparent asymmetry between NP MOVEMENT (which targets NPs) and WH MOVEMENT (which targets XPs) is in fact the consequence of some independent restriction, then the argument against conflating the two rules into a single rule collapses. But what kind of restriction might ensure that NP MOVEMENT only applies to NPs? Well, we might argue that the reason why other types of Phrase can't undergo NP MOVEMENT is that the rule involves movement into *Subject* position in sentences; and we might suppose that there is an independent restriction to the effect that only NPs can occur in Subject position. If so, then we might say that the possibility of NP MOVEMENT applying to move for example, an ADVP into Subject position is ruled out by a principle requiring that the target category of a substitution rule should match the landing-site category (e.g. only an NP can be moved into an empty NP position, not an ADVP, or PP, etc.). Given these assumptions, it might be perfectly possible to regard NP MOVEMENT as yet another manifestation of our generalised XP MOVEMENT rule.

An alternative way of defending the proposal to conflate NP MOVEMENT with XP MOVEMENT would be to question the observational adequacy of the claim that NP MOVEMENT only ever has NP constituents as its target. Sentences such as the following (from Radford (1981), p. 210) might be used to support the claim that NP MOVEMENT can indeed 'raise' constituents other than NP:

(23) (a) [AP *Rather plump*] seems — to be how he likes his girlfriends
    (b) [PP *In Paris*] seems — to be where they first met
    (c) [ADVP *A little too casually*] seems — to have been how he addressed the judge
    (d) [CP *For the Prime Minister to resign*] would seem — to be unthinkable

And examples such as (24) below would seem to suggest that NP MOVEMENT can likewise 'passivise' constituents other than NP:

(24) (a) [AP *Rather plump*] is said — to be how he likes his girlfriends
    (b) [PP *In Paris*] is said — to be where they first met
    (c) [ADVP *A little too casually*] is said — to have been how he addressed the judge
    (d) [CP *For the Prime Minister to resign*] is said — to be unthinkable

If it is indeed the case that the target of NP MOVEMENT is not NP but rather XP (so that the rule can apply not just to NPs, but to any kind of phrasal constituent), then the 'asymmetry' argument against subsuming NP MOVEMENT under our generalised XP MOVEMENT rule collapses.

So far, we have only looked at rules involving movement of Maximal Projections (i.e. phrase-level categories). But, as we saw in the Chapter 8, there are also rules moving Minimal Projections (= word-level categories). For example, V MOVEMENT moves a V out of VP and into an empty finite I, and I MOVEMENT moves an Auxiliary within I into an empty C. Perhaps these two rules could in turn be conflated into a more general rule which moves *Minimal Projections* (i.e. word-level categories) into other Minimal Projection positions? If we use the category variable 'X' to symbolise a word-level category, then we might call this generalised rule X MOVEMENT.

So now, we have two generalised movement rules: one which moves phrase-level categories (= XP MOVEMENT), and another which moves word-level categories (= X MOVEMENT). But in our quest for ever higher levels of generality, we might in turn ask if these two rules are different manifestations of a yet more general rule. Now at first sight, this might not seem plausible. After all, XP MOVEMENT moves phrasal categories into Phrase positions; whereas X MOVEMENT moves word-level categories into word positions. And yet, there are compelling similarities between the two generalised rules. For example, both XP MOVEMENT rules like NP MOVEMENT and WH MOVEMENT, and X MOVEMENT rules like V MOVEMENT and I MOVEMENT involve *substitution*, and more particularly, movement of the target category into an *empty* category position. But what is even more striking is that in each case the *target category* of the rule and the *landing-site category* have to 'match' in some sense. For example, NP MOVEMENT moves an NP (= the target category) into an empty NP position (= the landing-site category). And V MOVEMENT moves a V (= the target) into an empty I position (= the landing-site); but I is a 'verbal' position in a fairly obvious sense, since Modal Verbs are base-generated in I, so that V MOVEMENT can be regarded as movement out of one verbal position into another. In other words, the essential parallelism between XP MOVEMENT and X MOVEMENT is that *both involve movement of a target category into a matching empty category position*. This suggests that the two should be conflated as a single rule which can move any target category α ('alpha') into a matching empty category position. Following the terminology used by Chomsky in the past decade, we might accordingly refer to this generalised movement rule as 'Move α' (= Move Alpha), or α MOVEMENT (= ALPHA MOVEMENT), where α is a category variable which designates any random category you care to choose.

However, the generalised rule of ALPHA MOVEMENT which we have envisaged hitherto is a *substitution* rule. But we saw in the previous chapter that languages also have *adjunction* rules like EXTRAPOSITION. The obvious question to ask, therefore, is whether adjunction rules such as EXTRAPOSITION could also be particular cases of an even more general rule of ALPHA MOVEMENT. The answer to this question depends upon whether we can find some principled way of 'predicting' what type of operation (*substitution* or *adjunction*) a given movement of a given type of constituent may involve. Now, we saw in Chapter 8 that EXTRAPOSITION could not involve substitution, because there was no empty clause-final constituent for extraposed PPs to be moved into: thus, given that *substitution* was ruled out, *adjunction* was the only remaining possibility. And we might envisage the possibility of some more general principle which determines the type of operation that a given movement involves, to the effect that adjunction applies only where substitution is 'blocked' for some reason.

If speculation along these lines proves productive, then we open up the possibility that all substitution rules and all adjunction rules may be particular reflexes of a single, maximally general ALPHA MOVEMENT rule, which simply specifies:

(25)   ALPHA MOVEMENT

Move α (where α is a category variable, i.e. designates any random category you care to choose)

We might then suppose that independent principles will determine whether a given movement will involve *substitution* or *adjunction*; and likewise, we might posit that independent principles will also determine the landing-site of the rule (e.g. substitution always involves movement into a matching empty category, and adjunction always involves attachment to the first Maximal Projection 'above' the constituent out of which the moved element is being extracted; moreover, we might suppose that leftward adjunction rules involve adjunction to the left of the landing-site category, and rightward movement rules involve adjunction to the right of the landing-site category).

At first sight, the whole enterprise of reducing all movement rules in all languages to a single ALPHA MOVEMENT rule might seem to be absurd: after all, our ALPHA MOVEMENT rule (25) in effect says that *any* category in any sentence can be moved *anywhere*. And this in turn implies that words can occur in just about any order in any sentence. Yet we all know that this isn't true: there are severe restrictions on what kinds of constituents can be moved where in any language. So how do we square the relative rigidity of word-order in languages such as English with the postulation of a MOVE ALPHA rule which effectively says that any category in any sentence can be moved anywhere?

The answer Chomsky would give to this question is along the following lines. If we know that languages have rules moving a wide range of different constituents from one position in a sentence to another, then we ought to expect (as the simplest hypothesis) that *in principle* languages allow you to move *any constituent anywhere*; and if *in practice* this is not the case, then it is the linguist's task to discover the principles which determine why it's possible to move some constituents into some positions, but not others. Thus, the research programme which leads us to set ourselves the ambitious goal of conflating all movement rules into a single ALPHA MOVEMENT RULE also leads us to embark upon a voyage in search of the fundamental principles which restrict the operation of *movement* in natural language grammars. Our quest becomes all the more rewarding if we are able to uncover general principles of cross-linguistic validity (i.e. principles valid not only for English, but for other languages as well). For, as we have noted many times, the discovery of *universals* provides the key to attaining our ultimate goal of *explanatory adequacy*. What kind of universal principles might be involved? That's the question we address ourselves to in the remaining sections of this chapter. It's also the question which the greater part of Volume Two of our book will be devoted to.

10.4 Structure-preserving Principle

In our quest for generalisations governing the operation of transformations, let's begin by seeking to establish the general principles which determine the *landing-site* for movement rules, and the *derived constituent structure* produced by the operation of movement rules. An influential early attempt to resolve these issues is found in Emonds' (1970, 1976) work on *structure-preserving transformations*. Emonds argues that major transformations are of two types, namely *root* and *nonroot* transformations. A *root transformation* is one which is restricted to applying in a *root* Clause (viz. in a 'main', 'principal', or 'independent' Clause), and hence cannot apply, for example, in a Complement Clause. In this regard, it is interesting to contrast our familiar transformations of I MOVEMENT (alias Subject–Auxiliary Inversion) and WH MOVEMENT. As we see from (26) below, both rules may apply in 'direct questions' (i.e. in root clauses):

(26) (a)   You *will* do *what*? (echo question)
    (b)   *What will* [IP you — do —]?

But (setting aside the complex phenomenon of 'semi-indirect speech' Clauses, which seem to share some of the properties of their direct speech counterparts and thus to be *root* Clauses) only WH MOVEMENT, not I MOVEMENT can apply in indirect questions (i.e. in nonroot Clauses), as (27) below illustrates:

(27) (a)   He won't tell me [CP *what* [IP he *will* do —]]
    (b)   *He won't tell me [CP *what will* [IP he — do —]]

Thus, it follows that I MOVEMENT is a root transformation (i.e. can only apply in root clauses), whereas WH MOVEMENT is not (and hence can apply either in root or nonroot clauses).

In the wake of the distinction between *root* and *nonroot* transformations, Emonds (1976, p. 3) proposes the following principle governing the operation of transformations:

(28)   STRUCTURE-PRESERVING PRINCIPLE
          Major grammatical transformations are either root or structure-
          preserving operations

A Movement Transformation is structure-preserving if it moves 'a node C
into some position where C can otherwise be generated by the grammar'
(Emonds (1976), p. 3; note that he is using 'C' as a category variable here, not
to represent a Complementiser). (28) amounts to saying that nonroot transformations must be structure-preserving, though root transformations need
not be.

   To illustrate the principle (28), let's consider what it would mean for a *substitution* transformation to be *structure-preserving*. Emonds (1976, p. 3)
defines a *structure-preserving substitution* rule as one that 'substitutes a constituent C into a position in a phrase marker held by a C node'. Using category
and level variables, we might reformulate this as follows:

(29)   A substitution is structure-preserving if and only if it results in a
          constituent X^n being substituted for another constituent X^n of the
          same type

In the light of the definition (29), let's consider whether the substitution rules
with which we are familiar are structure-preserving.

   We'll begin by looking at NP MOVEMENT. Recall that this rule operates in
'Passive', 'Raising', and perhaps 'Ergative', and 'Middle' structures. For
example, in the case of a 'Passive' structure such as:

(30)   John is considered to be influential

the rule operates in the manner represented schematically in (31) below:

(31)   [NP e] is considered [IP *John* to be influential]
          └─ NP MOVEMENT ─┘

Since (as we see from (31) above) NP MOVEMENT moves an NP out of one NP
position into another NP position, and not, for example, into an N, N-bar, P,
PP, V, or VP etc. position, it should be obvious that the rule is a *structure-
preserving substitution* in the sense of (29) above. Moreover, since the rule can
apply freely in Complement Clauses (I hope you can devise your own
examples to illustrate this by this stage!), it is a nonroot transformation, and
satisfies the condition in (28) that nonroot transformations are structure-
preserving.

   Having looked at the structure-preserving character of NP MOVEMENT, let's
turn to consider the case of V MOVEMENT. Recall from our discussion in

Chapter 8 that this rule moves a V out of VP into an empty finite I. The operation of the rule in the case of a sentence such as:

(32)   John has no money

can be schematised as in (33) below:

(33)   John [$_I$ e] [$_{VP}$[$_V$ *have*] no money]
            ↑_____|
            V MOVEMENT

Since this rule obviously applies in root and nonroot Clauses alike, it is a non-root transformation, and thus required to be structure-preserving by principle (28). But is V MOVEMENT a structure-preserving substitution in terms of the definition given in (29) above? On the face of it, V MOVEMENT would not appear to satisfy the conditions imposed in (29), since it appears to move one category (V) into a position occupied by a *different* category (I). However, category labels like 'V' and 'I' can be deceptive, since (as we argued in Chapter 3) categories are in reality sets of features. What is significant about V MOVEMENT is that it can only move V into a *finite* I; and a finite I is the base position occupied by Modals. As we argued in Chapter 3, Modals are a subset of Verbs, and thus share with Verbs the features [+ V, − N]. Thus, we might argue that V MOVEMENT is simply movement from one [+ V, − N] position to another, and hence is structure-preserving, at least in respect of the *major* categorial features of the items concerned.

Let's now consider the case of I MOVEMENT. Recall that this is the rule responsible for 'inversion' in direct questions. The operation of the rule in a direct question such as:

(34)   Will John help you?

can be schematised as in (35) below:

(35)   [$_C$ e] John [$_I$ *will*] help you
            ↑_____|
            I MOVEMENT

Since the rule moves an Auxiliary from I into C, it might seem at first sight as if it is not structure-preserving, since I and C appear to differ in their categorial make-up: for example, C is marked for Mood as [± WH] (interrogative/noninterrogative) but not for Tense/Agreement, whereas I is inflected for Tense/Agreement but not for interrogative/noninterrogative mood. And indeed, given Emonds' contention (1976, p. 22) that (his counterpart of) the rule is a *root* transformation, then there is no reason (if we assume his principle (28)) to expect the rule to be structure-preserving.

However, it would seem unfortunate to simply reject the possibility that I MOVEMENT is structure-preserving, bearing in mind that it has some obvious structure-preserving properties: for example, the rule is not 'structure-building', because it moves I into an existing C position, rather than into some 'new' position. Moreover, movement takes place between categories *at the same level* – i.e. the rule moves a zero-level category (I) into a position where another zero-level category (C) is generated. And in addition, I and C share a considerable number of features in common, both in English, and more generally. For example, in English, both I and C contain items which are morphologically marked as finite/infinitival: e.g. *for* is an infinitival C, and *to* is an infinitival I. The finite/nonfinite parameter is a particularly important one, since the *finiteness* of I and C is obviously a crucial property in the operation of the rule, bearing in mind the fact that the rule only applies to move a *finite* I into a *finite* C, never to move a non-finite I into a nonfinite C (so that, for example, infinitival *to* doesn't get moved into C). And the similarities between I and C are even more marked in other languages. For example, Complementisers in C inflect for Tense in Irish (cf. McCloskey 1979), and for Agreement in Flemish (cf. Haegeman 1983); and Verbs in I inflect for declarative/interrogative mood in Eskimo (cf. Sadock 1984). The fact that C and I share obvious properties in common both in English and more generally suggests that it may be reasonable to maintain that movement from I to C is structure-preserving. This would be all the more so if we were to posit that structure-preserving rules do not require that the target category and the landing-site category should be *identical* in every respect, but rather only that the two should be *non-distinct* (i.e. should not conflict) in their featural make-up. This would allow a finite I constituent which is unmarked for interrogativity to move into a finite C constituent which is marked as interrogative; or, it would allow a 3rd person singular present tense finite indicative verb form such as *is* to move into a finite indicative C which is unmarked for Tense or Agreement.

One possible way in which we might seek to attain a structure-preserving formulation of I MOVEMENT might be by adapting a proposal made in Kayne (1982) along the following lines. Let us suppose that Complementisers may have the categorial properties of lexical categories. In particular, let us suppose that C may be nominal, prepositional, or verbal. We might then suppose that a prepositional C would be filled by the base-generated prepositional Complementiser *for*; and that a nominal C would be filled by a base-generated nominal Complementiser such as *that* (hence the fact that *that*-clauses are frequently referred to in traditional grammar as *Noun Clauses*). But how could a verbal C be lexicalised? Clearly it could not be filled by a base-generated

Complementiser, since English lacks verbal Complementisers (though there are languages which do indeed have verbal Complementisers, or at least Complementisers descended historically from Verbs, as Lord (1976) and Nylander (1985) have shown). Hence, in English, such a complex could only be filled *transformationally*, e.g. by movement of a V from I into C. Under this analysis, I MOVEMENT would involve movement from one verbal position (in I) to another (in C), and hence would clearly be structure-preserving.

It might seem perverse to devote so much space to defending a structure-preserving analysis of I MOVEMENT. Why should it matter whether the rule is or is not structure-preserving? Well, our ultimate goal is obviously to attain a *maximally constrained* Theory of Movement Rules; and clearly our theory would be far more constrained if we were able to argue that *all* major movement rules are structure-preserving, without exception. Now, the significance of I MOVEMENT is that this rule (or more precisely, its counterpart of SUBJECT–AUXILIARY INVERSION in Emonds' framework) is often taken as the canonical example of a major transformation which is not structure-preserving. But if, as we have maintained here, the rule responsible for 'inversion' in direct questions (= I MOVEMENT, in our framework) is indeed structure-preserving, then it opens up the (highly desirable) possibility of generalising Emonds' constraint so as to envisage the possibility that *all* substitution rules are structure-preserving, irrespective of whether or not they are root transformations. Although we lack the space to discuss the relevant issues here, it should be pointed out that all the rules argued by Emonds (1976, pp. 21–64) to be structure-building root transformations can be reanalysed as structure-preserving substitutions either into C, or into an empty Specifier of C.

One of the interesting consequences of the STRUCTURE-PRESERVING PRINCIPLE (28) is that it 'bans' a whole class of (nonroot) transformations which have been used widely in the relevant literature: these are what we shall call *attachment transformations*. A rule which *attaches* A to B results in a derived structure in which A is an immediate constituent (i.e. a daughter) of B. We can illustrate the notion of *attachment* in relation to our familiar EXTRAPOSITION rule (since this can apply freely in Complement Clauses, it is a nonroot transformation). Jacobsen (1986, p. 144) (writing within the earlier S/S-bar framework) assumes that the rule involves *attachment* of the extraposed constituent to S. Given this assumption, the bracketed S complement in (36) below:

(36)   I know that [a review will appear soon *of his latest book*]

would have a D-structure along the lines of (37) below (within the S/S-bar framework that Jacobsen uses, and omitting S-bar for the sake of clarity):

(37)

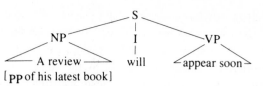

and (37) would be mapped into the S-structure (38) below by *attachment* of
the extraposed PP [*of his latest book*] to the S-node:

(38)

But any such *attachment* analysis of EXTRAPOSITION involves a *structure-building* operation which has the effect of 'creating' a PP node under S in the
derived structure (38) which was not there in the corresponding underlying
structure (37). And this obviously violates Emonds' condition that nonroot
transformations may only be *structure-preserving*, not *structure-creating*.
More generally still, Emonds' analysis outlaws *attachment rules* (except in the
case of root transformations).

Of course, the analysis of EXTRAPOSITION which we proposed in Chapter 8
involved an *adjunction* operation, under which material extraposed out of a
given containing Phrase is attached to the first Maximal Projection dominating the host Phrase out of which the extraposed constituent is being moved.
Under this alternative *adjunction* analysis, a PP extraposed out of a Subject
NP will be adjoined to the first Maximal Projection dominating the Subject
NP: and if we assume that S is the Maximal Projection of I (so that S = IP),
then it follows that a PP extraposed off a Subject NP will be adjoined to IP.
Thus, under this alternative analysis, the bracketed S Complement in (36)
above would have the S-structure (39) below:

(39)

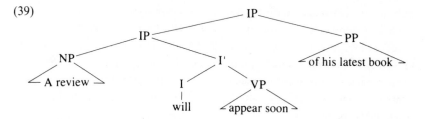

Is such an *adjunction* analysis structure-preserving (in Emonds' sense) or not?
Unfortunately, we can't tell whether Emonds would have considered such an

adjunction analysis structure-preserving, since he includes no detailed discussion of *adjunction* rules. However, in a fairly obvious sense, the adjunction analysis in (39) *is* structure-preserving: for example, the original IP survives intact, and the derived constituent created by the adjunction has the same categorial status (in this case, IP) as the constituent to which it is adjoined. Thus, in a fairly intuitive sense, any rule which adjoins material to an IP to form a derived IP is structure-preserving; whereas any rule which adjoins material to an IP to form a derived V, or N-bar, etc. would not be. More generally, we might suppose that adjunction of material to any constituent X^n to form a derived X^n is a structure-preserving operation: and that this is the only type of *adjunction* operation which transformations are permitted to perform. It is surely significant that the Categorial Component of our grammar allows for this type of adjunction operation: for example, we suggested in Chapter 5 that there might be three different types of base-generated Adjunct: (i) those which recursively expand X into X; (ii) those which recursively expand X-bar into X-bar; and (iii) those which recursively expand X-double-bar into X-double-bar. What these three different types of base-generated adjunction have in common is that they all result in a structure in which the Adjunct Phrase expands an X^n constituent into another X^n constituent. Thus, since transformationally generated Adjuncts produce the same derived structure as base-generated adjunctions, it seems clear that transformational adjunctions are structure-preserving in the relevant sense.

We might generalise these observations in terms of a condition on adjunction transformations such as the following:

(40)   An adjunction is structure-preserving just in case the material adjoined to a given category X^n results in the creation of a derived constituent with the same categorial status as the original X^n to which the material was adjoined

In accordance with the spirit (rather than the letter) of Emonds' constraint, we might suppose that all adjunctions are structure-preserving: this would seem to be a natural extension of the STRUCTURE-PRESERVING PRINCIPLE.

Given Chomsky's assumption in *Lectures* (1981d, p. 47) that 'There are two types of movement rules: substitution and adjunction', and given that we have argued here that both substitution and adjunction operations are structure-preserving, then this opens up the possibility of strengthening and generalising Emonds' original STRUCTURE-PRESERVING PRINCIPLE (28) along the lines indicated in (41) below:

(41)   GENERALISED STRUCTURE-PRESERVING PRINCIPLE
          All transformations are structure-preserving, and comprise either

structure-preserving substitutions of the form (29), or structure-preserving adjunctions of the form (40)

(41) imposes a strong constraint on the set of admissible transformations in natural language grammars, in keeping with our overall goal of devising a maximally constrained Theory of Grammar.

10.5   Explaining the Structure-preserving Principle

Thus far, we have argued that all transformations (both substitution and adjunction rules) are *structure-preserving* in the sense of the definitions given above in (29) and (40). However, any attempt to develop a Theory of Language which aspires to the ultimate goal of *explanatory adequacy* raises an important question of principle: namely, why should it be that transformations have the property of being structure-preserving? We shall argue here that the structure-preserving property of transformations follows largely (perhaps entirely) from more general principles. One of these is the ENDOCENTRICITY CONSTRAINT, familiar from our earlier discussions in Chapter 5. In its 'basic' form (i.e. ignoring modifications designed to block vacuous recursion, etc.) this can be outlined as:

(42)   ENDOCENTRICITY CONSTRAINT
          All Constituent Structure Rules are of the form:
          $X^n \rightarrow \ldots X^m \ldots (n \geqslant m)$

As formulated in (42), the ENDOCENTRICITY CONSTRAINT is a condition on the Base Rules used to generate D-structures, requiring them to be endocentric. Since the Base Rules generate D-structures, we might say that the ENDOCENTRICITY CONSTRAINT (42) *indirectly* constrains D-structures, so that the Categorial Component is restricted to generating endocentric D-structures. We might define an *endocentric structure* as follows:

(43)   A structure is *endocentric* if every non-terminal category X^n which
          it contains immediately dominates a proper head X^m $(n \geqslant m)$
          [a *non-terminal category* is a category which dominates one or
          more other category nodes]

Thus, the indirect effect of the ENDOCENTRICITY CONSTRAINT (42) is to require that D-structures should be endocentric in the sense of (43). Thus, *endocentricity* is a property of the *D-structures* generated by the Categorial Component, but not of the derived structures generated by the Transformational Component. If this is so, then it would allow for the possibility that Transformations could map *endocentric* D-structures into *exocentric* derived structures. But what kind of Transformations could produce exocentric structures?

Not *substitution rules*, obviously, since they move constituents into empty categories generated by the Categorial Rules (and the Categorial Rules are required to be endocentric by the constraint (42) above). Thus, if *substitution rules* can't generate exocentric structures, then since the only other type of Transformation are *adjunction rules*, the only potential source of exocentric structures are *adjunction* transformations. But can adjunction transformations produce exocentric structures? Chomsky seems to think that they can, since he remarks in *Barriers* (1986b, p. 3) that 'The X-bar constraints are satisfied at D-structure, but not at other levels of representation if adjunction has taken place'. The implicit import of his remark here is that *adjunction rules* produce *exocentric* derived structures which violate the endocentricity requirement. But this surely cannot be true in any restrictive theory of adjunction rules. To see this, consider how EXTRAPOSITION operates in the following case (familiar from our discussion in Chapter 8):

(44) (a)   John will [call [people *from Boston* NP] up VP]

    (b)   John will [call [people — NP] up VP] *from Boston*

In Chapter 8, we argued that in such cases the italicised PP is extracted out of the bracketed NP to be adjoined to the right of the bracketed VP. The result is the creation of a new VP node whose immediate constituents are the old VP together with the extraposed PP, as represented schematically in (45) below:

(45)

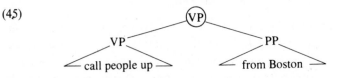

Note that the (encircled) derived VP constituent [*call people up from Boston*] produced by the application of EXTRAPOSITION in (45) satisfies the endocentricity requirement, insofar as it is properly headed by the subordinate (=lower) VP [*call people up*]. By contrast, the endocentricity requirement would not have been satisfied if the encircled derived constituent had been accorded the status of (e.g.) N, N-bar, NP, IP, etc.

The obvious conclusion to draw from this discussion is that (contrary to Chomsky's assertion), adjunction rules do indeed satisfy the endocentricity requirement. Moreover, as noted above, structure-preserving substitutions will also satisfy this requirement, since they don't 'distort' base-structures in any way (e.g. NP MOVEMENT moves a constituent from one NP position into another). Hence, if we want to attain a maximally constrained theory of constituent structure which applies not only to D-structures, but also to S-structures, then it would seem that a step in the right direction would be to extend the endocentricity requirement so that it holds not just at D-structure, but at *all stages of derivation.* This we might do in one of two ways. One possibility would be to require *endocentricity* to be a property not only of the Categorial Rules generating D-structures, but also of the Transformational Rules generating derived structures. However, a second possibility (and the one which we choose to adopt here) is to posit a general well-formedness condition on the Phrase-markers used to represent any (syntactic) stage of derivation of any sentence to the effect that they must be *endocentric.* This we might do in terms of a condition such as (46) below:

(46)   EXTENDED ENDOCENTRICITY CONDITION
        All syntactic representations are endocentric (i.e. must satisfy condition (43))

What (46) says is that any P-marker used to represent the syntactic structure of any sentence at any stage or level of derivation must satisfy the endocentricity requirement (43). Thus, (46) will apply not only to D-structures and S-structures, but to all stages of derivation intermediate between the two as well: in other words, (46) has the same status as our 'no crossing branches' condition (which is likewise a general 'global' condition on the well-formedness of Phrase-markers). Clearly, a linguistic theory which requires that *all* syntactic representations must be endocentric is far more constrained than one which simply stipulates that D-structures are endocentric (since the latter theory allows for transformations to distort D-structures in arbitrary ways). A principle such as (46) would obviously provide a partial account of the structure-preserving property of transformations: for it is quite obvious why transformations 'preserve' structure if both their input (= the structures they apply to) and their output (= the derived structures they produce) are subject to the same EXTENDED ENDOCENTRICITY CONDITION (46).

But although the EXTENDED ENDOCENTRICITY CONDITION provides a *partial* account of the structure-preserving property of transformations, *endocentricity* is not the whole story, since many kinds of illicit adjunction, substitution, and attachment operation result in endocentric structures. For example, suppose that in our earlier example (44) (a) [*John will call people from Boston up*] adjunction of the PP [*from Boston*] to the VP had resulted in the creation of a derived PP constituent, as in (47) below:

(47)

The resultant derived structure would have been endocentric, since the en-circled superordinate PP would be properly headed by the subordinate PP. So, an illicit adjunction such as (47) would not be ruled out by the EXTENDED ENDOCENTRICITY CONDITION. This being so, the obvious question to ask is what kind of principle does determine that the derived constituent [*call people up from Boston*] must have the status of VP (as in (45) above), and not that of PP (as in (47) above)?

One possible answer here would be to appeal to some principle requiring that *lexical structure* be preserved in the course of a derivation. Recall that in Chapter 7 we outlined just such a principle – namely the PROJECTION PRIN-CIPLE, repeated here as (48) below:

(48)   PROJECTION PRINCIPLE
         Syntactic Representations are projected from the Lexicon in that
         they observe the lexical properties of the items they contain

What (48) entails is (amongst other things) that the subcategorisation proper-ties of lexical items must be satisfied not only at D-structure, but also at S-structure (and arguably at all intermediate stages of derivation as well). The principle (48) must clearly be strengthened so as to specify that the relevant properties must be *uniformly* satisfied at each syntactic level, so as to preclude the possibility that a V which may take either an NP or a CP complement might take an NP complement at D-structure, but a CP complement at S-structure. Accordingly, we might revise (48) along the lines of (49) below, in such a way as to incorporate this *uniformity* condition:

(49)   PROJECTION PRINCIPLE (revised)
         Syntactic Representations are projected from the Lexicon in that
         they *uniformly* observe the lexical properties of the items they
         contain

It is the PROJECTION PRINCIPLE (49) which determines that the derived con-stituent produced by EXTRAPOSITION in (44) must have the status of VP accorded to it in (45) above, and cannot have the PP status posited in (47). The reason is quite simply that the derived constituent [*call people up from Boston*] functions as the complement of the Modal *will* in (44): and lexical properties of Modals specify that they subcategorise an infinitival VP Complement. Given the PROJECTION PRINCIPLE (49), it follows that a Modal such as *will* must subcategorise an infinitival VP Complement not only at D-structure, but also at S-structure. But the condition that *will* requires an S-structure VP comple-ment is met only by the analysis (45) in which the derived constituent pro-duced by application of EXTRAPOSITION is assigned VP status, and not by

548

analysis (47), which wrongly assigns it PP status. Generalising somewhat, we can say that the PROJECTION PRINCIPLE determines that the only type of adjunction operations permitted in natural language grammars are structure-preserving adjunctions (in the sense of (40) above). More generally still, we can say that the structure-preserving property of transformations follows in part from the PROJECTION PRINCIPLE, since this principle requires lexically-determined structural properties to remain constant in the course of a derivation.

We argued earlier that any theory which imposes the requirement (41) that all Transformations be structure-preserving substitutions or adjunctions would exclude the possibility of the existence of *Attachment Transformations*. Not surprisingly, perhaps, this ban on *attachment* operations follows in part from the PROJECTION PRINCIPLE. To see this, consider a typical Attachment Transformation which would be 'banned' within the present framework: and this is the rule known in earlier work (e.g. Postal 1974) as SUBJECT-TO-OBJECT RAISING, or RAISING-TO-OBJECT. The rule was supposed to apply to structures such as the following:

(50)   They may consider [$_{IP}$ *John* to be incompetent]

and to *raise* the NP *John* out of its underlying position as Subject of the bracketed subordinate IP complement into a higher position as Object of the main Clause Verb *consider*, resulting in a derived structure such as (51) below:

(51)   They may consider *John* [$_{IP}$ — to be incompetent]

in which *John* is no longer the subordinate Clause Subject, but is now the main Clause Object, and is *attached* as an immediate constituent of the main Clause V-bar constituent (so that SUBJECT-TO-OBJECT RAISING is an *attachment* rule, in our sense).

But why on earth posit that the NP *John* ends up as the Object of *consider*, even though it clearly originates as the Subject of [*to be incompetent*]? Well, the answer suggested by Postal was that *John* seems in many ways to behave as if it were the Object of *consider*. For example, just as Objects can 'passivise', so too can *John* in the relevant type of sentence, as we see from the grammaticality of (52) below:

(52)   *John* is considered to be incompetent

Postal (1974, p. 40) assumed that passivisation was a clause-internal operation (i.e. one that could not apply 'across' Clause boundaries). Part of the evidence on which he based this assumption was the fact that the Subject of a finite subordinate Clause cannot passivise, e.g. in structures such as (53) below:

(53) (a)   They consider [(that) *John* is incompetent]

(b)   **John* is considered [(that) — is incompetent]

According to Postal, the reason why (53) (b) in ungrammatical is that *John* has been moved out of its (bracketed) containing Clause, thereby violating the condition that passivisation is a clause-internal rule. Given the key assumption that passivisation can only apply internally within Clauses and not across clausal boundaries, then it would follow that passivisation cannot apply to a structure such as (50) above, since the rule would have to apply 'across' the bracketed Clause boundary. But if we assumed that the rule of SUBJECT-TO-OBJECT RAISING applied to 'raise' *John* out of subordinate Clause Subject position into main Clause Object position (resulting in the derived structure (51) above), then there would be nothing to prevent passivisation applying internally within the main Clause subsequently.

However, a rule such as SUBJECT-TO-OBJECT RAISING is objectionable on both *empirical* and *theoretical* grounds. The empirical objections are that the very facts which the rule purports to explain can be accounted for without the need to posit the rule. For example (as we argued in Chapter 8), we can account for the fact that passivisation is possible in (52) but not in (53) by supposing that passivisation is blocked only by an intervening CP (so that the subject of an Exceptional Clause or a Small Clause can be passivised, but not the subject of an Ordinary Clause). Since the bracketed Complement Clause in (50) is an *Exceptional Clause* and hence an IP, whereas the bracketed Complement Clause in (53) is an Ordinary Clause (and hence a CP), such an analysis would correctly predict that *John* can be passivised *directly* (viz. without the need for any rule of SUBJECT-TO-OBJECT RAISING applying) in (50), but not in (53).

An even more serious objection (in view of our ultimate goal of *explanatory adequacy*) is that the proposed rule of SUBJECT-TO-OBJECT RAISING has no explanatory force whatever. After all, what 'explains' why (52) is grammatical but (53) (b) is ungrammatical in the *Raising* analysis? The answer is that (52) is grammatical because RAISING applied prior to passivisation, whereas in (53) there was no application of RAISING, hence no possibility of passivisation (on the assumption that passivisation is a clause-internal rule). But this begs the whole question of why RAISING should be able to apply to structures such as (50), but not to structures such as (53). Thus, the burden of explanation is simply shifted from one rule to another: this is the linguistic counterpart of 'passing the buck'!

More directly relevant to our present discussion is the fact that there are also strong *theory-internal* objections to any rule of SUBJECT-TO-OBJECT RAISING. For (as Chomsky notes in *Lectures* (1981d), pp. 32–3), any such rule would violate the PROJECTION PRINCIPLE (49). Why? Because in the D-structure (50) above, *consider* subcategorises an infinitival IP Complement; but in the corresponding S-structure (51) which results from the application of RAISING, *consider* has both an NP Complement and an IP Complement. This means that SUBJECT-TO-OBJECT RAISING is a rule which illicitly 'changes' the subcategorisation properties of items during the course of a derivation. However, any such change of subcategorisation properties involves a violation of the PROJECTION PRINCIPLE (49), which requires that the subcategorisation properties of items should be *uniformly* satisfied at all syntactic levels. In other words, the PROJECTION PRINCIPLE (49) bans structure-building *Attachment Transformations* such as SUBJECT-TO-OBJECT RAISING. More generally, the structure-preserving requirement on transformations follows in part from the PROJECTION PRINCIPLE (49) (since this principle requires that lexical [e.g. sub-categorisation] properties be 'preserved' in the course of a derivation).

Of course, the PROJECTION PRINCIPLE (49) doesn't simply require that the *subcategorisation* properties of items must remain constant in the course of a derivation: it requires that *all* lexical properties remain constant. Among the other lexical properties of an item are its *categorial* features; so that another property of transformations which follows from the PROJECTION PRINCIPLE (49) is that they cannot change the categorial status of an item in the course of a derivation. Thus, the PROJECTION PRINCIPLE (49) subsumes the condition proposed by Jackendoff (1972, p. 13) that 'transformations cannot change node labels'. This means, for example, that the relationship between a Clause such as that bracketed in (54)(a) below and its bracketed Noun Phrase counterpart in (54)(b):

(54) (a)   They reported [CP *that the enemy had destroyed the city*]

(b)   They reported [NP *the destruction of the city by the enemy*]

cannot be a transformational one: that is to say, within the framework we are adopting here, we cannot assume that the NP in (54)(b) is derived from the Clause in (54)(a) by a NOMINALISATION transformation (of the type proposed in Lees 1960), since such a transformation would have the effect of changing the categorial status of the V *destroyed* into the N *destruction*, of the NP [*the enemy*] into the PP [*by the enemy*], of the NP [*the city*] into the PP [*of the city*], and of the bracketed CP in (54)(a) into the bracketed NP in (54)(b). But the PROJECTION PRINCIPLE (49) bars *category-changing* transformations such as NOMINALISATION.

Of course, the *lexical* properties of items include not only their categorial and subcategorisation properties, but also their *thematic* properties. It follows that one of the constraints subsumed under the PROJECTION PRINCIPLE (49) is that 'categories and positions are θ-marked in the same way at all syntactic levels' (Chomsky, *Lectures* (1981d), p. 39). This would mean that no transformation could have the power to change thematic structure in the course of a derivation. So, for example, if the Verb *murder* takes an AGENT Subject and a THEME Object at D-structure, then it must also have an AGENT Subject and a THEME Object at S-structure. We will explore one important consequence of this assumption in the next section.

However, there is one important respect in which the condition that thematic structure cannot be changed in the course of a derivation proves too weak. If we accept the assumption made in Chapter 7 that some Predicates have non-thematic subjects (e.g. Verbs like *seem*), then the PROJECTION PRINCIPLE (49) will not apply to these non-thematic subjects (since the principle requires that theta-marked Arguments be preserved, but says nothing about non-thematic constituents). This would mean that nothing would seem to preclude the possibility that a Clause could have a non-thematic Subject at one level, but be subjectless at another level. To exclude this possibility, we might follow Chomsky (*Lectures* (1981d), p. 27) in positing an independent 'structural requirement' to the effect that 'a Clause have a Subject' (ibid., p. 10). Since we are attempting to account for the structure-preserving property of transformations by assuming that structure (as determined by lexical properties of items) remains constant at all syntactic levels, we might assume that this *structural* requirement for Clauses to have Subjects also holds at all syntactic levels. Hence, we might outline the relevant structural principle informally as:

(55)   CLAUSAL SUBJECT PRINCIPLE
         Each Clause requires a uniform subject at all syntactic levels

We might then go even further and follow Chomsky (1982, p. 10) in positing that the PROJECTION PRINCIPLE (49) and the CLAUSAL SUBJECT PRINCIPLE (55) can be conflated into a single, more general principle, which Chomsky (1982, p. 10) terms the EXTENDED PROJECTION PRINCIPLE. We might characterise this principle informally in the following terms:

(56)   EXTENDED PROJECTION PRINCIPLE
         Lexical requirements (viz. categorial, subcategorisation and thematic properties) and structural requirements (viz. the requirement that a Clause should have a Subject) must be uniformly satisfied at all syntactic levels

In effect, (56) says that the Subject/Complement structure of a Predicate must satisfy lexical and structural requirements, and must remain constant in the course of a derivation. In the terminology of Chomsky, *Lectures* (1981d) p. 47

where Subject and Complement positions are said to be *A-positions* (i.e. positions in which theta-marked Arguments can, though need not occur), (56) can be understood as requiring that *A-structure* must remain constant in the course of a derivation, and must satisfy relevant lexical and structural requirements. So, for example, if a transitive V such as *devour* has an NP AGENT Subject and an NP THEME Object at D-structure, then it must have the same Subject and Object at S-structure also.

You should now be able to tackle exercise IV

10.6 Traces

Hitherto, we have formulated a number of principles which determine the derived constituent structure produced by transformations: initially, we formulated the GENERALISED STRUCTURE-PRESERVING PRINCIPLE (41); then we investigated the possibility that this principle might derive in part from the EXTENDED ENDOCENTRICITY CONDITION (46), and in part from the EXTENDED PROJECTION PRINCIPLE (56). So far, however, we have only considered how these principles determine the derived constituent structure produced at the *landing-site* of the rule. In particular, we have not considered the equally important question of what happens at the *extraction site* (i.e. the position out of which a constituent is moved) when a movement rule applies.

At first sight, it might seem as if the answer to this question is obvious: after all, surely if a movement rule applies to move a category and its contents from one position in a sentence (= the extraction site) to another (= the landing site), then won't the original category and its contents simply 'disappear' from the extraction site? However, more mature reflection shows that this cannot be so. To see why, consider the derivation of the following example:

(57)   [NP What] [C will] [IP you — [VP do —]]?

Given standard arguments, (57) will derive from an underlying structure in which the Modal *will* originates within IP in I, and in which the wh-NP *what* originates within VP as the complement of *do*: I MOVEMENT will then apply to move the Modal *will* from I into C, and WH MOVEMENT will move the wh-NP *what* into the empty NP (C-Specifier) position in front of C. The derivation of (57) can thus be represented schematically as in (58) below:

(58)   [NP e] [C e] [IP you [I will] [VP do [NP what]]]
                    └ I MOVEMENT ┘
         └────────── WH MOVEMENT ──────────┘

Now, let us suppose (for the sake of argument) that moved categories simply 'disappear' from their extraction site, and leave no trace behind, If this is so, then the resultant derived structure after I-MOVEMENT and WH-MOVEMENT will be (59) below:

(59)

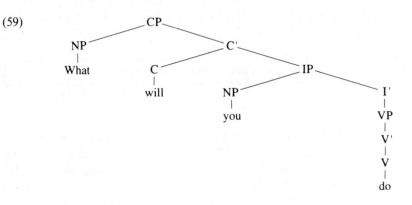

But any such structure would violate all three of the principles which we discussed in the two previous sections. For example, it is hard to see how we could consider rules like I MOVEMENT or WH MOVEMENT as structure-preserving if in fact they result in the loss of the original category at the extraction-site (such a rule would be *structure-effacing* rather than *structure-preserving*): so, there would be violation of our GENERALISED STRUCTURE-PRESERVING PRINCIPLE (41). Moreover, if I simply 'disappears' from I-bar when the Modal *will* is moved from I into C, then I-bar will be *headless*, in violation of the EXTENDED ENDOCENTRICITY CONDITION (46). And finally, if the wh-NP *what* simply 'disappears' from VP when WH MOVEMENT applies, then the transitive Verb *do* lacks an immediately following NP THEME Object at S-structure, in violation of the EXTENDED PROJECTION PRINCIPLE (56), which requires *do* to have an NP THEME Object at all syntactic levels, i.e. not just at D-structure, but also at S-structure.

It follows from the above discussion, therefore, that when a given category moves from its extraction-site to its landing-site, the category cannot simply 'disappear' from the extraction-site altogether, but rather must remain in some 'invisible' form at the extraction-site. But in what form? Let's assume that movement rules (whether *adjunction* or *substitution* rules) leave behind them at their extraction-site a 'ghost' copy of the category which is being moved: since this 'ghost' will obviously be *empty* of any lexical material (given that the material it used to contain has been moved elsewhere in the sentence), we might assume the following principle:

(60)   TRACE MOVEMENT PRINCIPLE

Any moved constituent X^n leaves behind at its extraction-site an identical empty category $[_{X^n}\ e]$. This empty category is known as a *trace*, and the moved constituent is said to be the *antecedent* of the trace

For obvious reasons, the theory that movement rules leave behind empty category 'traces' is known as the *Trace Theory of Movement Rules.*

At this point, when we are being asked to accept both that constituents can move into empty node positions, and that they leave behind empty nodes when they do move, we may begin to feel that the whole theory is getting so abstract and elaborate that it passes the comprehension of ordinary mortals (i.e. nonlinguists!) But perhaps a simple analogy will help to make things clearer. Just think of the problems of moving house. You can't move into a house unless it's *empty*; and when you move out of a house, you don't take your old house with you – rather, you leave it behind, *empty*. It's just the same with moved constituents: they too move into empty nodes (in the case of substitution rules), and leave behind them empty nodes.

Now, if we assume the *trace theory convention* outlined informally in (60) above, then the derived structure of our earlier example (57) *What will you do?* will not be (59) above, but rather (61) below:

(61)

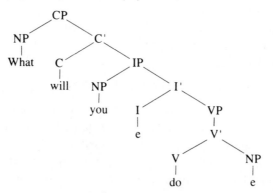

And note that the derived structure (61) satisfies all our three principles. Thus, the GENERALISED STRUCTURE-PRESERVING PRINCIPLE (41) is satisfied, since the D-structure I position held by *will* and the D-structure NP position held by *what* survive intact as empty categories at S-structure. Moreover, since I-bar is now headed by an empty I in (61), the EXTENDED ENDOCENTRICITY PRINCIPLE (46) is also satisfied. And since *do* still retains an NP Complement, its subcategorisation frame is satisfied by the S-structure (61), so that there is no violation of the EXTENDED PROJECTION PRINCIPLE (56).

The more general implication of our discussion here is that the GENERALISED

STRUCTURE-PRESERVING PRINCIPLE (41), the EXTENDED ENDOCENTRICITY PRIN-
CIPLE (46), and the EXTENDED PROJECTION PRINCIPLE (56) all require us to posit
that moved constituents leave behind an empty *trace* copy of the moved category. In other words, the Trace Theory of Movement Rules is a direct consequence of the independently motivated theoretical principles governing the
operation of Transformations which we posited earlier. That is to say, Trace
Theory has considerable theory-internal motivation.

However, an obvious question to ask at this point is whether there is independent *empirical motivation* for positing that moved constituents leave behind traces. Well, yes, there is indeed. Consider, for example, how we are to
account for the fact (noted in Chapter 8) that HAVE CONTRACTION is blocked in
cases such as:

(62) (a)   Should we have called the Police?

   (b)   *Should we've called the Police

We might assume that the Modal *should* here originates in I and is subsequently moved into C by the rule of I MOVEMENT, in the manner indicated
schematically in (63) below:

(63) $[_C e\,]$ $[_{IP}$We $[_I$ *should*$]$ have called the Police$]$
           $\llcorner$I MOVEMENT$\lrcorner$

Now if we further assume the Trace Theory of Movement Rules, then movement of I into C will leave behind an empty category *trace* of the moved
$[_I$ *should*$]$ constituent, resulting in the derived structure (64) below:

(64) $[_C$ *Should*$]$ $[_{IP}$ we $[_I$ e$]$ have called the Police$]$?

We might then argue that what blocks HAVE CONTRACTION from applying in
(64) is the fact that *we* and *have* are not immediately adjacent, but rather are
separated by the empty $[_I$ e$]$ trace of the preposed Modal *should*. For recall
that we argued in Chapter 8 that the presence of a 'gap' between the subject
Pronoun and *have* blocks contraction. But unless we posit that I MOVEMENT
leaves behind an empty I trace 'gap' between the Subject NP and the VP, we
will be left with no obvious account of why contraction is blocked in cases
such as (62).

A parallel *contraction* argument in support of Trace Theory can be formulated in relation to the WANNA CONTRACTION facts discussed in Chapter 9.
There, we argued that WANNA CONTRACTION is blocked (in standard dialects)
in cases such as:

(65) (a)   Who might you *want to* win?

   (b)   *Who might you *wanna* win?

But why should this be? If we suppose that the wh-NP *who* here originates between *want* and *to* as the underlying Subject of the *win*-clause, and if we further suppose that application of WH MOVEMENT to move the wh-NP *who* to the front of the overall sentence leaves an empty NP *trace* behind at the extraction site, then (65) would have the derived structure (66) below:

(66)   [NP Who] might you want [NP e] to win?

And we might then argue that it is the presence of the intervening empty NP trace between *want* and *to* which blocks contraction; for we argued in Chapter 8 that the presence of a 'gap' between *want* and *to* blocks WANNA CONTRACTION from applying, and clearly traces count as 'gaps' in the relevant sense.

In addition to the two *contraction* arguments outlined above, we can add a further range of empirical arguments in support of the claim that movement rules leave empty category *traces* behind: the arguments all make the general claim that such a convention considerably simplifies our account of certain grammatical phenomena, and in addition considerably simplifies the overall organisation of our grammar. In this connection, consider how we are to handle *Agreement* facts in sentences such as the following:

(67)   *Which one* do you think *seems* to be the best *candidate*?

Simplifying somewhat for expository purposes, we could say that (67) would have a derivation such as that outlined schematically in (68) below:

(68)

[NP e] [C e] You *do* think [CP C [NP e] [I e] [VP *seem* [IP *which one* to be ...]]]

       I MOVEMENT   V MOVEMENT

          WH MOVEMENT   NP MOVEMENT

That is, the wh-NP [*which one*] would originate as the Subject of the bracketed IP (= Exceptional Clause) Complement of *seem*: it would then be raised into the empty NP Subject position in the *seem* Clause by NP MOVEMENT; subsequently it is then moved into the empty NP (C-specifier) position at the front of the *think*-clause by WH MOVEMENT. In addition, the Modal *do* moves from I into C in the main Clause by I MOVEMENT; and *seem* moves out of VP into the empty I position in its Clause by V MOVEMENT.

Now, what interests us particularly here is the fact that the third person singular wh-NP [*which one*] agrees both with the Predicate Noun *candidate*, and with the verbal Predicate *seems*. How can we account for this? In a grammar without *traces*, we require an extremely complex AGREEMENT rule to handle the relevant facts. As we know, Agreement holds between the Subject of a Clause and its verbal or nominal Predicate. What poses problems for us in

(67) is how to account for the Agreement between [*which one*] and *seem*. The reason is that [*which one*] is neither the D-structure Subject nor the S-structure Subject of *seem*. Rather, [*which one*] is the final Subject of the *seem*-clause at the last point in the derivation where *seem* still had an overt Subject (i.e. after the application of NP MOVEMENT, but before the application of WH MOVEMENT). In other words, the relevant generalisation in a grammar without traces would be that:

(69)   A nominal or verbal Predicate agrees with the final Subject of its Clause (i.e. with the Subject of the Clause at the last stage of derivation where the Clause has a Subject)

It is easy enough to check for yourself that a rule like (69) would handle Agreement in cases like (67): for, as we can see from (68), [*which one*] would be the final Subject of the bracketed Exceptional Clause (IP), and hence trigger Agreement with the Predicate Noun *candidate*; and likewise [*which one*] would also be the final Subject of the bracketed CP, and hence trigger agreement with the verbal Predicate *seem* (once *seem* has moved from V into I by V MOVEMENT).

But if rule (69) works, what's wrong with it? The answer is that it is an extremely powerful *global* rule which requires us to scan all the various different stages of derivation of a sentence in order to see at what point (if any) its conditions of application are met. However, global rules are devices far too powerful to be allowed in any constrained theory of Syntax. Clearly, our overall model of grammar would be far more constrained if we were to impose the condition that particular types of rules operate *at a specified level* in the grammar. And one of the advantages of Trace Theory is that it allows us to specify that all morphosyntactic rules (i.e. syntactic rules which determine morphological properties of items, such as Agreement or Case-marking) operate at S-structure. Let's see how this assumption would help us handle our Agreement problem in the case of our earlier example (67). Given the assumption that movement rules leave traces, (67) would have the following S-structure (simplified by considering only traces of [*which one*], which are symbolised as *t*):

(70)   *Which one* do you think [$_{CP}$ C *t* seems [$_{IP}$ *t* to be the best candidate]]?

We can then say that a nominal or verbal Predicate agrees with the S-structure Subject of its Clause. Thus, the Predicate Noun *candidate* in the bracketed Exceptional Clause will agree with its empty NP trace Subject; and the verbal Predicate *seems* of the bracketed CP will agree with its own empty NP trace Subject. So, in both cases, the Predicate takes on the appropriate properties of its empty NP Subject. But what determines the Person and Number of an empty NP trace? We might assume a convention that a trace somehow inherits the grammatical properties of its *antecedent* (= the constituent whose movement gave rise to the trace). So, since the antecedent of both the empty NP traces in (70) is the third person singular wh-NP [*which one*], then it follows that both empty NP traces will also be third person singular, and will trigger appropriate agreement with the Predicate. Thus, the Predicate Noun *candidate* is singular because it agrees with its singular trace Subject, and the verbal Predicate *seems* is third person singular because its empty NP trace Subject is also singular.

A problem which arises with this account, however, is how we know what the antecedent of a given trace is. For example, how do we know that the two empty NPs in (70) are traces of [*which one*] rather than of *you*? It's obviously crucial to be able to pick out the right antecedent for a trace, otherwise we'll end up with the wrong Agreement pattern. This is particularly important in sentences involving more than one moved constituent – e.g. as in:

(71)   Which singers does he seem to be a fan of?

Given standard assumptions, (71) will have a simplified S-structure along the lines of (72) below:

(72)   *Which singers* does *he* seem [$_{IP}$ *t* to be a fan of *t*]?

The Predicate Noun *fan* here will agree with the trace Subject to its left: but how do we know whether this is the trace of the plural NP [*which singers*], or of the singular NP *he*? Of course, we could look back through the earlier stages of derivation and find out that *he* and not [*which singers*] originated as the Subject of the bracketed IP: but this would violate our earlier requirement that morphosyntactic rules cannot 'look back' to earlier stages of derivation, but rather operate uniquely at S-structure. So, what we need is some convention that will tell us what the antecedent of a given trace is at S-structure. Accordingly, we might posit a convention whereby whenever a constituent is moved, the moved category and its trace are *coindexed* – that is, assigned some unique subscript index (a letter, or a number) which they share. In the light of this proposal, we might replace our earlier principle (60) by its revised counterpart (73) below:

(73)   TRACE MOVEMENT PRINCIPLE
          Any moved category X^n is assigned a unique subscript index; each
          time it moves, it leaves behind a coindexed empty category *trace*

We assume that by convention whenever a given constituent moves several times, each of its traces is assigned the same index. Given this assumption, (67) above will have the S-structure:

(74)   [$_{NP_i}$ *which one*] do you think . . .

      . . . [$_{CP}$ C [$_{NP_i}$ e] seems [$_{IP}$ [$_{NP_i}$ e] to be the best candidate]]?

Since both empty NP traces here are assigned the same index as the moved wh-NP [*which one*], we assume that they inherit the Number and Person properties of their antecedent, and hence trigger singular Agreement on both *seems* and *candidate*. Similarly, if we assume the principle (73), then the S-structure of our earlier example (71) above will be:

(75)   [$_{NP_i}$ *which singers*] does [$_{NP_j}$ *he*] seem [$_{IP}$ [$_{NP_j}$ e] to be a FAN of [$_{NP_i}$ e]]?

And here the Predicate Noun *fan* will be singular, because it agrees with its empty Subject NP_j, and the index on this empty NP tells us that its antecedent is the singular NP *he*.

So, it seems clear that one advantage of Trace Theory is that it enables us to achieve a relatively straightforward account of *Agreement* in terms of properties of S-structure. Indeed, as we suggested earlier, we might claim that Trace Theory allows us to capture the generalisation that not just Agreement but *all morphosyntactic rules* apply at S-structure. In this connection, it is interesting to look briefly at *case-marking*. Simplifying in ways which do not prejudice the present discussion, let us suppose that English has the following two case-marking rules:

(76) (i)   Assign NOMINATIVE case to an NP which is the sister of an I-bar immediately dominating a finite I (= to the Subject of a finite Clause)

     (ii)   Assign OBJECTIVE case to an NP which immediately follows a transitive Verb or Preposition

Let us further suppose that all morphosyntactic rules (including case-marking rules) operate uniquely at S-structure.

The claim that all case-marking takes place at S-structure doesn't prove problematic in the case of sentences such as (77) below, where the italicised NP has undergone NP-MOVEMENT (i.e. 'Raising') out of the position marked —:

(77)   *John* must be likely [$_{IP}$ — to win]

After all, since *John* is the Subject of a finite I containing the Modal *must* at S-structure, then *John* in (77) will be assigned NOMINATIVE case by rule (76) (i).

More problematic, however, is S-structure case-assignment for NPs which have undergone WH MOVEMENT. Consider, for example, the OBJECTIVE case assigned to *whom* in (78) below:

(78)   *Whom* [$_C$ did] [$_{IP}$ you meet in town]?

Since *whom* here does not immediately follow the Verb *meet*, it cannot be assigned OBJECTIVE case by rule (76) (ii); neither does it satisfy the conditions in (76) (i) for NOMINATIVE case marking. In other words, S-structure case-marking would prove extremely problematic in a grammar without traces. By contrast, under the alternative Trace Theory account, no such problems arise. Assuming that *whom* here originates in postverbal position as the complement of *meet*, and is then moved in front of the C containing the preposed Auxiliary *did*, then (78) will have the S-structure (79) below, where t_i is the trace of the preposed wh-NP *whom*, and t_j is the trace of the preposed Auxiliary:

(79)   [$_{NP_i}$ *Whom*] [$_{C_j}$ did] [$_{IP}$ you t_j meet t_i in town]?

Our earlier case-marking rule (76) (ii) will assign OBJECTIVE case to the empty NP trace t_i which immediately follows the transitive Verb *meet*; and we might then assume that the antecedent of this case-marked trace (= the wh-NP *whom*) inherits OBJECTIVE case from its trace, and hence is indirectly (via its trace) assigned OBJECTIVE case. Thus, Trace Theory allows us to maintain the generalisation that all case-marking takes place at S-structure. Since we have already shown that Trace Theory also allows us to handle *Agreement* at S-structure, it follows that we can maintain the more general conclusion that *all morphosyntactic rules* apply uniquely at the level of S-structure. This results both in a vast reduction in the expressive power of the rules concerned (e.g. we no longer need global rules), and in a considerable simplification in the overall organisation of our grammar.

Before we leave *traces*, however, it is interesting to focus for a while on the nature of the relation between *traces* and their *antecedents*. As we saw in our discussion of agreement facts, traces have somehow to inherit the grammatical properties of their antecedents: for example, the trace of a third person singular NP has to count as a third person singular NP for Agreement purposes. This suggests that the inherent syntactic and semantic properties of antecedents are transmitted to their traces. But conversely, as we saw earlier, antecedents have somehow to inherit the case-marking of their traces. Since case-marking is an *assigned* property (i.e. one assigned by a rule) and not an *inherent* one, this suggests that traces transmit their assigned properties to their antecedents. So, what we need is a mechanism which will ensure that the

561

inherent properties of antecedents are transmitted to traces, and conversely that the assigned properties of traces are transmitted to their antecedents.

One mechanism which might serve our purposes is the notion of *chain* introduced by Chomsky in *Lectures* (1981d). Although this is a complex notion to which we shall subsequently devote lengthy discussions in Volume Two, for present purposes we can define a *chain* informally in the following terms:

(80)   A moved constituent and its coindexed traces form a movement
          chain

We might say the moved NP which forms the antecedent of the trace is the *Head* of the chain; and that two immediately adjacent constituents in a chain constitute a *link*. Given this terminology, we might then propose the following principle (with apologies to bike fans!):

(81)   CHAIN TRANSMISSION PRINCIPLE
          Grammatical properties are freely transmitted between the links
          of a movement chain

Given principle (81), it will follow that inherent grammatical properties of the head NP of a chain will be transmitted to its traces; and conversely that the grammatical properties assigned to traces will be transmitted to their Heads. Thus, in (74) above, both traces inherit the grammatical properties of their antecedent NP [*which one*], so that both traces are third person singular, and hence trigger singular Agreement on *candidate* and *seems*. Conversely, in (79), the trace t_i is assigned OBJECTIVE case by rule (76)(ii) (because it immediately follows the transitive Verb *meet*), and 'transmits' this case feature to the interrogative pronoun which is the Head of the movement chain, with the result that the case feature is morphologically marked on the pronoun *whom* (in the form of the OBJECTIVE inflection -*m*). Our discussion is necessarily somewhat sketchy at this point: we shall return to a full discussion of traces, chains, and case-marking in Volume Two.

You should now be able to tackle exercise V

10.7   C-command condition on Traces

Much of our discussion in this chapter has been concerned with formulating a principle to the effect that transformations must preserve lexical structure. This principle represents one way of *constraining* the operations performed by movement rules, in keeping with our overall aim of devising a maximally constrained model of grammar. But important though this principle is, it is not by any means the whole story: for, there is clear evidence that we have to constrain transformations in ways which go beyond the requirement that they should not 'distort' lexical structure in any way. In this connection, it is interesting to think about the properties of some of the movement rules we have already looked at. Take, for example, the case of NP MOVEMENT. In 'Passive' structures, the rule may move an NP out of Object position into Subject position in the same Clause, as in (82) (a) below; or else it may raise the Subject of a subordinate Exceptional Clause IP to become the Subject of a superordinate IP, as in (82) (b):

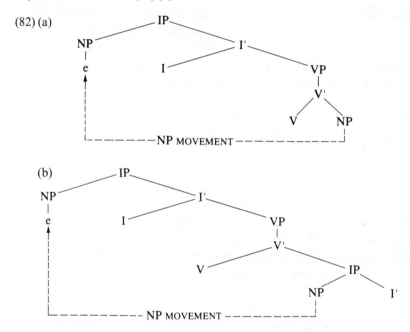

(82) (a)

(b)

In both cases, the rule operates in such a way as to move an NP from a 'lower' into a 'higher' position in the sentence. In the terminology of Chomsky (*Reflections* (1976), p. 107) we might say that NP MOVEMENT *upgrades* the moved NP. Interestingly, there are no cases in which NP MOVEMENT *downgrades* an NP – i.e. moves it from a 'higher' to a 'lower' position. We might wonder therefore if there is some general condition on Transformations 'that upgrading rules are permitted, but not downgrading rules' (Chomsky, ibid.)

To check whether *upgrading* is a general property of movement rules, we might examine the operation of other movement rules with which we are familiar. Consider, for example, the rule of I MOVEMENT which we discussed in Chapter 8. Recall that I MOVEMENT raises an Auxiliary out of I into C, in the manner indicated schematically in (83) below:

(83)

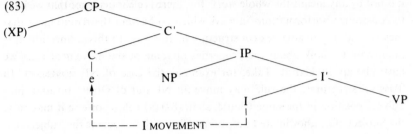

Thus, I MOVEMENT too is an *upgrading* rule which moves a constituent from a lower to a higher position. It is surely significant that English has an *upgrading* rule of I MOVEMENT *raising* Auxiliaries from I into C (as in (84) (a) below), but no converse *downgrading* rule of C MOVEMENT *lowering* Complementisers from C into I, as we see from the ungrammaticality of (84) (b):

(84) (a)   I wonder [C *will*] they [I e] like it (Semi-indirect Speech)
     (b)   *I wonder [C e] they [I *whether*] like it

Accordingly, it seems reasonable to conclude that it is a general property of movement transformations that they cannot *downgrade* constituents.

Given the key assumption of Trace Theory that a moved constituent leaves behind a coindexed trace, we might formulate the relevant principle that transformations cannot *downgrade* constituents in terms of an equivalent condition that a moved constituent cannot occupy a lower position than any of its traces. This principle might be stated more formally as in (85) below:

(85)   C-COMMAND CONDITION
          A moved constituent must c-command (= *constituent-command*) each of its traces at S-structure (X *c-commands* Y just in case the first branching node dominating X dominates Y, and neither X nor Y dominates the other)

If we look at (83) above, we see that C c-commands I by virtue of the fact that the first branching node above C is C-bar, and C-bar dominates I: by contrast, I does not c-command C, since the first branching node above I is I-bar, and I-bar does not dominate C. Hence, the C-COMMAND CONDITION (85) correctly predicts that movement is possible from I into C, but not from C into I. Thus, as desired, the principle permits upgrading, but not downgrading.

Moreover, the C-COMMAND CONDITION (85) helps to explain an apparent anomaly in the operation of EXTRAPOSITION. Recall that in Chapter 8 we saw that a CP extraposed off an Object NP is adjoined to VP (as in (86) (a) below), but a PP extraposed off a Subject NP cannot be adjoined to VP, but rather must be adjoined to IP (as in (86) (b) below):

(86) (a)   John will [vp call people — up] *who are from Boston*
   (b)   [ip Nobody — would ride with Fred] *who knew him*

The C-COMMAND CONDITION (85) provides a principled explanation for this otherwise rather puzzling asymmetry between EXTRAPOSITION off a Subject and off an Object. Thus, attachment of the extraposed Clause to VP in (86) (a) will result in the derived VP having the S-structure (87) below:

(87)

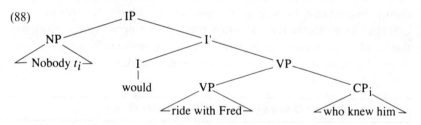

And it is easy enough to see that the extraposed Relative Clause [*who are from Boston*] in (87) c-commands its trace t_i. By contrast, adjunction of the extraposed Relative Clause to VP in (86) (b) would result in the relevant Clause having the (partial) superficial structure (88) below:

(88)

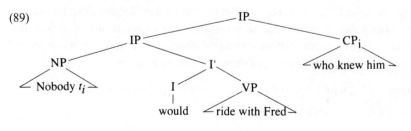

And it should be equally clear that the extraposed Clause [*who knew him*] does not c-command its coindexed trace t_i in (88). By contrast, if material extraposed off a Subject NP is adjoined to IP, the superficial structure of the S in (86) (b) will be:

(89)

And it is easy enough to see that the extraposed Relative Clause [*who are from Boston*] in (87) c-commands its trace t_i.

565

And in (89), the extraposed Clause CP$_i$ does indeed c-command its trace t_i – as I leave you to verify for yourself! So, the apparent asymmetry between Extraposition off Subject and Object NPs can be accounted for in terms of the C-COMMAND CONDITION (85): that is, EXTRAPOSITION adjoins an extraposed constituent to the minimal XP which will satisfy the C-COMMAND CONDITION.

What is interesting about the C-COMMAND CONDITION is that we have reformulated a *condition on transformations* (to the effect that transformations cannot 'downgrade' constituents) as a *condition on structures* (i.e. as a condition on the derived structures produced by transformations) to the effect that a trace must have a c-commanding *antecedent*. What is even more interesting is that the condition that a trace must be c-commanded by its antecedent has obvious parallels with our earlier condition (in section 3.3) that a Reflexive anaphor (like *himself*, etc.) must also be c-commanded by its antecedent. This suggests that there are significant parallels between the behaviour of *traces* on the one hand, and *anaphors* on the other. And in Volume Two, we shall explore this parallelism in much greater detail.

For the time being, however, it is sufficient to note the principle involved that incorporating *traces* into a grammar enables us to reformulate many conditions on transformations as structural conditions (i.e. as conditions which syntactic representations must meet in order to be well-formed). This is obviously reminiscent of our claim in section 10.5 that the ENDOCENTRICITY CONSTRAINT (42) – originally proposed as a constraint on Categorial Rules – should be replaced by a general condition on Phrase-markers (viz. the EXTENDED ENDOCENTRICITY CONDITION (46)). And it opens up the possibility that conditions on rules can in large measure be replaced by *structural conditions* (i.e. well-formedness conditions on Phrase-markers).

> *You should now be able to tackle exercise VI*

10.8 Bounding

Thus far, we've asked what principles determine where constituents can be moved *from* and *to*, but not what principles determine *how far* they can be moved. Most of the transformations we have looked at so far seem to be *bounded* in the sense that they can move constituents only a limited 'distance'. For example, NP MOVEMENT in passive structures can move an NP across a single IP boundary, as shown in schematic terms in (90) below:

(90)   [$_{NP}$e] was said [$_{IP}$*John* to believe [$_{IP}$ Mary to be wrong]]
        └─NP MOVEMENT ─┘

and this results in grammatical sentences such as:

(91)   *John* was said to believe Mary to be wrong

However, passivisation (= NP MOVEMENT) is not possible across two intervening IP boundaries, so that we cannot passivise *Mary* in the manner shown
informally in (92) below:

(92)   [$_{NP}$ e] was said [$_{IP}$ John to believe [$_{IP}$ *Mary* to be wrong]]
          └──×── NP MOVEMENT ──×──┘

as we see from the ungrammaticality of the resultant sentence:

(93)   *Mary* was said John to believe to be wrong

Not surprisingly, the same is also true of 'Raising' cases of NP MOVEMENT.
Thus, in a structure such as (94) below:

(94)   [$_{NP}$ e] is likely [$_{IP}$ *John* to believe [$_{IP}$ MARY to be wrong]]
          └NP MOVEMENT┘
          └──×── NP MOVEMENT ──×──┘

only the italicised NP *John* can be 'raised' to become the main Clause Subject,
not the capitalised NP *MARY*: hence the contrast in (95) below:

(95) (a)   *John* is likely to believe Mary to be wrong
     (b)   *Mary* is likely John to believe to be wrong

Why should this be? One plausible answer is that 'Raising' in the case of *John*
involves movement across a single IP, whereas 'Raising' in the case of *Mary*
involves movement across two IP nodes. And if we assume that NP MOVEMENT
is inherently *bounded* and hence can never move an NP across more than one
intervening IP node, we have a natural account of the ungrammaticality of
sentences such as (93) and (95) (b).

It should be obvious that I MOVEMENT is bounded in much the same way: for
example, it can move the italicised Auxiliary out of I into C across a single
intervening IP boundary, as in (96) below:

(96)   [$_C$ e] [$_{IP}$ John *might* suspect that [$_{IP}$ he will resign]]
          └I MOVEMENT┘

This results in the grammatical sentence (97) below:

(97)   Might John suspect that he will resign?

However, I MOVEMENT cannot move the subordinate Clause Auxiliary *will* across the two bracketed IP boundaries in (98) below:

(98)   [$_C$ e] [$_{IP}$ John might suspect that [$_{IP}$ he *will* resign]]

         └────── ✗ ── I MOVEMENT ── ✗ ────┘

since the resultant sentence is ungrammatical: cf.

(99)   *_Will_ John might suspect that he resign?

How can we account for the fact that both NP MOVEMENT and I MOVEMENT appear to be *bounded* in much the same way (i.e. they are unable to move a constituent out of more than one containing IP node)? The most principled answer to this question would be to posit that it is an inherent property of *all* movement rules that they are *intrinsically bounded*. That is to say, transformations can move constituents so far (e.g. out of a single containing IP node), but no further.

    However, there is an important qualification which needs to be made to this *bounding* condition. To see why, consider how we might derive a sentence such as the following:

(100)   The fur seems to be certain to fly

Given 'standard' arguments of the type we discussed in Chapter 8, it is clear that both *seem* and *certain* are Raising Predicates. Moreover, given that the NP [*the fur*] is an idiom chunk NP, it must originate as the subject of *fly*. This being so, then the NP [*the fur*] will originate as the Subject of *fly*, and be raised first to become the Subject of *be certain*, and then be raised again to become the Subject of *seems*, in the manner indicated schematically in (101) below:

(101)   [$_{NP}$ e] seems [$_{IP}$ [$_{NP}$ e] to be certain [$_{IP}$ *the fur* to fly]]

         └NP MOVEMENT┘ └─ NP MOVEMENT ─┘
              (2)   (1)

Now, at first sight it might seem as if a derivation such as (101) violates our *bounding* principle that no constituent can be moved out of more than one containing IP-node, since the NP [*the fur*] has crossed two IP boundaries in (101) during the course of its travels. But the key point is that the NP [*the fur*] here undergoes two different *successive movements*, and that each of these separate movements crosses only one single IP node boundary. Thus, if we say that nodes like IP which seem to act as 'boundaries' for movement are *bounding nodes*, we might formulate the relevant constraint on movement transformations in the following terms:

568

(102)   BOUNDING CONDITION

No constituent can be moved out of more than one containing bounding node *in any single movement*

The principle (102) is termed the SUBJACENCY CONDITION by Chomsky, the general idea behind the use of this term being that movement into a higher position is only possible out of an immediately subjacent (i.e. subordinate) bounding category. In Volume Two, we shall discuss in considerable detail the attempt to develop an adequate *Theory of Bounding*; but for the time being, principle (102) will suffice to illustrate the need to develop principles which determine *how far* a given constituent can be moved in any single rule-application. (In Volume Two, we shall also explain why structures like (92) and (94) result in ungrammatical sentences even if the italicised NP is not moved, and why 'double movement' of the italicised NP in structures like (101) is obligatory.)

So far, we have suggested that all movement rules are inherently *bounded*, in the sense that no constituent can be moved out of more than one containing bounding category in any single movement. However, at first sight, it would seem as if one of the transformations with which we are already familiar (WH-MOVEMENT) is an obvious counterexample to any such claim. To see this, consider a wh-question structure such as the following:

(103)   *What* did [IP you say that [IP you would do —]]?

In a structure such as (103), the wh-NP *what* originates within the Complement (= rightmost) IP in the position marked by the elongated dash, and is moved not only out of the Complement IP, but also out of the matrix (= leftmost) IP, into its superficial C-specifier position as the leftmost constituent of the overall sentence. Thus, it would appear from (103) that a wh-phrase can move not just out of one containing IP, but even out of two. And in fact, it is easy enough to construct examples in which a wh-phrase has apparently been moved across three, or four, or even more IP boundaries: cf.

(104) (a)   *What* did [IP you say that [IP you thought that [IP you would do —]]]?

(b)   *What* did [IP you say that [IP you thought that [IP it was likely that [IP you would do —]]]]?

In fact, there seems to be no theoretical upper limit on the number of Clause boundaries which a moved wh-phrase can cross (though there are obvious *performance* limitations: e.g. the longer the sentence gets, the harder it is to remember just how it started).

The question we have to address ourselves to here is: 'Just how does a wh-phrase move "across" Clause boundaries in complex sentences such as (103) and (104)?' For the sake of simplicity and clarity of exposition, we'll stick to simpler cases such as (103) for illustrative purposes (though the conclusions we reach here will generalise to more complex cases like (104)). So, in effect, we'll be asking how the wh-NP *what* comes to cross the two bracketed IP boundaries in (103).

Now, at first sight, the answer might appear to be obvious. Given the arguments developed in sections 9.2 – 9.5, it seems clear that the wh-NP *what* originates as the D-structure Object of the Verb *do*. Moreover, given the arguments of section 9.10, it also seems likely that it ends up in the C-specifier position outside the main (= leftmost) IP, to the left of the main-clause C containing the preposed Auxiliary *did*. We might therefore suppose that *what* is moved directly from its D-structure position into an empty NP position (= the specifier of C) to the left of C in the main Clause, so that WH MOVEMENT applies in the manner outlined schematically in (105) below:

(105)   [$_{NP}$ e] did [$_{IP}$ you say that [$_{IP}$ you would do *what*]]?
          |—————————— WH MOVEMENT ——————————|

Under this analysis, the wh-NP *what* moves from its underlying into its superficial position in a single step. And we might generalise this 'single step' analysis to more complex cases such as those in (104) above, so that WH MOVEMENT would apply in (104)(b) in the manner indicated schematically in (106) below crossing the four bracketed IP nodes:

(106)   [$_{NP}$ e] did [$_{IP}$ you say that [$_{IP}$ you thought that [$_{IP}$ it
          was likely that [$_{IP}$ you would do *what*]]]]?
          |—————————— WH MOVEMENT ——————————|

Under this 'single step' analysis, WH MOVEMENT can move a wh-phrase across a potentially *unbounded* (i.e. infinite) number of IP nodes in a single step: hence, we might refer to this as the *unbounded* analysis of WH MOVEMENT (since it claims that WH MOVEMENT is an *unbounded* rule, which can move wh-phrases indefinitely far in a single step).

However, there is an alternative derivation which we might consider for sentences such as (103), *What did you say that you would do?*: and this is to assume that WH MOVEMENT applies in successive steps (or, to use the relevant technical terminology, on successive *cycles*: hence, this second analysis is often referred to as the *successive cyclic* analysis). More precisely, we might posit that the wh-NP *what* is first moved into an empty NP C-specifier position in the Complement Clause, and then is subsequently moved from there into the empty NP C-specifier position in the main Clause, in the manner indicated in (107) below:

(107)   [CP [NP e] [C e] [IP you *did* say [CP[NP e] [C that] [IP you
              ↑   ↑   ↑   would do *what*]]]]
              | I MOVEMENT |
              └──── WH MOVEMENT ────────────┘ WH MOVEMENT
                       (2)   (1)

Thus, there would be two separate applications of WH MOVEMENT: the first would move *what* into the empty C-specifier position [NP e] in the Complement Clause (to the immediate left of the Complementiser *that*): the derived structure at this stage would be (108) below:

(108)   [CP [NP e] [C e] [IP you did say [CP [NP *what*] [C that] [IP you would do t]]]]

(where 't' is the trace of the moved wh-NP *what*). Subsequently, I MOVEMENT would apply to (108) to move the Auxiliary *did* out of I into the empty main Clause C position, thereby deriving:

(109)   [CP [NP e] [C did] [IP you — say [CP [NP *what*][C that] [IP you would do t]]]]

(where — represents the trace left behind by movement of *did*). And then, WH MOVEMENT would apply once again, to move *what* out of the Complement Clause C-specifier position into the empty main Clause C-specifier position, resulting in the following final derived structure (S-structure):

(110)   [CP [NP *What*] [C did] [IP you — say [CP *t* [C that] [IP you would do t]]]]

(where the italicised trace is the empty NP node left behind by this second movement of the wh-NP *what*). Note that under the 'successive steps' derivation schematised in (110) above, WH MOVEMENT is limited to crossing a single IP boundary *in each of its applications*: for obvious reasons, then, we might refer to this as the *bounded* analysis of WH MOVEMENT (though, as noted above, the analysis is also known as the *successive cyclic* analysis). Under the *bounded* analysis, the wh-phrase moves from its underlying position to its superficial position 'one Clause at a time' (in much the same way as people climb up a flight of stairs one step at a time).

The essential difference between the two different derivations which we have outlined for sentence (103) *What did you say that you would do?* reduces to this: is WH MOVEMENT a bounded rule which cannot move a wh-phrase across more than a single IP boundary in any one application (and so applies in successive steps in complex sentences, as in (107) above), or is it an *unbounded* rule which can move a wh-phrase across indefinitely many IP boundaries in a single application (and so applies in a 'single step' in complex sentences, as in (105) above)?

Although the issues are extremely complex, both theoretical and empirical considerations seem to favour the *bounded* analysis of WH MOVEMENT. The theoretical argument in favour of positing that WH MOVEMENT is *bounded* is that it enables us to severely constrain the class of possible movement rules in natural language by positing that *all* movement rules are intrinsically bounded (i.e. limited to crossing no more than one bounding node in any single application). And the importance of maximally constraining the technical devices used in grammars is a point which we emphasised at length in Chapter 1 (because of its implications for language acquisition, on the assumption that the more constrained a grammar is, the more 'learnable' it is).

So, it seems that metatheoretical considerations (relating to the need to maximally constrain the technical devices used in grammars) lead us to prefer the *bounded* analysis over the *unbounded* analysis of WH MOVEMENT. However, there is also important empirical evidence in support of this claim. One such argument in support of the assumption that WH MOVEMENT must be able to apply in a *bounded* fashion comes from structures such as (111) below in Spanish (from Chomsky, *Barriers* (1986b), p. 25), and its (rather more marginal) English counterpart (112):

(111)   Este es el autor del que no sabemos que libros leer
        This is the author of + the whom not we–know which books read
        'This is the author by whom we don't know which books to read'

(112)   'Emmanuelle 69' was the kind of film which the censor wasn't sure
        which parts of to cut

Let's consider how the Relative Clause in the English example (112) might be derived. Underlying (112), we might posit the structure (113) below (where C designates an empty Complementiser):

(113)   [CP C [IP the censor wasn't sure [CP C [IP PRO to cut *which parts of WHICH*]]]]

Assuming that WH MOVEMENT applies in a bounded fashion, it will first of all apply to move the italicised wh-NP [*which parts of WHICH*] into the C-specifier position immediately to the left of C in the rightmost Clause, resulting in the intermediate structure (114) below, where — marks the trace of the moved wh-NP:

(114)   [CP C [IP the censor wasn't sure [CP *which parts of WHICH* C [IP PRO to cut —]]]]

Subsequently, WH MOVEMENT will reapply to move the capitalised wh-NP *WHICH* out of the italicised position in (114) into the C-specifier position in the leftmost Clause, to the left of C, as in (115) below (where *t* marks the trace of *WHICH*):

(115)   [CP *WHICH* C [IP the censor wasn't sure [CP which parts of *t* to cut —]]]]

Thus, a sentence such as (112) can only be derived by allowing WH MOVEMENT to apply in two successive steps, moving a wh-phrase out of one C-specifier position into another. And it should be evident that the same kind of conclusion could be drawn in relation to Spanish examples such as (111) above. Thus, sentences such as (111) and (112) show that it has to be *possible* for WH MOVEMENT to apply in a bounded (= *successive cyclic*) fashion, moving a wh-phrase first to the front of one Clause, then to the front of another.

A second argument that WH MOVEMENT is a *bounded* rule can be formulated in relation to the syntax of multiple wh-questions (i.e. wh-questions which contain more than one wh-phrase) in complex sentences. Consider a multiple wh-question such as the following:

(116)   They might wonder [CP *what* he said to *who*]

It is not possible in such a question to move either the italicised wh-NP *who* or the wh-PP [*to who*], as the ungrammaticality of examples such as the following shows:

(117) (a)   *Who* might they wonder [CP what he said to]?
      (b)   *To whom* might they wonder [CP what he said]?

Now, why should this be? The *unbounded* analysis of WH MOVEMENT provides us with no principled answer to this question, since there seems to be no obvious reason why, for example, *who* shouldn't be moved directly from its underlying position to the C-specifier position in the main Clause, in the manner indicated in a simplified fashion in (118) below:

(118)   [CP [NP e] might [IP they wonder [CP what [IP he said to *who*]]]]
         |————————— WH MOVEMENT —————————|

By contrast, the *bounded* analysis of WH MOVEMENT provides us with an obvious answer to why *what* cannot be extracted out of the Complement Clause. On the assumption that WH MOVEMENT is bounded, 'direct' movement in a single step such as (118) is ruled out because it involves crossing two IP nodes. But what about 'indirect' movement in two successive steps, moving first to the C-specifier position in the embedded Clause, and then to the

573

C-specifier position in the main Clause? This too is ruled out, but for a different reason: namely, movement to the C-specifier position in the embedded Clause is impossible because this position is already filled by the preposed wh-NP *what*. Thus, the assumption that movement rules are intrinsically bounded together with the assumption that each Clause contains only a single C-specifier position (which can therefore be filled only by a single preposed wh-phrase) serves to account for the ungrammaticality of sentences such as (117) above.

A third empirical argument in support of a *bounded* analysis of WH MOVE-MENT (adapted from Kayne 1984) can be formulated in relation to *case-marking* facts. In this connection, consider the case-marking of the italicised relative pronoun in the following sentence:

(119)   He is someone [*who* I think it is obvious will be a problem]

Of course, given that in colloquial English *who* can function as both a Nominative and an Objective case-form, we can't tell from the superficial form of (119) what case *who* is assigned. So what case would be assigned to *who* by our existing grammar? We shall see that the answer to this question depends on whether we assume that WH MOVEMENT applies in a bounded or unbounded fashion.

Let's see first of all what would happen if WH MOVEMENT were to apply in an *unbounded* fashion. Given standard arguments, the Relative Pronoun in (119) would originate as the subject of *will*, and would be moved directly into the empty NP C-specifier position *in a single step*, as indicated in a simplified fashion in (120) below (where we indicate just the structure of the Relative Clause, and suppress a variety of details not directly relevant to the point at issue here):

(120)   *who* [$_{IP}$I think [$_{IP}$it is obvious [$_{IP}$*t* will be a problem]]]
                └─────────── WH MOVEMENT ──────────┘

The Relative Pronoun *who* originates in the position indicated by its trace *t* in (120) as the Subject of *will*, and then (assuming the unbounded analysis) moves *directly* into initial position in the overall Relative Clause, crossing three containing bounding nodes (= three IP nodes) on the way. What case will be assigned to the Relative Pronoun on the *unbounded* analysis? Recall that we are assuming (cf. (76) above) the following two case-marking rules for English:

(121) (i)   Assign NOMINATIVE case to an NP which is the sister of an I-bar immediately dominating a finite I (= to the Subject of a finite Clause)

(ii)   Assign OBJECTIVE case to an NP which immediately follows a transitive Verb or Preposition

And recall that we have argued that case-marking should take place at the level of S-structure. Given this assumption, it follows that the italicised trace in (120) will be assigned Nominative case, because it is the subject of a finite Clause. Moreover, given the CHAIN TRANSMISSION PRINCIPLE (81), the trace will 'transmit' this Nominative case-feature to its Relative Pronoun antecedent. Thus, the Relative Pronoun will (indirectly, via its trace) come to be assigned *Nominative* case. And since the form *who* which occurs in (119) can function as a Nominative Pronoun in both formal and informal registers of English, we might feel tempted to assume that our grammar has given us the right answer, and hence that an *unbounded* analysis of WH MOVEMENT is perfectly defensible.

Alas, not so! Why? Well, many speakers of English (myself included) accept the use of the (unambiguously OBJECTIVE) form *whom* in sentences such as (119), so that alongside (119) we find (122) below:

(122)   He is someone [*whom* I think it is obvious will be a problem]

Indeed, the widespread use of the OBJECTIVE FORM *whom* in this kind of construction is recognised by traditional grammarians (for example, Quirk *et al.* (1985), p. 368 describe it as 'common'). However, I take it as self-evident that the *unbounded* analysis of WH MOVEMENT provides no principled basis for accounting for the OBJECTIVE case assigned to the italicised Relative Pronoun in (122).

But does the *bounded* analysis fare any better? Well, let's see! Given the assumption that WH MOVEMENT is bounded, the Relative Pronoun will move first into the C-specifier position in the rightmost Clause, then from there into the C-specifier position in the 'middle' Clause, and finally from there into the C-specifier position in the leftmost (i.e. main) Clause. Assuming that each separate movement of the wh-pronoun leaves behind a coindexed trace, the resultant derived structure will be as in (123) below:

(123)   *whom* [IP I think t_3 [IP it is obvious t_2 [IP t_1 will be a problem]]]

We have numbered each of the traces for ease of reference here (these numbers have no theoretical significance: they are simply added for expository convenience). t_1 marks the original Subject position out of which the Relative Pronoun moved; t_2 is in the C-specifier position of the rightmost (*will*) Clause; t_3 is in the C-specifier position of the 'middle' (*is*) Clause; and *whom* is in the C-specifier position of the leftmost (*think*) Clause.

Given an S-structure such as (123), the OBJECTIVE case-marking of the Relative Pronoun *whom* no longer proves problematic. After all, t_3 occupies a position in (123) in which it immediately follows the transitive Verb *think*, so that this particular trace will be assigned Objective case by rule (121)(ii). Given the CHAIN TRANSMISSION PRINCIPLE (81), the Objective case assigned to t_3 will be transmitted automatically to the Relative Pronoun which functions as the Head of the chain, so that we correctly predict that the Objective form *whom* is used in (122). There are numerous theoretical and descriptive issues which the argument raises (e.g. how to ensure that the Objective case assigned to t_3 somehow 'cancels' the Nominative case assigned to t_1), but these can be resolved in a number of ways which need not concern us here (they are technical questions which we shall put aside until Volume Two). Suffice it to say that only a *bounded* analysis seems to provide a principled basis for accounting for Objective case assignment in structures such as (122).

The more general conclusion to be drawn from our discussion is that there is ample evidence that WH MOVEMENT is inherently *bounded* in English; and parallel evidence could be adduced to support the same conclusion for other languages (cf. Exercise VII at the end of this chapter). Since, as we saw earlier, NP MOVEMENT and I MOVEMENT are also inherently bounded, we might generalise our conclusion in an obvious way and hypothesise that *all movement rules are intrinsically bounded* (and hence cannot move any constituent out of more than one containing bounding category (e.g. IP node) in any single application). We shall devote a whole chapter of Volume Two to a discussion of *Bounding Theory*, so for the time being we shall put this issue to one side.

> **You should now be able to tackle exercise VII**

10.9 Rule interaction

As our discussion has progressed, we have become more and more concerned with complex problems of *rule interaction*. We might therefore wonder whether there are any general principles which determine how rules interact with each other, and with themselves.

We can demonstrate the clear need to establish just such a system of principles in relation to our earlier sentences (112), repeated as (124) below:

(124) (a)   **Who* might they wonder [CP what he said to]?

    (b)   **To whom* might they wonder [CP what he said]

Earlier, we suggested that if we posit that WH MOVEMENT is bounded, then our grammar will be unable to generate such sentences, and thus will correctly predict that they are ungrammatical. However, we deliberately simplified our discussion at that point by overlooking an important complication. For, there is indeed a way of generating sentences like (124), even if we posit that WH MOVEMENT is inherently bounded – as we shall now show in relation to (124) (a). Let's assume that underlying (124) is structure (125) below (where C is an empty Complementiser):

(125)   [CP C [IP they might wonder [CP C [IP he said what to *who*]]]]

Let's further assume that WH MOVEMENT applies in three successive steps. First of all, it moves the wh-NP *who* into the empty NP C-specifier position (to the left of C) in the subordinate (*said*) Clause, and thereafter moves it into the C-specifier position in the main (*wonder*) Clause: these two movements of *who* are schematised in (126) below:

(126)   [CP C [IP they might wonder [CP   C [IP he said what to *who*]]]]
         |_____ (2) _____| |_____ (1) _____|

Let's also assume that the Modal *might* undergoes I MOVEMENT, and thereby moves out of I into C in the main Clause. Given these assumptions, the resultant derived structure will then be as in (127) below, where *t* in each case marks a trace of the moved italicised wh-NP *who* (for the sake of simplicity, we omit the trace left behind by movement of *might*):

(127)   [CP *Who* [C might] [IP they wonder [CP *t* C [IP he said what to *t*]]]]

But now let us assume that WH MOVEMENT applies a third time, to move the wh-NP *what* out of its underlying position into the empty subordinate Clause C-specifier position occupied by the rightmost trace of *who*: this third movement might be schematised as in (128) below:

(128)   [CP *Who* [C might] [IP they wonder [CP *t* C [IP he said WHAT to *t*]]]]
                                                                    |_____ (3) _____|

The leftmost trace will thereby be obliterated, resulting in the derived structure (129) below, where — marks the trace of the moved wh-NP *what*:

(129)   [CP *Who* [C might] [IP they wonder [CP WHAT C [IP he said —
         to *t*]]]]

Thus, contrary to what we earlier claimed, there is indeed a way of deriving sentences like (124) even if we posit that WH MOVEMENT is intrinsically bounded: for, each of the three movements of wh-NPs in the derivation sketched above was *bounded* in the relevant sense, as we see from (126) and

(128) above. But, if our grammar provides us with a way of generating sentences such as (124), then since such sentences are ungrammatical, we have to find a principled way of 'blocking' the relevant derivations (i.e. making them impossible). But what kind of principle could we appeal to which would block the derivation we have sketched above?

One approach to this question is in terms of the STRICT CYCLICITY CONDITION proposed by Chomsky in 'Conditions' (1973). Central to this approach is the notion of the *domain* of a transformation. This we can define in the following terms:

(130)   The domain D of a given transformation (on a given application) is the minimal (i.e. 'lowest') category containing all the constituents affected by the rule

In Chomsky's terminology, when a rule is applying within domain D, then node D is said to be *being cycled*. A complete set of rule-applications in some domain D is called a *cycle* (more specifically, the *D-cycle*, or *the cycle on (node)* D). A node which can be the domain of application of at least some rules is called a *cyclic* node. Chomsky formulates the relevant principle as follows:

(131)   STRICT CYCLICITY CONDITION
         No rule can apply to a domain dominated by a cyclic node A in such a way as to affect solely a proper subdomain of A dominated by a node B which is also a cyclic node (Chomsky, 'Conditions' (1973), p. 243)

If we strip away some of the jargon in (131), we see that what the STRICT CYCLICITY CONDITION amounts to is the claim that rules must apply in subordinate ('lower') domains before they apply in superordinate ('higher') domains: in other words, rules apply from 'bottom to top' in Phrase-markers.

But how does a condition such as (131) block the 'illicit' derivation for the ungrammatical sentence (124)(a) sketched in (126) and (128) above? To see this, let's consider the domain of WH MOVEMENT on each of the three movements numbered in (126/128). On movement (1), the domain of the rule is the subordinate CP constituent, in the sense that the rule re-orders elements within the subordinate CP, and does not affect any constituent outside that CP. On movement (2), the domain of the rule is the main Clause CP, since the wh-NP *who* is being moved into the C-specifier position in the main Clause. And on movement (3), the domain of WH MOVEMENT is once again the subordinate Clause CP, since *what* is being moved into the subordinate C-specifier position. So, how has our derivation in (126/128) violated the STRICT CYCLICITY CONDITION (131)? The answer should be obvious. Since the domain of movement (2) is the main Clause CP, and since the domain of movement (3) is the subordinate Clause CP, we have (illicitly) allowed a rule to apply in a subordinate domain after it has already applied in a superordinate domain: that is, movements (1) and (2) satisfy the STRICT CYCLICITY CONDITION, but movement (3) violates it. Thus, *strict cyclicity* will rule out the derivation (126/128) as an impossible way of deriving the ungrammatical sentence (124) (a). Since (as we have already seen), there is no other way of deriving the sentence if we posit that WH MOVEMENT is inherently bounded, then our grammar does indeed correctly specify that sentences such as (124) are ungrammatical.

While the STRICT CYCLICITY CONDITION has the obvious merit that it solves our immediate problem, we might object to it on theoretical grounds. Why? Because it presupposes an extremely complex model of grammar in which rules have to apply *sequentially* (i.e. in an ordered sequence, one after the other), and in which stipulated conditions (such as the STRICT CYCLICITY CONDITION) have to be imposed on possible and impossible orderings of particular applications of particular rules in particular derivations. To the extent that the stipulated conditions seem to be *arbitrary*, we might question the explanatory force of any theory incorporating them.

Our misgivings about *strict cyclicity* might lead us to seek alternative explanations for the impossibility of a derivation such as (126/128) above. In a sense, we have already explored one alternative possibility. For, in section 8.3 we proposed a condition to the effect that the 'gap' left by a moved constituent cannot subsequently be filled by another constituent. Of course, what we meant by 'gap' was *trace*. Accordingly, we might formulate the 'no refilling of gaps' principle rather more precisely along the following lines:

(132)   TRACE ERASURE PRINCIPLE
        No moved constituent can erase the trace of another constituent
        (i.e. no constituent can be moved into an empty category position
        occupied by the trace of another moved constituent)

(adapted and modified from Freidin (1978), p. 524). To return to our earlier housing analogy, this amounts to saying that 'squatting' (i.e. the illegal occupation of a house left empty by someone else) is not allowed! For those of you who don't like the *squatting* metaphor (perhaps because of unfortunate canine connotations), I offer two more picturesque alternatives: (i) you can't move into a house haunted by the ghost (= trace) of someone else; or (ii) you can't follow in someone else's footsteps (= traces).

The obvious question to ask at this point is how the TRACE ERASURE PRINCIPLE (132) would block the derivation outlined in (126/128) above. The answer is that it would prevent the third application of WH MOVEMENT in

579

(128), since this involves movement of the wh-NP *what* into the subordinate Clause C-specifier position. Why? Because the subordinate C-specifier position is occupied by the trace of *who*, and the TRACE ERASURE PRINCIPLE (132) prohibits a moved constituent from filling a position which is already occupied by a trace. Thus, our triple assumptions (viz. (i) WH MOVEMENT is strictly bounded, (ii) Clauses have a single C-specifier position, and (iii) no constituent can be moved into a position occupied by a trace) suffice to block the derivation of sentences such as (124).

However, it is one thing to *stipulate* that *trace erasure* is not allowed, and quite another to *explain* why this should be so. Perhaps the key to solving this mystery lies with the notion of *chain* which we defined in (80) above. A typical chain will comprise a lexical head, and a series of 'empty' traces. The overall chain will have a single head, and will carry a single set of grammatical properties (e.g. a single case, a single theta-role, etc.) some of which will be inherent properties of the head, and others of which (e.g. case-marking) will be properties assigned to particular traces. We might therefore posit the following general well-formedness condition on *chains*:

(133)   CHAIN UNIQUENESS PRINCIPLE
          Each movement chain carries a unique set of grammatical features
          (a single case, a single theta-role, etc.)

Since the same conditions seem to be applicable to *unmoved* NPs (e.g. an unmoved NP can't have two cases, or two theta-roles), we might extend the notion *chain* to include not just *moved NPs and their traces*, but also unmoved NPs: this we could do by redefining *chain* as 'a lexical NP and any traces it may have' (so that an unmoved NP with no traces would also constitute a *chain* in this sense).

A condition such as (133) seems to be intrinsically plausible. For example, it is supported by the fact that no Pronoun in English can be inflected for more than one case. Thus, although the (italicised) passive subject of a gerund complement such as that bracketed in (134) below can be assigned either the Objective case-form *him* or the Genitive case-form *his*: cf.

(134)   I don't like [*him/his* being victimised —]

it cannot be doubly case-marked for both Objective and Genitive case, as we see from the ungrammaticality of (135) below:

(135)   *I don't like [*him's* being victimised —]

Hence, the CHAIN UNIQUENESS PRINCIPLE has obvious independent motivation. Of course, it will also follow from (133) that a Pronoun cannot be *caseless* (i.e.

cannot have *no case at all*): on the contrary, condition (133) will only be satisfied if a Pronoun (or, more generally, an overt NP) is assigned *one and only one case*. This condition turns out to have considerable explanatory force, as we shall see in Volume Two.

Now, it would seem reasonable to posit that when a constituent is moved into a position occupied by the trace of another moved constituent, this results in *interlinking* of the two different movement chains. But we might plausibly maintain that it follows from (133) that two different movement *chains* cannot be interlinked in any way. This is because if two different chains formed by movement of two different constituents are joined together, then the resultant interlinked composite chain will be double-headed, and will have more than one set of grammatical features, so violating the CHAIN UNIQUENESS PRINCIPLE (133). It should thus be obvious how a principle such as (133) would exclude the possibility of *what* being moved into the C-specifier position occupied by the trace of *who* in (128) above.

Moreover, we might argue that a number of other properties follow from the CHAIN UNIQUENESS PRINCIPLE (133). For example, if we regard subscript *indices* as 'grammatical properties', then it follows that a moved NP and all its traces must be assigned the same subscript index, since unless each constituent of a movement chain carries the *same* index, there will be an obvious violation of principle (133). Moreover, if we extend (133) to include *lexical* properties, then it will follow that a movement chain must contain a single set of lexical properties – i.e. that in general only one constituent of a movement chain can be *lexicalised*. This would provide the basis for explaining contrasts such as:

(136) (a) *Whose$_i$* don't [$_{IP}$ you much like t_i]?
   (b) **Whose$_i$* don't [$_{IP}$ you much like *his$_i$*]?

Structure (136) (a) would satisfy the CHAIN UNIQUENESS PRINCIPLE (133), since only one link of the movement chain has been lexicalised; but (136) (b) would not, because not only has the head of the movement chain been lexicalised (as *whose*), but also its trace (as *his*), in violation of the condition that only one link (the *head*) of a movement chain can be lexicalised.

Finally, we might extend (133) to include *categorial* features, so as to require that all the links of a movement chain have the same categorial status. This would then provide a partial account of the *structure-preserving* property of transformations. So, for example, if we ask why a substitution transformation can only move an NP into an empty NP position (and not, for example, into an empty VP position), the answer provided by the CHAIN UNIQUENESS PRINCIPLE would be that movement of an NP into an empty NP position results in a chain whose links all have the same unique categorial status (viz. that of NP); whereas movement of an NP into an empty VP position would result in a chain with a dual (and conflicting) categorial status (NP and VP).

While the CHAIN UNIQUENESS PRINCIPLE needs to be refined and developed in ways which go beyond the scope of our present discussion, it nonetheless serves to illustrate two important methodological issues. The first is that current research is moving away from postulating complex sets of conditions on the ways in which rules apply (such as the STRICT CYCLICITY CONDITION), and instead moving towards abstract conditions on *representations* (i.e. conditions on the P-markers used to represent syntactic structure), such as the CHAIN UNIQUENESS PRINCIPLE. A second conclusion to be drawn from our discussion here is that the remorseless search for the ultimate goal of *explanatory adequacy* demands that we should never be content with arbitrarily stipulated conditions (such as the STRICT CYCLICITY CONDITION), but should always seek to explain these in terms of more general, independently motivated principles (such as the CHAIN UNIQUENESS PRINCIPLE). And indeed, the quest for such general principles will guide us through most of the second volume.

You should now be able to tackle exercises VIII, IX, and X

10.10   Summary

We started off this chapter by looking at a number of movement rules (viz. NEGATIVE PREPOSING, VP PREPOSING, RESULTATIVE PREPOSING, and TOPICALISATION), and suggested in 10.2 that they too (like WH MOVEMENT) might involve movement into the C-specifier position. The obvious similarity between these rules and WH MOVEMENT led us to suppose that they might all be reflexes of a more general movement rule. Indeed, in 10.3 we went so far as to envisage the possibility that all substitution rules and all adjunction rules might be particular reflexes of a maximally general, putatively universal ALPHA MOVEMENT rule. However, we noted that this goal would only be attainable if the apparently idiosyncratic properties of individual transformations could be reduced to more general principles governing the way in which movement rules apply, and the type of derived structure they produce: and we set out to look for such principles.

In 10.4 we looked at the principles determining the landing-site of moved constituents: generalising Emonds' STRUCTURE-PRESERVING CONSTRAINT, we suggested that all major transformations are either structure-preserving substitutions, or structure-preserving adjunctions. In 10.5 we argued that the structure-preserving property of transformations follows from a number of independent principles, such as the EXTENDED ENDOCENTRICITY CONDITION (which requires that all syntactic representations be endocentric), and the EXTENDED PROJECTION PRINCIPLE (which stipulates that lexical and structural requirements must be uniformly satisfied at all syntactic levels). In 10.6 we presented arguments in support of the claim that moved constituents leave behind in the position out of which they move a coindexed empty category trace; we argued that traces and their antecedents form a *chain*, and that grammatical properties are freely transmitted between the links of a chain (so that moved constituents inherit the properties of their traces, and vice-versa). In 10.7 we attempted to account for the property of transformations that they may upgrade, but not downgrade, constituents in terms of a condition that a moved constituent must c-command its traces at S-structure. In 10.8 we argued that all transformations are intrinsically *bounded* in that they can move constituents over no more than a single bounding node (e.g. IP node) in any single movement: we examined the problems posed for this claim by apparently unbounded rules such as WH MOVEMENT, but we showed that there are strong empirical arguments in support of claiming that even WH MOVEMENT applies in successive steps and is thus inherently bounded. In 10.9 we looked at the way in which transformations interact, discussing Chomsky's STRICT CYCLICITY CONDITION that rules apply in subordinate domains before superordinate domains. However, we argued that this condition could be derived from Freidin's less arbitrary TRACE ERASURE PRINCIPLE. But we went on to argue that this condition in turn could be subsumed under an even more general principle, namely the CHAIN UNIQUENESS PRINCIPLE that each chain should carry a single, unique set of grammatical features.

Among the more important principles discussed in this chapter are the following:

(41)   GENERALISED STRUCTURE-PRESERVING PRINCIPLE
         All transformations are structure-preserving, and comprise either structure-preserving substitutions of the form (29), or structure-preserving adjunctions of the form (40)

(46)   EXTENDED ENDOCENTRICITY CONDITION
         All syntactic representations are endocentric (i.e. must satisfy condition (43))

(56)   EXTENDED PROJECTION PRINCIPLE
         Lexical requirements (viz. categorial, subcategorisation, and thematic properties) and structural requirements (viz. the requirement that a Clause should have a Subject) must be uniformly satisfied at all syntactic levels

(60)   TRACE MOVEMENT PRINCIPLE
        Any moved constituent X^n leaves behind at its extraction site a
        coindexed identical empty category $[_{X^n}$ e]. This empty category is
        known as a *trace*, and the moved constituent is said to be the ante-
        cedent of the trace (slightly revised)

(81)   CHAIN TRANSMISSION PRINCIPLE
        A moved constituent and any coindexed traces it has form a *chain*.
        Grammatical properties are freely transmitted between the links
        of a movement chain (revised, incorporating (80))

(85)   C-COMMAND CONDITION
        A moved constituent must c-command (= *constituent-command*)
        each of its traces at S-structure (X c-commands Y just in case the
        first branching node dominating X dominates Y, and neither X
        nor Y dominates the other)

(102)   BOUNDING CONDITION (alias SUBJACENCY CONDITION)
        No constituent can be moved out of more than one containing
        bounding node (e.g. IP) *in any single movement*

(131)   STRICT CYCLICITY CONDITION (simplified)
        Transformations apply in subordinate before superordinate do-
        mains (i.e. they apply from 'bottom to top')

(132)   TRACE ERASURE PRINCIPLE
        No moved constituent can erase the trace of another constituent

(133)   CHAIN UNIQUENESS PRINCIPLE
        Each chain carries a unique (i.e. single) set of lexical and gramma-
        tical properties

Our discussion of the principles determining the nature of the operations
which transformations can and cannot perform has of necessity been scant. So
much research in the past few years has been devoted to the search for universal principles governing the application of transformations that virtually the
whole of Volume Two (now in preparation) will be devoted to this issue.

What's that you say? You've decided to give up Linguistics and do Archae-
ology instead? Well, at least I've got you interested in *traces* ... even if it is
only *traces* of bygone civilisations! Anyway, congratulations on getting to the
end of the book: and don't forget to drop me a line with any comments, criti-
cisms, queries, suggestions ... or even fan mail!

EXERCISES

Exercise 1

Some linguists have argued in favour of positing a rule of THOUGH MOVE-MENT, whereby in sentences like:

(1)   *Very tall* though she may be —, few people look up to her
(2)   *Worthless parasites* though everyone says they are —, people still befriend them

the italicised AP and NP constituents originate in the position marked — and are subsequently moved in front of *though* by the transformation of THOUGH MOVEMENT. Try and develop a number of arguments parallel to those used in sections 9.3 – 9.6 in support of this claim.

**Exercise II

Chomsky in his (1977a) 'On Wh-movement' paper proposes an analysis of TOPICALISATION which is very different from the one adopted here. Using the S/S-bar framework, he suggests (ibid., p. 91) that Topic Phrases are base-generated by the following rule:

(1)   S'' → TOP S'

and that there is covert WH MOVEMENT within the S-bar which occurs to the right of TOP in (1). Adapting his proposal slightly, we might say that under this WH MOVEMENT analysis of Topic structures, a sentence such as:

(2)   This book, I really like

would be derived in the manner indicated schematically in (3) below:

(3)   S'' [$_{TOP}$ this book] [$_{S'}$ [$_C$ e] [$_S$ I really like O]]]
                               └— WH MOVEMENT —┘

(where O is a covert wh-NP). What theoretical and empirical objections might be raised against such an analysis?

**Exercise III

Discuss the problems posed for the analyses proposed in the text of the last two chapters of the book by sentences such as the following:

(1)   I know that never have I been so humiliated in all my life
(2)   I assure you that this kind of behaviour I will not stand for
(3)   We all know that weirdos, they give you the creeps
(4)   He's a man to whom liberty we could never grant (Baltin (1982), p. 17)
(5)   He protested that how could he have known that his office was bugged?

585

(6)   Me preguntaron que quién vio qué
        Me they-asked   that who saw what
        'They asked me who saw what' (Spanish, from Rivero (1978), p. 516)

(7)   María preguntaba que si no debieramos dejarlas   en paz
        Maria was-asking that if not we – should leave + them in peace
        'Maria was asking whether we shouldn't leave them in peace'
        (Spanish, from Plann (1982), p. 300)

How will we have to modify our grammar in order to be able to generate such sentences?

Exercise IV

Below we list a number of transformations (or particular versions of transformations) proposed in earlier work. Discuss whether or not each is compatible with the *structure-preserving* framework adopted here, and say why. In each case, say whether (and if so, how) the relevant rule could be modified so as to make it structure-preserving. (In all the Phrase-markers below, we include only the minimal structure relevant to the operation of the rule.)

(A)   DATIVE MOVEMENT (See Culicover (1982), pp. 177–84)
        The rule derives structures such as (1) (b) below from the structure underlying (1) (a)
        (1) (a) John will send a parcel to Mary
            (b) John will send Mary a parcel
        In schematic terms, the rule maps structures such as (2) (a) below into (2) (b):

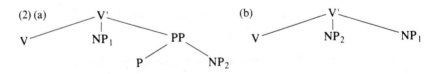

(2) (a) ... (b) ...

(B)   PASSIVISATION (See Akmajian and Heny (1975), pp. 88–95)
        Akmajian and Heny posit a PASSIVE transformation which directly maps an underlying structure such as (3) (a) below onto the derived structure (3) (b):

(3) (a)

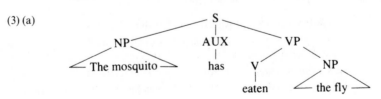

(b)

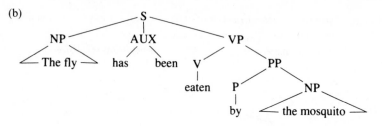

(Ignore the fact that mosquitoes don't eat flies!)

(C)   THERE INSERTION (see Emonds (1976), pp. 104–10)
We might suppose that this rule maps structures such as (4) (a) below onto
(4) (b):

(4) (a)

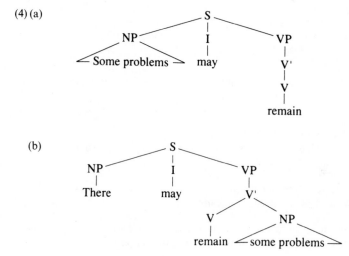

(b)

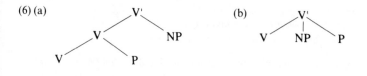

(D)   PARTICLE MOVEMENT (see Jacobsen (1986), pp. 151–2)
Jacobsen assumes that this rule derives structures such as (5) (b) below
from the structure underlying (5) (a):
(5) (a) John will take off his coat
    (b) John will take his coat off
The operation of the rule can be represented in schematic terms as mapping structures of the form (6) (a) into (6) (b):

(6) (a)

(b)

(E)   TOUGH MOVEMENT (alias OBJECT-TO-SUBJECT RAISING: see Postal and Ross (1971))

The rule maps structures such as (7) (a) below into (7) (b):

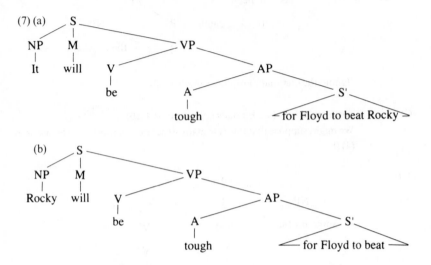

Exercise V

Discuss the role played by *traces* in accounting for the syntax of sentences such as the following:

(1) (a)   Who've you been out with?

(b)   *Who could you've gone out with?

(2) (a)   How many people do you wanna invite to your party?

(b)   *How many people do you wanna come to your party?

(3) (a)   Which film did you say they seem to consider the best one?

(b)   Which films did you say he seems to consider the best ones?

After you have done this, consider the following problem. It is often claimed that one of the advantages of Trace Theory is that it allows us to posit that all RULES OF CONSTRUAL (i.e. rules which determine the coreference relations between constituents, and hence e.g. 'find' the antecedents of anaphoric expressions such as Reflexives) operate at S-structure. Show how incorporating traces into our grammar would simplify any account of the interpretation of Reflexives in sentences such as:

(4)   John seems to have perjured himself

(5)   John seems to himself to be invincible

(6)   John is likely to seem to himself to be invincible

(For the purpose of the second part of this exercise, make the simplifying assumption

588

that non-subject reflexives require a clausemate antecedent – i.e. require an antecedent within the minimal IP containing them.)

Finally, consider what (real or apparent) problem is posed for the trace-theoretic account of case-marking by dialects which show contrasts such as:

(7) (a)   *Who/*whom* did you give the book to?
    (b)   *To whom/*to who* did you give the book?

What solutions might be explored to this third problem?

Exercise VI

In section 8.2 we discussed the problem posed by the fact that the Tense/ Agreement properties associated with a finite I are realised on the leftmost V of VP if I is underlyingly empty; and we suggested two alternative rules which might account for this. One of these was V MOVEMENT (moving V into an empty finite I), proposed in Chomsky's (1986b) *Barriers* monograph. The second alternative was the rule of AFFIX MOVEMENT proposed in Chomsky's (1981d) *Lectures*, 'transferring' the Tense/Agreement properties of an empty finite I onto the leftmost V of VP. Discuss why the rule of AFFIX MOVEMENT would be incompatible with the framework being assumed here.

A variety of alternative analyses of the operation of WH-MOVEMENT have been proposed in the relevant literature, including those listed below:

(A)   WH MOVEMENT involves movement (by substitution) of a wh-phrase into an empty C (Baker (1970), p. 209)
(B)   WH MOVEMENT involves adjunction of the moved wh-phrase to C (Chomsky, 'On Binding' (1980): cf. section 9.10)
(C)   WH MOVEMENT involves adjunction of the moved wh-phrase to C, with erasure of the original C if C is empty (Chomsky, *Lectures* (1981d): cf. section 9.10)
(D)   WH MOVEMENT involves movement of the wh-phrase into an empty phrasal category to the left of [±WH] within COMP (Chomsky, 'Conditions' (1973): cf. Chapter 9, exercise VI)
(E)   WH MOVEMENT involves adjunction of the moved wh-phrase to CP (Bresnan (1976b): cf. Chapter 9, exercise VI)
(F)   WH MOVEMENT involves movement of the wh-phrase into an empty C-specifier position within CP (Chomsky, *Barriers* (1986b): cf. section 9.10)

Discuss which of these analyses would (or would not) be compatible with the various conditions proposed in this chapter (the EXTENDED ENDOCENTRICITY CONDITION, the C-COMMAND CONDITION, etc.) and why.

*Exercise VII

In section 9.7 we saw that STYLISTIC INVERSION (alias 'Subject Postposing') in French applies in an indicative Clause *only if the Clause contains a preposed wh-phrase.* However, the rule can apply to postpose the italicised subject NP in the rightmost bracketed indicative complement Clause in (1) below:

(1) (a)   Je me demande [CP QUI elle a dit [CP que *Paul* avait vu?]]
            I me ask WHO she has said that Paul had seen
            'I wonder who she said that Paul had seen'

   (b)   Je me demande [CP QUI elle a dit [CP qu'avait vu *Paul*]?
            I me ask WHO she has said that had seen Paul
            'I wonder who she said that Paul had seen'

Show how such sentences can be used to support the claim that WH MOVEMENT of the capitalised wh-NP QUI 'who' out of the rightmost CP applies in a bounded fashion, if we assume the italicised condition on STYLISTIC INVERSION given above. (Concern yourself only with the structure of the bracketed Clauses, not with the structure of the main Clause.)

Now try and construct a second argument in support of a bounded analysis of WH MOVEMENT, in relation to the facts of *Complementiser Selection* in Irish (as described in McCloskey (1979) and Zaenen (1983)). The Complementiser which normally introduces the Irish counterpart of *that* Clauses is *goN* (where N marks the fact that it triggers nasalisation of the first segment of the following word): cf. the following example (from McCloskey (1979), p. 17):

(2)   Deir siad *goN* síleann an t-athair *goN* bpósfaidh Síle e
          Say they that thinks the father that will-marry Sheila him
          'They say that the father thinks Sheila will marry him'

However, in 'operator' relatives in Irish (i.e. relatives containing an empty wh-operator), all the Complementisers over which the empty wh-operator 'O' moves when it undergoes WH MOVEMENT change to *aL* (where L marks the fact that this word triggers lenition of the first segment of the following word): cf. the following example (from McCloskey (1979), p. 17):

(3)   an fear *aL* deir siad *aL* shíleann an t-athair *aL* phófaidh Síle
          the man that say they that thinks the father that will-marry Sheila
          'the man that they say the father thinks will marry Sheila'

What is interesting about this 'change' of Complementiser from *goN* to *aL* is that it affects all the Complementisers in the movement path of WH MOVEMENT (i.e. all the Complementisers between the extraction site and landing site of the rule). Show how a bounded analysis of WH MOVEMENT (assuming movement of a zero wh-pronoun) would provide a simple account of this phenomenon.

Exercise VIII

Williams (1975, pp. 257–60) claims that the STRICT CYCLICITY CONDITION determines the order in which transformations apply in a derivation. Consider how this principle would determine the order of application of the various transformations which apply in the derivation of sentence (1) below:

(1)   How much heed is thought to seem likely to be paid to his advice?

**Exercise IX

It is reported in the Language Acquisition literature (e.g. Menyuk (1969, p. 73), Hurford (1975), and Kuczaj (1976)) that some young children acquiring English as their mother tongue go through a stage (at around the age of 30 months) when they produce sentences such as the following:

(1) (a)   Where does the wheel goes?
   (b)   What did you bought?

Discuss how such child sentences appear to be derived, and why they are ungrammatical in adult speech. Comment on the apparent differences between the child and adult grammars.

**Exercise X

For my last exercise in this volume, I'm going to outline a number of potential problems which face the *bounded* analysis of WH MOVEMENT outlined in the text. Discuss the nature of the problems, and see if you can work out any coherent solutions. To start you off, I've given you hints about how to solve the first two problems . . . but don't expect me to do them *all* for you!

Problem A
Discuss how WH-MOVEMENT would apply in structures such as the following:

(1) (a)   *Which one* do you consider [— is the best]?
   (b)   *Which one* do you consider [— to be the best]?
   (c)   *Which one* do you consider [— the best]?

Which structure(s) prove(s) problematic for the assumption that WH-MOVEMENT is bounded – and why?

How would it help if we made the following assumption in (2) below?

(2)   The only type of clausal constituent which acts as a bounding node is an IP immediately contained within a CP (i.e. an IP which is the complement of a C)

Problem B
Consider how we might account for the dual case-marking of the italicised Relative Pronoun in structures such as:

(3)   He's someone *who/whom* it's obvious will be a problem

in such a way as to satisfy the CHAIN UNIQUENESS PRINCIPLE.

How would it help if we were to assume that case-marking rules like those discussed in the text apply *optionally*?

Problem C

Discuss the problems posed for the analysis of the *who/whom* distinction in the text by sentences such as the following (assuming the judgments given, which are my own):

(4)   He is someone *who/whom* I am sure is innocent

(5)   He is someone *who/whom* it is obvious is innocent

(6)   He is someone *who/whom* it seems is innocent

(7)   I don't know *who/*whom* will win the election

(8)   He asked me about *who/*whom* would be coming to the party

Problem D

Discuss the apparent problems posed for the trace-theory account of WANNA CONTRACTION by sentences such as the following, if we assume that WH MOVEMENT is intrinsically bounded, and if we also assume that the complement of *want* is an Ordinary Clause (CP) containing an empty prepositional Complementiser:

(9)   *Who does he wanna come to his party

(10)   Who does he wanna invite to his party?

(11)   Who does he wanna be sure is dead?

Problem E

WH-MOVEMENT is optional in direct questions in French, so that we find contrasts such as:

(12) (a)   Tu   crois QUE je préfère *laquelle*?
            You think that I prefer which?

     (b)   *Laquelle* crois-tu   QUE je préfère?
            Which   think-you that I prefer?
            'Which one do you think that I prefer?'

However, when the Subject of a Complement Clause introduced by the Complementiser QUE 'that' is extracted by WH MOVEMENT, the Complementiser QUE takes on what appears to be the *Nominative* form QUI: cf.

(13) (a)   Tu   crois QUE *laquelle* va gagner?
            You think that which   will win?

     (b)   *Laquelle* crois-tu   QUI va gagner?
            Which   think-you that will win?
            'Which one do you think will win?'

In such cases, it is often said that the Complementiser QUE has 'absorbed' the Nominative case assigned to the trace of the moved wh-NP subject *laquelle* 'which'. But absorbed case from *which* trace of the moved subject, and how? Consider this problem in the light of sentences such as (13) above and (14) below:

(14) (a)   Tu   as   dit QUE tu   crois QUE *laquelle* va   gagner?
You have said that you think that which   will win

(b)   *Laquelle* as-tu   dit QUE tu   crois QUI va   gagner?
Which   have-you said that you think that will win
'Which one did you say that you think will win?'

Note in particular that only the righthand QUE changes to QUI in (14) (b), not the lefthand one. (It should be noted that the *qui* construction is a fairly literary one; the colloquial counterpart of (14) (b) would have an empty Complementiser in place of QUI. For the purposes of the exercise, concern yourself only with the literary QUI construction.)

Problem F
Given a D-structure such as (15) below:

(15)   [CP He might claim [CP (that) you quarrelled with who]]?

show how a *bounded* analysis of WH MOVEMENT will allow us to derive not only the grammatical sentences (16) below:

(16) (a)   *Who* might he claim (that) you quarrelled *with*?
(b)   *With whom* might he claim (that) you quarrelled?

but also the ungrammatical sentences (17) below:

(17) (a)   *Might he claim *who* (that) you quarrelled *with*?
(b)   *Might he claim *with whom* (that) you quarrelled?
(c)   * *Who* might he claim *with* that you quarrelled?

Show how sentences such as (16) and (17) would be derived by our existing grammar, and suggest principled ways of blocking (17). (Ignore the *who/whom* contrast for the purposes of this exercise.)

Problem G
In section 9.7 we claimed that sentences such as:

(1)   *He is someone [that I don't know what Mary said to]

provide us with strong evidence in support of claiming that *that* relatives involve preposing of a zero relative pronoun operator 'O'. Why should this be so?

Problem H
In the text of this chapter, we deliberately simplified the derivation of sentence (67) *Which one do you think seems to be the best candidate?*, for expository purposes. In what way(s)?

Bibliographical background

The function of this part of the book is to provide a brief outline of some of the key books and articles on which the ideas outlined in each chapter are based, and in some cases to present alternative ideas which the interested reader can follow up.

However, two words of caution need to be sounded. For the most part, the works cited here constitute the *primary* literature in the field (i.e. they are original works written for experts, not introductory survey articles written for beginners): hence, they often presuppose knowledge of technical concepts and constructs which will not be familiar to the beginner. Moreover, some of the works cited are written from a different theoretical perspective (e.g. an earlier model of TG), and thus will be based on assumptions rather different from those adopted here. For these two reasons, it will not always be easy for the beginner to follow the argumentation in many of the works cited below. It would be sensible to read *all* of this book before attempting to tackle any of the primary literature cited.

The bibliographical guidelines provided here are organised into sections by chapter (though because of the close overlap between the X-bar literature on Noun Phrases and on other Phrases, we have merged the bibliographical background material for Chapters 4 and 5 into a single section).

Chapter 1

For a clear introduction to many of the topics covered in this chapter, see Smith and Wilson (1979, pp. 1–74). For an introduction to Chomsky's views on the goals of Linguistics and the nature of language, see his *Rules and Representations* (1980, pp. 3–140). The distinction between *competence* and *performance* is presented in Chomsky's *Aspects* (1965, pp. 3–15). For a discussion of levels of adequacy in grammars, see Chomsky, *Current Issues* (1964, pp. 28–55), and *Aspects* (1965, pp. 18–27). For a defence of the Innateness Hypothesis, see Chomsky, *Language and Mind* (1972a, pp. 65–99), and *Reflections* (1976, pp. 3–77). For Chomsky's views on language acquisition, see *Aspects* (1965, pp. 47–59). For a defence of the *Autonomous Syntax* position, see Newmeyer (1983, pp. 2–34), and (for a more technical work) Chomsky's *Essays* (1977a, pp. 36–59). For a discussion of the distinction between language as an *internalised* or *externalised* phenomenon, see Chomsky's *Knowledge* (1986a, pp. 1–50). For a (technical) discussion of the concepts of *Markedness* and *Core Grammar*, see

Chomsky (1981a), and other papers in Belletti *et al.* (1981). As noted in the text, Chomsky has little to say about Pragmatics: for an introduction to the topic, see Levinson (1983) and Leech (1983); for a more advanced text, see Sperber and Wilson (1986).

Chapter 2

By way of background reading, you might find it useful to read a good introduction to traditional grammatical concepts and terminology, such as Palmer (1983, pp. 1–120), Simpson (1982), Aarts and Aarts (1982), or Young (1984). You may find a good dictionary of linguistic terminology useful, such as Crystal (1985). (Smith and Wilson (1979) has a useful glossary of technical terms.)

Although we have not placed much faith in notional definitions of categories here (because they are dangerous in inexperienced hands), see Lyons (1966) for a competent attempt to characterise categories in notional terms. Many of the constituent structure tests used here date back to pre-generative work. For example, Bloomfield (1935) justifies his constituent structure analyses on the basis of phonological criteria (stress, pauses), morphological criteria (inflections), and syntactic criteria (distribution, pronominalisation, and ellipsis). By contrast, Harris (1946) bases his constituent structure analysis purely on distributional criteria (which he terms 'substitution'); and Wells (1947) makes use of criteria relating to distribution, pronominalisation, and structural ambiguity, as well as phonological criteria (viz. the location of stress, pitch, pauses, juncture).

Early generative work used similar criteria. For example, Chomsky's *Logical Structure* (1955/1975) makes use of the *simple coordination* test (1975, p. 224), the *adverb distribution* test (1975, p. 228), *phonological* criteria such as the location of stress and potential pauses (1975, pp. 229–30), and the *structural ambiguity* test (1975, p. 238). For a discussion of some of the problems surrounding the use of the coordination criterion, see Matthews (1981, pp. 195–219). The distinction between S-adverbs and VP-adverbs is discussed at length in Jackendoff (1972, pp. 47–107).

We have assumed here that a tripartite analysis of Clauses in which the three major constituents of S are [NP M VP]. It should be noted, however, that there are a number of alternative descriptions which appear in the published literature. One (which we shall return to in Chapter 9) is a *binary* analysis of Clause structure in which M and VP together form a larger phrasal constituent similar to the Predicate Phrase constituent of Chomsky's *Aspects* (1965, p. 106). Yet another analysis (adopted e.g. in Matthews (1981) and Huddleston (1984)), is to assume that the Verb and any (Modal etc.) Auxiliaries which modify it together form some kind of verbal complex which is sometimes (confusingly) called a Verb Phrase. For a brief discussion of some of the differences between Phrasal Verbs and Prepositional Verbs, see Kilby (1984, pp. 99–113), and Quirk *et al.* (1985, pp. 1150–67).

Useful further reading at this point would be an elementary textbook treatment of the constituent structure of a range of construction types in English: e.g. Brown and Miller (1980), or Burton-Roberts (1986) – though it should be noted that their analyses differ from ours in some ways (e.g. in the treatment of Auxiliaries). A non-theoretical cross-linguistic account of a wide range of construction types is found in Shopen (1985).

Chapter 3

For an early discussion of Phrase Structure Grammars, see Chomsky's *Syntactic Structures* (1957, pp. 26–33), as well as his *Logical Structure* 1955 (1975, pp. 171–291). However, the version of Phrase Structure Grammar given here (incorporating a Lexicon, is based more closely on the model presented in Chomsky's *Language and Mind* (1972a, pp. 139–55); see also Chomsky's *Aspects* (1965, pp. 84–127) for a more technical discussion of lexical insertion.

The system of Categorial Rules presented in this chapter are *context-free* Phrase Structure Rules; we have not dealt with *context-sensitive* PS rules, since they are largely only of historical interest within the context of contemporary TG: for relevant discussion concerning the distinction between *context-free* and *context-sensitive* PS rules, see early textbooks such as Kimball (1973, pp. 1–28), Grinder and Elgin (1973, pp. 45–67), Bach (1974, pp. 37–57), or Huddleston (1976, pp. 35–46).

The claim that Particles and Subordinating Conjunctions are Prepositions is defended in Emonds (1976, pp. 172–6). The analysis of Adverbs as positional variants of Adjectives is likewise suggested by Emonds (1976, p. 12). For a discussion of Auxiliaries in English and other languages, see Steele (1981), and the collection of articles in Heny and Richards (1983). The system of major categorial features presented here is based on Chomsky's (1974) Amherst lectures: see Jackendoff (1977a) for an alternative feature-based analysis of categories, and Stowell (1981, pp. 21–51) for a defence and extension of Chomsky's system. For further discussion of features, see the articles in Muysken and Van Riemsdijk (1986). Stuurman (1985, pp. 120–73) presents an extensive critique of the use of categorial features.

The c-command condition on anaphors discussed here derives from work by Reinhart (1976, p. 1983). The conventional 'no crossing branches' constraint on Phrase-markers is attacked in McCawley (1982), but defended in Baltin (1984). We have tacitly assumed the so-called *Single Mother Condition* on Phrase-markers, to the effect that no node may have more than one mother. There have been occasional proposals in the literature to abandon this condition, and thus allow nodes to have multiple mothers (this is sometimes called the *multi-domination* approach): cf. e.g. the proposals in Morin and O'Malley (1979), Sampson (1975), and Jacobson (1977).

The view that Grammatical Relations (e.g. 'Subject', 'Object', etc.) are not primitive terms but are derivative from tree structure configurations is defended at length in Chomsky's *Aspects* (1965, pp. 68–74); for a more technical treatment of Grammatical Relations, see Marantz (1984). In some other theoretical frameworks, Grammatical Relations are analysed as primitive relations – see for example the collections of articles on *Relational Grammar* in Perlmutter (1983), and Perlmutter and Rosen (1984), and the articles on *Lexical-Functional Grammar* in Bresnan (1981).

Chapters 4 and 5

The version of X-bar theory presented here is the 'classical' theory which Chomsky has consistently adopted, from his earliest 'Remarks' paper on the subject (1970) to his most recent *Barriers* monograph (1986b). We have referred to this as the *three-level* theory, since it presupposes three different categorial levels, viz. the zero-bar level, the single-bar level, and the double-bar level: it should be noted however that Jackendoff (1977a) employs a different system of counting levels, under which the classical theory would be a *two-level* theory (because it posits two different phrasal expansions (X' and X'') of any head category X.

Jackendoff (1974) presents a comprehensive introduction to the classical theory. Although the 'classical' symmetrical three-level theory (symmetrical in the sense that all categories are assumed to permit the same range of phrasal expansions) is the one generally adopted, there are several other versions of X-bar theory: for example, Jackendoff (1977a) in his seminal $\bar{X}$-*Syntax* book argues for a symmetrical four-level X-bar theory (though, as noted above, because he uses a different system of counting levels, he calls it a *three-level* theory); and a similar analysis is adopted in Halitsky (1975), and Binkert (1984). Moreover, a four-level theory is presupposed by numerous descriptive studies of particular constituents – e.g. in the analysis of NPs by Selkirk (1977), of VPs by Akmajian Steele and Wasow (1979) (though see the critique of this latter analysis in Pullum (1981b), Gazdar, Pullum and Sag (1982), and Takezawa (1984)), and of PPs by Van Riemsdijk (1978). At the other end of the scale, Stuurman (1985) has argued in favour of a symmetrical two-level X-bar theory.

However, some proponents of X-bar Syntax have argued in favour of an *asymmetrical* Theory of Categories (i.e. one in which different categories permit a different range of phrasal expansions). For example. Emonds (1985) presents an asymmetrical theory in which the Maximal Projection of V is assumed to be V^3, but the maximal projection of other categories is assumed to be X^2. And Jacobsen (1986, p. 90, fn. 2) posits an asymmetrical theory in which the maximal projection of V is V^2, but the maximal projection of other categories is X^3.

There are a vast number of descriptive studies of particular Phrase types within the classical X-bar framework assumed here. Among those we might mention are the analysis of NPs in Hornstein and Lightfoot (1981a, pp. 17–24), Lightfoot (1982, pp. 51–66), and Woolford (1983, pp. 526–8); and the analysis of VPs in Culicover and Wilkins (1984, pp. 26–31). Our claim that English has a class of Adjuncts and Attributes which function as recursive modifiers of X-bar is in keeping with parallel claims made in Andrews (1983). Our claim that there is a further class of Adjuncts which recursively modify double-bar constituents is supported by Haik (1983, p. 323). Although we did not deal with postnominal genitive NPs here (e.g. that chair *of Bills*), we might note in passing that Anderson (1983) argues that they are nominal Specifiers and thus sisters of N-bar and daughters of NP. Although we took N to be the ultimate head of NP here, it should be noted that Hellan (1986) (using Norwegian data) argues that the ultimate head of NP is D(eterminer), not N, so that Noun Phrases in effect have the categorial status of DP (Determiner Phrase). While we purposely concentrated on the internal structure of NPs in *English* in Chapter 4, it should be noted that NPs in other languages may have a very different internal structure; see, for example, Szabolsci (1983) for Hungarian. The analysis of the Aspectual Auxiliaries *have/be* as Specifiers of V presented in the text follows Jackendoff (1977a); however, an alternative analysis of Aspectuals as full Verbs heading an independent VP and taking a VP complement is found in Emonds (1976), Baltin (1982), and Andrews (1982).

Stowell (1981) argues that many central tenets of X-bar theory can be derived from more general principles of grammar. Farmer (1984) attempts to derive the ENDO-CENTRICITY CONSTRAINT from a more fundamental FEATURE PERCOLATION CONVENTION. Pullum (1985) is an attempt to characterise some of the formal properties of X-bar grammars. The suggestion that ordering and constituency relations between categories should be handled by two different rule subsystems dates back to early work by Staal (1967) and Sanders (1969, 1970a, 1970b, 1971, 1972a, 1972b), though it has taken more than a decade for this to find its way into the conservative corridors of mainstream Transformational Grammar, and to be 'borrowed' into other models (e.g. the model of Generalised Phrase Structure Grammar of Gazdar *et al.* (1985)). The claim that Categorial Rules should be replaced by category-neutral rule schemas formulated entirely in terms of category variables (thereby eliminating traditional category-specific Phrase Structure rules) is made most forcefully in Stowell (1981), and is adopted in Chomsky's more recent works (e.g. *Knowledge* (1986a), and *Barriers* (1986b)).

We have concentrated here primarily on the structure of English (a typical *configurational* language): for some thoughts on the structure of *nonconfigurational* languages, see Chomsky (1981d), pp. 127–35, Hale (1983), and Farmer (1984).

Chapter 6

The S-bar analysis of Ordinary Clauses is due to Bresnan (1970, 1972, 1979), who assumes that S-bar is the Maximal Projection of S. There have been occasional claims in the linguistic literature to the effect that S-bar can be projected into S-double-bar by the addition of some other constituent (e.g. Chomsky (1977a), McCloskey (1979), Kiss (1981), Bayer (1984), Haegeman (1984), Gunnarson (1986)), and even into S-treble-bar (cf. Hornstein (1977), pp. 160, fn. 23)); but these have generally been treated with scepticism by the TG community at large. The assumption that Ordinary Clauses which lack overt C, NP, I, or VP constituents actually have empty constituents occupying the relevant positions is an extension of early work by Emonds (1976, p. 67) on empty categories: see Bouchard (1984) and Bennis (1986) for a more recent (but highly technical) treatment of empty categories.

We have argued here that subjectless ('Control') infinitives have the status of 'Ordinary Clauses' (= S-bar) containing an empty Complementiser and an empty PRO subject: the analysis of Control Predicates outlined here essentially follows Chomsky *Lectures* (1981d, pp. 74–9, 98–100). It should be pointed out, however, that an alternative analysis of 'subjectless infinitives' as bare VPs has been proposed by a number of linguists such as Brame (1975, 1976, 1978, 1979, 1981), Bresnan (1971, 1978, 1982), and

Bibliographical background

Borsley (1986). Arguments against the VP analysis and in favour of the S-bar analysis assumed here are found in Koster and May (1982), and Chomsky (1982, p. 97).

The postulation that there is a subset of Complement Clauses which have the status of a complementiserless S is likewise due to Bresnan (1972, 1979, Chapter 3). However, the analysis of Exceptional Clauses adopted here is modelled more closely on Stowell (1981, pp. 188–97), and Chomsky's *Barriers* (1986b). There are a number of alternative analyses of Exceptional Clauses. Some linguists analyse them as S-bar complements, though they differ as to what makes Exceptional Clauses different from Ordinary Clauses. Kayne (1981b) claims that the 'exceptional' feature of such Clauses is that they contain a null prepositional Complementiser. Van Riemskijk and Williams (1986, p. 237) argue that their 'exceptional' characteristic is the fact that their S-bar constituent is 'transparent' to various syntactic operations. Chomsky, in *Lectures* (1981d) argues that they are 'exceptional' by virtue of undergoing a rule of S-BAR-DELETION which reduces them to S-complements.

Implicit in all four analyses of Exceptional Clauses mentioned in the preceding paragraph is the key assumption that the postverbal NP (*John* in 'I consider [John to be highly intelligent]') is the superficial Subject of a Complement Clause. However, this is by no means an uncontroversial analysis. Others have claimed that in such cases the postverbal NP (*John*) is the superficial main Clause Object, not the Complement Clause Subject: see Postal (1974), and Cole and Hermon (1981) for one such analysis (attacked in Bresnan (1976c)), and Bresnan (1982) for another (in a nontransformational framework).

The analysis of Small Clauses presented here derives from work by Stowell (1981, pp. 257–67; 1983), and Chomsky's *Lectures* (1981d, pp. 106–12, 169). It should be emphasised, however, that by no means all linguists are happy to treat sentences such as 'John considers [*Mary intelligent*]' as involving a structure in which *Mary* is the Subject of a Small Clause (cf. Pullum's (1986, p. 409) remark that 'If you believe in Small Clauses you probably eat steak with a spoon'). An alternative analysis of *Mary* as the main Clause Object of which the AP *intelligent* is predicated is found in Williams (1980, 1983), and Napoli (1987): for obvious reasons, this is known as the *Predication Theory* analysis. For a defence of the Small Clause analysis against the Predication Theory analysis, see Safir (1983). Stowell 1981 and Burzio (1986) extend the Small Clause analysis to copula constructions such as 'There are [*some people sick*]'; but see Williams (1984) for arguments against this. The Small Clause analysis is extended to Absolute Prepositional Phrases in Beukema and Hoekstra (1984), and Beukema (1984). Cattell (1984) considers (but rejects) the possibility of a Small Clause analysis for the bracketed sequence in sentences such as 'Overwork gave [*Harry a heart-attack*]'. Kayne (1985) extends the Small Clause analysis to Verb + Particle constructions such as [*look something up*]. Hornstein and Lightfoot (1987) argue that Small Clauses are headed by an empty I constituent. In Radford (1986), I argue that the earliest clausal structures produced by young children (at around two years of age) resemble adult Small Clauses.

The claim that Modals and infinitival *to* are different members of the same category (termed AUX in earlier work, and INFL in more recent work) has been made by

599

Bibliographical background

numerous linguists over the years – e.g. Stockwell, Schachter and Partee (1973), Akmajian and Wasow (1975), Bresnan (1976a), Emonds (1976, p. 221), Chomsky, *Essays* (1977a, p. 157), Fiengo (1980), Stowell (1981), and Pullum (1981a, 1982). The claim made here that all finite Clauses have an I constituent (filled or empty) is in marked contrast to the claim made by Baltin (1982, p. 32) that subjunctive Clauses have no I constituent at all.

We have not dealt here with the Syntax of gerund Clauses (i.e. Clauses headed by a Verb carrying the inflectional suffix *-ing*). The interested reader might look at the analyses proposed for a variety of gerund structures in Wasow and Roeper (1972), Horn (1975), Williams (1975), Akmajian (1977), Gee (1977), Stowell (1982), Reuland (1983), Williams (1983), and Battistella (1983).

Chapter 7

The first model of generative grammar incorporating an independent Lexicon was outlined in Chomsky's *Aspects of the Theory of Syntax* in 1965. Chomsky assumed there that among the syntactic information included in lexical entries should be categorial, subcategorisation, and selectional information. Most syntactic work on the Lexicon in this era concentrated on a detailed specification of the subcategorisation properties of items. In this connection, it is instructive to look at various textbook treatment of the Lexicon in the *Aspects* era, e.g. Jacobs and Rosenbaum (1968, pp. 59–69), Akmajian and Heny (1975, pp. 51–61), Huddleston (1976, pp. 147–57), etc.

Within the *Aspects* model, it was assumed that Predicates were assigned selectional features which restricted their choice of Arguments. Subsequently, however, McCawley (1968) and Jackendoff (1972) argued that Selection Restrictions were determined in part by the semantic properties of Predicates, and in part by pragmatic factors (e.g. personal beliefs), and hence should not properly be included in lexical entries.

The proposal that lexical entries should include a specification of the theta-role which Predicates assign to each of their arguments is associated with the pioneering work of Gruber (1965, 1976), and Fillmore (1966, 1968a, 1968b, 1969, 1971a, 1971b, 1972, 1977) in the latter half of the 1960s. The earliest systematic attempt to develop a set of rules correlating thematic and syntactic structure is to be found in Fillmore's SUBJECT SELECTION and COMPLEMENT SELECTION rules: a more recent attempt is found in the *Realisation Rules* developed by Edwin Williams (e.g. 1981): for a discussion of relevant problems see Woolford (1984). Other attempts are to be found in Carter (1976), and Carrier-Duncan (1985). For a critical discussion of some problems underlying the assumption that the subcategorisation properties of items directly reflect their thematic properties, see Jackendoff (1985). We have not here dealt with the assignment of theta-roles by head Ns to their modifiers within NP: for some discussion, see Anderson (1983). Constraints on theta-role assignment such as the THETA CRITERION and the PROJECTION PRINCIPLE are discussed in considerable technical detail in Chomsky (1981d, 1982).

Another issue not touched upon here is how word-formation rules operate within the Lexicon: this is because we have adopted the 'classical' view here that word-formation rules fall within the domain of a Theory of Morphology, and not within the domain of a Theory of Syntax (which is concerned solely with the principles of phrase-formation). For some discussion of word-formation rules, see Aronoff (1976), Selkirk (1982), Scalise (1984).

Chapter 8
The rule of AFFIX MOVEMENT dates back to the very earliest work in TG, in its earlier incarnation as AFFIX HOPPING – e.g. Chomsky's *Logical Structure* (1955) and *Syntactic Structures* (1957). The precursor of the rule of V MOVEMENT was the rule of BE/HAVE SHIFT proposed in Jackendoff (1972) (though attributed by him to unpublished lectures by Edward Klima in 1966), and Akmajian and Wasow (1975). The more general formulation assumed in the text was argued for by Koopman (1984), and adopted in Chomsky's (1986b) *Barriers* monograph. The claim that SUBJECT–AUXILIARY INVERSION involves preposing Auxiliaries into an empty Complementiser position is made by den Besten (1978), Koopman (1983a), Rizzi (1984), and Chomsky (1986b).

The claim that both 'Passive' and 'Raising' are reflexes of a single NP MOVEMENT rule is first made in Chomsky's (1973) 'Conditions' paper, and extended in Chomsky (1977a). A transformational analysis of the 'Middle' construction essentially along the lines of the analysis sketched in the text was proposed in Chomsky (1962), and adopted in Emonds (1976, pp. 89–90). The claim that 'Ergative' structures involve NP MOVEMENT is defended at length in Burzio (1986). Chomsky suggests in his 'Remarks' paper (1970) that the Passive case of NP MOVEMENT applies not only within the domain of S, but also within the domain of NP, so that an NP such as [the city's destruction by the enemy] would derive from [e destruction *the city* by the enemy], with NP MOVEMENT applying to move the italicised object NP into the empty NP subject position marked by 'e': but cf. Williams (1981b) for a critical attack on the claim that NP MOVEMENT can apply within the domain of NP.

The analysis of 'prepositional passives' adopted here follows Van Riemsdijk's (1978) REANALYSIS proposal (which in turn is based on Chomsky (1974)): see Hornstein and Weinberg (1981) for a rather different formulation of the rule. On the differences between *transformational* and *lexical* passives, see Wasow (1977), and Roeper and Siegel (1978); for arguments that *un*-passives are lexical, see Siegel (1973) and Hust (1977). On the more general issue of the relative scope of *transformational* and *lexical* rules, see the various papers in Hoekstra *et al.* (1981), and Moortgat *et al.* (1981).

The EXTRAPOSITION rule discussed here dates back to work by Ross (1967): for more recent discussion of the rule, see Reinhart (1980), Guéron (1980), Baltin (1981, 1984), McCawley (1982), and Guéron and May (1984).

Chapter 9
The arguments for WH MOVEMENT given here are an expanded version of those presented in Radford (1981). On AUXILIARY CONTRACTION, see King (1970), Baker (1981), Kaisse (1983), and Schachter (1984); on WANNA CONTRACTION, see the references given below for Chapter 10.

Bibliographical background

On the status of relative *that*, see Van der Auwera (1985), and the extensive references given there. On *Free Relatives*, see Bresnan and Grimshaw (1978), Groos and Van Riemsdijk (1981), Harbert (1982, 1983), Hirschbühler and Rivero (1983a,b), Suñer (1984), and Rivero (1984). On Appositive Relatives, see Jackendoff (1977a), Emonds (1979), Perzanowski (1980), and Stuurman (1983). On Cleft and Pseudocleft sentence structures, see Declerk (1984) and Rochemont (1986, pp. 127–70).

There have been a very large number of different analyses of the operation and landing-site of WH MOVEMENT. Katz and Postal (1964, p. 104) suggest that wh-questions involve movement of a wh-phrase to become a *right* sister of an initial Q morpheme (which can be thought of as an abstract interrogative Complementiser). Baker (1970, p. 209) suggests that WH MOVEMENT may involve substitution of the moved wh-phrase into an empty C. Chomsky (1973) maintains that WH MOVEMENT is movement into a base-generated empty XP position to the left of C within COMP (as described in exercise VI in the text). Bresnan (1976b) analyses WH MOVEMENT as adjunction to S-bar: Baltin (1982) does likewise, and attempts to integrate this analysis into a generalised landing-site theory for movement rules. Chomsky (1980b) analyses WH MOVEMENT as adjunction to C, with concomitant erasure of C if C is empty (1981d, p. 53). Koopman (1984) and Chomsky (1986b) argue that the rule involves movement into a base-generated empty XP C-specifier position within CP.

Although, as we have seen, languages like English don't allow more than one preposed wh-phrase in wh-structures (arguably, because such languages have only C-Specifier position), other languages appear to allow *multiple wh-movement* – preposing of more than one wh-constituent. Among such languages are Czech and Polish (see Toman (1981)), and Romanian (Adams (1984), Comorovski (1986)). It would appear that in such languages we shall have to allow to the Complementiser constituent to permit more than one Specifier. Thus, it may be that there is parametric variation across languages with respect to the number of Specifiers which C permits (viz. only one/more than one). Also interesting is the fact that languages like Spanish allow (a counterpart of) sequences such as 'I asked *that whether/that why he was leaving*' (see Plann (1982)): in our terms, the italicised structures are probably to be analysed as C-bar constituents of the form [C CP] (where C takes a CP rather than an IP complement). Much more problematic for the supposed universality of the C-specifier analysis is the claim in Horvath (1986) that WH MOVEMENT in Hungarian interrogatives involves substitution of the preposed wh-phrase into an empty preverbal XP position within V-bar.

We have assumed in our analysis of interrogatives here that *whether* is an interrogative Complementiser. However, an alternative analysis of *whether* as a wh-word which undergoes WH MOVEMENT like other wh-constituents is put forward in Bolinger (1978), and Larson (1985). An issue not touched on here is the question of whether subject wh-NPs in simple wh-structures such as 'Who went home?' undergo vacuous WH MOVEMENT from subject into C-specifier position or remain in subject position. Clements *et al.* (1983) argue in favour of vacuous movement in such cases, whereas Chomsky (1986b) suggests that movement may be optional.

Although there is general agreement in more recent work that clausal constituents

602

like S, S-bar and SC cannot be primitive categories but must each be projections of some word-level category, there is very far from being any general consensus on the question of which clause-type is a projection of which word category. The text analysis of I as the head of S, and C as the head of S-bar follows Stowell (1981), Koopman (1984), and Chomsky's (1986b) *Barriers* monograph: cf. Everaert (1986) for an adaptation of this analysis to Dutch. However, there have been numerous alternative analyses of both S and S-bar. For example, a number of authors have analysed S as the Maximal Projection of V: thus, if VP is V-double-bar, then we might follow Jackendoff (1977a) and Emonds (1985) in positing that S is V-treble-bar. Alternatively, we might follow Bresnan (1976a, p. 20) in positing that VP plus I together form a V-treble-bar constituent, and that the NP subject together with this V-treble-bar form a V-quadruple-bar constituent corresponding to S. We should also note that there have been some proposals in the literature to the effect that S is double-headed, and is thus a projection both of the Subject and the Predicate: e.g. Williams (1980, 1981b, 1982), and Taraldsen (1984).

Among alternative analyses of S-bar found in the relevant literature, we might cite two obvious alternatives to the CP analysis: one is that V is the head of S-bar, as proposed in Jackendoff (1974, 1977a), Williams (1975), Bresnan (1976a), and numerous other works of that era. The second is to suppose that S-bar is a projection of I: one version of this analysis is to posit that I together with its subject NP and VP complement form an I-bar (= S) constituent, which in turn can be expanded into an I-double-bar (alias S-bar) by the addition of a C(omplementiser) Specifier: under this analysis, S would be an I-bar of the schematic form [NP I VP], and S-bar would be an I-double-bar of the canonical form [C I']. The analysis is suggested as a possibility in Chomsky's *Lectures* (1981d), and is advocated in Freidin (1983), Suñer (1984), Hoekstra (1984, p. 75) and Safir (1985). An alternative analysis is proposed by Hoekstra (1983) for Dutch, under which S = V-double-bar, and S-bar = I-double-bar: a similar analysis for Spanish is proposed by Groos and Bok-Bennema (1986).

The analysis of Small Clauses as projections of the head category of their Predicate Phrase derives from work by Stowell (1981, pp. 257–67; 1983), and Chomsky's *Lectures* (1981d, pp. 106–12, 169): the suggestion that Small Clauses are X" constituents of the structure [NP X'] is made in Chomsky's *Barriers* (1986b, p. 16). The alternate possibility that Small Clauses with Subjects are triple-bar expansions of the Head category of their Predicate (so that they are X''' constituents of the schematic form [NP X''] is suggested by Van Gestel's (1986) claim that Complements are daughters of X-bar, Specifiers are daughters of X-double-bar, and Subjects are daughters of X-treble-bar: see the references given for Chapter 6 for further literature on Small Clauses.

We have concentrated here on the structure of Clauses in English, a typical configurational language. In so-called nonconfigurational languages which have a 'flatter' constituent structure, however, it is generally claimed that Clauses are single-bar projections of the head V of the Clause: see Hale (1983) and Jelinek (1984) on Warlpiri, and Farmer (1984) on Japanese. It follows that nonconfigurational languages lack a VP constituent. However, it is often difficult to decide whether a given language is configurational or nonconfigurational: e.g. Kiss (1981) claims that Hungarian is nonconfigurational, whereas Farkas (1986) claims that it is configurational.

Chapter 10

On Topicalisation and Dislocation, see Chomsky (1977b), Rivero (1978, 1980), Bowers (1981), Maling and Zaenen (1981), Baltin (1982), and Greenberg (1984). It is often claimed that 'Verb Second' (V2) structures involve preposing of V into C, and of some phrasal constituent into the C-specifier position: see Adams (1987) for such an analysis of V2 in Old French, and various papers contained in Haider and Prinzhorn (1986) for a similar analysis of V2 in the Germanic languages.

The proposal to conflate individual movement transformations into ever more general rules leads to the suggestion in Chomsky's *Essays* (1977a, p. 205) that core movement transformations can be reduced to just two generalised rules – NP MOVE-MENT and WH MOVEMENT. In Chomsky (1980a, p. 145; 1980b, p. 3, and subsequent work) we find this process of conflation taken to its logical extreme, with the proposal that these two rules in turn are different instantiations of a maximally generalised, universal rule of ALPHA MOVEMENT. The STRUCTURE-PRESERVING PRINCIPLE (as a constraint on substitution rules) derives from work by Emonds (1970, 1976). The EXTENDED PROJECTION PRINCIPLE derives from Chomsky (1981d, 1982).

An early defence of Trace Theory is presented in Lightfoot (1976). Chung (1982) presents evidence that WH MOVEMENT leaves behind traces in Chamorro, arguing that traces of moved wh-phrases trigger a special agreement morphology on the Verb of the clause out of which the wh-phrase has been moved. A great deal of the literature on Trace Theory has centred on the adequacy of the trace-theoretic account of WANNA CONTRACTION: for a blow-by-blow account of the ongoing debate, see Lightfoot (1976), Postal and Pullum (1978), Andrews (1978), Chomsky and Lasnik (1978), Pullum and Postal (1979, 1982, 1986), Jaeggli (1980), Carden (1983), Aoun and Lightfoot (1984), Bouchard (1986), and Lightfoot (1986).

The suggestion that transformations cannot downgrade constituents appears in an early form in Chomsky's *Reflections* (1976, p. 107). There have been occasional challenges in the literature to the claim that there are no *downgrading* rules in natural language: for example, Horvath (1986) argues that Hungarian has a FOCUS rule which downgrades focussed constituents; but this claim is rebutted in Farkas (1986).

Evidence in support of a bounded analysis of WH MOVEMENT comes not only from the sources cited in the text, but also from Torrego (1983, 1984) and Chung (1982). There is a vast amount of literature on the question of what constitutes the set of *bounding nodes* in English and other languages: for some relevant discussion, see e.g. Chomsky (1977b), Koster (1978), Baltin (1981, 1982, 1983), Sportiche (1981) (for French), George and Kornfilt (1981) (for Turkish) Rizzi (1982) (for Italian), Cole (1982), Adams (1984), Chomsky (1986b) for various proposals.

Although we have not focussed on this question here, the *bounded* analysis of WH MOVEMENT does raise a few problems. One such is how to prevent a moved wh-phrase from remaining in an 'intermediate' non-wh C-specifier position: see Lasnik and Saito

(1984, p. 240) for one solution to this problem. Postal (1972) points to an interesting complication which arises from the bounded analysis, to do with 'dangling Prepositions': see Hornstein and Weinberg (1981) for one solution to the problem.

The STRICT CYCLICITY CONDITION was proposed in Chomsky (1973, p. 243). Williams (1975, pp. 257–60) argues that the principle determines the order of application of transformations. Freidin (1978) attempts to derive the condition from independent principles. A detailed discussion of *chains* is found in Safir (1985).

Bibliography

Where a book is cited in the text under an abbreviated title, the abbreviated title is given in square brackets [. . .] after the main title.

Aarts, F. and Aarts, J. (1982) *English Syntactic Structures*. Pergamon, Oxford

Adams, M. (1984) 'Multiple Interrogation in Italian', *The Linguistic Review*, 4, pp. 1–27

    (1987) 'From Old French to the Theory of Pro-Drop', *Natural Language and Linguistic Theory*, 5, pp. 1–32

Akmajian, A. (1977) 'The Complement Structure of Perception Verbs in an Autonomous Syntax Framework' in Culicover, P. W. *et al.* (eds.) *Formal Syntax*, pp. 427–60

    (1984) 'Sentence Types and the Form-Function Fit', *Natural Language and Linguistic Theory*, 2, pp. 1–23

Akmajian A. and Heny, F. W. (1975) *An Introduction to the Principles of Transformational Syntax*. MIT Press, Cambridge, Mass.

Akmajian, A. and Wasow, T. (1975) 'The Constituent Structure of VP and the Position of the Verb BE', *Linguistic Analysis*, 1, pp. 205–45

Akmajian, A., Steele, S. and Wasow, T. (1979) 'The Category AUX in Universal Grammar', *Linguistic Inquiry*, 10, pp. 1–64

Anderson, J. M. (1977) *On Case Grammar*. Croom Helm, London

Anderson, M. (1983) 'Prenominal Genitive NPs', *The Linguistic Review*, 3, pp. 1–24

Andrews, A. D. (1978) 'Remarks on *To* Adjunction', *Linguistic Inquiry*, 9, pp. 261–8

    (1982) 'A Note on the Constituent Structure of Adverbials and Auxiliaries', *Linguistic Inquiry*, 13, pp. 313–17

    (1983) 'A Note on the Constituent Structure of Modifiers', *Linguistic Inquiry*, 14, pp. 695–7

Aoun, J. and Lightfoot, D. W. (1984) 'Government and Contraction', *Linguistic Inquiry*, 15, pp. 465–73

Aronoff, M. (1976) *Word Formation in Generative Grammar*. MIT Press, Cambridge, Mass.

Bach, E. (1974) *Syntactic Theory*. Holt, Rinehart and Winston, New York

Bach, E. and Harms, R. T. (eds.) (1968) *Universals in Linguistic Theory*. Holt, Rinehart and Winston, New York

606

Baker, C. L. (1970) 'Notes on the Description of English Questions: The Role of an Abstract Question Morpheme', *Foundations of Language*, 6, pp. 197–219

(1978) *Introduction to Generative-Transformational Syntax*. Prentice-Hall, Englewood Cliffs, New Jersey

(1981) 'Auxiliary–Adverb Word Order', *Linguistic Inquiry*, 12, pp. 309–15

Baker, C. L. and McCarthy, J. J. (eds.) (1981) *The Logical Problem of Language Acquisition*. MIT Press, Cambridge, Mass.

Baltin, M. (1981) 'Strict Bounding' in Baker, C. L and McCarthy, J. J. (eds.) *The Logical Problem of Language Acquisition*, pp. 257–95

(1982) 'A Landing Site Theory of Movement Rules', *Linguistic Inquiry*, 13, pp. 1–38

(1983) 'Extraposition: Bounding versus Government-Binding', *Linguistic Inquiry*, 14, pp. 155–62

(1984) 'Extraposition Rules and Discontinuous Constituents', *Linguistic Inquiry*, 15, pp. 157–63

Battistella, E. (1983) 'A Subjacency Puzzle', *Linguistic Inquiry*, 14, pp. 698–704

Bayer, J. (1983) 'COMP in Bavarian Syntax', *The Linguistic Review*, 3, pp. 209–74

(1984) 'Towards an Explanation of Certain That-*t* Phenomena: the COMP-node in Bavarian' in De Geest, W. and Putseys, Y. (eds.) *Sentential Complementation*, pp. 23–32

Belletti, A., Brandi, L. and Rizzi, L. (eds.) (1981) *Theory of Markedness in Generative Grammar*. Scuola Normale Superiore di Pisa, Pisa

Bennis, H. (1986) *Gaps and Dummies*. Foris, Dordrecht

Bennis, H. and Van Lessen Kloeke, W. U. S. (eds.) (1983) *Linguistics in the Netherlands 1983*. Foris, Dordrecht

Bennis, H. and Hoekstra, T. (1984) 'Gaps and Parasitic Gaps', *The Linguistic Review*, 4, pp. 29–87

Berko, J. (1958) 'The Child's Learning of English Morphology', *Word*, pp. 150–77

Beukema, F. (1984) 'Small Clauses and Free Adjuncts' in Bennis, H. and Van Lessen Kloeke, W. U. S. (eds.) *Linguistics in the Netherlands 1984*. Foris, Dordrecht, pp. 13–21

Beukema, F. and Hoekstra, T. (1984) 'Extractions from *With*-Constructions', *Linguistic Inquiry*, 15, pp. 689–98

Binkert, P. J. (1984) *Generative Grammar Without Transformations*. Mouton, Berlin

Bloomfield, L. (1935) *Language*. George Allen and Unwin Ltd, London

Bolinger, D. (1978) 'Yes–No Questions are Not Alternative Questions' in Hiz, H. (ed.), *Questions*. Reidel, Dordrecht, pp. 107–150

Borsley, R. D. (1983) 'A Welsh Agreement Process and the Status of VP and S' in Gazdar, G. *et al.* (eds.) *Order, Concord and Constituency*, pp. 57–74

(1986) 'Prepositional Complementizers in Welsh', *Journal of Linguistics*, 22, pp. 67–84

Bouchard, D. (1984) *On the Content of Empty Categories*. Foris, Dordrecht

(1986) 'Empty Categories and the Contraction Debate', *Linguistic Inquiry*, 17, pp. 95–104

Bibliography

Bowers, J. (1981) *The Theory of Grammatical Relations*. Cornell University Press, Ithaca, New York

Brame, M. K. (1975) 'On the Abstractness of Syntactic Structure: the VP-Controversy, *Linguistic Analysis*, 1, pp. 191–203

   (1976) *Conjectures and Refutations in Syntax and Semantics*. North Holland, Amsterdam

   (1978) *Base Generated Syntax*. Noit Amrofer, Seattle

   (1979) *Essays Toward Realistic Syntax*. Noit Amrofer, Seattle

   (1981) 'Trace Theory with Filters vs. Lexically Based Syntax Without', *Linguistic Inquiry*, 12, pp. 275–93

Brandon, F. R. and Seki, L. (1981) 'A Note on COMP as a Universal', *Linguistic Inquiry*, 12, pp. 659–65

Bresnan, J. W. (1970) 'On Complementisers: Toward a Syntactic Theory of Complement Types', *Foundations of Language*, 6, pp. 297–321

   (1971) 'Sentence Stress and Syntactic Transformations', *Language*, 47, pp. 257–81

   (1972) *Theory of Complementation in English Syntax*. Ph.D dissertation, MIT, Cambridge, Mass. (published as Bresnan 1979)

   (1976a) 'On the Form and Functioning of Transformations', *Linguistic Inquiry*, 7, pp. 3–40

   (1976b) 'Evidence for a Theory of Unbounded Transformations', *Linguistic Analysis*, 2, pp. 353–93

   (1976c) 'Nonarguments for Raising', *Linguistic Inquiry*, 7, pp. 485–502

   (1978) 'A Realistic Transformational Grammar' in Halle, M. *et al.* (eds.) *Linguistic Theory and Psychological Reality*. MIT Press, Cambridge, Mass.

   (1979) *Theory of Complementation in English Syntax*. Garland, New York (published version of Bresnan 1972)

   (ed.) (1981) *The Mental Representation of Grammatical Relations*. MIT Press, Mass, New York

   (1982) 'Control and Complementation', *Linguistic Inquiry*, 13, pp. 343–434

Bresnan, J. W. and Grimshaw, J. (1978) 'The Syntax of Free Relatives in English', *Linguistic Inquiry*, 9, pp. 339–91

Brown, E. K. and Miller, J. E. (1980) *Syntax: A Linguistic Introduction to Sentence Structure*. Hutchinson, London

Burton-Roberts, N. (1986) *Analysing Sentences*. Longman, London

Burzio, L. (1986) *Italian Syntax*. Reidel, Dordrecht

Carden, G. (1983) 'The Debate about *wanna*: Evidence from Other Contraction Rules' in Richardson, J. F., Marks, M. and Chukerman, A. (eds.) *Papers from the Parasession on Interplay of Phonology, Morphology, and Syntax. Chicago Linguistic Society*, University of Chicago, pp. 38–49

Carrier-Duncan, J. (1985) 'Linking of Thematic Roles in Derivational Word Formation', *Linguistic Inquiry*, 16, pp. 1–34

Carter, R. (1976) 'Some Linking regularities' in *Recherches Linguistiques*, Vincennes University, Paris, pp. 3–4

Cattell, R. (1984) *Composite Predicates in English, Syntax and Semantics,* Vol. XVII, Academic Press, New York

Chisholm, W. S. (1984) (ed.) *Interrogativity.* Benjamins, Amsterdam

Chomsky, N. (1955) 'The Logical Structure of Linguistic Theory' [*Logical Structure*], unpublished manuscript; published as Chomsky 1975 (see below)

(1957) *Syntactic Structures.* Mouton, The Hague

(1962) 'A Transformational Approach to Syntax' in Hill, A. A. (ed.) *Proceedings of the Third Texas Conference on Problems of Linguistic Analysis in English.* University of Texas Press, Austin, Texas, pp. 124–58; also in Fodor, J. A. and Katz, J. (eds.) *The Structure of Language: Readings in the Philosophy of Language.* Prentice-Hall, Englewood Cliffs, New Jersey (1964), pp. 211–45

(1964) *Current Issues in Linguistic Theory* [*Current Issues*]. Mouton, The Hague

(1965) *Aspects of the Theory of Syntax* [*Aspects*]. MIT Press, Cambridge, Mass.

(1966) *Topics in the Theory of Generative Grammar* [*Topics*]. Mouton, The Hague

(1968a) *Language and Mind.* Harcourt Brace Jovanovich, New York

(1968b) Interview with S. Hamshire in *The Listener,* May 1968

(1970) 'Remarks on Nominalisation' [Remarks] in Jacobs, R. A. and Rosenbaum, P. S. *English Transformational Grammar,* pp. 184–221

(1972a) *Language and Mind* (enlarged edition). Harcourt Brace Jovanovich, New York

(1972b) *Studies on Semantics in Generative Grammar* [*Studies*]. Mouton, The Hague

(1973) 'Conditions on Transformations' [Conditions] in Anderson, S. R. and Kiparsky, P. (eds.) *A Festschrift for Morris Halle.* Holt, Rinehart and Winston, New York, pp. 232–86

(1974) 'The Amherst Lectures', unpublished lecture notes distributed by Documents Linguistiques, University of Paris VII

(1975) *The Logical Structure of Linguistic Theory* [*Logical Structure*]. Plenum, New York

(1976) *Reflections on Language.* Fontana, London

(1977a) *Essays on Form and Interpretation* [*Essays*]. North Holland, Amsterdam

(1977b) 'On Wh-movement' in Culicover P. W. *et al.* (eds.) *Formal Syntax,* pp. 71–132

(1980a) *Rules and Representations.* Blackwell, Oxford

(1980b) 'On Binding', *Linguistic Inquiry,* 11, pp. 1–46

(1981a) 'Markedness and Core Grammar' in Belletti, A. *et al.* (eds.) *Theory of Markedness in Generative Grammar,* pp. 123–46

(1981b) 'Principles and Parameters in Syntactic Theory' in Hornstein, N. and Lightfoot, D. (eds.) *Explanation in Linguistics,* pp. 32–75

(1981c) 'On the Representation of Form and Function', *The Linguistic Review,* pp. 3–40

(1981d) *Lectures on Government and Binding* [*Lectures*]. Foris, Dordrecht

(1982) *Some Concepts and Consequences of the Theory of Government and Binding* [*Concepts*]. MIT Press, Cambridge, Mass.

(1986a) *Knowledge of Language: Its Nature, Origin, and Use* [*Knowledge*]. Praeger, New York

(1986b) *Barriers*. MIT Press, Cambridge, Mass.

Chomsky, N. and Halle, M. (1968) *The Sound Pattern of English*, Harper and Row, New York

Chomsky, N. and Lasnik, H. (1977) 'Filters and Control', *Linguistic Inquiry*, 8, pp. 425–504

(1978) 'A Remark on Contraction', *Linguistic Inquiry*, 9, pp. 268–74

Chung, S. (1982) 'Unbounded dependencies in Chamorro Grammar', *Linguistic Inquiry*, 13, pp. 39–77

Clahsen, H. and Smolka, K.-D. (1986) 'Psycholinguistic Evidence and the Description of V-Second Phenomena in German' in Haider, H. and Prinzhorn, M. (eds.) *Verb Second Phenomena in Germanic Languages*, pp. 137–67

Clements, G. N., McCloskey, J., Maling, J. and Zaenen, A. (1983) 'String-Vacuous Rule Application', *Linguistic Inquiry*, 14, pp. 1–17

Cole, P. (1982) 'On Defining Bounding Nodes for Subjacency', *Linguistic Inquiry*, 13, pp. 139–45

Cole, P. and Hermon, G. (1981) 'Subjecthood and Islandhood: Evidence from Quechua', *Linguistic Inquiry*, 12, pp. 1–30

Comorovski, I. (1986) 'Multiple *Wh* Movement in Romanian', *Linguistic Inquiry*, 17, pp. 171–7

Comrie, B. (1981) *Language Universals and Linguistic Typology*. Blackwell, Oxford

(1984) 'Russian' in Chisholm, W. S. (ed.) *Interrogativity*, pp. 7–46

Crystal, D. (1985, 2nd edn) *A Dictionary of Linguistics and Phonetics*. Blackwell, Oxford

Culicover, P. W. (1982, 2nd edn) *Syntax*. Academic Press, New York

Culicover, P. W., Wasow, T. and Akmajian, A. (eds.) (1977) *Formal Syntax*. Academic Press, New York

Culicover, P. W. and Wilkins, W. K. (1984) *Locality in Linguistic Theory*. Academic Press, New York

Czepluch, H. (1982) 'Case History and the Dative Alternation', *The Linguistic Review*, 2, pp. 1–38

De Geest, W. and Putseys, W. (eds.) (1984) *Sentential Complementation*. Foris, Dordrecht

Declerk, R. (1984) 'Some Restrictions on Clefts that Highlight Predicate Nominals', *Journal of Linguistics*, 20, pp. 131–54

de Haan, G. and Weerman, F. (1986) 'Finiteness and Verb Fronting in Frisian' in Haider, H. and Prinzhorn, M. (eds.) *Verb Second Phenomena in Germanic Languages*, pp. 78–110

den Besten, H. (1978a) 'On the Interaction of Root Transformations and Lexical Deletive Rules', paper presented at the 1978 GLOW conference, Amsterdam

(1978b) 'On the Presence and Absence of *Wh*-Elements in Dutch Comparatives', *Linguistic Inquiry*, 9, pp. 641–71

den Besten, H. and Moed-van Walraven, C. (1986) 'The Syntax of Verbs in Yiddish' in Haider, H. and Prinzhorn, M. (eds.) *Verb Second Phenomena in Germanic Languages*, pp. 111–35

Dougherty, R. C. (1970) 'A Grammar of Coordinate Conjoined Structures', *Language*, 46, pp. 850–98

Emonds, J. E. (1970) *Root and Structure-preserving Transformations*, mimeographed paper circulated by the Indiana University Linguistics Club

(1976) *A Transformational Approach to English Syntax*. Academic Press, New York

(1979) 'Appositive Relatives have no Properties', *Linguistic Inquiry*, 10, pp. 211–43

(1985) *A Unified Theory of Syntactic Categories*. Foris, Dordrecht

Engdahl, E. (1986) *Constituent Questions*. Reidel, Dordrecht

Everaert, M. (1986) *The Syntax of Reflexivization*. Foris, Dordrecht

Farkas, D. (1986) 'On the Syntactic Position of Focus in Hungarian', *Natural Language and Linguistic Theory*, 4, pp. 77–96

Farmer, A. K. (1984) *Modularity in Syntax: A Study of Japanese and English*. MIT Press, Cambridge, Mass

Fiengo, R. (1980) *Surface Structure*. Harvard University Press, Cambridge, Mass.

Fillmore, C. J. (1966) 'A Proposal Concerning English Prepositions', Monograph Series on Language and Linguistics, 19, Georgetown University, Washington, pp. 19–33

(1968a) 'The Case for Case' in Bach, E. and Harms, R. T. (eds.) *Universals in Linguistic Theory*, pp. 1–88

(1968b) 'Lexical Entries for Verbs', *Foundations of Language*, 4, pp. 373–93

(1969) 'Toward a Modern Theory of Case', in Reibel, D. A. and Schane, S. A. (eds.) *Modern Studies in English*. Prentice-Hall, Englewood Cliffs, New Jersey, pp. 361–75

(1971a) 'Types of Lexical Information' in Steinberg, D. D. and Jakobivits, L. A. (eds.) *Semantics*, pp. 370–92

(1971b) 'Some Problems for Case Grammar', Monograph Series on Language and Linguistics, 22, Georgetown University, Washington, pp. 35–56

(1972) 'Subjects, Speakers and Roles', in Davidson, D. and Harman, G. (eds.) *Semantics of Natural Language*, Reidel, Dordrecht

(1977) 'The Case for Case Reopened' in Cole, P. and Sadock, J. M. (eds.) *Syntax and Semantics*, 8, pp. 59–81

Frantz, D. (1973) 'On Question Word Movement', *Linguistic Inquiry*, 4, pp. 531–4

Freidin, R. (1978) 'Cyclicity and the Theory of Grammar', *Linguistic Inquiry*, 9, pp. 519–49

(1983) 'X-bar Theory and the Analysis of English Infinitivals', *Linguistic Inquiry*, 14, pp. 713–22

Gazdar, G., Klein, E. and Pullum, G. K. (1983) *Order, Concord, and Constituency*. Foris, Dordrecht

Gazdar, G., Pullum, G. K. and Sag, I. (1982) 'Auxiliaries and Related Phenomena in a Restricted Theory of Grammar', *Language*, 58, pp. 591–638

Bibliography

Gazdar, G., Klein, E., Pullum, G. and Sag, I. (1985) *Generalised Phrase Structure Grammar*. Blackwell, Oxford

Gee, J. P. (1977) 'Comments on the Paper by Akmajian' in Culicover, P. W. *et al. Formal Syntax*, pp. 461–81

George, L. M. and Kornfilt, J. (1981) 'Finiteness and Boundedness in Turkish' in Heny, F. (ed.) *Binding and Filtering*, pp. 105–27

Gérard, J. (1980) *L'Exclamation en Français*. Niemeyer, Tübingen

Goldsmith, J. (1981) 'Complementizers and Root Sentences', *Linguistic Inquiry*, 12, pp. 541–74

Greenberg, G. R. (1984) 'Left Dislocation, Topicalization, and Interjections', *Natural Language and Linguistic Theory*, 2, pp. 283–7

Grimshaw, J. (1975) 'Evidence for Relativisation by Deletion in Chaucerian English', *University of Massachusetts Occasional Papers in Linguistics*, I

Grinder, J. T. and Elgin, S. H. (1973) *Guide to Transformational Grammar*. Holt, Rinehart and Winston, New York

Groos, A. and Van Riemsdijk, H. (1981) 'Matching Effects in Free Relatives: A Parameter of Core Grammar' in Belletti, A. *et al.* (eds.) *Theory of Markedness in Generative Grammar*, pp. 171–216

Groos, A. and Bok-Bennema, R. (1986) 'The Structure of the Sentence in Spanish' in Bordelois, I., Contreras, H. and Zagona, K. (eds.) *Generative Studies in Spanish Syntax*. Foris, Dordrecht, pp. 67–80

Gruber, J. S. (1965) 'Studies in Lexical Relations', Ph.D dissertation, MIT, Cambridge, Mass.

(1976) *Lexical Structures in Syntax and Semantics*. North Holland, Amsterdam

Guéron, J. (1980) 'On the Syntax and Semantics of PP-Extraposition', *Linguistic Inquiry*, 11, pp. 637–78

Guéron, J. and May, R. (1984) 'Extraposition and Logical Form', *Linguistic Inquiry*, 15, pp. 1–31

Guéron, J., Obenauer, H.-G. and Pollock, J.-Y. (eds.) (1985) *Grammatical Representation*. Foris, Dordrecht

Gunnarson, K.-A. (1986) 'Predicative Structures and Projections of Lexical Dependencies', *Linguistic Inquiry*, 17, pp. 13–47

Haegeman, L. (1983) '*Die* and *dat* in West-Flemish Relative Clauses' in Bennis H. and Van Lessen Kloeke, W. U. S. *Linguistics in the Netherlands, 1983*, pp. 83–91

(1984) 'Definite NP-Anaphora and Adverbial Clauses', *Linguistic Inquiry*, 15, pp. 712–15

Haider, H. (1986) 'V-Second in German' in Haider, H. and Prinzhorn, M. *Verb Second Phenomena in Germanic Languages*, pp. 49–75

Haider, H. and Prinzhorn, M. (eds.) (1986) *Verb Second Phenomena in Germanic Languages*. Foris, Dordrecht

Haïk, I. (1983) 'Indirect Binding and Referential Circularity', *The Linguistic Review*, 2, pp. 313–30

Hale, K. (1983) 'Warlpiri and the Grammar of Nonconfigurational Languages', *Natural Language and Linguistic Theory*, 1, pp. 5–47

Halitsky, D. (1975) 'Left-Branch S's and NP's in English: A Bar Notation Analysis', *Linguistic Analysis*, 1, pp. 279–96

Harbert, W. (1982) 'On the Nature of the Matching Parameter', *The Linguistic Review*, 2, pp. 237–84

   (1983) 'A Note on Old English Free Relatives', *Linguistic Inquiry*, 14, pp. 549–53

Harmer, L. C. and Norton, F. J. (1935) *A Manual of Modern Spanish*. University Tutorial Press, London

Harris, Z. S. (1946) 'From Morpheme to Utterance', *Language*, 22, pp. 161–83

Hawkins, J. A. (1983) *Word Order Universals*. Academic Press, New York

Hellan, L. (1986) 'The Headedness of NPs in Norwegian' in Muysken, P. and Van Riemsdijk, H. (eds.) *Features and Projections*, pp. 89–122

Heny, F. (ed.) (1981) *Binding and Filtering*. Croom Helm, London

Heny, F. and Richards, B. (1983) *Linguistic Categories: Auxiliaries and Related Puzzles*. Reidel, Dordrecht

Hinds, J. (1984) 'Japanese' in Chisholm, W. S. (ed.) *Interrogativity*, pp. 145–88

Hirschbühler, P. and Rivero, M.-L. (1983a) 'Non-matching Concealed Questions in Catalan and Spanish and the Projection Principle', *The Linguistic Review*, 2, pp. 331–63

   (1983b) 'Remarks on Free Relatives and Matching Phenomena', *Linguistic Inquiry*, 14, pp. 505–20

Hoekstra, T. (1983) 'The Distribution of Sentential Complements' in Bennis, H. and Van Lessen Kloeke, W. U. S. (eds.) *Linguistics in the Netherlands 1983*, pp. 93–103

   (1984) *Transitivity: Grammatical Relations in Government-Binding Theory*. Foris, Dordrecht

Hoekstra, T., Van der Hulst, H. and Moortgat, M. (eds.) (1981) *Lexical Grammar*. Foris, Dordrecht

Horn, G. M. (1975) 'On the Nonsentential Nature of the POSS-ing Construction', *Linguistic Analysis*, 1, pp. 333–88

Hornstein, N. (1977) 'S and X' Convention', *Linguistic Analysis*, 3, pp. 137–76

Hornstein, N. and Lightfoot, D. (1981a) 'Introduction' to Hornstein and Lightfoot 1981b, pp. 9–31

   (1981b) *Explanation in Linguistics*. Longman, London

   (1987) 'Predication and PRO', *Language*, 63, pp. 23–51

Hornstein, N. and Weinberg, A. (1981) 'Case Theory and Preposition Stranding', *Linguistic Inquiry*, 12, pp. 55–91

Horvath, J. (1986) *FOCUS in the Theory of Grammar and the Syntax of Hungarian*. Foris, Dordrecht

Huddleston, R. (1976) *An Introduction to English Transformational Syntax*. Longman, London

   (1984) *Introduction to the Grammar of English*. Cambridge University Press

Bibliography

Hurford, J. (1975) 'A Child and the English Question Formation Rule', *Journal of Child Language*, 2, pp. 299–301

Hust, J. R. (1977) 'The Syntax of the Unpassive Construction in English', *Linguistic Analysis*, 3, pp. 31–63

Jackendoff, R. S. (1972) *Semantic Interpretation in Generative Grammar* [*Semantic Interpretation*]. MIT Press, Cambridge, Mass.

  (1974) 'Introduction to the X̄ Convention', mimeographed paper circulated by the Indiana University Linguistics Club

  (1977a) *X̄ Syntax: A Study of Phrase Structure*. MIT Press, Cambridge, Mass.

  (1977b) 'Constraints on Phrase Structure Rules' in Culicover, P. W. *et al. Formal Syntax*, pp. 249–83

  (1985) 'Multiple Subcategorisation and the θ Criterion', *Natural Language and Linguistic Theory*, 3, pp. 271–95

Jacobs, R. A. and Rosenbaum, P. S. (1968) *English Transformational Grammar*. Ginn, Waltham, Mass.

  (1970) *Readings in English Transformational Grammar*. Ginn, Waltham, Mass.

Jacobsen, B. (1986) *Modern Transformational Grammar*. North Holland, Amsterdam

Jacobson, P. (1977) 'Some Aspects of Movement and Deletion', Chicago Linguistic Society, University of Chicago, Illinois, 3, pp. 347–59

Jaeggli, O. (1980) 'Remarks on *To* Contraction', *Linguistic Inquiry*, 11, pp. 239–46

Jelinek, E. (1984) 'Empty Categories, Case, and Configurationality', *Natural Language and Linguistic Theory*, 2, pp. 39–76

Jespersen, O. (1927) *A Modern English Grammar on Historical Principles*, Vol. III. Carl Winter, Heidelberg

  (1937) *Analytic Syntax*. Levin and Munksgaard, Copenhagen

  (1940) *A Modern English Grammar on Historical Principles*, Part V. Ejnaar Munksgaard, Copenhagen

Kaisse, E. (1983) 'The Syntax of Auxiliary Reduction in English', *Language*, 59, pp. 93–122

Katz, J. J. and Postal, P. M. (1964) *An Integrated Theory of Linguistic Descriptions*. MIT Press, Cambridge, Mass.

Kaufman, E. (1975) 'Theoretical Responses to Navajo Questions', unpublished Ph.D dissertation. MIT, Cambridge, Mass.

Kayne, R. S. (1972) 'Subject Inversion in French Interrogatives' in Casagrande, J. and Saciuk, B. (eds.) *Generative Studies in Romance Languages*. Newbury House, Rowley, Mass. pp. 70–126

  (1976) 'French Relative *que*' in Hensey, F. and Luján, M. (eds.) *Current Studies in Romance Linguistics*. Georgetown University Press, Washington DC, pp. 255–99

  (1981a) 'ECP Extensions', *Linguistic Inquiry*, 12, pp. 93–133

  (1981b) 'On Certain Differences Between French and English', *Linguistic Inquiry*, 12, pp. 349–71

  (1982) 'Predicates and Arguments, Verbs and Nouns', *GLOW Newsletter*, 8, p. 24

  (1984) *Connectedness and Binary Branching*. Foris, Dordrecht

(1985) 'Principles of Particle Constructions' in Guéron, J. *et al.* (eds.) *Grammatical Representation*, pp. 101–40

Kayne, R. S. and Pollock, J.-Y. (1978) 'Stylistic Inversion, Successive Cyclicity, and Move NP in French', *Linguistic Inquiry*, 9, pp. 595–621

Keyser, S. J. (1968) Review of S. Jacobson *Adverbial Positions in English*, *Language*, pp. 357–74

Keyser, S. J. and Roeper, T. (1984) 'On the Middle and Ergative Constructions in English', *Linguistic Inquiry*, 15, pp. 381–416

Kilby, D. (1984) *Descriptive Syntax and the English Verb*. Croom Helm, London

Kimball, J. P. (1973) *The Formal Theory of Grammar*. Prentice-Hall, Englewood Cliffs, New Jersey

King, H. (1970) 'On Blocking the Rules for Contraction in English', *Linguistic Inquiry*, 1, pp. 134–6

Kiss, K. E. (1981) 'Structural Relations in Hungarian, a "Free" Word Order Language', *Linguistic Inquiry*, 12, pp. 185–213

Koopman, H. (1983a) 'ECP Effects in Main Clauses', *Linguistic Inquiry*, 14, pp. 346–50
(1983b) 'Control from COMP and Comparative Syntax', *The Linguistic Review*, 2, pp. 365–91
(1984) *The Syntax of Verbs*. Foris, Dordrecht

Koster, J. (1975) 'Dutch as an SOV Language', *Linguistic Analysis*, 1, 111–36
(1978) *Locality Principles in Syntax*. Foris, Dordrecht

Koster, J. and May, R. (1982) 'On the Constituency of Infinitives', *Language*, 58, pp. 116–43

Kuczaj, S. (1976) 'Arguments against Hurford's *Aux Copying Rule*', *Journal of Child Language*, 3, pp. 423–7

Kuno, S. (1973) *The Structure of the Japanese Language*, MIT Press, Cambridge, Mass.

Lakoff, G. and Ross, J. R. (1966) *A Criterion for Verb Phrase Constituency*, Report NSF 17, Harvard University Computation Laboratory, Cambridge, Mass.
(1971) 'Presupposition and Relative Well-formedness' in Steinberg, D. D. and Jakobovits, L. A. *Semantics*, pp. 329–40

Langacker, R. W. (1969a) 'Mirror Image Rules I: Syntax', *Language*, 45, pp. 575–98
(1969b) 'Mirror Image Rules II: Lexicon and Phonology', *Language*, 45, pp. 844–62

Larson, R. K. (1985) 'On the Syntax of Disjunction Scope', *Natural Language and Linguistic Theory*, 3, pp. 217–64

Larsson, E. (1979) *La Dislocation en Français*. Etudes Romanes de Lund, C. W. K. Gleerup

Lasnik, H. (1981) 'Restricting the Theory of Transformations: a Case Study' in Hornstein, N. and Lightfoot, D. *Explanation in Linguistics*, pp. 152–73

Lasnik, H. and Saito, M. (1984) 'On the Nature of Proper Government', *Linguistic Inquiry*, 15, pp. 235–89

Leech, G. (1983) *Principles of Pragmatics*. Longman, London

Bibliography

Lees, R. B. (1960) *The Grammar of English Nominalizations*. Mouton, The Hague

Lefebvre, C. (1979) 'Réanalyse de Que/Qui, Inversion Stylistique et Mouvement de WH en Français', *Montreal Working Papers in Linguistics*, 13, pp. 73–90

Lefebvre, C. and Muysken, P. (1979) 'Comp in Cuzco Quechua', *Montreal Working Papers in Linguistics*, 11

(1982) 'Raising as Move Case' *The Linguistic Review*, 1, pp. 161–210

Levinson, S. (1983) *Pragmatics*. Cambridge University Press

Li, C. N. and Thompson, S. A. (1984) 'Mandarin' in Chisholm, W. S. *Interrogativity*, pp. 47–61

Lightfoot, D. (1976) 'Trace Theory and Twice-Moved NPs', *Linguistic Inquiry*, 7, pp. 559–82

(1979) *Principles of Diachronic Syntax*. Cambridge University Press

(1982) *The Language Lottery*, MIT Press, Cambridge, Mass.

(1986) 'A Brief Response', *Linguistic Inquiry*, 17, pp. 111–13

Lord, C. (1976) 'Evidence for Syntactic Reanalysis: From Verb to Complementizer in Kwa' in Steever, C., Walker, C. and Mufwene, S. (eds.) *Papers from the Paresession on Diachronic Syntax*, Chicago Linguistic Society

Lyons, J. (1966) 'Towards a "Notional" Theory of the "Parts of Speech"', *Journal of Linguistics*, 2, pp. 209–36

(1968) *Introduction to Theoretical Linguistics*. Cambridge University Press

Maling, J. M. (1978) 'The Complementizer in Middle English Appositives', *Linguistic Inquiry*, 9, pp. 719–25

Maling, J. and Zaenen, A. (1981) 'Germanic Word Order and the Format of Surface Filters' in Heny, F. (ed.) *Binding and Filtering*, pp. 255–78

Marantz, A. (1984) *On the Nature of Grammatical Relations*, MIT Press, Cambridge, Mass.

Matthews, P. H. (1981) *Syntax*. Cambridge University Press

McCawley, J. D. (1968) 'The Role of Semantics in a Grammar', in Bach, E. and Harms, R. T. (eds.) *Universals in Linguistic Theory*, pp. 124–69

(1982) 'Parentheticals and Discontinuous Constituents', *Linguistic Inquiry*, 13, pp. 91–106

McCloskey, J. (1979) *Transformational Syntax and Model Theoretic Semantics*. Reidel, Dordrecht

McNeil, D. A. (1966) 'Developmental Psycholinguistics' in Smith, F. and Miller, G. A. (eds.) *The Genesis of Language*. MIT Press, Cambridge, Mass.

Menyuk, P. (1969) *Sentences Children Use*. MIT Press, Cambridge, Mass.

Moortgat, M., Van der Hulst, H. and Hoekstra, T. (eds.) (1981). *The Scope of Lexical Rules*. Foris, Dordrecht

Morin, Y. C. and O'Malley, M. (1969) 'Multi-rooted Vines in Semantic Representation', in R. I. Binnick et al. (eds.), *Papers from the Fifth Regional Meeting*, Chicago Linguistic Society, University of Chicago, Illinois

Muysken, P. and Van Riemsdijk, H. (eds.) (1986) *Features and Projections*. Foris, Dordrecht

(1986) 'Projecting Features and Featuring Projections' in Muysken, P. and Van Riemsdijk, H. (eds.) *Features and Projections*, pp. 1–30

Nanni, D. L. and Stillings, J. T. (1978) 'Three Remarks on Pied Piping', *Linguistic Inquiry*, 9, pp. 310–18

Napoli, D. J. (1987) 'Prediction Theory: A Case Study for Indexing Theory', unpublished manuscript, University of Michigan, Program in Linguistics

Newmeyer, F. J. (1980) *Linguistic Theory in America*. Academic Press, New York

(1983) *Grammatical Theory*. University of Chicago Press

Nylander, D. K. (1985) 'ECP Effects in Krio', *Linguistic Inquiry*, 16, pp. 152–5

Palmer, F. R. (1983) *Grammar*. Penguin, London

Perlmutter, D. M. (ed.) (1983) *Studies in Relational Grammar 1*. University of Chicago Press

Perlmutter, D. M. and Rosen, C. G. (eds.) (1984) *Studies in Relational Grammar 2*. University of Chicago Press

Perzanowski, D. (1980) 'Appositive Relatives Do Have Properties', *Cahiers Linguistiques d'Ottowa*, 9, pp. 355–68

Plann, S. (1982) 'Indirect Questions in Spanish', *Linguistic Inquiry*, 13, pp. 297–312

Platzack, C. (1986) 'The Position of the Finite Verb in Swedish', in Haider, H. and Prinzhorn, M. (eds.) *Verb Second Phenomena in Germanic Languages*, pp. 27–47

Postal, P. M. (1972) 'On Some Rules That Are Not Successive Cyclic', *Linguistic Inquiry*, 3, pp. 211–22

Postal, P. M. (1974) *On Raising*. MIT Press, Cambridge, Mass.

Postal, P. M. and Pullum, G. K. (1978) 'Traces and the Description of English Complementizer Contraction', *Linguistic Inquiry*, 9, pp. 1–29

(1982) 'The Contraction Debate', *Linguistic Inquiry*, 13, pp. 122–38

(1986) 'Misgovernment', *Linguistic Inquiry*, 17, pp. 104–10

Poutsma, H. (1928) *A Grammar of Late Modern English*. P. Noordhoff, Groningen

Pullum, G. K. (1981a) 'The Category Status of Infinitival *to*' *Working Papers in Linguistics*, University of Washington, Seattle, pp. 55–72

(1981b) 'Evidence against the "AUX" node in Luiseño and English', *Linguistic Inquiry*, 12, pp. 435–63

(1982) 'Syncategoremacity and English Infinitival *to*', *Glossa*, 16, pp. 181–215

(1985) 'Assuming Some Version of X-bar Theory', Chicago Linguistic Society, University of Chicago, Illinois, 21, pp. 323–53

(1986) 'Footloose and Context-free', *Natural Language and Linguistic Theory*, 4, pp. 409–14

Pullum, G. K. and Postal, P. M. (1979) 'On an Inadequate Defense of Trace Theory', *Linguistic Inquiry*, 10, pp. 689–706

Quirk, R., Greenbaum, S., Leech, G. and Svartvik, J. (1985) *A Comprehensive Grammar of the English Language*. Longman, London

Radford, A. (1978) 'Agentive Causatives in Romance: Accessibility versus Passivisation', *Journal of Linguistics*, 14, pp. 35–58

(1981) *Transformational Syntax*. Cambridge University Press

Bibliography

(1986) 'Small Children's Small Clauses', *Research Papers in Linguistics*, University College of North Wales, 1, pp. 1–38

Ramsden, H. (1959) *An Essential Course in Modern Spanish*. Harrap, London

Reinhart, T. (1976) 'The Syntactic Domain of Anaphora', Ph.D dissertation, MIT, Cambridge, Mass.

(1980) 'On the Position of Extraposed Clauses', *Linguistic Inquiry* 11, pp. 621–4

(1983) *Anaphora and Semantic Interpretation*. Croom Helm, London

Reuland, E. (1983) 'Governing -*ing*', *Linguistic Inquiry*, 14, pp. 101–36

(1986) 'A Feature System for the Set of Categorial Heads' in Muysken, P. and Van Riemsdijk, H. (eds.) *Features and Projections*, pp. 41–88

Rivero, M.-L. (1978) 'Topicalization and *Wh* Movement in Spanish', *Linguistic Inquiry*, 9, pp. 513–17

(1980) 'On Left Dislocation and Topicalization in Spanish', *Linguistic Inquiry*, 11, pp. 363–93

(1984) 'Diachronic Syntax and Learnability: Free Relatives in Thirteenth-century Spanish', *Journal of Linguistics*, 20, pp. 81–129

Rizzi, L. (1982) *Issues in Italian Syntax*. Foris, Dordrecht

(1984) *Spiegazione e Teoria Grammaticale*. CLESP, Padova

Rochemont, M. S. (1986) *Focus in Generative Grammar*. Benjamins, Amsterdam

Roeper, T. and Siegel, M. E. A. (1978) 'A Lexical Transformation for Verbal Compounds', *Linguistic Inquiry*, 9, pp. 199–260

Rohdenburg, G. (1970) 'Zum Persönlichen Subjekt im Englischen', PAKS Arbeitsbericht 6, University of Stuttgart, pp. 133–64

Ross, J. R. (1967) 'Constraints on Variables in Syntax', Ph.D dissertation, MIT, Cambridge, Mass.; circulated by IULC in 1968; published as *Infinite Syntax!* by Ablex Publishing Corporation, Norwood, New Jersey, 1986

(1970) 'On Declarative Sentences' in Jacobs, R. A. and Rosenbaum, P. S. (eds.) *Readings in English Transformational Grammar*, pp. 222–72

Sadiqi, F. (1986) 'The Notion of COMP in Berber', unpublished paper, University of Fès, Morocco

Sadock, J. M. (1984) 'West Greenlandic', in Chisholm, W. S. (ed.) *Interrogativity*, pp. 189–214

Safir, K. (1983) 'On Small Clauses as Constituents', *Linguistic Inquiry*, 14, pp. 730–5

(1985) *Syntactic Chains*. Cambridge University Press

Sag, I. A. (1978) 'Floated Quantifiers, Adverbs, and Extraction Sites', *Linguistic Inquiry*, 9, pp. 146–50

Sag, I. A., Gazdar, G., Wasow, T. and Weisler, S. (1985) 'Coordination and How to Distinguish Categories', *Natural Language and Linguistic Theory*, 3, pp. 117–71

Sampson, G. (1975) 'The Single Mother Condition', *Journal of Linguistics*, 11, pp. 1–11

Sanders, G. (1969) 'On the Natural Domain of Grammar', mimeographed paper circulated by the Indiana University Linguistics Club

(1970a) 'Invariant Ordering', mimeographed paper circulated by the Indiana University Linguistics Club

(1970b) 'Constraints on Ordering', *Papers in Linguistics*, 2, pp. 460–502

(1971) 'On the Symmetry of Grammatical Constraints', Chicago Linguistic Society, University of Chicago, Illinois, 7, pp. 232–41

(1972a) *Equational Grammar*. Mouton, The Hague

(1972b) 'Precedence Relations in Language', mimeographed paper circulated by the Indiana University Linguistic Club

Scalise, S. (1984) *Generative Morphology*. Foris, Dordrecht

Schachter, P. (1984) 'Auxiliary Reduction: An Argument for GPSG', *Linguistic Inquiry*, 15, pp. 514–23

Selkirk, E. O. (1977) 'Some Remarks on Noun Phrase Structure' in Culicover, P. W. *et al.* (eds.) *Formal Syntax*, pp. 185–316

(1982) *The Syntax of Words*. MIT Press, Cambridge, Mass.

Shopen, T. (ed.) (1985) *Language Typology and Syntactic Description* (3 vols), Vol. I *Clause Structure*; Vol. II *Complex Constructions*; Vol. III *Grammatical Categories and the Lexicon*. Cambridge University Press

Siegel, D. (1973) 'Nonsources of Unpassives' in Kimball, J. (ed.) *Syntax and Semantics*, Vol. II. Seminar Press, New York

Simpson, J. M. Y. (1982) *A Reference Book of Terms in Traditional Grammar for Language Students*. University of Glasgow

Smith, N. V. and Wilson, D. (1979) *Modern Linguistics*. Penguin, London

Soames, S. and Perlmutter, D. M. (1979) *Syntactic Argumentation and the Structure of English*. UCP, Berkeley

Sperber, D. and Wilson, D. (1986) *Relevance*. Blackwell, Oxford

Sportiche, D. (1981) 'Bounding Nodes in French', *The Linguistic Review*, 1, pp. 219–46

Staal, J. F. (1967) *Word Order in Sanskrit and Universal Grammar*, Foundations of Language supplementary series no. 5, Dordrecht

Steele, S. (1981) *An Encyclopedia of AUX*. MIT Press, Cambridge, Mass.

Steinberg, D. D. and Jakobovits, L. A. (eds.) (1971) *Semantics*. Cambridge University Press

Stockwell, R. P., Schachter, P. and Hall Partee, B. (1973) *The Major Syntactic Structures of English*. Holt Rinehart and Winston, New York

Stowell, T. (1981) 'Origins of Phrase Structure', unpublished Ph.D dissertation, MIT Cambridge, Mass.

(1982) 'The Tense of Infinitives', *Linguistic Inquiry*, 13, pp. 561–70

(1983) 'Subjects Across Categories', *The Linguistic Review*, 2, pp. 285–312

Stuurman, F. (1983) 'Appositives and X-bar Theory', *Linguistic Inquiry*, 14, pp. 736–44

(1985) *Phrase Structure Theory in Generative Grammar*. Foris, Dordrecht

Suñer, M. (1984) 'Free Relatives and the Matching Parameter', *The Linguistic Review*, 3, pp. 363–87

Szabolcsi, A. (1983) 'The Possessor That Ran Away From Home', *The Linguistic Review*, 3, pp. 89–102

Takezawa, K. (1984) 'Perfective *Have* and the Bar Notation', *Linguistic Inquiry*, 15, pp. 675–87

Bibliography

Taraldsen, K. T. (1978) 'The Scope of *Wh* Movement in Norwegian', *Linguistic Inquiry*, 9, pp. 623–40

(1984) 'The Internal Structure and External Distribution of Tensed Clausal Complements in English, French and Norwegian' in De Geest, W. and Putseys, Y. (eds.) *Sentential Complementation*, pp. 239–46

(1986) 'On Verb Second and the Functional Content of Syntactic Categories' in Haider, H. and Prinzhorn, M. (eds.) *Verb Second Phenomena in Germanic Languages*, pp. 7–25

Thráinsson, H. (1986) 'V1, V2, V3 in Icelandic' in Haider, H. and Prinzhorn, M. (eds.) *Verb Second Phenomena in Germanic Languages*, pp. 169–94

Toman, J. (1981) 'Aspects of Multiple Wh-movement in Polish and Czech' in Koster, J. and May, R. *Levels of Syntactic Representation*. Foris, Dordrecht, pp. 293–302

Torrego, E. (1983) 'More Effects of Successive Cyclic Movement', *Linguistic Inquiry*, 14, pp. 561–5

(1984) 'On Inversion in Spanish and Some of Its Effects', *Linguistic Inquiry*, 15, pp. 103–29

Traugott, E. C. (1972) *A History of English Syntax*. Holt, Rinehart, Winston, New York

Travis, L. and Williams, E. (1982) 'Externalization of Arguments in Malayo-Polynesian Languages', *The Linguistic Review*, 2, pp. 57–77

Van der Auwera, J. (1985) 'Relative *That* – a Centennial Dispute', *Journal of Linguistics*, 21, pp. 149–79

Van Gestel, F. C. (1986) *X-bar Grammar: Attribution and Predication in Dutch*. Foris, Dordrecht

Van Riemsdijk, H. (1978) *A Case Study in Syntactic Markedness: The Binding Nature of Prepositional Phrases*. Foris, Dordrecht

Van Riemsdijk, H. and Williams, E. (1981) 'NP-Structure', *The Linguistic Review*, 1, pp. 171–217

(1986) *Introduction to the Theory of Grammar*. MIT Press, Cambridge, Mass.

Vat, J. (1978) 'On Footnote 2', *Linguistic Inquiry*, 9, pp. 695–716

Wasow, T. (1977) 'Transformations and the Lexicon' in Culicover, P. W. *et al.* (eds.) *Formal Syntax*, pp. 327–60

Wasow, T. and Roeper, T. (1972) 'On the Subject of Gerunds', *Foundations of Language*, 8, pp. 44–61

Wells, R. S. (1947) 'Immediate Constituents', *Language*, 23, pp. 81–117, reprinted in Joos, M. (ed.) (1957) *Readings in Linguistics I*. University of Chicago Press, pp. 186–207

Williams, E. (1975) 'Small Clauses in English' in Kimball, J. P. (ed.) *Syntax and Semantics*, Vol. iv, pp. 249–73

(1980) 'Predication', *Linguistic Inquiry*, 11, pp. 203–38

(1981a) 'Argument Structure and Morphology', *The Linguistic Review*, pp. 81–114

(1981b) 'On the Notions "Lexically Related" and "Head of a Word"', *Linguistic Inquiry*, 12, pp. 245–74

(1982) 'The NP Cycle', *Linguistic Inquiry*, 13, pp. 277–95

(1983) 'Against Small Clauses', *Linguistic Inquiry*, 14, pp. 287–308

(1984) '*There*-Insertion', *Linguistic Inquiry*, 15, pp. 131–53

Woolford, E. (1983) 'Bilingual Code-switching and Syntactic Theory', *Linguistic Inquiry*, 14, pp. 520–36

(1984) 'Dative Verbs with Unspecified Objects', *The Linguistic Review*, 3, pp. 389–409

Young, D. (1984) *Introducing English Grammar*. Hutchinson, London

Zaenen, A., Engdahl, E. and Maling, J. (1981) 'Resumptive Pronouns Can Be Syntactically Bound', *Linguistic Inquiry*, 12, pp. 679–82

(1983) 'On Syntactic Binding', *Linguistic Inquiry*, 14, pp. 469–504

Zubizaretta, M. L. (1982) 'Theoretical Implications of Subject Extraction in Portuguese', *The Linguistic Review*, 2, pp. 79–96

Index

Index

nonthematic Subject, 387–8
notional criteria, 57, 595
Noun, 59, 60
Noun Phrase, 52–6, 64–105, 167–225, 597–8
NP MOVEMENT, 420–56, 534–5, 539, 563, 566–7, 601, 604

objective, 291–2, 318, 327, 471–3; *see also* case
obligatory constituent, 230, 243, 244, 348
observational adequacy, 28–30, 63
one, 175, 186–7, 189, 198, 200, 294, 211, 221–2, 224–5
operator, 485–92, 593
optional constituent, 127–8, 179–87, 229, 230, 266–7, 348
order, 120–32, 143, 177–8, 199, 211–12, 234, 236, 244, 250, 273–8, 348–53, 453, 598
Ordinary Clause, 301 ff., 598–600
orphaned Preposition, 496–9
overgeneration, 267, 369

parameters, 43, 272–8, 368
paraphrase, 176
particle, 133–7, 596
particular grammar, 2–3, 37–8
passive, 233, 288, 318, 327, 376, 420–35, 444–6, 459, 549–51, 601; *see also* NP MOVEMENT
performance, 3–7, 594
peripheral rule, 41–2
PERIPHERY PRINCIPLE, 350, 368
phrasal categories, 64–89, *and passim*
phrasal Verbs, 70–1, 75, 77, 90–101, 107–8, 257, 344, 427–30, 459–60, 496–9, 523–4, 595, 601
phrase-markers, 109–22, *and passim*
Phrase Structure Rules, 123–32, 160, 177–89, 198–203, 208–11, 216, 232, 258–80, 367–9, 596
pied piping, 496–9
pleonastic pronouns, 319–20, 440–1
postmodifiers, *see* Adjunct *and* Complement
postposing, 71–2; *see also* EXTRAPOSITION *and* STYLISTIC INVERSION
pragmatics, 595
precedence, 110–11
predication theory, 599
premodifiers, *see* Attributes, Determiners, *and* Specifier
preposing, 69–71, 88, 92, 95, 100, 168, 191, 231, 244, 322, 452, 517–8
Preposition,, 57, 59, 62, 133–7, 273, 328–9, 363–4, 596
Prepositional Phrase, 52–6, 64–105, 167–96, 204–7, 246–52, 254, 280
Prepositional Verbs, 90–101, 107–8, 345, 427–30, 496–9, 523–4, 595, 601
prescriptivism, 7–9, 12, 46–7

PRO, 313–17, 320–4, 327, 356, 362; *see also* control
proconstituent, 78–82, 88, 92–3, 98–9, 168, 175, 180, 186–7, 189, 234, 243, 244, 247, 248, 249; *see also* one
proform, *see* proconstituent
PROJECTION PRINCIPLE, 369, 391–2, 548–9, 551–6, 600, 604
Pronoun, *see* proconstituent
pseudo-cleft sentences, 493, 602

Quantifier, 223, 470

Raising, 435–46, 461, 601; *see also* NP MOVEMENT
RAISING-TO-OBJECT, 549–50
realisation rules, 382–3, 600
REANALYSIS, 429–32, 459–60, 496–9, 601
reciprocal, 116–20
recursion, 128–31, 169–70, 183–4, 189, 200–2, 211, 242, 245, 256, 261, 453, 532–3
redundancy, 347–61, 366–9, 383–4
reflexive, 25–7, 116–20, 238–9, 315, 318, 322, 325, 327–8, 377, 436–8, 476–7
Relative Clause, 15–16, 218–9, 490–92, 522–3, 602
RESULTATIVE PREPOSING, 529, 533
root transformation, 538–42
R-suppletion, 328–9
rule-governed nature of language, 18–22

S, 52 ff., 508–15, 603
S-bar, 293 ff., 499–508, 603
Selection Restrictions, 94–5, 144, 369–72, 374–5, 387–92, 425, 443, 447, 479, 600
semi-indirect speech, 299, 415, 538
sentence fragments, *see* fragment
sister, 113–14, 192
Small Clause, 324–31, 335, 358–60, 426, 444, 515–20, 599–600, 603
sociolect, 9–10
Specifier, 227 ff., 251–3, 273–4, 503–8
spoken language, 8–9
S-structure, 401 ff.
stranded Preposition, 496–9
stress, 56, 215
strict adjacency, *see* adjacency
strict cyclicity, 578–82, 590, 605
structure, 50 ff., 595–6
structure-dependence, 32–5, 41–2
STRUCTURE-PRESERVING PRINCIPLE, 538–6, 604
STYLISTIC INVERSION, 488–90, 589–90
subcategorisation, 192–3, 231, 235, 250, 252, 339–69, 383–4, 396–7, 421, 449–50, 467–8, 516–17, 600–1
SUBJACENCY CONDITION, 569 *see also* bounding
Subject, 112–13